Nietzsche in the Nineteenth Century

INTELLECTUAL HISTORY
OF THE MODERN AGE

Series Editors
Angus Burgin
Peter E. Gordon
Joel Isaac
Karuna Mantena
Samuel Moyn
Jennifer Ratner-Rosenhagen
Camille Robcis
Sophia Rosenfeld

Nietzsche *in the* Nineteenth Century

*Social Questions
and Philosophical Interventions*

Robert C. Holub

UNIVERSITY OF PENNSYLVANIA PRESS

PHILADELPHIA

Copyright © 2018 University of Pennsylvania Press

All rights reserved. Except for brief quotations used for purposes of review or scholarly citation, none of this book may be reproduced in any form by any means without written permission from the publisher.

Published by
University of Pennsylvania Press
Philadelphia, Pennsylvania 19104-4112
www.upenn.edu/pennpress

Printed in the United States of America on acid-free paper
1 3 5 7 9 10 8 6 4 2

Library of Congress Cataloging-in-Publication Data

Names: Holub, Robert C., author.
Title: Nietzsche in the nineteenth century : social questions and philosophical interventions / Robert C. Holub. Other titles: Intellectual history of the modern age.
Description: 1st edition. | Philadelphia : University of Pennsylvania Press, [2018] | Series: Intellectual history of the modern age | Includes bibliographical references and index.
Identifiers: LCCN 2018002984 | ISBN 978-0-8122-5023-7 (hardcover : alk. paper)
Subjects: LCSH: Nietzsche, Friedrich Wilhelm, 1844–1900. | Nietzsche, Friedrich Wilhelm, 1844–1900—Political and social views. | Philosophy, German—19th century.
Classification: LCC B3317 .H5725 2018 | DDC 193—dc23
LC record available at https://lccn.loc.gov/2018002984

Contents

A Note on Citations	vii
Introduction: The Timely Meditator	1
Chapter 1. The Education Question	19
Chapter 2. The German Question	75
Chapter 3. The Social Question	125
Chapter 4. The Women's Question	173
Chapter 5. The Colonial Question	218
Chapter 6. The Jewish Question	260
Chapter 7. The Evolution Question	313
Chapter 8. The Cosmological Question	360
Chapter 9. The Eugenics Question	408
Concluding Remarks	454
Notes	461
Index	507
Acknowledgments	523

A Note on Citations

All citations from Nietzsche's writings and correspondence are noted parenthetically in the text according to the standards established in current Nietzsche scholarship. Abbreviations used in this study are given below.

When there is no indication in the text, parenthetical citations for published and unpublished writings will include the abbreviation for the work, an indication of where in the work the citation occurs, and the volume and page number in the critical edition. Letters will include the addressee or sender, the date of the letter, the number of the letter, and the volume and page number in the critical edition.

I have consulted various sources for translations, modifying for the sake of accuracy and consistency. In cases where no translation exists, I translated myself.

Editions Used

BAW — Beck'sche Ausgabe Werke = Nietzsche, Friedrich. *Historisch-kritische Gesamtausgabe. Werke.* 5 vols. Munich: Beck 1933–42.

KGW — Kritische Gesamtausgabe der Werke = Nietzsche, Friedrich. *Werke. Kritische Gesamtausgabe.* Planned ca. 50 vols. Ed. Giorgio Colli, Mazzino Montinari et al. Berlin: de Gruyter, 1967– .

KGB — Kritische Gesamtausgabe Briefwechsel = Nietzsche, Friedrich. *Briefwechsel. Kritische Gesamtausgabe.* 24 vols. Ed. Giorgio Colli, Mazzino Montinari et al. Berlin: de Gruyter, 1975–2004.

KSA — Kritische Studienausgabe = Nietzsche, Friedrich. *Sämtliche Werke. Kritische Studienausgabe.* 15 vols. Ed. Giorgio Colli and Mazzino Montinari. Berlin: de Gruyter, 1980.

KSB — Kritische Studienausgabe Briefe = Nietzsche, Friedrich. *Sämtliche Briefe. Kritische Studienausgabe.* 8 vols. Ed. Giorgio Colli and Mazzino Montinari. Berlin: de Gruyter, 1986.

Published Works

SGT — Sokrates und die griechische Tragoedie [Socrates and Greek Tragedy]
GT — Die Geburt der Tragödie [The Birth of Tragedy]

NJ	Ein Neujahrswort [A Message for the New Year]
MD	Mahnruf an die Deutschen [Admonition to the Germans]
UB	Unzeitgemässe Betrachtungen [Untimely Meditations]
DS	David Strauß, der Bekenner und der Schriftsteller [David Strauß, the Confessor and the Writer]
HL	Vom Nutzen und Nachtheil der Historie für das Leben [On the Advantage and Disadvantage of History for Life]
SE	Schopenhauer als Erzieher [Schopenhauer as Educator]
WB	Richard Wagner in Bayreuth [Richard Wagner in Bayreuth]
MA	Menschliches, Allzumenschliches (I und II) [Human, All Too Human]
VM	Vermischte Meinungen und Sprüche [Mixed Opinions and Sayings]
WS	Der Wanderer und sein Schatten [The Wanderer and His Shadow]
M	Morgenröthe [Dawn]
IM	Idyllen aus Messina [Idylls from Messina]
FW	Die fröhliche Wissenschaft [The Gay Science]
Za	Also sprach Zarathustra [Thus Spoke Zarathustra]
JGB	Jenseits von Gut und Böse [Beyond Good and Evil]
GM	Zur Genealogie der Moral [On the Genealogy of Morals]
WA	Der Fall Wagner [The Case of Wagner]
GD	Götzen-Dämmerung [Twilight of the Idols]
AC	Der Antichrist [The Antichrist]
EH	Ecce homo
NW	Nietzsche contra Wagner
DD	Dionysos-Dithyramben [Dionysian Dithyrambs]

Unpublished Writings and Fragments

Nachlass	Nachlass [Literary Remains]
WM	Die Nachlass-Kompilation "Der Wille zur Macht" [The Compilation from the Literary Remains "The Will to Power"]
GMD	Das griechische Musikdrama [The Greek Music Drama]
ST	Socrates und die Tragödie [Socrates and Tragedy]
DW	Die dionysische Weltanschauung [The Dionysian Worldview]
GG	Die Geburt des tragischen Gedankens [The Birth of Tragic Thought]
BA	Ueber die Zukunft unserer Bildungsanstalten [On the Future of Our Educational Institutions]
CV	Fünf Vorreden zu fünf ungeschriebenen Büchern [Five Prefaces to Five Unwritten Books]

PHG   Die Philosophie im tragischen Zeitalter der Griechen [Philosophy in the Tragic Age of the Greeks]
WL   Ueber Wahrheit und Lüge im aussermoralischen Sinne [On Truth and Lies in an Extramoral Sense]

Introduction: The Timely Meditator

Friedrich Nietzsche made a conscious effort to present himself as an "untimely" thinker.[1] As he began to transition out of his career as an academic in the early 1870s, he started writing books that he believed placed him in opposition to, or even outside, the dominant tendencies of his time. Certainly his initial nonphilological study, *The Birth of Tragedy* (1872), was a treatise that violated the norms of classical scholarship, and its support of the cultural mission of the composer Richard Wagner (1813–1883) placed it outside the usual works dealing with ancient Greece. Nietzsche's next project emphasized even more his opposition to his era, and in particular to Germany's recently proclaimed Second Empire. The four reflections received the series title "Untimely Meditations," and they were composed in harmony with the views of Wagner and against many of the prevailing tendencies in German society. The first piece, *David Strauß, the Confessor and Writer* (1873), polemicized against a popular author and his celebration of the cultural and political accomplishments of his era. This polemic was followed by *On the Advantage and Disadvantage of History for Life* (1874), which criticized the role of historical thought in contemporary culture and education. In the "Preface," he explains why his views are out of fashion in his era: "These thoughts are 'untimely' because I am trying to represent something of which the age is rightly proud—its historical culture—as a fault and a defect in our time, believing as I do that we are all suffering from a malignant historical fever and should at least recognize the fact" (HL, Vorwort, KSA 1.246). The third and fourth *Meditations* extolled the virtues of Arthur Schopenhauer (1788–1860) and Richard Wagner, the philosophical and musical inspirations for what Nietzsche considered the cultural renaissance Germany so desperately needed. In Schopenhauer he finds the "true philosopher as educator," who elevates him above his "inadequacies" and teaches him "again to be *simple* and *honest*"; for these qualities, he is "untimely in the deepest sense of the word" (SE 2, KSA 1.346). And in *Richard Wagner in Bayreuth* (1876), where the opening of Wagner's *Festspiele* was the occasion for Nietzsche's text, he describes the spectators—and Nietzsche was among them—as "untimely people: they have their home elsewhere than in the present time and seek their explanation and justification elsewhere as well" (WB 1, KSA 1.432–33). In his notebooks, Nietzsche reinforces the untimeliness of the Meister: his "art does not belong to our *present* art: he is far *ahead* or *above* it. One should not credit his existence to our age, since it has done everything it could to hinder his existence" (Nachlass 1875, 11[19], KSA 8.205). He is against the "clever ones, the cold ones, the contented ones" as well as the frivolous and the elegant, and for that reason he is "untimely" (Nachlass 1878, 27[27], KSA 8.491). Nietzsche partakes of the untimeliness of his mentor through his advocacy for his movement. Later, after he has broken with Wagner, he continues to be untimely, affirming in 1885 that he is today what he was then: "untimely" (Nachlass 1885, 36[17], KSA 11.559). Nietzsche's self-stylization as untimely continues right through to his last year of published works: In *Twilight of the Idols* (1888), he includes a long section with a series of observations on culture, art, and morality titled "Expeditions of an Untimely Man" (GD, Streifzüge eine Unzeitgemässen, KSA 6.111–53).

Nietzsche's cultivation of an "untimely" status for the Wagnerian movement to which he belonged, and then later for himself alone, acquires another dimension in his final years of sanity. His opposition to his times undergoes a slight transformation, and he begins to consider his untimeliness as a confirmation that his contemporaries are not yet able to appreciate or comprehend what he is writing. Nietzsche was sensitive to his lack of readers, especially in Germany, and part of his censure of Germany in his later works stems from the meager sales of his books and the scant reception of his thought in German intellectual life. In his writings from 1887 and 1888, he begins to refer to individuals—and to himself—as someone who will be read and understood only at a later time. To supplement the untimely individual and his meditations, he develops the notion of a "posthumous" man. In *Twilight of the Idols*, he writes: "Posthumous men—like me, for instance—are not so well understood as timely men, but they are *listened to* better. More precisely, we are never *understood*—and *hence* our authority" (GD, Sprüche und Pfeile 15, KSA 6.61). In *The Gay Science*,[2] he poses as a hermit who extolls the posthumous men who will only come to life after their death, "oh very much alive" (FW 365, KSA 613–14). But the *locus classicus* for his posthumous essence occurs in his autobiographical account, *Ecce Homo*, in the section in which he is explaining why he writes such great books:

> I am one thing, my writings are another.—Here, before I speak of these writings themselves, I shall touch on the question of their being understood or *not* understood. I shall do so as perfunctorily as is fitting: for the time for this question has certainly not yet come. My time has not yet come, some are born posthumously.—One day or other, institutions will be needed in which people live and teach, as I understand living and teaching: perhaps even chairs for the interpretation of Zarathustra will be established. (EH, Warum ich so gute Bücher schreibe 1, KSA 6.298)

In this passage and in the initial section of "Why I Am a Destiny" (EH, Warum ich ein Schicksal bin 1, KSA 6.365), Nietzsche supplies a megalomaniacal depiction of himself as the untimely philosopher whose importance will be recognized only in an unspecified future era. In his later writings, he is more than an untimely critic of contemporary life in the Second Reich; he is the misunderstood, solitary prophet whose explosive vision ("I am dynamite" [EH, Warum ich ein Schicksal bin, KSA 6.365]) will find an enthusiastic following long after his earthly demise.

Nietzsche was certainly prescient regarding his fame. Although he started to gain acclaim after his mental breakdown in 1889 and prior to his death in 1900, his celebrity really begins full force in the twentieth century, when he became perhaps the most celebrated philosopher of the modern era. But his self-stylization as untimely is surely open to question. If we consider again his *Untimely Meditations*, we can understand them as critical of tendencies of his era, but the very fact that he is engaging with these tendencies makes these works timely. In the first *Meditation*, he was preoccupied with a popular book dealing with current trends in culture, science, and religion. In the second, Nietzsche examined contemporary education and cultural movements; his dissatisfaction with the intellectual directions of the new Reich was not unique, and the discontent extended well beyond the Wagnerian circle. In writing about Schopenhauer, he took as his subject an extremely popular philosopher of the post-1848 period, and many prominent contemporary thinkers shared Nietzsche's fascination with him. Finally, Wagner, the inspirational and charismatic leader of a movement to resurrect cultural greatness in a united Germany, was a well-known composer with a musical following of European dimensions. These themes, persons, and perspectives signaled an active involvement with the new Reich; in this sense, the *Meditations* were anything but untimely. Indeed, Nietzsche himself recognized his timeliness in these early works in a notebook entry from the mid-1880s: "When I once wrote the word 'untimely' on my books, how much youthfulness, inexperience, provinciality is expressed in this word! Today I understand that with this sort of plaint, enthusiasm, and discontent, I actually belonged to the most modern of the moderns" (Nachlass 1885–86, 2[201], KSA 12.165). The same holds true for the later reflections of the "posthumous" man. Throughout the two decades of his writing, Nietzsche was always in dialogue with theories, movements, and events of his era. As his biographer Curt Paul Janz noted, Nietzsche is "enmeshed in his times, to a certain extent he is even conditioned by his times."[3] Nietzsche's self-fashioning as a philosopher outside or ahead of his contemporaries belies the fact that a great deal of what he wrote is part of diverse conversations in Western Europe in the latter half of the nineteenth century.

This study argues that Nietzsche was very much involved in the discourses of his time, that he can be regarded as a contributor to these discourses—although one who was not heard very well during his own lifetime—and that an understanding of several of his main convictions and propositions is possible only if we pay sufficient attention to the discourses in which he participated. Nietzsche's self-presentation as a man unconcerned with the mundane matters of society and politics, or with the most recent theoretical developments in the natural sciences, is misleading and steers us away from the issues with which he was grappling. Nietzsche's sister Elisabeth was partially responsible for perpetuating this view when she emphasized his isolation and loneliness, and sought to depict him as an individual touched by genius and immense wisdom. But many commentators in the first century of Nietzsche scholarship and criticism have been equal contributors to the Nietzsche myth. In some regards, Nietzsche's gradual acceptance as a philosopher assisted in an ahistorical and decontextualized understanding of his works. Philosophy has always had the tendency to deal with matters on an abstract level, to disconnect thought from its embeddedness in socio-historical structure, and to consider the writings of great philosophers to be in dialogue solely with a tradition of other great minds. When this study was first conceived about a quarter of a century ago, most of the books and articles on Nietzsche dealt with him in this fashion: he was abstracted from his times and regarded as a philosopher who was at most in conversation with other noted philosophers of the past, or as anticipating philosophical movements of the future. The various books and articles composed by students and associates of the editors of the authoritative Nietzsche edition, Giogio Colli and Mazzino Montinari, and some essays appearing in *Nietzsche-Studien*, were the exceptions that proved the rule. In the Anglophone world, the situation was even more dismal than in Germany. But in the past two and a half decades, there has been a remarkable change in some corners of Nietzsche scholarship, and there now exist a half dozen or more volumes whose goal is to situate Nietzsche in one or another of the discourses of the late nineteenth century.[4] This turn recognizes the starting point for, and impetus behind, the research that went into this book: It affirms that Nietzsche was not a student of great philosophers—indeed, from his library we can discern that he possessed and read remarkably little from the philosophical tradition, with the exceptions of the ancients and Schopenhauer. The works of Hegel, Descartes, Kant, Spinoza, and Leibniz—to name just a few—are nowhere to be found in his library, and from the marginal notes and comments in the volumes he did consult, we have to conclude that he was in direct dialogue not with the most stellar thinkers of the philosophical tradition, but with such lesser dignitaries as Léon Dumont (1837–1877), Harald Höffding (1843–1931), William Lecky (1838–1903), James Sully (1842–1923), Otto Liebmann (1840–1912), Afrikan Spir (1837–1890), and William Henry Rolph (1847–1883).[5] Nietzsche's knowledge of the great tradition came largely from secondary sources; even his philosophical conversations were conducted with, and with the help of, contemporaries, not with the primary sources. In his philosophical reflections, as in his views on social and scientific matters, Nietzsche was very much the "timely meditator."[6]

To a certain extent Nietzsche disguises his indebtedness to contemporary sources, leading readers and subsequent commentators away from the conversations in which he was involved, and suggesting to them that he was, as he describes it in his second *Untimely Meditation*, one of the "giants" speaking to other giants "across the desolate expanses of time," "undisturbed by the wanton, noisy dwarfs who crawl about beneath them" (HL 9, KSA 1.317).[7] Nietzsche's use of sources is somewhat deceptive. He rarely gives credit to the material he adopts, and he frequently leaves unmentioned the names of the authors and books he is culling or the individuals against whom he is writing.[8] One illustration will have to stand for many cases: In the 1880s, in preparation for the composition of *On the Genealogy of Morals* (1887), Nietzsche read several works by the eminent and prolific legal historian Josef Kohler (1849–1919), at the time a professor of law at the University of Würzburg. His scholarship on comparative law was especially interesting for Nietzsche, and of the three works by Kohler in his library, *Law as a Cultural Phenomenon* (1885), which was a brief introduction to the topic, is the most heavily marked. In this slim volume, Nietzsche read about legal customs surrounding debt [*Schuld*], a topic that occupies a central place in the second essay of the *Genealogy*. Kohler writes that in Old Norse law the notion of liability originally involves the body and life itself. The debtor who could not pay was therefore at the mercy of the creditor and could be made a slave or even killed. The creditor could also take a limb from the debtor, but it had to be a part of the body that was equivalent to the debt. He continues: "It was a kind of progress when the twelve tables of Rome[9] put an end to this unworthy calculation, in that they determined that in such cases of concurrence it did not matter whether the individual creditor cuts off a larger or a smaller piece: the creditors are permitted to cut the debtor into pieces, if they wish; the details were no longer important to the legal system: si plus minusve secuerunt, se fraude esto."[10] Nietzsche covers much of the same ground. He observes that formerly the debtor would pledge to the creditor something that he possesses: "his body or his wife or his freedom or even his life," but adds that the creditor could subject the debtor to humiliation and torture: "For this purpose, there have existed from the earliest times precise and in part horrifically detailed measurements, *legal* measurements, of the limbs and parts of the body." Nietzsche continues, referring to the same Roman law he found in Kohler: "I take it as already a sign of progress, as proof of a freer, *more Roman* conception of law, one grander in its calculations, that the twelve-table legislation of Rome decreed the amount which creditors excised in such cases a matter of indifference, 'si plus minusve secuerunt, ne fraude esto'" (GM, Zweite Abhandlung 5, KSA 5.299). Nietzsche embellishes Kohler's account, but it is identical in substance to the remarks of the legal scholar, right down to the Latin citation from the twelve tables.[11] Nowhere in the *Genealogy* does Nietzsche credit Kohler as his source. Indeed, Kohler's name is absent from anything Nietzsche wrote, whether published or unpublished, in books or in correspondence. The way in which Nietzsche dealt with Kohler, however, was no different from the way he treated dozens of contemporaries and their works. Nietzsche's "timeliness," his participation in the discourses of his era, which were often more evident to his earliest critics, is difficult for later commentators to discern, since only on rare occasions does he allow us direct access to the participants in the conversations into which he inserts himself.

The chapters in this study examine Nietzsche's relationship to nine different discourses he encountered in the late nineteenth century. The word "discourse" is meant in its normal and neutral sense, as written or spoken communication or debate. It encompasses the various written items in circulation at the time, as well as the oral communications surrounding these items, as far as these items can be determined for Nietzsche and the circles around him. This study is therefore not an example of discourse analysis in the sense used by Michel Foucault (1926–1984) in his *The Archaeology of Knowledge* (1972); while power is surely involved in discourses, as Foucault maintained, "discourses" in this book refer more simply to the conversations in which Nietzsche implicitly participated. In some cases, the chapters explore the sources he used to formulate his views, but the emphasis is never on the derivative nature of Nietzsche's thought: there is no attempt to provide a full account of influences and readings. In most instances, what is more important is the way in which Nietzsche engaged with his sources, but in a much wider sense how he engaged with larger discussions of issues composed of various voices, some of which were directly familiar to Nietzsche, others forming part of a background or foundation for discussions in the public sphere. The main concern is therefore always the manner in which Nietzsche understood the stakes of discourses and the way in which he offered his own contributions to the discussion. The goal is to ascertain the contributions he made to these conversations, whether they were widely known to his contemporaries or not. Like any social being, Nietzsche was born into a world in which various discussions were ongoing, and he could hardly have avoided contact with them. Nietzsche was certainly not unique in his broad exposure to social and scientific discourses of his times—every educated German of his generation encountered a similar set of discourses—but he was unusual at times in the way he understood discussions of issues, and the manner in which he responded or contributed to the conversations that constituted the intellectual landscape of the 1870s and 1880s. Despite his insistence that he was untimely in his contributions, we often find, even in his early writings, that he articulated positions shared by many contemporaries. An oppositional status was hardly unique to him in the 1870s, since there were many individuals who likewise harbored similar concerns and fears about what was occurring in the newly unified German nation. And in his later writings, when he began to believe that he would have only a posthumous effect on a German and European readership, we also find that the issues that impacted him most, as well as many of the solutions he proffered, circulated quite freely in the general discussions of his times. The aim of this study is thus to situate Nietzsche in the discursive universe of the late nineteenth century in Europe, but in particular in Germany, and to understand how and what Nietzsche learned from these discourses, and how his thought then participated in the larger concerns of the era.

Some Nietzsche enthusiasts might wonder why anyone should be concerned with the context of Nietzsche's writings. The discourses of the late nineteenth century may hold little interest for philosophers who do not value context, and who assess Nietzsche solely as he relates to the great issues of the philosophical tradition, or as an abstract thinker unconcerned with contemporary issues and writings. There are at least three reasons why situating Nietzsche in the context of his own times produces something significant. The first concerns the nature of Nietzsche's writings. Implicit in many commentaries on Nietzsche is the assumption that part of his work is philosophical and serious, while other passages or sections of his writings deal with peripheral issues that have no real import. When Nietzsche writes about topics relating to epistemology or ethics, or includes mention of eternal recurrence or the will to power, he is a philosopher worthy of treatment. When he reflects on women or workers, or polemicizes against Wagner or anti-Semitism, he is a mere historical curiosity and not appropriate for philosophical consideration. Nietzsche himself, however, did not draw such a distinction in philosophers and their thoughts. His characterization of philosophy in *Beyond Good and Evil* (1886) as "the personal confession of its author, a kind of unintended and unwitting memoir" (JGB 6, KSA 5.19) indicates a belief that "high philosophy" is inseparable from more mundane factors and interests. He is even more explicit in *Twilight of the Idols* (1888). He writes disparagingly of philosophers' "lack of historical sense, their hatred of the idea of becoming, their Egyptianism. They think they are doing a thing *honor* when they dehistoricize it, *sub specie aeterni*—when they make a mummy of it. All that philosophers have handled for millennia has been conceptual mummies; nothing actual has escaped from their hands alive. They kill, they stuff, when they worship, these conceptual idolaters—they become a moral danger to everything when they worship" (GD, Die "Vernunft" in der Philosophie 1, KSA 6.74).[12] And in *Ecce Homo*, he writes that the "the little things," by which he means the concrete dimensions of life—nutriment, place, climate, recreation—are the "fundamental affairs of life," while the more abstract ponderings of humankind "are not even realities, merely imaginings, more strictly speaking *lies* from the bad instincts of sick, in the profoundest sense injurious natures" (EH, Warum ich so klug bin, 10, KSA 6.295–96). Indeed, Nietzsche's own writings confirm his refusal to distinguish between the abstract and the historical, the philosophical and the mundane. In all his collections of aphorisms, we find a mixture of considerations on diverse topics, from epistemological reflections to social observations. Situating Nietzsche in conversations of the late nineteenth century serves to dispel the notion that we should take one part of his thought more seriously than another.

Second, contextualization is important because it corrects the erroneous notion that Nietzsche was first and foremost in dialogue with the great thinkers in the philosophical tradition, and that he can be best understood and appreciated solely for his commentary on this tradition. As we have already seen, Nietzsche had little firsthand knowledge of modern philosophy from Descartes through German idealism, with the notable exception of Arthur Schopenhauer's writings.[13] We are fortunate to have detailed knowledge of Nietzsche's library and also a very good idea of the volumes he borrowed from various libraries, as well as the books he requested from his publisher and friends.[14] With a great degree of confidence, we can assert that he never undertook a systematic study of any major modern philosopher, but that he did read and appreciate many books from contemporary thinkers. Context therefore assists us in determining what he knew firsthand and how he gained knowledge of philosophy as well as other matters, and in placing his own reflections within actual, rather than imagined, conversations. But perhaps the most important reason for considering the timely meditations of Nietzsche is that, by citing and analyzing works Nietzsche read, and by considering the conservations in which he participated, we gain a more precise understanding of his thought. The contextualization in this study gives us a better feel for Nietzsche's concerns, his thinking, his engagement with works and ideas of his time, his development during the 1870s and 1880s, and his reaction to contemporary issues, all of which find their way with regularity into his published writings. The context of his thought provides us with insight into the intellectual universe he inhabits, which is an essential background and prerequisite for comprehending the "personal memoir" that was his philosophy. The major contribution of thick contextualization stems from its illumination of Nietzsche's thought as it relates to currents in late nineteenth-century German and European intellectual life.

Chapter 1 examines issues surrounding education and schools in Germany. The Education Question was one of Nietzsche's central concerns in the 1870s, second only to his commitment to the Wagnerian renaissance. His thoughts on education were defined largely by the institutions he had attended, which included a village school in Röcken, an elementary school in Naumburg, a preparatory institute in Naumburg directed by Carl Moritz Weber, the Cathedral *Gymnasium* in Naumburg, the boarding school Schulpforta or Pforta—one of the premier secondary schools in Germany—and the universities in Bonn and Leipzig. He also had experience in Basel both as a classical philologist at the university and as an instructor in the advanced classes of the secondary school or *Pädagogium*. He was thus personally acquainted with various educational institutions, but had no experience as a pupil or teacher with *Realschulen*, which were secondary schools that included more extensive training in modern languages and science than the *Gymnasium*. In 1872, he collected his thoughts on the philosophy of education and the structure of the current school system in a series of five lectures titled "On the Future of our Educational Institutions," and presented them to the general public in Basel from January through March. In doing so, Nietzsche entered into an area that was addressed by many contemporaries; we have evidence that he read several authors who likewise criticized aspects of the school system and made suggestions for change, although Nietzsche's lectures differ in their lack of specific propositions for reform. Many of his peers made more concrete suggestions that included specific revisions in curriculum, including the number of hours devoted to certain subjects. Nietzsche, who in his activity as a faculty member at the university and the *Pädagogium*, made suggestions for change that contained a great deal of specificity, recommending, for example, the grammar book that should be used for Greek instruction and deliberating on the introduction of chemistry into the curriculum, provided only a broad discussion of principles in his lectures. Like other commentators, Nietzsche is reacting primarily to momentous changes in German education during the latter part of the nineteenth century: the demand for greater attention to general education for the entire population and the appropriate content of this instruction for the masses; the advent of the more practically oriented *Realschulen*, which only recently acquired the status of preparatory schools for admission to university training; the concomitant devaluation and decline of the humanistic *Gymnasium*, which Nietzsche valued as the sole institution for genuine *Bildung*; the watering down of curriculum in advanced institutions of higher education; and the tendency to connect even elite education with "job training" and the marketplace. Nietzsche's opposition to the tendencies in the educational system relates directly to his advocacy for *Bildung* and educational institutions that foster cultural excellence. Nietzsche's second *Untimely Meditation*, which deals with historical thought and education in the Second Empire, reinforces many of the themes from the lectures and promotes even more strongly the production of a cultural elite at the expense of mass education. This topic continues to be important in *Schopenhauer as Educator*, but as Nietzsche proceeds into the 1880s, we find that the educational imperatives he developed in the early 1870s are no longer a central focus. As Nietzsche begins to regard the human being from the perspective of biology, his enthusiasm for education and other factors in the realm of "nurture" cede to a conviction that the destiny of individuals and even groups is determined by "nature" and not subject to great modification through the school system.

The topic of the second chapter is the German Question. Like most Germans after the failed 1848 revolutions, Nietzsche was concerned with the political and cultural aspects of Germany and what it meant to be German. Born in Prussian Saxony, he was initially a Prussian patriot who championed a unified Germany under Prussian rule well into his mid-twenties. We find his early notebooks filled with references to German themes and myths, and he was the co-founder and inspiration for a club of high school students called "Germania." Even when Nietzsche left Prussian soil for the first time and matriculated as a student at the Saxon University of Leipzig, he retained his Prussian loyalties and engaged in a political campaign for a candidate that represented Prussian interests. This chapter documents his early involvement with Germany as it moved toward unification, as well as his personal involvement with patriotism and unification as a volunteer in the German army. We can detect a shift of emphasis in Nietzsche's thought during the 1870s as he assumes the role of Wagnerian acolyte and adopts many of the views advocated by the Meister. Like Wagner, Nietzsche remained an enthusiastic supporter of the new Reich as a political entity, but he began to recognize that political unity was worthless if it was not accompanied by a cultural renaissance. Accordingly, he became more skeptical of the Second Empire and critical of individuals like David Strauß (1808–1874) who are inattentive to the deficiencies that still exist in German culture. Nationalism is in evidence in all the writings of Nietzsche's Wagnerian period, from his praise of German art as the inheritor of the Dionysian impulse in *The Birth of Tragedy* to his *Untimely Meditations*, where he admonishes his compatriots that the victory on the battlefield may be a defeat for what really matters in the cultural arena. After his break with Wagner, however, Nietzsche's views on the German Question change radically. Reacting to Wagner's promotion of an unalterable German essence, Nietzsche begins to consider Germany as a nation that is in transition and not completed, tentative and subject to future modification. During the latter part of the decade, Nietzsche abandons his former identification with Germanness and the Wagnerian mission and begins to propose Europeanness and a European identity as a salutary alternative to the narrow nationalism espoused by the politics of National Liberalism, which he had embraced in the 1860s, and by Wagner during the period of their friendship. He becomes increasingly critical of Otto von Bismarck (1815–1898) and the German state; political parties of all stripes, especially those that embrace nationalism, are considered a problem to be overcome, not a possible solution to Germany's problems. In his final years, Nietzsche violently rejects German jingoism as a symptom of decline and *ressentiment*. In part, his annoyance with Germany is the consequence of a perceived lack of appreciation for his writings. But it also entails a perspective that becomes dominant in Nietzsche's thought, and that views Germany and Germans as a major hindrance to past and present endeavors to achieve cultural greatness. This chapter thus traces Nietzsche's transition from a supporter of German national unity to a critical promoter of a Wagnerian version of cultural Germanness to a Europeanist who vehemently repudiates German nationalism as the very antithesis of everything he advocates.

The Social Question, the topic of the third chapter, involves the German response to the organization of the working class during the rapid industrialization of the economy occurring in the second half of the nineteenth century. The formation of working-class parties coincides with Nietzsche's years as a student in Leipzig and his initial years as a professor at Basel. The passing of the Socialist Laws in 1878, which barred many organizational activities of the Social Democrats, in the effort to damage its election campaigns and discourage membership, is coterminous with the publication of Nietzsche's first post-Wagnerian book, *Human, All Too Human*. The surprising growth of Social Democracy during the 1880s occurs as Nietzsche is composing some of his most seminal works. Nietzsche, like many of his contemporaries, was thus compelled by his times to take a stance toward the working people of Germany, their organizational structures, and their ideological convictions, and he did so often during his lifetime. There was no period in Nietzsche's life when he came into close contact with workers or working-class culture, but in the 1860s he initially showed interest in the "fourth estate"[15] and one of its recognized leaders, Ferdinand Lassalle (1825–1864). He shared this interest with his closest friend at the time, Carl von Gersdorff (1844–1904), and he was acquainted with the history of socialist parties through his readings. Under Wagner's influence in the early 1870s, he became concerned that the working class posed a threat to cultural achievements, and his reaction to the Paris Commune indicates how seriously he felt culture endangered by a crude mass movement. Indeed, we find that consideration of the Commune is pivotal for his views of the Social Question, and he frequently returns to the perils the masses represent for civilization. Although Nietzsche grew to dislike all parties, including the Social Democrats, he is not an advocate of capitalism, and at various points in his middle period he demonstrates an abhorrence of the nouveau riche of the Second Empire and occasionally understanding for the plight of the proletariat that opposed bourgeois domination. In general, Nietzsche's comments on capitalism, the bourgeoisie, and the working class during the late 1870s and early 1880s are moderate and dispassionately argued; they belie the frequent claim, especially from Marxists, that Nietzsche was an advocate of capitalist imperialism and an unremitting enemy of the working class. But as Nietzsche began to observe the growing strength of Social Democracy in the 1880s, he came to a different understanding of its historical significance. In his writings of the late 1880s, he turns more sharply against the working class and its representatives; he begins to regard the socialist alternative embraced by the working class as a violation of basic human psychology and a sign of cultural decline. We suspect that

Nietzsche identified socialist theory in these years with the Berlin philosopher Eugen Dühring (1833–1921), and we can therefore understand why he considers it part of a larger complex of rancor that includes anarchism, vengefulness, and anti-Semitism. The solution to the Social Question is not socialism, which, similar to Christianity, is itself a manifestation of decadence and degeneration, but a variation on slavery or at least a renewed passivity in the working class.

Nietzsche's preoccupation with the egalitarian movements of his time led to a concern with women, women's rights, and women's emancipation, all of which is collected under the rubric the Women's Question in Chapter 4. Once again we are dealing with a phenomenon that arose at the time Nietzsche was most active in writing, and it was, like socialism, a topic that attracted the attention of many of Nietzsche's contemporaries, both in Germany and throughout Europe. Nietzsche's exposure to this question was mediated by his reading, as well as his personal contacts: he was familiar with works by male authors on the Women's Question, including John Stuart Mill's (1806–1873) *The Subjection of Women* (1869), and was acquainted with several women who championed women's education, most of whom studied at the University of Zurich, among them some of the first female recipients of degrees from that institution. One of his closest friends was Malwida von Meysenbug (1816–1903), who was, like Nietzsche, a devotee of Richard Wagner, but who had a history of progressive thought starting with activities in the 1840s. She is often considered today the mother of the first women's movement in Germany. In his personal life, Nietzsche could be supportive of women and their advancement; in his contact with women, he was evidently polite and respectful. In the early twentieth century, he was often praised by many of the leaders of the first women's movement in Germany, and by some feminist thinkers in the United States. In recent years, adherents to poststructuralism and deconstruction have managed to fashion him as a "feminist" because of his putative opposition to "male," rationalist paradigms of thought. But many remarks in his works are still considered part of the misogynist philosophical tradition. Examining his entire oeuvre in this chapter, we find that he was largely unconcerned with issues surrounding women until his aphoristic writings, when he reflected on courtships, women, and marriage. In this period, his reflections on women were not devoid of bias, but they were composed as witty observations on conventions and habits. A drastic change occurs in Nietzsche's attitude only in the 1880s. This change was possibly precipitated by his disappointment in Lou Salomé (1861–1937), in particular the manner in which she abandoned him for his friend Paul Rée (1849–1901). From the first book of *Zarathustra* (1883–1885), we clearly see a different perspective on women's issues, one that is overtly misogynist and often accompanied by deprecatory rhetorical flourishes. In *Beyond Good and Evil*, Nietzsche adds a series of aphorisms to the section on "Our Virtues" (JGB 231–39, KSA 5.170–78), all of which ridicule and denigrate women, their intelligence, their desire to attain equality with men, and the men and women who have advocated for women's emancipation. In his final works, we encounter some of his most abrasive passages on women: emancipated women are considered to be those unable to accept their biological destiny as mothers; feminism is categorized as just another redemptive movement that is a symptom of decline in contemporary life. Still, despite the harshness of his views, Nietzsche's consideration of the Women's Question, as offensive as it may be at times, was part of his ongoing dialogue with important socio-political phenomena in the late nineteenth century.

Chapter 5 deals with a slightly different set of issues that arose during Nietzsche's lifetime: colonialism and German overseas settlements, especially in the Americas. Germany was a late European entrant in the competition for colonies, finally managing to secure a small colonial empire in 1884. Discussions about colonization were particularly intense at that time, but they occurred in various forms during the previous decade as well. Nietzsche was involved with the discourse on colonies in two ways. First, he became acquainted with colonial movements through his brother-in-law, Bernhard Förster (1843–1889), who, in 1885, along with Nietzsche's sister Elisabeth (1846–1935), founded a German colony in Paraguay, Nueva Germania. Although emigration colonies such as Nueva Germania were different from colonies controlled and administered by a European power, such as German Southwest Africa, in many publications of the era, both were considered part of the larger colonial enterprise. They share a nationalist sentiment, one that Nietzsche came to abhor, and a large part of Nietzsche's reaction to colonization must be considered part of his rejection of German nationalism. But a further dimension of Förster's colony was the anti-Semitism of its founder. Förster was a member of the extended circle of Wagnerians, and, sharing Wagner's views on contemporary Jewry, he helped organize the Anti-Semites' Petition in 1881–82. His colonial venture was in large part a consequence of his anti-Semitism, since he sought to establish a settlement free from the influence of Jewry, which he believed dominated contemporary Europe. This chapter deals in the first instance with Nietzsche's connection with this colonial effort, his ambivalence toward the colony in remarks to correspondents, and his reaction to news about colonies and colonialism as a result of his sister's involvement. But it also takes up Nietzsche's larger and more philosophical response to the colonial movement, encapsulated in the notions of the "good European" and "great politics," both of which became prominent in his writings of the 1880s. The former concept refers explicitly to Nietzsche's alternative to the nationalism dominant in the Europe of his era, and it can be found in writings already in the late 1870s. Although it functions in most of his works as a counter to the pettiness and chauvinism in contemporary Europe, at times it also encompasses a desire for European nations to produce a ruling caste to reign over the entire world. "Great politics" appears in his writings primarily as a response to the political pretensions of Otto von Bismarck and the German Second Empire, but on occasion it also partakes of hegemonic demands to exercise unrestrained power across the globe. While Nietzsche thus eschewed the nationalist, mercantile, and utopian/idealist versions of colonization, he developed along the lines of his own philosophy a conceptual framework that entailed a rudimentary and Eurocentric geopolitical perspective. Good Europeanism and great politics are untimely in negating the nationalist and class ideologies of his era, but they partake in dimensions of contemporary colonial discourse in advocating a hierarchical structure for a new, non-national world order in which the European continent will dominate the world.

In the sixth chapter, we return to Germany to examine one of the most controversial issues of the day, the Jewish Question. Nietzsche lived at a time when anti-Jewish sentiments were growing, in part owing to the nationalist fervor emerging from German unification, and in part owing to the rapid industrialization of Germany, in which Jews played a role in industry and finance. Jews were also identified as leading members of the National Liberal Party, which ruled Germany with Bismarck in the 1870s. Nietzsche's familiarity with Jews and Judaism in his early years was probably not very extensive: there were few Jews living in Prussian Saxony, and the information he obtained about Jews was likely mediated by the church and local lore. There are almost no mentions of the topic in his early notebooks. Nietzsche's first real encounter with Judeophobic sentiments occurs when he matriculated at Leipzig in 1865, where there was a resident Jewish population and an increase in Jewish presence at the annual fairs. For the first time, we read anti-Jewish remarks from Nietzsche and his friends. Nietzsche's acquaintance with Richard Wagner in 1868 increased his exposure to racist ideology. Wagner had harbored racial prejudice against the Jews since the 1840s, and in 1869 he republished his Judeophobic diatribe *Judaism in Music*. Nietzsche was a frequent visitor in the Wagner household and witnessed much of the public reaction to this anti-Jewish tract. Indeed, Nietzsche endeavored to emulate the Meister by making his own comments about the deleterious nature of the Jewish press, but Wagner and his future wife Cosima (1837–1930) discouraged Nietzsche from direct references to contemporary Jewry. Accordingly, his published works of the 1870s contain no direct references to Jews, but there are obvious allusions to Jewry in the barely concealed Judeophobic "cultural code" he adopted. After breaking with Wagner, Nietzsche's published remarks become more favorable toward Jews, but ambivalence remains in his sentiments and is more easily discerned in his notebooks and in his relations with Jewish acquaintances. The 1880s brought the rise of a political anti-Semitic movement to Germany, and Nietzsche was exposed to it through his publisher, a leader of the movement in Saxony; his brother-in-law, one of the notorious anti-Semites in

Germany; and the Wagnerians with whom he still had contact. Nietzsche was vehemently opposed to political anti-Semitism because of the personal damage it caused his reputation through his publisher and sister, and on principle because it was associated in his mind with Christian, socialist, anarchist, and other modern movements of *ressentiment*. His opposition to anti-Semitism did not alter his anti-Jewish sentiments, however; he continued to believe there was a Jewish Question that needed a solution, and in most cases he proposes intermarriage, which would foster good Jewish traits, while eliminating those that were unfavorable. In his later works, he develops theories that connect ancient Jewry with the rise of slave morality. Judaism is thus considered the root cause of the decline of noble values and the resulting predominance of ascetic ideals and decadence in the contemporary world.

The last three chapters focus on Nietzsche's forays into the natural sciences and the philosophical conclusions supported by his understanding of scientific theories. Undoubtedly the most important scientific event of the nineteenth century was the publication of Charles Darwin's (1809–1882) *On the Origin of Species* in 1859 and the acceptance of evolution as an explanation for the development of organic life, including *Homo sapiens*. The Evolution Question was very much alive by the time Nietzsche graduated from Pforta in 1864 and started his studies at the University of Bonn, and we find that during the 1860s he gained exposure secondhand to Darwin's hypothesis, as well as to objections to natural selection on the part of numerous scientists of the time. Important for the mediation of evolutionary theory in these early years was Friedrich Albert Lange's (1828–1875) *History of Materialism* (1866), which was generally a source for much of Nietzsche's early knowledge about scientific developments in the nineteenth century. But Nietzsche also came into contact with Ludwig Rütimeyer (1825–1895) and with texts by other biologists who commented on Darwin. Important for Nietzsche at this early stage was not simply natural selection, but the alternatives and modifications to this hypothesis posited by the scientific community. We find that Nietzsche, at an early age, following various discourses on evolution, harbors doubts about the mechanism for development proposed by Darwin. Even in his earliest writings, however, he was just as interested in the ethical and philosophical implications of evolution, and these aspects continued to occupy his attention into his more mature work in the 1880s. At the beginning of the decade, he read three books that had a significant impact on his understanding of evolution and its ramifications. The first was *The Struggle of the Parts in the Organism* (1881), written by the German anatomist and embryologist Wilhelm Roux (1850–1924). Roux postulates that adaptation can be observed in embryonic development and involves struggles internal to the organism, a hypothesis that resonates with Nietzsche's vitalist philosophy. A second book that influenced Nietzsche was William Rolph's (1847–1883) *Biological Problems*

(1884), which maintains that evolution does not receive its major impulse from scarcity, but from superfluity; Nietzsche refers directly to this thesis in *Beyond Good and Evil* (JGB 262, KSA 5.214–17), and Rolph's work supported his notion of the will to power, which similarly proposes an expansionist perspective on change. Nietzsche was also influenced by Carl von Nägeli's (1817–1891) *A Mechanical-Physiological Theory of Organic Evolution* (1884). A Swiss botanist noted for his study of cell formation and plant physiology, Nägeli believed that Darwin offered only a partial solution to the mechanism for evolution, and his positing of an internal drive to supplement the external factors in Darwin's hypothesis was appealing to Nietzsche, who rejected a process based solely on determinants outside the organism. Nietzsche's interaction with evolutionary theory is perhaps most evident in his hypothesis of an "overman" as a further evolutionary step beyond the human being. The criticisms of Darwin in his writings are not due to a rejection of evolution, but to philosophical differences relating to perceived implications of natural selection. That Nietzsche's biologism of the 1880s has been so often ignored is in part the consequence of philosophers like Martin Heidegger (1889–1976) removing him from the discourses with which he was so intimately involved and interpreting him solely as a thinker preoccupied with purely speculative concerns in ontology and metaphysics.

A similar neglect of Nietzsche's involvement with the scientific theories of his age is remedied in the eighth chapter, which deals with his views on cosmology and their implications for his late philosophy. Lange's *History of Materialism* again plays a major role in the 1860s in his understanding of the physical nature of the universe, but Nietzsche devoted himself more assiduously to topics dealing with thermodynamics, matter, and force only in the 1880s, when he posited two of the most important concepts for his mature philosophy: the eternal recurrence of the same and the will to power. Eternal recurrence is introduced in *The Gay Science* (1882) and in *Zarathustra*, and Nietzsche claims that it was the result of a revelation in August 1881. But we can find theories of recurrence frequently articulated in works Nietzsche must have known prior to that summer. Heraclitus is the most obvious source from antiquity, although we could also cite, as Nietzsche does at one point, the Pythagoreans. In Nietzsche's era there are many illustrations, from the poet Heinrich Heine, whom Nietzsche read and admired, to various French thinkers contemporaneous with Nietzsche. Although Nietzsche's discussion of eternal recurrence in his published writings is often framed as a hypothetical and presented with metaphorical language, in his notebooks it is obvious that Nietzsche was reflecting on the first and second laws of thermodynamics when he contemplated the possibility of all things repeating in exactly the same manner throughout all eternity. In the 1870s, we already find Nietzsche reading about the conservation of energy, but he intensifies his scientific study just prior to his "revelation" of 1881. Nietzsche accepts the notion of a finite amount of energy in the universe and an infinite duration of time. The first law of thermodynamics thus poses no difficulties for his hypothesis, but the second principle, which involves entropy in a system, does. Nietzsche's notebooks during the 1880s frequently argue against stasis or equilibrium as an end stage, since, Nietzsche reasons, in an infinite amount of time, if equilibrium could have been attained, it would have already occurred. Thus Nietzsche joins a large chorus of scientists and intellectuals in the nineteenth century disputing what was called "heat death"; for Nietzsche, it cannot obtain because it contradicts eternal recurrence. For eternal recurrence to function properly, however, Nietzsche needs to have recourse to energy as the sole content of the universe, and for energy to be expansive rather than static. Nietzsche found the sort of theory he needed for recurrence and for the will to power, which made recurrence function, in Roger Boscovich (1711–1787), the eighteenth-century Jesuit scientist Nietzsche read in the early 1870s and extols in *Beyond Good and Evil*. But in the 1880s, we find Nietzsche frequently consulting works by writers who embrace, as he does, monistic dynamism as an alternative to traditional, mechanistic materialism. The writings of Johannes Vogt (1843–1920), Otto Caspari (1841–1917), Otto Schmitz-Dumont (1835–1897), and Maximilian Drossbach (1810–1884) serve for Nietzsche as confirmation of a cosmology that incorporates the will to power and eternal recurrence.

The final chapter in this study deals with the pseudoscience of eugenics. In the wake of evolutionary theory, there arose considerable commentary reflecting on social engineering. This commentary was fueled by the increasing attention accorded to hypotheses of degeneration. The earliest nineteenth-century text dealing with degeneration was Bénédict-Augustin Morel's (1809–1873) *Traité des dégénérescences de l'espèce humaine* (1857), but since it predates Darwin, its focus is less on positive and negative eugenic regimes than on treatment of the observable manifestations of degeneration, in particular alcohol, but also other maladies associated with modern life. After Darwin, we encounter an optimistic and a pessimistic version of the progress of the species: for Darwin, Herbert Spencer (1820–1903), and many other scientists, as well as scientifically inclined philosophers, the human species appeared to be improving, becoming more moral and more civilized. But even the optimistic evolutionist had to admit occasionally that under current conditions in society the "fittest" do not always survive best, and that humanity runs the risk of declining as a species because of wars, which remove the best men from procreation, and the tendency to protect lives that were formerly unable to survive the harshness of disease or the ravages of nature. Nietzsche was among those who were convinced that egalitarian movements in modern society militated against an improvement of the species, but he was certainly not alone in this belief. Several of the English and French sources available to him reached similar conclusions. We find in Nietzsche's thought of the 1880s an increasing concern with degeneration as a biological phenomenon and an attraction to books that deal with these issues. Especially important for Nietzsche in his most mature works were the role of Christianity and its advocacy of charity toward those less fortunate in the social order. Many of his most forceful arguments are directed against a religion that preserves individuals who are unfit for procreation and the embrace of pity, which serves only to direct our sympathies toward those unworthy of life. Like many contemporaries, Nietzsche latched onto the larger European discourse that linked criminality, social disorder, alcoholism, prostitution, and sexual "perversions" as part of a complex that must be eliminated if the human species is going to reach its true potential. Nietzsche was fascinated by eugenic solutions, writing in his notebooks about who should have the right to procreate, how we can make certain that the sexual impulses of the masses are satisfied without procreation, and what the rules should be for promoting an improvement of the species through taxations of various sorts and alternatives to traditional marriage, for example, term marriages. Nietzsche showed great interest in the writings of Francis Galton (1822–1911), Darwin's cousin and the inventor of the term eugenics, and in eugenic speculation in books he read. He even read an anonymous treatise devoted entirely to the topic: *The Aristocracy of the Spirit as a Solution to the Social Question* (1885). Increasingly, remarks in published and unpublished writings of his last sane years view the world and its ills in terms of biological solutions, and endorse past social orders that regulated marriage and procreation.

A brief conclusion discusses the interconnectedness of the topics in these nine discourses and what other issues might have been included in a study of his timeliness. I then turn to three sets of questions concerning the relevance of social and scientific concerns for what has been understood as his philosophy, the use of unpublished materials to examine Nietzsche's views, and how the conclusions in this study might affect the prevailing views on Nietzsche and his importance as a great philosopher.

Chapter 1

The Education Question

During the early 1870s, Nietzsche was preoccupied with two large areas of interest, as he drifted away from the academic life and his professional studies in classical philology. The first was the perceived renaissance in German and European culture spearheaded by the genial and charismatic personality of the composer Richard Wagner (1813–1883). Indeed, much of Nietzsche's writing and thought during the first half of the 1870s was directly related to Wagner and to mutual concerns, such as the philosophy of Arthur Schopenhauer (1788–1860). During these years, the effect on Nietzsche of Wagner as a person and of the Wagnerian cult on his life can hardly be exaggerated. After Nietzsche ceased activity in classical scholarship, almost everything he published until the appearance of *Human, All Too Human* (1878) was directly or indirectly inspired by his association with the composer. Although his first nonphilological work, *The Birth of Tragedy* (1872), can be conceived as an attempt to unite his classical education with his veneration of Wagner, it resonated only with Wagner and Wagnerians, and was almost completely neglected by conventional scholars of ancient Greece. The first *Untimely Meditation*, which was an attack on the liberal Hegelian David Strauß (1808–1874), can be conceived as a commission from Wagner: it seems Strauß had supported one of Wagner's musical rivals in Munich for the post of orchestral conductor [*Kapellmeister*], and the Meister had convinced his enthusiastic young supporter to act as a tool for revenge because Strauß had opposed him.[1] *Schopenhauer as Educator* (1874), although not about Wagner, was an essay on the philosophical link between Nietzsche and Wagner; indeed, at their very first meeting in 1868 Schopenhauer had been one of the topics of conversation, and their mutual admiration for the philosopher of pessimism continued until their friendship ended. The final *Meditation*, *Richard Wagner in Bayreuth* (1876), which was sent special delivery to Wagner in July of 1876, a month before the opening of the new opera house, is obviously celebratory in character—although the attentive reader can already detect some of the misgivings that would surface more openly in Nietzsche's later writings on the composer.

In Nietzsche's private life, Wagner assumed a prominent place almost immediately. Two months after he met Wagner, Nietzsche wrote to his friend and fellow classicist Erwin Rohde (1845–1898) about his experience and expressed an admiration that would last well into the mid-1870s: "I have extreme confidence that we can agree entirely about a genius who appears to me like an insoluble problem and whom I make new efforts to understand year in and year out: this genius is Richard Wagner." For Nietzsche, Wagner is the "living illustration" of what Schopenhauer meant when he used the word genius, and it is evident that his worship of Wagner goes hand in hand with his adulation of Schopenhauer (9 December 1868, Nr. 604, KSB 2.352). In his correspondence during the next eight years, Nietzsche would frequently allude to his visits to Wagner and his wife Cosima,[2] the plans for Bayreuth, and Wagnerian music. Nietzsche's entire mental economy and social life were arranged for many years around Wagner and Wagnerians. Nietzsche reported to Rohde in January 1869 that upon learning of his appointment to the extraordinary professorship at Basel, he spent the entire afternoon walking around singing melodies from Wagner's *Tannhäuser* (Nr. 608, KSB 2.359). A few years later, obviously feeling that as a professor he was not contributing enough to the "cause," he contemplated resigning his position at Basel to embark on a lecture tour throughout Germany promoting Wagner and his works. Nietzsche traveled to Bayreuth in May of 1872 for the official ceremony laying the cornerstone for the Bayreuth opera house. In early October of 1873, he was evidently asked to provide some written material that could be used for fundraising, and although he first tried to convince Rohde to undertake this task (18 October 1873, Nr. 319, KSB 4.167), he actually did compose an "Admonition to the Germans" in late October as a propaganda piece for the Wagnerian mission. In this pamphlet, which was evidently rejected by the Wagnerians,[3] Nietzsche tried to convince his reader that the building of the Bayreuth opera house is not simply the enterprise of a small group, but rather an important cultural undertaking for the "benefit and the honor of the German spirit and of the German name." Wagner is apostrophized as "the great, valiant, indomitable, unflagging warrior," whose ideas, as they are manifested in Bayreuth, have reached "their last and final form and a truly victorious perfection" (MD, KSA 1.893–94). Indeed, most of Nietzsche's closest friends in the 1870s—and even some people with whom he remained on good terms after his break with Wagner—he either met through Wagner or Wagnerians, or himself introduced to the Wagner circle. In these years of Wagnerian discipleship, the relationship between Nietzsche and Wagner was not one of equals, however, as it may appear today. Although Nietzsche's last essay on Wagner, *Nietzsche contra Wagner*, produced in 1888 and published after Nietzsche had lapsed into insanity, would try to convince the reader that the two men possess equal stature, this parity existed only in Nietzsche's mind. When they met, Wagner was fifty-five years old and had already completed several major operas known throughout Europe; Nietzsche was a twenty-four-year-old philology student. When Wagner died in 1883, Nietzsche was still identified chiefly as a Wagnerian, no matter how much in his own mind he had distanced himself from Bayreuth. Much has been written on the relationship between the two men, but the fact is that Wagner was considerably more important for Nietzsche, right up until his final moments of sanity, than Nietzsche was for Wagner.[4]

A second and related large area of concern that occupies Nietzsche's thoughts and activity during the early and mid-1870s is education and the educational system. That Nietzsche was concerned with schools and universities is really not very surprising: outside of his brief stints in the military in 1867–68 and in 1870, he had been either a student or a teacher at a high school or at a university since he enrolled in a German *Gymnasium* in 1855. For many years, Nietzsche's life had an academic trajectory: educated in a private preparatory institute and then for three years at Naumburg's Cathedral *Gymnasium* before transferring to Pforta, where young men were groomed for university studies and often for careers as scholars,[5] Nietzsche was set on a path, even before he reached his teens, that involved an intimate involvement with traditional educational institutions. Furthermore, his concern with education was intimately connected with his cliquish and—at times—fanatic enthusiasm for Schopenhauer and Wagner. We can best understand the connection between Nietzsche's two primary areas of interest if we consider the German notion of *Bildung*. Translated often as "education" and connected intimately with the goals of the German educational system, *Bildung* actually refers to a general acculturation that may or may not be achieved through formal institutions. It was the central goal for the neo-humanist educational philosophy of Wilhelm von Humboldt (1767–1835), who was the founder of the University of Berlin and the chief architect of educational reform in Prussia at the beginning of the nineteenth century. For Humboldt and for Nietzsche, *Bildung* relates to the culture of a society as much as it does to its system of training and instruction, and Nietzsche was certainly not alone in measuring the achievements of Germany in the 1870s by examining the quality of *Bildung* among his peers. Indeed, the deficiencies Nietzsche noted in the culture of the Second Reich were in large part responsible for his embrace of Richard Wagner and a cultural mission he believed would rival the excellences of the ancient world that he had come to admire so much in his studies. *Bildung* thus forms a bridge between culture and pedagogy, and these latter two notions are intimately connected in the German mind, even today the ministry in charge of education is most commonly called the "cultural ministry" [*Kultusministerium*]. In devoting himself to the spread of Schopenhauer's philosophy and Wagner's music, Nietzsche was convinced that he was promoting a culture worthy of the newly established Second Empire and its political power. In criticizing the present condition of the schools—in particular those devoted to higher education and the preparation for university study—and in suggesting the necessity for a drastic reorientation, he was affirming a cultural objective consonant with his philosophical perspective.

This cultural objective was in harmony with his philological views as well, and although Nietzsche had largely abandoned activity in scholarship surrounding the ancient world by 1872, his admiration for central aspects of the classical tradition remained undiminished. In *The Birth of Tragedy* (1872), Nietzsche's notion of cultural excellence was largely defined by his views of ancient Greece prior to the advent of Socrates as a philosopher and Euripides as a playwright. His hope for the newly unified German Reich, as well as his later criticism of Germany, was always connected with a cultural ideal derived from the Hellenic world. Nietzsche, as much as anyone in his generation, is the heir of a German "Grecophilia" that had been such an important feature in the intellectual atmosphere since the latter part of the eighteenth century.[6] This tradition, which had been established in the writings of the art historian Johann Joachim Winckelmann (1717–1768) and the classicism of Johann Wolfgang von Goethe (1749–1832) and Friedrich Schiller (1759–1805), was taken on a somewhat different path by Nietzsche, who emphasized *agon* (struggle), inequality, and slavery in Greek life, as well as Dionysian excesses. But Nietzsche, like his idealist predecessors, looked to the ancients for a paradigm of excellence and achievement in the contemporary world. Any time he wants to cite a counterillustration to the cultural depravity or pretentiousness he felt was pervasive in his own era, he looks to the ancient world. A large part of Nietzsche's frustration, particularly in his early years, is thus related to the disappointment he feels when Germany falls short of realizing the reincarnation of Greek culture in the modern world. His impatience with his contemporaries stems from their failure to understand that their recently achieved political unity means nothing if it is not accompanied by cultural achievements that will rival those of Hellenic society. Thus in the second of his *Untimely Meditations, On the Advantage and Disadvantage of History for Life* (1874), he upbraids his compatriots[7] for their myopic and smug contentment with the unification following the Franco-Prussian War and the attendant superficiality in cultural values. "I shall explicitly set down my testimony here," he writes at the close of the fourth section, "that it is German unity in that highest sense for which we strive and strive far more ardently than political reunification, the unity of the German spirit and life after the annihilation of the opposition of form and content, of inwardness and convention" (HL 4, KSA 1.278). This essay—to which we shall turn in more detail later in this chapter—is thus an admonition to Germany—although Nietzsche was a resident of Switzerland at the time, he obviously still felt himself to be a German—that the real work remained unaccomplished despite victory on the battlefield. Unlike his Enlightenment predecessors, he is centrally concerned not with a regeneration of humankind or the propagation of democratic institutions, but with a rebirth of "true culture," the restoration of health, and the recovery of instincts and integrity (HL 4, KSA 1.275) in Germany. In this *Meditation* from early 1874, he is still exhorting and agitating for Germany to become Greece; as the years progressed and his disappointment with his countrymen mounted, his invectives against Germany became sharper, and his tolerance for the failure to effect a modern turn toward ancient values diminished drastically.

Nietzsche's Experience with Educational Institutions

The thematic concentration in Nietzsche's university training and subsequent scholarship, as well as his musical enthusiasm and cultural engagement for the Wagnerian cause, intersect conveniently with his pedagogical critiques and reveilles. Already in November of 1870, we find him contemplating a critique of the Prussian educational system. Writing to his friend Carl von Gersdorff (1844–1904) following his own discharge from military service as a medic—shortly after joining the military, Nietzsche contracted dysentery and diphtheria and spent most of September and October 1870 recuperating—he confesses that he has grave concerns about cultural developments in Germany. He recognizes that Prussia is the leading political power in the German federation and in what will become a newly united German state, but writes that he considers "Prussia a highly dangerous power for culture." His determination to "expose" Prussian education "publicly" is obviously conceived as a way to counter or correct the perils he senses in Prussian hegemony (Nr. 107, KSB 3.155). Nietzsche's critique was not produced immediately; he first had to complete work on *The Birth of Tragedy*, but immediately after its publication at the beginning of 1872, he returns to the project he had evidently conceived while recuperating from the illnesses contracted during the Franco-Prussian War. Nietzsche kept his word: he did "expose" Prussian education "publicly." His critique of contemporary education and his suggestions for reform were delivered forcefully and provocatively in a lecture series Nietzsche agreed to give with the title "On the Future of Our Educational Institutions."[8] Delivered from January to March in 1872[9] in the auditorium of the university museum in Basel as public and popular events—not university and academic lectures—these five lectures were his first sustained effort to deal with education, its possibilities, and its importance for the creation of greatness in German culture.[10] By all accounts they were a huge success.[11] According to Nietzsche, approximately three hundred people attended each lecture, and this enthusiastic response probably contributed to his initial intention to publish them as a small volume.[12] Although he eventually decided that they were not ready for dissemination in print, the notions he develops in them are echoed often in his subsequent writings, especially the second and third essays of his *Untimely Meditations*. These lectures, therefore, provide important insight into perhaps the most important facet of Nietzsche's early professional life, his pedagogical engagement at institutions in Basel, and his main cultural concern, the Wagnerian rebirth of German and European art; and despite his resignation from the teaching profession in 1879 and his increasing pessimism with regard to educational reform, we can still find echoes of his early critique of education and of his adherence to the notion of *Bildung* in his writings from the last year of his life. It is probably fair to say that he never relinquished this Humboldtian ideal, although he gradually became convinced that it could not be achieved through the state and its educational institutions.

The fact that Nietzsche was delivering public lectures for the citizens of Basel and that he was taking up topics related to educational institutions was neither unusual nor untimely. It was common for professors to offer presentations to the general public, and Nietzsche himself had already done so with his inaugural lecture in 1869 on "Homer and Classical Philology," which was likewise given in the auditorium of the city museum, and with two subsequent lectures in 1870 on classical topics in the identical venue.[13] In Basel there was a significant patrician and highly educated class that attended lectures on various learned topics. Nietzsche's specific theme, educational institutions and how they can be improved, was a quite common topic in his era, especially with the rapidly shifting patterns of education in Germany during the nineteenth century. There were scores of articles, essays, and pamphlets dealing with the *Gymnasium*, as well as the *Realschule*,[14] and although Nietzsche makes no reference to specific essays, we know that he was familiar with at least a portion of the vast literature on education produced in his time. Nor was it exceptional that a noted philosopher or scholar would deal with these issues. A few years after Nietzsche's lecture series in Basel, Eduard von Hartmann (1842–1906), the target of Nietzsche's derision in the second *Untimely Meditation*, advocated in print for a unified type of secondary school that would combine the traditional, classical *Gymnasium* and the more practically oriented *Realschule*;[15] noted scientists, such as Hermann von Helmholtz (1821–1894) or Emil du Bois-Reymond (1818–1896), contributed their views urging more attention to the natural sciences in secondary schools;[16] Heinrich von Treitschke (1834–1896), like Nietzsche, wrote about the need for genuine education to counteract the wayward tendencies of modernity;[17] and the philosopher and later Nobelist Rudolf Eucken (1846–1926), who had been Nietzsche's colleague at Basel in 1871 before moving to Jena three years later, wrote several essays collected under the title "The Struggle for the Gymnasium," in which he defends the focus on the ancient world in secondary education.[18]

What was perhaps a bit unusual in Nietzsche's lectures is that they do not culminate in concrete plans for the reform of the educational system. As Nietzsche notes in the preface to his lectures, his auditors should not expect "at the close, as a result, tables. I do not promise," he continues, "tables and new hourly course plans for the *Gymnasium* and the *Realschulen*," and while he professes to admire those who have acquired such a sovereign overview that they can produce "the most sterile regulations and the most elegant tables," he will not similarly satisfy "table enthusiasts" in his book.[19] With these remarks, Nietzsche is referring to the many contemporary articles and essays on education that argue for modification of the attention devoted to one subject or another and include a course plan in a tabular conclusion to a discursive argument. But Nietzsche's contribution to educational theory and practice differs most from those he read in the narrative he constructs for critiquing current practice and discussing directions for reform. The lectures are framed as a modification on Socratic dialogues. Nietzsche portrays himself as a young student at Bonn, who goes with a friend on a late summer day to practice shooting pistols.[20] Arriving at the edge of a forest, the friends encounter an older man accompanied by a dog and a younger companion. The older man, who is referred to as "the philosopher," and who is very likely modeled on Nietzsche's image of Schopenhauer, convinces the friends to cease their shooting and to cede to him their rights to this area. The lectures purport to record various conversations conducted by the philosopher with his companion and with the students. It is not immediately apparent how this framework contributes to Nietzsche's goals. Placing the bulk of the discussion in the mouth of an older and wiser man may give his ideas more weight, and the dialogic nature of the text permits an airing of objections to arguments and correction of details. But this frame, as we shall see, also presents us with some indication of what real education should be, and certainly one of Nietzsche's points is that genuine *Bildung* is not necessarily imparted as part of university attendance and student activities, which in these lectures are characterized by the nonintellectual and almost pointless sport of shooting pistols, but entails the encounter with, and the encouragement of, geniality.

Nietzsche's own educational experience was in many ways elite, and it certainly included a rigorous contact with ancient texts and cultures, but the institutions in which he was enrolled appear in retrospect to have fallen short of what Nietzsche in 1873 considered schools that would promote genuine *Bildung*. After spending some time at the local elementary school after his family moved to Naumburg in 1850, Nietzsche received instruction at a private institute whose purpose was to prepare him for entrance to the city's Cathedral *Gymnasium* [*Domgymnasium*]. The Naumburg Cathedral *Gymnasium* was an excellent school, and although it did not carry the prestige associated with Pforta, the boarding school about four miles from Naumburg that Nietzsche attended from 1858 to 1864, it had an outstanding faculty and an academic rigor that rivaled the more renowned institution. After examining the source materials for these institutions, Thomas Brobjer has concluded that "the difference between the *Domgymnasium* and Schulpforta was not as great as has been assumed," and even in the area of classical antiquity, for which Pforta was justly celebrated, the hometown school had extremely high standards. The main difference between the two institutions was that Pforta attracted a more eminent faculty, if we evaluate eminence by the number of teachers with a doctorate, or who carry the title of "Professor." If we believe Nietzsche's own accounts, he worked extremely hard at the *Domgymnasium*, often studying until late in the evening. Most of the earlier biographical accounts of Nietzsche's youth emphasize his brilliance as a student, and they explain his transfer to Pforta with a scholarship after three years at the Cathedral *Gymnasium* as the result of his accomplishments and superior intelligence. It turns out, however, that Nietzsche was a rather mediocre pupil in Naumburg; indeed, in his third semester he received an average of "4," which would be the equivalent of a letter grade of "D" or the grade just above passing in the American system.[21] The only area in which Nietzsche consistently achieved the highest marks was conduct. The offer Nietzsche's mother received for her son to attend Pforta with a scholarship was the consequence of the premature death of Nietzsche's father, Carl Ludwig Nietzsche (1813–1849), and his service as a village pastor in Röcken. Pforta was a boarding school that drew students from across Germany, and it offered many scholarships to young men who were orphaned or whose fathers were deceased. Nietzsche's good fortune in gaining admission therefore has little to do with his achievements in Naumburg, where he worked hard, but was evidently not a particularly inspiring or inspired student.[22]

We should continue to view Nietzsche's six years at Pforta as extremely important for him and his personal development, but educationally they represent a continuation rather than a rupture with his previous experience. Schulpforta or Pforta is situated on the grounds of a former Cistercian monastery, but it had been a boarding school since the middle of the sixteenth century. It was well known for its devout Christianity, as well as its excellence in classical antiquity, and sported a long list of distinguished graduates, including the poet Friedrich Gottlieb Klopstock (1724–1803), the philosopher Johann Gottlieb Fichte (1762–1814), and the historian Leopold von Ranke (1795–1886). There were approximately two hundred students at Pforta during the years Nietzsche attended; his class contained just over forty pupils, but there was fairly steady attrition over the next few years, and by the time Nietzsche graduated not more than twenty had achieved their diploma [*Abitur*].[23] Nietzsche had to repeat a semester in his initial year, which may simply indicate the higher standards at Pforta, but may also be related to his rather mediocre performance at the *Domgymnasium*. Nietzsche continued to be a hard worker at Pforta, and here his diligence paid off since he was the number-one student in his class [*Primus*] several times over the next six years. Whether his success was attributable to the preparation he received at the *Domgymnasium* or simply to him coming into his own is impossible to ascertain. We do know that he was educated at Pforta in the humanist tradition, which meant that a large number of hours was devoted to the study of ancient languages. If we judge by weekly hours in the class plan, Latin was by far the most important subject; pupils took ten or eleven hours per week. They also had six hours of Greek throughout their education, and in the upper classes two hours of Hebrew. Disciplines that became increasingly important for the nineteenth century, and that were taught more intensively at *Realschulen*, mathematics and natural sciences, or modern foreign languages (French), were of minor concern at Pforta. Although four hours per week were devoted to mathematics, the only science taught at Pforta was physics, which the pupils attended for two hours in their final year, the same amount of time allotted to lessons in French. According to Nietzsche's sister Elisabeth, his "4" (or "D") in mathematics threatened his graduation, but the Greek instructor purportedly put the mathematics teacher in place by telling him: "Do you really want to fail the most talented pupil that Pforta has had since I've been here?"[24] Nietzsche would come to regret many of the deficiencies in natural science and modern languages that he experienced at Pforta, and much of his reading during the 1870s and 1880s was intended to redress these educational shortcomings. But the training he received in Naumburg and at Pforta prepared him well for his university studies in classical philology and aided him in securing the position of professor at Basel.

Nietzsche had one other experience in secondary education that was important for his lecture series in 1873. When he was appointed professor in Basel in 1869, the position entailed not only eight hours of instruction at the university, but also six hours at the *Pädagogium*, which during the years 1817–80 was the designation for the Basler institution that comprised the last three years of the *Gymnasium*. The *Pädagogium* was therefore the primary preparatory school for Basler students who intended to enroll at the university, although it also had the official function of training "judicious" civil servants so that they would be "educated men" in their professional circles. Many of the students came from the patrician class in Basel—several Burckhardts, for example, were at one point or another enrolled in Nietzsche's courses in the *Pädagogium*—and most pursued, or intended to pursue, careers in one or another profession. We should not consider teaching at the *Pädagogium* to be a punishment or a sign that Nietzsche was not highly regarded as a teacher and a scholar. Most members of the instructional staff were professors; a university regulation from 1818 committed faculty to devote a significant amount of their teaching to the *Pädagogium*.[25] When in 1869 Wilhelm Vischer-Bilfinger (1808–1874), the Basler professor in charge of finding a new classical philologist, contacted Friedrich Ritschl (1806–1876), Nietzsche's doctoral adviser, Ritschl spoke with Nietzsche and received assurances from his student that he was willing to teach six hours in the *Pädagogium* along with his professorial duties at the university.[26] Jacob Burckhardt (1818–1897), perhaps the most illustrious faculty member in Basel during this period, taught history at this preparatory school for thirty-five years, but he was only one of many distinguished scholars to engage in instruction at the secondary level. The *Pädagogium* was therefore unusual in the European world of secondary education, rivaled in the German-speaking countries perhaps only by an institution such as Schulpforta, and Nietzsche was fortunate to have experienced as a student and a teacher two of the most outstanding secondary schools in all of Europe.

Nietzsche was charged with instruction in Greek, teaching six hours to the most advanced students. At the *Pädagogium*, ancient languages usually occupied almost half the total hours of instruction in a week, and although only Latin was obligatory, most students also enrolled in Greek. Those who did not were nicknamed "barbarians," a word the Greeks themselves used to designate those who did not speak their language, and most students who opted out of Greek were by this point in their careers attending the *Realschule* or a trade school. By all accounts, Nietzsche was a diligent, inspiring, and beloved teacher. He himself comments on his success in *Ecce Homo*: "During the seven years in which I taught Greek to the top form of the Basel preparatory school [*Pädagogium*], I never once had occasion to mete out a punishment; the laziest were industrious when they were with me" (EH, Warum ich so weise bin 4, KSA 6.269). Although his autobiographical reports are often self-serving and should not be taken at face value, his assertions are confirmed by various independent sources. He joined a faculty, on which he was the youngest instructor; the Latin professor, Franz Dorotheus Gerlach (1793–1876), had already taught at the *Pädagogium* for a half century when Nietzsche arrived. Nietzsche was therefore closer in age and interests to his young charges, and was less old-fashioned in his dress, manners, and relationship to the pupils. He also brought with him new ideas, but in contrast to the lectures he presented in 1873, Nietzsche did not hesitate to engage himself on a more concrete and mundane level in suggesting reforms at the *Pädagogium*. In a letter sent to educational officials in the summer of 1875, Nietzsche makes five proposals for changes in the instruction of Greek. He suggests first that pupils do not have enough exposure to the language and would recommend an additional year of mandatory study, for which he suggests the name "Selecta." He also proposes that pupils who want to study medicine, who were hitherto required to take only Latin, be obliged to receive training in Greek. Furthermore, he recommends that all classes of Greek use one grammar book, Ernst Koch's (b. 1839) *Griechische Schulgrammatik* (1869). And he concludes his petition to the authorities by providing a list of the writings a pupil must have read to be considered educated in Greek, and the curriculum for each of the three grade levels.[27] Nietzsche was unsuccessful in his overly ambitious program for an additional year of, and a more exhaustive training in, Greek, but his suggestion that all pupils, including prospective medical students, enroll in Greek was eventually accepted, and Koch's grammar was adopted for all forms. Nietzsche's activities were not restricted to substantive issues of curriculum. The same professor who disdained including tables in his discussion of future educational institutions delved into considerable details of school organization while an active pedagogue. During his very first term in Basel, he suggested that the arrangement of Greek instruction be modified so that no more than two hours would occur on any given day. In 1873, he proposed that attendance be kept by the top student in the class [*Primus*]. The following year he was appointed to a committee to explore the introduction of chemistry into the curriculum, and in the same year he advocated unsuccessfully that the rubric "diligence" be eliminated from report cards. Indeed, in August of 1871 Nietzsche engaged himself in the battle to eliminate the disturbance coming from wagon noise on the square adjacent to the school, suggesting to city officials that they undertake pavement of the road and introduce speed limits. The petition went through bureaucratic channels, but was ultimately rejected; the city recommended instead that the school try to reach an understanding with the owners of the vehicles in question.[28]

Expansion of Education

Nietzsche obviously turned his thoughts to loftier questions when he lectured on education to the Basel citizenry in early 1872. The title of this lecture series merits some attention, since it indicates the higher and more ideal focus of his discussions. Nietzsche uses the word *Bildungsanstalten*, which has usually been translated, somewhat inaccurately and following past precedent, as "educational institutions" to avoid the clumsier, but more accurate "institutions for *Bildung*."[29] In the lectures themselves, Nietzsche is careful to distinguish *Erziehunganstalten* [educational institutions] from *Bildungsanstalten* [institutions for *Bildung*], and we should therefore note that in the very title these lectures, putatively about education, are concerned primarily with a "higher" notion of cultural achievement and personal development, and how the institutions associated with education can contribute to attaining this goal. However, the title may have posed additional difficulties for Nietzsche's audience in 1872, since auditors in Basel had good reason to expect a discussion of Swiss institutions. But Nietzsche's concerns regarding culture, in 1872 and throughout his life, were more closely tied to his native country than to his present residence. To avoid any misunderstandings, he therefore explains in his "Introduction" to the series that, despite his audience and his domicile, he will be addressing issues connected to the German institutions of his time. "With our educational institutions I therefore understand neither the special Basler institutions nor the countless forms of contemporary institutions encompassing all nations; rather I mean the types of *German institutions* that we also enjoy here. The future of these German institutions will be our topic; i.e., the future of the German elementary school, the German *Realschule*, the German

Gymnasium, the German university" (BA, Einleitung, KSA 1.644). Nietzsche continues by stating that he will not be entering into invidious comparisons concerning the educational system currently found in different parts of Germany, and he will certainly avoid the "flattering insanity" that considers the German institutions far superior to those of other civilized nations. Educational institutions are connected to a people and its history; discussion of the future of these institutions necessarily involves an embrace of the ideal spirit that gave them birth. But his lecture series also entails a sober look at the directions they are taking in the contemporary world, and in this regard Nietzsche senses danger and deficiency. He is convinced that "the numerous changes that the present day has allowed to occur in these educational institutions in order to make them 'timely,' are for the most part only distorted paths and deviations from the original, sublime tendencies of their foundation"[30] (BA, Einleitung, KSA 1.645). Nietzsche's lectures will both expose the false direction the educational system has taken and endeavor to steer it onto its proper and preferred course.

On the most general level, Nietzsche opposes two tendencies of his time. The first, reflected in the Enlightenment demand for "universal education," calls for an extension of *Bildung* into ever widening circles of society. Responsible for this widening of the educational system, according to Nietzsche, is the German state, which thereby endeavors to subsume culture and education as *Bildung* under its auspices. Throughout Nietzsche's writings, we find derogatory references to the state as an institution that is self-serving and promotes mediocrity. During the years when Nietzsche was writing, the newly unified German state was ruled by Otto von Bismarck (1815–1898), the conservative Prussian Junker nicknamed the "Iron Chancellor," and while Germany during the 1870s and 1880s could hardly have been viewed as the vanguard of European democracy, it is consistently imagined by Nietzsche as a leveling agent, destroying natural hierarchies and unnecessarily upholding civil rights. With his reference to the "widening of *Bildung*," Nietzsche is alluding to a number of phenomena in contemporary German education, including the proliferation of public high schools of various types and the generally increased access to education during the latter part of the nineteenth century. Indeed, by European standards, German elementary education is a success story in Nietzsche's era. Since the end of the eighteenth century, the *Volksschule* or elementary school had been defined as a state institution with the obligation to provide a foundational level of knowledge to all German citizens. Although the relationship between church and state was never properly settled, and the church retained authority over education in many areas, the education of the population increased tremendously in the first half of the nineteenth century. Chiefly responsible for this burgeoning of national education were the educational reformers in Prussia, in particular Karl von Altenstein (1770–1840), who implemented necessary improvements in professional teacher training. The conservative minister Friedrich Eichhorn (1779–1856), who succeeded Altenstein in 1840, advocated policies that promoted church involvement with school administration and validated confessional organization of elementary education. Nonetheless, the success of the generation of reform was obvious: from 1816 to 1846 the number of teachers increased by 40 percent to accommodate the additional million school-aged children; attendance grew by over 100 percent (although the population increased only 44.7 percent), and by 1849 over 80 percent of eligible children were enrolled in school, a greater percentage than in England or France.[31] Despite relative declines in school attendance in the decades following the Revolution of 1848, and the almost complete confessionalization of schools throughout the country, we can understand why Nietzsche might have believed that the educational mandate from the state, which called for universal access and participation, had been largely fulfilled.

In the first lecture and in his notebooks from 1872, Nietzsche outlines three explanations for this deleterious expansion of education. The first concerns the need for a greater number of educated individuals to perform the tasks of an increasingly complex society. For Nietzsche, the claim that education is essential for the economy is not convincing; indeed, he calls it one of "the favorite nationaleconomic dogmas of the present day" (BA 1, KSA 1.667). Nietzsche regards this explanation for the expansion of *Bildung* as an outgrowth of utilitarian thought: "As much knowledge and *Bildung* as possible—leading to the largest amount of production and demand—leading to the greatest happiness"; "humankind has a claim to happiness on earth—therefore *Bildung* is necessary" (BA 1, KSA 1.667–68). Education, as conceived by his contemporaries, is a means to maximize economic activity and the production of wealth. In this facet of his presentation, Nietzsche seems to be responding not only to the general changes that were occurring in an industrializing German society during the course of the nineteenth century, but, more specifically, to the increased economic activity in Germany following the Franco-Prussian War. At this point in his intellectual development, Nietzsche was still enthralled in idealist thought, although he already took an interest in materialist philosophical arguments, as evidenced by his admiration for Friedrich Albert Lange's (1828–1875) *History of Materialism* (1866). But even when Nietzsche had abandoned the metaphysical trappings of Schopenhauer and Wagner in the 1880s, he never turned to a materialism of the sort we associate today with economic materialism. In this early phase of his development, he views economic activity and the educational focus on production as the antithesis of *Bildung* for higher and less instrumental goals. In this sense, his project is "untimely," since it opposes educational practices that promote integration into the economic order to the exclusion of more worthy goals. Nietzsche disagrees with an expansion of educational opportunities to make people "*courant*" (BA 1, KSA 1.667), and he heaps ridicule on institutions that "train everyone to convert his innate capacity for knowledge and science, whatever it may be, into the greatest amount of happiness and pecuniary gain" (BA 1, KSA 1.667–68).³² This "union of intelligence and possession" loathes any sort of education "that isolates, that sets goals beyond money and gain, that requires time." These sorts of educational practices and institutions, which Nietzsche considers predominant in the Second Reich, are disparaged as tendencies promoting "higher egotism" or categorized disdainfully as "unethical educational Epicureanism" (BA 1, KSA 1.668). Genuine culture is allowed in contemporary society, according to Nietzsche, only insofar as it accords with the interests of earning money. Nietzsche summarizes this "source" of "the greatest possible generalization of *Bildung*" in his notebooks as a "complete secularization," "a subordination of *Bildung* as a means to material gain under a crudely understood earthly happiness" (Nachlass 1870–72, 8[57], KSA 7.243).

Nietzsche's second explanation or source of expanded educational opportunities relates to a perceived fear of religious oppression. He may very well be referring to the *Kulturkampf* [cultural struggle], which began shortly after German unification and which involved a state-supported attack on activities of the Catholic Church and the Center Party, dominated by Catholics. For the National Liberal Party, on which Bismarck depended for his rule, the assault on Catholics was partly a reaction to the papal declaration of infallibility, issued by the Vatican Council on 19 July 1870, the day France declared war on Prussia, and from the perspective of the Iron Chancellor, the *Kulturkampf* was initiated by the Catholic Church. Ideologically, the Catholic Church and its institutions were considered an enemy of Prussia and the newly formed German nation. The practical consequences of the *Kulturkampf* were perhaps most manifest in the educational system.³³ Shortly after Prussia's victory in the Franco-Prussian War, Bismarck eliminated the Catholic Section in the Prussian Ministry of Culture; nine months later, in March 1872, the Prussian parliament passed legislation that placed the supervision of all schools under the state; and shortly thereafter the Prussian minister of education, Adalbert Falk (1827–1900), issued the May Laws, which placed all public aspects of Catholic life, including the education of theologians, under state control.³⁴ In effect, shortly after German unification the state was asserting its hegemony in the area of general education, especially in the elementary schools. The laws asserting the state's authority over education applied not only to the Catholic Church, but to Protestant denominations as well, although the enforcement was uneven. Still, the legislation and measures undertaken as part of the *Kulturkampf* occurred precisely at the time that Nietzsche was preparing his lectures on education, and these governmental actions contributed to the continuing tension between public and church control of education that had existed for many decades. Nietzsche's presentation is somewhat odd, however, since he presents the state measures as the result of actions on the part of all social classes fearing or recalling former instances of religious tyranny (BA 1, KSA 1.668–69). In the expansion of *Bildung*, the state is implicitly claiming that it can satisfy "the metaphysical needs" (Nachlass 1870–72, 8[58], KSA 7.244) over which religion had claimed a monopoly. In this regard, Nietzsche assumes an unusual position in the *Kulturkampf*: on the one hand, his arguments can be read as a defense of the actions Bismarck has taken against church interference in public affairs; but since Nietzsche is also criticizing this expansion, he might also be viewed as promoting a continuation of religious involvement in educational institutions. The philosopher's companion, who articulates these views, confesses that whenever he hears a call for general education, he cannot discern whether its source is "a greedy lust of gain and property, the memory of a former religious persecution, or the prudent egotism of the state itself" (BA 1, KSA 1.669).

In his notes for the composition of his lecture series, Nietzsche lists a third explanation or source for educational broadening: "the belief in the masses, the disbelief in genius" (Nachlass 1870–72, 8[59], KSA 7.244; 14[11], 378). He does not include this explanation in his original discussion of the expansion of *Bildung* in the initial lecture, but instead refers to it at several critical points throughout his presentation. The notion that education is aimed at a large and increasing portion of the society and that in this expansion the genuine nature of *Bildung* has been lost is a pervasive theme in the lecture series. In an early exchange between the philosopher and his companion, the former accuses him of acting as if he had never heard the "cardinal principle" of all education. The companion is quick to issue the following rejoinder:

> I remember ... you always said that no one would strive to attain *Bildung* if they knew how incredibly small the number of truly cultured people [*Gebildeten*] actually was, or ever could be. But that it was impossible to attain even this small number of truly cultured people unless a great mass of people were tricked, seduced, into going against their nature and pursuing *Bildung*. As a result, we must never publicly betray the ridiculous disproportion between the number of truly cultured people and the size of our monstrously overgrown educational system. That is the real secret of *Bildung* you said: Countless people fight for it, and think they are fighting for themselves, but at bottom it is only to make *Bildung* possible for a very few. (BA 1, KSA 1.665)

The philosopher gives his assent, but adds in a deprecatory fashion that his companion may have forgotten the true sense of this principle is the belief that he himself is one of the chosen few. This belief is only part of the "signature of our educated [*gebildeten*] times." Contemporary society encourages people to believe that they can achieve *Bildung* and that they need not strive to foster true *Bildung*.

"The rights of genius have been democratized, so that people may be relieved of the task of acquiring culture and of their own deficiencies in *Bildung*" (BA 1, KSA 1.666). The chief characteristic of the current German educational system is the delusion that *Bildung* is a goal for the masses, and that the genius, the only truly educated or cultured individual, is superfluous.

In his early years, Nietzsche was very likely adopting the emphasis on genius he had found in Schopenhauer's philosophy.[35] Like Nietzsche, Schopenhauer differentiated between the vast multitude of people, "the countless millions who use their head only in service of their belly," and those exceptional individuals, the "truly noble, the real *noblesse* of the world."[36] In *The World as Will and Representation* (1818/1819, 1844), he had developed a philosophically oriented account of genius: in the great chain of being, the intellect gradually separates itself from its origins in the will, and this separation reaches its greatest point in the genius, where it becomes completely distinguished from its roots and achieves autonomy. In a normal person, the intellect is clearly subservient to the will and is likened to the threads that control every movement of a puppet. The genius, by contrast, is a sovereign individual, able to perceive everything and therefore able to leave the puppet stage and enjoy the show.[37] In *Parerga and Paralipomena*, he distinguishes the multitudes from the genial few as follows:

> Those who emerge from the multitude, who are called geniuses, are merely the *lucida intervalla* of the whole human race. They achieve what others could not possibly achieve. Their originality is so great that not only is their divergence from other men obvious, but their individuality is expressed with such force, that all the men of genius who have ever existed show, every one of them, distinguishing peculiarities of character and mind; so that the gift of his works is one which he alone of all men could ever have presented to the world.[38]

Nietzsche shares this vision of men of genius and their utter distinction from the populations from which they emerge. But while Schopenhauer concerns himself almost exclusively with descriptive accounts of the genius and his intellect,[39] Nietzsche is preoccupied with how education can contribute to fostering genius. In his notes he remarks that nature proceeds toward perfection (a teleological view he repudiates in his later years), and the goal of *Bildung* is then to assist nature in its own aims, in the same way that medicine supports the drive toward wellness. The task of *Bildung* is clearly delineated: "to complete the creation of genius, to smooth his paths, to make possible his effects through reverence, to discover him." Likewise, the educational goals of non-geniuses are evident: "(1) obedience and modesty (2) correct insight into the narrowness of each vocation (3) service for the genius, collecting material." Educational institutions should be organized so that they perform the "service of midwives" for the birth of the genius (Nachlass 1871–72, 18[3], KSA 7.413).

The "disbelief in genius" has resulted in a perspective on, and an organization of, education that is the very antithesis of the task of institutions devoted to genuine *Bildung*. But the other half of Nietzsche's formula—"the belief in the masses"—gives us a better indication of perhaps his greatest source of discontent with German society in the nineteenth century: the spread of educational opportunities among large segments of the population and their gradual acquisition of rights and privileges formerly reserved for the elite. At the outset, we should consider that Nietzsche's view of the circumstances in the nineteenth century is very likely to be completely different from ours today. Even with the increased educational access we have noted in the elementary schools and the burgeoning of public education in secondary institutions, the educational system in nineteenth-century Germany remained rigidly hierarchical and restrictive. Children from lower-class backgrounds rarely reached the higher levels of the system; middle-class parents often preferred to enroll their children in *Realschulen*, where their sons could acquire useful knowledge, but not much in the way of what Nietzsche considered genuine *Bildung*. Women were excluded from universities until 1908. Only those who aspired to higher government service or sought to become professionals found their way into a *Gymnasium* and later matriculated at a university. The results were a stratified and relatively static social structure. In the academic year 1886–87, for example, over 70 percent of the student body at Prussian universities came from what we would now call the upper-middle class or upper class; only one-quarter of 1 percent were children of workers or servants.[40] The extension of *Bildung*, to which Nietzsche refers pejoratively, hardly reached the lower classes in any form except the elementary school or *Volksschule*, and education in these institutions was traditional and limited, focused on religion and basic skills, and largely devoid of anything that resembled higher culture. In pure numbers, there may have been an expansion of education in Nietzsche's short lifetime; over the course of the nineteenth century there was certainly an increase of pupils, teachers, and educational institutions. The philosopher comments on this proliferation of institutions, asserting that "a much smaller number of educational establishments would suffice" for the purposes of a genuine process of *Bildung* (BA 3, KSA 1.697). But it is difficult to reconcile the actual expansion of education and institutions with Nietzsche's phrase "belief in the masses" in any way that would substantiate it as a dramatic shift in the educational focus away from the privileged segments of German society, which had enjoyed it in former times.

What concerned Nietzsche was not so much the inclusion of previously excluded groups in higher education as the process of state-sponsored democratization that he identified with this expansion and the way in which this emphasis of the state detracts from the apposite goals for education. When the philosopher formulates his criticism of contemporary teachers and their activities in the third lecture, he is especially incensed at their promotion of *Volksbildung* or education of the people. Nietzsche does not allow the philosopher to define *Volksbildung*, but we must presume that it entails the sort of instruction advocated by numerous educational reformers of Nietzsche's era for the curriculum and instruction in elementary schools. According to the philosopher, however, like universal education, *Volksbildung* is encouraged by those who favor a "saturnalia of barbarity" and "fetterless freedom," while opposing the "sacred order of nature." The philosopher leaves no doubt concerning his contempt for the promoters of such an unnatural and demophilic pedagogy, as well as his disdain for the masses, who "are born to serve and to obey, and every moment during which their creeping or grallatorial or lame-winged thoughts are active only confirms what kind of stuff they are made of and what trademark they have branded on them" (BA 3, KSA 1.698). The appropriate relationship of the genius to the masses has been violated in contemporary Germany, and in his notes Nietzsche attempts to set the record straight: "only in its geniuses does a people achieve the right to exist, its justification; the masses do not produce the real individual; quite the contrary, they oppose him. The masses are a raw block of stone that is difficult to hew; tremendous work is necessary on the part of the individual to make the masses resemble something human" (Nachlass 1870–72, 8[59], KSA 7.244). The orientation of educational institutions must then necessarily be altered to accommodate what should be important for great individuals as well as their followers:

> *Bildung* for the masses cannot be our goal, but rather *Bildung* for the select few, for people equipped to produce great and durable works: we know very well that the judgment of posterity concerning the status of *Bildung* among a given people will be based solely on those great heroes of the time, who stride in solitude; and that it will evaluate according to the manner in which these heroes are recognized, promoted, honored, or segregated, abused, and destroyed. (BA 3, KSA 1.698)

Volksbildung is thus the very antithesis of authentic *Bildung*. It seeks to reverse the "natural hierarchy in the realm of the intellect," to arouse the masses from a slumber that is their true lot, and thereby to disrupt the noble and natural goal of promoting genius (BA 3, KSA 1.699). Instead of "breeding great leaders" (BA 3, KSA 1.710), the educational system, under the auspices of a state whose real goals are vocational training and the production of an intelligent civil service, nurtures the pretension of culture, deceiving the masses into believing that they too can partake in genuine *Bildung*.

This vehement repudiation of the notion of *Volksbildung* or general education, and the utter disparagement of the masses, can be understood fully only when we consider Nietzsche's reflections on the "Social Question" of his era. We will have an opportunity to examine this dimension of Nietzsche's thought in more detail in Chapter 3, but here we should note that in the early 1870s the most important moment for his views of the masses was very likely connected with the Paris Commune.[41] Indeed, in his notes on the lecture series he clearly delineates the connection between education and the brief outbreak of what was perceived as "communism," which Europe witnessed in France's capital in the spring of 1871. "Universal education," Nietzsche wrote as his first remark on the topic of education in his notebooks, "is only a prelude to communism: in this way education is so weakened that it can no longer grant any privilege. Even less so is it then a means against communism. Universal education, i.e. barbarism, is precisely the prerequisite for communism" (Nachlass 1870–72, 8[57], KSA 7.243). He continues by categorizing contemporary education as "instant" education, by which he means the crude grasping of momentary utility. We have already seen that Nietzsche criticized the broadening of education as an outgrowth of utilitarian thought, but in his notebooks he emphasizes its connection with communism and the masses. General education stands opposed to "true *Bildung*"; culture is no longer the goal for the masses, but rather luxury and fashion—in other words, momentary and transitory pleasures. Nietzsche even makes direct reference in this passage to Ferdinand Lassalle, stating that the socialist leader had asserted "not to have any needs is the greatest misfortune for the people," and he connects this claim with the rise of working-class educational associations [*Arbeiterbildungsvereine*], which were fostered by the socialist party across Germany to counteract the Socialist Laws, but, according to Nietzsche, arose to promote "needs." Nietzsche's anticommunism finds only a faint echo in the actual lectures, but it can be discerned in the philosopher's remarks about the masses and their happiness. Responding to his companion's comment on humanity's desire for earthly bliss, he speaks of "the tremendous danger that at some time or other the great masses may overleap the middle class and spring headlong into this earthly bliss. That is what people today call the 'Social Question'" (BA 1, KSA 1.668). The Social Question, which was understood at the time as a direct reference to the working-class movement, is intertwined here with the instrumentalization of education for the purposes of attaining "earthly bliss." Extending education entails a weakening of education so that "it can no longer confer privileges or inspire respect." The result is "barbarism" (BA 1, KSA 1.668). This interjection of the philosopher reveals the threat that Nietzsche felt from the demands and actions of the masses: the barbarism he observed in 1871 with the brief rule of the working class in the Paris Commune is conceived as the logical extension of the German expansion of instruction into "general education" and *Volksbildung*.

Narrowing of Education

The second tendency that Nietzsche detects in contemporary education is a narrowing and weakening. To some extent this tendency is a natural consequence of the expansion of *Bildung* into hitherto uneducated sectors of society, since the rigor with which certain topics were treated could not be consistently maintained when extended to a mass audience. But Nietzsche is more concerned about another aspect of the alleged impoverishment of education: the increasing specialization of scholarly and scientific endeavor.[42] A young man with moderate abilities, claims Nietzsche, is compelled to devote himself to one subject and exclude all others if he is to accomplish anything. In the process, he loses any connection to *Bildung* and becomes a mere academic drone. He may be able to raise himself above the vulgar masses in his area of concentration, but he does not rise above them in all other topics, and thus really belongs among them. Indeed, the comparison Nietzsche uses is revealing: "An exclusive specialist in a discipline is then similar to the factory worker who spends his entire life making one particular screw or lever on a particular instrument or machine, an activity at which he attains an incredible virtuosity" (BA 1, KSA 1.670). The image of mindless and mechanical work carried out by members of society who likely enjoyed only schooling at an elementary level indicates how problematic Nietzsche regards the trend toward specialization among his contemporaries. He considers it most unfortunate that in Germany these single-minded scholars are revered for their attention to erudition and minutia, while their ignorance of anything that resembles real culture outside of their specialty is considered "a sign of noble satisfaction" (BA 1, KSA 1.670). Practices at modern educational institutions have led to the radical separation of learned from cultured individuals (*Gelehrten* versus *Gebildeten*), so that now the two designations, formerly referring to the same sort of person, are not even related. The scientific division of labor is no longer even questioned; learned individuals are exploited by the vampire-like demands of disciplines; and like religions in some other societies, this fragmentation of scholarly effort leads to the minimization, or even the complete annihilation, of *Bildung*. It has reached a point where the narrowly, but highly educated individuals in contemporary society have nothing more to contribute to discussions about the most important philosophical problems (BA 1, KSA 1.670).

The vacuum created by the dearth of truly cultured individuals is filled by journalism. It occupies the interstices between the various fragmented disciplines, but, as Nietzsche points out, it does so, as the etymology of its name suggests, in the fashion of a day laborer. Like many conservative writers of the late nineteenth century, Nietzsche has a particular animus against the press and newspapers, which he regarded as deleterious manifestations of a burgeoning modernity.[43] In his writings about ancient Greece, the press is identified with the dialectic and with Socrates—in other words, with the forces that destroyed the felicitous duality of the Dionysian and Apollonian that produced the great works of Attic drama.[44] In his notebooks, it is placed in a field of association with "timely knowledge," the degenerated cultural individual, hastiness, immaturity, historical thought, and acting for the moment (Nachlass 1870–72, 8[87], KSA 7.255). Among Wagnerians and in wider circles throughout Europe, however, the press was also associated with Jews, who were presumed to be in control of the major journalistic organs, and whose nature was similarly considered deracinated, unsettled, transient, and essayistic.[45] Writing in 1874 in his notebooks about Wagner's political mistakes, Nietzsche remarks that he has insulted the Jews, "who possess the most money and the press in Germany" (Nachlass 1874, 32[39], KSA 7.766). As we shall see in Chapter 6, Nietzsche also associated Jews with the press in public, only to earn a rebuke from the Wagners for his openness. In his draft copy of the lecture "Socrates and Tragedy," Nietzsche wrote curtly: "this Socratism is the Jewish Press" (Drafts of ST, KGW III 5/1.670). Cosima Wagner, to whom Nietzsche had sent the draft, cautioned the young professor "in maternal fashion" not "to stir up a hornet's nest": "Don't mention the Jews," she admonished, "and especially not in passing" (6 February 1870, Nr. 72, KGB II 2.140). Cosima assures Nietzsche that she agrees with him, but if he chooses to take up the "gruesome fight," he should not do so in this manner. Nietzsche obediently removed the offensive passage, and this episode had an impact on the ways in which Jews were included in—and excluded from—his published works during his Wagnerian period.[46] In the lecture series on education, Nietzsche does not include any readily identifiable anti-Semitic remarks when he writes about journalism. It is portrayed as a consequence of both the expansion and the minimization of education; it is the culmination of the educational intentions of the times and is juxtaposed with genuine *Bildung*. The journalist is the "servant of the moment," who has replaced "the great genius, the leader for all times, the redeemer of the momentary" (BA 1, KSA 1.671). But many of the associations with journalism and its putatively Jewish character that Nietzsche had imprudently made explicit in the draft of his earlier and more academic lecture would certainly have been recognized by the Basler audience that attended his lectures in 1872.

In his criticism of the narrowing of education in his own era, Nietzsche is undoubtedly also reflecting on a conflict that had persisted in German educational circles for the greater part of the nineteenth century. This conflict involved the role of more practically oriented education in German secondary schools and was therefore related to the appearance and growth of the *Realschule*. Although the *Gymnasium* continued to expand and prosper in Nietzsche's era, throughout the nineteenth century the *Realschule* had gained increasing legitimacy and had many advocates. A book like August Beger's (1802–1859) *The Idea of the*

Realgymnasium, published the year after Nietzsche's birth, gives us a sense of how progressively minded educational theorists viewed these issues. Although he himself was classically trained and professes a love of ancient languages, Beger understands that with the changing times and needs of society, educational priorities and institutions must also undergo modification. Recognizing that the establishment of more practically oriented secondary education was considered for a long time as "an attack on philology and humanity, on the study and worth of classical antiquity," Berger notes that fewer critics subscribe to this view in 1845, and that many contemporaries now recognize "the high value in recent times of scientific and literary achievement" and the "perspective and needs" of education for young individuals in the present.[47] Others were less sanguine about the appropriateness of more practically oriented education offered by the *Realschule*. Heinrich von Treitschke, for example, considers the *Gymnasium* constricted by the "modish sickness of the century": "the demand for a so-called realistic education." His description of the type of education offered in *Realschulen* makes it evident that his real concern, like Nietzsche's, is the threat to genuine *Bildung*:

> The barbarian gathers together an unsystematic pile of secret teachings and empirical impressions and preserves them in order to use them on occasion for the purposes of practical life. Genuine scholarship thrives only in nations that have recognized that formless knowledge is no knowledge. Therefore the instruction of young people by all cultured peoples involves preparatory, formal education. . . . It teaches not knowledge, but the ability to know; it does not inculcate a sum of half-comprehended fragments of knowledge, but rather strengthens their will, schools their cognitive powers, and places them later in the position, as soon as they are ready for productive scholarship, to acquire a well-formed, coherent body of knowledge.[48]

Although Treitschke concedes that both practical education in the *Realschule* and classical humanistic *Bildung* in the *Gymnasium* are necessary, he was concerned, as were Nietzsche and other contemporaries, that schools preparing pupils exclusively for employment were beginning to infringe on the privileges formerly accorded to schools designed to train for civil service careers and for study at the university.[49]

At the time Nietzsche was delivering his lecture series, the controversy surrounding the *Realschule* was particularly acute in German discussions. During the 1840s, there was a noticeable push toward raising the status of the *Realschule* and making it somewhat equal with education at the *Gymnasium*. Originally designed to provide a practical educational alternative in disciplines such as mathematics, natural sciences, modern languages, German, history, and geography, Prussia had recently, in 1859, established a "*Realschule* of the First Order" that included instruction in Latin, a key element in justifying matriculation at universities. In 1870 these schools were then allowed to award a diploma [*Abitur*] that secured admission to certain fields within the university system. Thus, shortly before Nietzsche delivered his lectures in Basel, the *Gymnasium* had lost its monopoly on access to the university; in certain fields such as medicine, successful completion of the program at a *Realschule* without instruction in Latin was sufficient for admission to university study. In 1882, the process was extended further when these *Realschulen* became known as *Realgymansien*, an institution Treitschke calls "as misguided as its name."[50] Continuing to exist alongside these elite *Realschulen* were the more ordinary "high schools," called *Oberrealschulen* and "*Realschulen* of the Second Order." To an educational purist this tendency in secondary education must have appeared as a dilution of requirements for university study and hence a disregard for the task of the transmission and promotion of *Bildung*. The "solution" to this comingling and confounding of roles in secondary education was a frequent topic during Nietzsche's lifetime: Treitschke, for example, proposes quite simply that *Realschulen* no longer be considered as preparatory schools for any subject studied at the university, a prohibition that would result, he believes, in the disappearance of Latin as a subject at *Realschulen* and a renewed focus on training for middle-class professions and technical universities. Many other commentators, however, recognized that both society and the university were changing, that natural sciences were assuming an increasingly important role in higher education, and that therefore universities should expand the number of fields in which pupils trained at the *Realschule* qualify for admission to higher education. Still others proposed the creation of a "unified school" [*Einheitschule*], which would offer both the subjects taught traditionally at the classical *Gymnasium* and training in the natural sciences and modern foreign languages.

Nietzsche's contribution to this ongoing and timely discussion about secondary-school education is a combination of realism and traditionalism. In the fourth lecture, the philosopher tells the students from Bonn that individuals must learn a great deal in order to survive in the "struggle for existence," but at the same time he cautions them that everything one learns for this practical purpose "has nothing to do with *Bildung*." Genuine *Bildung* only begins "in a sphere that lies far above the world of necessity, scarcity, and struggle for existence." It has nothing to do with individuals in their state of need and craving, and anyone who believes that he has achieved true *Bildung* and can make a living from it finds that it vanishes "with silent footsteps and an air of derisive mockery" (BA 4, KSA 1.713–15). Nietzsche thus establishes completely separate realms for any education that, on the one hand, enables someone to secure a living or gainful employment and, on the other hand, deals with authentic cultural achievement. At the same time, he expresses admiration and understanding for the types of educational institutions devoted to the "struggle for existence," a notion borrowed from evolutionary discourse, but he believes that the regulations and standards of institutions that produce "civil servants or merchants or officers or wholesale dealers or farmers or physicians or technicians" are different from those at institutions of *Bildung*. He praises *Realschulen* and advanced middle-class schools, where pupils learn "the language of commerce," geography, and natural science. Furthermore, he recognizes the tendency of the past few decades that has added legitimacy to these practically oriented institutions and accorded them a status equal to the classical *Gymnasium*: "I am quite willing to say further that those students prepared by the better class of *Realschulen* are perfectly entitled to the same privileges as our fully-fledged graduates of *Gymnasien*; and it will surely not be long before such pupils will be everywhere freely admitted to universities and positions in state government, which has hitherto been the case only for graduates of the *Gymnasien*" (BA 4, KSA 1.716–17). The realism Nietzsche evidences in his public lectures is modified with a somewhat more critical and analytical attitude in unpublished comments. In notebook entries, he views the *Realschule* as a "protest" against the *Gymnasium*, and to a great extent its ascendancy is regarded as the consequence of failings in humanistic education to realize its appropriate place among institutions (Nachlass 1871–72, 14[20], KSA 7.382–83). The *Realschule* is considered to be a hybrid form that combines some aspects of humanistic education with practically oriented knowledge, but as "an attack on what has existed previously," it is really a $\mu\eta\delta\grave{\epsilon}\nu\ \check{\alpha}\gamma\alpha\nu$ [not too much of anything] (Nachlass 1870–72, 8[86], KSA 7.255), a mélange of knowledge that does not efficiently accomplish any task. Nietzsche's more sober and considered evaluation is that Germany needs a "large number of vocational schools," which will give training not only in middle-class occupations, but also in academic preparation for teaching. Like Treitschke, Nietzsche believes that the university and the *Gymnasium* are one unified level of education, while the *Realschule* exists in the same educational realm as the technical universities and advanced vocational institutions. This division of education into a sphere of genuine *Bildung* and one of practical life is consistent with what the philosopher articulates at the start of the fourth lecture and with the chief distinction Nietzsche is drawing in his lectures between institutions devoted to "mere education" [*Erziehung*] and those dedicated to higher cultural achievement [*Bildung*].

Gymnasium and University

After he has noted that pupils of the *Realschule* will soon be admitted to the university on an equal basis with "graduates of the *Gymnasien*," Nietzsche qualifies by stating: "it should be noted, the graduates of the modern *Gymnasien*" (BA

4, KSA 1.717). Perhaps one of the reasons that Nietzsche does not include his misgivings about the nature of the *Realschule* in his lectures is that it would detract from his main goal, which is the critique of the *Gymnasium*, and to a lesser extent, the university, for abandoning the concentration on *Bildung* and succumbing to the practical and myopic ideals of the late nineteenth century. Nietzsche recognizes that there have been significant changes to the social order during the nineteenth century, and that to a large degree the evolution of the German school system, in particular the flourishing of more practically oriented institutions—the *Realschulen*, the technical universities, and trade schools—is only an accommodation to the new realities of modern society. But we must recall that Nietzsche is primarily concerned with institutions of *Bildung*, not merely institutions of education, since only the former foster what is ultimately worthwhile and important for humanity. Thus the confluence of secondary education captured by both the suggestions for a unified secondary school and the gradual movement of the *Realschule* into territory formerly occupied by the *Gymnasium* is a troubling tendency. Nietzsche is justified in maintaining: "if it is true that the *Realschule* and the *Gymnasium* are now nearly identical in their present goals, and differ from each other only in such a slight degree, so that they may be considered completely of equal rank before the tribunal of the state, then that means we are fully lacking another species of educational institution: the species of a *Bildung* institution!" (BA 4, KSA 1.717). Throughout the lecture series, Nietzsche addresses issues pertaining to both the *Volksschule* and the *Realschule*, but there can be little doubt that his real focus, as one might expect, is the traditional bastion of German elite education, the *Gymnasium*, since in his mind the *Gymnasium* is charged with the important task of fostering *Bildung* in those capable of attaining it, and its appreciation in those who are not. Comparable to a French *lycée* and attended by pupils as a preparatory school for higher education, the *Gymnasium* provided the strict classical education that Nietzsche had enjoyed in his formative years, and in which he participated as an instructor in the *Pädagogium* in Basel. Its role as the bearer of culture, however, is what makes it of central importance, and the philosopher's companion appropriately marks it as the key to the entire education system: "if the struggle here leads to victory, all other institutions of *Bildung* must follow suit." The philosopher confirms its centrality:

> Every other institution is measured against the educational goals of the *Gymnasium*; whatever errors of judgment *it* may commit, they suffer from too, and its purification and rejuvenation will purify and rejuvenate them as well. Even the university can no longer claim this importance as the center of influence, considering that, as they now exist, they are, at least in *one* important aspect, only an extension of the propensity in the *Gymnasium*. (BA 2, KSA 1.674–75)

Nietzsche's lectures bemoan the fact that the *Gymnasium* has abandoned its role as the promoter of genuine *Bildung* and as the focal point of the German educational system, becoming instead the breeding ground for the spurious and insipid culture of the Second Reich or a machine for producing the pedantic and irrelevant trivialities of scholarly learning (BA 4, KSA 1.712–13). As the key to the deficiencies in German education and to overcoming the present state of affairs, the *Gymnasium* quite appropriately occupies the bulk of Nietzsche's presentation.

We know that Nietzsche's thought on contemporary education, and in particular on the *Gymnasium*, was informed by the ongoing debate in secondary literature. His borrowings from the library at Basel indicate a familiarity with many of the seminal texts for these discussions in the 1870s, and both the central concepts and "the structure of argumentation" found in the lectures can be traced to sources dealing with pedagogical treatises.[51] Slightly unusual, however, is Nietzsche's emphasis on German language instruction as the centerpiece of education in the *Gymnasium*. While other contemporaries—for example, Tycho Mommsen (1819–1900) and Heinrich von Treitschke—mention German as one element that requires more attention in secondary schools, they do not accord it the central role that Nietzsche does in his lectures. Indeed, the first topic that the philosopher broaches when considering whether the *Gymnasium* can be purified and renewed is German instruction, which is clearly not being taken seriously enough.[52] The criticisms are far-reaching. They extend from the demand that teachers prohibit their pupils from using specific phrases and expressions deemed substandard, and that these same teachers emphasize how carefully authors of German classicism constructed their sentences to express with utmost precision their thoughts; to the criticism of the historical manner in which German is being taught, which treats German as if it were a dead language, and the contradictory expectations in assigning German essays. With regard to this last topic, Nietzsche points out that the assignment of a German composition is conceived as an "appeal to the individual," and that most pupils at that stage of their development are unable to produce the sort of originality called for in this assignment. The teachers then criticize their students for exactly those types of excesses and indulgences that, at their stage of development, are the only measure of their originality, and they prefer bland mediocrity and conformity, which then becomes the paradigm for expression in their native language (BA 2, KSA 1.675–80). The exercise is a "farce," continues the philosopher, since there is the tacit assumption that pupils can hold and formulate opinions on important subjects that are valid and mature, when in fact a proper education should strive most zealously to suppress this ridiculous claim regarding independent judgment, and to accustom these young men "to obedience under the scepter of genius" (BA 2, KSA 1.680). German composition thus steers pupils away from genuine *Bildung* and perpetuates the false notion of an "'autonomous personality,' which is nothing more than the hallmark of barbarism" (BA 2, KSA 1.681). These deficiencies in the instruction of German disqualify the current *Gymnasium* as an institution that can contribute to authentic cultural renewal: "as long as the German *Gymnasien* continue to promote despicable, unconscionable scribbling by assigning German essays, as long as they do not regard the immediate and practical discipline of speaking and writing as their most sacred duty, as long as they treat the mother tongue as if it were nothing but a necessary evil or a dead body, I cannot regard these establishments as institutions of true *Bildung*" (BA 2, KSA 1.681).

Behind this focus on German language instruction in the schools and its deficient mediation in the classroom is the more general concern about the deterioration of German associated with the rise of journalism. Once again we are dealing with a familiar motif in the criticism of modernity on the part of conservative ideologues and anti-Semitic agitators. According to Nietzsche, in an age dominated by "newspaper-German," it is an essential duty of the *Gymnasium* to facilitate in "the maturing, noble and talented youth" the development of elegance in his own language, and this task should be accomplished with strict linguistic training if necessary (BA 2, KSA 1.675). This demand for improved and more stringent instruction in German actually reflects Nietzsche's own experience, expressed frequently in early letters, that he had not received adequate instruction in his mother tongue. The *Gymnasium*, however, is failing miserably in its obligation to its pupils and is thereby inflicting damage on the national culture. Although the *Gymnasium* was perhaps not originally established to promote the highest cultural achievement, it was at least supposed to further learning and erudition, but in the present day it has even turned away from this more noble calling and educates now exclusively for journalism (BA 2, KSA 1.677). It has furthermore neglected the finer, classicist authors of the German tradition, placing the "repulsive stamp of our aesthetic journalism" (BA 2, KSA 1.678) on the unformed minds of German youths. Severely deficient in disciplining pupils in the German language, the *Gymnasium* fails to inculcate the compulsory disgust at the inappropriately admired "elegance" of Germany's "newspaper factory workers and novelists" (BA 2, KSA 1.684); as a result, the youth of the nation are unable to distinguish their creative geniuses from the tabloid hacks.[53] Indeed, the defective education of German youth in their own language is ultimately responsible for numerous pernicious manifestations in popular culture, the press, and belletristic:

> Given all this, who could possibly doubt that the exercise [the German essay assignment] stamps each rising generation with everything that ails our literary and artistic public sphere: the hasty overproduction driven by self-regard; the shameful churning out of books; the complete lack of

style; immature formulations that miserably sprawl or lack character altogether; the loss of any aesthetic canon; the reveling in anarchy and chaos; in short, the literary traits of our journalism, and no less of our scholars. (BA 2, KSA 1.681)

As the key institution for the transmission of German culture, the *Gymnasium* is failing miserably. Instead of facilitating a renaissance of genuine *Bildung* and assuming an exalted place as the pivotal institution of *Bildung*, it is succumbing to the worst tendencies of modern German society, providing shoddy training in the German language and thereby contributing to a debased culture founded on journalistic standards.

Part of the remedy to this unfortunate state of affairs is a renewed emphasis on classical antiquity and on those parts of the German tradition that evidence a genuine understanding of that tradition. As we know, Nietzsche enjoyed a comprehensive training in classical languages at the Cathedral *Gymnasium* in Naumburg, at Pforta, and at the universities in Bonn and Leipzig, and there is no doubt that he believed that the cultures of antiquity provided a sound basis for *Bildung* in contemporary Germany. In advocating for a more thorough focus on the great writers of Greece and Rome, he was lending his voice to a growing chorus of German intellectuals, many of whom disapproved of the same sort of watering down of education in secondary schools Nietzsche detected and objected to the recently introduced regulations allowing graduates of the *Realschule* to matriculate at universities. Treitschke and Rudolf Euken, who wrote about secondary education in the 1880s, certainly shared Nietzsche's respect for the classics, as did Tycho Mommsen, the director of the city *Gymnasium* in Frankfurt-am-Main. Mommsen also concurs with the sentiment behind Nietzsche's lectures: that there is a noticeable decline in the rigor of secondary education, in the preparation of teachers, and in the quality of pupils enrolled at the *Gymnasium*. His recommendations are for stricter controls and examinations, no texts with footnotes in anything but Greek and Latin, a prohibition on the use of German translations, and a more extensive study of Greek.[54] Nietzsche was even more decisive in his remarks about the pretensions toward classical education in his era: "The claim put forward by the *Gymnasium* concerning the 'classical education' they provide is nothing more than an embarrassing excuse; it is trotted out whenever there is any question raised as to the competence of the public schools to impart culture and to educate" (BA 2, KSA 1.682). Nietzsche grants that the *Gymnasium* provides adequate instruction in ancient languages (BA 2, KSA 1.688), but unlike many commentators of his time, he recommends that pupils should be led to the ancients via the authors of German classicism. He cites with admiration the pedagogical activities of Friedrich August Wolf (1759–1824), who helped establish the *Gymnasium* as a genuine institution of *Bildung*, but he points out that Wolf was a contemporary of those very German authors for whom the ancients were a living inspiration.[55] That spirit of antiquity is absent in his time, and for this reason, the endeavor to foster classical education has become a hollow and meaningless exercise. "Classical education" is a "cultural ideal that hovers freely in the air," disconnected from the foundation of the current educational system; it has become a "pretentious illusion" whose major value is that the phrase "classical education" continues to be uttered and has not yet lost its pathetic ring (BA 3, KSA 1.693). At fault in this educational farce are the instructors of classics, whose sterile philology fails to convey the value of the subjects they are supposed to teach. The *Gymnasien* may be "academic greenhouses," but they are not contributing to a healthy and flourishing culture directed toward "noble goals." Rather, the culture promoted might be compared to the "hypertrophic swelling of an unhealthy body": "Scholarly obesity is what the *gymnasium*-nurseries of today produce, if indeed they have not degenerated into wrestling schools for the elegant barbarism that nowadays fancies itself 'contemporary German culture'" (BA 3, KSA 1.702–5). The revival of the German *Gymnasium* will not result from a continued artificial focus on the ancients, but only from recapturing the spirit that made classical studies in former epochs the foundation of the educational system.

Although Nietzsche's reflections on the *Gymnasium* share important traits with pedagogical commentary from the nineteenth century and draw at various key points from contemporary treatments of the topic, the educational question for Nietzsche had quite different stakes. While most educational reformers sought to recapture something they imagined had been lost, or to introduce learning that was more rigorous, Nietzsche was chiefly moved in his lectures, as he was in *The Birth of Tragedy* and in his *Untimely Meditations*, by more encompassing thoughts about a renewal of contemporary German culture. At this point in his intellectual development, education was important insofar as it could contribute to the cultural renaissance Nietzsche associated largely with Richard Wagner and the Wagnerian movement, and with Schopenhauer's elitist notions of genius as the highest value in human society. Given Wagner's chauvinism, we should not be surprised to find a passionate nationalism informing Nietzsche's assertions about the direction of secondary schools and a xenophobic reaction to anything that resembles foreign intervention into German cultural life. Discussing the failure of Wolf's model of classical education to take hold, Nietzsche's philosopher attributes it ultimately to the "un-German, almost foreign or cosmopolitan character of these efforts at *Bildung*." One simply cannot ignore the native soil in which culture takes root; in order to truly mediate the magnificence of the Hellenic world, one must proceed from the German and national spirit; not, of course, from the spirit that informs the modern culture of the Second Reich, but a genuine German spirit, which is now somewhat hidden and must be excavated from the rubble of the present: "What presumes to pass for 'German culture' today is a cosmopolitan composite, having the same relation to the German spirit as a journalist to Schiller, as Meyerbeer to Beethoven" (BA 2, KSA 1.689–90). The negative use of "cosmopolitan," in opposition to German, and the conjuring of Giacomo Meyerbeer, Wagner's "French" and Jewish operatic adversary,[56] give a good indication of the agenda behind these remarks. The *Gymnasium* is revealed to be the site of an ongoing struggle for German culture and is thus a pedagogical continuation of the Franco-Prussian War, where "brave German soldiers" recently vanquished the French adversary: Nietzsche desires now "a victory over that modish, pseudo-culture of the present" (BA 3, KSA 1.694). In order to achieve this triumph, however, it will be necessary to establish the proper relationship between the state and culture. In his lectures Nietzsche consistently depicts the state as overstepping its role in education and in cultural activities. It has become the "mystagogue of culture," influenced by a "tendency in Hegelian philosophy" to subsume all endeavors in the realm of *Bildung* under its auspices. The philosopher points out that the Greek state demonstrated the ideal relationship: "The state was not the culture's border patrol and regulator, its watchman and warden, but the culture's sturdy, muscular, battle-ready comrade and companion, escorting his admired, noble, and so to speak transcendent friend through harsh reality and earning that friend's gratitude in return" (BA 3, KSA 1.707–9). Nietzsche's discussions of the deficiencies and reforms of the *Gymnasium* are part of a larger discourse that extends beyond educational policy. While some critics and reformers similarly conceived of their contributions as part of a discourse on a more encompassing notion of German culture, Nietzsche's relate more specifically to the Wagnerian mission to which he had dedicated himself so thoroughly in the early years of his Basler professorship.

In the first four lectures, Nietzsche has his philosopher discuss issues related primarily to general education in the *Volksschule* or elementary school and to issues involving secondary schools (*Realschule* and *Gymnasium*). Only in his final lecture does he broach the topic of university training. Nietzsche was familiar with the workings of higher education from the institutions he had attended as a student, Bonn and Leipzig, as well as the institution where he was currently employed, the University of Basel. At Bonn, Nietzsche began as a student of theology; he was expected to follow in the footsteps of his father and relatives on both sides of the family and become a Lutheran minister. Instead of devoting himself to his theological studies, he appears to have passed his two semesters in the Rhineland in a fashion akin to that of American first-year students. He sampled from various disciplines, attending a variety of lectures, including a course given by Heinrich von Sybel (1817–1895), the well-known historian and political figure. He joined a student fraternity, Franconia; went to pubs, concerts, and plays; fought in a duel, obtaining the obligatory scar; and spent more money than he had at his disposal. Only in his second semester did he announce that he was changing his major to classical philology. At Leipzig, where he arrived in the fall of 1865, he led a more orderly existence. He devoted himself to his studies assiduously, attending lectures by Friedrich Ritschl, who had also moved from Bonn to Leipzig, and his student, Georg Curtius (1820–1885), on a variety of topics from antiquity. He soon became a favorite of Ritschl, who was responsible for his rapid advancement and appointment at Basel,[57] and he participated in two philological clubs. Convinced already that he was on the path to becoming a professor, he focused not only on the substance of classical studies, but also on scholarly methods and how to communicate his knowledge effectively to students.[58] When he began at Basel in 1869, he had the opportunity to put his pedagogical thoughts into practice, and by all accounts, he was a popular and successful teacher. Although some of his courses may have contained material related to his unconventional views about ancient Greece, the seminars and lectures he offered are not unusual for a classicist.[59] Nietzsche led something of a schizophrenic existence as a faculty member at Basel; on the one hand, performing the duties of a more traditional professor and philologist, and, on the other, authoring writings that departed from scholarly and academic norms. This dichotomy was not simply the result of a struggle between philology and philosophy, which had begun already in Leipzig when Nietzsche discovered Schopenhauer and began to feel that his classical studies were at odds with his philosophical ambitions. It was part of Nietzsche's belief that the university, like the *Gymnasium*, was not accomplishing the real business of education as acculturation and was instead turning out narrow specialists, proficient, but lacking in an appreciation of genuine culture.

In his lectures on education, the philosopher's auditors are university students from Bonn, and it is likely that Nietzsche is reliving in a fictionalized format his experiences as a student and the kind of encounter and sage advice he wished he had received in his initial year. When the philosopher asks the students to relate something about their educational experience, they express the belief that the fundamental task of the *Gymnasium* is to prepare its pupils for independence, and that, in their view, the essence of university education is self-sufficiency in learning and research. These seemingly laudable goals of a liberal pedagogy, recognizable as the ideals of early nineteenth-century educational reformers such as Wilhelm von Humboldt, meet with the disapproval of the philosopher. He agrees that his interlocutors have achieved independence: "Yes, my good friends, you are finished, you are mature; nature has cast you and broken the mold, and your teachers must surely gloat over you. What freedom, certitude, and independence of judgment; what novelty and freshness of insight!" But this apparent independence possesses a dubious worth when it is measured against the yardstick of genuine culture, and the university as an institution for the propagation of *Bildung* fails its essential task by promoting this illusion of self-sufficiency. The philosopher continues by advancing a scathing attack on contemporary higher education, railing against a system where professors are nothing more than mouths spouting knowledge, and students are reduced to ears that listen to the faculty and hands that write down what their professors say. Students and professors are indeed self-sufficient, but their independence means only that the former are free to close their ears to whatever they do not want to hear, while the latter can speak about anything that they choose. Nietzsche's philosopher calls this method of teaching and learning "acroamatic," derived from the Greek word ἀκροάομαι, "to listen to": "One speaking mouth plus many ears and half as many writing hands: that is the academic system as seen from the outside—the educational machinery of the university in action." Although the state oversees the "purpose, aim, and content of the strange speech and auditory procedures," the entire arrangement is artificial, arbitrary, and antithetical to acculturation. The "double independence" is hailed as "academic freedom," but the philosopher insists that students are unable to achieve a genuine education without a more encompassing and disciplined bond to a real institution of *Bildung*. Training at the university is thus regarded as the continuation of a pernicious deception fostered in the *Gymnasium*, namely, that young people are mature enough and have sufficient insight to learn, judge, and act with self-sufficiency and to disregard the "dependence, discipline, subordination, and obedience implanted by former generations" (BA 5, KSA 1.737–40). If one requires proof of the abject state of education as it relates to genuine *Bildung*, one need only look at the three "categorical imperatives" of culture: the need for philosophy, the instinct for art, and the appreciation of Greek and Roman antiquity. In all three areas, the individuals who currently pride themselves on their academic self-sufficiency have failed miserably to convey and to value the seminal achievements of a truly cultured existence.

    Nietzsche's ultimate goal in this lecture on the aberrant ways of the university is identical to his larger concern during the first half of the 1870s: the renaissance of German culture. The failure of the university to assume the role ascribed to it by the philosopher and by all advocates of genuine *Bildung* has resulted in a culture of pedantic scholarship, pretentious journalism, the appearance of a "degenerate literary art," and the annihilation of the drive toward true learning. Behind the "degenerate man of culture," however, lies an individual who was destined for something nobler, but who has been forced into this miserable state of affairs by a system of education that has lost a higher focus and purpose. Although these individuals have been captured by the momentary and the transient, Nietzsche suggests that they have not entirely lost their hunger for something better and more substantial. They are victims of the general decline in nineteenth-century values: "Oh these miserable guilty innocents who are held to account! There is something they do not have, and every last one of them must have felt the lack of it: a genuine educational institution [*Bildungsinstitution*], which could provide them with goals, masters, methods, models, companions and the invigorating, uplifting breath of the true German spirit welling up from within it" (BA 5, KSA 1.747). The fear of the true German spirit has allowed a heavy and stifling atmosphere to develop at universities, where noble young men struggle to breath fresh air and many eventually perish from suffocation. There is a need to promote once again the noble and beautiful traits for which the German nation has been so admired: "German erudition, German ingenuity, the honest German drive for knowledge, qualifying German hard work capable of any sacrifice," and Nietzsche's philosopher suggests that contemporary Germany look to its recent past, when there was an attempt to revive a genuine German spirit with the formation of the nationalist German fraternities or *Burschenschaften*. Nietzsche's membership in Franconia may have inspired this favorable portrayal of nationalist fraternities, although by the time Nietzsche had affiliated, the *Burschenschaften* no longer evidenced the same ideals that inspired their formation in the wake of the Napoleonic Wars. Nietzsche was well aware of the erstwhile spirit of these fraternities, however. As a response to French domination, both on the battlefield and in European culture, the original *Burschenschaften* are extolled for their "internal renewal and inspiration of the purest moral capacities" (BA 5, KSA 1.747–49). The young man of the early nineteenth century suddenly recognized "the un-German barbarism" hidden in the guise of learning and saw "that his own leaderless comrades were abandoned to a repulsive youthful intoxication." Their experience on the battlefield taught them an important lesson forgotten in Nietzsche's time: "that great leaders are necessary, and that all *Bildung* begins with obedience" (BA 5, KSA 1.749). They learned through martial engagement that Germany can regain a position of cultural dominance when it discards the false notion of academic freedom and returns to a solid foundation for cultural excellence: "All *Bildung* begins with the exact opposite of what everyone today esteems as 'academic freedom.' It begins with obedience, with subordination, with discipline, with servitude. And just as leaders must have followers, so too must followers have a leader. A certain reciprocal predisposition prevails in the hierarchy of spirits, a kind of pre-established harmony" (BA 5, KSA 1.750).[60] The recrudescence of German culture that Nietzsche so desperately sought in Wagnerian opera is here conjured up in an allusion to one of the most militant and nationalist movements of the early nineteenth century, opposed resolutely to the vapid pseudoculture of the present, and defined as the antithesis of the ideals of liberal education developed by an earlier, more cosmopolitan generation of educational reformers.[61]

The Disadvantage of Historical Education

Nietzsche's continued concern with problems of education and *Bildung* is reflected in his writings published in the next two years after his public lectures. Indeed, pedagogical reforms as they relate to educational practices in contemporary Germany are an important subtext of all his *Untimely Meditations*, the series of essays that appeared in four installments from 1873 to 1876. They are particularly important for the second essay, *On the Advantage and Disadvantage of History for Life*, which appeared almost exactly a year after the public lectures, in February of 1874. Composed rapidly during a three-month period at the end of 1873, it is, like the first *Untimely Meditation* on David Strauß, part of Nietzsche's conscious shift away from the philological studies that were the foundation for his chair in classical philology in Basel, and the concomitant turn toward a preoccupation with more general cultural and contemporary affairs. Once again Nietzsche was intervening in the public sphere and taking aim at a popular author. In the first *Untimely Meditation*, he had focused on Strauß's recently published volume *The Old Faith and the New* (1871), criticizing its author for his naïve belief in historical progress and his pseudocultural pretensions. In *Advantage and Disadvantage*, the target in key passages was Eduard von Hartmann's *Philosophy of the Unconscious* (1869), an extremely popular book that was sometimes viewed as a continuation of Schopenhauer's views.[62] In short, Nietzsche hoped to insert himself in the public sphere by criticizing writers and works of particular renown during the first few years of the Second Reich. But as is common in all Nietzsche's work from this initial period of his nonphilological writing, classical Greece continued to play an important role, even if it recedes somewhat into the background and completely disappears from Nietzsche's active research program. The images Nietzsche harbored of classical Greece continued to inform his thought until the last days of his conscious life. In *Advantage and Disadvantage*, Nietzsche credits his classical training with his self-proclaimed status as an "untimely" meditator. In the "Preface," he informs us: "only so far as I am the nursling of more ancient times, especially the Greek, could I come to have such untimely experiences about myself as the child of the present age" (HL, Vorwort, KSA 1.247). Greece continues to serve him as a paradigm for cultural excellence and appropriate educational practices, while contemporary Germany of the *Gründerzeit*[63] or Second Empire constitutes the negative example that should be corrected by the confrontation with the ancient world. From *The Birth of Tragedy* onward, Nietzsche's views of Greece inform his works primarily in this *ex-negativo* fashion.

Much more important for him are his perceptions of his own society, its cultural aspirations and failings, and the way in which the educational system neglects to instruct young men in the spirit of genuine *Bildung*. Much of the latter part of *Advantage and Disadvantage* deals with these topics in a rhapsodic fashion.

Indeed, the last seven of the ten sections in the essay consist of remarks directed at institutions and assumptions in contemporary German society. The essay can therefore be divided into two parts: in the first, which encompasses the initial three sections, Nietzsche presents an abstract parsing of two sets of categories. We first encounter a discussion of three types of human being—the historical, the unhistorical, and the superhistorical—followed by a consideration of three approaches to historical material: the monumental, the antiquarian, and the critical history.[64] Thereafter we find the aforementioned extended and sometimes rambling, albeit much more spirited, diatribe against the present age, organized loosely around five "dangers" listed at the start of the fifth section. Although Nietzsche does return briefly to his original considerations at the close of the work, the essay is apt to leave the impression of disunity in tone and purpose. What nonetheless unifies this work is a theme common to both the conceptual sections and the extended critique of contemporary society: the pernicious character of "historical" education. This unity is signaled in the prefatory remarks, where Nietzsche states that his goal is to criticize the acquisition of knowledge, in particular, historical knowledge, which is not relevant for something vital or actual. "Our aim," he writes, "will be to show why instruction which fails to quicken activity, why knowledge which enfeebles activity, why history as a costly intellectual excess and luxury must ... be seriously hated; for we still lack what is most necessary, and superfluous excess is the enemy of the necessary" (HL, Vorwort, KSA 1.245). Nietzsche goes on to observe that "we need history," and from the title of the work down to the individual discussions, he will insist that we need it insofar as it promotes "life." But the history that Nietzsche allegedly values turns out to be a rather strange variety; in many cases it resembles rather a lack of history, or a negation of what we normally consider historical thought. The title itself and the several discussions concerning the necessity of history are slightly misleading in suggesting a balance between advantages and disadvantages of historical study. Ultimately the central reason for studying history or for introducing historical perspective into our study of culture and human endeavor is to overcome history, to move beyond the recounting of the past, in order to engage in a more meaningful and vital present, and to forge a future of cultural preeminence.[65]

Nietzsche begins his treatise on historical education with a familiar distinction. The question he implicitly poses is what characteristic or characteristics separate human beings from animals. In the tradition of German idealism and even in materialist philosophy of the nineteenth century, the answer to this question is usually formulated in terms of consciousness or thought or some other variant of mental activity. Nietzsche does not totally disagree with this view, but he frames the issue in a slightly different fashion. Important for Nietzsche is not simply consciousness, but other, related qualities and states such as forgetting, happiness, dissimulation, honesty, and truth.[66] In one of the most amusing passages in the essay, he implores us to consider the herd grazing in the field, claiming that these animals have no sense of history. They are "enthralled by the moment" and are therefore neither melancholy nor bored. The human predicament is to long for this blissful state, yet at the same time to reject it: the human being "is proud of being human and not an animal and yet regards its happiness with envy because he wants nothing other than to live like the animal, neither bored nor in pain, yet wants it in vain because he does not want it like the animal" (HL 1, KSA 1.248). In other words, human beings would like the same result that animals achieve—freedom from pain and boredom, happiness and contentment with life—but they cannot give up consciousness, nor do they want to. The animal is happy, but not conscious, at least not historically conscious, and therefore does not have a memory of happiness, a consciousness of happiness, or even a mechanism to express this happiness. Or, as Nietzsche observes in a more humorous fashion: "Man may well ask the animal: why do you not speak to me of your happiness but only look at me? The animal does want to answer and say: because I always immediately forget what I wanted to say—but then it already forgot this answer and remained silent: so that man could only wonder" (HL 1, KSA 1.248). Consciousness in Nietzsche, which is assimilated more closely to memory than in his idealist and historical materialist predecessors, is a barrier to fulfillment, a hindrance to the implicit goal of human existence: happiness. Previous thinkers arrived at very different conclusions: In the thought of Immanuel Kant (1724–1804), for example, the telos for humanity was conceived as a development of the natural faculty of reason;[67] in G. W. F. Hegel (1770–1831), the goal is freedom conceived as perfect self-consciousness;[68] Karl Marx (1818–1883) projects a state of affairs in which we achieve the conscious control of human society. In Nietzsche, by contrast, consciousness and reason seem to be the very items that prevent us from a biologically conceived state of bliss. Education that is based on historical premises thus leads away from happiness and thwarts the attainment of our chief objective as a species.

The difference in consciousness between animals and humans, phrased in terms of forgetting and memory, forms the basis for three relationships to history. The human being who cannot learn to forget and remains attached or chained to the past lives a historical life. In Nietzsche's poetic phrasing, the page in the scroll of time loosens and falls, but falls into his lap. The animal, by contrast, immediately forgets; the page from the scroll of time flutters off into oblivion. The animal lives unhistorically and is therefore happy. Humankind is condemned to historical existence, but this very historical consciousness robs human beings of happiness and fulfillment. Nietzsche affords us at least the possibility for some modicum of happiness in this life when he indicates that we can achieve a temporary happiness if we seek to imitate the animal and live unhistorically. At various points, in fact,

Nietzsche declares that the human being must live both historically and unhistorically, that both are necessary "for the health of an individual, a people and a culture" (HL 1, KSA 1.252). The historical element that he admits as necessary, however, is limited insofar as it must contribute to "life." Since he repeatedly declares that the unhistorical is necessary for life, his limited concept of the historical appears to approach its very antithesis, and Nietzsche's work therefore flirts continuously with contradiction. Only by shrinking our horizon to a point, as animals do, can we achieve happiness, or at least live, like a child, without boredom and dissimulation. More importantly, the unhistorical is the prerequisite for action. "All acting requires forgetting" (HL 1, KSA 1.250), Nietzsche claims, and everything great that has occurred in history, from the painting of great artists to the winning of great battles, results from an unhistorical condition. The man of action is one who is able to forget. Historical thought and historical education are thus inimical to the metaphysics of genius from the lecture series: since genuine culture arises only from the activities of genial individuals, and since genial individuals act only when they are unhistorical, instruction based on historical method negates both the achievement and the appreciation of *Bildung*.

Nietzsche's third category, the "superhistorical," appears to have been developed to account for those individuals who, like Nietzsche and his colleague Jacob Burckhardt, stand above the historical fray and philosophically reflect on the paradoxes of the human condition. Like the historical and the unhistorical, the superhistorical is clearly an ideal type. Nietzsche describes it initially as follows: "If someone could, in numerous instances, discern and breathe again the unhistorical atmosphere in which every great historical event came to be, then such a one might, as a cognitive being, perhaps elevate himself to a superhistorical standpoint" (HL 1, KSA 1.254). We recognize the superhistorical individual as an observer of the historical process, as a sovereign meditator; this status seems to result from the study of history, from observing history and appreciating its lessons, not from action itself. It is derived from an unusual merger of the unhistorical, the central category of historical action, and the historical, the chief impediment to historical action. In the sovereign demeanor, the superhistorical man partakes in features of the unhistorical, while at the same time resembling the historical man in his refusal or inability to participate in the historical process. This unusual combination of features may help us to understand why both the historical and the superhistorical man would answer negatively Nietzsche's hypothetical question about the desirability of reliving the last ten or twenty years of one's life. The former answers "no," because he naïvely and optimistically looks forward to a more pleasant future. The superhistorical men answer "no" to the same question because from their vantage point above the historical process, yet conscious of it ("as a cognitive being"), there is no essential distinction between past and present: "the past and the present is one and the same, that is, typically alike in all manifold variety and, as omnipresence of imperishable types, a static structure of unchanged value and eternally the same meaning" (HL 1, KSA 1.256). Since the next ten or twenty years will bring nothing different from the past ten or twenty, there is no reason to relive them. We note that the superhistorical thus shares in the suffocating surfeit of memory which characterizes the historical; the result in this case is not knowledge, however, but wisdom; but this wisdom can easily lead to nausea when too much of the same thing is consumed: the superhistorical men become beings who have overconsumed historical knowledge and threaten to regurgitate it. Their wisdom, like the knowledge of the historical men, is ultimately unproductive since "a historical phenomenon clearly and completely understood and reduced to an intellectual phenomenon, is for him who has understood it dead." Thus the superhistorical man is also involved in a paradox, which potentially applies to Nietzsche and Nietzsche's reader as well: "As far as he is a knower, this power has now become powerless for him: not yet perhaps so far as he is a living being" (HL 1, KSA 1.257). History, Nietzsche suggests in this passage, is only productive when it is subordinated to an ahistorical power; paradoxically it becomes important for us only when it is no longer reflective, no longer a goad to memory and remembrance, no longer a recollection of the past: in short, when it ceases to be history as the word is normally understood.

The pedagogical ramifications of Nietzsche's distinctions in this early portion of his essay are significant, although they were perhaps more obvious for Nietzsche's contemporaries than they are for us today. From remarks in other published writings and in his notebooks, it is evident that Nietzsche conceived of his own education as thoroughly historical. Training in the *Gymnasium* and at the university involved careful attention to the past, in particular in Nietzsche's own area of expertise. In his lectures, the philosopher asserts that the chief means employed "to suppress and to cripple," "to divert or to deform" the natural proclivities of young men is "to paralyze that natural philosophic impulse by the so-called 'historical culture.'" Nietzsche identifies this historical culture with Hegelianism, a system of thought against which Schopenhauer directed his philosophical ire throughout his career, and which we find espoused by the neo-Hegelian David Strauß in the book denounced in the first *Untimely Meditation*. Nietzsche's claim is that "the historical vantage point" is assimilating the irrational to the rational and real, and it is the effective irrational that is the real driving force in "historical education." Nietzsche's allusion here is obscure, but it is likely another reference to the naïve optimism and the cultural affectations of the Second Empire. Nietzsche even blames "historical education" for deficiencies associated with philological training, and his criticism demonstrates that for him "history" and "historical education" are descriptive terms with much wider fields of meaning than what we might suspect.[69] The "balancing and questioning" in instruction, the attempt to determine what a philosopher really thought or which works should be attributed to him, or whether one or another variant is preferred are all items subsumed under a pernicious historical perspective (BA 5, KSA 1.742). His criticism of the historical in *Advantage and Disadvantage* is thus a reaction to his own educational experience as well as to the dominant perspectives Nietzsche associates with education in the Second Empire. At the same time, Nietzsche arrives at his predominantly antihistorical position only because he has had the good fortune of a classical training. In his study of antiquity, he identifies a model for an unhistorical culture that promoted action and fostered "life." Finally, Nietzsche's notion of a superhistorical position, which appears to have been more of an afterthought to the original dichotomy, is a partial validation of select sage university professors who have achieved a detached standpoint and no longer validate a facile progress and optimism. Ultimately, these superhistorical men are unable to further the goals of "life," but they at least recognize the debilitating effects of the hegemonic historical culture. The criticism that predominated in the lectures thus differs from the critique of historical education in the second *Untimely Meditation* in that the latter has a wider purview, focusing less on specific institutions than on a spirit that permeates the entire culture.

Three Types of Historical Pedagogy

Nietzsche's objections to historical education form the background for his discussion of three types of history or three relationships to historical knowledge. This discussion is usually considered the most pellucid portion of his essay because the terms Nietzsche introduces appear to be straightforward. But the complexity and contradictoriness of Nietzsche's undertaking have been vastly underestimated. Initially, Nietzsche distinguishes among three types of historical activity: the monumental, the antiquarian, and the critical, each of which would have had easily recognizable illustrations in his own time. In each case, he employs an identical approach, outlining first the advantages and then the disadvantages of each type of history with respect to the enigmatically defined notion of "life." Although Nietzsche had emphasized in his initial remarks that "the unhistorical and the historical are equally necessary for the health of an individual, a people and a culture" (HL 1, KSA 1.252), his explications do not evidence the even-handed treatment he promises in this statement or in his title. The bulk of his treatise does not, in fact, seek to establish the dual contribution of the historical and the unhistorical to "life"; rather, implicit in his arguments is an opposition between history and life—or at the very least an economy dominated by an inverse relationship between history and life. "Life," the least clearly defined term in the essay—which may give us some suspicion that it is related to other metaphysical notions that appear in his earliest writings, such as the Dionysian in *The*

Birth of Tragedy—is clearly identified with the unhistorical, as Nietzsche himself concedes when he writes: "History, so far as it serves life, serves an unhistorical power" (HL 1, KSA 1.257). Since "life" is the ultimate beneficiary of both the historical and the unhistorical and the *raison d'être* for any sort of educational practice, the balance Nietzsche establishes rhetorically is substantively and decidedly tilted toward the unhistorical. If we wish to make sense of the discussions of the individual approaches to history, we must remember that they partake in the general paradox that informs the essay: only where history belies its own nature—that is, where it becomes unhistorical or contributes to the unhistorical—does it serve life in the fullest manner.

Nietzsche demonstrates the greatest affinity for a monumental approach to history, since monumentality is intimately related to "great individuals" and their momentous achievements, which, as we have seen from the discussion of the "metaphysics of genius" in the lectures, should be the ultimate goal of human endeavor. Monumental history celebrates "the great moments in the struggle of individuals" as "the high points of humanity" (HL 2, KSA 1.259). Its "advantage" is a reaffirmation of existence over against the flux of historical events and thus the assertion of the ahistorical against a historical flux. "It is the knowledge," Nietzsche writes, "that the great which once existed was at least possible once and may well again be possible sometime" (HL 2, KSA 1.260). The actual historical occurrence of an event, Nietzsche suggests, is less significant than its effect. Greatness as it is reported to us in fictional genres would be just as efficacious as an actual occurrence, and Nietzsche concedes that "aesthetic criteria" may be introduced into the historical record: "there are even ages which are quite incapable of distinguishing between a monumental past and a mythical fiction: for precisely the same incentives can be given by the one world as by the other" (HL 2, KSA 1.262). What appears to be of paramount importance is only that some feat of greatness be recorded and transmitted, not that it actually happen. For this reason, in monumental history the "past itself" suffers damage, since it may distort the accuracy of the historical record. To this "disadvantage" Nietzsche adds other liabilities: monumental history may lead to a celebration of effects without causes and thus to a facile celebration of historical phenomena and a failure to recognize the uniqueness and import of historical actions. Indeed, monumental history may even distort greatness and, in some cases, become a weapon in the hands of the weak instead of an inspiration for the strong. Monumental history can take desirable characteristics and encourage inappropriate individuals into false emulation, thus making these characteristics unwelcome: "with tempting similarities the courageous are enticed to rashness, the enthusiastic to fanaticism; and if one thinks of this history as being in the hands and heads of talented egoists and enraptured rascals, then empires are destroyed, princes murdered, wars and revolutions instigated and the number of historical 'effects in themselves,' that is, of effects without sufficient causes, is further increased" (HL 2, KSA 1.262–63). But monumental history also deceives others who are not blessed with greatness into thinking that they too can be great or significant in the historical process. The "feebly artistic natures," perhaps encouraged by a reading of monumental history, may strike against what is truly great in art. These iconoclasts make manifest a disadvantage in monumental history because they destroy, rather than imitate and honor, superior achievement. They "let the dead bury the living," by disparaging "the mighty and great of their time" in admiring "the mighty and great of past ages" (HL 2, KSA 1.264). For Nietzsche, this instrumentalization of monumental history by epigones represents its worst perversion.

One of the abuses of monumental history—the disregard for the integrity of the past—can be corrected by the second approach to historical knowledge: antiquarian history. The beneficial dimension of the antiquarian is related to the preservation of roots and of personal, communal, or national histories. "By tending with loving hands what has long survived he [the antiquarian historian] intends to preserve the conditions in which he grew up for those who will come after him—and so he serves life" (HL 3, KSA 1.265). Although hundreds of "antiquarian" historians from Nietzsche's era would have agreed on the value of their contributions, the contentment with small and local accomplishments and the minutia of quotidian existence contradicts Nietzsche's embrace of greatness and geniality in this work and in other writings from this period. The very metaphors that Nietzsche employs to describe the advantages of the antiquarian indicate a passivity or, at most, a patient evolutionary procedure that conflicts with his stated aspirations for education and "life": "The contentment of a tree with its roots, the happiness of knowing oneself not to be wholly arbitrary and accidental, but rather as growing out of a past as its heir, flower and fruit and so to be exculpated, even justified in one's existence—this is what one now especially likes to call the proper historical sense" (HL 3, KSA 1.266–67). There exists a faint connection with the lectures since antiquarian history confronts the rootlessness of modern life, the growth of urban centers, and the "restless cosmopolitan choosing and searching for novelty and ever more novelty" (HL 3, KSA 1.266). Otherwise, Nietzsche's notion of the antiquarian appears to possess more liabilities than benefits. Indeed, patient preservation, for which it was lauded, can easily delude us into thinking a tradition is important when it is not. We lose a sense of proportion; everything seems to be of equal significance; consequently, we neglect what is really important. Moreover, the antiquarian spurns true greatness. If everything is worthy of preservation, then the truly great achievements of the past do not receive their due. Finally, the antiquarian approach to historical knowledge threatens to stifle anything new and promising. We may lose sight not only of the significance of past accomplishments, but also of the promise of future achievements. In this fashion, the antiquarian threatens "to undermine further and especially higher life, when the historical sense no longer preserves life but mummifies it" (HL 3, KSA 1.268). Nietzsche states at one point that antiquarian history "merely understands how to preserve life, not how to generate it; therefore it always underestimates what is in process of becoming because it has no instinct for discerning significance—unlike monumental history, for example, which has this instinct" (HL 3, KSA 1.268). Nietzsche appears to withdraw all "advantage" by such unqualified criticisms, which are ultimately more consonant with his general argument for dynamic action and genial feats.

The final type of history that Nietzsche delineates is the critical, to which he dedicates only a sparse discussion. Nietzsche characterizes it as iconoclastic: Man "must have the strength, and use it from time to time, to shatter and dissolve something to enable him to live: this he achieves by dragging it to the bar of judgment, interrogating it meticulously and finally condemning it." The liberating moment for the present is purchased at the expense of the past. "Life" alone, which Nietzsche here describes in a manner resembling Schopenhauer's notion of "will," as "that dark, driving, insatiably self-desiring power," delivers the unjust, merciless verdict. The verdict is unjust because there is no absolute standard for justice, and for that reason what matters is the result itself, not the justification. Life as the measure for action does not take into account justice in asserting itself; as Nietzsche writes: "it takes a great deal of strength to be able to live and to forget how far living and being unjust are one." It is apparent that critical history is less a historical sense or an approach to knowledge of the past, than an imperative to reject the past. The critical historical sense does not endeavor to construct history; its function is to condemn, to tear down, to destroy: occasions arise when life recognizes that a tradition or a dynasty is worthy of destruction; then "its past is considered critically, then one puts the knife to its roots, then one cruelly treads all pieties under foot." Nietzsche's misgivings about critical historiography are related to the attendant distortions of our true origins. Nietzsche affirms that we are not only the results of the crowning achievements of earlier generations, but also "the results of their aberrations, passions and errors, even crimes." And he further reminds us that "it is not possible quite to free oneself from this chain" (HL 3, KSA 1.269–70). In employing the critical sense of history for life, we simultaneously condemn life—or at least that part of the past that is always a part of the present. It is as if in affirming ourselves, we are compelled to deny ourselves as well. Nietzsche expresses this process as an attempt to impart a second nature, to give ourselves *a posteriori* a past that is a fiction. Thus his discussion of the critical perspective ends in a paradox that resembles the paradoxical stance he has taken toward history as a general phenomenon. While we cannot act without tearing down the past, we cannot tear down the past without injuring ourselves and our ability to act.

Historical Learning and Cultural Criticism

Nietzsche's parsing of these two sets of three abstract concepts relating to history and historical approaches to knowledge makes it clear that his treatise is less about a balance between advantages and disadvantages of history than it is about how history is a detrimental force for "life." But the conceptual framework in the first three sections is a mere propaedeutic to Nietzsche's central concern: how the pervasive historical consciousness found in contemporary Germany, and in particular the historical education that is the foundation for this consciousness, has had an adverse effect on German *Bildung*. The distinctions that Nietzsche draws and the evenhandedness with which he treats each category in the first part of the treatise are uncharacteristic for the remainder of the essay and for the pedagogical imperative to rescue German culture. The discussion in sections four through ten consists, in large measure, of a harangue against various abuses of history in the recently unified German state and the deficiencies found in the education of German youth, many of which recapitulate shortcomings noted in his lecture series from the previous year. As we read through Nietzsche's diatribe, it becomes evident that the disdained historical approach to knowledge has a wider field of meaning than we would normally ascribe to it today. We have already seen that in his lecture series, "history" was associated with an antiphilosophical attitude and with unproductive philological practices, and these associations continue and are expanded in the second *Untimely Meditation*. Nietzsche questions the activity of scholarly examination and careful consideration of historical phenomena as destructive for these phenomena and therefore antithetical to life's genuine purposes. Christianity, for example, when historicized in an excessive fashion becomes "blasé and unnatural" and ultimately is annihilated by this historical treatment. But this process is identical for anything that has life: "it ceases to live when it has been dissected completely and lives painfully and becomes sick once one begins to practice historical dissection on it" (HL 7, KSA 1.297). Moreover, the notion of history is brought into the proximity of all "science" [*Wissenschaft*], a term that for Nietzsche entails any sort of scholarly activity involving objectivity and the establishment of systems of knowledge. We might note that the distinction between historical knowledge involving human activity and knowledge of the external world of matter and its properties was a frequent theme in the nineteenth century—for example, in the writings of Wilhelm Dilthey (1833–1911). But Nietzsche, although he deals almost exclusively with the "human sciences," fails to draw this distinction in his critique of "history."

His point is that all scientific pretensions in the academy establish an artificial yardstick by which to measure the value of research and knowledge, and ignore the measure that truly matters: the ability to further life. He bemoans, in short, the penchant on the part of educators and educational institutions to promote irrelevant knowledge: "Now life is no longer the sole ruler and master of knowledge of the past: rather all boundary markers are overthrown and everything which once was rushes in upon man." We recognize again that Nietzsche is not primarily concerned with a viable approach to historical knowledge as much as he is focused on condemning its stranglehold on education and culture. The motto he associates with the academic historical attitude, *fiat veritas pereat vita* [let there be truth, even if life perishes], reverses the cultural and educational priority that he espouses (HL 4, KSA 1.271–72). The current preference for history, science, objectivity, philology, and truth, on the one side, versus life, on the other, must be reversed if culture is going to flourish in the new empire.

One of Nietzsche's chief objections to the historical education that predominates in Germany of the *Gründerzeit* is that it teaches that contemporaries, as the product of earlier ages, are old and no longer vital. "Historical education is a kind of inborn grayheadedness, and those who bear its mark from childhood on surely must attain the instinctive belief in the *old age of mankind*" (HL 8, KSA 1.303). Some insightful individuals who possess an advanced historical consciousness may recognize how absurd it is to continue to educate in a historical fashion, and may also understand that other, stronger peoples have been educated in another fashion and have achieved greatness. They, however, are enveloped by a cynicism about their own age and, as themselves the product of a thinking that places them at the end of a lineage, are comfortable with that knowledge and do not act to counter it. The philosophy behind historical education, as we have already noted, is Hegelian, and in the latter part of the essay Nietzsche attacks Hegel and his historical outlook more directly. Indeed, although most academic philosophers had turned away from Hegel by the time Nietzsche was writing his *Untimely Meditation* on history,[70] Hegel appears to be singlehandedly responsible in Nietzsche's argument for the deleterious path of German education:

> I believe that there has been no dangerous change or turn in the German education of this century which has not become more dangerous through the enormous influence, continuing to the present moment, of this philosophy, the Hegelian. Truly the belief that one is a late arrival of the ages is paralyzing and upsetting: terrible and destructive it must seem, however, if one day such a belief, by a bold inversion, defies this late arrival as the true meaning and purpose of all that has happened earlier, if his knowing misery is equated with a consummation of world history. (HL 8, KSA 1.308)

In Nietzsche's view, the historical perspective attributed here to Hegel has led to a general state of enervation. Individuals in the nineteenth century believe that their times are the necessary consequence of a "world process"; they worship history as the sole driving force for their current plight, ignoring other powers, such as art and religion. Nietzsche's antipathy to this historical determinism helps to explain his assault on Eduard von Hartmann. Citing almost exclusively passages from Hartmann that refer optimistically to the progress of the "world process," Nietzsche characterizes Hartmann as a "parodic monster" spouting a philosophical message that negates creative thought and individual initiative, casting contemporary humanity as workers "in the vineyard of the Lord" who are participating in the redemptive process ordained by history (HL 9, KSA 1.314–15).[71]

Hartmann's educational imperatives are even more repugnant because they contradict the hierarchic and elitist notions that Nietzsche endorsed so heartily in his lectures and similarly advocates in *Advantage and Disadvantage*. We have seen that Nietzsche disparaged "general education" in his lectures because of its egalitarian aspirations, and his remarks in the treatise continue to voice his disapproval. In *Advantage and Disadvantage*, he contends that general education teaches modern man to deceive himself about his true needs, thus making him "a walking lie," while also claiming that "the most sincere of all the sciences, the naked goddess philosophy" cannot thrive "in an age which suffers from general education" (HL 5, KSA 1.282). Nietzsche takes exception to Hartmann, however, for opposing the metaphysics of genius that lay at the heart of the educational enterprise in his lecture series. Hartmann's contentions that geniuses are no longer needed in the contemporary world and that we are approaching an era in which each worker will be able to lead a comfortable existence with an ample amount of leisure are reproduced by Nietzsche and subjected to derision. Citing Schopenhauer as his source and inspiration, Nietzsche writes of the geniuses, the giant intellects, who call to each other "across the bleak intervals of ages" and are "undisturbed by the wantonly noisy dwarfs who creep away beneath them," while they carry on "the lofty conversation of the spirits."[72] For Nietzsche, history does not entail a "world process" that produces satisfaction for the common man, but rather a few select geniuses, who are all that really matter: "The task of history is to be the mediator between them and so again and again to provide the occasion for and lend strength to the production of greatness. No, the *goal of humanity* cannot lie at the end but only *in its highest specimens*" (HL 9, KSA 1.317). Nietzsche is disdainful toward the rest of humankind, and he scorns the "mania for education" that produces a history "from the standpoint of the *masses*." The masses are worthy of notice, Nietzsche asserts, for only three reasons: "as blurred copies of great men, produced on bad paper with worn plates," as "resistance to the great," and as "the tools of the great" (HL 9, KSA 1.319–20). The pedagogy of his contemporaries, exemplified in *Advantage and Disadvantage* by Hartmann, can only lead to a mediocre existence precisely because it has adopted a false and pernicious historical foundation.[73]

The "untimeliness" of Nietzsche's essay on history derives from its opposition to one important current in German intellectual life associated with Hegelian notions of progress, the popular philosophical writings of Eduard von Hartmann, and the way in which young men were educated in the *Gymnasium* and at the university. But in many regards, his message partakes of criticisms and perspectives that were often articulated in Bismarckian Germany. Although we may not find writers who are as rhetorically skilled and as openly hostile to "historical education," Nietzsche's elitist notions were hardly uncommon in more conservative circles in the Second Empire. We have witnessed in connection with his lectures that Nietzsche also evidenced a Germanophilic antimodernism shared by many contemporaries, and we find it apparent in *Advantage and Disadvantage* as well. In connection with his ridicule of Hartmann, for example, he alludes to newspapers in a deprecatory fashion, and we will recall that one of his chief objections to educational institutions of his era was that journalistic virtuosity was valorized over true culture. But other negative manifestations of modernity appear in the essay as well. "The education of German youth," Nietzsche asserts, using the metaphors of the conservative critique of modernity, produces "the historico-cultural Philistine, the precocious newly wise chatterbox on matters of state, church and art, the sensorium of thousands of sensations, the insatiable stomach which yet does not know what honest hunger and thirst are" (HL 10, KSA 1.326). At another point, Nietzsche implores us to "walk around any German city" and observe that everything is "colorless, worn down, badly copied, careless," and that we notice "a general haste" and "a general craving for comfort." Even German fashion is not authentically native, but "borrowed from foreigners and copied as carelessly as possible." Nietzsche exudes some sense of accomplishment in the recent victory over France and the resulting unification, but Germany has been disappointing in failing to emulate its military achievement in the sphere of culture. As we noted at the outset of this chapter, Nietzsche juxtaposes German military and political prowess with discouraging cultural accomplishment: "it is *German unity* in that highest sense for which we strive and strive for more ardently than political reunification, the *unity of the German spirit and life after the annihilation of the opposition of form and content, of inwardness and convention*" (HL 4, KSA 1.275–78). This disharmony in the German spirit, this disjunction of purposes in spite of the external, political unity, is another sign of the hegemony of modernity. In Nietzsche's presentation, Germany becomes a paradigm for the ills of the modern age, and he likens it to Rome in its period of decline: it is characterized by "the influx of the foreign and the degenerated in the cosmopolitan carnival of gods, customs, and arts" (HL 5, KSA 1.279). Ultimately, "historical education," which is itself a product of this modern mentality, bears responsibility for Germany succumbing to the enervating and pernicious symptoms of a modernist, superficial pseudoculture.

Historical education is culpable because it advocates attitudes and behaviors antithetical to the instincts of German youth. Its goal, Nietzsche claims, is to produce either pedantic scholars or pseudo-cultured Philistines, both of which counter the natural proclivities of young men desiring a new, vital, German spirit: "That an education with that aim and this result is contrary to nature is felt only by the man who is not yet completely fashioned by it, it is only felt by the instinct of youth because it still has the instinct of nature which is first broken artificially and violently by that education" (HL 10, KSA 1.326). With the introduction of nature and instinct as foils to historical education, however, Nietzsche has moved beyond the agenda of the lecture series. In speaking about the "future of educational institutions," Nietzsche was making a contribution to the vast literature on educational reform, in particular on the role of the *Gymnasium* and secondary schooling as an essential part of the educational system. In *Advantage and Disadvantage*, he begins to set up an opposition between formal education, now disqualified as "historical" and detrimental to the very nature of German youth, and learning through instinctual activity, through experience with culture, and through "life." "Breaking" historical education entails moving away from the strictures of formal education entirely; Nietzsche advocates "destroying a superstition, the belief in the *necessity* of that educational procedure." His reflections on the educational literature he had read in preparation for his lecture series now assume a different meaning: the bankruptcy of the entire educational enterprise:

> It is, after all, a prevailing opinion that there is no other possibility at all than just our present tiresome reality. Just examine the literature of secondary and higher education in the last decade with that in mind: the examiner will, with indignant astonishment, become aware how uniformly the whole intent of education is conceived in all the fluctuating proposals and vehemence of disagreement, how thoughtlessly the prevailing product, the "educated man" as he is understood at present, is accepted as the necessary and rational foundation of all further education. (HL 10, KSA 1.326–27)

The present system starts by teaching cultural as historical knowledge; the youth have their heads filled with "an enormous number of concepts which are drawn from the highly mediate knowledge of past ages and peoples, not from the immediate perception of life." The desires of youth to gain experience, to grow in living and expand their horizon is thereby "anaesthetized" or even "intoxicated" with the illusion that knowledge of the ancients and their experiences can be internalized in a few years. The revised educational mission Nietzsche conceives in this essay is not to impart formal education to youth at the outset of their careers, but rather to enable them to experience life as a practice of living and learning: "As though life itself were not a craft which has to be learned from the beginning and continuously practiced without stint if it is not to breed a crawling brood of botchers and babblers!" (HL 10, KSA 1.327). We see that in one short year Nietzsche has made the transition from educational reformer of institutions of learning to advocate of a vitalistic alternative outside the confines of formal instruction.

At the close of his essay, Nietzsche's brief return to the three categories he had analyzed in the first section—the historical, the unhistorical, and the superhistorical—confirms this transition. He no longer writes in a balanced fashion of the necessity for both the historical and the unhistorical, but instead seeks to cure the historical illness of his age with the "antidotes" of the unhistorical and the superhistorical. To counter scientific observation and historical knowledge, he recommends two powers that possess "an eternal and stable character": art and religion. Along with "life," which is to "rule over knowledge, over science," these powers perform a "hygienic" function in the contemporary world; the unhistorical and the superhistorical "are the natural antidotes to the stifling of life by history, to the historical malady." At some point, after they are cured of their historical sickness, men may return to history, now dominated by life, and benefit from the monumental, the antiquarian, and the critical approaches. But at that time, "they will have unlearned much and moreover will have lost all inclination even to look at what those educated ones want to know above all." From the perspective of today, they will be characterized precisely by their "lack of education, their indifference and reserve toward much that is famous, even toward much that is good" (HL 10, KSA 1.332). It is interesting to note in the last sections of *Advantage and Disadvantage* the introduction of biological and medicinal metaphors that reinforce Nietzsche's arguments, since sickness, health, and related terms, often used in a literal sense, will be employed in later writings to attack religion, art, and the putative "eternal" power they possess—in opposition to the late Nietzsche's preferred hypothesis of eternal becoming or recurrence. In 1874, however, Nietzsche continues to extol a metaphysical regime into which he incorporates his philological interests. Greek antiquity, no longer the object of tedious academic studies, persists in Nietzsche's writings as the foil to a wayward modernity. The Greeks provide proof that "a man can be very educated and yet be historically quite uneducated" (HL 4, KSA 1.273). Nietzsche implores his age to strive for an emulation of Hellenic culture, "to seek our standards of the great, the natural and the human in the ancient Greek world. But there we will also find the actuality of an essentially unhistorical culture, and a culture which is nevertheless, or rather therefore, unspeakably rich and full of life" (HL 8, KSA 1.307). Germans of the Second Reich must imitate Greeks, who were also threatened at one point "of perishing through 'history,'" and throw off everything that is "alien or past," organizing the "chaos of all foreign countries, of all antiquity" and realizing their own "genuine needs," "letting their sham needs die out" (HL 10, KSA 1.333). At the close of the essay, we therefore encounter once again a contradictory tension in Nietzsche's thought: he is calling on a particular understanding of history, on historical thought, to convince his contemporaries of the damage inflicted by historical education and of the necessity to embrace the unhistorical and the superhistorical. But only when Germany has learned this historical lesson and asserts its own values, its own "ethical nature," its own instincts, and its own cultural preeminence, will it achieve an educational perspective that fosters what really matters in the course of human affairs.

The Paradigm of Anti-Institutional Education

The tensions and paradoxes in *Advantage and Disadvantage* are very likely the result of Nietzsche's transition away from institutional reform and practical issues involved with instruction to a stance that believes education of German youth for genuine cultural achievement and appreciation cannot be accomplished within the current—or perhaps within any—institutional framework. The balance that we find asserted and then belied throughout the first three sections of the essay reflects uneasiness with the very categories of analysis. Ultimately, the historical is revealed not as one side of an equilibrium with unhistorical forces, but as the bane of contemporary German life and a barrier that must be overcome if greatness is going to be achieved. The historical also becomes in this treatise a shorthand for numerous ills in German society; it relates not only to the way in which the youth are educated in schools and at the university, or to the cultural veneration of the past in monumental or antiquarian form, but to a more encompassing mentality that permeates the Second Empire. What Nietzsche has come to realize is that while the current school system may be part of the problem, education in any traditional sense can no longer be part of the solution. The position he appears to reach by the middle of the decade is that genuine education is not—or is rarely—connected to an actual university or secondary school because institutions are arranged to cater to the needs of the state and to the economic exigencies of the public. The alternative that Nietzsche envisioned in his early lectures—an instruction arrangement that would accommodate the needs of the select few and produce a renewal of German culture—disappears and is replaced by a demand that the youth be allowed to develop and express their "instincts" outside institutional boundaries. Since schooling hinders, rather than promotes, the development and expression of instincts, the pedagogical lesson is that institutional education is antithetical to the values and aims of genuine *Bildung*. In contrast to the Enlightenment tradition of pedagogy still very alive in the nineteenth century, the goal of education is not a knowledgeable, well-informed, or well-trained citizenry, but the production of exceptional individuals. Nietzsche shares some educational views with conservatives of his era, but as the decade progresses, his positions become those of an outsider to any accepted pedagogical direction. Nietzsche gradually came to understand education as it had been institutionalized in the Germany of his era as a perversion of the real purpose of knowledge and learning. Just as the highest purpose of history is ultimately embodied in the unhistorical, so too the highest pedagogical goal becomes the anti-educational.[74]

Nietzsche's third *Untimely Meditation*, *Schopenhauer as Educator*, confirms its author's anti-institutional turn. The ostensible subject of the essay, the philosopher Arthur Schopenhauer, had himself a rather precarious relationship with the educational institutions of his time. Having received his doctorate from Jena in 1813, and having composed the first version of *The World as Will and Representation* from 1814 to 1818, Schopenhauer decided to demonstrate his pedagogical prowess by disseminating his philosophical teaching at the University of Berlin in 1820. Although he held no chair, he received nevertheless permission to hold lectures as an adjunct, but he had the audacity to schedule his course at the same time at which G. W. F. Hegel was accustomed to teach. The newcomer Schopenhauer was evidently no match for Hegel, who enjoyed widespread popularity among the student body. Attendance for Schopenhauer's offering was so poor—his course on "general philosophy" drew only five students—that he did not even complete the term. Although he had announced lectures through the winter semester of 1831–32, he decided abruptly to abandon a career in higher education and devote himself to a life of learning outside the institution, an alternative he was fortunate and wealthy enough to be able to pursue.[75] Nietzsche's selection of the word "educator" [*Erzieher*] in his title thus contains an irony of which the author was undoubtedly aware—and is thus simultaneously a commentary on the German educational establishment in the nineteenth century. In terms of an institutionalized educational system, Schopenhauer hardly qualifies as an educator at all. He was engaged as a regular instructor at no school or university and had no students studying with him. Having devoted his life to a pursuit of truth outside the confines of establishment pedagogy, however, Schopenhauer becomes, in Nietzsche's portrayal, the paradigm for education in his new sense of this word. Like the philosopher in the frame of Nietzsche's pedagogical lectures of 1872, Schopenhauer instructs outside the institution, imparting wisdom for life, rather than "historical knowledge" for the sake of convention and in the service of the state or a career. Schopenhauer becomes for Nietzsche an "educator" whose objective is consonant with the real meaning of the word, since he strives through his philosophy to impart *Bildung* in accord with a superior and elitist cultural mission.

Nietzsche makes the reader aware of his unusual characterization of Schopenhauer and the peculiar nature of the educational process early in the essay. We might note first, however, that Nietzsche was one of many individuals who derived inspiration from Schopenhauer's philosophy in the second half of the nineteenth century. Although Schopenhauer had not attained great prominence in the Romantic era in which his philosophy had its roots, after the failed revolutions of 1848 he began to attain considerable acclaim in Germany, in particular among young German intellectuals like Nietzsche. The partisanship for Schopenhauer was thus hardly "untimely" for educated circles in the 1870s; indeed, most of Nietzsche's peers were similarly enthusiastic about Schopenhauer, and Paul Deussen (1845–1919), Nietzsche's closest friend while he was studying at Bonn, was the founder of the Schopenhauer Society and became the first editor of the *Schopenhauer Yearbook*. For Nietzsche, however, Schopenhauer assumed a very special role as an anti-institutional educator. Addressing a "young soul" in the first section of *Schopenhauer as Educator*, Nietzsche comments that the "true educators and cultivators" [*Erzieher und Bildner*] impart "the true primeval sense and elementary material of your being, something that is not subject to education or acculturation at all." Nietzsche's conception of education is thus resolutely anti-institutional, but also elemental and attuned to the innermost core of his "students'" being. In this essay, Nietzsche conceives of the authentic educator as a personal emancipator, someone who allows disciples to free themselves from the shackles of convention. A particularly descriptive passage portrays the liberation involved in genuine education by applying horticultural metaphors: it is the "removal of all weeds, rubble, and vermin that seek to harm the plant's delicate shoots, a radiance of light and warmth, the loving rush of nocturnal rain" (SE 1, KSA 1.341). What appears to be even more important for Nietzsche is that the student does not encounter the educator as a member of the teaching profession, but rather seeks him out for his philosophical wisdom. Nietzsche emphasizes that he found Schopenhauer the philosopher and made him his educator. The task that he assigns to Schopenhauer therefore has nothing to do with integration into the social order or training for a profession—this role was the one Friedrich Ritschl played in Nietzsche's life. The educator has the much more difficult task of disclosing to his pupil how one becomes an authentic human being. In contrast to institutionalized education, where knowledge and scholarship are the primary goal, Nietzsche's educational goal is humanity. Schopenhauer is especially impressive in this regard because he was rejected by his own era as a university instructor, because he conducted a philosophical existence independent of the state, and because he constantly harangued the most eminent members of the teaching profession, in particular Hegel. The very qualities that disqualified him as an actual teacher at a Prussian university make him more suitable for Nietzsche's revised pedagogical imperative.

Nietzsche's stylization of Schopenhauer into the prototypical noninstitutional educator is nowhere more apparent than in Nietzsche's typology of three images of man in contemporary society. The first type is identified with the French philosopher Jean-Jacques Rousseau (1712–1778). This individual advocates hasty revolutions and socialist upheavals under the guise of a return to nature. Nietzsche despises individuals who conform to this type and regards them as repressed creatures who secretly loathe themselves. It is not insignificant that Rousseauian man is viewed so negatively, since Rousseau himself is commonly identified with Enlightenment ideals of education. In opposing this type so categorically, Nietzsche once again rejects the naïve optimism he came to associate with certain strands in Enlightenment thinking. As a counterbalance to Rousseauian man, Nietzsche posits an individual modeled on Goethean principles. Throughout his works, Nietzsche displays a great deal of respect for Goethe, in particular for his literary abilities and aristocratic tastes. In *Schopenhauer as Educator*, however, Goethean man is depicted as a contemplative and quietist corrective to the rebelliousness of Rousseauian individuals. Two characteristics stand out: First, Goethean man is patiently evolutionary; in contrast to Rousseauian man, he dislikes violence, jumps, and discontinuities. Although in his youth Goethe had evidenced features consonant with Rousseauian revolutionaries, his Faust metamorphoses from world revolutionary to world traveler. Second, this type of man prefers contemplation to action; he is "a conserving and conciliatory force." The danger Nietzsche detects in the Goethean individual is that once he ceases to strive in a Faust-like fashion, he can easily degenerate into the prototype of a cultural Philistine. His virtues would be greater, Nietzsche contends, if they had a bit more "muscle and natural wildness." The final image of man, the Schopenhauerian, contains the hope for the future. By accepting voluntarily the suffering of earthly existence, the Schopenhauerian individual can accomplish a complete alteration of his being and thereby reach a higher stage of humanity. Although Schopenhauer's philosophy would seem to qualify him as a model for the contemplative and resigned individual of Goethean province, Nietzsche maintains that his pessimism and negativity lead to a "powerful yearning for sanctification and salvation." Ultimately, Schopenhauerian man is considered a model for a heroic life and for "the great individual," and by following his teaching, by subscribing to a nobler vision of mankind and the quasi-Platonic ideal in Schopenhauer's philosophy, Nietzsche believes that human beings can achieve the highest goals (SE 4, KSA 1.369–74).

Nietzsche often speaks as if every individual had equal access to a Schopenhauerian education, as if this antiestablishment pedagogy had as its goal a society replete with great individuals. But as in his lecture series and his *Untimely Meditation* on history, his further reflections indicate that what we learn from Schopenhauer's educational and cultural philosophy is the necessity of hierarchy in human affairs. The basic thought of any culture, Nietzsche claims, should be "the production of the philosopher, the artist, and the saint in ourselves and outside of us" (KSA 1.382), since the appearance of these three types of exceptional human beings would signify the perfection of nature. It is possible, of course, that any individual could be taken into that sublime order of philosophers, artists, and saints, that the multitudes could participate in the transition to a higher order of humanity. But the lesson we have to learn and the consequences we have to face are that most human beings will never attain this lofty status, and that the happiness of the "mass of specimens" is of no consequence in this scheme. Nietzsche again makes his elitist proclivities evident when he poses the following question for his reader: "How does your life, the life of an individual, obtain the highest value, the most profound significance? How is it wasted as little as possible? Certainly only by living for the advantage of the most seldom and most valuable specimens, not for the advantage of many, that is, of the most worthless specimens, when considered individually" (SE 6, KSA 1.384–85). Nietzsche's critique of culture and his praise of Schopenhauer's educational program are consonant with the conclusions he draws in *Advantage and Disadvantage*. Germany must cease training individuals exclusively for the pecuniary advantages of middle-class life, or for service to the state as mediocre civil servants, or for tedious and myopic scholarly activity; and concentrate instead on the true mission for any higher education: the production of genius. Nietzsche recognizes the practical limitations of his alternative vision of pedagogy and does not delude himself into believing it could be implemented under current circumstances. His suggestion that all philosophical education be removed from the auspices of the state—since it and its academies are unable to evaluate true philosophy (SE 8, KSA 1.421–22)—is clearly untenable. But if a Nietzschean pedagogy inspired by a Schopenhauerian "education" was going to produce anything of lasting value, higher education would have to liberate itself from "third and fourth-rate scholarship" (SE 8, KSA 1.424) and embrace a loftier mission for itself and for the sake of German society.

This liberation, of course, did not take place, and as the years passed, an educational agenda gradually disappears from Nietzsche's writings. Part of its disappearance stemmed doubtless from Nietzsche's own disenchantment with the teaching profession. The summer semester of 1876 was his last as a teacher at the *Pädagogium*, and poor health compelled him to take a yearlong leave from all teaching obligations in 1876–77. Indeed, persistent illness forced him to resign his professorship entirely after the winter semester 1878–79, but we can sense from his correspondence and from the courses he offered that he was no longer fully engaged in the academic enterprise. His remarks about education in his aphoristic period are sparse and mostly critical of the role education was playing or could play in German life. In the first volume of *Human, All Too Human,* he writes that "in the case of the individual human being, the task of education is to imbue him with such firmness and certainty that he can no longer as a whole be in any way deflected from his path" (MA 224, KSA 2.188), a rather modest and rigid task that contrasts starkly with the aim of fostering genius. Later he ascribes to the schools the rather standard charge of teaching "rigorous thinking, cautious judgment, and consistent reasoning," and likens the preoccupation with the classics to a "higher gymnastics for the head" (MA 266, KSA 2.220–21). In the second volume of *Human, All Too Human,* he composes an aphorism with the title "education contortion," whose main contentions are that educators themselves are not educated, that they compliantly pass on useless knowledge to their pupils, and that an individual seeking to obtain a real education must twist himself around the stunted trees that are his teachers, and in the end wind up "contorted and deformed" (VM 181, KSA 2.458–59). He later asserts baldly that there are no educators, and that any "thinker" desiring an education must acquire it autodidactically. Traditional education is either an "experiment" on an unknown subject or a "fundamental leveling" to achieve conformity with social norms (WS 267, KSA 2.667–68). By the time we reach the 1880s, Nietzsche has begun to assimilate education to a biological register. In *Dawn,* he considers education to be "a continuation of procreation, and often a kind of supplementary beautification of it" (M 252, KSA 3.252). And in *The Gay Science,* he conceives of education as an almost scientifically prescribed method that destroys individuality and compels social conformity: "Education always proceeds as follows: it seeks to determine an individual through a series of stimuli and biases to adapt a way of thinking and action, which, when they have become habit, drive, and passion, will dominate him externally and internally *to his ultimate disadvantage,* but 'for the general good'" (FW 21, KSA 3.392). In his late writings, he regards education as a force that can at most deceive an individual about his genetic inheritance. In *Beyond Good and Evil,* after asserting that it is "simply impossible that a person would *not* have his parents' and forefathers' qualities and preferences in his body," he turns to the role of education and *Bildung*: "In our very populist, or rather, very plebeian age, 'education' and '*Bildung*' *must* be essentially the art of deceiving—deceiving with regard to origin, with regard to the inherited rabble in body and soul" (JGB 264, KSA 5.219). In his last notebooks, education is viewed only as a means of leveling and a tool to achieve mediocrity: "*Education*: a system of means to ruin the exceptions in favor of the rule. *Bildung*: a system of means to direct taste against the exception in favor of the ordinary" (Nachlass 1888, 16[6], KSA 13.484). In sharp contrast to his earlier exhortations, education in his later writings no longer holds the promise of transcending the limitations of social constraints and promoting cultural greatness; it has been reduced to either a handmaiden of biological destiny, a means to assimilate genuine achievement to a pseudocultural mediocrity, or a measure to convince individuals that they can escape their genetic fate.

There exists only one point in Nietzsche's writings after 1874 where he devotes extensive attention to matters of education. It occurs in *Twilight of the Idols* in the section entitled "What the Germans lack." Fundamentally, Nietzsche returns to his earlier criticism, adding very little besides heightened rhetoric. Higher education in Germany, by which Nietzsche means both the *Gymnasium* and the university, is dominated by the state and the "Reich," whose goals are antithetical to those of genuine *Bildung*. Lacking are educators, "superior, noble spirits," for both types of institutions; instead we find only "learned boors" who function as "higher nursemaids." The sole objective for German "higher education" is the brutal preparation of countless young men for the civil service. Indeed, the very fact that "countless" students are engaged in "higher education" indicates that it cannot achieve any worthwhile purpose: "All higher education belongs to the exceptions alone: one must be privileged to have a right to so high a privilege. Great and fine things can never be common property." And this sad state of educational affairs has led directly to a decline in German culture, which is attributed to the fact that "'higher education' is no longer a privilege—the democratism of 'culture' made 'universal' and *common*" (GD, Was den Deutschen abgeht 5, KSA 6.107). Thinking is absent from schools and universities: "even among students of philosophy themselves, the theory, the practice, the *vocation* of logic is beginning to die out" (GD, Was den Deutschen abgeht 7, KSA 6.109). As we have seen in earlier critiques, universities are censured for a useless and dull learning: "what an atmosphere prevails among its scholars, what a barren, self-satisfied, and lukewarm spirituality." The slavish state of scholarship in all disciplines has destroyed any trace of genuine culture and "is one of the main reasons why education *and educators* appropriate to fuller, richer, *deeper* natures are no longer forthcoming." The end result is that German universities have become the breeding grounds for "instinct atrophy of the intellect" (GD, Was den Deutschen abgeht 3, KSA 6.105).

Significant in this late diatribe against the German educational system is only the total absence of any redeeming feature for institutional education. Nietzsche is at pains to convince his reader in 1888 that he had been consistently asserting the deleterious nature of German education since his writings of the early 1870s: "For seventeen years I have not wearied of exposing the *despiritualizing* influence of our contemporary knowledge factories" (GD, Was den Deutschen abgeht 3, KSA 6.105). But, as we have seen, Nietzsche had not begun his commentary on the Education Question with the same vehement disconsolateness that we find in *Twilight of the Idols*. His earliest remarks on the German educational system were composed in an ongoing dialogue with the pedagogical literature of his era, which

Nietzsche consulted in preparation for his lecture series, but never cites in his presentations. His initial perspective was critical of what was transpiring in Germany, but his motivation in broaching this topic was a reform of the institutions responsible for imparting instruction to German youth, and his hope was that these reforms would contribute to a rejuvenation of German culture along Wagnerian and Schopenhauerian lines. Although his positions were not derivative from any single source or tradition, they resemble at times those of neo-humanists writing in the spirit of the early nineteenth century and, in some passages, conservative critics in the Second Reich, who likewise averred a decline in German educational practice and general cultural achievement. Reinforcing his views on education were his own experiences as a student at Pforta, Bonn, and Leipzig, and his professional positions as both a university professor and a teacher at a *Gymnasium* in Basel, where he was an engaging classroom instructor as well as a concerned contributor to practical and administrative matters. His gradual turn from a reformist to a strictly condemnatory agenda coincides with significant changes in his personal and professional life: his disenchantment with Wagner and the Wagnerian cause; his recognition of fundamental philosophical differences with Schopenhauer and the metaphysical tradition; his discontent with teaching and classical philology as a profession; and his growing interest for, and adherence to, modes of thought associated with nineteenth-century biology, a topic we will revisit in Chapters 7 and 9. In his later thought, Nietzsche may have been able to convince himself of a consistent seventeen-year campaign against the German educational establishment. But in fact his actual discussions and criticisms of educational institutions and practices occurred primarily during the years 1872–74 and changed considerably from the mid-1870s until his final writings in 1888.

Chapter 2

The German Question

A nineteenth-century German intellectual could not have avoided the German Question. In the eighteenth century, Germany existed as a patchwork of principalities, states, and free cities in central Europe, but the overriding structure of the Holy Roman Empire of the German Nation,[1] a multi-ethnic entity whose origins dated to the reign of Charlemagne in the ninth century and whose boundaries extended well beyond what anyone considered "Germany," provided a loosely centralized governance and identification point for its inhabitants. The rise of the modern German Question was coincidental with the demise of the Holy Roman Empire in 1806, and it continued to be a central issue for Europe until the unification of Germany under the auspices of Prussia and the declaration of the Second Empire in 1871. Indeed, as we shall see, for some individuals, including Nietzsche, it persisted as an open question even after the formation of the Second Reich. Napoleon Bonaparte had considerable responsibility for the emergence of the German Question, not only because he dissolved the First Empire, but also because he simplified German politics for easier administration. More than three hundred governmental units that could be identified in some regard as German were reduced to fewer than forty under his rule, and although his goal was not one of creating a modern unified German nation-state, he provided an example of how such a state might operate, as well as an enemy around which German sentiments could rally in their own drive toward unity. This drive was thwarted to some extent by the territorial settlements of the Congress of Vienna (1814–15). While some Germans had hoped to achieve a modern and unified nation, the powers of Europe and the rulers of the separate German domains opted for a German Confederation consisting of thirty-nine separate entities. While this solution represented a significant change over the Holy Roman Empire, the lack of any centralized power or executive force meant that the real authority in Central Europe would remain in the hands of the two rival powers, Austria and Prussia.[2] The dream of a unified nation, however, did not die in 1815, and the independence movements of other European nations in the 1830s gave it renewed impetus. The formation of a Customs Union in 1834 provided some economic unity under the leadership of Prussia and is usually regarded today as an important step in the ultimate unification of Germany following the Franco-Prussian War. The hopes of liberals for "unification from below" in the revolution of 1848 and the deliberations of the democratically elected National Assembly in Frankfurt's St. Paul's Church were ultimately dashed, and the Confederation was restored. But the march toward a modern nation-state was only postponed. With the appointment of Otto von Bismarck (1815–1898) as Prussian chancellor, his alliance with the National Liberals seeking a unified nation, and the succession of wars against Denmark (1864), Austria (1866), and France (1870–71), the process of unification "from above" was completed in the "small German" format.[3] The way in which Germany achieved nationhood and the nature of the new Germany were not what most intellectuals and enthusiasts during the nineteenth century had envisioned, but the results did provide a tentative resolution to political and economic aspects of the German Question, while stimulating a great deal of intellectual and cultural activity on the meaning of Germanness in the new nation.

Reflections on Germanness had been a frequent theme throughout the century. They were particularly intense during the Napoleonic invasion and occupation of Germany, and during the so-called Wars of Liberation against the French. The radical national spirit of the times is captured in many forms, from the administrative activities of Baron von Stein (1757–1831) to the engaged journalism of Joseph Görres (1776–1848) and the patriotic fervor of the philosopher Johann Gottlieb Fichte (1762–1814) in his *Addresses to the German Nation* (1808). The sentiments of this generation were perhaps captured in their most concise form in the celebrated poem "What Is the Fatherland of the Germans?" ["Was ist des Deutschen Vaterland?"], composed by Ernst Moritz Arndt (1769–1860) in 1813. The poem is directed against German particularism, negating in strophe after strophe the notion that the German Fatherland is embodied in any of the individual German states. It also contains a heavy dose of anti-French animus, as well as a condemnation of the German leaders who are obstacles to a unified nation. The solution to the question posed by its title is the famous proclamation that Germany consists of all areas in which German is spoken ("As far as the German tongue sounds" ["So weit die deutsche Zunge klingt"]); Arndt, like most members of his generation, conceived of Germany as an entity that included both Austria and Prussia, as well as significant parts of Switzerland. The poem, which was set to music as a popular song, was influential for August Heinrich Hoffmann von Fallersleben (1798–1874), who, almost thirty years after Arndt, composed "The Song of the Germans" ["Das Lied der Deutschen"] (1841) in another era of patriotic enthusiasm. Hoffmann is reiterating many of the points in his predecessor's verse: his call for "Germany, Germany above everything" ["Deutschland, Deutschland über alles"] is meant to oppose separatist German regimes, not to promote aggression against foreign nations. Only when the "Song of the Germans," under pressure from conservative forces, became the German anthem in 1922 and was retained after Adolf Hitler rose to power in 1933 did it assume its association with German militarism. The nationalist writings from the first half of the nineteenth century would certainly have been common fare for a schoolboy like Nietzsche, growing up in the 1850s and 1860s, and Arndt in particular was someone with whom he was familiar. After two decades during which Prussian authorities prohibited his participation in university life at Bonn, Arndt was rehabilitated in 1840, regaining his professorship, and the following year he was even appointed rector of the university. After he retired from the university, he remained active in the civic life of Bonn until his death in 1860, just four years before Nietzsche began his studies at the Rhineland University. Nietzsche was certainly conscious of Arndt's reputation and views. Indeed, shortly after his arrival in Bonn he made a visit to the recently deceased poet's gravesite, and in the following year he mentions in several of his letters his attendance at the 1865 "national Arndt festival," where a memorial monument depicting the celebrated German patriot was dedicated (to Franziska and Elisabeth Nietzsche, 29 May 1865, Nr. 468, KSB 2.59; to Franziska Nietzsche, June 1865, Nr. 470, KSB 2.69; to Carl von Gersdorff, 1 August 1865, Nr. 476, KSB 2.76).[4]

Nietzsche's enthusiasm for Arndt and the nationalist tradition occurs in his youthful period, and his views on the German Question would evolve over the next decade and a half from a Wagner-inspired German patriotism through a cosmopolitan stance toward German affairs before ending in an overt rejection of almost everything associated with Germany in the last years of his sane life. Before turning to a more detailed consideration of Nietzsche's dealing with this timely concern, however, we should briefly take up two issues that have indirect bearing on his sentiments about the German Question: Nietzsche's nationality and his oft-repeated claim of Polish ancestry. Nietzsche was never a German in the legal sense of that word. He never obtained citizenship in the newly formed German Empire, and he had no German passport. At his birth and during his childhood, he was Prussian, since Röcken, the town in which he was born; Naumburg, the city in which he spent his formative years; and Pforta, the secondary boarding school he attended, were all on Prussian territory. Traditionally this area had been part of Saxony, and three of Nietzsche's grandparents had been subjects of the Electorate of Saxony, the fourth hailing from the nearby Duchy of Saxe-Meiningen.[5] But Saxony had been an ally of the French in the Napoleonic Wars, and when the Congress of Vienna redrew the map of Europe, granting Prussia additional territories, the places of Nietzsche's birth and youth were ceded to Prussia. In negotiations in 1815, Prussia had wanted to gain all of Saxony, but the European powers decided to give Prussia only the northern sections of the recently established Kingdom of Saxony, and as compensation for this loss,

Prussia received lands along the Rhine River, including the city of Bonn. Nietzsche thus did not take up residence outside Prussian soil until he left Bonn in 1865 and moved to Leipzig, which was still part of Saxony. Nietzsche remained a Prussian citizen throughout his university career, however, and when he received the offer of a professorship in Basel, one of the concerns was his political inclination and residential status: the Swiss were reluctant to hire someone who had allegiances to a foreign power. Friedrich Ritschl (1806–1876), Nietzsche's mentor in Leipzig, wrote to Wilhelm Vischer-Bilfinger (1808–1874), the head of the commission charged with making the appointment in Basel, that Nietzsche "was not an especially political type," and that despite his general feelings concerning the "growing greatness of Germany," he was not particularly beholden to Prussia.[6] Ritschl was referring only to how Nietzsche might acclimate himself to the atmosphere in the free city of Basel, but he was probably also aware that Basel preferred that its younger "German" appointees relinquish their German citizenship so that compulsory military service would not disrupt the academic calendar. Thus, although the appointment at Basel did not require Nietzsche to give up his Prussian citizenship, Nietzsche announced to Vischer-Bilfinger that he was prepared to do so in March of 1869 (Nr. 626, KSB 2.381); documentary confirmation occurred in April.[7] Nietzsche could have applied for Basler citizenship after a period of residence, but he never did so, although he traveled over the next two decades using a temporary passport issued from Basel. After 1879, when he dissolved his residence in Basel, he never resided long enough in any place to apply for citizenship. He returned to Germany only in insanity, first in an institution in Jena, then at his mother's home in Naumburg, and later with his sister at Villa Silberblick in Weimar, but no one sought to apply for German citizenship on his behalf. In effect, from April 1869 until his death in August 1900 he was a man without a country, and while he was still of sound mind, he showed no inclination to alter this state of affairs.

That Nietzsche went so many years without formal citizenship may be the outcome of his unusual situation: he was not a Basler in spirit or origin, and was a resident of the city merely by dint of his appointment at the university. He relinquished his Prussian citizenship as a courtesy to his new employer and prior to the founding of the Second Empire. He would not have been eligible for reinstated German citizenship unless he established a domicile in the country; his position prevented his departure from Basel for a number of years, and by the time he could have returned to Germany, his feelings about the country had begun to change. Nonetheless, it is fair to conclude that he subjectively considered himself a German, and that he regarded Germans and Germany as the main audience for his writings. We have seen that the school system and the general public for his lectures on education were German—even though he delivered them in Basel—and surely his four *Untimely Meditations* were meant as a contribution to German, not Swiss, intellectual life. Although he was always delighted to learn of translation possibilities for his writings, he produced his works in German and for Germany. Indeed, in *Ecce Homo*, he claims that he is probably more German than "current Germans, the 'Reichsdeutsche' [Germans in the Empire]" (EH, Kommentar, Warum ich so weise bin, KSA 14.472), indicating that for Nietzsche, citizenship meant less in determining national identity than other, undefined qualities. Nonetheless, in his revisions to the same text, he insists that he is a "pure-blooded Polish nobleman, in whom there is no drop of bad blood, least of all German" (EH, Warum ich so weise bin 3, KSA 6.268). This assertion matches several similar utterances in notebooks[8] and especially in letters, mostly from the 1880s. In the biography of her brother, Elisabeth reproduces Nietzsche's contention and writes of their aunt's account that their ancestors arrived in Germany from Poland fleeing religious persecution.[9] Nietzsche even engaged someone to investigate his alleged Polish heritage; a document was reportedly produced, but it was not found among Nietzsche's papers, and even Elisabeth casts doubt on its existence. Subsequent research has proven that the Nietzsche family was German for many generations, extending back into the seventeenth century, and that there is no indication of any Polish ancestry or noble lineage.[10] We can probably assume that the myth of Polish nobility was a product of the young Nietzsche's fertile imagination—there is already some indication of it in a letter from 1862 (to Raimund Granier, 28 July 1862, Nr. 324, KSB 1.217)—and that it reappears in the last decade of Nietzsche's sane life to foster the notion of aristocratic origins and to distinguish Nietzsche from a nation that had squandered its opportunity for greatness and was unappreciative of his writings. The seemingly antithetical assertions that he is more German than the current Germans and that he is a pureblooded Pole without a drop of German blood amount to the same thing in Nietzsche's psychic economy in 1888.

Nietzsche's Prussian and Germanic Phase

In his youth, Nietzsche was not denying his German heritage, nor asserting a Polish ancestry, but rather, like many of his contemporaries, advocating for German unity through Prussia. It is unlikely that all of Nietzsche's classmates in Naumburg or Pforta shared his political inclinations, even if they were nationalistically inclined. Some citizens no doubt viewed Prussia as an illegitimate sovereign force in the northern areas of what was formerly Saxony, and some inhabitants were not enthusiastic about the rising influence of Prussia in German affairs at the expense of Austria. From the documents we possess, however, in his youth Nietzsche never waivered from his adherence to Prussia and a "small-German" solution to the German Question. Indeed, he was named Friedrich Wilhelm in honor of the reigning Prussian king, with whom he shared a birthday, and he identified with his nephew, Friedrich III (1831–1888), right into the

1880s.[11] As a teenager, he participated eagerly in the general celebrations surrounding Prussia and the German national spirit. In an extended autobiographical sketch written shortly before his fourteenth birthday, and therefore prior to his departure for Pforta, Nietzsche relates his enthusiasm for the visit of Friedrich Wilhelm IV (1795–1861) to Naumburg. All of the local pupils were assembled and appropriately garbed to receive their sovereign [*Landesvater*]. The king was apparently expected in the late morning hours, and Nietzsche describes how the gathering was first drenched by a cloudburst before the day cleared and the king arrived at around 2:00 in the afternoon. Despite their long wait and wet clothes, the crowd greeted him with a boisterous "hurrah!," and Nietzsche along with his friends swung their caps in the air, roaring at the top of their lungs. He goes on to describe with enthusiasm the fireworks and general celebration, as well as the king's visit to the cathedral (Nachlass 1858, 4[77], KGW I 1.302–3). A little over a year later, when Nietzsche was at Pforta, he writes about a different event: the centennial celebration of the birth of Friedrich Schiller (1759–1805). Unlike Goethe, who was consistently viewed as a cosmopolitan and even an antinationalist writer, Schiller was widely considered a poet of the German people. The 1859 commemoration was celebrated throughout German-speaking lands and was part of the reawakening of nationalist sentiment after the failed revolutions in 1848. Nietzsche apostrophizes Schiller as "the great German" and emphasizes that all segments of society participated in this memorial festival: "not only the educated stratum, no, also the lower classes of the people partook in a lively manner in this national festival." He reports further that classes were canceled the next day, and that in the school gymnasium Schiller songs were performed by the choir, after which Professor Koberstein, the literary historian at Pforta, impressed on the young men in attendance Schiller's "literary importance for the German nation," concluding with the assertion that "this national festival is a significant omen for the reawakened feeling of German nationhood," and that "one could attach to this celebration fine hopes for the future" (Nachlass 1859, 7[3], KGW I 2.175–77). At this point in his development, Nietzsche considered events of this nature, containing public displays of fealty to Prussia, general feelings of German pride in its most celebrated representatives, and hopes for future German unification, part of a patriotic feeling toward his Fatherland that he shared with many of his peers.

In his teenage years, Nietzsche did not distinguish enthusiasm for political unity from cultural aspirations of the nation, and in the early 1860s, we find Nietzsche as the leading force in establishing a cultural club called "Germania." There were only three members of this exclusive association: Nietzsche; Wilhelm Pinder (1844–1928), the son of a prominent Naumburg lawyer; and Gustav Krug (1844–1902), Pinder's cousin and an avid musician, who first introduced Wagner's music to Nietzsche. The name Germania was likely drawn from the celebrated history text by Tacitus, *De origine et situ Germanorum* (98 AD), an ethnographic account that praises Germans (in contrast to the Romans of Tacitus's times), which became perhaps the central work from antiquity for German nationalists. In the summer of 1860, when the club was founded, Nietzsche was already a student at Pforta, while Pinder and Krug, with whom Nietzsche had attended the Cathedral *Gymnasium* in Naumburg, had remained in their home city. The club was thus a means for Nietzsche to maintain connections with his friends and for all three of them to find expression for their budding creativity outside of the school environment. Nietzsche was very likely alluding to Germania in the first lecture on German educational institutions, when he refers to a small club whose purpose was to find an outlet for creative energies in art and literature: "each of us would pledge to present an original piece of work to the club once a month, either a poem, a treatise, an architectural design, or a musical composition, upon which each of the others, in a friendly spirit, would have to pass free and unrestrained criticism" (BA 1, KSA 1.653). Since Nietzsche faithfully recorded all the submissions that the three members made to their association, we can see that the main emphasis was literature and music, consisting of original contributions as well as criticism (Nachlass 1862, 13[28], KGW I 2.475–83). Nietzsche reports, however, that the members were aware of the limited nature of their exchanges within the club and desired to extend their reach beyond the "exclusivity of previous accomplishments" into the area of "politics and contemporary history." At the same time, the club's chronicler notes in September 1862 that members have not regularly submitted their contributions, in part owing to "political agitation" (Nachlass 1862, 13[28], KGW I 2.475); at that point, the club was obviously on a precipitously downward path, and it would disband entirely in 1863. In his final listing of the desired submissions from October 1862 through June 1863, only Nietzsche himself had complied with the club's rules and written something (Nachlass 1863, 15[16], KGW I 3.143).[12] Leaving the cultural pretentiousness of this undertaking aside, we can discern that Nietzsche and his friends regarded artistic and literary achievement, whether or not it was directly connected with German themes or persons, as an essential element of a loosely conceived nationalist movement. For many members of the more educated stratum of society, the German Question could not be separated from cultural accomplishment, elite schooling, and the course of German *Bildung*.

In his pre-university years, we find Nietzsche interested in topics that were the usual fare of German nationalism. In 1858, for example, he composes a poem to Theodor Körner (1791–1813), a celebrated figure from the Wars of Liberation. Körner was well known for his fiery patriotic verse, as well as his heroic participation in the Lützow Free Corps, a volunteer unit in the Prussian army fighting against Napoleon. Körner's death on the battlefield in 1813 only enhanced his posthumous reputation as a symbol of German unity, and he was frequently celebrated by nationalists in the ensuing half century. Nietzsche's poem is the usual fare: Körner is the "youthful hero" who fought valiantly for the cause, suffered for freedom from the French invaders, and conducted a life filled with noble deeds. Nietzsche also includes the mandatory notion that he did not perish in vain, that his patriotic vision will find fulfillment: "the bloody daybreak is already dawning" (Nachlass 1858, 4[9], KGW I 1.222). The poem dedicated to Körner refers back to a key period for nineteenth-century nationalism. Nietzsche returns to the anti-Napoleonic wars in other celebratory lyrics, such as the commemoration of the Battle of Leipzig, where coalition forces defeated the French army. They have the same tenor: an admonition to contemporaries to draw inspiration from the struggle for freedom in the Wars of Liberation. In the first, composed on 6 October, 1862, Nietzsche conjures up the bloody days of Leipzig, which, although they seem to be long past, should sound the knell for Germans in the 1860s to struggle for the "freedom" not yet realized.

> O Germans, do you want to, already exhausted,
> Lay your hands in your laps,
> While freedom painfully wrests itself
> From contemptuous slavery?
> The organ chord of the world powers[13]
> Can wake you from your dreams:
> You are the eternal refuge of freedom,
> The chosen warrior of the spirit. (Nachlass 1862, 14[4], KGW I 3.10)[14]

In the second poem, composed ten days later, Nietzsche writes of his "German Fatherland" initially in chains, but then rising up to defeat its oppressor (Nachlass 1862, 14[7], KGW I 3.17–18). Again the lesson for contemporaries is evident. In 1863, Nietzsche returns to these themes on the fiftieth anniversary of the battle. The lengthy poem on this topic in his juvenilia was probably commissioned by Krug, who on 30 September asked his friend, who was at school in Pforta, for assistance with an assigned school presentation. He complains of illness and flatters Nietzsche by telling him that he can produce something easily in a few hours with little effort (Nr. 65, KGB I 1.404). On 15 October, he thanks Nietzsche for sending the poem (Nr. 69, KGB I 1.408). Entitled "Over Fifty Years," it is an unusual piece, in that it views the battle retrospectively from the vantage point of the defeated Napoleon. But this conceit allows it to comment on important issues, such as how the aftermath of the battle thwarted the real desires of the German people: "They thought they were chasing away the tyrant, and thousands of small ones still remained." Napoleon's final vision then reveals more precisely the direction in which Nietzsche is driving the German Question in 1863: Voices cry out "Hail Germany, Hail united Germany," and Napoleon concedes that he saw this moment coming fifty years ago (Nachlass 1863, 16[1] and 16[2], KGW I 3.231–39).

Some of Nietzsche's preoccupation with patriotic topics resulted from school assignments. In one instance, he was asked to write an essay on the benefits young people draw from dealing with the history of the Fatherland, an assignment that he carries out very properly, but without any special zest for the theme (Nachlass 1864, 16[19], KGW I 3.292–97). In other instances, he acts on his own initiative, for example, in 1858, when he composed a poem about Barbarossa, Friedrich I (1122–1190), emperor of the Holy Roman Empire from 1152 to 1190. Barbarossa was an especially beloved symbol for German nationalists because of the legend that he is merely asleep beneath Kyffhäuser Mountain and one day will rise and restore Germany to its former greatness. Heinrich Heine (1797–1856) satirized this legend in *Germany: A Winter's Tale*,[15] but there is no hint of irony in Nietzsche's treatment, which offers a straightforward account (Nachlass 1858, 4[57], KGW I 1.268–69). Most teenagers in the 1850s and 1860s demonstrated their adherence to a German nationalist spirit by delving into the rich heritage of Germanic epics, and Nietzsche is no exception in this regard either. Perhaps the central text in this tradition is the epic poem *Song of the Nibelungs* (c. 1200), which relates the story of Siegfried's exploits, his treasonous death, and the ultimate revenge of his wife Kriemhild. Unlike many other medieval German narrative poems, it does not draw from the Romance originals of Chrétien de Troyes, but from Germanic legends and historical accounts. Writing to his sister and mother, Nietzsche requests a specific edition of the *Song of the Nibelungs* for his birthday in 1863 (Nr. 382, KSB 1.257), but we know that he, like most of his peers, was quite well acquainted with the text at a much earlier age. Fascinated by the tale and its characters, he occupied himself with it extensively in his spare time. In the first months of 1862, he composed a poem on Siegfried's death at the hands of perfidious Hagen (Nachlass 1862, 12[20], KGW I 2.376–80). In October of the same year, he wrote a character analysis of Kriemhild for Germania, depicting her personality as full and profound, and passionately dedicated to the goal of avenging her husband's death (Nachlass 1862, 14[18], KGW I 3.38–44). And just before he requests his birthday copy of the *Song of the Nibelungs*, he spends the "dog days" of 1863 making extensive notes on this Middle High German epic (Nachlass 1863, 15[24], KGW I 3.148–67).

But Nietzsche's real passion from the Germanic tradition in his Pforta years was another, less known hero, Ermanaric, the fourth-century king of the Goths whose life and death are depicted in various Latin and Germanic sources. This historical figure is credited with driving the Vandals out of Dacia, a region of Central Europe, and with ruling over an empire comparable to that of Alexander the Great. Legends grew around him, and in one he purportedly had a woman named Swanhilda torn asunder by horses because of her husband's treachery, and her brothers avenged her, wounding Ermanaric, who eventually died of the injuries at the age of one hundred and ten. In alternative accounts, Ermanaric takes his own life when he recognizes that he cannot repel the invasion of the Huns. Nietzsche was fascinated by the gory legends surrounding this figure, and in July of 1861 he completed a historical sketch of Ermanaric (10[20], KGW I 2.274–84). In the following years, he wrote a poem titled "Ermanaric's Death" (Nachlass 1862, 12[17], KGW I 2.370–75), a symphonic piano composition for four hands (*Ermanarichsymphonie*), which he describes in his notebooks (Nachlass 1862, 14[2], KGW I 3.4–8), a sketch for a drama based on Ermanaric (Nachlass 1863, 14[28], KGW I 3.54–57), and finally, as the culmination of his preoccupation with the Gothic king, an extensive scholarly consideration of the sources for the Ermanaric legend (Nachlass 1863, 16[3], KGW I 3.239–69). We should recall that the emphasis at Pforta was classical antiquity, and that the greatest part of Nietzsche's classroom instruction and assignments related to the Greek and Roman tradition. That he, nonetheless, devoted so much time to the Germanic heritage and to topics central to the nationalist movement among German intellectuals indicates his enthusiastic participation in, and concern for, discourses surrounding the cultural aspects of the German Question.

With the beginning of his university studies, Nietzsche eliminated most of the creative writing and commentary about the German tradition. At Bonn, but in particular at Leipzig, he was heavily invested in classical studies, and the volumes of juvenilia containing writings from 1866 to 1869 focus almost exclusively on themes from Greek antiquity. His activities and remarks in his correspondence indicate, however, that he still harbored the same political beliefs, that he still evidenced sympathy for what we would today consider the National Liberal position in German politics, and that he was actively engaged in supporting the Prussian version of German national unity. As we have seen from his lectures on education in 1872, Nietzsche held the German nationalist student fraternities or *Burschenschaften* in high regard as bearers of a genuine German spirit, and we should not be surprised to find that in his first semester at Bonn, he became a member of the student fraternity Franconia. When he announces to his mother his membership in Franconia, he mentions that he is one of eight former Pforta students to join, and to impress his family further, he adds that former members of Franconia include the historian Heinrich von Treitschke (1834–1896) and the noted novelist Friedrich Spielhagen (1829–1911) (24–25 October 1864, Nr. 449, KSB 2.14–15). A few months later, he still professes admiration for Franconia, but he claims that both Bonn and the fraternity are too expensive, and that he has decided that next Michaelmas (29 September) he will go to Berlin to serve in the army along with his closest friend, and the future Indiologist, Paul Deussen (1845–1919). Nietzsche obviously sees the destiny of Germany in the strategic actions of Prussia at this point in his life. He may have been assisted in this conviction by Heinrich von Sybel (1817–1895), whose lectures at Bonn he attended along with two or three hundred other auditors (to Franziska and Elisabeth Nietzsche, 10–17 November 1864, Nr. 451, KSB 2.18). Sybel was both a noted historian and a political figure who, as early as 1850, had belonged to a party that promoted the unification of Germany under the influence of Prussia. In the 1860s, he was a National Liberal of conservative bent, a description that approximates well Nietzsche's political position in his university years, and although for a time Sybel opposed the policies of Bismarck, he, like most members of the party, was eventually forced to reconcile his convictions with the Iron Chancellor's actions.[16]

The following year, after Nietzsche had transferred to Leipzig and was living in Saxony, he was still a Prussian nationalist. Although he expresses a deep admiration for King Johann of Saxony (1801–1873) on the occasion of the monarch's visit to Leipzig in January 1866 (to Franziska Nietzsche, Nr. 493, KSB 2.109), when hostilities erupt between Prussia and Austria, he declares himself resolutely on the side of the former, even though Saxony became an ally of Austria. Writing to his mother and sister shortly after the Prussian invasion of Saxony, he praises Bismarck's "program" for German unification: "To found the unified German state in this revolutionary way is Bismark's [sic] strong suit: he possesses courage and unbending consequentiality, but he underestimates the moral powers of the people" (July 1866, Nr. 509, KSB 2.135–36). This mild criticism of Bismarck is rather typical for the romantic nationalism of Nietzsche's generation, which valued the ideal of a people's army, such as the one established to defeat Napoleon in 1813, in contrast to the diplomatic maneuvering and the professional military of the Prussian leadership. But he is unequivocal in his adherence to Prussia and unconcerned with who bears responsibility for the war: "Our position is very simple. When a house is burning, one does not first ask, who is guilty of setting the fire, one extinguishes it." And he continues, by contrasting his own blind loyalty to Prussia with his cousin's to Saxony: "From the moment the war began, all other considerations became secondary. I am a Prussian just as enraged as, for example, my cousin, who sides with Saxony." Indeed, Nietzsche reveals his proclivity for the small-German solution when he observes that the war is a perfect means for consolidating German power in Prussia by eliminating the princes of smaller states. He is thankful that Hanover and Hessen have not joined the Prussian coalition since otherwise "we would not be able to get rid of these gentlemen for all eternity." He himself anticipates being called into service—he never was, perhaps because the war lasted only seven weeks—and states that it is "dishonorable" to sit at home "when the Fatherland is beginning a life-and-death struggle" (Nr. 509, KSB 2.135–36). To Pinder a few days later, he rationalizes his noncombatant role, claiming "we are really serving the Fatherland even in our studies." He has only praise for the actions of the Prussian government and

Bismarck; the measures taken by Prussia over the past six weeks have his unmitigated approval; Bismarck is "talented and energetic" or even a "revolutionary" (Nr. 510, KSB 2.137). To Hermann Mushacke (1845–1905) in Berlin, he writes: "Who wouldn't be proud in these times to be a Prussian," since Prussia, after "a lengthy period in which history was stalled, has moved it forward and overthrown countless circumstances with its positive momentum" (Nr. 511, KSB 2.140). To his friend Carl von Gersdorff (1844–1904), an officer in the Prussian army whose brother was wounded in the fighting, he expresses similar enthusiasm a week after the battle of Sadowa (Königgrätz): "We have to be proud to have such an army, yes even—*horribile dictum*—to have such a government, one that has a national program not just on paper, but that supports it with the greatest energy, with a great expenditure of money and blood, even against the great French tempter, Louis *le diable*." He writes further of the nationalist task of changing European conditions, and of the honor he would have to be struck by a French bullet and to fall on the battlefield should the nationalist cause fail (Nr. 512, KSB 2.142–43). In these letters, Nietzsche not only celebrates the Prussian victory over Austria, which had occurred on 3 July, but also anticipates the outbreak of the Franco-Prussian War in 1870, which would lead to the establishment of the Second Empire.

In this context of German nationalist feelings surrounding the Austro-Prussian War, Nietzsche engaged himself for the first and only time in an actual political campaign. Inspired by Treitschke, a spearhead of the ascendant nationalist movement, who would later become a noted conservative and anti-Semitic political figure in Berlin, Nietzsche lent his support to the National Liberal candidate for a seat in the newly formed parliament of the North German Confederation, in which Saxony, despite its opposition to Prussia in the recently fought war, became a member. Treitschke's pamphlet, entitled "The Future of the North German Middle States," which was evidently forbidden in Saxony for a period of time, articulated a political position that received Nietzsche's concurrence. Treitschke argues that the northern German states allied with Prussia should be treated with respect and integrated carefully into a unified Germany. Those states that opposed Prussia—Saxony, Hanover, and Hessen—and fought on the side of Austria, however, should be forcibly annexed and their leaders should be summarily deposed. Treitschke's animus toward Saxony is remarkable considering that he was a native Saxon, born in Dresden, and that he was the son of a military officer and later government official in Saxony. The ruling house of Saxony is a "thorn in the side of Prussia," Treitschke asserts; it has promoted a hatred of Prussia and its politics, and sought to thwart German unification. Elimination is the only acceptable action for Prussia. When Treitschke learns, during the composition of this pamphlet, that French and Austrian pressure has secured the preservation of the royal house in Saxony, he urges Prussia to reconsider and eradicate the Albertine dynasty.[17] Nietzsche read Treitschke's pamphlet in August 1866, and he supported the vote of National Liberals in Saxony, who, like Treitschke, demanded unconditional annexation. Nietzsche adds that he hopes King Johann, whom he had praised just seven months earlier, is stubborn enough to force this outcome by resisting and provoking his own demise (to Carl von Gersdorff, August 1866, Nr. 517, KSB 2.159). The ensuing election campaign at the beginning of 1867 was thus conducted in an atmosphere of controversy about the very existence of Saxony and was tantamount to a referendum on Prussian politics. Nietzsche describes the political process in detail to his friend Gersdorff. In the first round of voting, the National Liberal candidate, Eduard Stephani (1817–1885), supported by Nietzsche, won handily over the chief representative of Saxon particularism, Karl Georg von Wächter (1797–1880). But the smaller parties, whose candidates had been eliminated, then threw their weight behind von Wächter. Among the defeated candidates specifically mentioned by Nietzsche were Heinrich Wuttke (1818–1876), who advocated the "greater German solution" and was associated with the leading German socialist Ferdinand Lassalle (1825–1864); and Ludwig Wükert (1800–1876), who was likewise connected to the German workers' movement. As a result, Stephani lost by a thousand votes in the second and decisive round of voting. We can detect in Nietzsche's lengthy account a sardonic perspective on the election process, but he nonetheless appears to be genuinely disappointed that the German cause has been so severely damaged by electoral politics: "We were defeated," he informs his friend. "Particularism hoists the victory flag" (20 February 1867, Nr. 538, KSB 2.198–200).[18]

Nietzsche did not contribute to the war effort as a combatant, and his first stint in the military occurs after his brief flirtation with German electoral politics. He reported to his family in March 1864 that he had registered for the draft, and that he must enter active service by October 1867 (Nr. 411, KSB 1.275). Although, as we have seen, he demonstrated pride in being a Prussian citizen and was supportive of the war, writing shortly before the fighting began that he is "someone who is ready for war" (to Franziska and Elisabeth Nietzsche, 22 April 1866, Nr. 502, KSB 2.126) and, after the war started, that it was "dishonorable" not to assist the "Vaterland" (to Franziska and Elisabeth Nietzsche, July 1866, Nr. 509, KSB 2.136), he did not seek to fulfill his obligation in the spring or summer of 1866. Instead, he waited until the last possible moment in October of 1867 to serve his country. In a letter to Mushacke in Berlin in October of 1867, Nietzsche writes of how seldom one is the master of one's fate and of the "music of the entr'acte that I had hoped no longer to hear in this life. Drums and fifes, warlike sounds!" And he continues: "The sword does not hover over my head, but on my side; this quill in my hand will soon be a lethal weapon; these papers covered with notes and drafts will probably acquire a somewhat musty smell. The god of war wanted me, that is, I have been found fit for volunteer service, while I believed when I departed for Halle to attend the philologists' convention that this chalice would pass me by" (Nr. 549, KSB 2.225). A few weeks later, he writes to Ritschl that he has fallen victim to the god of war despite his myopia and goes on to complain about the long hours in the stables, in the *manège*, and in the barracks: "That is quite a new and foreign foodstuff, which once chewed remains sometimes stuck between my teeth" (Nr. 550, KSB 2.227). And to Deussen he confesses that he resigned himself "to becoming an artillerist after he had tried in vain to climb up and over the walls of my destiny" (Nr. 551, KSB 2.228). These sentiments hardly reflect an enthusiasm for serving Prussia and furthering the glories of the beloved Fatherland. Over the next few months, however, military service starts to grow on Nietzsche; he enjoys riding and fancies himself proficient with horses, and he appears to devote himself to instruction for becoming an officer with dedication and good humor.[19] He begins to value the "courage, fortitude, and manliness" of the military, and he regards his military service as a means of overcoming a one-sided education and a foil to "rigid, pedantic, narrow-minded scholarship" (to Hermann Mushacke, 13 February 1868, Nr. 561, KSB 2.253). Having reconciled himself to Prussian service, he even reports that he experienced "enormous pleasure" in reading Bismarck's speeches, and castigates his opponents as petty, parochial, partisan, and obtuse (to Carl von Gersdorff, 16 February 1868, Nr. 562, KSB 2.258). After sustaining a severe chest injury, which ultimately led to his discharge, he claims to Ritschl that he longs for his horse and for the military, but otherwise he does not seem overly disappointed at the prospect of abbreviated service.

Nietzsche's attitude toward the more practical aspects of the German Question—political engagement and military service—is considerably less passionate than his response to Prussian leadership in moving Germany toward unification and the nationalist rhetoric that surrounded the National Liberal acquiescence to Bismarck's plans. We may be able to account for this difference by observing that, despite the vitalist rhetoric in the second *Untimely Meditation*, he was already more a man of the mind than a man of action, and that the abstract idea of a united Germany under Prussian hegemony appealed to him intellectually, while the dirty and mundane work of accomplishing this unification was somewhat less desirable for him. We might also observe that Nietzsche had the tendency to want to please the recipients of his correspondence: if he wrote to someone invested in German nationalism, he was more likely to include a positive evaluation of the Austro-Prussian War, National Liberal positions, and Bismarck's politics. As we shall see, he maintained this pattern of tailoring his letters to the views of the addressee throughout his life, although he becomes more independent in his thought in the latter part of the 1870s and during the last decade of his sane existence. Even in these early years, however, we can draw some tentative conclusions regarding how he deals with the German Question. After an initial period when he seems to have shunned military service, he became more enthusiastic about the army and activities involved in training and discipline. At the very least, he appears to have reconciled himself to the life of a soldier, but there are also indications that he admires the "manly virtues" involved with military life.

With regard to politics, however, we recognize a rejection of processes associated with democracy and parliament, and sometimes impatience with the sorts of compromises necessary to conduct governmental business. It is quite possible that Nietzsche's disappointment with the election in Saxony contributed to his disengagement from politics; or perhaps he simply became preoccupied with other more pressing personal issues. But his involvement in this electoral contest and his ardent, unequivocal pro-Prussian and patriotic utterances disappear shortly thereafter. In October 1868, he was renting a room from Karl Biedermann (1812–1901), a fervent advocate for workers' rights, free speech, and equality, who was earlier active in the 1848 revolution, a major political figure in Saxony in the 1860s, and subsequently a member of the German Reichstag in the 1870s.[20] Nietzsche writes to his friend Erwin Rohde (1845–1898), however, that Biedermann is really quite a family man, and that he is delighted to report that at his present domicile "to his relief politics is almost never discussed," and that "he is no ζῷον πολιτικόν[political being]" (27 October 1868, Nr. 596, KSB 2.331). Two years before, he had welcomed Biedermann's political advocacy for Prussia as editor of the *Deutsche Allgemeine Zeitung*; six months prior to his remarks to Rohde, he was lauding Bismarck's speeches. Nietzsche does not relinquish his advocacy for Germany and German greatness entirely, especially its potential cultural distinction, but he becomes increasingly critical of Prussia, Bismarck, electoral campaigns, and parliamentary politics. Nietzsche was obviously undergoing a change in his thinking about politics and about the German Question, and the person who assisted him most in reconceptualizing these issues was the composer Richard Wagner.

Wagner, Culture, and German Values

Nietzsche fell under Wagner's influence soon after they met in November 1868, and until the mid-1870s, he was the dominating force in his intellectual universe. With regard to the German Question, Wagner was very likely responsible for Nietzsche's shift from the more conventional focus on politics and German unification to the general area of culture and the arts. To a great extent, Nietzsche was predisposed for this shift, since his education and his personal predilections were in the realm of classical antiquity, philosophy, and music; his dalliance with the military and with political campaigns was fleeting and quickly abandoned. It would be false to assume, however, that Nietzsche forsook entirely his German and Prussian allegiances and turned to a more cosmopolitan preoccupation with cultural achievement.²¹ Rather, he recognized that national unity under the hegemony of Prussia was not the ultimate answer to the German Question, but merely a possible step toward the real and more essential goal of cultural renewal. And the person who both embodied and theorized this cultural goal in a new Germany was Richard Wagner. It was Wagner, after all, who had successfully incorporated German myth into his "music dramas," in many cases the very German traditions that Nietzsche had studied as a pupil at Pforta. The operas *Lohengrin* (1850), *Tannhäuser* (1845), and *The Mastersingers of Nuremberg* [*Die Meistersinger von Nürnberg*; 1868] had each incorporated parts of a German heritage that was familiar to educated German youth growing up in the mid-nineteenth century. *Tristan und Isolde* (1865), although ultimately derived from the French medieval romance, was conceived by Wagner as the product of Gottfried von Strassburg's "improved" medieval German version; indeed, in his essay "What Is German?" Wagner specifically mentions that while the French "originals" [of *Parsifal* (1882) and *Tristan*] have become mere curiosities" that are of no importance to the history of literature, their German counterparts are "poetic works of imperishable worth."²² And the tetralogy *The Ring of the Nibelungs* [*Der Ring des Nibelungen*] (1876), which was composed over several decades, is derived from what had become the core Germanic source for nationally minded youth, *The Song of the Nibelungs*. Wagner had written most of the libretto in the 1850s, but the musical score was left incomplete while he worked on *Tristan und Isolde* and *Die Meistersinger*. He completed work on the *Ring* and oversaw its first productions in the years Nietzsche was closest to him. Wagner's Germanness in his creative works was matched by his advocacy for a positive resolution to the German Question in the political and ideological sphere, and his essays from the period of the late 1860s and 1870s frequently broach topics surrounding the essence of Germans, the history of Germany from the time of Charlemagne to the present, and the greatness of German cultural achievement. Nietzsche may not have agreed with everything that the Meister wrote about these various topics, but he certainly strove to please his new mentor by incorporating positive motifs of Germanness and ideas about German cultural supremacy into his writings of the period.

Wagner's influence on Nietzsche was enormous and pervasive during the first few years Nietzsche spent in Basel, and it is quite possible that Cosima and Richard Wagner hold the key to Nietzsche's odd and hitherto insufficiently explained actions at the outbreak of the Franco-Prussian War. Nietzsche's sudden and seemingly unmotivated decision to volunteer for military service on the side of the Germans in August of 1870 is an episode that has not received much attention in biographical accounts, and when it has been discussed, the reasoning provided has been strained and unconvincing. Since Nietzsche was no longer a Prussian citizen and therefore had no military obligation to Prussia, he could have taken advantage of his status as a non-citizen of any country—the Swiss would have considered him *heimatlos* or "homeless"—and simply continued to discharge his teaching obligations at the *Pädagogium* and the university. The start of the war obviously took Nietzsche by surprise, but in this regard he did not differ very much from his friends and acquaintances, or for that matter the general public in Europe. Prior to mid-July of 1870, however, when war was declared, Nietzsche did not indicate that he would consider reenlisting if Prussia fought France, even though he, like his contemporaries, anticipated hostile actions between the two states at some point. As we have already seen, he relinquished his Prussian citizenship when he received the appointment at Basel specifically to reassure Swiss authorities that he would not be fulfilling the military obligation to which he would have been obliged if he had remained a Prussian, and he did not appear to harbor any second thoughts in making this decision in the spring of 1869. He states explicitly to Wilhelm Vischer-Bilfinger that he considers it his duty to the University of Basel not to make his instructional engagement dependent on war and peace (Nr. 626, KSB 2.381). In his correspondence from 1869, we do not encounter any overtly pro-Prussian sentiments; nor do we find any indication that he desires to continue his aborted military career if a war should occur. We can assume, of course, that he still supported Prussia and that he favored German unity: although he never expresses dissatisfaction with the German Confederation formed after the Austro-Prussian War, he, like most German patriots of his generation, very likely considered that the political goal Germans had longed for since the early years of the century had not yet been fully realized. But his thoughts in the late 1860s were obviously more focused on his classical studies and, after April 1869, on his new life as a faculty member in Basel. His notebooks from the last year of his student days and the first months of his professorship are devoid of patriotic topics and thoughts, in contrast to the notebooks from the mid-1860s.

When Nietzsche learned of the declaration of war, he did not immediately react by asking the Swiss authorities to allow his participation in the Prussian army. The letter he wrote to Vischer-Bilfinger requesting permission for a leave of absence is dated 8 August, over three weeks after the war began. In the interim, he vacationed with his sister at a Swiss resort, interrupting his stay only to visit the Wagners in Tribschen, but without giving any indication to Cosima or Richard, or to any correspondent, that he was considering military service. Cosima wrote in her diary on 18 July that Nietzsche was traveling to Axenstein "in order to escape both the French and the Germans,"[23] which would indicate that Nietzsche was trying to avoid military service, not engage in it. Biographers have speculated that Nietzsche may have been stirred to patriotism by Adolf Mosengel (1837–1885), a Hamburg painter he and Elisabeth met at their hotel, but there is no evidence in Mosengel's letters to Nietzsche or in Nietzsche's remarks about Mosengel that the painter played any role in Nietzsche's military service.[24] From the evidence we possess, it is just as likely that Nietzsche persuaded Mosengel to join him in enlisting as the other way around. In the biography of her brother, Elisabeth takes credit for Nietzsche's re-enlistment: She claims that after hearing about battles and heavy losses, and conferring with Mosengel, her brother asked her what she would do if she were a man. When she responded that she would do her duty to her country, he agreed that he should do the same.[25]

More likely than the intervention of Mosengel or Elisabeth is that Nietzsche gradually began to consider it his duty to Wagner's cultural mission to serve the pro-German cause. His remarks indicate he was interested less in German political or military greatness than in a renaissance of European culture. Writing to perhaps his closest friend at the time, Erwin Rohde (1845–1898), he comments on 16 July 1870: "Here a fearsome thunderbolt: the French-German War has been declared, and our entire shabby culture is toppling with the horrible demon at its throat." He continues by suggesting that he and Rohde may have to go into seclusion to preserve culture: "We could already be at the beginning of the end! What a wilderness! We will need cloisters again. And we will be the first fraters" (Nr. 86, KSB 3.130). He signs the letter "a loyal Swiss," which suggests at this point a non-identification with the Prussian cause. The same day, however, he exclaims to his mother: "Now I too am saddened by being Swiss! It's a question of our culture! And for this there is not a sacrifice that would be great enough! This accursed French tiger!" (Nr. 87, KSB 3.131). And a few days later, writing to Sophie Ritschl (b. 1820), Friedrich Ritschl's wife, he again foregrounds his cultural concerns:

> What a shameful feeling, to have to be inactive now; now, when it would be the appropriate time for even my field-artillery studies!
> My consolation is that for the new cultural period at least a few of the old elements have to remain: and to what extent even the traditions of culture can be annihilated in such a national war of embitterment, one can imagine for today from sorrowful analogies in history. (Nr. 88, KSB 3.132–33)

Nietzsche's tone in these three letters is very different, and he obviously composed his correspondence very carefully to accommodate the views of each recipient. But common to all three letters is a focus on the preservation of culture. Unlike Cosima and Richard Wagner, who harbored an animus against France and beat the Prussian drums as much out of revenge as patriotism,[26] Nietzsche is rather restrained in his pro-German and anti-French sentiments, concentrating instead on the task of maintaining and promoting cultural excellence. But the shift in Nietzsche's thinking on the German Question from the politics of German unification to German cultural accomplishment was directly attributable to his recent appreciation for, and association with, Wagner. Thus, although Cosima in several of her letters expresses dismay at Nietzsche's decision to join the military, even as a medical orderly,[27] it is likely that the ultimate reason for his enlisting was a desire to march to the Wagnerian cultural drumbeat. Indeed, Nietzsche's most overtly nationalist statements come in the context of promoting Wagnerian opera and the Bayreuth project as a sacred task of German cultural renewal. His relationship to the German Question, after his personal acquaintance with Wagner, even in his military service, is ultimately a matter of *Bildung* in the service of the Wagnerian cause and not political power.

Nietzsche's experience in the war did nothing to shift his focus back to military glory and the primacy of the political in the German Question. His second stint in the military was even shorter and more miserable than his first. Sent to Erlangen for ten days to train for fieldwork as a medic, he very soon encountered firsthand the horrors of war: "Yesterday a Prussian died in the hospital, shot in the lung, today a second one. A Prussian named Liebig is doing well, good appetite, sleeps well, but there is little hope, arm bones shattered, impossible to use plaster for a cast" (Nachlass 1870, 4[1], KSA 7.88). From Erlangen he was sent to Ars sur Moselle to accompany a transport of wounded soldiers back to Karlsruhe. He describes his ordeal to Wagner on 11 September:

> In Ars sur Moselle, we assumed the care of the wounded and returned to Germany with them. Being together with severely wounded soldiers for three days and three nights was the high point of our efforts. I had to care for, bandage, and nurse a miserable cattle wagon in which there were six men immensely suffering. Each had shattered bones, several with four wounds; moreover I found that two had contracted gangrene. That I was able to survive in this pestilent miasma, even sleeping and eating there, seems to me now to be a miracle.[28] (Nr. 100, KSB 3.143)

As a result of this unsanitary exposure to infectious disease among wounded soldiers, Nietzsche himself fell ill. Shortly after his arrival in Germany, he was diagnosed with dysentery and diphtheria and had to cut short his military tour having served only a few weeks on active duty; for most of September until his return to Basel in late October, he convalesced at the family residence in Naumburg. Nietzsche thus had personal experience with the misery of war. To Ritschl, however, he still feigned regret that he could not participate more actively in battle: "All my military passions are again aroused, and I could not satisfy them. If I had been with my battery, I would have experienced practically and perhaps also passively the days of Rezonville, Sedan and—Laon. But my Swiss neutrality tied my hands" (Nr. 101, KSB 3.145). To his friend Gersdorff, whom he is not making so much of an effort to impress, he writes more candidly that the "atmosphere of these experiences envelopes me like a dismal fog; for a long time I heard plaintive cries that seemed never to end" (Nr. 103, KSB 3.149). This ambivalence toward the experience of combat was shared by many of his generation, including Gersdorff and Rohde, who write similarly about the gruesome war and its deleterious effects.[29] They did not regret the outcome of the hostilities, especially the unification of Germany that was its result, but the horrors of the battlefield led Nietzsche and his friends to a more sober consideration of the realities of this dimension of the German Question.

What troubled Nietzsche's generation most, however, was what would ensue after the war, and to a large extent Rohde and Gersdorff shared with their friend an apprehension about the cultural future of Germany. Rohde writes that he does not foresee the advent of a new Middle Ages, since he detects no mysticism, but at the "present time" [*Jetztzeit*] he fears a withering of "all the most profound powers, all artistic, creative capabilities" (11 December 1870, Nr. 138, KGB II 2.280). Gersdorff conjures up the years 1814 and 1815 as a period of cultural stagnation and disappointment following the last national victory over the French, and presents a list of empty, ultra-patriotic manifestations that could result from a militaristic and Prussian cooptation of the German Question, including a book market swamped with military potboilers and a school system devoted to jingoistic rhetoric (23 November 1870, Nr. 132, KGB II 2.268–69). Nietzsche harbored similar misgivings about the period following the successful conclusion of the Franco-Prussian War, and his writings in the first two years after the cessation of hostilities can be interpreted as his contribution to securing a positive outcome for German culture in the new Reich. For Nietzsche and many of his closest friends, the philosophical cicerone who would lead them into a richer and greater cultural prominence was Schopenhauer. In one letter, Gersdorff writes of a four-day furlough from the army in which he renews his strength and resolve by reading the philosopher. Later he speaks of two artists to whom he introduced Schopenhauer's works and who have already become admirers. And he even makes reference to "a great number of genuine Schopenhauerians" who perhaps do not yet know the name of "the master" (25 October 1870, Nr. 126, KGB II 2.254–55): some individuals are obviously natural disciples. Schopenhauer's pessimistic philosophical outlook might seem an odd inspiration for a generation seeking cultural renewal and a future in which Germany realizes its greatness in genial works of art. But the combination of his aesthetic predilections, especially his valorization of music, and their central place in his philosophy, as well as the implied admonition in his philosophy not to accede to the superficial and momentary optimism of political achievements, made him an appropriate guide for the elite in the postwar era. Nietzsche's *Untimely Meditation* on *Schopenhauer as Educator* (1874) was untimely only for those who believed that the German Question had already been resolved by the victory over France and the ensuing unification in a Second German Empire. For the cognoscenti who were Nietzsche's closest friends, however, this essay expressed, as we saw in the previous chapter, precisely their hopes and aspirations for the renewal of *Bildung* in a country threatened by complacency and pseudocultural accomplishment.

While Schopenhauer may have been the background philosophical inspiration, there is no doubt that for Nietzsche and his circle of friends, Wagner, himself a Schopenhauer disciple since the 1860s, was the focal point of hope for a positive resolution to the newly conceived German Question. Almost immediately after his appointment at Basel, Nietzsche had begun work on integrating Wagner's practical activity and theoretical insights into his own work on antiquity. In doing so, Nietzsche was endeavoring to support a program for renewal of German culture, returning it to its essence and purging it of foreign influences, under the guise of classical scholarship. Prior to the Franco-Prussian War, Nietzsche had already delivered a lecture in Basel entitled "The Greek Music Drama," which clearly indicates the extent of Wagner's impact on his intellectual development. Like Wagner in his seminal theoretical work *Opera and Drama* from 1851, Nietzsche wants to distinguish opera from a preferred form that combines dramatic action with musical composition. The Greeks are thus regarded as practitioners of "music drama," of which opera is but a crude distortion. Just as Wagner had castigated Giacomo Meyerbeer (1791–1864) for producing "effects without causes," Nietzsche characterizes "the first thought of opera" as straining with artificial means to achieve an effect. The natural German roots of drama, found in the carnival or Shrovetide play [*Fastnachtspiel*] during the time of the Reformation, has been gradually subverted, thereby destroying the important national foundation and introducing foreign roots and models (GMD, KSA 1.516). This lecture from January 1870, along with "Socrates and Tragedy," delivered publicly the following month, formed the basis for Nietzsche's first "Wagnerian" publication, *The Birth of Tragedy*, in 1872. Indeed, Nietzsche gave private readings of the two lectures to Cosima and Wagner in Tribschen and had special presentation copies made for them as gifts. They in turn suggested to Nietzsche that he pursue the themes of these lectures in a book-length study, a suggestion with which their enthusiastic disciple was more than willing to comply.[30] Wagner undoubtedly recognized his own thoughts in Nietzsche's writings and was eager to see them legitimated in the publication of a scholar. At the end of July in 1870 after the outbreak of the war, Nietzsche began work on "The Dionysian Worldview," which contained material that would eventually find its way into the first sections of *The Birth of Tragedy*. He had to interrupt his work on this essay for military service, but a revised version with the title "The Birth of the Tragic Concept" was presented to Cosima in December as a birthday gift when Nietzsche visited Tribschen for Christmas.[31] In February and March, he continued work on the project, reading an almost final version to the Wagners on 5 April; he completed the manuscript later in April, submitting it to a Leipzig publisher.[32]

The Birth of Tragedy is thus a book composed largely at the time of the Franco-Prussian War, and it is not surprising that it partakes in the patriotic spirit of that conflict. In the published version Nietzsche includes a brief foreword to Richard Wagner, which argues that the reader should not approach his thoughts with an opposition between "patriotic excitement and aesthetic indulgence" in mind. Rather, if the reader examines closely what Nietzsche has written, he will be perhaps astounded to learn "what a serious German problem is being dealt with here, one which we place in the center of German hopes, as the point around which they twist and turn" (GT, Vorwort an Richard Wagner, KSA 1.24). The close connection between Nietzsche's apparently aesthetic and academic concerns and his activities—both on the battlefield and in his scholarship—in dealing with the German Question is made even more apparent in the original foreword to Wagner composed in February 1871. This piece was published with sections 8–15 of the completed book in a limited private edition in 1871 with the title *Socrates and Greek Tragedy*. Thirty copies of this pamphlet were produced in June exclusively for friends, and Nietzsche's decision for partial publication of his first significant non-philological text may have resulted from his doubt that he could secure a publisher for the entire work.[33] In the February foreword, Nietzsche extolls a "future hero of tragic knowledge" who will "inaugurate a rebirth of antiquity, a *German* rebirth of the Hellenic world" (Nachlass 1871, 11[1], KSA 7.353). He goes on to write that he identifies this rebirth intimately with "the present bloody glory of the German name," thereby making explicit the connection with the still ongoing Franco-Prussian War.[34] There can be little doubt that the hero to whom Nietzsche refers is Wagner himself, but he proceeds to recount again, as Wagner did in his essay on Beethoven from 1870, the hopes that he harbors from current military and political developments:

> The only productive *political* power in Germany, which we do not need to delineate for anyone, has now arrived at a victory in the most enormous fashion, and from now on will dominate the essence of Germany in its most minute parts. This fact is of tremendous value because something is perishing through this power, something that we hate as the real opponent of every profound philosophy and artistic reflection; a state of sickness on which the essence of Germany has suffered since the great French Revolution, and which afflicts even the best constituted German souls in ever repeating swollen convulsions—not to mention the great masses, for whom one calls this affliction "liberalism," with contemptuous desecration of this innocuous word. (Nachlass 1871, 11[1], KSA 7.355)

Nietzsche appears to be counting on the new German state—he is writing only a month after the proclamation of the Second Empire in Versailles on 18 January 1871—to redress a situation that he attributes to French cultural "interference" in German affairs. In this draft of a foreword, he still views the new Germany as an ally in the pursuit of greatness and superior individual accomplishment: "And what purpose does that unbending power serve, with its centuries of continuing birth from coercion, conquest, and bloodbaths, if not to prepare the path for the genius?" (Nachlass 1871, 11[1], KSA 7.356). At the time of the writing of *The Birth of Tragedy*, Nietzsche had already begun to conceptualize the German Question in nonpolitical terms, but prior to the establishment of the Second Reich, he was still convinced that political unity was the first stage of a more encompassing transformation that would restore German cultural preeminence.

The argument in *The Birth of Tragedy* entails the origins of tragedy in the fortuitous amalgam of the Dionysian and the Apollonian, the demise of tragedy owing to the development of Socratic rationalism and Euripidean realism, and the hope for a rebirth of tragedy in contemporary Germany in Wagnerian opera. Only the last topic, which is treated in a somewhat unsystematic fashion in the last ten sections, would seem to relate to the nationalist spirit conjured up in the actual, as well as the draft, foreword to Wagner. But Nietzsche conceived of the entire essay, the early discussions dealing with Hellenic drama, as well as the later sections focusing on Wagner and contemporary issues, as a contribution to a more broadly conceived German Question. In doing so, Nietzsche was hardly different from his contemporaries, who also associated classical studies with a German tradition of scholarship and culture. In Wagner's essay on Beethoven, for example, he claims that Germany assimilated "the classical form of Roman and Greek culture," imitated their language and poetry, appropriated the views of the ancients, but accomplished everything in a manner that allowed Germany to express its "own internal spirit."[35] *The Birth of Tragedy* likewise partakes in the long tradition of German veneration for Greece that dates back to the eighteenth century, and Nietzsche consciously cites this Grecophilic heritage in his work. At the beginning of section twenty, he asks in which era and in which individuals had "the German spirit" learned most from the Greeks, and his answer is not surprising. He finds that German classicism has previously done the most to unite the Greeks with the German spirit, and specifically cites Johann Winckelmann (1717–1768), Johann Wolfgang von Goethe (1749–1832), and Friedrich Schiller (1759–1805) as the chief proponents of that movement. Nietzsche maintains, however, that German classicism did not go far enough and did not achieve a thorough and profound understanding of antiquity: "Should we, in order not to have to despair completely of the German spirit, not conclude that in some essential point or other those participants in the struggle might have failed to penetrate to the core of the Hellenic character and to establish a lasting bond of love between German and Greek culture?" Since the time of Goethe and Schiller, the German preoccupation with Greece has shown definite signs of regression: the combination of a superficial understanding of antiquity found in the schools and universities, a focus on "historical" education that levels the achievements of Greece to those of other civilizations, and a dominant journalistic culture that values quick and facile knowledge have led to a deterioration in the German appropriation of Greece. But in a thinly veiled reference to Wagner and in a brazen promotion of his own theory developed in earlier sections, Nietzsche detects a "reawakening of the Dionysian spirit and the rebirth of tragedy." He holds firm to the conviction that a genuine understanding of Greece is at hand and that it is a specifically German project. He writes defiantly: "Let no one seek to stunt our belief in a forthcoming rebirth of the ancient Hellenic world; for in it alone we find our hope for a renewal and purification of the German spirit through the fiery magic of music" (GT 20, KSA 1.129–31). Nietzsche's conviction of a "rebirth of the Hellenic world" in contemporary Germany (Nachlass 1871, 9[36], KSA 7.285) explains his response to a group of students in Prague who had requested a copy of his treatise on Greek tragedy. He sent the book, along with information on two favorable evaluations of it by his friend Erwin Rohde and Richard Wagner,[36] and adds: "Finally it will be permitted, my dear sirs, to utter the heartfelt wish that my book is also able to have the effect of increasing and strengthening your enthusiasm for truly German efforts in art and scholarship."[37] Nietzsche believed that his concern for ancient Greece and a Greek renaissance in postwar Germany was a logical and necessary continuation, and an appropriate expansion, of the German Question, which to that point had been solved only in the military and political arenas.

The connection between Germany and the Hellenic world was also fostered in *The Birth of Tragedy* by a framework and terminology that Nietzsche applied equally to both ancient and modern concerns. The concepts that he developed to explain the original birth of tragedy and its decline were also operative in German developments in the nineteenth century. We have already seen in the previous chapter that Socratism, which is responsible for the demise of tragedy in the ancient world, manifests itself in contemporary Europe in the Jewish press, and we will examine the ramifications of this position in greater detail in dealing with the Jewish Question. Although Nietzsche does not return directly to the Judeophobic associations with Socratism, he does invite us to think of an ongoing struggle between Socratic tendencies, which have held the upper hand since the fifth century BC, and Dionysian impulses, which have had sporadic appearances in previous centuries, but now appear poised for a final ascendency and reassertion of dominance. With regard to specifically German developments, in large part Nietzsche adopts the historical scheme he found in Wagner's essay on Beethoven, which was composed, like *The Birth of Tragedy*, at the time of the Franco-Prussian War, and uses his terminology as an overlay to elucidate the antagonisms and progress in the German spirit. In this Wagnerian-Nietzschean interpretation of history, Luther assumes a prominent role as someone who grasped the essence of the German people and opposed a culture dominated by foreign influences. He is credited with the "Germanic talent" of reintroducing Dionysian elements in music and of introducing again "the artistic view of art, myth," which is opposed to opera, "the form of Latin [*romanisch*] inartistic people" (Nachlass 1871, 9[10], KSA 7.275). Luther's chorale is a turning point for the revival of the Dionysian: "So deep, courageous, soulful and so effusively good and tender, this chorale of Luther's rings out from the thick undergrowth as the first Dionysian luring call at the approach of spring. It was answered in a competing echo by that solemnly arrogant festival procession of Dionysian enthusiasts, to whom we owe German music—and to whom we shall owe the *rebirth of German myth*!" (GT 23, KSA 1.147). By contrast, Socratism is cast as an overly rationalist tendency with no real relationship to the genuine German spirit. As Nietzsche writes in his notes from the fall of 1869: "Socratism in our time is the belief in things having been already finished: art is finished, aesthetics is finished. The dialectic is the press, ethics the optimistic putting into place of the Christian worldview. Socratism without any sense for the Fatherland, but only for the state. Without compassion for the future of Germanic art" (Nachlass 1869, 1[8], KSA 7.13). We find here the motifs of antimodernism that we noted previously in Nietzsche's lectures on education and his second *Untimely Meditation*, in this instance connected with the vocabulary he employs specifically to deal with phenomena in antiquity. The struggle between these two tendencies, the Socratic and the Dionysian, is eternal; only the manifestations of the conflict and the respective representatives differ as we progress from Attic Greece through the Reformation and the Enlightenment to Germany in the final decades of the nineteenth century.

For both Nietzsche and Wagner, music was the artistic form in which the German spirit manifested itself most fully and significantly. The focus on music is self-serving for both men, and it contradicts a commonsense approach to artistic forms, which would view music as more universal than any literary or even pictorial forms because the nature of tones, melodies, harmonies, and rhythm does not seem to have obvious national dimensions. But Wagner's "Beethoven" essay, written to commemorate the composer's centennial and fortuitously to celebrate the apparent German victory in the Franco-Prussian War, argues that the connection between a composer and his nation lies deeper than any literary or painterly association. In the process, he also manages to bring Beethoven into proximity of the nationalist sentiments of 1870; indeed, Wagner had evidently contemplated entitling the piece "Beethoven and the German Nation":[38]

> The idiosyncrasy that marks the musician as belonging to his nation must in any case be seated deeper than that whereby we recognize Goethe

and Schiller as Germans, Rubens and Rembrandt as Netherlanders, even though we must take it that both have sprung, at bottom, from the selfsame cause. To follow up that cause might be every whit as attractive as to explore the depths of music's essence. On the other hand, it may prove easier to obtain a glimpse of what has hitherto eluded the grasp of a dialectical method, if we set ourselves the more definite task of inquiring into the connection of the great musician, whose hundredth anniversary we are now about to celebrate, with the German nation which has lately undergone such earnest trials of its worth.[39]

Wagner goes on to detail the decay of literature, art, and music in non-German countries, singling out for particular condemnation the "artificial formalism of Jesuit observance" in music, the "Jesuit architecture of the last two centuries," and French classicism, "in whose spirit-deadening laws we may trace a speaking likeness to the laws of construction of the operatic Aria and the Sonata." Germans came to the rescue—Wagner mentions specifically Lessing, Goethe, and Schiller—but it is Beethoven who is chiefly responsible for redeeming the German spirit. The *"unique relation of great Beethoven to the German people"* lies in his lifting the status of music to a level where it became a "sublime vocation" able to communicate a profundity equal to that of any philosophically abstract thinker.[40]

The trajectory Nietzsche sketches for music is very similar, except that he places these developments within his own conceptual framework. The Dionysian worldview declines under the "disastrous influence of opera" and its culture of optimism, which is identified with Socratism. But the "transformation and degeneration" of the Greek ideal is now being subjected to a reversal with the "gradual awakening of the Dionysian spirit":

> From the Dionysian ground of the German spirit a power has risen up which has nothing in common with the original conditions of Socratic culture, a power which it rather senses as something horrifically inexplicable, something overpoweringly hostile: *German music*, as we have to understand it principally in its powerful solar course from Bach to Beethoven, from Beethoven to Wagner. What, under the most favorable circumstances, can the Socratic system of our time with its lust for knowledge even begin to do with this daemon rising from the unfathomable depths? (GT 19, KSA 1.126–27)

In section twenty-three, he expresses his faith in the "pure and strong core of the German character" to excise the foreign elements that have been "forcibly implanted"; the war, he suggests, was an "external preparation and encouragement" to such activity, whose pioneers were Luther and the great German artists and poets. If the German seeks a leader, he need only listen to the "beckoning call of the Dionysian bird, which hovers above him and wants to show him the way" (GT 23, KSA 1.149). Shifting metaphorical registers in the next section, Nietzsche makes more explicit the leader to whom he has referred. Here the German spirit is likened to a sleeping knight, "dreaming peacefully in an inaccessible abyss, in magnificent health, depth, and Dionysian strength." Then, in a series of unmistakable allusions to Wagner's *Ring*, he conjures the image of a violent and virile rousing of Germany from its prolonged lethargy: "Let no one believe that the German spirit has lost its mythical home for all eternity, when it can still understand so clearly the birdsong that tells it of that home. One day it will awaken in the morning freshness that follows a great sleep: then it will slay dragons, annihilate the spiteful dwarves, and awaken Brünnhilde—and Wotan's spear itself will not be able to bar its way!" (GT 24, KSA 1.153–54). The solution to the German Question following the conquest of the French and the establishment of a new political unity lies in the renewal of cultural greatness in music and culminates in the works of Richard Wagner, the worthy heir to the Dionysian tragedy of fifth-century Athens.

The realization of the newly defined German Question was endangered externally by the French and the Jews, especially by the rationalist or Socratic practices inspired by these "foreign" elements. Wagner's writing emphasizes in greater detail the deleterious effects of the "tyranny of the mode,"[41] but Nietzsche too makes frequent reference in texts and notes from the early 1870s to the threats to the German spirit from non-native sources. Internally Germany faced a different peril: the smug optimism of patriotic countrymen who believe that the attainment of German unity is the final stage in the resolution to the German Question. This internal opposition to the Wagnerian program so dear to Nietzsche is the subject of his first *Untimely Meditation*: it is embodied in David Strauß and his recently published volume *The Old Faith and the New* (1872), and labeled with the moniker "cultural Philistinism." The first sections of the essay elucidate the problem. While *The Birth of Tragedy* suggests that cultural achievements are likely to be a consequence of military prowess and political pursuits, *David Strauß, the Confessor and Writer* (1873) begins by juxtaposing the triumph on the battlefield with victorious culture. The latter does not follow from the former; in fact, here military prowess is regarded as a grave danger for cultural achievement. The delusion that cultural supremacy was automatically realized with military conquest is "extremely pernicious," not only because it is a delusion, but because it is capable of turning victory into utter defeat: "*into the defeat—indeed, the extirpation—of the German spirit for the sake of the 'German Reich'*" (DS 1, KSA 1.159–60). The postwar reality is that the nation is still dependent on French culture, and that the elements that contributed to victory on the battlefield have nothing whatsoever to do with the cultural realm. What Nietzsche witnessed around him in the first years of the Second Reich was a cultural enthusiasm that vastly overestimated its own stature and accomplishments, and that reveled in newspaper accounts, novels, and histories that are of little value. Real culture, Nietzsche asserts, is manifested above all in a "unity of artistic style in all vital expressions of a people"; contemporary German culture, however, is characterized by an absence of style, "a chaotic hodgepodge of all styles." The Germans are still barbarians in the cultural realm, while the French, no matter how we may regard their achievements, have at the very least "a real, productive culture." In the Franco-Prussian cultural struggle, we could consider it a German triumph only if "we had imposed on them an original German culture." But since Germany has no unified culture, since it is still dependent on Paris "in all matters of form," the ultimate and essential outcome of the German Question has yet to be determined (DS 1, KSA 1.163–64). These thoughts are not dissimilar to those of other German intellectuals of the 1870s—for example, Heinrich von Treitschke, who likewise points out that the young German nation is lacking a "national style" in "our whole essence."[42] Those who blindly assert otherwise and proclaim optimistically the arrival of cultural preeminence are, in Nietzsche's view, "cultural philistines [*Bildungsphilister*]," who are in reality more detrimental to Germany and its genuine goals than foreign armies. David Strauß, "a true *satisfait* with the state of our cultivation and a typical philistine" (DS 2, KSA 1.171) becomes in Nietzsche's presentation the prototype for naïve native forces working against the Wagnerian cultural vision. Only by overcoming the internal obstacles to genuine cultural achievement can the German Question, answered hitherto only in military and political terms, find a worthwhile, meaningful, and ennobling resolution.

Rethinking the Question: What Is German?

Nietzsche's understanding of the German Question underwent a further evolution in the middle of the decade. This change was precipitated by his break with Wagner and his alienation from the cult-like following surrounding the Meister. It is difficult to pinpoint the moment when Nietzsche became disenchanted with Wagner and the Wagnerian project of cultural renewal. Most likely it occurred gradually during the period from 1873 to 1878, and culminated in his shock at the opening of the Bayreuth opera festival. But we cannot be certain regarding Nietzsche's views about Bayreuth in 1876: there is little evidence in his correspondence of disappointment or of any obvious affront. His most extensive description of happenings in the summer of 1876 appeared only in the retrospective sketch from 1888 designed for the autobiographical text *Ecce Homo*. In this passage, he describes events surrounding the grand opening in a contemptuous fashion: "Even to those most intimately concerned, the 'ideal' was not what mattered most. . . . Then there was the pathetic crowd of patrons . . . all very spoilt, very bored and unmusical as yowling cats. . . . The whole idle riff-raff of Europe had been brought together, and any prince who pleased could go in and out of Wagner's house as if it were a sporting event. And fundamentally it was nothing more" (EH, Kommentar, Warum ich so gute Bücher schreibe, KSA 14.489–90). Written a dozen years after the actual occurrence, this passage may not be an accurate reflection of Nietzsche's sentiments in 1876; we have seen already that Nietzsche often reinterprets the past in light of his present attitudes, and we can suspect the same thing occurs in this description. A further clue to Nietzsche's break with Wagner comes in correspondence with Franz Overbeck (1837–1905) on 22 February 1883, less than ten days after Wagner's death. In this letter, Nietzsche mentions a "deadly insult" [*tödliche Beleidigung*] on the part of Wagner, and there has been much speculation concerning what the insult was and whether it was responsible for Nietzsche's distancing himself from his former friend. There was some speculation that Wagner had offended Nietzsche in mocking or rejecting his "Hymn to Friendship" [*Hymnus auf die Freundschaft*], which Nietzsche had composed in 1873–74 and played for Wagner on a visit to Tribschen. Nietzsche was evidently extremely proud of this composition and thought it the best he had ever produced. Cosima mentions in 1887 that the break may have occurred because of criticism that occurred thirteen years earlier, but there is no hint of any offense in Nietzsche's writings from that period. It is also possible that "the deadly insult" occurred as a result of Nietzsche's visit to a doctor in Frankfurt named Otto Eiser, whom he consulted for his symptoms of a nervous disorder and depression, and that it had to do with Wagner's intrusion into Nietzsche's sexual life, which was evidently Wagner's diagnosis of his disciple's difficulties, and which he did not hesitate to communicate directly to Eiser. This incident has been well researched,[43] but ultimately what exactly occurred, whether it was *the* "deadly insult" to which Nietzsche later refers, and how this "deadly insult" contributed to Nietzsche's estrangement from Wagner still remain something of a mystery. Nietzsche also ascribes his break with Wagner to the latter's turn toward Christianity, as evidenced in his opera *Parsifal*, and Nietzsche directly references Wagner's embrace of religion in connection with the "deadly insult." In his late works, Nietzsche mentions often and critically Wagner's piety, but Nietzsche must have known about the plans for *Parsifal* at a much earlier date since Wagner had included material about it in his autobiography, which Nietzsche proofread. We are left with some uncertainty surrounding the growing enmity between the two men, and we can verify only that a break did occur, but not exactly when it occurred or why.[44]

We can be fairly confident, however, in asserting that Nietzsche began to distance himself from Wagner in the mid-1870s, and that his turn from Wagner was coterminous with a modification in his views of Germany, its politics, and its cultural aspirations. As we have seen, in his pre-Wagnerian stage Nietzsche had resembled many Germans of his time in embracing National Liberal desires for unity in a modern state, but had shifted this view once unification was achieved and, under the influence of the Wagnerian movement, began to regard cultural renewal as the only worthy goal for the new German Empire. To a certain extent, this first shift was in harmony with Nietzsche's natural proclivities: even in his school years, we saw that he was more of a cultural enthusiast than a political being. His shift away from German nationalism in the wake of his break with the Wagnerian cause also seems in accord with his own inclinations. After the 1860s, Nietzsche rarely exhibited signs of ardent nationalism. He differed significantly from Wagner, whose adherence to German traditions in his musical compositions and essays, and to an essence he imagined in the German spirit, was apparent and frequently articulated. Despite some nationalist sentiments expressed in letters—usually to individuals who themselves harbored patriotic views—and the bow toward nationalist goals in some of his writings in the Wagnerian period, Nietzsche seemed less attached to the typical nationalist traditions of his contemporaries and more interested in general aesthetic, cultural, and philosophical themes. We should therefore not be surprised to find that after 1876, when he began to identify even the minority and oppositional Wagnerian project with a betrayal of genuine cultural ideals, his ardor for the German Question diminished. Betrayed by Wagner's "crawling to the cross" in his religiously infused opera *Parsifal*, surrounded by cultural philistines [*Bildungsphilister*] without the requisite appreciation for grandeur and excellence, and rejected by both Wagnerians and their adversaries for his adversarial tone and position, Nietzsche's frustration with his Fatherland, which may have had psychological dimensions as well, reverberates through all his "mature" writings, from the aphoristic texts starting with *Human, All Too Human* (1878) to the last frenzied works composed in 1888. Having embraced the German cause primarily for its cultural promise, Nietzsche gradually unleashed his venom on the country and the people responsible for his disappointment. Unlike Wagner, who would publish an essay extolling German virtues titled "What Is German?" in 1878, Nietzsche could only ridicule endeavors to regard German achievements, whether they were in the political or the cultural arena, as exemplary.

To some extent, Nietzsche's rethinking of the German Question after 1876 is a response to Wagnerian themes and more specifically to the composer's exploration of the essence of the German in his essay from 1878. Most of this piece was composed in 1865, Wagner informs the reader; he added only a brief preface and conclusion when it appeared in the initial issue of the *Bayreuther Blätter*. The thrust of Wagner's argument is that there is a German essence, that there is something original about it, that it has survived periods in which it was subject to foreign elements, and that the German essence manifests itself most apparently, and even after suffering extreme hardships, in "German poetry, German music, and German philosophy." The external facts of the German essence are clear:

"German peoples," Wagner writes, "is the title given to those Germanic races which, upon their natal soil, retained their speech and customs." These peoples have definite characteristics: "In rugged woods, throughout the lengthy winter, by the warm hearth-fire of the turret-chamber soaring high into the clouds, for generations he [the German] cherishes the memories of his forefathers; the myths of native gods he weaves into an endless web of sagas." The German assimilates foreign influences in his own fashion; he is characterized by a "native bent to the phlegmatic"; he is prone to fantasticalness; he withdraws himself from mundane public life; he does not feel at home abroad, but he loves to travel and to observe.[45] This stereotype of the German that Wagner constructs contrasts sharply with Nietzsche's refusal to recognize anything essential or original in Germans. Already in 1873, he had commented in his notebooks that what is German had not yet been established, that it is still in flux: *"The German essence is not yet there; it must first come into being; at some point it must be born, so that above all it can be observable and honest for itself. But every birth is painful and violent"* (Nachlass 1873, 29[123], KSA 7.687). This theme of Germans being unfinished and not yet identifiable would persist in Nietzsche's writings well into his final year of sanity. Indeed, at one point Nietzsche asserts that to be a good German means to "de-Germanize" oneself, that is, to grow more and more beyond what has been hitherto considered as German: "a *change into the un-Germanic* has always been the mark of the most able of our people" (VM 323, KSA 2.511–12). Nietzsche is therefore less kind to the notion of the search for origins that Wagner implicitly advocates in his essay. In the second volume of *Human, All Too Human*, in an aphorism entitled "Original German," he ridicules the endeavor to excavate some essence of the German stripped of all foreign influence: "German prose, which is in fact not based on some foreign model and ought no doubt to be accounted an original product of German taste, might offer a signpost to the zealous advocates of a future original German culture as to how, without imitation of foreign models, a truly German costume, for instance, a German social gathering, a German furnishing of a room, a German luncheon, would look." Nietzsche concludes his derisive musings on an "original German culture" with the remark: "Someone who had reflected long on this prospect finally cried out in horror: 'But, for heaven's sake, perhaps we already *have* this original culture—only we don't like to talk about it!'" (WS 91, KSA 2.594). By the late 1870s, the German Question for Nietzsche is no longer framed in terms of a solution that entails political unity or the recruitment of a purified German spirit or essence as the hope for future artistic achievement; instead, the belief in an "original essence or spirit" that has to be restored politically or aesthetically is regarded as part of a foolhardy and vapid exercise.

Nietzsche's move away from the magnetic force field of Wagnerian ideology is easily detected in his reevaluation of noted individuals in the German tradition.

At one point in his notebooks from 1872, Nietzsche lists six names: Schopenhauer, Wagner, Goethe, Schiller, Luther, and Beethoven. From our examination of his writings during the early years of the decade, it is fair to say that at that point he regarded each as an exemplary representative of a genuine German culture. This evaluation changes significantly over the next fifteen years. Schopenhauer, Goethe, and Beethoven are simply stripped of their nationality and regarded as European phenomena.[46] In an aphorism from *The Gay Science* entitled "On the Old Problem: 'What Is German?'", Nietzsche reviews three significant philosophical occurrences: Leibniz's insight that "consciousness is merely an *accidens* of experience," Kant's questioning of causality, and Hegel's notion that "species concepts develop *out of each other*," and concludes that each of them contains "a thoughtful piece of German self-knowledge, self-experience, self-understanding." Schopenhauer, by contrast, is dissociated from Germanness, since his pessimism is a consequence of "a generally European event in which all races had their share and for which all deserve credit and honor" (FW 357, KSA 3.597–99). In an aphorism on German theater from *Human, All Too Human*, he argues similarly that Goethe, unlike other dramatists, should not be identified with Germany: "Goethe stood above the Germans in every respect and still stands above them: he will never belong to them." He continues by citing the non-German identity of the triumvirate whose works he now appreciates as European: "Just as Beethoven composed music above the head of the Germans, just as Schopenhauer philosophized above the heads of the Germans, so Goethe wrote his *Tasso*, his *Iphigenie*, above the heads of the Germans" (VM 170, KSA 2.448–49). Remaining on the roster of individuals exemplifying Germanness are Wagner, Schiller, and Luther, but in each case Nietzsche's evaluation of their accomplishment and excellence changes markedly during the late 1870s and 1880s. Lauded in the early works as an exemplar of the German spirit and associated with Goethe in their joint endeavor to shepherd Greek values and aesthetics into the modern German world, Schiller is viewed increasingly critically and dissociated from Goethe in both artistic accomplishment and ideological temperament. He is called a merely theatrical being (MA 176, KSA 2.161); he is an idealist (Nachlass 1886–1887, 7[6], KSA 12.274); in his dealings with Greece, he embraced "a false antiquity," too smooth and soft (Nachlass 1879, 41[67], KSA 8.593); he is overly didactic and moralistic, scornfully called "the moral trumpeter of Säckingen"[47] (GD, Streifzüge eines Unzeitgemässen 1, KSA 6.111). "Goethe," Nietzsche writes in his notebooks in 1885, "is an exception: he lived among Germans, sheltered and clothed in a fine manner. Schiller belongs to those Germans who love the great, grandiloquent phrases and the pompous gestures of virtue" (Nachlass 1885, 36[38], KSA 11.567). Luther, who was somewhat bizarrely associated with the Dionysian in 1872, is still credited with reforming the German language, and opposing the Roman Catholic Church, especially its ascetic tendencies. But as the years go by, he becomes the prototypical German responsible for the "cultural crime" of reintroducing a more resilient form of Christianity (AC 61, KSA 6.251–52). The same can be said for Wagner, who increasingly becomes associated with decadence and illness. His stage, Nietzsche asserts, "requires only one thing: *Teutons!* ... Definition of the Teuton: obedience and long legs." Although, as we shall see, Nietzsche later brings Wagner into proximity of the French or even the Jews to mock his Francophobic and anti-Semitic former friend, until his final works in 1888 more than perhaps any other artist he is identified with the Second Empire and its racist patriotism: "It is full of profound significance that the arrival of Wagner coincides in time with the arrival of the 'Reich': both events prove the very same thing: obedience and long legs" (WA 11, KSA 6.39). The worldview Wagner had propagated, now seen as dilettantish, German, and unclear (Nachlass 1885, 36[14], KSA 11.555), but to which Nietzsche also adhered in his early writings, is thoroughly revised by Nietzsche after his estrangement from the composer: German artists of quality become, like Nietzsche, European in outlook and import, while those who retain their Germanness are devalued and regarded as part of a sick and degenerate culture emanating from the Fatherland.

Nietzsche's turn away from Wagner and from the nationalism Wagner continued to embrace, even as he, Wagner, also became critical of the Second Empire as a political entity, does not mean that he abandoned all interest in politics and affairs of state. In 1895, Richard Reuter (1840–1904) reported about a visit to Nietzsche in the summer of 1876, where politics in Germany became the main topic of conversation. The discussion became livelier, according to Reuter, only when Nietzsche mentioned a recently published pamphlet, "National Liberal Party, National Liberal Press and Higher Gentlemanliness," which contained "the first shriek and angry outburst of public opinion against that Party's increasingly mindless and characterless servility toward Prince Bismarck." This pamphlet obviously struck a chord with Nietzsche because of his growing disillusionment with political developments and the continued failure of the recently unified Germany to promote a culture worthy of support. Reuter goes on to give a short sketch of Nietzsche's position on the German Question, from his childhood embrace of the Germanic tradition and his initial enthusiasm for the possibilities in the new Reich to his disillusionment with the subsequent course of events. At the end of the evening, Reuter mentions that Nietzsche lent him an essay "by the Göttingen theologian Paul de Lagarde," which appeared to him to have expressed thoughts similar to those found in the anonymous pamphlet. Reuter does not mention the title of the Lagarde (1827–1891) essay, and it is impossible to say with certainty the exact piece to which he is referring. In January of 1873, Nietzsche had recommended to Erwin Rohde an essay written by Lagarde, *On the Relationship of the German State to Theology, Church, and Religion* [*Über das Verhältniss des deutschen Staates zu Theologie, Kirche und Religion*] (Nr. 294, KSB 4.121), but this piece, written mostly in 1859 and published separately as a small book in 1873, deals primarily with issues relating to the Evangelical and Catholic Churches; it contains some interest for the present study because of Lagarde's negative treatment of Saint Paul, a topic to which we will return in Chapter 6, and his mention of "Judaism free from 'Judaine,'"[48] but it has little in common with the political pamphlet of the National Liberals. Nietzsche may have given Reuter a short book by Lagarde that appeared in September of 1875 entitled *On the Present Situation in the German Reich* [*Über die gegenwärtige Lage des Deutschen Reiches*], which begins by stating that "the situation of the Fatherland is entirely not what it should be" and goes on to analyze the perils the Second Reich will face in the coming years.[49] No matter which piece Nietzsche lent, Reuter proceeds in his account by claiming that Lagarde was responsible for Nietzsche's change of thinking in 1876 and that he "was practically a disciple of Lagarde."[50] Known today for his seminal contributions to the anti-Semitic ideology that culminated in National Socialism, Lagarde was ridiculed by Nietzsche in 1887 as a "sentimental crank" (to Theodor Fritsch, 23 March 1887, Nr. 819, KSB 8.46), which hardly suggests discipleship. The contention of pervasive influence appears hyperbolic even for the mid-1870s, but it is not insignificant that Nietzsche demonstrated a continued interest in writers who shared his disappointment with developments in Germany. Wagner, similarly disappointed, tried to attract Lagarde's participation in the *Bayreuther Blätter*, but Lagarde demurred, although he enjoyed continued praise from Wagnerians.[51] What is more important for our concerns is that Nietzsche retained an interest in the German Question and in works on German politics. Despite his embrace of Europeanism and his rejection of the nationalist views he had harbored in the early 1870s, he continued to follow political developments in Germany and sought writers who similarly expressed skepticism about Bismarck and the German state.

However, by the latter part of the decade, Nietzsche had largely abandoned the German Question conceived as a cultural mission of Wagnerian provenance. Elements retained from this discarded ideology are either Europeanized, if they are exemplary, or incorporated into a negative perspective on Germany, if they are not. Similarly, Nietzsche rejects the central aspects of the original German Question, which dealt with the creation of a unified nation-state under the auspices of Prussia. Indeed, from about the mid-1870s onward Nietzsche turns against the modern state as a phenomenon of contemporary life and portrays the newly established German state as a promoter of decline and decadence. Arguing that it is the protector of the rights of the masses and the sign of a creeping democracy, he places the state in strict opposition to the hallowed goal of culture achievement. We have seen in Nietzsche's discussions of education that he considers the Prussian state partially responsible for the decline in the quality of educational institutions, and that education for the civil service and genuine philosophical *Bildung* should be strictly separated. This antagonism between state and culture that Nietzsche detects in Germany of the 1870s has a much longer tradition in the Western world. Nietzsche traces it back to ancient Greece: "Like every organizing political power," he writes in *Human, All Too Human*, "the Greek polis was mistrustful of the growth of culture and sought almost exclusively to paralyze and inhibit it." In this aphorism, he continues by contending that the ancient *polis* was a conservative entity hampering further development of culture and seeking only to affirm itself through restrictive education. Culture evolves *in spite of* the *polis*, not because of it (MA 474, KSA 2.308). In modern Europe, Nietzsche is not insensitive to the function of the modern state in protecting its population; particularly in his more enlightened, middle period, he recognizes some benefits that have accrued to the citizenry. But the advantages threaten to turn into disadvantages when the state becomes too expansive: "The state is a prudent institution for the protection of individuals against one another: if it is completed and perfected too far it will in the end enfeeble the individual and, indeed, dissolve him—that is to say, thwart the original purpose of the state in the most thorough way possible" (MA 235, KSA 2.197). In his later works, however, Nietzsche becomes less tolerant of state activities and less differentiated in considering the benefits of its institutions. By the time he wrote *Twilight of the Idols*, he had begun to reject all modern forms of government: "All our political theories and constitutions—and the 'German Reich' is by no means an exception—are consequences, necessary consequences, of decline; the unconscious effect of decadence has assumed mastery even over the ideals of some of the sciences" (GD, Streifzüge eines Unzeitgemässen 37, KSA 6.138). Although many today identify Bismarck's Germany with an autocratic regime in which the military and the aristocracy exercised an inordinate amount of influence under pseudo-parliamentary rule, in his late writings Nietzsche consistently views the Second Reich as the symptom of a baneful democratizing movement that threatens to drag all Europe into mediocrity. While he had advocated German unification in a national state as the solution to the German Question in his youth, in his final statements Nietzsche regards the unified Germany of the late 1880s—and, indeed, the entire German Question—as part of the decadence enveloping European culture.

One of the chief reasons for Nietzsche's dismissive attitude toward the modern state has to do with its promotion of a system of political parties. It is quite possible that Nietzsche's early involvement with electoral politics soured him to the parliamentary system in general, and his hostility became increasingly apparent in his writings. He could easily be identified as a National Liberal in the 1860s, but any sympathies he had for party platforms disappeared soon after the establishment of the Second Empire. Although during the 1870s and 1880s his published views occasionally coincide with a plank or sentiment identified with one or another of the major German parties, he remained a staunch opponent of politics as such. This antipolitical stance does not mean that his writings have no political implications or that he desired no political effects—in the broader sense of the word "political"—but only that he disdained day-to-day political activity. Indeed, Nietzsche's celebrated claim that he was "the last antipolitical German" (EH, Kommentar, Warum ich so weise bin, KSA 14.472) refers specifically to his antagonistic attitude to parliamentary politics and to the hegemony of politics over more important areas, such as cultural affairs.[52] Again Nietzsche's views are partially attributable to an antipathy to what he perceives as a democratizing tendency in governance. In *The Gay Science*, he points out that at one time politics, like the military, was the domain of the nobility, and that Europe has gradually witnessed a shift away from aristocratic control. He continues: "And it is quite possible that some day one may find it [politics] so common and vulgar that, along with all party literature and journalism, one would classify it as 'prostitution of the spirit'" (FW 31, KSA 3.403). His larger, "philosophical" objections have to do with what we might call the necessity to compromise and to reach consensus. Political parties, because they are organizations of many individuals, are based on falsehood and self-deception; they are an affirmation of another pernicious collective phenomenon, slave morality, and as such, they perpetrate (self-)deceit and decadence. In *The Antichrist,* Nietzsche contends that lying to oneself is the precondition for any party: "of necessity, the party man becomes a liar" (AC 55, KSA 6.238). And in his initial remarks in the section on the state in *Human, All Too Human,* he suggests that the necessity to pander to the populace compels parties into simplistic propaganda: "The demagogic character and the intention to appeal to the masses is at present common to all political parties: on account of this intention, they are all compelled to transform their principles into great al fresco stupidities and thus to paint them on the wall" (MA 438, KSA 2.285). Nietzsche's objection to parties is thus intimately related to his rejection of the new German state: instead of promoting greatness and genius, two ideals he had not relinquished from his Wagnerian years, they cater to the rabble and destroy the hierarchy that is so essential for cultural achievement. Nietzsche's political position, narrowly defined, becomes increasingly unclear in the 1880s. But the lack of clarity does not stem from an inability to assign him to a political direction, to see him as a conservative or a liberal or a socialist, but rather from his rejection of politics as such and everything that involves political parties, parliaments, and elections.

The increasingly dismissive attitude toward the state and political parties extends to the political leadership of Germany as well. We will recall that in his National Liberalist phase, Nietzsche, like many of his contemporaries, was a staunch proponent of Bismarck and his government. As we move into the 1870s, however, Nietzsche begins to resemble many individuals in a small group of oppositional figures who become skeptical of Bismarck on cultural grounds, and this oppositional perspective perseveres even after he distances himself from Wagnerian circles. In *Human, All Too Human,* we still find Nietzsche remaining neutral or even supportive with regard to Bismarck's political activities and achievements. In aphorism 445, he writes: "to be able to act with complete ruthlessness, a statesman will do best to perform his work not on his own behalf but on behalf of a prince." Four aphorisms later he contends that even "the learned and cultivated" display "superstitious faith" in crediting a statesman with "all the important changes and turns of events that take place during their term of office as being their own work." And shortly thereafter, in aphorism 453, he refers to the statesman who "excites public passions so as to profit from the counter-passions thereby aroused," and speaks directly of foreign affairs that can only pertain to Germany (MA 445, 449, 453, KSA 2.289–94). For much of his aphoristic period, Nietzsche continues to credit Bismarck, referred to often with the transparent moniker of "the statesman,"[53] with politically astute maneuvers. He appreciates that Bismarck is not a zealous nationalist, but that he acts out of political calculation. The fact that he has "no principles" but only "strong drives" is viewed as not very German, but is also not regarded as an unfavorable trait (M 167, KSA 3.148–49). Even in 1884, he observes that Bismarck created parliament as a "lightning rod," a protection against the crown and under certain circumstances a lever for exerting pressure internationally (Nachlass 1884, 25[272], KSA 11.82). He is associated at one point with the "Europeans" Goethe and Beethoven as part of an elite vanguard for a stronger future. His distrust of scholars and ignorance of philosophy, which Nietzsche could have considered objectionable, are adjudged an advantage: "I like that about him. He has thrown away what our stupid German education (with *Gymnasium* and university) wanted to teach him" (Nachlass 1884, 26[402], KSA 11.256). Eventually, however, Bismarck as the German who created the nation-state, thereby impeding Europeanism, and who shows no understanding for cultural greatness, earns Nietzsche's scorn. In a wholesale revision of his views at the time of the *Untimely Meditations,* in *Ecce Homo* Nietzsche uses his discussion of the last two essays in that series to associate Bismarck with Reich, culture, Christianity, and success as an enemy of "Schopenhauer and Wagner *or,* in *one* word, Nietzsche" (EH, Warum ich so gute Bücher schreibe, Die Unzeitgemässen 1, KSA 6.317). Increasingly in 1888, Bismarck comes to stand for the Reich itself, the new Kaiser, and despised German "virtues," including anti-Semitism. In his final letters, Nietzsche states that he will be sending Bismarck and the young Kaiser the first copies of his latest "anti-German" book, *Ecce Homo,* with "a declaration of war" (to August Strindberg, 8 December 1888, Nr. 1176, KSB 8.509);[54] Bismarck is regarded as a tool of the Hohenzollerns (to

Ruggero Bonghi [draft], December 1888, Nr. 1231, KSB 8.569); and he reports that he has ordered Bismarck shot along with Wilhelm II (1859–1941) and the noted anti-Semitic court preacher Adolf Stöcker (1835–1909) (to Meta von Salis, 3 January 1889, Nr. 1239, KSB 8.572). In his last notebook before the outbreak of insanity, he calls "Prince Bismarck" the "idiot par excellence among all statesmen" (Nachlass 1888–89, 25[13], KSA 13.643). Mirroring his turn from nationalist to antinationalist politics, Nietzsche's image of Bismarck undergoes a transformation from heralded hero of unification to reluctantly admired statesman to reviled proponent of revanchist nationalism.[55]

Because of Nietzsche's consistent objections to the state and its chief institutions, his reception among various anarchist and libertarian groups has been generally favorable. There are several obvious thematic connections between Nietzsche and the anarchist tradition, especially the German branch associated with Max Stirner (pseudonym for Johann Kaspar Schmidt, 1806–1856). Even during Nietzsche's lifetime, there was some speculation that he had been influenced by the author of *The Ego and Its Own* (1845). Nietzsche's sister Elisabeth, who had a proprietary interest in maintaining her brother's originality, and who certainly did not desire his works placed in the circle of left-Hegelian individualism, maintained that he had never read Stirner.[56] Franz Overbeck, however, who was Nietzsche's closest associate during his Basel years, and who was actively engaged in a dispute with Elisabeth over her brother's legacy, asserts the contrary and estimates that the influence was considerable.[57] Curiously, we find no reference to Stirner in any of Nietzsche's writings or notebooks; nor does his name appear in his correspondence, and several of his closest acquaintances, when queried by Elisabeth, stated that Nietzsche had never mentioned Stirner.[58] Whether Nietzsche read Stirner or not, he, like Stirner and other anarchist writers, advocates—at least implicitly—an abolition of the state or, at a very minimum, the reduction of state interference in individual affairs. This impression is furthered by the veritable absence of an alternative suggestion for government. While we can be certain that Nietzsche disdains parliamentary democracy—in his literary remains he calls parliamentarianism and journalism "the means by which a herd animal makes himself into a master" (Nachlass 1885, 34[177], KSA 11.480)—he posits no recognizable alternative. Unlike reactionary political thinkers of the nineteenth century, he does not propose a return to feudal or semifeudal forms of government, despite his advocacy of "aristocratic radicalism."[59] It does not appear, however, that he can be recruited for an anarchist or libertarian cause without significant distortion of his writings. Nowhere does he embrace a doctrine of individual liberties or rights, and he never espouses anything that would suggest the freedoms and equality usually found in anarchist doctrine. From the few hints we can gather in his texts and notes, it would seem that he prefers either an oligarchic rule—headed by an elite of "spirit" rather than a nobility of blood, as we shall see in Chapter 9—or a dictatorship of one genial individual. The former alternative would conform in a vague sense to Nietzsche's conception of Greek society before the decline precipitated by Socratism; the latter can be gleaned from Nietzsche's frequent laudatory comments about Caesar, Napoleon, Charlemagne, Cesare Borgia, and Machiavelli. If we extrapolate his most often expressed thoughts on leadership, we would conclude that his "solution" to the German Question would be embodied in one or more strong leaders who would stem the democratic tide and promote a genuine culture of the elite.

Nietzsche's self-designation as a "good European" and his advocacy of "great politics" are likewise subject to the same type of misunderstanding. While there is little doubt that his "Europeanism" is meant to contrast with a narrow German nationalism, and that "great politics" is juxtaposed to the petty parliamentary maneuvers and election campaigns of the Second Reich, neither position can be viewed as viable or desirable from the perspective of twenty-first-century realities. We should recall that at about the time Nietzsche was writing, the first discussions of German colonies were in progress, and we will have occasion to examine his thoughts on the Colonial Question in more detail in Chapter 5. For now we will observe only that Nietzsche had frequent fantasies regarding a European hegemony over the earth (JGB 208, KSA 5.137–40),[60] but what role Nietzsche ascribes to Germany in this "new world order" is not always apparent or consistently maintained. Despite his deprecation of German nationalism and his disappointment at Germany's political and cultural direction under Bismarck, Nietzsche occasionally harbors hope for a significant German contribution to the new united Europe. A feature that Nietzsche frequently associates with Germans is their diversity. Composed of a great mixture of races, this "people of the middle" has multiple identities and a multivalent personality. German nature, Nietzsche avers, is still in the process of becoming. As a not-yet-finished people, it loves everything that is obscure and uncertain, but it has the possibility to evolve into something great and dominant: "'Development' is therefore the essentially German discovery and hit in the great domain of philosophical formulas:—a ruling idea, which, together with German beer and German music, is laboring to Germanize all Europe" (JGB 244, KSA 5.185). Nietzsche's thoughts here are tongue-in-cheek, yet there remains a serious residue to his favoring of Germans, as we see evidenced in other passages. Wagner, for example, could never have been possible without "super-German" sources, but his "German nature" provided the requisite "strength, daring, severity, and elevation" for his thought. Nietzsche takes pride in the fact that "we Germans are as yet nearer to barbarism than the French" (JGB 256, KSA 5.203), a statement whose significance lies not only in the affirmation of a "barbaric"—that is, antireligious and amoral dimension of cultural achievement—but also in the identification signaled by the first-person plural pronoun. Indeed, in some of his more generous moments, Nietzsche fantasizes about Germans breeding "a ruling caste" (Nachlass 1885, 34[11], KSA 11.457) or expresses the faint hope that with "will, effort, discipline, and breeding" Germans can progress beyond their present condition and become something great (Nachlass 1885, 36[53], KSA 11.572). The sheer amount of ink Nietzsche devoted to Germans and Germany indicates that even after his break with Wagner, the German Question was not a settled matter in his mind. That Germans had not realized their potential and that the jingoism of the Second Reich is contemptible are propositions that Nietzsche propounded for the last decade and a half of his conscious life. But there are also faint hints that he believed Germany could overcome its nationalism, its parliamentary imbecility, its journalistic culture, and its philistinism, and become a cultural leader in the new Europe he envisioned.

Anti-German Tirades

Nonetheless, the last writings Nietzsche penned before his fall into insanity most often evidence a violent rejection of anything associated with Germans and Germany. Although Nietzsche had many reasons, both philosophical and political, to attack German developments during the *Gründerzeit* [Founders' Age],[61] we should not discount his personal animus against the Germans for not appreciating his writings. Nietzsche mentions it in his published works, his notebooks, and his correspondence too often to consider it irrelevant. We should recall that from the fourth part of *Zarathustra* onward, Nietzsche had begun to publish his own books, unable to find a publisher who would promote him to his satisfaction and convinced that he could do better acting on his own behalf. He still used the same printer, Georg Naumann in Leipzig, but Nietzsche funded publication costs from his limited university pensions. He did everything he could to augment the sales of his writings—including, for example, composing the book *On the Genealogy of Morals* as a stimulus to purchases of *Beyond Good and Evil* and earlier works—but his efforts came to naught. Nietzsche remained virtually unknown—or at least his books went unsold—in Germany during his own lifetime. There were few reviews of his writings, and those that did appear Nietzsche believed misunderstood what he was trying to accomplish. In 1887 he laments to Heinrich Köselitz (1854–1918) that he is forty-three years old and has written fifteen volumes, but no German publisher wants to promulgate his works (Nr. 878, KSB 8.113), and in a letter to his former colleague, Franz Overbeck, he remarks that despite distributing sixty review copies, sales of *Beyond Good and Evil* have barely exceeded a hundred (Nr. 900, KSB 8.140).

Eventually this lack of attention among his compatriots turns to anger toward them, and he begins to develop the fiction that his popularity internationally far outstrips his native appeal. After complaining in *Ecce Homo* that in the Prussian *Nationalzeitung* [National Newspaper] his work was erroneously regarded as a "sign of the times" and as an example of *"Junker philosophy,"* he writes, as if to prove that only Germans do not understand him: "This was said for Germans: for I have readers everywhere else—nothing but *choice* intelligences of proved character brought up in high positions and duties; I have even real geniuses among my readers. In Vienna, in St Petersburg, in Stockholm, in Copenhagen, in Paris and New York—I have been discovered everywhere: I have *not* been in Europe's flatland Germany" (EH, Warum ich so gute Bücher schreibe 2, KSA 6.301). Later in his autobiography, he again takes up his poor treatment at the hands of his countrymen: "Up to now, they [the Germans] have compromised themselves with me, I doubt if they will do better in the future. . . . The readers and auditors most natural to me are still Russians, Scandinavians, and French" (EH, Warum ich so gute Bücher schreibe, Der Fall Wagner 3, KSA 6.360). These sentiments are repeated with regularity in his correspondence during 1888. The grain of truth in the claims concerning his reputation in foreign lands stems largely from his attempt to ingratiate himself with a few notable foreign authors: he corresponded with August Strindberg (1849–1912) and Hippolyte Taine (1828–1893), writing them obsequious letters that feigned a nonexistent intimacy, but there is little evidence that their opinions of his writings matched Nietzsche's own megalomaniacal self-evaluation. Nietzsche did attract the positive attention and assessment of Georg Brandes (1842–1927), the noted Danish critic and scholar, and Nietzsche often mentions in his correspondence, with considerable pride, that Brandes held lectures about his work, in contrast to scholars in Germany, where he has gone unnoticed.[62] He laments accordingly in *Ecce Homo*: "Ten years: and no one in Germany has made it a question of conscience to defend my name against the absurd silence under which it has lain buried: it was a foreigner, a Dane, who was the first to possess sufficient refinement of instinct *and courage* for that, who inveighed against my supposed friends" (EH, Warum ich so gute Bücher schreibe, Der Fall Wagner 4, KSA 6.363). Nietzsche also had occasional followers in other European countries, as well as in the United States: for example, the German-American author Karl Knortz (1841–1918) evidently read and appreciated his writings.[63] But he exaggerates vastly his international fame in contrasting it with his neglect in Germany, and despite the frequent assumption of a haughty attitude toward Germans and Germany, he longed for readers and disciples among his compatriots. At one point, Nietzsche asks plaintively in a letter to Reinhart von Seydlitz (1850–1931), "how long will it be before my peripheral impact (—for I have followers in North America and even in Italy) initiates an effect back on the beloved Fatherland?" (13 May 1888, Nr. 1034, KSB 8.314). Nietzsche's disappointment at the lack of a reading public in the "Fatherland" likely stimulated his claim that he was not German at all, but descended from Polish nobility, an assertion, as we have seen, that was articulated with increasing frequency and vehemence in 1888. It also accounts for his recurrent allusions to posthumous acclaim, another repeated motif in his late notes and works. We should likewise consider that in his last sane year Nietzsche often expresses satisfaction that in public he is not recognized as a German. These frequent signs of dissociation from his country of birth stem, at least in part, from an intense feeling of estrangement resulting from the conviction that he was largely unappreciated and misunderstood by his countrymen.

Nietzsche's assaults on Germans and Germany in his final year of writing took account of more than his own lack of popularity, however, and they signal the final stage in the development of the German Question in his thought. It is not surprising to find Wagner as a central figure in Nietzsche's reflections on the German Question, since Wagner had been involved directly or indirectly with his conception of Germany since the late 1860s.[64] Some of the longest passages about Germany occur either in his final two short works on Wagner, or in the discussion of *The Case of Wagner* in *Ecce Homo*. But it is somewhat unusual that Nietzsche, who had repeated many of the nationalist motifs from Wagner's Germanophilic essays, makes an effort in his final works to separate Wagner from the very Germanness that Wagner advocated and that he had earlier embraced. In almost all discussions of Wagner from 1888, Nietzsche identifies Wagner with French culture. In *Nietzsche contra Wagner*, after finding both Schopenhauer and Heine only "coincidentally" German, and asserting that they have a far more intimate relationship to France, he turns to his former friend: "As regards Richard Wagner, finally, it is so plain that one could grasp it with hands, though perhaps not with fists, that Paris is the real soil for Wagner: the more French music develops according to the needs of the 'âme moderne,' the more it will Wagnerize." Is Nietzsche merely poking fun at Wagner by associating him with the French, against whom Wagner had written so much and so vehemently, or is he rescuing him from a Germany that is incapable of appreciating Wagner's true greatness? Evidence for the latter is Nietzsche's hypothetical query a bit further on in the same section: "Who could be more incapable of understanding Wagner than, for example, the young Kaiser?" He proceeds to claim an intimate link between Wagner and French romanticism (NW, Wohin Wagner gehört, KSA 6.427–28). In *Ecce Homo*, we find similar passages, which, again, may have been composed tongue-in-cheek, but which also may be an attempt to situate Wagner outside a national tradition Nietzsche considers inartistic and uncultured.

> There is in Germany absolutely no conception of the tremendous ambition that dwells in the soul of a Parisian artist. The German is good-natured—Wagner was by no means good-natured.... But I have already said enough (in 'Beyond Good and Evil' ß 256) about where Wagner

belongs, in whom he has his closest relatives: the French late romantics, that high-flying and yet exhilarating kind of artists such as Delacroix, such as Berlioz, with a *fond* of sickness, of incurability in their nature, sheer fanatics for *expression*, virtuosi through and through. (EH, Warum ich so klug bin 5, KSA 6.289)

Certainly Wagner would not have been flattered by the company with whom Nietzsche associates him or the characteristics Nietzsche assigns to his music. But even if we consider Nietzsche's compliments backhanded and his descriptions insincere, there is still something odd about his removal of Wagner from the German patriotism and tradition he so revered.

Perhaps his remarks about Wagner and his denial of Wagner's Germanness are all part of a twisted revenge on the celebrated composer for allegedly betraying the ideals to which both had adhered during their period of friendship. Certainly Nietzsche's attacks on Wagner in the texts from 1888 are numerous and vicious. He is associated with illness, sexual perversion, and a feminine weakness; with degeneration and *décadence*; with being a mere actor and a hypocrite; with narcotics and the deleterious effects of alcohol; and with abandoning the healthy sensualism of his youth for a chaste and debilitating Christian piousness. He is Nietzsche's antipode, a danger for European art, an idiot, the mistake of Nietzsche's youth, someone from whom Nietzsche had to escape, and someone against whom he has declared war. Although these characteristics and accounts are often associated with Germans in 1888, Nietzsche refuses to make this connection. Quite the contrary. In a footnote inserted in the first "Postscript" to *The Case of Wagner*, he writes: "Was Wagner a German at all? There are some reasons for this question. It is difficult to find any German trait in him." This statement is remarkable if only because the "traits" he has just associated with Wagner are typically also ascribed to Germans in his late writings. As several commentators have pointed out, the main purpose of this footnote is to suggest—in a rather obvious fashion—that Wagner was of Jewish origins and displays Jewish attributes. Like a Jew, he imitates his host nation: "Being a great learner, he learned to imitate much that was German—that's all. His own nature *contradicts* that which has hitherto been felt to be German—not to speak of a German musician." Nietzsche casts aspersions on Wagner's birth, averring that Ludwig Geyer, Wagner's stepfather, who perhaps had Jewish blood, was his real father. "His father was an actor by the name of Geyer. A Geyer is practically an Adler." Nietzsche plays with the two birds of prey, *Geyer* [vulture] and *Adler* [eagle], the latter being a very marked Jewish patronym. And he goes on to accuse him of prevarication in his autobiography (WA, Nachschrift, KSA 6.41). Nietzsche is obviously repaying Wagner for his anti-Semitism in a passage that would have angered the composer about sensitive issues. But he is also dissociating him from Germans and Germany.

Nietzsche recognizes, of course, that Wagner promoted Germanic themes in his operas (NW, Eine Musik ohne Zukunft, KSA 6.424), that, as he writes in *The Case of Wagner*, Wagner and the Second Reich are simultaneous (WA 11, KSA 6.39), that once in Germany, he succumbed to some of the worst tendencies of the Second Empire, including anti-Semitism (NW, Wie ich von Wagner loskam 1, KSA 6.431).

But in passages that indicate his profound ambivalence toward the composer, he evidences respect for him and his works, frequently in the middle of anti-German tirades. After asserting his own apocryphal Polish origins, and stating that he would not allow the German Kaiser to serve as his coachman, Nietzsche claims Cosima Wagner as his equal, and then continues: "Richard Wagner was by far the most closely related man to me" (EH, Warum ich so weise bin 3, KSA 6.268). In a later passage, in which he maintains that no German could know what genuine music is, he excludes from this general condemnation of native composers Wagner's "Siegfried Idyll" (EH, Warum ich so klug bin 7, KSA 6.291). In a fierce diatribe against Germans of every sort, he qualifies his blanket censure as follows: "If I subtract my commerce with a few artists, above all with Richard Wagner, I have experienced not a single good hour with Germans" (EH, Warum ich so gute Bücher schreibe, Der Fall Wagner 4, KSA 6.362). And in a section where he declares that he was "*condemned* to Germans," he states that "Wagner is the counter-poison to everything German *par excellence*," that he is "the greatest benefactor of my life," and that he "is among Germans merely a misunderstanding, just as surely as I am and always will be" (EH, Warum ich so gute Bücher schreibe 6, KSA 6.289–90). This late identification with Wagner and the dissociation of him from German culture and politics exist uneasily with frequent deprecatory remarks in the final writings. Considering Nietzsche's anti-German sentiments in his final year of sanity, and his numerous assaults on Wagner, his removal of Wagner from an essential Germanness pays a great tribute to the composer and indicates Nietzsche's tremendous psychological ambivalence toward him even during his final moments of lucidity.

Nietzsche harbored no such ambivalence toward the movements in German history he and Wagner had formerly extolled. The German Reformation is a primary example. In the early 1870s both Nietzsche and Wagner had lauded Luther for his activities against Rome and for the implicit sensualism in his efforts. Nietzsche even considered him Dionysian; Wagner worked on an opera entitled "Luther's Marriage." But from the perspective of 1888, Nietzsche views the Reformation completely differently. In his published works and notebooks, it is considered solely in opposition to the Renaissance, as the German alternative to a movement that was artistically superior and that held the hope of overcoming Christianity. The Reformation is not praised for its criticism of foreign dominance in the religious sphere, but castigated for its reinforcement of Christian doctrine.

The German Reformation amounts to nothing more than the "recrudescence of Christian barbarism" (Nachlass 1888, 15[8], KSA 13.409); it is a "barren and plebian counterpoint to the Italian Renaissance" (Nachlass 1888, 15[23], KSA 13.419), a "*dark* curse" for which Germans should not be pardoned (Nachlass 1888, 22[9], KSA 13.587).[65] In *Ecce Homo*, Nietzsche discusses the relationship between the Renaissance and Reformation by ridiculing a statement from Friedrich Theodor Vischer (1807–1887), the noted author and aesthetician, who considered the two movements "the aesthetic rebirth *and* the moral rebirth." Nietzsche feigns an end of patience with such ludicrous sentiments, which are devoid of psychological insight, and proceeds to inform Germans about their pernicious role in historical development: "*Every great cultural crime of the centuries is what they have on their conscience!*" The Renaissance and the Reformation were in Nietzsche's revised notion of world history antithetical, not complementary, movements:

> The Germans deprived Europe of the seriousness, of the meaning of the last *great* age, the age of the Renaissance, at a moment when a higher order of values, when the noble, life-affirmative values which guarantee the future had achieved victory at the seat of the antithetical values, *the values of decline—and even into the instincts of him who sat on it.* Luther, that fatality of a monk, restored the church and, what is a thousand times worse, Christianity, at the moment *of its defeat.*

Nietzsche regards the Renaissance as a missed opportunity to overcome the old ideals of the Catholic Church and its moral valuations. The Reformation, however, thwarted this chance for humankind to "progress," and under the guise of opposition to the Catholic Church, "Germans have known how to discover secret paths to the old 'ideal,' reconciliations between truth and 'ideal,' at bottom formulas for a right to reject science, for a right to *lie*" (EH, Warum ich so gute Bücher schreibe, Der Fall Wagner 2, KSA 6.359–60). Evangelical freedom amounts to a formula for retaining and enhancing the "lust for revenge and envy in an insatiable fury." Eventually the Renaissance and the Reformation both exhausted themselves; using the words of Tacitus witnessing the fall of the Roman Republic, Nietzsche claims that European man plunges back into slavery ("*ruere in servitium*"); and then "the *indecent* century of Germany arrives" (Nachlass 1888, 15[23], KSA 13.420). In a decade and a half, the Reformation has been transformed from a seminal moment in the realization of the German Question into a Germanic barrier to overcoming Christian morality. Formerly embraced as part of a German tradition of national pride, and as exemplary for the superiority of the German spirit, the Reformation in 1888 becomes an obstruction to the very changes that might have overcome degeneracy and moral decadence in contemporary Europe.

The German Wars of Liberation suffer a similar fate. They were an integral part of German nationalist thought for anyone of Nietzsche's generation, and we have seen that as a teenager Nietzsche himself expressed admiration for the heroic struggles of German free corps volunteers fighting the French invaders. They were especially important because they represented the first time that Germans had united against a common enemy, and had conceived of the possibility of unification in a modern nation-state. The spirit of these wars was continued after the disappointment at the Congress of Vienna by the *Burschenschaft* movement, which kept alive the patriotic ardor squelched by Metternich's *Realpolitik*. Again Nietzsche was a more than willing participant in this German jingoism, joining the student fraternity Franconia and praising the movement with lofty phrases in his lectures on education. In 1888, Nietzsche mentions the same events and persons he had included in his early years when discussing the German Question, but they are valued in an antithetical fashion. He recognizes that he would not be who he has become "without an oppositional racial type, without Germans, without *these* Germans, without Bismarck, without 1848, without 'Wars of Liberation,' without Kant, without Luther himself" (Nachlass 1888–89, 25[7], KSA 13.641), but these high points of the German spirit, formerly extolled for their momentum toward a positive solution to the German Question, are now recast as the foil for his own personal development and as "great moments of fatal destiny" for the progress of European culture (Nachlass 1888, 22[9], KSA 13.587). Similar to the Reformation, the negative valence of the Wars of Liberation results from what they prevented, from their historical role in destroying the possibility of genius and greatness:

> When on the bridge between two *décadence* centuries a *force majeure* of genius and will became visible, strong enough to forge Europe into a political and *economic* unity for the purpose of ruling the earth, the Germans with their "Wars of Liberation" deprived Europe of the meaning, of the miracle of meaning of the existence of Napoleon—they thereby have on their conscience everything that followed, that exists today, this sickness and unreason the *most inimical to culture* there is, nationalism, that *nervose nationale* with which Europe is sick, that eternalizing of the petty-state situation of Europe, of *petty* politics: they have deprived Europe itself of its meaning, of its *reason*—they have led it into a blind alley. (EH, Warum ich so gute Bücher schreibe, Der Fall Wagner 2, KSA 6.360)

Napoleon is no longer the individual whose presence accelerated the movement toward German unity as a positive goal, but the hope for a better European future.

Napoleon, whom Nietzsche calls a synthesis of inhuman and the superhuman [*Unmensch und Übermensch*] (GM, Erste Abhandlung 16, KSA 5.288), represents the powerful and ruthless unifier of Europe and the adversary of nationalism. Nietzsche associates him with the great European spirits of the nineteenth century: Goethe, Beethoven, Stendhal, Heine, Schopenhauer, and Wagner (JGB 256, KSA 5.202), and he frequently uses Goethe to triangulate Napoleon and Germany: "Goethe's heart opened up at the phenomenon of Napoleon—it *closed* up to the 'Wars of Liberation'" (GD, Was den Deutschen abgeht 4, KSA 6.106). Just as the Reformation reinstated Christianity at the very moment the Renaissance was preparing to do away with it, so too the Germans with their Wars of Liberation reinforced nationalism against an individual whose mission was to unite Europe beyond petty patriotic interests. Nietzsche's hatred for the Germans is caused by his recognition that they, "as stragglers" (Nachlass 1884, 25[115], KSA 11.43), have perverted every positive impulse in European affairs for over a millennium, depriving Europeans of true geniality in the political realm, happiness in the private sphere, and new possibilities for a renewal of culture.

Although we encounter severe criticism of Germans and Germany in most of Nietzsche's late works, his anti-German sentiments reach a climax in *Ecce Homo*. We have already reviewed some of his more reasoned accusations about the course of German history and Germany's pernicious role in opposing preferred individuals or movements. But we also witness in his autobiographical text remarks that may strike the normal reader as unbalanced rants against his compatriots and their nation. Germans are "the horned cattle among my acquaintances," Nietzsche writes (EH, Warum ich so gute Bücher schreibe 3, KSA 6.303). He himself is "a stranger in my deepest instincts to everything German"; "the mere presence of a German hinders my digestion" (EH, Warum ich so klug bin 5, KSA 6.288). At one point, he equates the adjective "German" with "mediocre," and comments on the detrimental effects of life in Germany on individual accomplishment: "the German climate alone is enough to discourage strong and even heroic intestines," and he continues by contrasting German "air" with that found in other global localities: "Paris, Provence, Florence, Jerusalem, Athens—these names prove something: that genius is *conditioned* by dry air, clear sky—that is to say by rapid metabolism, by the possibility of again and again supplying oneself with great, even tremendous quantities of energy" (EH, Warum ich so klug bin 2, KSA 6.282). Nietzsche's sensitivity to weather and climate, and his notion that they have a determinative effect on individuals, is well known and anything but metaphorical: he was convinced that a real connection exists. Important in this passage is that Germany is singled out as an environment unconducive to genius and superior achievement. In another section, he states that he "can do everything," but "to think German, to feel German" is "beyond my powers" (EH, Warum ich so gute Bücher schreibe 2, KSA 6.301). While he—and Wagner—had formerly considered German music and German philosophy the stellar achievements of the German mind and the hope for a cultural solution to the German Question, in his late writings Nietzsche dismisses this dual heritage. With regard to music, he claims bluntly: "I shall never admit that a German is *capable* of knowing what music is." We have already seen that Nietzsche removes Beethoven from German composers and considers him European. Other noted Germans, "what one calls German musicians, the greatest above all, are *foreigners*, Slavs, Croats, Italians, Netherlanders—or Jews." This reference to "Jews" probably alludes to Felix Mendelssohn, although, as we have seen, Nietzsche could be subsuming—with some irony—Wagner under that rubric as well. German composers from earlier centuries are placed in a Germanic racial category that has died out: they are called "Germans of the strong race, *extinct* Germans, like Heinrich Schütz, Bach and Handel" (EH, Warum ich so klug bin 7, KSA 6.290–91). Philosophers fare even worse. Leibniz and Kant are deemed the "two greatest impediments to the intellectual integrity of Europe!" Indeed, the entire tradition becomes suspect in Nietzsche's anti-German rage: "In the history of knowledge, the Germans are represented by nothing but ambiguous names, they have always produced only 'unconscious' counterfeiters (—Fichte, Schelling, Schopenhauer, Hegel, Schleiermacher deserve this description as much as Kant and Leibniz: they are all mere veil makers—)"[66] (EH, Warum ich so gute Bücher schreibe, Der Fall Wagner 3, KSA 6.361). These characterizations of the German tradition, of Germans and their essential features, and of Germany's place in Europe not only contradict his earlier, Wagnerian views; they also reveal something of the bitterness, frustration, and anger Nietzsche felt about the German Question shortly before his descent into insanity.

In his discussion of *The Case of Wagner* in *Ecce Homo*, Nietzsche unleashes his most venomous and furious assaults. In addition to excoriating Germans for their deficiencies in music and philosophy, Nietzsche finds their historiography completely defective, because it is informed by precisely the type of patriotism he formerly embraced: "'German' is an argument, '*Deutschland, Deutschland über alles*' a principle, the Germans represent the 'moral world-order' in history; in relation to the *imperium romanum* the bearers of freedom, in relation to the eighteenth century the restorers of morality, of the 'categorical imperative'" (EH, Warum ich so gute Bücher schreibe, Der Fall Wagner 2, KSA 6.358). A few pages later, in the following passage, his invectives reach a climax: "the German" comes to embody all qualities antithetical to good breeding and aristocratic behavior:

> And why should I not go on to the end? I like to make a clean sweep. It is even part of my ambition to count as the despiser of the German *par excellence*. I expressed my *mistrust* of the German character already at the age of twenty-six (third untimely essay)—the Germans are impossible for

me. Whenever I picture to myself a type of man that goes against all my instincts it always turns into a German. . . . The Germans are *canaille*. . . . One lowers oneself by commerce with Germans . . . . Supposing the profoundest spirit of all the millennia appeared among the Germans, some goose of the Capitol would opine that its very unbeautiful soul came at least equally into consideration. I cannot endure this race, with which one is always in bad company, which has no finger for *nuances*—woe is me! I am a *nuance*!—which has no *esprit* in its feet and cannot even walk. . . . In the end, the Germans have no idea whatever how common they are; but that is the superlative of commonness—they are not ever *ashamed* of being mere Germans. (EH, Warum ich so gute Bücher schreibe, Der Fall Wagner 4, KSA 6.362–63)

The struggle we sense in the composition of these passages results from Nietzsche's endeavor to find phrases harsh and abusive enough to apply to his subject. Even if we discount a large part of this vituperation as the ravings of a half-insane man, it seems evident that Nietzsche had a good deal of pent-up anger and malice against "the German" in him. We must suspect, therefore, that more than the dashing of a cultural dream is at stake for Nietzsche. Such emotional outbursts indicate not only disappointment and the resulting antipathy of a Germanophile apostate, but also the violation of a strong and powerful psychological bond. Without wanting to subscribe to an amateurish psychoanalytic procedure, we can readily observe that the force of Nietzsche's denunciation is directly related to the strength of his own former identification with "the German spirit," especially in its Wagnerian variant. Nietzsche is distancing himself—at the very least—from his Protestant upbringing and his family, from the many German critics and readers who have not given him his due, and from the Wagnerians, who have succeeded in capturing the public attention that he deserves. At this point in his life, the German Question is inseparable from the complex mixture of personal, philosophical, and cultural factors that structured Nietzsche's life, his aspirations, and his disappointments.

We might be tempted to conclude that at the end of Nietzsche's sane life the German Question undergoes its final transformation into the "Anti-German Question." But is that conclusion accurate? In his writings of 1888, it is apparent that Nietzsche went out of his way to make Germans the chief protectors and propagators of Christian morality, and the central impediment to any value system more supportive of Nietzsche's vision of geniality and the highest achievements of culture. As we have seen, any German in whom he still finds value is no longer considered a representative of the Fatherland, but rather a European. And he spares no words of abuse and censure for compatriots of whom he does not approve, or for the stereotype of Germans he establishes. But the sharpness of his criticism may conceal, even in 1888, a more favorable attitude toward his countrymen and toward the role that Germans can play in the future. Despite his devastating condemnation, Nietzsche recognizes that Germany occupies a special role among nations. In the section entitled "What the Germans Lack" in *Twilight of the Idols*, Nietzsche begins his discussion by citing the enormous achievements and potential in the Second Empire. "The new Germany represents a great quantity of inherited and inculcated ability, so that it may for a time be allowed even a lavish expenditure of its accumulated store of energy." Germans lack a worthwhile culture, but they possess "more manly virtues than any other country of Europe can exhibit." Among these virtues are "courage and respect for oneself," "self-confidence in social dealings and in the performance of reciprocal duties, a good deal of industriousness, a good deal of endurance," "inherited moderation," and a tradition where "people can still obey without being humiliated by obeying." They have succumbed to the twin European narcotics of alcohol and Christianity, and have therefore not produced anything in philosophy or culture that matches their positive virtues. But Nietzsche asks pointedly: "Who has not pondered sadly over what the German spirit *could* be!" (GD, Was den Deutschen abgeht 1, KSA 6.103–4). Even in his harshest criticism, Germany still retains the possibility for leadership in the new Europe that Nietzsche had envisioned since the mid-1880s. Indeed, what other nation could rival Germany's supremacy if his compatriots took seriously his assessment of their country, harnessed the virtues that enabled it to succeed militarily and politically, and realized its potential in a Napoleon-like regime that simultaneously valued culture and philosophy?[67] In a revealing comment in his notebooks from September of 1888, shortly before he began writing *Ecce Homo*, Nietzsche replies to the question of why he writes his books in German: "My answer is always the same: I love the Germans. . . . What does it matter to me if the Germans don't read me? I try even harder to do *justice* to them.—And, who knows? Maybe they will read me the day after tomorrow" (Nachlass 1888, 19[1], KSA 13.539). The German Question, which had preoccupied Nietzsche's compatriots in the nineteenth century for so many years, and which had been a pivotal moment in his own development, may not have become simply a rejection of earlier visions for the glory of the Fatherland. If Germans utilize their vast resources and their many virtues, if they overcome European narcotics and narrow chauvinism, and, above all, if they come to appreciate the prophet they have hitherto scorned, they may yet realize a grander resolution to the German Question, which, as we have seen previously, entails a military, political, and cultural hegemony in a united Europe.

Chapter 3

The Social Question

The Rise of the German Working Class

Germany's late political unity—in comparison to England and France—contributed to tardiness in industrial development as well. As we have seen in the previous chapter, after the Napoleonic Wars, Germany consisted of some three dozen separate principalities, and after various attempts at overcoming their economic isolation with tariff unions, the customs union or *Zollverein*, under Prussian leadership, finally came into being in 1834. But this economic federation had several disadvantages in comparison to a unified federal system, and the development of industry proceeded haltingly during the middle of the century. Gradually road and railway infrastructure began to unite the separate German states, and industries developed in major urban centers. Coal and lignite resources contributed significantly to the growth of heavy industries, and Germany showed evidence of progress in textiles, chemicals, and electrical production in the years following the 1848 revolution. But the turning point for industrial development occurred only shortly after Nietzsche began his short career as a professor in Basel, with the defeat of France in the Franco-Prussian War, and the establishment of a unified nation. In the early 1870s, Germany entered a process of modernization that, by the dawn of the twentieth century, made it one of the most powerful nations on earth, both militarily and economically. Spurred on by the unification of currencies, the standardization of weights and measures, the annexation of Alsace-Lorraine, which provided the country with access to new supplies of iron ore, and the exorbitant reparation of some 200 million pounds it exacted from France, Germany experienced an unprecedented prosperity in a period that came to be known as the "Founders' Age" [*Gründerzeit*]. During the decades Nietzsche was publishing his writings, between 1870 and 1890, Germany doubled its production of coal and increased its output of steel by a factor of ten. Indeed, the fact that industrialization came to Germany later than it did to England and France proved to be an advantage, since Germany could avoid the mistakes of its competitors in promoting more efficient methods of production.

The population steadily increased from 41 million at the founding of the Second Reich to 67 million at the outbreak of the First World War. Urbanization accompanied the large demographic increases; Berlin alone nearly doubled in size during the years Nietzsche was publishing. In the first three years of the 1870s, when economic activity was perhaps most intense, the industrial production of Germany rose by more than 40 percent. The Ruhr region became a center of coal mining, as well as iron and steel production, essential industries for economic development in the late nineteenth century. In 1872, almost twice as many corporations were established in Prussia as in the entire period from 1801 to 1870 combined. The founding of major financial institutions, the Deutsche Bank in 1870 and the Dresdner Bank in 1872, were further signs of an expanding and confident economy. There was, of course, a rather severe economic downturn in 1873, known as the "Founders' Crash" [*Gründerkrach*], which dampened spirits to some degree and which, as we shall see in Chapter 6, played a major role in the Jewish Question, but in general the economic and political strength of Germany was greater during the 1870s and 1880s than at any other time in the century.

The process of modernization in Germany, as elsewhere in Europe, produced simultaneously and necessarily severe and lasting social problems. The shift from a rural to an urban population, the role of industry in government and politics, and the relationship to other industrialized and non-industrialized nations were all matters that demanded increased attention. Many manifestations of modernity had an impact on the social fabric. In the Germany of Nietzsche's time, however, when one referred to "the Social Question," it was understood to mean quite specifically the situation of the working class and the issues surrounding workers in the new Germany. There was good reason for the working class to become a concern in the very years Nietzsche was maturing as a philosopher. In the first place, the size of the industrial proletariat had multiplied dramatically during Nietzsche's lifetime. When he was born in 1844, there were about one million individuals who could be classified as workers in Germany, but by the time he began writing the first volume of *Zarathustra*, this figure had increased over seventeenfold. Accompanying this proliferation of workers was the restructuring of the German social order that accompanied rapid industrialization and urbanization. The political parties that had existed in the middle of the century were focused either on religion or on interests of the aristocracy or the bourgeoisie. Although the revolutionary fervor of 1848 did include some measure of working class participation, it was carried largely by the middle class and its economic and ideological interests. Certainly Karl Marx (1818–1883) recognized that the proletariat was not the major force for change at midcentury when he advised in the *Communist Manifesto* that the Communists in Germany should "fight with the bourgeoisie whenever it acts in a revolutionary way, against the absolute monarchy, the feudal squirearchy, and the petty bourgeoisie."[1] But one of the major ramifications of the rapid industrialization in the second half of the nineteenth century was that the proletariat suddenly became a significant political and economic power. Labor unions and unionized workers became increasingly frequent; between 1860 and 1865 alone, the number of workers' organizations doubled, and unions began to exert an influence on industrial affairs and decisions. As we shall see in a moment, this increase in the activity of the working class was reflected in items Nietzsche was reading in the late 1860s, and he no doubt learned of disturbances and work stoppages from newspapers as well. In the political realm, the formation of the General German Workers' Association [Allgemeiner Deutscher Arbeiterverein] in 1863 under the leadership of Ferdinand Lassalle (1825–1864) and, six years later, the rival Social Democratic Workers' Party of Germany (SDAP), headed by August Bebel (1840–1913) and Wilhelm Liebknecht (1826–1900), thrust the working class into the political arena more strongly than ever before. Lassalle, whose organization was oriented more toward the crafts and journeymen than factories and industrial workers, even met a few times with Chancellor Otto von Bismarck (1815–1898), and his politics were openly pro-Prussian and statist. The organization led by Bebel and Liebknecht appealed more to the newly industrialized workforce in Saxony and had an anti-Prussian bias. But when Lassalle was killed in a duel in 1864, it took about a decade before the two workers' organizations merged and were renamed the Socialist Workers' Party of Germany (SAPD).

The Social Democrats, as they were popularly known, were a constant concern for Bismarck and the parties that supported him: immediately after unification, the National Liberal Party, with which Nietzsche had affinities in the 1860s; and then, from 1879 until the end of his chancellorship, various conservative factions in the Reichstag. Accustomed to patriarchal relations with the lower classes and fearing the breakdown of the social order, the parties representing the bourgeoisie and the aristocracy exhibited the dual strategy of patronizing and proscription to restrain and control the working-class party. During Nietzsche's lifetime, workers received benefits that went far beyond what even the most advanced Western nations provided for their lower classes; by the time of Nietzsche's mental breakdown in 1889, laborers in Germany enjoyed some form of health insurance, accident insurance, and social security. This "carrot" was balanced by a rather large and powerful "stick," especially after Bismarck broke with the National Liberals and the "Cultural Struggle" [Kulturkampf] against the Catholic Church became a less important policy objective in the Second Empire. Already in the early 1870s, the Socialists had been considered enemies of the new Reich because of their opposition to the Franco-Prussian War and their support for the Paris Commune. In 1878, at about the time Bismarck was shifting his governmental base of support from the National Liberals to the Conservatives, he used the pretext of two assassination attempts on Kaiser Wilhelm I (1797–

1888) to enact legislation "against the subversive strivings of the Social Democrats."[2] Although neither perpetrator had been a member of the party,[3] the unsuccessful assassinations provided the government with a pretext to eliminate the potential power of the working class in the German parliament. The "Socialist Laws" [*Sozialistengesetz*],[4] as they came to be known, did not proscribe the Socialist Workers' Party of Germany (SAPD)[5] as such, but it officially criminalized organizations that strove for socialism, and generally made it difficult for the Socialists to participate in election campaigns by suppressing their newspapers, prohibiting open party meetings, and by exiling key socialist leaders. If we judge by election returns, then the Socialist Laws, however, were largely ineffective; they may have even assisted the workers in election campaigning as a rallying point. In addition, the proletariat continued to expand with increased industrial development, and in a country where political parties were frequently formed along class lines, workers believed the Social Democrats were their natural representatives. Through legal and semilegal activities the leadership was able to maintain communication with its constituents, and as a result, the voting totals and representation of the party increased throughout the 1880s. In 1881, there were just over 300,000 ballots cast for the Socialists, but by 1887 that number had more than doubled, and by 1890 the Socialist Democrats received over 1.4 million votes. Although the law was debated and extended four times by the German Parliament in the 1880s, by the time the insane Nietzsche was taken to Naumburg by his mother in May of 1890, the Socialist Laws had been repealed, as the Socialist Workers' Party of Germany, rechristened as the Social Democratic Party of Germany (SPD), had emerged from quasi-legality as perhaps the strongest party in the German parliament.

The precipitous rise in industrialization in Germany, the increased prominence of the working class, the rapid urbanization of society, and the controversies surrounding the Socialists were all occurrences during the period when Nietzsche was most intellectually active. They seemed to take place, however, on the periphery of Nietzsche's interests. It would be an exaggeration to claim that he actively engaged with the Social Question in any of its manifestations. At no time in his life was Nietzsche compelled to deal with the proletariat or with industrialized urban centers. His early years in Naumburg would not have brought him into extensive contact with the lower classes, except perhaps with rural poverty, and none of the educational institutions he attended—Pforta and the universities in Bonn and Leipzig—were likely to bring him into the proximity of workers. Basel did have a class-conscious proletariat, and Leipzig was an organizational center for Lassalle's party, but Nietzsche, like most of his colleagues in higher education, kept his distance from any involvement with such matters. Predominant in the circles that Nietzsche frequented as a Basler professor was a patrician attitude that was typified by the Burckhardts or the Bachofens. After

Nietzsche relinquished his teaching position, his preferred domiciles were resort areas where he was unlikely to meet anyone except the middle and upper echelons of European society. Throughout his life, most of Nietzsche's friends or close associates had no substantial connection with the working class or the Social Democrats,[6] and Nietzsche's own insistence that he was a descendant of Polish nobility, as well as his friendships with women who held aristocratic titles, suggests his own desire to climb the social ladder, rather than to sympathize with the downtrodden.

Nor does Nietzsche's reading indicate any sustained interest in socialist theory or the Social Question.[7] Although at one point he requests a catalogue of books that are promoted by the socialist bookstore in Zurich (to Franz Overbeck, 28 April 1880, Nr. 25, KSB 6.17), there are few works in his library that indicate a desire to explore leftist thought. Aside from volumes written by the self-proclaimed socialist (and anti-Semite) Eugen Dühring (1833–1921), whose views Nietzsche came to dislike intensely, Nietzsche neither possessed nor read many books that were written by socialists or socialist sympathizers.[8] It would be equally foolish to maintain, however, that Nietzsche had no acquaintance at all with the Social Question and no interest in its solution. Friedrich Albert Lange's (1828–1875) *History of Materialism* (1866), a work Nietzsche certainly knew well and thoroughly admired, contained long passages on materialist philosophy in the nineteenth century, including discussions of political economy. It is not possible to say exactly what knowledge Nietzsche had from his exposure to Lange's great historical work, since we do not know, for example, whether he read the second edition where Marx figures prominently in several long footnotes.[9] But he certainly would have been introduced to some aspects of the Social Question in the *History of Materialism*, as well as in Lange's later study, *The Workers' Question: Its Significance for the Present and the Future* (1875), or Albert Eberhard Friedrich Schäffle's (1831–1903) *The Quintessence of Socialism* (1879), both of which are found in his library.[10] Indeed, almost any book Nietzsche read that addressed issues in contemporary society would have mentioned something about socialism, the working class, or the political economy of the era. For example, David Friedrich Strauß's (1808–1874) *The Old and the New Beliefs* (1872), which Nietzsche lambasted in his first *Untimely Meditation*, contains sections on "The Fourth Estate and the Workers' Question" and on "Social Democracy and the Inequality among Human Beings."[11] Although he lived outside the industrial regions of Germany and avoided for the most part the major urban centers of Europe, he, like his contemporaries, could not help feeling the effects of the economic revolution. The Social Question thus forms a background for his reflections on the social order, a topic he could not entirely avoid, even if it occupied his interests on an intermittent basis.

Early Interest in the Fourth Estate

As we have seen, Nietzsche's greatest interest in conventional politics occurred while he was a university student in the late 1860s, when he, like many of his peers, was enthusiastic in supporting Bismarck and the drive toward German unification. Some of this interest was mediated by Carl von Gersdorff (1844–1904), his close student friend at the University of Leipzig and, like Nietzsche, a graduate of Schulpforta. Many biographical accounts of Nietzsche have attributed his transfer from the University in Bonn to the University in Leipzig to the "Bonn philological war" between Friedrich Ritschl (1806–1876) and Otto Jahn (1813–1869); he is often regarded as following his eventual mentor Ritschl in moving from the Rhineland university to the Saxon institution. More likely, however, is that Nietzsche was seeking to reunite with his friend, who had graduated from Pforta a half year after Nietzsche had left that preparatory school for Bonn to study theology, while Gersdorff enrolled in Göttingen to study law. Since both Nietzsche and Gersdorff were unhappy with student life and their majors at their respective institutions, they decided to matriculate in the fall of 1865 at the University of Leipzig, where they both began as students of philology.[12] Of interest for the Social Question is the exchange of letters between Nietzsche and Gersdorff a few years later when the former was starting his military service in Naumburg, while the latter was carrying out his officer training in Berlin. Gersdorff informs Nietzsche that he has engaged a Dr. Schmidt to assist him with Roman law, but he is also instructing him in economics, a discipline for which Gersdorff is gaining considerable respect. It supplies a purview over what motivates human actions and satisfies human needs, Gersdorff remarks; it is an indispensable aid in understanding history, especially recent historical movements; indeed, history is "only a servant of national economy." But most of all, Gersdorff extols it for providing insight into contemporary events in Europe: "All the struggles in the present day are of an economic nature. Capital and labor struggle against each other in France, in England, in America, and at home. All theories of our century: socialism, communism, cooperative associations, have been invented in order to address this struggle, to do away with the proletariat, this cancerous damage for all higher culture." Gersdorff continues by noting that the progressive party for which both he and Nietzsche have affinity at this time is really economically based, since it presupposes a minority class and a large number of workers, which it does not try to impress with political ideas, but rather with the promise of material satisfactions, which, however, it cannot deliver. Despite his remark on the enmity between the proletariat and higher culture, Gersdorff received from Schmidt, or perhaps from readings he has done with Schmidt, a distinctly socialist perspective on the class struggle, which he then conveys to his friend: for the past forty years, he continues, we stand under a law that has taught us that capital concentrates itself in the hands of increasingly smaller numbers, while the proletariat increases in size, but not in welfare. "Where there is plenty, more comes; whoever has something will receive more until he is completely sated, but anyone who has nothing will lose even what he has. This motto is also a truth in the realm of economic thought" (30 December 1867; Nr. 175, KGB I 3.224–25). Gersdorff closes this section of his letter urging Nietzsche to take up the study of economics. It is an empirical science, but it is logical and there are connections with philosophy, and even with Schopenhauer's thought.

Gersdorff had written this letter from his familial estate in Ostrichen (today: Ostróżno) bei Seidenberg. In February, prior to receiving a response from Nietzsche, he wrote to his friend again from Berlin. His pretext is to thank him for the recommendation of a novel that Nietzsche had mentioned to him in a letter composed at the end of November, and that, presumably, Gersdorff had since acquired and read. The book in question is Friedrich Spielhagen's (1829–1911) *In Rank and File* [*In Reih' und Glied*] (1867), a work of over a thousand pages that provides a somewhat contrived panorama of German society and the shifts in power occurring among the various classes in the post-1848 period. In these years, Spielhagen was perhaps the foremost prose author in the German world, having established his reputation in 1861 with the novel *Problematic Characters* [*Problematische Naturen*]. He was a resolute democrat and nationalist, and thus there were some affinities between his views and those of Nietzsche and Gersdorff in these years. Known mostly for his prose, Spielhagen also wrote plays, edited the important journal *Westermann's Illustrated German Monthly*, and expounded on realism theoretically in several longer essays. In the 1870s, Spielhagen's fame expanded into international circles: his novels were translated often into many different languages, and he gained particular fame in Russia, where most of his enormous oeuvre was translated and where he achieved considerable success. In Germany and most of the world, however, he gradually fell out of favor and out of the canon as the century proceeded toward its close, and today his works are rarely cited.[13] We must recall, however, that in 1867, for Nietzsche and his peers the appearance of a new work by this author was cause for considerable excitement. In his recommendation to Gersdorff, Nietzsche associates the novel somewhat perversely with his own current philosophical interests, calling it the "first product of a literature in that tragic, almost ascetic sense of Schopenhauer." The heroes of this book are driven through "the red flame of samsara" to a sudden change of their wills; it has a high artistic value, a great richness of ideas, and it is written in a "beautiful, pleasant style." Nietzsche even includes an endorsement from his dissertation director, who claims the novel is worth ten times more than the entire oeuvre of Gustav Freytag (1816–1895), an author likewise popular at the time, but almost completely forgotten today (Nr. 554, KSB 2.239). There is really no justification for Nietzsche's bringing *In Rank and File* into association with Schopenhauer; in biographical accounts of Spielhagen, we find no evidence that the author had any sustained interest in the pessimistic philosopher, and if the ending is tragic for many of the chief characters—there are several protagonists and subplots—it has more to do with the machinations resulting from change in the German social order or with unhappy love affairs than from an adherence to Schopenhauerian principles. What Nietzsche's recommendation reveals is probably that at this point in time he was so preoccupied with Schopenhauer's philosophy that it colored his views of everything he read.

We should probably not be surprised that Gersdorff's reception is quite different from Nietzsche's, although he too is lavish in his praise of the novel. His recent readings in national economy conditioned him to interpret Spielhagen's book as a reflection of the socioeconomic disruptions occurring in German society, a perspective that is certainly more evident in the text than Nietzsche's association with pessimistic philosophy. *In Rank and File* deals in a schematic way with the class structure in Germany in the mid-nineteenth century: there are characters representing the monarch and his associates, the lower levels of the nobility, the middle class, including the professional and intellectual strata of the bourgeoisie, the agricultural sector, and even the industrial working class. Intrigues, schemes, love affairs, seductions, and secret liaisons occur throughout, but if we abstract from the romance and personal animosities, we encounter something of the dynamics operating in Germany during the 1850s and 1860s. The lower nobility displays loyalty to its subjects, but eventually gets involved in a dubious manufacturing venture, which ends with the impoverishment of the aristocrats and the enrichment of the banker, who also happens to be a recently ennobled man of Jewish heritage. The ascendancy of the middle class advances by a logic that destroys the personal bonds that formerly tied together members of different classes. The logic of capital appears to be all powerful, and inherited titles are less important than the ability to deal effectively with the new realities of the financial world. Gersdorff recognizes that his economic studies have influenced his reading of the novel; indeed, he was uninterested in the novel until he understood that it reflected his current interests. "In the last lessons prior to Christmas and in the first hours of instruction in the New Year we discussed precisely the questions that form the center of the novel: the so-called Social Question, the question of capital and labor" (15 February 1868, Nr. 177, KGB I 3.229). Gersdorff's reduction of the work to the Social Question is also an exaggeration, although not quite as far from the novel's center as Nietzsche's interpretation: the working class appears in very few scenes, and capitalism is present as a force that changes the social structure. But, in fact, the novel deals much more with the interpersonal relationships between various sets of young men and women situated within this social structure, sometimes relationships that involve violating class boundaries, than it does with the class struggle.

Despite the partial views of the novel expressed by both friends in their letters, we can be certain that Nietzsche was at least exposed to the Social Question in the novel *In Rank and File*. He read, for example, the view of one protagonist that the liberal party, which represents the bourgeoisie, when it has recognized that it is not strong enough to take the reins of government and requires support, disdains its natural ally in the fourth estate, the working class, and instead flirts with the "party of the prince." Or he encountered passages in which the Jewish banker and industrialist recognizes that the "workers' question is again moving into the foreground." Or he could find sentiments that claim that "it is not the impotent nobility, not the crumbling church" that opposes a humane existence, "but the party of the bourgeoisie, the party of omnipotent capital, of the malicious, boundless exploitation of the working class."[14] Most of all, the novel presented him with a character modeled on the erstwhile leader of the working-class movement in Germany, Ferdinand Lassalle. As the organizer of the first socialist party in Germany, Lassalle had abandoned the liberal party of the bourgeoisie, hoping to gain advantage for the proletariat by negotiating with Bismarck for universal suffrage and state support of workers' cooperatives. Even if Nietzsche did not recognize that Lassalle was the model for Leo Gutmann in *In Rank and File*, Gersdorff alerted him to the fact that Spielhagen had drawn on Lassalle to create this figure, using a great deal of poetic license. In his letter to Nietzsche from the beginning of February, Gersdorff mentions that the novel coincided with reading he had done with Schmidt.

> A few weeks ago on the recommendation of Dr. Schmidt I made the acquaintance of Ferdinand Lassalle by acquiring and reading with great interest his classical text *Mr. Bastiat-Schulze von Delitzsche, the Economic Julian, or, Capital and Labor*.[15] From this text, I have gotten to know a man who is one of the rare cases in our century. I think that since Lessing there is no one who has delivered such a sharp, logical, and convincing polemic as Lassalle delivered in his work against Schultze Delitzsch [*sic*]. If you want to spend a few pleasant hours in a special way at some point, then read this book; you will learn from it at the same time more about national economy than you will from any voluminous professorial compendium.

Lassalle is important for Gersdorff because he came to recognize as he read *In Rank and File* that Spielhagen had Lassalle in mind when he created Leo Gutmann: "you can imagine that this doubled my interest" (Nr. 177, KGB I 3.230).[16] For Gersdorff, Spielhagen's novel was centrally about the encroachment of capital in German social life and the aborted attempt of Lassallean tactics to derail the inexorable power of this new economic force.

In the novel, Leo Gutmann is orphaned at an early age and taken in by his uncle, who serves as the forester on the estate of a kindly and virtuous baron. A restless and unstable character, who at an early age exhibits a strong sense of justice, Gutmann becomes radicalized through his contact with a teacher, Conrad Tusky, who has connections with radical circles in Germany. He eventually becomes a physician, but he associates secretly with the growing working class to foment revolt. Throughout the novel, it is never entirely clear whether Gutmann is more interested in promoting social equality and a just political order, or whether he is egotistically seeking to attain and exercise power through a manipulation of social unrest. He articulates his plans in the first part of the novel, when he describes two types of revolutionary action that both lead to the same result. The first entails a "revolution from below," where the masses organize and seize control. The second and preferred path for Gutmann is a "revolution from above," that employs the reigning power of the king to break the hegemony of the bourgeoisie. When Gutmann explains these revolutionary options to the representatives of the workers, they are astounded and at first feel betrayed, but Gutmann claims to have gathered the experience and insight necessary to formulate this unusual second alternative and eventually to put it into action. His views were heavily influenced by his distrust of liberals, who betrayed the revolutionary ideals they possessed during the revolution of March 1848, and are now responsible for the oppression of the working class.[17] Gutmann's insights are an obvious reflection of Lassalle's strategy of abandoning the liberal party and negotiating with Bismarck to try to effect revolutionary change. By the time Gutmann returns to his Thuringian origins in the second half of the novel, he is recognized by the inhabitants as the "herald of a new world order, in which the omnipotence of capital will be broken just as surely as one no longer hears about the robber-knights of the Middle Ages."[18] He attempts to convince the king to liberate the workers and become the sovereign of the people,[19] and he instigates a violent strike, but he is ultimately unsuccessful in gaining power for himself or in attaining any improvement in the life of the proletariat of the region. Like Lassalle, Guttmann dies in a duel stemming from a private love affair. In this figure, Nietzsche was thus able to learn a good deal about Lassalle, the Social Question, and the incipient working-class movement. But the message conveyed by Spielhagen, despite occasional admiration for the ideals espoused by Gutmann/Lassalle, is that the solution to the Social Question does not lie with violent agitation from below or with the endeavor to secure favor from above. If there is a pessimism that pervades *In Rank and File*, it is not of the Schopenhauerian variety; rather, it is a political pessimism that casts doubt on the ability of any political entity—the monarch and conservatism, national liberalism, as well as socialist parties—to solve in adequate fashion the Social Question.

Nietzsche's familiarity with Lassalle was not limited to his putative fictionalization as Leo Gutmann in Spielhagen's *In Rank and File*. In his response to Gersdorff's letter in February 1868, he passes over the Lassalle reference in the novel and tells his friend about a book he has recently read that deals with issues surrounding the actual Lassalle and the Social Question: Joseph Edmund Joerg's *History of the Social-Political Parties in Germany*.[20] He states that he appropriated a great deal from this book, although it is a dubious monograph because of the reactionary and Catholic sentiments of its author. But he did gain insight into the "irrational greatness" of Lassalle, whom he does not have time to read at present, but indicates he will return to at a later point.[21] Joerg's interest in Lassalle, who figures prominently in the book and who is cited at length on numerous occasions, is his opposition to liberalism, which Joerg repeatedly emphasizes and which corresponds to some degree with his own criticisms of the National Liberals. For Joerg, liberalism has effected a reduction of people to isolated individuals and deprived them of the spirituality formerly associated with religious belief. The bourgeoisie is opposed to Christianity and to the teaching of revelation, and therefore the teachings of "liberal economism," which is the term he repeatedly employs as the ideological basis of the liberal movement, are inimical to the church. His viewpoint is supported in various places by citations from the Bishop of Mainz. On the whole, however, there is much more in this monograph about Lassalle and the Social Question than about religion. At the outset Joerg states the importance of the working-class movement and strikes, and he regards the Social Question as the fundamental question in German society (V). Already in the preface, he adverts to Lassalle as a "genial agitator" (VI), and, in a series of subsequent chapters, Lassalle is the key referent and the individual who is seen as the most authoritative commentator on contemporary German affairs. Joerg subscribes to an economic outlook that draws heavily on socialist analysis. For him, the crux of the Social Question is whether capital or labor should profit from the work performed by the proletariat (18), and like Marx and Lassalle, he regrets the reduction of personal relations to a purely cash nexus (29). He uses Lassalle to further the argument that the growth of industry results in the immiseration of the working class, and that the natural tendency of an economy based on the principles of supply and demand is the sinking of wages to the minimum necessary for survival (35–36). His analysis of the bourgeoisie since the French Revolution of 1789 similarly depends heavily on Lassalle, who recognized that along with the emancipatory tendencies of those times there was a negative side in the triumph of private property. The goal of the present working-class movement is therefore the realization of the ideals of freedom and equality without property. Joerg devotes a chapter to the stages in Lassalle's development from a critic of liberal economism to revolutionary enthusiasm, points to his meteoric rise as a leader of the socialist movement, and lauds him as the "messiah" of a new church (130–61). From this monograph, which Nietzsche mentions to Gersdorff and which is found in his library, the philosopher gained valuable information about, and insight into, the Social Question and the chief proponent of a socialist alternative to liberal economic thought in the person of Ferdinand Lassalle. Indeed, when Nietzsche refers to socialism in the 1860s and 1870s, it is very likely that he is referencing Lassalle and his thought.[22]

Nietzsche's preoccupation with Joerg's book occurs at a time when he evidenced a passing interest in political economy and in German politics prior to unification.[23] With few exceptions, however, he did not follow up on the main themes he encountered in the monograph from 1867: in the next decade, we find little evidence of concern for socialist parties, the economic and polemical writings of Lassalle, or questions surrounding the growing importance of the working class in Germany. He focused at first on his philological studies, and, after he met Richard Wagner, he began to shift his attention, as we have seen, to a possible renaissance in German culture and to issues related to education and *Bildung*. The name Lassalle appears only once in his writings, in his notebooks written in preparation for his lectures on education in 1873. We have already examined this passage, which deals with general education as a precursor to communism, in the first chapter; by this point in his development Nietzsche was obviously unsympathetic to socialist thought, so that Lassalle, who was praised by Joerg and grudgingly regarded as possessing "irrational greatness" by Nietzsche, is no longer viewed as a positive force, despite the fact that Nietzsche, like Lassalle and Joerg, had also come to reject liberalism and its economics. In this passage, Nietzsche regards general education as opposed not only to genuine *Bildung*, but as a promoter of materialist needs and mundane desires.

> General education [*Die allgemeine Bildung*] passes over into hatred of genuine acculturation [*Bildung*]. The task of the people is no longer culture, but luxury, fashion. To have no needs is the greatest misfortune for a people, Lassalle once declared. For that reason the workers' education associations, whose tendency to create needs has been indicated to me many times. For national economists Christ's parable of the rich man and poor Lazarus is turned on its head: the rich man merits Abraham's bosom.—Thus the drive toward the largest possible spread of general education has its source in complete secularization, in the subordination of *Bildung* as a means to acquisition, to crudely conceived happiness on earth. (Nachlass 1870–72, 8[57], KSA 7.243)

This passage makes reference to Joerg's text in a most unusual fashion.[24] Joerg points out that Lassalle and social democracy agree with liberal economism in juxtaposing an ascetic lifestyle to luxury. They do so, however, for very different reasons. Lassalle wants workers to enjoy the fruits of their labor; the bourgeoisie, represented by the liberal economists, promote luxury for themselves along with the exploitation of the working class. In Joerg's text, Lassalle does not assert that the greatest misfortune for a people is to have no needs; that sentiment Lassalle attributes to the national economist. Lassalle does not mention in this connection anything about the workers' education associations [*Arbeiterbildungsvereine*], and the connection with general education is entirely absent as well in Joerg's discussion. The opposition between a genuine culture and materialism promoted by education of the masses is Nietzsche's framework from his lecture series, not something that reproduces Lassalle's thought. The sentence about Christ's parable is directly lifted from Joerg, but it is clear that Nietzsche attributes to Lassalle from his reading of Joerg several ideas to which he did not necessarily subscribe. The Social Question in Nietzsche's notebook becomes part of a complex that interested him at the time, relating to mass education, its affinity to communism, and barbarism, while the chief representative of the working class is transformed into an advocate of luxury, fashion, consumption, utility, and crude materialism, and the enemy of higher culture and genuine *Bildung*.

Communards and Slaves

From this early exchange with Gersdorff and the reading of Spielhagen's novel and Joerg's treatise, it is difficult to draw any conclusions about Nietzsche's early views on the Social Question. He recognized it as an important issue of his era, but he does not indicate how he believes the issues around the working class can or should be solved. His position at this time is perhaps best characterized by ambivalence as it is captured in his reference to Lassalle's "irrational greatness." Indeed, even after Nietzsche has decided and declared publicly that general education is counterproductive for the public weal, he retains a modicum of ambivalence about the education of the fourth estate. In a note composed in 1873, after Nietzsche had completed his lectures on education, he writes: "When at some point the working class discovers that it can surpass us by means of education and virtue, then we're done for. But if that doesn't happen, then we're really done for" (Nachlass 1873, 29[216], KSA 7.715). It would be tempting to conclude from this statement that Nietzsche had gained familiarity with and respect for the working class since the time he and Gersdorff corresponded about Lassalle, but most of Nietzsche's remarks indicate a lack of interest in the Social Question and an increasing disdain for the lower classes of society. Nietzsche did have the opportunity for firsthand knowledge of Lassalle's party, since Leipzig was the site of the founding party congress of the General German Workers' Association, which took place in May of 1863 before Nietzsche had transferred to the University of Leipzig, and was the venue for a national meeting in June of 1866, after Nietzsche had relocated. In September of 1868, Leipzig police officials evidently disbanded the Association, although it reconstituted itself the next month in Berlin.[25] But we find no trace of any of these matters in Nietzsche's notebooks or letters; his concern in 1866 was the impending conflict between the Confederation of German states under Prussian leadership and Austria, and in 1868 he was making plans for what he would do after his release from military service. In general, we find no references to working-class German political parties in Nietzsche's writings and letters, and the proletariat similarly escapes his attention. After his enlistment in the Wagnerian cultural cause, he took note of current events only insofar as they had an impact on Wagner's self-imposed mission to revitalize German culture, and it is in this realm that we have to understand his comments on the socialist and communist movements of his times in the early 1870s. We also find a sober and harsh interpretation of the conditions that produce greatness in culture, and his views in this area are also no doubt related to the Wagnerian enterprise. Thus, as we have already seen, education for the vast majority of people is disdained because it does not promote genuine cultural achievement; the masses are regarded as incapable of appreciating the renaissance Nietzsche identified with Wagner and his "total work of art."

Within the context of his growing admiration for Wagner and his increasing participation in the Wagnerian mission, we can understand better Nietzsche's reaction to the Paris Commune. At first, Nietzsche took little note of the civil war that was raging in France; at least we find nothing about the happenings in Paris in his correspondence of March and April in 1871. We have to assume that he kept himself informed about events in France through newspapers or through associates. We know that the Commune was a topic broached in letters he received during this period. Gersdorff, who was with the conquering German army that defeated France and thus precipitated the rise of the Commune, comments most extensively at the end of March, and he was unsympathetic to the revolutionary cause. He writes of the "gates of hell" in Paris, stating that he sees no end to the developments that have occurred since the outbreak of civil unrest. The fighting continues unabated with both sides claiming to gain the advantage. It is clear that the chief danger for him is the fourth estate, and he asks rhetorically: "where is the man of action, who has both the knowledge and the means to put a stop to the movement of the reds—which has spread over the entire civilized world—here, where this movement strives to usurp power with such furious audacity?" He reports further of the reign of terror initiated by the Commune from which thousands are fleeing the city, and the horrors of the regime growing more gruesome by the day. The refined classes of Paris are characterized as decadent poltroons whose resistance is entirely ineffective (Nr. 174, KGB II 2.349).

On 2 April, Cosima Wagner (1837–1930) reports to Nietzsche that her mother had been traveling about since the outbreak of the war, and has had to remain with her in Tribschen because of the present uncertainties surrounding the resolution of the conflict. She has some sympathy with a portion of the French population, but the advent of the Commune has had disastrous consequences: "The French—I mean the good ones—are really pitiable; they really can't be helped, and they have to tolerate the dissolution of their country like a natural disaster, an earthquake, or a flood" (Nr. 175, KGB I 2.351). And Gersdorff writes further a few days later about the prolongation of war and bloodshed: "*homo homini lupus*," and the fact that the Germans are waiting patiently to begin peace negotiations outside of Paris, while the civil war continues. But he adds that the sentiments among the Germans are that "they [the French] should rip one another to shreds: let Paris, this abscess of France, burst from its own fervor" (Nr. 176, KGB II 2.353–54). These reports could hardly have elicited any understanding or compassion for the cause of the Commune on Nietzsche's part, and they certainly did not suggest that revolution was a solution to the problems of the fourth estate.

Nietzsche's correspondents fall silent about the civil war and the Commune until the end of May, when the rebellion was suppressed by French troops. At that point, Nietzsche begins to mention the Commune, primarily because newspapers carried the erroneous report that the Communards, under attack by French army troops, had set fire to parts of the city and destroyed the Louvre. It is difficult to ascertain what precisely occurred, and who set fire to which buildings, but we know for certain that the Tuileries Palace was destroyed by flames and that the Louvre suffered some fire damage; the rumor of the museum's destruction, however, was false. Nietzsche and many others, however, believed it to be true in late May 1871, and his reaction sets the tone for his enmity toward any type of popular uprising of the working class in subsequent writings. In a letter from 27 May addressed to Wilhelm Vischer-Bilfinger (1808–1874), the classical philologist who was responsible for hiring Nietzsche in 1869, he writes of his shock upon hearing of the destruction of culture at the hands of the Communards:

> The news from the last few days was so terrible that I am no longer able to put myself into even a tolerable mood. What are you as a scholar against such earthquakes of culture! How infinitesimally small you feel! You spend your entire life and your greatest effort to understand one period of culture better and to explain it better; what kind of profession is this, when on one unfortunate day the most valuable documents of such periods are burned to ashes! It is the worst day of my life.—(Nr. 134, KSB 3.195)

The next day finds Nietzsche in Tribschen with the Wagners. Cosima notes in her diary that Nietzsche remarked somewhat hyperbolically that "for the scholar such events mean the end of all existence." Wagner was less concerned with the reported loss of cultural artifacts and uses the occasion to lash out at the French and their artistic deficiencies: "If you are not capable of painting pictures again, you are not worthy of possessing them."[26]

Almost a month later, Nietzsche continues to be haunted by the actions attributed to the Communards, but there are slight changes in his interpretation of the events. Writing to Gersdorff, he points ominously to the "international hydra-head" that appeared so suddenly and that portends an entirely different sort of battle in the future. But Nietzsche does not place the blame for the threat to European civilization entirely on "those unfortunate ones" who purportedly set fire to the Louvre. We are all guilty of "such terrors that are coming to light." For Nietzsche, who is relying on a Wagnerian framework,[27] the struggle is one against culture as it has been preserved for us, a culture that has become predominately "Romanic" or "Latin" [welsch] and for a future culture that will result from appropriate measures and real genius. For this reason, the fourth estate, despite its horrific actions, is not solely responsible. Nietzsche closes his reflections on this issue with a summary of his personal shock, but also his sense of shared responsibility:

> When I learned about the fires in Paris, I felt for several days annihilated and was broken up with tears and doubts; the entire scholarly and philosophical-artistic existence seemed to me an absurdity, if a single day could wipe out the most glorious works of art, even whole periods of art; I clung with earnest conviction to the metaphysical value of art, which cannot exist for the sake of poor human beings but which has higher missions to fulfill. But even in my greatest pain, I could not cast a stone against those blasphemers, who were to me only carriers of the general guilt, which gives much food for thought. (Nr. 140, KSB 3.203–4)

In this passage, we find an allusion to section five in *The Birth of Tragedy*, where Nietzsche contends that "the whole comedy of art is not in any way performed for our benefit," but has a metaphysical purpose beyond the purview of mere mortals (GT 5, KSA 1.47–48). Absent from all Nietzsche's reactions is any concern for the loss of life, for the murder of prisoners of war and hostages, or the general loss of property and destruction in the French capital. His sole focus is culture, and he has begun already to identify the fourth estate as the enemy of genuine accomplishment in art; in his notes for his lectures on education, he associates general education of the masses with "barbarism" (Nachlass 1870–72, 8[57], KSA 7.243). The change in perspective from his student years is significant. By the early 1870s, under the sway of Wagnerian imperatives, the Social Question has been transformed from issues of social-democratic parties and liberal economics into yet another manifestation in the struggle for control of culture.

By the time the Commune had been suppressed by the French military, Nietzsche had a distinctly negative view of revolutionary activities as a way to advance the cause of the fourth estate. Indeed, Nietzsche's mother even contributes to her son's aversion in her letter from the end of May in 1871. She copies a statement about the Commune penned by Giuseppe Mazzini (1805–1872) that had appeared in the local Naumburg newspaper. Nietzsche and his sister had met the Italian politician and activist in February of that year when they traveled in the same compartment to Lugano, and Franziska Nietzsche felt it important to tell her son that Mazzini also condemned the Parisian revolutionaries. They act as if they were drunk, proclaiming victory while flaying themselves; they remind Mazzini of the horrible faces in Dante's *Inferno*. "The actions of the Commune should be damned eternally; they have neither love of the fatherland, nor a principle of humanity. To mow down hostages when their death can gain no advantage for the cause of the Commune; to burn down buildings that were the pride of the city is unspeakable infamy" (Nr. 189, KGB II 2. 379). Whenever the Commune or its reported actions are mentioned in any piece of writing after this time, it is a cause for condemnation and grief. In 1879 Nietzsche writes in a notebook entry that he cried when he heard about the Commune (Nachlass 1879, 40[24], KSA 8.583). In 1878, in a section of his notebooks entitled "Memorabilia," he includes as the first item a reflection on his feeling of "cultural autumn"—"never a deeper pain"—upon hearing about the fate of the Louvre at the hands of the Communards (Nachlass 1878, 28[1], KSA 8.504), and later in the same year, he writes of the endangerment of culture: "War. Greatest pain, *Fire in the Louvre*" (Nachlass 1878, 30[166], KSA 8.552). In 1885, he contends that the Commune is a first indication of what we can expect from the future. Under the rubric of "socialism," he discusses the occasional conflicts that occur in Europe, citing the Commune and its defenders in Germany—he names specifically "the philosophical grimace-faced swamp salamander E[ugen] D[ühring]"—as perhaps only a slight bout of indigestion compared with what will come later (Nachlass 1885, 37[11], KSA 11.586). In *On the Genealogy of Morals*, where the Commune makes its sole appearance in a published piece of writing, Nietzsche cites it as an example of how slave morality associated with inferior, dark-haired races has conquered the blond Aryans: "Who can say whether modern democracy, the even more recent phenomenon of anarchism, and particularly that tendency, now common to all European socialists towards the 'Commune,' the most primitive form of society, does not for the most part represent a huge *atavistic throwback*—and that the race of conquerors and *masters*, the Aryan race, now finds itself physiologically in an inferior position?" (GM, Erste Abhandlung 5, KSA 5.264). Again in this passage, Nietzsche evidences the significant impact that the Commune had on his psyche, long after he recognized that the Louvre had not suffered irreparable damage. The Paris Commune remains for him an indication of the decline in European man, the destruction of what is valuable and worth preserving in past human experience. The fourth estate thus assumes the role of a vanguard in decadence, an agent in his contemporary society and in future eras that will promote the demise of civilization and enforce mediocrity in cultural attainment.[28]

Nietzsche's reaction to the Commune also finds more immediate inclusion in *The Birth of Tragedy*. As we shall see in Chapter 6, in his early lectures that contributed to his first major book publication, especially in "Socrates and Tragedy," Nietzsche had already sought to relate his insights into Greek culture to contemporary tendencies in German and European society. In a similar fashion, he demonstrates to the readers of *The Birth of Tragedy* that his discussions of the ancients are relevant for concerns in the nineteenth century. This claim is made more explicit in the last ten sections of the text, where Wagner emerges as the key figure in a modern rebirth of tragedy, but section eighteen is significant for its indirect reference to recent revolutionary developments in the French capital. Nietzsche focuses on Alexandrian culture, which is the outgrowth of the Socratism he has explicated in the first fifteen sections. "The whole of our modern world," Nietzsche writes, "is caught in the net of Alexandrian culture and takes as its ideal the *theoretical man* who is equipped with the highest powers of knowledge, works in the service of science, and whose archetype and progenitor is Socrates." Contemporary education and scholarship are signs of this Alexandrian culture in the nineteenth century; Goethe's *Faust*, in which the eponymous hero strives for knowledge, is its exemplary literary work. It is also characterized by optimism, as opposed to tragic culture, which rejects optimistic religions and cultures in favor of the realism of pessimism. The social structure of Alexandrian culture is the feature that brings it into direct association with the Social Question of Nietzsche's time. "Alexandrian culture," Nietzsche asserts, "needs a slave-class in order to be able to sustain its existence over any length of time, but in its optimistic view of existence, it denies the necessity of such a class and therefore, when the effect of its beautiful words of seduction and reassurance about the 'dignity of man' and the 'dignity of labor' is exhausted, it gradually drifts towards its end in horrific annihilation." It is not difficult to recognize the slogans of bourgeois ideology in these internal citations, and to discover in the "slave-class" the working class of nineteenth-century Europe. At an earlier point in his book, Nietzsche had associated the slave class with the advent of Attic comedy (GT 11, KSA 1.78), but in this later passage, he uses the slave class to allude to recent events in Paris: "There is nothing more fearful than a barbaric slave-class which has learnt to regard its existence as an injustice and is preparing to take revenge not just for itself but for all generations" (GT 18, KSA 1.116–17). Neither religion nor myth, the traditional powers that hold the lower classes in check, retains any efficacy against the ascending force of Socratic rationalism and its attendant optimism. The Commune appears in *The Birth of Tragedy* as a countervailing tendency to the tragic Greek spirit, as a revolt of modern slaves representing an advanced stage of Alexandrian culture.

We do not find any further direct or indirect reference to the Commune or working-class revolt in *The Birth of Tragedy*. But we can see from the passage just referenced that Nietzsche was giving thought to the social structure underlying Greek culture and its implications for a modern renaissance of culture in Germany and Europe. He was not a philosopher who focused a great deal on the economy of ancient or modern societies, on how the necessities of life are procured and what sort of labor force was needed to sustain a city or a nation. He showed sporadic interest in economic theory, but economics was never well integrated into his philosophical thought. In his work around *The Birth of Tragedy*, however, he does appear to have developed ideas about these matters, and the fundamental conclusions he reached would persist into the 1880s, where they became infused with reflections on morality and value systems. Essentially, Nietzsche comes to recognize, or at least to emphasize in writing, that slavery is a necessary component of Greek society, that it is a prerequisite for the production of great art, and that, extrapolating to modern times, a "slave"-like class is a necessity if we are again to achieve the greatness he associated with the ancient world of tragedy. He claims to have garnered this insight from Friedrich August Wolf (1759–1824), the great German philologist who taught at Göttingen in the late eighteenth and early nineteenth centuries (Nachlass 1870–1871, 7[79], KSA 7.156),[29] but by Nietzsche's era this premise could be found in writers from Schopenhauer to Marx. In various notes around the composition of *The Birth of Tragedy*, Nietzsche contrasts slavery with the clichés "dignity of work" and "dignity of the human being," citing the latter phrases as deceptive verbal compensation for the indignity of physical labor. In one note, he states that the "'dignity of work' is a modern delusion of the most stupid kind. It is the dream of slaves." The only work that really possesses dignity is work done by a subject whose will is free:[30] "Thus an essential part of genuine cultural work is a well-founded being freed from the cares of the world; inversely, slavery is an essential part of culture" (Nachlass 1870–71, 7[16], KSA 7.140). The artist can only exist if society has a class that will do the drudgery of necessary work and release certain individuals from these mundane and demeaning activities. Nature, Nietzsche declares in an extended note on this topic, is "something dreadful." The crowning achievements of culture are available to an unbelievably small minority of privileged mortals, while service as slaves is a necessity for the great masses. Modern man has invented the palliatives in linguistic usage attaching dignity to work and to all human beings and their endeavors. But, Nietzsche asks, "what else should we find in the necessity of labor of all those millions besides the drive to vegetate further at any price; and who does not see in stunted plants that stick their roots into barren stones the same all-powerful drive?" (Nachlass 1871, 10[1], KSA 7.336–37). We recognize in this passage that the Social Question for Nietzsche in the early 1870s has become confounded with the cultural imperatives to which he subscribes in his Wagnerian discipleship. The Social Question does not have a solution because what we require is a class of laborers, whether they are called slaves or proletarians, to continue their activity so that the elite may create and enjoy a superior culture.

The passage just cited from Nietzsche's notebooks comes from a section entitled "Fragments to an expanded form of the 'Birth of Tragedy.'" We might think of these pages in Nietzsche's notes from early in 1871 as the foundational material on Greek society that did not make its way into the final version of the text published at the end of the year. They supply a crude economic basis that otherwise appears only in the very few brief remarks we have reproduced from the published work. In this entry, Nietzsche asserts that the Greeks did not mince words about physical labor; they spoke about it directly as a disgrace that occasions shame, not "because existence itself is a disgrace, but from the feeling of the impossibility that a human being struggling for his bare survival could be an artist." He then repeats sentiments we have encountered in other passages from his notebooks:

> In order to prepare the ground for a greater development in art, the vast majority have to be subjected in a slave-like fashion in the service of a minority *beyond* the measure of their individual necessity. At their expense, through their surplus labor the privileged class is released from its struggle for existence, and now produces a new world of needs. Accordingly, we have to understand and include as a cruel and fundamental condition of every *Bildung* that slavery belongs to the essence of a culture: an insight that can already cause an appropriate shudder in the face of existence. These are the vultures that gnaw at the liver of the Promethean promoters of culture. The misery of the toiling masses has to be increased even more in order to make possible for a number of Olympian individuals the production of a world of art. (Nachlass 1871, 10[1], KSA 7.339)

The greatness of tragic art in *The Birth of Tragedy* would not be possible without the sacrifice and excess production of laborers, whether they are slaves or free workers. Nietzsche sketches very vividly the essence of great art and the exclusivity that great art entails. It is produced at the expense of the vast majority for a select few; it has nothing to do with the flourishing of democracy or freedom; indeed, the ideology-laden platitudes of democracies only conceal the basic economic nexus of slavery. Later Nietzsche employs the metaphor of a war hero and his slaves to reinforce this thought: "we should be allowed to compare splendid culture with a conqueror dripping blood, who drags with him on his triumphant procession the conquered ones chained to his wagon as slaves, and who a beneficent power has blinded so that they, almost crushed by the wheels of the wagon, yet cry out 'dignity of work! dignity of human beings!'" (Nachlass 1871, 10[1], KSA 7.340–41). Nietzsche regards the socioeconomic institution of slavery as the prerequisite for the production of great art, and he considers it as a model still viable for the present if we are to achieve once again the pinnacles of culture the ancients attained. Slaves, however, have to know and accept their place in this social order. For this reason, he writes that it is an "unfortunate age" in which the slave begins to contemplate about himself and becomes agitated about his condition, a reference to mass education as well as to working-class organizations such as the workers' cultural associations of his own era. And the misguided "seducer," like Lassalle, who has led the slave away from his "state of innocence" by supplying him with fruit from the tree of knowledge, is similarly "unfortunate." Nietzsche readily draws conclusions about his present time from the knowledge he has gained about the necessity of slavery for cultural achievement among the ancients. The source of furious disregard for superior art on the part of "communists, socialists, and their paler descendants, the white race of liberals of all times" is ultimately linked to the knowledge that greatness is possible only on the basis of the enslavement of other human beings. In these passages from the "expanded" *Birth of Tragedy*, the inordinate concern for the "enormous social misery of the present day," which was the essence of the Social Question, is attributed to the "coddling" of a nineteenth-century world that, unlike antiquity, original Christianity, or the Teutonic past, cannot tolerate slavery, even under its current euphemistic labeling (Nachlass 1871, 10[1], KSA 7.337–41).

The views on social structure Nietzsche developed from his observations of ancient society while he was writing his treatise on the origins of Greek tragedy remained with him throughout his sane life. In 1884, for example, he remarks laconically in his notebooks: "The necessity of slavery" (Nachlass 1884, 25[232], KSA 11.74), and two years later he again comments on this topic in passing: "Slavery and the division of labor: the higher types are only possible through the *oppression* of the lower types to one function" (Nachlass 1886, 2[76], KSA 12.96). In the 1880s, Nietzsche appears to be less concerned with the existence of slavery or the exploitation of the working class than with the existence of a class that will be able to profit from this stratification of society—not in the sense of monetary gains, of course, but with an eye toward the creation of a superior culture. He writes that "slavery should not be eliminated; it is necessary." But he wants to make certain that there are appropriate individuals for whom others work "so that this enormous mass of political-commercial forces is not wasted" (Nachlass 1881, 11[221], KSA 9.527). In 1882, he points to the various forms of slavery that have existed—it is not a category that applies solely to the lower classes for Nietzsche—and the many justifications and concealments of slavery. He advises not to bother opposing views that promote compassion for slaves, but to remember that slavery has its social function and rationale in those who can take advantage of their release from laboring: "Always keep in mind that this enormous effort, the sweat, dust, and the noisy work of civilization, exists for those who know how to use all of this without working themselves: that there have to be people who constitute an excess, supported by the general surplus labor; and that these 'excess individuals' are the sense and the apology for the entire business." All states and societies are only different forms of slavery, Nietzsche observes; only those who are self-sufficient, who are also those who do not labor, are important; the rest are always merely "accessories" (Nachlass 1882, 16[23], KSA 9.664–65). In the 1880s, slavery assumes additional importance in Nietzsche's writings in his discussion of morality and values: slave morality is juxtaposed with master morality in his later thought to emphasize the degeneration and decline of European civilization. In these passages, which occur frequently in Nietzsche's books and notes from the last two years of his creative life, in particular in *On the Genealogy of Morals*, the economic dimension of slavery and its necessity in supporting a "master" caste is rarely emphasized. But the socioeconomic dimension of slavery, developed in writings from the early 1870s, never disappears entirely from Nietzsche's concerns and exists as a complement to the discussions of value systems.

We have seen thus far that the Social Question, which originally interested Nietzsche as a university student, is transformed in the works of the mature philosopher into a series of observations on the necessity of some form of slavery. The work that must be accomplished for a society to survive must be done by the vast majority so that a small elite group can have the leisure to create a great culture. This vast majority may be called slaves or serfs or proletarians; they may be subject to overt oppression or ideological coercion; what is important is that they work for the benefit of others who are genial and great. To this extent, the Social Question is a pivotal one for Nietzsche throughout the 1870s and 1880s, since advocacy of geniality and superior achievement in the arts was a constant for him from his Wagnerian years until his mental collapse. Nietzsche comments on the Social Question infrequently in his published works, but in his last writings, he includes a brief reflection on these issues that demonstrates very clearly where he stands. The passage in question occurs in the section "Expeditions of an Untimely Man" in *Twilight of the Idols* (1888), and it carries the title "The Workers Question," which is synonymous with the Social Question in Nietzsche's time.[31]

> The stupidity, fundamentally the instinct degeneration that is the cause of *every* stupidity today, lies in the existence of a workers question at all. About certain things *one does not ask questions*: first imperative of

instinct.—I simply cannot see what one wishes to do with the European worker now that one has made a question of him. He is doing too well not to go on asking for more, and to ask more impudently. After all he has the great majority on his side. There is absolutely no hope anymore that a modest and self-sufficient kind of human being, a type of Chinaman, could be formed itself into a class: and this would have been sensible, this was actually a necessity. What has one done?—Everything designed to nip in the bud even the prerequisites for it—through the most irresponsible thoughtlessness one has totally destroyed the instincts by virtue of which the worker becomes possible as a class, possible *for himself*. The worker has been declared fit for military service; he has been given the right to form labor unions and to vote in political contests: no wonder that the worker today already feels his existence to be a state of emergency (expressed in moral terms as *injustice*). But what does one *want*—to ask it again. If one wants a given result, then one has to want the means to it as well. If one wants slaves, then one is a fool if one raises them to be masters. (GD, Streifzüge eines Unzeitgemässen 40, KSA 6.142–43)

Europe has ignored what is necessary for great cultural achievement: a subservient class of slaves or workers who labor for an elite caste that has complete domination over the social order. Nietzsche suggests in this passage that the Social Question has been solved, but that its solution has been to the detriment of everything he has desired and his readers should desire. Noteworthy is that Nietzsche does not direct his anger completely at the working class itself; he suggests that the proletarians are acting in a rational and expected fashion in making more and greater demands, and in taking advantage of the social privileges they have been granted. At fault are the rulers of Europe, the social elite, the potential master caste, whose dulled instincts have led them to extend rights and opportunities to those who are inferior. The Social Question thus continues to be an important issue for Nietzsche right up until his last works. The increased importance of the working class—and Nietzsche may also be thinking of the working class political party, which was gaining strength despite the Socialist Laws—means that Europe in general and Germany in particular will not enjoy the type of social structure most conducive to artistic and cultural excellence. In *Twilight of the Idols*, the Social Question is less an issue or series of issues to be solved than a further sign of the general decadence, cowardice, and mediocrity of the nineteenth century.

Workers and Capitalists

Nietzsche's increasing hostility toward the Social Question, his advocacy of slavery even in modern times, his lack of compassion for poverty and exploitation, and, as we shall see in a moment, his antagonism toward socialism might suggest that he was a supporter of the bourgeoisie and of an aggressive form of capitalism. Although this conclusion is unwarranted by Nietzsche's writings, in recent times we can find Nietzsche associated with twentieth-century advocates of capitalism such as the economist Friedrich Hayek (1899–1992) or the writer Ayn Rand (1905–1982). For the first hundred years of commentary on Nietzsche, however, the only critics who consistently embraced this position were adherents to Marxism. At a time shortly before Nietzsche's death, when he had already begun to attract considerable critical acclaim, the socialist theorist Franz Mehring (1846–1919) wrote one of the first reviews of the philosopher's writings from a left-wing perspective. While Mehring distinguishes various periods in Nietzsche's works and recognizes different themes emerging in these periods, he feels compelled at one point to situate him in the overarching ideological struggle between capitalists and the working class. Using a critical vocabulary drawn from Marx and Engels, he separates the subjective tendency in his oeuvre, which is the apparent or outward character of his thought, from its objective dimension, which relates to the class his philosophy supports: "Subjectively a desperate delirium of the intellect, this so-called philosophy is objectively a glorification of big capitalism and as such it has found a large reading public."[32]

With considerably more critical acumen, but within the same generally restrictive evaluative framework, Georg Lukács (1885–1971) in the mid-twentieth century came to a similar assessment of Nietzsche's place in the history of the class struggle. Although Lukács concedes that Nietzsche never read a single word from Marx and Engels, he still feels entitled to characterize his "entire life's work" as a "continuous polemic against Marxism, against socialism" (10).[33] Nietzsche's writings are not completely consistent; they contain numerous contradictions and a variety of perspectives. But Nietzsche remains for the Hungarian Marxist the leading philosopher of the imperialistically inclined bourgeoisie. Lukács is relying here to some extent on Vladimir Lenin's (1870–1924) definition of "imperialism" as the highest stage of capitalism, a theory the Russian revolutionary explicated during the last years of the First World War,[34] but also the constellation formed in the Cold War during the 1950s, when he published *The Destruction of Reason*. Nietzsche's philosophy is attractive for various strata in bourgeois society, including "parasitic intellectuals" fascinated by his aphoristic style and the hyper-revolutionary rhetoric. But his response to fundamental questions remains, despite nuanced and subtle discussions, "the robust-reactionary class content of the imperialist bourgeoisie" (12). The specific task that Nietzsche's philosophy receives is one of showing bourgeois intellectuals a path that obviates the need to break with their class by displacing any rebellion from the real world, any actual feelings of social revolution into a "more fundamental, cosmic-biological" realm (14). He is an "indirect apologist" for capitalism (16) in particular in his ethical theory, since he defends the "bad side" of modern economies. While the usual "vulgar" apologists idealize the fate of individuals under capitalist relations, Nietzsche places "everything bad" in capitalism "in the center of his observations." He emphasizes "the egotistical, the barbaric and bestial aspects of capitalism" and affirms them as the essence of human nature (49). If we consider the Social Question of Nietzsche's time, Lukács and, before him, Mehring would regard the philosopher as the mouthpiece of the most aggressive sectors of the bourgeoisie.

Nietzsche, however, had no particular affinity with the bourgeoisie or the capitalists in Germany or European nations. The framework of capitalist and proletariat was foreign to his thought; to a large extent his chief adversaries in the initial years of the Second Empire were precisely those members of the ruling party and ruling elite—many of whom we would consider capitalists—who did not appreciate that their role was not simply to promote national unity or prosperity in German industry and finance, but to foster cultural greatness. The group he abhorred most consisted of those smug *nouveaux riches* who believed that wealth, party politics, and military victories automatically signaled German cultural superiority. His early texts are replete with invectives against the accumulation of wealth and the neglect of genuine cultural achievement. As we have seen in Chapter 1, Nietzsche's early discussions of education were usually directed precisely against those individuals who sought to instrumentalize education for bureaucratic or exclusively practical ends. In his very first lecture, Nietzsche expounds on his objections to the expansion of education, which constitutes not only a criticism of greater access to education on the part of the lower classes, but also the purposes he detects behind this increased availability of educational opportunity. Democracy and capitalism are in these lectures equally important targets of Nietzsche's observations regarding the deficiencies in German educational institutions. Expansion of education is part of the usual "national economic dogmas of the present." The objective appears to be an increase in production and needs, which are conceived as a contribution to the greatest possible happiness for the nation. Nietzsche is obviously attributing utilitarian goals to modern education and connecting both to the fostering of a capitalist economy that aims at producing wealth. "In this case, utility is made the object and goal of education, more precisely acquisition, the greatest possible monetary gain." Education in the modern era seems designed to foster the ways that one can "earn money most easily"; the aim is the maximization of "happiness and profit." Education that strives to go beyond these mundane objectives is despised and considered "higher egotism" or "immoral cultural Epicureanism." "According to the ethics that reign here the very opposite is demanded: namely, *speedy* education in order to produce as quickly as possible a money-making creature and yet such a thorough education that the creature can earn a great deal of money. Individuals are allowed only as much culture as is commensurate with the interest in earnings" (BA 1, KSA 1.667–68). These remarks relate indirectly to the Social Question insofar as they indicate that Nietzsche's antipathy for the working class does not stem from a partisanship for National Liberalism, bourgeois economics, or the capitalist class. His position entails an opposition to the evolving capitalist economy as such and encompasses a disdain for both the oppressor and the oppressed.

In assuming this position, Nietzsche is again evidencing his adherence to principles associated with the Wagnerian cultural enterprise. Although the Meister was preoccupied during the years he and Nietzsche were close with accumulating monetary support for the construction of Bayreuth, we should recall that Wagner's "revolutionary" past included a healthy dose of anticapitalism. Remnants of his disdain for vulgar capitalism find their way into many of his operas, perhaps most obviously in the first part of *The Ring* tetralogy, *The Rhinegold* (1869), where the repulsive dwarf Alberich enslaves the Nibelungs with his golden ring and forces them to accumulate a huge pile of gold. Thus Nietzsche's own disdain for amassing riches that do not support genuine cultural achievement is part and parcel of Wagnerian themes in his operatic works as well as in his theoretical writings. We should not be surprised to find further evidence of Nietzsche's aversion to wealth and an economy that values only the accumulation of money in the third *Untimely Meditation*, *Schopenhauer as Educator*, whose subject is the philosophical link between the young academic from Basel and the famed composer. In the fourth section of that essay, Nietzsche is contrasting the concerns of a real philosopher like Schopenhauer with philosophy professors as they currently exist at institutions in contemporary Germany. The main contention is that philosophers are no longer involved with genuine culture; religious belief is declining with nothing to take its place; national hostilities are rising. All firm beliefs are dissolving, and "the educated classes and states are being swept away by a grandly contemptible monetary economy" (SE 4, KSA 1.366). These remarks are reminiscent of the celebrated passage in the *Communist Manifesto*, when Marx characterizes the effects of capitalism: "all that is solid melts into air."[35] A bit later in this essay, Nietzsche includes "moneymaking" as one of the distractions to which we succumb instead of tending to "our true task" (SE 5, KSA 1.379). And in a third passage, Nietzsche connects the "*misused and exploited culture*" of contemporary Germany with individuals who have ulterior motives: "There is, first of all, the *selfishness of the moneymakers*, who require the assistance of culture, and who gratefully offer their assistance in return, whereby, of course, they would at the same time like to dictate the goal and standards of culture." In this passage, Nietzsche repeats almost verbatim the sentences cited above from his lecture series on education relating to a "speedy education" that aims at producing money-making individuals (SE 6, KSA 1.387–88). We should also recall that for both Wagner and Nietzsche in the years around the establishment of the Second Empire capitalism, the concern with accumulating wealth and the opposition to genuine culture were often associated with Jewry. Indeed, several scholars discern in select Wagnerian operatic figures associated with greed and exploitation further evidence of Wagner's anti-Judaism.[36] Nietzsche provided a similar connection in a Christmas present he gave to the Wagners in 1872. In his discussion of "The Greek State" in "Five Prefaces to Five Unwritten Books," he writes of the "international, homeless, money hermits" who manipulate the stock exchange, the state, and society for their own avaricious ends. The "stateless money aristocracy" and the "modern money economy" are clearly the enemies of the Wagnerian cause to which he subscribes (CV 3, KSA 1.774). Whether identified with Jewish interests or seen simply as greedy, uncultured industrialists and financiers, however, it is clear that in these early years, under the influence of various Wagnerian ideological leitmotifs, capitalism and the class of exploiters it produced did not find favor with Nietzsche. He was not against solutions to the Social Question because he sided with the bourgeoisie, but because he came to regard the Social Question itself as a manifestation of an inappropriate modern focus on money and wealth that he detested.

As we have seen and will continue to see, Nietzsche's views on social issues moderate in his middle or aphoristic period. The extreme stance he takes toward workers and slavery, and toward capitalists as the accumulators of wealth in the early 1870s, becomes less pronounced in the decade from 1876 to 1885, and the aggressive rhetoric accompanying his comments in the early and late writings is largely absent in these years. The views do not seem to change a great deal—exploitation of workers is usually seen as a necessary element in a social order striving for greatness, and capitalist wealth does not constitute a positive social goal—but Nietzsche is more thoughtful and reflective in his pronouncements. Noteworthy in quite a few remarks, mostly in his notebooks, is the similarity between the working class and the bourgeoisie. Although they are considered adversarial from the standpoint of economic interests, Nietzsche appears to believe that their participation in an economy defined by monetary interests brings them closer together. Thus he notes that workers "complain about being overworked," but that overwork is widespread in contemporary society and is common to "salesmen, scholars, civil servants, and the military: in the wealthy classes overwork appears as an internal drive toward every greater activity; among the workers it is compelled externally: that is the difference" (Nachlass 1876, 19[21], KSA 8.335). In discerning what is necessary for cultural achievement, Nietzsche observes that there must be a "surplus of leisure," and for one class to enjoy this sort of surplus, "those who are active (whether they be workers or bankers or civil servants) must supply them with their surplus work" (Nachlass 1876, 19[27], KSA 8.337). At another point, Nietzsche comments that in Europe the culture of the worker and of the employer enjoy a close proximity (Nachlass

1877, 25[1], KSA 8.482), and he asserts that aside from the reservoir of genuine culture all other movements are inimical to culture, "the socialist as much as the culture of the large states, or of the moneyed powers, and even the scholarly world" (Nachlass 1876, 17[22], KSA 8.300). In other passages, Nietzsche writes about a mercantile spirit, which has the task of implanting a passion in individuals who are incapable of higher aspirations, and these individuals form a new sort of species of human being akin to the slaves in antiquity (Nachlass 1880, 6[200], KSA 9.248). In a notebook entry from 1884, Nietzsche characterizes both the bourgeoisie and the worker as intermediate stages (25[178], KSA 11.61); they both belong to an order that will eventually pass out of existence. And in *The Gay Science,* Nietzsche suggests that a common economic interest reigns over all classes in the modern world: "Looking for work in order to be paid: in civilized countries today almost all men are at one in doing that. For all of them work is a means and not an end in itself. Hence they are not very refined in their choice of work, if only it pays well" (FW 42, KSA 3.408). In all of these passages, Nietzsche suggests a fundamental equality of desires, beliefs, and habits in modern society due to the dominance of money and wealth. The proletariat and the bourgeoisie adhere to the same system of values. They are opposed by the genuine artists and creators of great culture, but bound to each other by the mercantile mentality that pervades modernity.

The Social Question thus has a very different meaning for Nietzsche. It no longer involves the struggle between two classes, both seeking to gain advantage over the other, to increase the share of the social product they receive, or to ameliorate the poverty that results from the oppression of the working class under capitalist conditions. Rather, the Social Question becomes one more facet of modernity, which is itself the target of Nietzsche's critique. There is no way to solve the issues raised by the proletariat since the problem is not one of class conflict but of an economic system that is based on the "dignity of labor" and on mercantile gain. As Nietzsche makes clear in an aphorism from *Dawn,* work itself, whether accomplished by the worker or the bourgeois, is a negative factor in the modern world, and its "glorification," like the praise of altruistic acts, expresses a "fear of everything individual. Fundamentally, one now feels at the sight of work—one always means by work that hard industriousness from early till late— that such work is the best policeman, that it keeps everyone in bounds and can mightily hinder the development of reason, covetousness, desire for independence" (M 173, KSA 3. 154). The exploitation of the working class is not condemned, but rather the notion of industriousness as a diversion from individuality. We should not be surprised, therefore, to find in Nietzsche's writings that the factory is consistently used as a metaphor for the pernicious effects of modernity. He employs it frequently in reference to educational institutions in his early writings, but wherever it appears, it signals the kind of uniformity and mindless discipline that negates the development of genius.[37] Similarly, Nietzsche recognizes the degrading impact of machines on human labor. He appreciates advances that industrialization has brought, but he deplores the loss of individuality that "machine culture" fosters.[38] Machines bring workers together and simplify the tasks that they have to do; they are the paradigm for the organization of political parties and the military. But the machine "does not teach individual autocracy; it makes of many *one* machine, and of every individual an instrument to *one* end" (WS 218, KSA 2.653). It is credited with being the product of intellect and considerable intellectual energies, but "it sets in motion in those who serve it almost nothing but the lower, non-intellectual energies." As Marx would also note, it enhances production, but it does not enhance the individual, it does not promote the individual as an artist. "It makes men *active* and *uniform*," and ultimately engenders "a despairing boredom of the soul" (WS 220, KSA 2.653). In a longer aphorism touching on consumer demand and the appearance of commodities, Nietzsche notes the tendency in modern society for products that have an "effect on the eye" and are inexpensive, and that these goods are often produced by machine work; machines thus produce "*saleable*" merchandise. But what is important is the appearance of quality, and therefore machines are involved with a modern deception (WS 280, KSA 2.675–76). Nietzsche's conclusion about machine production demonstrates a preference for older forms of labor, for handicrafts, where individual workmanship is still embodied in the final product:

> *To what extent the machine abases us.*—The machine is impersonal, it deprives the piece of work of its pride, of the individual *goodness* and *faultiness* that adheres to all work not done by a machine—that is to say, of its little bit of humanity. In earlier times, all purchasing from artisans was a *bestowing of a distinction on individuals*, and the things with which we surrounded ourselves were the insignia of these distinctions: household furniture and clothing thus became symbols of mutual esteem and personal solidarity, whereas we now seem to live in the midst of nothing but an anonymous and impersonal slavery.—We must not purchase the alleviation of work at too high a price. (WS 288, KSA 2. 682–83)

The claim is that modern industry debases individuals; that it deprives us and the products of our labor of any individuality and humanity; that it produces uniformity and ignores distinction in workmanship; that it destroys the relationship between the laborer and his product, and between individual producers; that it fosters the anonymity of commodities: these sorts of insights bring Nietzsche closer to Marx and socialist theorists than to apologists for capitalism. Nietzsche, however, is less interested in taking the side of the proletariat against the bourgeoisie; industrial work, factories, and technology, as manifestations of modernity, debase the entire culture. Indeed, Nietzsche even expresses a proto-ecological thought in commenting on the hubris of his contemporaries in their application of technology: "Today our whole attitude towards nature is one of hubris, our violation of nature with the aid of machines and the thoughtless ingenuity of technicians and engineers" (GM, Dritte Abhandlung 9, KSA 5.357). In his reflections on workers, work, capitalism, and technology, Nietzsche appears to be more critical of the general influence on culture than on the exploitation of one class by another. In an aphorism from *Human, All Too Human*, he objects to the way individuals use one another without a purpose: "Mankind mercilessly employs every individual as material for heating its great machines: but what then is the purpose of the machines if all individuals (that is to say humankind) are of no other use than as material for maintaining them? Machines that are an end in themselves—is that the *umana commedia*?" (MA 585, KSA 2.336-37). What Nietzsche appears to deplore more than the exploitation and misery of the lower classes is the purposelessness of this exploitation and misery, the lack of any higher goal to which a hierarchically based social order should aspire. Once again the Social Question is reconceived from a Nietzschean perspective, where classes have little meaning except insofar as they are unfortunate symptoms of modernity and their members are not cognizant of alternatives to the debased, mundane, mercantile order of contemporary Europe.

On occasion, however, Nietzsche does offer more specific observations on issues associated with what was generally understood as the Social Question of his era. One of these instances occurs in the second book of *Human, All Too Human*, in an extended reflection titled "The Value of Work." He begins by questioning the ability to ascertain a precise value for work: "If we wanted to determine the value of work by how much time, effort, good or ill will, compulsion, inventiveness or laziness, honesty or deception has been expended on it, then the valuation can never be *just*; for we would have to be able to place the entire person on the scales, and this is impossible." Like Marx, Nietzsche assumes that value is a measure corresponding to the input of the worker, not to the market as it determines the cash value of a commodity. From this perspective, all the various inputs of the worker, both physical and mental, cannot be reduced to a common measure—they resist calculation—and only the totality of the individual, which similarly is incalculable, could account for true value. Nietzsche alludes to those who are discontent with the evaluation of work, and who consider this evaluation unjust; he likely means socialist theorists who consider the worker's rewards for their labor to be insufficient. But from his own definition of value, they too are wrong, since they are already entwined in the struggle for the proceeds of work, and are not really concerned with its "value" in the larger sense in which Nietzsche uses the term. Nietzsche contrasts this usage, according to which one cannot derive any stance on "*merit*" since "all work is good or bad as it must be given this or that constellation of strengths and weaknesses, knowledge and desires," with utility, which can attach a valuation to work. Utility creates value because it abstracts from the input and considers only the social dimension of labor. But even from this rather different perspective, Nietzsche notes that society has not proceeded in its own best interests. Utility includes not only the momentary actions of a worker, but also the need of the worker to procreate, producing future generations of workers. We must consider "the wellbeing of the worker, his contentment of body and soul—so that he and his posterity shall work well for our posterity too and be relied on for a longer span of time than a single human life." The pronouns are significant: the future generations of workers will work for "our posterity." The class structure in Nietzsche's thought does not admit of upward or downward mobility. But for just that reason, it is in the interests of those for whom the workers labor to treat them with more consideration than is currently the case. "The *exploitation* of the worker was, it has now been realized, a piece of stupidity, an exhausting of the soil at the expense of the future, an imperiling of society. Now we already have almost a state of war," Nietzsche continues, referring not only to the frequent labor disruptions of his era, but also to the rise of socialism and the antisocialist legislation Bismarck has been compelled to impose on Germany. And Nietzsche closes his reflection by noting that the harshness of current and past injustice will be difficult to overcome: "the cost of keeping the peace, of concluding treaties and acquiring trust, will henceforth in any event be very great, because the folly of the exploiters was very great and of long duration" (WS 286, KSA 2.681–82). In this aphorism, we can discern various bits and pieces of socialist theory that Nietzsche picked up from his readings over the years. But his solution to the Social Question is definitely not related to socialist doctrine. He chides the bourgeoisie for their excesses in exploiting the working class, but his goal is the continuation and reproduction of a social structure that contains a class of less exploited laborers and those who live from the fruits of others' labor. He advocates a cessation of exploitation not to promote equality or a just distribution of wealth, but to assuage a restive proletariat, whose discontent and potency he clearly recognizes and fears.

A few years later, in *Dawn*, Nietzsche again takes up the Social Question and arrives at somewhat different conclusions. The title of the aphorism—"The Impossible Class"—already indicates Nietzsche's perspective: that the working class as it currently exists cannot maintain its existence in its current form. Nietzsche ponders at the start that an individual can be "poor, happy, and a slave" and that this description may be accurate for contemporary "workers of factory slavery" provided they accept their miserable fate: "that is, they do not feel it to be in general a *disgrace* to be thus used, and *used up*, as a part of a machine and as it were a stopgap to fill a hole in human inventiveness." Nietzsche then lists the beliefs that deceive the workers into thinking that their situation can be ameliorated: "that higher payment could lift from them the *essence* of their miserable condition"; that the enhancement of production within a "machine-like operation" in a new society "could transform the disgrace of slavery into a virtue"; that setting a price for themselves and their work could eliminate the fact that workers have become a mere cog in a large machine. Obviously, Nietzsche believes none of these "solutions" will resolve the Social Question. As we have already seen in other passages, Nietzsche maintains that workers are actually complicit with the general aims of the exploiters against whom they sometimes protest, since they too advocate increased production and wealth as the ultimate goals of society. Workers ought to counter the status quo by asserting their individuality against the dominant mercantile ethos, pointing out "how great a sum of *inner* value is thrown away in pursuit of this external goal." But the working class has no internal value if it no longer knows how to "breathe freely"; if it no longer has any power over itself; if it has become so integrated into the present order that it mimics the wealthy and aspires to similar material comforts; and if it no longer recognizes the virtues of a spiritual, philosophical existence, lived in poverty and isolation. The propaganda of the "Socialist pied-pipers" is a deception for the proletariat, since they only "design to inflame you with wild hopes," to "bid you *to be prepared* and nothing further, prepared day upon day, so that you wait and wait for something to happen from outside and in all other respects go on living as you have always lived—until this waiting turns to hunger and thirst and fever and madness, and at last the day of the *bestia triumphans* dawns in all its glory." Nietzsche perceives very little chance for change in a working class thoroughly assimilated into a capitalist order, coopted by the value system of the bourgeoisie, and misled by socialist demagogues.

The last half of this aphorism, however, offers an unusual alternative to the plight of the proletariat: emigration. It was, as Nietzsche knew all too well, the path taken by many Germans from the lower classes in the second half of the nineteenth century, and Nietzsche presents it as an opportunity for workers to become "*masters* in new and savage regions of the world and above all master over myself." Similar thoughts, as we shall see in Chapter 5, animated Nietzsche's brother-in-law, Bernhard Förster (1843–1889), a few years later when he established Nueva Germania in Paraguay as a refuge for industrious Germans. A life of real freedom can only be achieved, Nietzsche suggests, outside the confines of Europe and the narrow class struggle that defines contemporary society. This radical change can be achieved only with a radical change in consciousness: "This would be the right attitude of mind: the workers of Europe ought henceforth to declare themselves *as a class* a human impossibility and not, as usually happens, only a somewhat harsh and inappropriate social arrangement." The colonists would flourish since European virtues, suppressed by their current social situation, would be liberated. And although Europe would lose a large percentage of its inhabitants, it could perhaps compensate for this lost population by importing "numerous *Chinese*," who would bring with them "the modes of life and thought suitable to industrious ants" and would contribute to Europe "Asiatic calm and contemplativeness and—what is probably needed most—Asiatic *perseverance*" (M 206, KSA 3.183–85). Noteworthy in Nietzsche's strange and fantastic reflection on the Social Question is the recognition of the misery of the working class, as well as the near impossibility of any significant relief within European parameters. The class struggle, no matter how it is decided, cannot provide any real relief. Only a revolution in consciousness that would encourage workers to leave Europe for new adventures in foreign climes can liberate the proletariat from their enslavement. And if the modern "slaves" of Europe would abandon their respective nations, Nietzsche conjures up a vision of importing a new docile class/race that will provide labor without discontent, and new stability for the social order.

A final consideration of the Social Question from Nietzsche's aphoristic middle period is found in *The Gay Science*. Nietzsche begins his observations in "On the Lack of Noble Manners" by comparing the military and the industrial realm, in particular the relationships that are formed within these two social settings. "Soldiers and leaders still have a far higher relation to one another than do workers and employers. So far, at least, all cultures with a military basis are still high above so-called industrial culture: the latter in its present form is altogether the most vulgar form of existence there has ever been." The contrast between the two hierarchical organizations highlights an oft-noted feature of capitalist economies: while the relationships between superiors and their followers are often based on a personal bond, or at least on personal contact, capitalism fosters an anonymous hierarchy in which a base mentality brings together the bourgeois and the proletariat. Nietzsche clarifies: "Here it is simply the law of need operating: one wants to live and has to sell oneself, but one despises those who exploit this need and *buy* the worker." Capitalism degrades both ruler and ruled: the workers must sell themselves in order to live, but the capitalists who control industry do not gain respect for their actions, since they are seen as participants in a fundamentally crude and ignoble economic system. Nietzsche notes further that subservience to powerful individuals, even to tyrants, is not considered as distressing as "submission to unknown and uninteresting persons, which is what all the greats of industry are: the worker usually sees in the employer only a cunning, bloodsucking dog of a man who speculates on all distress and whose name, figure, manner, and reputation are completely indifferent to him." Nietzsche is analyzing the psychology of subjects and arguing that submission to the powerful is less problematic when the powerful have achieved real distinction, when they exhibit the signs of a "*higher race*," when they "legitimize themselves as *born* to command." Indeed, Nietzsche asserts that workers would willingly surrender themselves to the bourgeoisie—"the masses are basically ready to submit to any kind of *slavery*"—if they detected the necessary distinction of legitimate leaders. Since workers do not detect this distinction, they are more susceptible to opposition and to socialist alternatives:

> The commonest man senses that nobility cannot be improvised and that one has to honor in it the fruit of long ages—but the absence of the higher demeanor and the notorious manufacturer's vulgarity with ruddy, plump hands give him the idea that it is only accident and luck that elevated one above the other in this case: well, then, he infers, let *us* try accident and luck! Let *us* throw the dice!—and socialism begins. (FW 40, KSA 3.407–8)

The problem for Nietzsche is not one of equality or breaking down hierarchies; it is one of sustaining hierarchical structures that are meaningful and that promote the nobility of spirit that can produce greatness. As we have seen, the workers can solve their situation only by removing themselves from the mercantile mentality dominating Europe. Nietzsche has no admiration for the capitalist oppressors, not because he is averse to oppression, but because the capitalist class lacks the substance of real leadership and nobility. As Nietzsche had observed in *Human, All Too Human*, in the mercantile and industrial world, we can detect something similar to previous ruling classes, but at present "they lack nobility in obedience" found in former social constellations, where it is an "inheritance from the feudal ages and will no longer grow in our present cultural climate" (MA 1, 440, KSA 2.287).[39] Again we find confirmation that for Nietzsche the issues surrounding the Social Question cannot be resolved within the confines of class struggle since they are products of a "cultural climate" and a capitalist mentality that must be overcome.

The Socialist Alternative

Socialism as a form of economic organization in which the working class controls production and distribution is thus no solution to the Social Question, although many regarded it in Nietzsche's era as the most promising way to eliminate the misery and oppression of the lower classes. Nietzsche's objections to socialism, which he occasionally views as an inevitable stage in European development, differ over time as his understanding of what socialism entails changes. It is somewhat difficult to know with precision what Nietzsche had in mind when he referred to socialist and socialism at any particular point in time from the mid-1860s to the end of the 1880s. The names we may identify today as the main theorists of the nascent socialist movement in Germany, Karl Marx and Friedrich Engels (1820–1895), appear nowhere in Nietzsche's writings; only August Bebel, the leader of the Socialist Workers' Party of Germany (SAPD), is referenced by Nietzsche on a single occasion, but not for his views on the economy or socialism.[40] We have already seen that Nietzsche seems to have taken an interest in Ferdinand Lassalle in the mid-1860s, and that he would have learned a great deal about this socialist leader from his reading of Joerg's book. But Nietzsche showed no inclination to follow up on this early interest. Nietzsche could have easily read about socialist theories in Friedrich Albert Lange's *History of Materialism* and, more specifically, about socialism in Lange's later book *The Workers' Question* (1875). The former volume Nietzsche praised as a young man and consulted on numerous occasions and in various editions starting in the 1860s, and the latter book is found in Nietzsche's library and contains an entire chapter dedicated to the explication of Marx's theory.[41]

But again there is no real evidence in his writings or notes that these discussions of socialist theory were important for his understanding of socialism. In the 1880s, we can assume that Nietzsche read thoroughly John Stuart Mill's (1807–1873) essay titled "Socialism," as well as his article "Thornton on Labour and Its Claims," whose German title was simply "Die Arbeiterfrage" [The Workers' or Labor Question]. Both were collected in the twelfth volume of the translation of Mill's *Collected Works*, which also contains his essay on the "Subjection of Women."[42] All three pieces were translated from the English by the young Viennese medical student Sigmund Freud (1856–1939). As we already saw, Nietzsche also had in his library a short pamphlet written by Albert Eberhard Friedrich Schäffle with the title *The Quintessence of Socialism* (1879).[43] Not all of these writings are sympathetic to socialism, but important for our purposes is that they did not appear to leave much of a mark on Nietzsche's views concerning the working class, capitalism, or socialist politics. We find some potential contact with socialists or communists—or at least former socialists of various stripes—in Nietzsche's biography. The fourth Congress of the International took place in Basel just five months after his arrival in 1869, and the parades and festivities, as well as the appearance of Mikhail Bakunin (1814–1876), an old friend of Richard Wagner, might have drawn Nietzsche's attention. Indeed, both Wagner and Malwida von Meysenbug (1816–1903) had exhibited socialist leanings in the 1840s, and both had friends and acquaintances that continued to identify with socialism. Leipzig, as we have seen, was an important hub for working-class organizational activity, and the local newspapers must have carried reports of meetings as well as strikes in the area.[44] But we find scant mention of these sorts of occurrences in Nietzsche's correspondence or in the reminiscences of friends and relatives.

Ultimately, we gain the impression that after his student years, Nietzsche probably had a variety of sources for his views of socialism, some advocating socialism, some opposed to it, but that for many years no one book or theoretical direction was foremost in his mind as representative for this working-class movement. In the 1880s, however, when he mentioned socialism he was most likely referring to the writings of the prolific Berlin professor, philosopher, and anti-Semite Eugen Dühring (1833–1921), whom Nietzsche had read and appreciated in the 1860s, but whose thought Nietzsche gradually came to disdain. As we shall see, socialism in Nietzsche's later works is often associated with *ressentiment*, which would bring it into the proximity of Dühring's views on ethics and justice.

During his Wagnerian period, socialism was likely seen as a theoretical position advocated by Lassalle, explicated by Joerg, and put into practice by the Paris Commune. Nietzsche concerned himself less with the liberation of the working class from demeaning tasks or the implications of socialism for the political economy of the new German Reich than with the relationship of socialism to the Wagnerian enterprise. We have seen that perhaps the decisive moment in his evaluation of socialism was therefore the erroneous report of the Commune's arson of the Louvre, but from what he knew about socialism and its advocates, he would likely have concluded anyway that socialist practice was not consonant with the renaissance in culture that he and Wagner envisioned. Socialism appealed to the lowest common denominator in society. It aimed at overcoming the hierarchy that in Nietzsche's view was essential for the production of any genuine artistic accomplishment. Socialism as the basis for a social order is thus diametrically opposed to the kind of society required for significant accomplishments in culture. Nietzsche's references to socialism are few in his early writings, and even in his notebooks, but he does mention it in section nineteen of *The Birth of Tragedy*. He is discussing opera, which he, like Wagner, opposes to music drama. Accordingly, opera incorporates all the anti-Wagnerian features in cultural activity. It is a modern phenomenon, part of "Socratic culture" and "Alexandrine culture," invented to oppose pessimism and propound the idea of inherent goodness in humanity. In doing so, Nietzsche claims it satisfies "a completely unaesthetic need," since its aim is to glorify "man himself" and to portray the natural and the primitive "as the naturally good and artistic man." Nietzsche concludes his discussion of the purpose of opera with a remark on the socialism of his own times: "this operatic principle has gradually transformed itself into a threatening and terrible *demand*, which we with respect to the present socialistic movement can no longer overlook. The good primitive, the 'noble savage' demands his rights. What paradisiacal prospects!" (GT 19, KSA 1.120–23). The socialist campaign for equal rights, for a cessation of exploitation, and for an equitable distribution of the fruits of the labor process is considered an outgrowth of the principles that form the basis of opera and that now pose a threat to Western civilization.

The reference to "the noble savage" is echoed in *Schopenhauer as Educator*, where Nietzsche identifies one of his three fundamental types of human beings, the Rousseauian, with all revolutionaries, "for in the instances of all socialist upheavals and tremors, it is always Rousseau's human being that is doing the shaking" (SE 4, KSA 1.369). The Rousseauian individual is juxtaposed with the more preferable types: the Goethean and the Schopenhauerian. Significant for Rousseau is an optimistic view of life, the emphasis on nature as good, and a thoroughly unaesthetic attitude. Socialism in the early writings of Nietzsche is thus situated in the camp opposed to Greek tragedy and to the Wagnerian mission. It exhibits no appreciation for greatness and no understanding of cultural excellence.

An incident that occurred less than a year after the appearance of *The Birth of Tragedy* demonstrates the extent to which Nietzsche's evaluation of socialism was tethered to his Wagnerian partisanship. In October 1873, he appears to have gotten the impression that "the International" was threatening the Wagnerian Bayreuth enterprise. In a letter to Gersdorff, he writes of "a weird machination that demands my immediate, personal intervention in Leipzig." He states further that he cannot write about it in his letter because he fears putting it on paper. But he affirms that "an entirely unexpected horrible danger threatens the Bayreuth undertaking" and that he is responsible for the "countermines" (Nr. 318, KSB 4.165). He suggests that a certain "ghost R[osalie] N[ielsen]" is involved. The same day he writes to Erwin Rohde (1845–1898) about the "weird machination to bring the - - - Leipzig Publishing House into the hands of the International." Ernst Fritzsch (1840–1902), Wagner and Nietzsche's publisher, is allegedly already "compromised." "Our cause," Nietzsche continues, "will be destroyed the moment when only a word about this is heard in the public sphere." And he tells Rohde that he is seeking to intervene personally in this matter, again mentioning the "ghost R[osalie] N[ielsen]" (Nr. 319, KSB 4.168).[45] When Nietzsche visited the Wagners at the end of the month, he was still unsettled about this matter. Cosima reports on 1 November: "Our friend also relates how he is being tormented in connection with the International; a Frau Nilsson [*sic*], a friend of Mazzini's, announced herself to him as a servant of the cult of Dionysus, she wants to advance Fritzsch money and if possible also to take over his business. Our friend greatly agitated by these curious happenings!"[46] It is not easy to understand precisely what had transpired and why Nietzsche was so concerned about "the International" and its involvement with the Wagnerian cultural mission. From the evidence we possess, it seems that Nietzsche believed that his publisher Fritzsch had already taken money, presumably from the socialists represented perhaps by Rosalie Nielsen, who either wanted to take control of the Bayreuth project or to subvert it. Nietzsche's reasons for such suspicions are not clear. Aside from the general atmosphere of labor agitation and social unrest in the early 1870s, Fritzsch's publishing house had been affected by typographers' strikes, which delayed the publication of books by Wagner, Nietzsche, and Overbeck.[47] An additional alarm signal for Nietzsche was the appearance in 1873 of an admirer, the mysterious Rosalie Nielsen, an older woman evidently enthralled by the Dionysian in *The Birth of Tragedy*. Not much is known about Nielsen. She is reported to have been acquainted with the Italian revolutionary Giuseppe Mazzini (1805–1872), and she contrived at one point to meet Nietzsche himself, which appears to have been an unpleasant experience for both of them.[48] We have only one letter from her to Nietzsche, and it contains nothing about the "International," just remarks pertaining to their meeting and to the Dionysian (17 June 1873, Nr. 440, KGB II 4.262).[49] For whatever reason, Nietzsche associated her with the socialist conspiracy he imagined was threatening Bayreuth, since he writes to both Gersdorff and Rohde of her involvement, and obviously mentioned it to the Wagners as well. The entire cabal was, it appears, the product of Nietzsche's (and perhaps Overbeck's) fantasy and paranoia, perhaps assisted by Nielsen's "overactive imagination."[50] But the very fact that Nietzsche could leap to such a quirky theory of socialist intrigue indicates how unrealistically he regarded the International, and how much he believed genuine culture was threatened by it. As the product of a petty-bourgeois family with bourgeois pretensions who feigned aristocratic lineage and frequented patrician parlors, Nietzsche was not a likely candidate for socialist sympathies. But his reaction to this minor incident shows the extent to which socialism irrationally became associated in his mind with opposition to Wagner, Bayreuth, and the renaissance of cultural greatness.

Once Nietzsche had broken away from the Wagnerian dogmatism that informs a good deal of his early writings, he exhibits a more differentiated and broader view of socialism. It is no longer seen exclusively connected to cultural imperatives, but encompasses a spectrum of attitudes and convictions about the social, legal, and political order. We see in the middle or aphoristic period that Nietzsche is less polemical than in his early and late writings, and that in the various aphorisms and notes from the mid-1870s until the early 1880s he is able to regard aspects of socialism with more objectivity and equanimity. He never becomes an advocate of socialism, but he occasionally admits it as useful or necessary or inevitable for the progress of human development. A case in point is aphorism 446 from *Human, All Too Human*, titled "A question of power, not justice." Nietzsche begins by making exactly that argument: even if we assume that socialism is a rebellion of the oppressed against their oppressors, we would be wrong to conclude that it represents a "problem of *justice*"; for Nietzsche, anticipating perhaps his turn to theories of power in his later years, it is clearly a "problem of *power*." Nietzsche conceives of this rebellion in terms of the demands made by socialists for change, and the willingness of those in power to deal with these demands. Thus the question is not how far we should accede to the demands, which turns the issue into a moral decision for the oppressors, but "how far *can* we exploit its demands?" He likens socialism to a force of nature and uses the example of steam, which can be harnessed for production in machines if appropriately captured and contained, or, if the "machine is faulty," will lead to the destruction of both man and machine. Nietzsche is likely reflecting on the strength of the socialist movement in his own time and what should be done to channel this strength in the most productive fashion. "To solve this question of power one had to know how strong socialism is, with what modification it can still be employed as a mighty lever within the existing play of political forces; under certain circumstances one would even have to do all one could to strengthen it." Nietzsche recognizes socialism as a great force, and a potential threat, but it may also be regarded as beneficial: "mankind has to make of it an instrument for the attainment of its objectives." Nietzsche further envisions socialism as attaining rights only if a war between the old and the new powers appears to be imminent. But he believes that prudence will lead both parties to a compact, which will secure rights, presumably for the working class that socialism represents (MA 1, 446, KSA 2.289–90). At this point—and Nietzsche is writing prior to the Socialist Laws in 1878—we have neither conflict nor a compact, both of which would secure rights for socialists, and the situation is unstable and unsatisfactory. Socialism in this aphorism is not relegated to its role as a threat to cultural achievement, but seen as a more generalized power that has potential and unstated benefits, provided a suitable arrangement renders it productive.

Nietzsche's associations with socialism during his post-Wagnerian phase are often unexpected. In the aphorism "Socialism with Regard to Its Means," he discusses it as a movement that promotes despotic state power. His understanding of socialism in this period was certainly not based on Marx and Engels and their writings, since they clearly state that the legal and juridical apparatus of the state supports the class in power, and that the proletariat, after a period of transition in which it captures the functions belonging to the state, will no longer need it, since class hegemony will be abolished and the state will no longer have any purpose. Thus the state will "wither away."[51] Nietzsche was most likely thinking of the type of socialism advocated by Ferdinand Lassalle, who had broken with Marx and Engels over this issue and other disagreements about strategy and tactics. Lassalle no longer believed a revolution possible, so he placed his hope in an alliance with the quasi-feudal entities in the German state. He approached Bismarck with his plans, but achieved very little. His hope was that with something approaching universal suffrage, the working class could gain control of state power, and that the state could in turn be used to support cooperative movements so that the economy could gradually become socialized. The state was thus at the very center of his socialist thought, and Nietzsche is very likely alluding to theories like Lassalle's when he calls socialism "the fanciful younger brother of the almost expired despotism whose heir it wants to be." For Nietzsche, then, socialism is "reactionary" in the strict sense of that word, since it wants to move away from the democratizing tendencies of contemporary Europe and reintroduce "an abundance of state power such as only despotism has ever had." He claims further that it outdoes earlier despotism in its desire to annihilate the individual and to become the legitimate successor to the tyrannical court of Sicily in Plato's time and "the Caesarian despotic state of the present century." Socialism requires "a more complete subservience of the citizen to the absolute state than has ever existed before," and since it cannot appeal to "ancient religious piety toward the state," it must rely on "the exercise of the most extreme terrorism." For this reason, Nietzsche suggests it cannot exist for an extended period of time. Socialism of his era thrives on fear and on brainwashing the "half-educated masses" with notions of "justice" in order "to rob them of their reason" and prepare them for the "evil game they are to play." The only positive aspect of socialism is thus that it can serve as a lesson regarding the dangers of an accumulation of state power: it can teach us to mistrust the state. The watchword of socialism for Nietzsche is "*as much state as possible*," but he seems confident that it will engender the opposing cry with even more force: "*as little state as possible*" (MA 1, 473, KSA 2.307–8).

Nietzsche is especially concerned in other aphorisms to elaborate on the relationship between socialism and justice. We have already seen that in his earlier reflections on the working class, Nietzsche ridicules notions of the dignity of man and the dignity of labor as the vacuous and deceptive slogans of bourgeois ideology. The same can be said for the socialist insistence that their struggle entails justice for the working class. This perspective is false, Nietzsche argues, because it operates with a limited and inadequate understanding of history, psychology, and the forces that initiate change. It is possible within the ruling class to practice a notion of equality and justice, but it would involve voluntary "sacrifices and self-denials" of those in power. A demand for equality of rights on the part of socialists, by contrast, is a manifestation of greed, not justice, and in these reflections we again see Nietzsche's anticipation of theories of power. He invokes the following comparison to emphasize his point: "If one holds up bleeding chunks of meat to an animal and takes them away again until it finally roars: do you think this roaring has anything to do with justice?" (MA 1 451, KSA 2.293). Socialists, here likened to wild animals demanding that food be restored to them, are in essence demonstrating a material desire and are unconcerned about abstract notions like justice. They cloak reality in high-minded phrases to incite and attract followers. Their idealist justifications of their own activities are just as much a part of ideology as the catchphrases of the bourgeoisie. Socialists may persist with arguments for rebellion and change, pointing out that the distribution of property in society has been the result of "countless acts of injustice and violence," and that this unjust foundation delegitimizes the current state of affairs. Nietzsche points out, however, that this allegedly unjust foundation must be regarded as an essential and "natural" part of our heritage: "The entire past of the old culture was erected upon force, slavery, deception, error; but we, the heirs and inheritors of all these past things, cannot decree our own abolition and may not wish away a single part of them." Nietzsche suggests in this passage, as he did in commenting on critical history in the second *Untimely Meditation*, that we are too much a product of our past to separate ourselves artificially from it, or to excise artificially only a portion of that past. Furthermore, he asserts that even those who lack property and possession have inherited "the disposition to injustice," and are no better than those who have been advantaged by the injustices of the past. What is required for the future is not a redistribution, but "a gradual transformation of mind: the sense of justice must grow greater in everyone, the instinct for violence weaker" (MA 1, 452, KSA 2.293–94). Significant about these aphorisms is not necessarily the solutions Nietzsche proffers—it remains unclear what would transpire in the distribution of property if the sense of justice in everyone were heightened—but that Nietzsche addresses concerns associated with the working-class socialist movement. He is neither dismissive nor polemical; he evidences genuine concern with examining and parrying the most prominent theoretical premises of the socialist movement.

Indeed, Nietzsche's most thorough and thoughtful discussions of socialism stem from this period, which is marked historically in Germany by the growing power of the socialists just prior to the implementation of the Socialist Laws. *Human, All Too Human* contains several aphorisms that are devoted to socialism and related topics, and in his notes from the autumn of 1877, at the same time he was composing his first book of aphorisms, we find a sustained consideration of socialism in eight points. As in aphorisms 451 and 452 in *Human, All Too Human*, Nietzsche seeks to counter prevailing sentiments regarding socialism in European society:

1. Nietzsche asserts that the sufferings and deprivations of the working class are misunderstood because they are inappropriately measured. As one climbs in the social hierarchy there is greater susceptibility to suffering; the senses of the lower classes are dull. If the situation of the lower classes improved—something advocated by socialism—it would only make them more vulnerable to suffering. In 1887, Nietzsche makes a similar claim with regard to "Negroes" in *On the Genealogy of Morals* (GM, Zweite Abhandlung 7, KSA 5.303).
2. If we consider not the individual, but the greater goals for humanity as a whole, we find socialism deficient. Nietzsche doubts that an ordered society, such as the socialists propose, could produce great results, since he believes it probable that great individuals arise "only in the freedom of

the wilderness." This objection to socialism is predicated on Nietzsche's conviction that humanity has no goals other than "great individuals and great works," a view Nietzsche held throughout his lifetime.

3. Nietzsche turns to the economic necessity of having someone do the hard and unappealing work. If the working class receives a higher level of education, which is something socialism demands, then workers will seek to free themselves from these unpleasant tasks that must be done. Nietzsche speculates that this liberation could be accomplished if there were a mass importation of "barbarian peoples from Asia and Africa, so that the civilized world would continuously make serviceable the uncivilized world." We have already seen that in a comment from *Dawn*, Nietzsche suggests importing Chinese to take the place of European laborers (M 206, KSA 3.183–85). Nietzsche concludes his thought by noting that the culture of the worker and the employer is often so proximate that there is already incipient protest against forms of exhausting mechanized tasks.

4. Nietzsche dismisses abstract appeals to fairness and justice, as we have already seen. The slogan "what's good for the goose is good for the gander" is not a sentiment that accords with conditions in nature. Power is operative, not fairness. Only when the new social order becomes as powerful as the old order can we conceive of contracts that will establish justice in equal measure: in contrast to socialist propaganda, "there are no human rights."

5. Nietzsche agrees with the sentiment expressed by some members of the working class about their wealthy factory owners: "You do not deserve your happiness." But he does not draw the same conclusions from this statement. Nietzsche does not advocate a more equitable distribution so that everyone has the same chance for happiness. Rather, he claims that this statement is true because no one merits happiness or, for that matter, unhappiness. The socialist appeals to a moral value system that Nietzsche rejects.

6. Following on his fifth point, Nietzsche claims that to increase happiness on earth does not imply a change in institutions, but rather a change in temperament, which has very little to do with external factors of class differences. In fact, socialists, who exhibit a disagreeable sort of temperament, decrease in all circumstances earthly happiness, and that will be true even if they succeed in altering the current social order.

7. Nietzsche argues that contentment on earth is possible only "within traditions, firm customs, limitations." Since socialists strive to destroy these very things, they cannot solve the social problems they seek to remedy. And new constitutive abilities are not yet perceptible in the socialist program.

8. Nietzsche saves his only favorable remark about socialism for last. Because socialism injects into the lowest strata of society a practical-philosophical discourse, it fosters a type of excitement or arousal. To this extent, "it is a vital source of intellect." (Nachlass 1877, 25[1], KSA 8.481–83)

Nietzsche's remarks in these notes from 1877, as well as his comments in the aphorisms in the first volume of *Human, All Too Human,* reveal someone who is trying to come to terms with a phenomenon he confronts in contemporary Europe. Nietzsche is no more favorably disposed toward socialism in 1877 than he was during his Wagnerian period. But he conceives socialism less as a direct threat to a cultural enterprise he must defend than as a philosophical challenge. Socialism may claim that it will solve the Social Question, but Nietzsche maintains that it has not been able to work through the real issues confronting the working class, its sufferings, its happiness, and the nature of social development. From Nietzsche's perspective, socialism offers some minor advances for the most disadvantaged members of the social order, but it proposes nothing that can lead to a permanent solution to the conditions it detects, and certainly nothing that will result in the realization of the genuine goals of any social order: individual and cultural greatness.

These remarks from 1877, as well as the aphorisms contained in the first book of *Human, All Too Human,* were composed prior to the implementation of the Socialist Laws. During the course of 1878, however, as Nietzsche was writing the continuation of his first aphoristic work, subtitled *Assorted Opinions and Maxims,* there had been two assassination attempts directed at Kaiser Wilhelm I, a new parliamentary election that reduced the power of the Social Democrats, and several drafts and the eventual enactment of laws directed at weakening Social Democracy in Germany and outlawing certain kinds of socialist activities. Although, as we noted earlier, neither of the perpetrators was a member of the Socialist Workers' Party of Germany, Bismarck used these incidents as a pretext to persuade the National Liberals to join conservative parties in this restrictive legislation. Nietzsche never commented directly on these various events, but the aphorisms dealing with socialism in *Human, All Too Human II* refer unmistakably to what had occurred in German politics in 1878. In perhaps his most revealing comment on this legislation, Nietzsche claims that the Socialist Laws are really part of a larger antidemocratic campaign: "The socialist movements are now more welcome than fear-inspiring to the dynastic governments, because through them the latter can get into their hands *the right and the weapons* for taking the exceptional measures with which they are able to strike at the figures that really fill them with terror, the democrats and anti-dynasts." The public disdain for socialism disguises a "secret inclination and affinity," since it gives the government a reason to take action against democracy. Socialists are therefore the "desired enemies," which is the title of this aphorism (VM 316, KSA 2.506–7). Nietzsche directs his most bitter attack against the wealthy bourgeoisie of the National Liberals, whose betrayal of their own principles allowed the passage of the Socialist Laws. Addressing them directly, Nietzsche writes: "The only weapon against socialism you still have at your command is not to challenge it: that is to say, yourselves to live modestly and moderately, as far as you can prevent the public display of extravagance and assist the state when it imposes heavy taxes on all superfluities and things that resemble luxuries." This emphasis on luxury items may well have been influenced by Nietzsche's reading of Lange's book on *The Workers' Question*, which suggests that a solution to the Social Question lies in the cessation of producing luxury items for the wealthy.[52] It is in keeping with Nietzsche's general plea and preference for a modest life style. Nietzsche's point is that the wealthy are responsible for the workers' revolutionary ardor, since they are only adopting the values of the bourgeoisie. The only thing that separates the wealthy from the proletariat is the "possession of property." If the wealthy, who are identified with the "liberals," seek to solve the Social Question with legal restraints and prohibitions, they will be unsuccessful. The opulence and grandeur they ostentatiously display, detailed by Nietzsche in this aphorism, are the root cause of socialist unrest: they are "the poison-bearing propagators of that sickness of the people which, as socialist scabies of the heart, is now spreading faster and faster among the masses but has its primary seat and incubator in *you*" (VM 304, KSA 2.304). Nietzsche's reaction to the Socialist Laws immediately after their enactment is that they are a vain attempt to contain the spread of socialism in Germany. Since the bourgeoisie has flaunted its wealth and instilled vulgar materialist values in the envious working class, only a radical change in value systems can be effective in quelling socialist demands for the acquisition of goods.

Although Nietzsche suggests at times that socialism is inevitable and in some regards a desirable development, in most instances he considers it impossible because it violates basic human psychology. In one aphorism, he posits that democracy will destroy socialism. Again alluding to the Socialist Laws, he maintains that "all political powers nowadays try to exploit the fear of socialism in order to strengthen themselves." But the result is increasing concessions to the "people," which Nietzsche translates into a strengthening of democratic rule. He continues:

> As socialism is a doctrine that the acquisition of property ought to be abolished, the people are as alienated from it as they could be: and once they have got the power of taxation into their hands, through their great parliamentary majorities they will assail the capitalists, the merchants and the princes of the stock exchange with a progressive tax and slowly create a middle class which will be in a position to forget socialism like an illness it has recovered from. (WS 292, KSA 2.683–84)

Nietzsche evidently believes that the natural inclination of the people in favor of owning property will make them reject socialism, whose highest command is "you shall not possess" (Nachlass 1879, 42[19], KSA 8.599). Even if the innate psychological disposition of the people were not against socialism, the problems posed by the abolition of property are insurmountable. Nietzsche cites two ways in which property relations can be altered radically. The first and nonsocialist alternative is to distribute it equally among members of society. Practical difficulties make this option unfeasible. No two pieces of land are really equal, Nietzsche notes, and even if they were, in a generation or two with families having unequal numbers of offspring, inequality would be reestablished. The socialist abolition of property, which in Nietzsche's view cedes all ownership to the community, is equally problematic, but for psychological reasons: "For upon that which he possesses only in passing man bestows no care or self-sacrifice, he merely exploits it like a robber or a dissolute squanderer." Plato, Nietzsche notes, had opined that the abolition of property would lead to the elimination of egoism. But without egoism, humankind would eradicate its cardinal virtues, "for it has to be said that the foulest pestilence could not do so much harm to humankind as would be done him if his vanity disappeared. Without vanity and egoism —what are the human virtues?" Thus socialist solutions "rest on a defective knowledge of man." Nietzsche's solution is more modest, less radical: we should simply prevent individuals from amassing too much wealth. But we should affirm property and the accumulation of a "*moderate* wealth through work." Those who possess too much wealth—and Nietzsche does not address what amount of wealth he means—are as much a threat to the social order as those who live in penury (WS 285, KSA 2.279–81). In posing a radical solution to the Social Question, socialism ignores individual psychology and propounds an alternative that violates human nature.

Nietzsche's late reflections on socialism assume a different tenor than the comments from his aphoristic writings of the middle period. Absent are the reasoned arguments against socialism as a faulty psychology, the discussions of practical difficulties in abolishing private property, and the reflections on connections between socialism and justice. We also find that the rhetoric is often different. Nietzsche evidenced no affinity for socialism in any phase of his life, but in his late writings his remarks are harsher, more derogatory, more dismissive. It also appears that Nietzsche has somewhat different associations with socialism and depends for his understanding on sources that diverge from the readings of earlier years. Eugen Dühring becomes for him the paradigm for a socialist thinker, and he may also begin to associate it with individuals like his brother-in-law, the anti-Semitic agitator Bernhard Förster (1843–1889), whose diatribes against capitalism as something Jewish and his embrace of German community could be mistaken for socialist proclivities. Above all, Nietzsche begins to identify socialism with other pernicious phenomena he has come to detest in contemporary

Europe. Thus we find in his late writings the frequent mention of similarities between socialism and Christianity. In a note from 1887, for example, when he is elaborating on Christian morality, he writes that the "socialist *ideal*" is "nothing other than a clumsy misunderstanding of that Christian moral-idea" (Nachlass 1887, 10[170], KSA 12.558). The following year, under the general heading of "The Nihilist," he begins with a review of the main lessons of the Gospels: "The message that the lowest and poorest have open access to happiness;—that one only has to free oneself from the institution, the tradition, the tutelage of the ruling classes: to this extent the lineage of Christianity is nothing other than the *typical teaching of socialism*." He continues his reflections by citing several factors common to socialism and Christianity, all of which hinder earthly happiness: "property, acquisitions, fatherland, status and rank, tribunals, police, state, church, education, art, the military: everything just as many obstacles to happiness, errors, entanglements, devil's work, which the Gospels pass judgment on . . . everything typical for the teaching of socialism" (Nachlass 1888, 11[379], KSA 13.178). The tendencies that Nietzsche comes to identify with socialism are the same ones he finds in his consideration of Christianity; indeed, socialists "appeal to Christian instincts, which is their most subtle cunning" (Nachlass 1888, 15[20], KSA 13.424). In contrast to the portrayal of socialism in *Human, All Too Human*, socialists are not seeking to emulate the bourgeoisie and enjoy material pleasures; rather, they have become, like Christians, ascetics. Both Christianity and socialism, "the latent Christianity" (Nachlass 1887, 10[2], KSA 12.453), take the side of the lower classes, favoring "the poor, the 'illegitimate,' the despised ones" (Nachlass 1888, 11[383], KSA 13.181). In these passages, socialism, conceived as "the residue of Christianity and Rousseau in the de-Christianized world" (Nachlass 1887, 10[5], KSA 12.456), becomes the economic and political correlate of the long history of religious asceticism.

Christianity and socialism are similar because both are manifestations of the decadence and degeneration of European society. They are different expressions of an identical decline. As Nietzsche develops a history of moral systems in his later writings, according to which a slave morality replaces a noble morality identified with masters or aristocrats, he begins to consider within this framework the import of socialism, which, like Christianity, is fundamentally an expression of *ressentiment* in the powerless strata of the social order. Like slave morality or ascetic values, it has some positive dimensions: socialism is "useful and therapeutic" for a degenerating Europe insofar as it "forces the Europeans to retain spirit, namely cunning and cautious care, not to abjure manly and warlike virtues altogether, and to retain some remnant of spirit, of clarity, sobriety, and coldness of the spirit—it protects Europe for the time being from the *marasmus femininus* that threatens it" (Nachlass 1885, 37[11], KSA 11.587). By challenging the status quo, in other words, socialism keeps the ruling classes alert, preventing complacency and encouraging Europeans to be prepared for struggle and antagonism. For the most part, however, Nietzsche rails against socialism as a deception, a negation of healthy instincts, and a sign of nihilism. In the very same aphorism, which Elisabeth incorporated into *The Will to Power*, Nietzsche characterizes socialism as "the logical conclusion of the *tyranny* of the least and the dumbest, i.e., those who are superficial, envious, and three-quarters actors"; it follows from "modern ideas and their latent anarchism"; it is "on the whole a hopeless and sour affair." It disregards and contradicts the will to power, perhaps the central philosophical tenet Nietzsche develops in the 1880s. The will to possess something is innate in the human being, but Nietzsche adds that "one must want to have more than one has in order to *become* more." To this extent, socialism represents the very antithesis of the will to power, evidencing instead "a will to negate life." He attributes the theories of socialism to "degenerate men and races," since in socialism "life negates itself, cuts off its own roots" (Nachlass 1885, 37[11], KSA 11.586–87). In authorized published writings, he employs similarly vituperative language. At the close of a section on the history of morals in *Beyond Good and Evil*, Nietzsche writes of the rare individual who can detect "that 'the human being' is itself *degenerating*" and understands "what kind of things have usually caused the finest example of an evolving being to shatter, break apart, sink down, become wretched." This perceptive individual knows that socialism is the logical extension of this modern tendency: "The *overall degeneration of man*, right down to what socialist fools and flatheads call their 'man of the future' (their ideal!); this degeneration and diminution of man into a perfect herd animal (or as they call it, man in a 'free society'); this bestialization of man into a dwarf animal with equal rights and claims is *possible*, no doubt about that!" (JGB 203, KSA 5.127–28). This vilification of socialism reaches a climax in *The Antichrist* in a passage that discusses initially the *Law Book* (or *Traditions*) *of Manu*. Nietzsche finds much to his liking in this ancient Sanskrit text on customs and morals, in particular "the order of castes, the *order of rank*," and the *"inequality* of rights." When he turns to mediocrity and its advocates, he refers directly to socialism: "Whom do I hate most among the rabble of today? The Socialist rabble, the Chandala apostles, who undermine the worker's instinct, his pleasure, his feelings of contentment with his little state of being, who make him envious, who teach him revengefulness" (AC 57, KSA 6.244). Socialism comes to represent the fulfillment of a value system that negates life, and the antithesis of the value system Nietzsche extols. Socialists embody the degenerate spirit of contemporary Europe and the essence of a caste of social pariahs.

Nietzsche was never an advocate for socialism, but his views on what socialism entailed changed at various stages of his life. As a young man studying at the University of Leipzig, he evidenced interest in political alternatives to the National Liberals, including the parties of socialism, and at the time he showed begrudging admiration for one socialist leader, Ferdinand Lassalle. After his incorporation into the Wagnerian community, he became a strong detractor from anything that resembled the real socialist movements of his era. Especially disturbing for him was the Paris Commune, which he suspected of destroying the artworks in the Louvre, and he came to associate socialism with a force inimical to Wagner's grand schemes for Bayreuth and a renewal of genuine culture. His views moderated somewhat after his break with Wagner, and we find him both better informed and more differentiated in his discussions while he was composing his books of aphorisms in the so-called middle period. In the last four years before his mental breakdown, however, he returned to stronger condemnations of socialism and socialists, associating them with a degenerating social order in general and, at times, with Christianity in particular. He rejected socialism throughout his lifetime as a solution to the Social Question, and on occasion Nietzsche appears to ignore that the largest impetus for the growth of socialism in Germany and Europe was the misery and exploitation of the working class. When he does address socialism as an outgrowth of the Social Question, he rejects it strongly. For the most part it is considered an inadequate response to the problems it is confronting because it has a faulty understanding of human psychology and the history of societal development. Throughout his writing career, Nietzsche is persuaded that only hierarchically organized societies can produce greatness, and that equality in any of its multiple guises is undesirable. Not only should slavery, exploitation, and discrimination not be eliminated; they are in Nietzsche's view the very prerequisites for the type of social order he believes will foster great individuals and superior culture. At the same time that he rejected socialism and its ideological principles, he remained fairly impartial regarding the bourgeoisie and the proletariat. He sometimes demonstrates sympathy with the latter, more often accusing socialist leaders of duping the working class with their false and deceptive rhetoric. Workers are only made discontent and rebellious by the rants of socialist agitators. The wealthy are frequently taken to task for failing to understand the true goals of humankind. Nietzsche is more consistently hostile toward capitalism, its emphasis on material wealth, and those who celebrate acquisition than toward the working class. Thus Nietzsche's discussions of the Social Question engage the discourses of the late nineteenth century, but do not replicate any of the most popular positions. He does not fit conveniently into any category, although a tendency toward conservatism and an outspoken elitism are most apparent. The conglomeration of unusual views we can attribute to him demonstrates not only his preoccupation with one of the key issues of his times, but also his inability to come to terms fully with the complexities of the Social Question.

Chapter 4

The Women's Question

Like his remarks on socialism and democracy, Nietzsche's comments on women and the feminist movement would appear to allow for scant controversy. Even those who have only a fleeting acquaintance with Nietzsche's views know that the most notorious comments he made about women were hardly flattering, and his deprecation of women and the struggle for equal rights for women has led the vast majority of commentators to condemn his misogynist attitudes. Although his late writings are replete with utterances that confirm Nietzsche's denigration of women as inferior human beings, perhaps the most frequently cited remark about women in Nietzsche's oeuvre occurs in the first part of *Zarathustra*, where the reader encounters the following shocking piece of advice: "You are going to women? Do not forget the whip!" (Za 1, Von alten und jungen Weiblein, KSA 4.86). Our first response may be to consider this statement a call for the subjugation of women, suggesting actions ranging from taming and training to physical abuse or the infliction of punishment. It is possible, however, to read this piece of counsel in another fashion, one that suggests bringing a whip to women so that they can use it on the man.¹ Even if we follow a more traditional suggestion in the literature on Nietzsche and attribute to the "whip" a metaphorical sense, the citation still advocates attitudes antithetical to our conventional sensibilities. Complicating the most obvious interpretation is the fact that this outburst does not belong to Zarathustra, Nietzsche's mouthpiece in this work, but to a little old woman whom he meets on his travels. This maxim is the "little truth" that she gives to Zarathustra about her own sex. But Zarathustra's comments on women are hardly more complimentary. In the section "On Little Old and Young Women," in which the citation about the whip occurs, Zarathustra makes frequent assertions that belong to the traditional canon of misogyny. He maintains, for example, that "everything about woman is a riddle, and everything about woman has one solution: that is pregnancy"; he asserts that man wants woman as "the most dangerous plaything" and insists that "man should be educated for war, and woman for the recreation of the warrior; all else is folly." And a bit further on, he comments tersely: "The happiness of man is: I will. The happiness of woman is: he wills" (Za 1, Von alten und jungen Weiblein, KSA 4.84–85). These statements have been frequently admonished by feminist writers from the nineteenth through the twenty-first centuries, as well as by men sympathetic to women's causes and gender equality. Most commentators have accordingly placed Nietzsche in a long tradition of philosophers who have disparaged women, contending that his view of women is "as radical and thorough-going as it was consistent with the inherited prejudice of centuries of philosophers before him." If he is accorded any originality, it is only in representing a modern and pernicious variant to an ancient bias: he is "the founder of peculiarly modern patriarchy and the inventor of one of the crassest and most subtle misogynies."[2]

Defending Nietzsche for Feminism

Despite the overwhelming evidence, especially in his late writings, that Nietzsche was a fierce opponent of women's rights and women's emancipation, there have been at least two instances of Nietzsche's adoption by writers who claim him for feminism. Shortly after Nietzsche lapsed into insanity we find that he began to attract attention from women whom we today associate with the first wave of the women's movement in the late nineteenth and early twentieth centuries. These women were conscious of Nietzsche's published vituperative remarks against women. But they either ignored Nietzsche's misogyny because they found other areas of his works so important for women and women's plight at the turn of the century, or they expressed incredulity that someone who was so perspicacious about philosophical issues of great import could be so conventional about his attitudes toward women.[3] Typical for this direction of disappointed advocacy was Hedwig Dohm (1831–1919), a woman of Jewish heritage who had agitated for women's rights and equality already in the 1870s and continued as a central figure in the radical feminist movement until her death shortly after the First World War. In her 1902 book "defending" women, titled *The Antifeminists*, Dohm includes Nietzsche among the "orthodox" with regard to issues of women's rights, but the manner in which she writes about him indicates her high regard for his thought. She wonders why "even the noble, most daring thinkers, as soon as they pick up the pen to write about the women's question, momentarily stop their thought processes and resort to feelings, instincts, intuitions, and eternal truths." It is astounding for her to observe the complete abandonment of all logic, science, and conscientiousness when men like Nietzsche begin to reflect on the women's movement. She observes that Nietzsche himself delivers an apt explanation for his own failings when he comments in *Dawn* about his lack of exposure to certain areas of life: "Even great spirits have only their five-fingers' breadth of *experience*— just beyond it their thinking ceases and their endless empty space and stupidity begins" (M 564, KSA 3.328). Thus for Dohm, the absence of any intimate relationship with women in Nietzsche's life accounts for his fatuous comments, but she still marvels that the "most noble, most profound of our adversaries," Schopenhauer and Nietzsche, despite their admitted dearth of contact with women, can utter such apodictic certainties about "woman as such."[4] Dohm recognizes that Nietzsche is a "genial, electrifying poet" as well as a "passionate thinker," whose thoughts are often precise and "golden arrows" that hit their target, illuminating, "like the sun," entire worlds or crashing down like Zeus's thunder. She also acknowledges Nietzsche's close relationship with "free-thinking" women, such as Lou Andreas-Salomé (1861–1937) or "Malvida von Meysenburg" [sic].[5] But these personal associations and abilities only heighten her displeasure. "O Nietzsche," she apostrophizes, "you high sacerdotal spirit, profound revealer of secrets, and yet an ignoramus with regard to the most simple truths." For Dohm, it is almost incomprehensible that the "greatest poet of the century" could write about women "so entirely beyond good." Ultimately, Nietzsche is a personal disappointment: a "deep, deep heartbreak," that makes her "even more lonesome, older, and distant."[6] Only Dohm's high regard for Nietzsche keeps her from turning completely against him on account of his antifeminist remarks.

Not every feminist thinker, however, regarded Nietzsche's views as antithetical to women or to a progressive stance on the Women's Question. A more consistent supporter of Nietzsche among early feminist thinkers was Helene Stöcker (1869–1943), who, in contrast to Dohm, excuses the philosopher's frequent misogynist remarks and views him almost entirely as a liberating force for women. This difference is attributable in large part to their diverging positions in the feminist movement. While Dohm promoted traditional civil liberties and opportunities for women, and recognized in Nietzsche a man opposed to these demands for equal treatment, Stöcker was more focused on emancipation from traditional religious and moral values, and on sexual liberation. One of the first German women to earn a doctorate degree, Stöcker is known for her leadership of the League for the Protection of Mothers. But the work she did in connection with this organization and its journal *Protection of Mothers*, as well as her later activities, entails less a confirmation of the traditional role of women in the home than the movement toward a "New Morality" that was in essential ways opposed to the conventional image of motherhood and women's subjection in marital relations. For these radical notions, Stöcker borrowed liberally from Nietzsche's thought, sometimes crediting him with emancipatory impulses that were foreign to his writings. In her most concentrated work on Nietzsche, the book *Love and Women* (1908), Stöcker immediately demonstrates her reliance on the philosopher. Cited in the introduction as the source for a new humanity,[7] Nietzsche becomes the central figure for "the new Renaissance" that has manifested itself in the first decade of the twentieth century because of his insistence on a revaluation of values.⁸ According to Stöcker, Nietzsche proclaimed a "religion of joy,"⁹ that raises everything earthly into the realm of beauty, and his "higher men" are tantamount to the announcement of a new humanity in which we say "yes" to life and to ourselves, while exhibiting "a strong, unbroken will to life" involving "the courage of great responsibility." Stöcker's method of appropriating Nietzsche is to borrow key phrases and concepts from his philosophy and, because they contain rhetorically liberationist overtones, insert them into her own thoughts on the emancipation of women. She returns to Nietzsche toward the end of her reflections on "our revaluation of values," referencing primarily passages in *Zarathustra*. "If man were something absolutely superior," she writes, "how could we bear not being a man. Therefore man is not something absolutely superior." In this passage, Stöcker has transformed a passage from the second book of *Zarathustra* that calls into question the divine realm: "*if* there were gods," Zarathustra states, "how could I stand not to be a god! *Therefore* there are no gods." She cites further the apothegm: "become who you are" (Za 4, Das Honig-Opfer, KSA 4.297) and strings together familiar notions from the Nietzschean arsenal that foster "our own feminine-human nature" [*weibmenschlichen Natur*]: "learn to give ourselves laws, to define the order of rank of values through us and for us; *that* is the emancipation from the authority of ascetic morality of past or declining cultures and traditions." Stöcker thereby adapts Nietzsche's thought for feminist purposes, for "liberation from the masculine worldview." The overman becomes the product of both sexes in equal measure, and the lessons of *Zarathustra* apply as much to women as men. Nietzsche, Stöcker admits, never drew these conclusions, largely because "woman" never became a "*personal* problem" for him. Citing Nietzsche's favorable judgment on women from *Human, All Too Human*— "The perfect woman is a much higher type of human being than the perfect man" (MA 377, KSA 3.265)—Stöcker concludes that Nietzsche supported a fundamental gender equality whose motto is succinctly captured by Zarathustra's dictum: "Only he who is man enough will *redeem the woman* in woman" (Za 3, Von der verkleinernden Tugend 2, KSA 4.214).¹⁰

Stöcker could not completely ignore Nietzsche's misogynist remarks and the reputation he had acquired from them. Accordingly, in a later section devoted to Nietzsche's writings she mounts a spirited defense against the "legend" that Nietzsche was "a hopeless despiser of women." Part of his undeserved reputation comes from a failure to understand Nietzsche's humor and self-parody. The famous citation about the whip, which has been his most celebrated derogatory remark about women, even in his own era,¹¹ was something we should not take seriously, since Nietzsche himself did not. She points to "The Other Dance Song" in the third book of *Zarathustra*, where we find the following reflection on the original remark dealing with the whip from the first book: "To the beat of my whip you will dance for me and cry! But did I forget the whip?—Not I!" Answering this refrain is life itself, which scolds the eponymous hero: "Oh Zarathustra! Don't crack your whip so fearfully! You know too well: Noise murders thought" (Za 3, Das andere Tanzlied 1, KSA 4.284). Anyone who takes the "whip" statement so literally, Stöcker insists, "lacks any sense of humor." As further evidence against alleged misogyny she refers to Nietzsche's relationships with women throughout his life. Although he, like Schopenhauer, may have uttered horrible invectives against women, in his contact with women we find the tenderest signs of considerateness, "an almost ceremonial admiration of women." The individual women he knew never spoke about a hatred of, or contempt for, women, and in the early 1870s he longed for a wife to fulfill his life's wishes. When in the following years he did write disparagingly about women, especially famous women, it was really "a reaction against the exaggeration on the part of modern women" that accounts for his harsh words. Nietzsche's genuine appreciation of women can be found in sections such as "Woman and Child" from *Human, All Too Human* (1878), from which Stöcker quotes liberally. Nietzsche's most important contribution to women and the Women's Question, however, comes from his opposition to the "old ascetic morality of the church fathers, who found in love between the sexes something sinful, and who viewed women as something base and impure." Stöcker then sketches a philosophy of mutual sensual and intellectual appreciation between men and women, attributing its inspiration to Nietzsche's philosophy. It may be true, she concedes, that Nietzsche did not validate everything about women in precisely the way we would have wanted him to, but we would be viewing his contribution to women's liberation in a narrow and restricted fashion if we simply rejected him and discarded the high and incomparably beautiful thoughts contained in his writings.[12]

Feminist thinkers and activists beyond German borders shared this early admiration for Nietzsche. In the United States, several of Nietzsche's most ardent early supporters were progressive women. Perhaps the best known of these American Nietzsche enthusiasts was Emma Goldman (1869–1940), who had to overlook not only the passages in Nietzsche's writings that denigrated women, but also his frequent and unrelenting polemics against anarchism and socialism. She was evidently willing to ignore these transgressions because she believed, as Stöcker did, that Nietzsche's more encompassing worldview had a tremendous emancipatory potential for the causes in which she believed. For this reason, Goldman included an essay by Stöcker in the March 1907 issue of *Mother Earth*, a leading journal of the anarchist movement that Goldman edited. The piece is titled "The Newer Ethics," and it follows closely the types of arguments about Nietzsche that Stöcker had included in *Love and Women*.[13] Zarathustra is the emblem of newer ethics, since he endorses a healthier attitude toward sexuality and morals. Stöcker's views on Nietzsche are somewhat unusual for an anarchist publication and clash in important areas with those of Goldman and other contributors: she considers Nietzsche's teachings to be a continuation and development of Christianity, not a rejection of it, and she remarks at one point that his philosophy "is identical with certain underlying principles of Christianity." Nietzsche advances beyond religious doctrine in his advocacy of a freer sexual life. "To Nietzsche," she writes, "as to the Greeks, sex was symbolic of all the inner and deeper meaning of ancient piety, and everything pertaining to the procreative act, pregnancy and birth, awakened only the highest and purest emotions." Stöcker is extremely short on evidence for these claims in Nietzsche's writings, but she is for that reason even more expansive in her assertions. Nietzsche not only endorsed sexual liberation; he also supported childhood education in sexual matters: "Nietzsche was one of the first to satisfy our moral feelings upon the sex question in relation to children. He realized the danger of letting the latter grow up in entire ignorance of the most vital subject, and of allowing women to marry without the least preparation for, or realization of the meaning of, the most important questions of life." Nietzsche believed, we are told, that women "should be treated with the greatest gentleness"; his very idea of love was founded on the feminine. In Stöcker's presentation, Nietzsche also becomes an incisive critic of contemporary marriage, as well as an earnest exponent of reform. "Nothing seemed to Nietzsche more despicable or more detrimental to the interests of the race than marriage for money or position. That children of such origin are apt to be worthless is easily realized" (22). For Stöcker, and for the readers of *Mother Earth* in 1907, Nietzsche is likely to be regarded as a contributor to enlightened thought about women, as a writer who, like Stöcker and Goldman, was concerned with their liberation as well as the institutions that kept them in a subservient social position. For many early feminists in the Western world, Nietzsche was thus considered an ally in their struggle against patriarchal oppression, traditional religious values, and a repressive morality.

Philosophical Feminism and the Figure of Woman

Until the second wave of feminist thought in the Western world in the last three decades of the twentieth century, Nietzsche remained categorized as a misogynist, if there was any attention at all directed toward his thoughts on women. Walter Kaufmann's (1921–1980) judgment is typical of the attitude of many commentators: Nietzsche expresses views on women that are hostile and irrational, but they have no import for an evaluation of his philosophy. "Nietzsche's writings contain many all-too-human judgments—especially about women—but these are philosophically irrelevant; and *ad hominem* arguments against any philosopher on the basis of such statements seem trivial and hardly pertinent."[14] Nietzsche's rehabilitation for the feminist cause is an almost direct confrontation with this sort of perspective. His remarks on women are viewed as not only relevant, but frequently as the very center of his philosophical enterprise. Chiefly responsible for this turnaround in the thinking about Nietzsche and women/feminism was an essay by Jacques Derrida (1930–2004) titled "Éperons: Les styles de Nietzsche," which was the printed version of a lecture he presented at a conference on "Nietzsche: aujourd'hui?" in 1972.[15] It appeared in French in 1978 and in a dual-language French-English edition the very next year. Many subsequent observations on Nietzsche and women—in both France and the United States—drew heavily on this lecture, using the reasoning in Derrida's essay as well as the identical citations from Nietzsche's writings. Indeed, it would not be an exaggeration to say that *Spurs: Nietzsche's Styles*, the English rendition of this central lecture, supplied something akin to a canonical list of passages that occur with great frequency whenever Nietzsche was treated as a philosopher with positive implications for the cause of feminism. The two key texts from the French deconstructive camp in this tradition are the rhapsodic and somewhat disjointed reflections of Luce Irigaray (b. 1930) in *Marine Lover of Friedrich Nietzsche*,[16] originally published in 1980, and Sarah Kofman's (1934–1994) *Nietzsche et la scène philosophique* from 1979,[17] which has appeared only in partial English translation. Kofman had written an earlier and influential study on Nietzsche titled *Nietzsche und Metaphor* (1983; orig. 1972), but she began to connect Nietzsche with feminist concerns only after hearing Derrida's lecture "Éperons."[18] With a delay of a little more than a decade, the Anglophone world responded to the new feminist Nietzsche with a series of books: the collections *Nietzsche, Feminism and Political Theory* (1993), *Nietzsche and the Feminine* (1994), *Feminist Interpretations of Friedrich Nietzsche* (1998), and, in parts, *Feminism and Deconstruction* (1994) belong to this wave of renewed recruitment of Nietzsche for the cause of women, as does Kelly Oliver's *Womanizing Nietzsche* (1995).[19] Some of these volumes contain excerpted translations from the French, but all of them depend heavily on Derrida, Kofman, and Irigaray for their connection between Nietzsche and women. Indeed, at times it appears that the main texts these American disciples are analyzing are not Nietzsche's, but Derrida's, Kofman's, or Irigaray's reflections on Nietzsche.

We can discern three basic strategies employed to diminish the more obvious passages of misogynistic sentiments in Nietzsche's works. The first we might call philosophical mitigation and contextualization, a strategy that juxtaposes the derogatory comments on women with other, less objectionable statements; or else that regards these oppositions to be part of a larger "economy" that negates their apparently antithetical nature. This strategy allows the commentator to concede that there are overtly misogynist remarks found in Nietzsche's writings, but to determine that they are only one dimension of Nietzsche's sentiments regarding women and the feminine. Ultimately, his views must be considered ambivalent or, in more deconstructive parlance, undecidable. Derrida authorizes this type of reading when he cites the allegedly favorable evaluation of woman, starting with the preface to *Beyond Good and Evil*, where Nietzsche playfully associates truth with woman, and then references the many passages in which the philosopher writes disparagingly about women. "Must not these *apparently feminist* propositions be reconciled with the overwhelming *corpus* of Nietzsche's venomous anti-feminism?" Derrida asks. And he concludes that "their congruence . . . although ineluctably enigmatic, is just as rigorously necessary. Such in any case, will be the thesis of the present communication."[20] Invariably the undecidability of woman is linked to Nietzsche's reflections on truth and falsehood, where the former cannot be conceived without the latter.[21] Passages such as the following are typical for the confounding of this antithesis and their connection with woman: "Because, indeed, if woman *is* truth, *she* at least knows that there is no truth, that truth has no place here and that no one has a place for truth. And she is woman precisely because she herself does not believe in truth itself, because she does not believe in what she is, in what she is believed to be, in what she thus is not." At one point, to harmonize Nietzsche's allegedly positive remarks with his misogyny, Derrida is compelled to support the odd—and Nietzschean—argument that women feminists are actually men:

> For it is the man who believes in the truth of woman, in woman-truth. And in truth, they too are men, those women feminists so derided by Nietzsche. Feminism is nothing but the operation of a woman who aspires to be like a man. And in order to resemble the masculine dogmatic philosopher this woman lays claim—just as much claim as he—to truth, science and objectivity in all their castrated delusions of virility. Feminism too seeks to castrate. It wants a castrated woman. Gone the style.[22] (64–65)

This dizzying display of rhetorical flourishes, where women are men and truth is falsehood, and therefore neither can be determined as one or the other, becomes a commonplace of Nietzschean philosophical feminist critique during the 1990s. As Peter Burgard asserts in his introduction to *Nietzsche and the Feminine*, "there is probably no area in Nietzsche's philosophy where one finds less unity and univalence than on the question of the feminine." Citing again passages from *Beyond Good and Evil* that associate woman with truth as well as with dissimulation and lies, Burgard concludes: "Through the association of the figure of woman with both sides of this hierarchically inscribed binary opposition, we might say that woman comes to be a figure of Nietzsche's subversion of that opposition as such." In this view, there is an "irreducible ambivalence about woman," and the "countless, competing meanings to woman" militate against definitive statements regarding Nietzsche's position on the Women's Question.[23]

A second strategy to recruit Nietzsche for concerns of feminism regards his philosophy as generally hostile to a patriarchal framework and therefore an indispensable aid to a reinterpretation of women, regardless of what Nietzsche actually wrote about women. Sometimes this appropriation of Nietzsche takes the form of drawing inspiration from the general liberationist tenor of his discourse. Much like the first wave of feminists in Germany, these feminists of more recent vintage find Nietzsche's philosophical outlook to be conducive to their own concerns. Thus the iconoclasm of Zarathustra is appealing to one critic, who notes parallel aims between Nietzsche's most celebrated philosophical spokesman and feminists of the twentieth century: "If we take seriously the feminist ideal of a nonoppressive society, and if the creation of such a future involves the destruction of old norms and patterns of being and relating, then we may still have something to learn from Zarathustra, who was also attempting to prepare the way for something better." This writer is able to "ignore the way in which Nietzsche's texts exclude or belittle women" and to consider him "a feminist" because his philosophy "gives me some suggestions as to how to transform the often ugly and nauseating 'truths' that are my cultural resource into something I can affirm in the present."[24] A more frequent and philosophically sophisticated tactic in considering Nietzsche an advocate of the cause of women is to regard the feminist implications of passages in which Nietzsche argues that oppositions are part of a metaphysical delusion of previous philosophies. The second aphorism in the initial section of *Beyond Good and Evil* is an important foundational text in dealing with metaphysical oppositions, but we should note that calling into question putative oppositions and their hierarchical ordering of terms, then reversing or subverting this hierarchy, is also part of the standard practice of deconstruction from its very inception. Indeed, to a large extent deconstruction drew its inspiration for the subversion of dualistic hierarchy from a close reading of Nietzsche's texts. In *Beyond Good and Evil*, Nietzsche begins by interrogating the notion that something cannot arise from its opposite. These sorts of judgments, he asserts "constitute the typical prejudice by which we can always recognize the metaphysicians of every age." Oppositions are foundational for metaphysical thought, and it follows that to go beyond metaphysics we must overcome *"the belief in the opposition of values"* (JGB 2, KSA 5.16). Although Nietzsche is writing specifically about matters such as "truth" and "falsehood," or "radiant contemplation" and "covetous desire," if we extend his aversion to oppositions from the realm of philosophical values into the arena of gender roles, then we could postulate Nietzsche might oppose the antithesis between man and woman and, in keeping with his valorization of the putatively inferior term, become an advocate for the feminine. Thus even if we admit that Nietzsche wrote in a derogatory fashion about women, women's rights, and feminism, we can claim that his philosophy contains "the seeds of a deconstruction of that misogyny." This sort of reasoning can lead to rather strange assertions. If we believe that Nietzsche's most fundamental insight was his "attack on dualism," then we may be forced to conclude that his misogynist remarks "miss the point," that they violate his own philosophy. One commentator was therefore driven to claim that Nietzsche was not "philosophically entitled to hold" the negative view on women he often expressed.[25] There are other areas of appeal in Nietzsche's philosophy: his materialism and discussion of the body, or his remarks on style and metaphor. The inference contained in this second strategy, however, is clear: if Nietzsche's philosophy possesses an internal consistency, such that his epistemological and ethical claims operate with the same sort of logic as his statements on social issues and gender, then he must go beyond the philosophically facile, misogynist positions he propounds with regard to woman and the feminine.[26]

A final and culminating strategy to associate Nietzsche with positions more favorable to feminism combines the first two strategies. The ambivalence associated with his views on woman becomes its defining role in deconstructive philosophy. Woman, or the figure of woman, is regarded as one of the key "non-concepts" so central to deconstruction. Like "writing" (or "arche- or proto-writing"), "différance," "supplement," or "pharmakon," as well as other terms Derrida developed in his endeavor to discuss a non-metaphysical philosophical position, woman can be conceived as a "non-concept" informing the binary opposition of man and woman, male and female. In *Spurs*, Derrida outlines three fundamental propositions about woman. In the first, which we recognize as the tradition of philosophical misogyny, she is "censured, debased and despised." In the second proposition she continues to be censured, debased, and despised, but "only in this case it is as the figure or potentate of truth." Derrida is referring to the Nietzschean identification of the "true world" with woman and Christianity in *Twilight of the Idols* (GD, Wie die "wahre Welt" endlich zur Fabel wurde, KSA 6.80). In the third proposition ascribed to Nietzsche, woman is no longer negative; she is "recognized and affirmed as an affirmative power, a dissimulatress, an artist, a dionysiac."[27] She has escaped the pernicious dichotomy of man and woman, and reached the stage of self-affirmation. Luce Irigaray expresses a similar thought when she connects woman and truth; her more psychoanalytic approach includes the dichotomy of pleasure and pain as well. "If error becomes the 'truth' of pleasure, the 'idea' becomes woman. Woman becomes the possibility of a 'different' idea, which amounts to a store of strength."[28] The notion of woman as a non-concept that informs a conceptual realm of metaphysical oppositions is more clearly articulated in the collection *Nietzsche and the Feminine*. One contributor explains the position of woman outside of binary pairs quite lucidly: "Excluding 'woman' both from the traditionally male and the traditionally female realm and including 'woman' in his philosophical discourse as both truth and deception (the negative side of truth), Nietzsche undercuts a bivalent or Aristotelian logic that operates on distinctions like male and female, truth and deception, or being and appearance."²⁹ And focusing more on the psychoanalytic topos of woman as castrated, but also castrating, a topos that Derrida and Irigaray both develop in their writings, another critic notes that Nietzsche can be harnessed for "a covert, and (pro)creative, feminism: in depicting woman as subversive metaphor, as a liberating, deceitful *différance*. Nietzsche is thereby shown to propose the creation of a metafeminine, namely, the figure of a woman who is supremely—if perhaps somewhat too neatly—transvalued beyond all passive, castrated good as well as overactive, castrating evil."³⁰ In all of these revaluations of woman or the figure of woman in Nietzsche's writings, her ambivalent position within, but also outside of, the commonplace binary terms of the metaphysical tradition transforms her into a philosophical dynamo that disrupts and overturns the status quo of thought. Her essence is to have no essence, but rather to occupy a place in a deconstructive universe of non-concepts that underlies and informs conventional philosophical discourse.

At this point, we might be tempted to ask why in the two instances we have examined feminist thinkers strained to incorporate a writer who has been identified as a misogynist by so many readers, even by those who are sympathetic to women's issues. The feminist movement of the late nineteenth and early twentieth centuries certainly had many writers and thinkers, both male and female, they could select as models or precursors. Similarly, feminists of the late twentieth century have numerous men and women who have been engaged on the side of equality for women in word and deed. We should note that feminists are hardly the only individuals who have managed to interpret and adopt Nietzsche for their own purposes despite his open hostility to what they advocate. As we have already seen, despite the fact that Nietzsche was unreservedly hostile to anarchism, his most vocal initial supporters in the United States were involved with the anarchist press, and socialists were among early enthusiasts for Nietzsche, although Nietzsche's "aristocratic radicalism"³¹ was unequivocally opposed to socialism and even to parliamentary democracy. Nietzsche's attraction obviously goes well beyond his stated positions and is occasionally contrary to what we imagine might result from the views he expresses. It appears that Nietzsche's general popularity as a writer and thinker often trumps the statements he makes about political or gender issues, and part of his appeal is no doubt related to his brilliant style and the generally provocative nature of his expression. The overall impression that Nietzsche's message is emancipatory and his obvious superiority as a rhetorician can help us account for the urgency to claim Nietzsche for the feminist camp. Common to feminists at the beginning and end of the past century is the attractiveness of a celebrated thinker whose writings bristle with suggestive and stimulating implications. But uniting the first and second waves of feminism is also a neglect of the context in which Nietzsche makes his statements about women, the feminine, and feminism. Nietzsche's connections with actual women and his own familial situation were still occasionally mentioned in the early period of enthusiasm for his thought. But the tradition to which Nietzsche was responding, as well as the contemporary discourse into which he was venturing with his remarks on women, is ignored by almost all feminist commentators. For issues surrounding gender, women's rights, and the feminist movement, there was a rich biographical and historical context without which his remarks and reactions are difficult to understand. As we have seen in his comments on other social phenomena of his era, Nietzsche is an active participant in an ongoing conversation that has personal, social, and political dimensions. It is certainly possible to abstract from Nietzsche's texts a lesson that may be consonant with certain tenets of feminism and in this fashion to rescue him from remarks that are obviously misogynistic. But if we are going to comprehend Nietzsche's views and their apparent contradictions, we have to eschew philosophical abstractions and seek to discover the ways in which Nietzsche was responding to exigencies of his times.

The Women's Movement and Nietzsche

Nietzsche lived at a time when men and women were becoming conscious of the subordinate position of women in the social order and began to do something about this inequity. Scholarship on the women's movement is fairly unanimous in its verdict that the first wave of activity in Germany is a phenomenon occurring during the last third of the nineteenth century, during the very years when Nietzsche was intellectually active. Nietzsche was personally acquainted with many women who were quite aware of the women's movement and who were to an extent pioneers in advocating women's rights, especially in the realm of higher education. Through these women or through his own reading, Nietzsche had some familiarity with the "first women's movement," its demands, and the chief proponents of women's emancipation. Indeed, Leipzig, about fifty kilometers from Naumburg, where Nietzsche was raised, and the city in which he studied classical philology at the university, was a central location for the early women's movement in Germany. Although there were important precursors to the first wave of activities around women's rights—notably in the wake of the French Revolution and in the German *Vormärz* (the "Pre-March" period between 1840 and 1848)—the birth of the modern women's movement in Germany is usually considered the first conference of the General German Women's Association (ADF) [*Allgemeiner deutscher Frauenverein*], which took place from 15 to 18 October 1865 in Leipzig. This gathering was the first large public meeting organized by women: Louise Otto-Peters (1819–1889) and Auguste Schmidt (1833–1902) were the most important members of the newly formed organization and the driving force behind the conference.[32] These two women had established the Women's Educational Organization [*Frauenbildungsverein*] in Leipzig on 24 February 1865, and it grew rapidly from its initial membership of thirty-five to over one hundred by the summer. In contrast to other organizations that dealt with women's issues, the ADF was not directed solely toward charity and support for women, but was meant from the outset to promote a fuller integration of women into German society. It emphasized education, employment, and the expansion of opportunities for women to improve their lot in the male-dominated social order. As chair of the Women's Educational Organization and the organizing committee for the conference, Otto-Peters delivered the welcoming address on Sunday evening, 15 October, in the hall of the booksellers' association of Leipzig. Schmidt followed her on the podium and spoke at greater length on work.[33] Indeed, the connection between the ADF and the incipient workers' movement was obvious from the very outset when the singers from the workers' educational association [*Arbeiterbildungsverein*] opened the festivities. Although Schmidt gave due consideration to the traditional work of women in the home, she argued that changes in society have now demanded a greater and different role for women. "Work," she asserted, "is the purest and highest happiness that we can achieve on earth." Family and motherhood are noble activities, but she demanded that women be granted "the right to participate in the great labor market of life." If they are not accorded this right, they will deteriorate intellectually and physically. In preparation for their appearance as equals in work, "it is necessary that women be given a general human education," whose purpose is not to confound the differences of the sexes, but "to provide women with the possibility and ability to recognize and achieve the ideal of the highest femininity."[34] As modest and deferential as this inaugural speech may appear to us today, it represented in its context a departure from norms that predominated in German society and that appeared to many men and women as the natural course of life.[35]

While Otto-Peters was opening the conference in Leipzig and Schmidt was delivering her address to the group, Nietzsche was celebrating his twenty-first birthday. He was in Berlin, having traveled there from Bonn to the home of his friend Hermann Mushacke (1845–1905), and was fast becoming close to Mushacke's father Eduard (d. 1873), a *Gymnasium* teacher in Berlin.[36] The two students left Berlin shortly thereafter, and on 17 October, while the "First German Women's Conference" was still debating various matters, they arrived in Leipzig, where they found housing and made plans for the continuation of their studies at the city's celebrated university. The great historical event concerning women occurring in Leipzig went completely unnoticed by Nietzsche, if we judge by his correspondence and the retrospective account of his initial days in Leipzig found in his notebooks (Nachlass 1864–68, 60[1], KGW I 4.506–28). More important for the budding classical philologist was the fact that Goethe had enrolled at the same university a hundred years before him (to Eduard Mushacke, 19 October 1865, Nr. 481, KSB 2.88); he also needed to settle accounts from his previous university life by withdrawing officially from the student fraternity "Frankonia" (to Convent der Burschenschaft Frankonia, 20 October 1861, Nr. 482, KSB 2.88–89). The concerns of women in German society were far from his thoughts, although we should note that there were a large number of men who engaged themselves in the struggle for women's rights even in these early years. Chief among them was Philipp Anton Korn (1810–1866), a retired officer in the Austrian army, who was essential in promoting the conference, served with Otto-Peters and Schmidt as a featured speaker on the evening of 15 October, and even offered his newspaper as the public organ for the ADF. Indeed, so many men took an active interest in this organization that the second statute of the ADF had to account for their official status. Evidently, after a protracted debate in which many women favored the same level of membership for both sexes, the men agreed (and had supported) a subsidiary and honorary role "with advisory vote."[37] Nietzsche's lack of interest and concern for these matters was more typical in the male world, however, but his indifference to the Women's Question in 1865 is not of central importance. What matters is that Nietzsche's mature life and the beginnings of the women's movement in Germany and throughout Europe were coincidental. Unlike philosophers from the long tradition of misogyny who commented in a derogatory fashion about women—from Plato to Schopenhauer[38]—Nietzsche's remarks were always formulated in the context of an actual social movement for women's rights. His comments are thus in dialogue with more than a philosophical heritage hostile to women; they are responses to women (and men) and movements flourishing in Europe of the late nineteenth century.

During Nietzsche's lifetime, the women's movement was hardly monolithic. There were various goals depending on the radicalness of the proponents, and there were obvious differences that resulted from class distinctions. The ADF was part of a liberal, middle-class women's movement that resembled to a certain degree analogous groupings in Western Europe and the United States, but, as Richard Evans has argued, it lagged noticeably behind its counterparts because of the politically fragmented nature of Germany and the pervasive tenacity of patriarchal conditions, especially in the eastern regions of the nation. In Evans's judgment, organizations like the ADF "had already retreated from the radicalism of 1848 and in the following decades as liberalism in Germany . . . withdrew even further and compromised more and more with the existing order, the General Association followed suit."[39] The socialist women's movement was of a somewhat different nature, focusing on the working conditions of women, rather than their integration into the workforce, and on labor practices and wage rates, rather than educational opportunities. It is unlikely that Nietzsche took note of the breadth and diversity of women's concerns. He was obviously less familiar with the socialist women's movement and generally ignorant of the main writings of the leaders of German socialism; as we saw in the previous chapter, frequent remarks in his writings indicate that he considered Eugen Dühring (1833–1921) the central theoretician of socialist thought.[40] But we do have evidence that he was acquainted with August Bebel's (1840–1913) writings on women, specifically the book *Woman in the Past, Present, and Future*, which was an early version of the extremely popular title *Woman and Socialism*.[41] This evidence appears in a letter written to Heinrich Köselitz in August 1885, when Nietzsche asks his friend to send him a citation from Elizabeth Blackwell, to whom Bebel refers in his book (Nr. 624, KSB 7.86–87).[42] We can conclude from this request that Nietzsche had probably read at least parts of Bebel, perhaps during the previous spring, when he had visited Köselitz in Venice. Bebel had been present at the inaugural conference of the ADF, and in 1869 he founded the Social Democratic Workers' Party of Germany (SDAP), which, as we saw in the previous chapter, in 1875 merged with the German Workers' Association to form the Socialist Workers' Party of Germany (SAPD). His book on women went through fifty-three editions during his lifetime and was the most popular socialist text of the nineteenth century. Nietzsche was not interested in Bebel, however, or his views on women, or the socialism he advocated, but only in the citation from Elizabeth Blackwell (1821–1910), an interesting figure in her own right. She was not only the first woman to receive a medical degree in the United States (from Geneva Medical College, later Hobart College), but also the founder of the New York Infirmary in New York City (1857), a hospital staffed solely by women, as well as the London School of Medicine for Women (1869). Nietzsche vaguely recalls that Bebel cites Blackwell concerning the urgency of sexual needs in women, and he requests the exact quotation from Köselitz. Köselitz, cooperative as always, produces the only two Blackwell citations he finds in Bebel's text, but neither of them deal with the topic Nietzsche had recalled, and so he assumes that Nietzsche is referring to a passage in which Bebel writes about this topic without citing Blackwell. It appears, however, that Köselitz misses a passage in which Bebel cites Blackwell referring to the sexual drive as an indispensable condition of life and the foundation of society.[43] It is possible that Nietzsche was recalling another passage from a Dr. Hegerich, which appears directly after the citation from Blackwell and refers to the deleterious effects of sexual abstinence on women. In either case, he is less interested in issues of women's rights or equality than in women's sexual drives and desires. Köselitz offers to send him Bebel's book, remarking in a derogatory fashion that "it can easily be dumped where the bookcase is deepest" (Nr. 292, KGB III 4.50–51), but Nietzsche responds that he meant another quote and that the entire matter is not very important (22 September 1865, Nr. 430, KSB 7.94). As far as we can ascertain, this reference to Bebel's book marks the extent of Nietzsche's preoccupation with the socialist women's movement of his time. There is no indication that he had any greater interest in the problems of working women than he had in the problems of the working class in general.

The bourgeois women's movement played a larger role in Nietzsche's life, in particular the discussion of women and education, which, along with marriage, divorce, and other legal issues, was a central point of contestation. As Evans points out, the bourgeois women's movement during Nietzsche's lifetime focused largely on two concerns: "the improvement of women's education and the admission of women to the medical profession."[44] With regard to higher education, which was Nietzsche's particular preoccupation since his own entrance to university studies in 1864, it is noteworthy that in Switzerland, where Nietzsche taught and lived for the first half of the last twenty years of his sane existence, he was confronted directly with emancipatory tendencies. At the time of his tenure in Basel, Swiss universities were in the forefront of the European movement for women's integration into higher education, in particular for women who could speak German. Although the United States seems to have taken the lead in both the matriculation of women— Oberlin College admitted both women and African Americans from its inception in 1833[45]—and in the establishment of women's institutions of higher education—for example, the women's medical colleges established in Philadelphia and Boston in 1850 and 1856—in Western Europe, women's admission to a formerly male bastion began to become a reality with increasing frequency during the last four decades of the nineteenth century. Beginning with France in 1863, which matriculated women in all fields except theology, the barriers prohibiting women from higher education gradually fell across the continent: in Switzerland in 1864; in Sweden, Denmark, England, Italy, and the Netherlands in the 1870s; and in Norway in the 1880s. In Germany, women were not officially admitted to university studies until 1908, although women did attend courses as auditors and petitioned to take examinations in various disciplines before that time. In 1905, there were eighty full-time women students at German universities, but once they were allowed to matriculate more easily, the numbers rapidly grew. By 1910, there were 1,867, and four years later, 4,126 women were enrolled.[46] This central issue of the middle-class women's movement touched Nietzsche's life in a very palpable fashion. Although Basel was the most conservative Swiss university with regard to admitting women—the first woman student was admitted only in 1890—he was aware of the fact that women were either being educated or demanding education in neighboring schools. Many of his closest women friends, as we shall see in a moment, were pioneering female students at Swiss institutions. Indeed, Nietzsche himself in his early years as a professor seems to have supported the demand for women to obtain a university degree. In 1875, he voted on the side of the faculty members who proposed to extend permission for a woman to pursue her examinations at Basel, but the petition was turned down by a vote of six to four, Jacob Burckhardt being among those who voted with the majority.[47]

Nietzsche's Women Friends

Although Nietzsche took little interest in the women's movement and its demands, it is noteworthy that many of the women he knew personally were pioneers in breaking the gender barrier in higher education. The best known of these women is Lou Salomé, who arrived in Zurich in the fall of 1880 and audited courses in theology, philosophy, archaeology, and art history at the University of Zurich during both the winter semester 1880–81 and the summer semester 1881. Salomé was the daughter of a Huguenot family that had immigrated northward from Strasbourg, eventually settling in St. Petersburg. The family was ennobled by Czar Nicholas I, and Lou's father rose in the ranks of the military to general. Her mother was a woman from northern Germany of Danish extraction, and in order to honor their heritage, French and German were the languages in the Salomé household.[48] Lou also learned Russian, and as an inhabitant of Russia she is illustrative of the scores of Russian women who flocked to Zurich during the 1870s and 1880s to receive an education. Statutes in Russian universities in 1863 made it clear that women would be excluded from universities and that the government had no plans to establish separate institutions for the higher education of women. Zurich became a destination for Russian women, many of them Jewish, because higher education was closed to them in their country, but also because there was already a colony of Russian men studying in Zurich, and the university was one of the only European institutions that was prepared to matriculate women. Indeed, between 1867, when the first Russian women graduated with a degree in medicine, and 1914, Zurich hosted five to six thousand Russian women. Salomé thus traversed a well-traveled route from Russia to Zurich, but she differed from the typical Russian student in two regards. Most of her fellow women students had entered Switzerland to obtain a degree in medicine, many of them harboring the hope of returning to Russia and practicing what they had learned in the service of their motherland.[49] Salomé had apparently no interest in this career path: she had received instruction in Russia in what we would call today the liberal arts from a Danish pastor, Henrik Gillot (1836–1916), who, like many men she met, fell in love with her and precipitated her departure for foreign lands. At the university, Salomé was seeking not a professional degree, but a philosophical education; for that reason, once she left Zurich because of illness after her initial year, she found it attractive to be together with educated men, such as Nietzsche or his friend Paul Rée (1849–1901), to continue her education. Unlike most of the Russian women who came to Switzerland, Salomé was also not officially matriculated in a degree program in Zurich. She was something like an auditor, and had her weak lungs not caused an interruption in her university training, it is difficult to determine what her further course of studies would have entailed. Much has been written about Nietzsche and Salomé, the triangle with

Paul Rée, and the ultimate separation of Nietzsche from both his friend and the young woman he imagined as his protégé.[50] Salomé's intelligence is beyond question, but the judgments concerning her relationship to feminism and the women's movement have always been rather ambivalent. Hedwig Dohm, whom we met above, considered her an adversary of women's rights.[51] During her year in Zurich, Salomé had studied with the leftist intellectual Gottfried Kinkel (1815–1882), whose views certainly supported women's emancipation, but she was at best skeptical of feminism, as she understood its manifestation in the nineteenth century. In many ways, she was an example of a liberated woman in her own actions, but her views on women are not easily integrated into the progressive movements for women's rights that were flourishing in Europe of the late nineteenth century. Although, as we shall see, as a person she may have played a decisive role for Nietzsche in his attitude toward women and women's emancipation, her intellectual interactions with the philosopher do not appear to have had a bearing on his attitude toward the Women's Question.

Salomé was not an isolated example of an academic woman in Nietzsche's life. Most of the women he knew and who were attracted to him were highly educated, especially for the era, and Nietzsche related to these women as intellectual equals. One such acquaintance was Resa von Schirnhofer (1855–1948), an Austrian woman who, like Salomé and so many other women, studied at the University of Zurich. Nietzsche met her in Nice during the spring of 1884 while she was on Easter break from her university studies, and they spent time together on several occasions over the next few years discussing various topics of mutual interest. In 1889, Schirnhofer became one of the first Austrian women to obtain a doctorate in philosophy, completing a dissertation on "A Comparison Between the Teachings of Schelling and Spinoza." Schirnhofer never became active as a feminist, but Nietzsche recognized that many of her friends were champions of women's rights, and he was aware that his own published remarks against women were regarded as offensive. In a letter to Schirnhofer from May 1884, he writes that regarding geniuses one has to be "properly humane, *even* if they are women [*Weiberchen*]," and in using the diminutive Nietzsche realizes the derogatory nature of his comment and adds: "But I know how you yourself think about this" (Nr. 510, KSB 6.502). And in a letter from June 1885, he reports that Louise Röder-Wiederhold, a woman serving briefly as his secretary through the recommendation of Heinrich Köselitz, is still tolerating his "anti-democratic attitude," but he fears she will flee him and Sils Maria because she is "baptized in the blood of 1848." He then adds: "It is also pretty bad with my views on women 'per se.' Enough, I suspect that no one will be able to stand me much longer" (Nr. 607, KSB 7.59). Although she remained on good terms with Nietzsche and, after his lapse into insanity, his sister Elisabeth, Schirnhofer did not write about her experiences with the philosopher until 1937. In her recollections, she clearly places herself in the position of a deferential admirer of Nietzsche—she was eleven years his junior and a student, while he was a "retired" professor and the author of many books—but she does emphasize that he treated her with respect and without condescension.[52] The single passage where Schirnhofer reports that she and Nietzsche broached the topic of women relates to the notorious comment about the whip from *Zarathustra*. "At one point he told me I should not take offense at the passage about the whip—which later became so infamous—in *Zarathustra*," Schirnhofer reports, "which would not have occurred to me since I did not consider it a general judgment about women, but rather a poetic generalization of individual cases."[53] Nietzsche evidently explained cursorily the origins of the counsel the old woman gives Zarathustra and about whom Nietzsche was thinking when he wrote it, but she does not reveal any names and refers the reader instead to the explanation Förster-Nietzsche supplies in her book on Nietzsche and women.

Förster-Nietzsche complains that the whip remark has unfairly made her brother appear to be a misogynist and that, in part at least, the writing of her book on *Friedrich Nietzsche and the Women of His Time* was meant to correct this misconception. The origin of the remark about the whip, according to Nietzsche's sister, lies in a novella by Ivan Turgenev (1818–1883), "First Love" (1860), in which we encounter a flirtatious young woman of twenty-one, a boy of sixteen who falls in love with her and later narrates the tale, and the boy's father, with whom the young woman is infatuated. In a final meeting between the young woman and the father, the older man strikes her with a riding crop, leaving a red welt on her white arm. Nietzsche, according to his sister, shared with her various humorous remarks about this story, but resolutely condemned the father's brutal treatment of the woman who loved him. Förster-Nietzsche reports, however, that in discussing this plot with her brother, she told him of several cases where only forceful action on the part of a man could hold a woman in check, and that if the "symbolic whip" was no longer a threat to her, a woman would take unfair advantage of a man. Nietzsche concurred and was able to cite several cases himself where such treatment was appropriate. Nietzsche then exclaimed facetiously that his sister was advising men to use a whip on women, which she denied, and he responded by claiming that the whip was certainly inappropriate "for llamas and for all reasonable, virtuous women,"[54] who must be treated with love and tender consideration. The following year, when Nietzsche included the advice about the whip in the first part of *Zarathustra*, the two siblings spoke about it as an inside joke. Although it is difficult to see how anyone else could have understood the source of this remark, she claims that Nietzsche was nonetheless upset about the inability of his readers to fathom the novelty and originality of his writings and also the deadly seriousness that caused them to misunderstand his intentions, in particular with regard to this section of his book. Many women, Förster-Nietzsche adds, "especially the emancipated ones and their champions at that time blundered regarding the whip passage."⁵⁵ Förster-Nietzsche's explanation, which can never be fully trusted, has several obvious functions: It transfers the responsibility for her brother's most notorious misogynistic statement from Nietzsche to her, thus making her the furtive source for this utterance and removing any stain from her brother. It also accounts for the scandalous passage in *Zarathustra* by claiming its origins in a private, intimate conversation between two siblings, thus allowing her to appear privy to Nietzsche's innermost thoughts in the early 1880s.

That Schirnhofer was apparently so willing to accept this explanation indicates perhaps her gullibility in her dealing with Förster-Nietzsche, but also her readiness to absolve Nietzsche, whom she deeply respected, from any association with attitudes that were antiwoman. Indeed, we find in the writings of many women with whom Nietzsche associated an unwillingness to acknowledge his misogyny or at least a sense of bafflement that the man they knew could have penned such derogatory statements about their sex and the women's movement. A chief reason for this attitude was that in his comportment with women, every account we possess agrees that Nietzsche was polite, accommodating, and thoughtful. In his letters to Schirnhofer, for example, he always expresses concern with her academic progress and dissertation topic, not giving a hint that in his writings he characterized women who strive for education and autonomy as an unwarranted departure from true femininity or a contribution to the "uglification" of Europe (JGB 232, KSA 5. 170). In her report, Schirnhofer writes of his "tone of utmost admiration" for Malwida von Meysenbug (1816–1903), their mutual friend who was responsible for their friendship, and how Nietzsche spoke of Lou Salomé's "extraordinary discernment." In relating their brief rendezvous in Zurich, Schirnhofer refers to "an old, ailing, intelligent English woman, Mrs. Fynn," who was a devout Catholic whom Nietzsche greatly admired. Schirnhofer is referring to Emily Fynn, who summered with her daughter, also named Emily, in Sils Maria and knew Nietzsche in the 1880s. Nietzsche, Schirnhofer continues, begged Mrs. Fynn "with tears in his eyes" not to read his books because he knew that so much of what he had written would be deeply offensive to her. For her part, Fynn wrote in defense of Nietzsche's attitude toward women some eight years after the philosopher's death:

> Our philosopher has also been falsely accused of hating and disrespecting feminine individuals. On the contrary, he had a sincere admiration for the capacities of women; for their heart, their intelligence, the force of their will and resistance. Nietzsche's sincere friendship for diverse distinguished women, the deference that he showed for all women, no matter who they were, young or old, beautiful or ugly, intelligent or not, proves conclusively that Nietzsche did not despise women.⁵⁶

Helen Zimmern (1846–1934), an early translator of Nietzsche's writings, supplies further confirmation of Nietzsche's exemplary behavior around women. In an interview, she was asked about Nietzsche's attitude toward women, and she immediately understands that this question was posed because of his reputation for hostility to women and women's emancipation. But she too denies any misogynistic tendencies: "According to my experiences I can only say that Nietzsche always was of the most perfect 'gentilezza.' There are apparently men who have theories about women that they never put into practice. There are apparently others who can combine brutal practice with the most beautiful theories. Nietzsche certainly belonged to the first category." She continues in her account, citing an incident with an old Russian woman, Madame de Mansuroff (1830–1899), who refused to leave her room for a coach that would convey her to a warmer climate in Italy. Nietzsche intervened with her and "appeared at the front door of the hotel with the sick lady, who followed him obediently like a little dog, whereas she otherwise used to fly into a rage at the very mention of the journey."[57] The testimony we possess from women with whom Nietzsche was acquainted is unanimous in its verdict: Nietzsche evidenced no trace of misogyny in his social intercourse with women. In personal interactions, he was a gentleman whose conduct with the opposite sex was beyond reproach.[58]

To this point, we have considered women who had a marginal association with feminism and the women's movement. Nietzsche's relationship with women more dedicated to women's rights and equality evidences some similarities, but there are more periods of friction. Meta von Salis (1855–1929) provides a good illustration of a woman Nietzsche knew well and who admired his work, but who was still committed to positions on women with which Nietzsche disagreed in his writings. By the time she met Nietzsche in July 1884, she was already familiar with his writings since she frequented the circle of women around Malwida von Meysenbug. She was also already outspoken in her advocacy of women's issues and pursuing an advanced degree at Zurich. As she writes in her memoir on Nietzsche,[59] which is actually less about the philosopher than about Salis herself, she had come to understand that men accorded to women limited opportunities for self-realization: "Not only my father, almost all men with whom I came into contact during the first 24 years of my life imposed on women a position that I found unworthy of them, or at least of me" (18). Salis's experiences—being sent away to a boarding school to train for appropriately female pursuits; her exclusion from any demanding educational path—turned her against men in general: "So I grew into a position of complete opposition to men. Wherever I found myself—in the second boarding school, at home, at social gatherings, in my first situation abroad—everywhere I stood in opposition against men and tried to awaken in women the feeling for their individual self-esteem" (19). Indeed, she reports that in a conversation with Nietzsche she informed him that the doctorate had little meaning for her, but that "in the interest of the women's question" she "did not want to leave the university without obtaining it" (14). Despite her radical views, we should recognize that Salis was an unusual sort of feminist. She was somewhat of an elitist and individualist, believing that it would be the accomplishments of individual women that would advance the Women's Question, not the large congresses of the women's movement, which she demeans by associating it with the "happiness of the herd" and a "deceptive superficiality" (20). Her feminism had therefore a Nietzschean tinge, which perhaps explains her ability to overlook his misogyny. She recognizes and appreciates, as other women did, his courtesy toward women, especially older women, and although she sees the "increasing sharpness of tone in his judgment" of women as a shortcoming, she grants him "the right to err in this one area" (20). Besides, she reasons, the worst things he wrote are accurate for the majority of women today and do not originate in a negative assessment of women (21). She goes on to cite some of the passages we have seen quoted earlier that praise women. Finally, she notes that although she cannot completely forgive his remarks about women, he made comments no less harsh about men (22). Nietzsche, for his part, shows some respect and perhaps even admiration for Meta von Salis, but in his correspondence to others he does make several snide remarks about her. When she fails to receive permission to study with Jacob Burckhardt (1818–1897) in Basel, he likens her to an "agent provocateur" who got exactly what she wanted with the rejection: something she could use to agitate for the movement (to Franz Overbeck, 31 March 1885, Nr. 589 KSB 7.35).[60] He gossips with his sister about other women's dislike of her, including Schirnhofer's, although he voices his approval because she values "good manners" even if she is "Swiss-rigid" (5 July 1885, Nr. 611, KSB 7.65). At one point, he doubts that she can understand his *Beyond Good and Evil* (to Franziska Nietzsche, 15 January 1887, Nr. 791, KSB 8.10). And on two occasions, he indicates that he does his best to tolerate conversations with Salis, implying that she is of little interest for him (to Franziska Nietzsche, 3 August 1887, Nr. 885, KSB 8.120; to Elisabeth Förster, 15 October 1887, Nr. 925, KSB 8.166–67).[61] Whether Salis's overt commitment to women's issues precipitated Nietzsche's ambivalence is impossible to determine. But we can establish that her unwavering admiration for him[62] and his respect for her in personal interaction were not always matched by his privately expressed opinions.

Undoubtedly the most important woman proponent of emancipation with whom Nietzsche was acquainted was Malwida von Meysenbug. Nietzsche met her first at the groundbreaking ceremony for the Bayreuth opera house in May 1872, and their friendship lasted until the end of Nietzsche's sane life with only one brief period of estrangement. Aside from Nietzsche's family, his colleague Franz Overbeck (1837–1905), and the composer Heinrich Köselitz (1854–1918), her correspondence with Nietzsche is the longest and most substantial; it lasted from the early 1870s until the outbreak of Nietzsche's insanity and contains over fifty communications from Nietzsche's side alone. Meysenbug was extremely important for Nietzsche's social life during the 1870s and 1880s: her circle of friends and acquaintances supplied Nietzsche with many of his social contacts, especially the educated women he knew, whom Meysenbug refers to at one point as the "troop of Amazons" (26 March 1887, Nr. 447, KGB III 6.40). Although by the time Nietzsche met her, she, like Wagner, whom she had met in the early 1860s and greatly admired, had already begun to exhibit more conservative proclivities, she was widely known for her progressive views on women's education and admired by the younger generation who began their studies at Swiss institutions. Her belief that women should be encouraged to develop themselves as autonomous individuals and her rejection of religion also brought her into contact with leading socialists of her time, including Giuseppe Mazzini (1805–1872) and Alexander Herzen (1812–1870), so that she had a reputation as a somewhat radical supporter of women's emancipation. Her three-volume autobiography, *Memoirs of an Idealist* (1869–1876),[63] was acknowledged as a foundational work for middle-class women struggling to achieve equality of opportunity in a male-dominated educational system. It contains numerous passages in which Meysenbug champions the emancipation of women and equal educational access for women. In the preface, she writes expectantly of the day "on which the emancipation of the woman will be a completed task; on which she will have without any objection the same right to development of all her capabilities through instruction and study as any man; on which she will be an equal in the eyes of the law and liberated from the yoke of ignorance, superstition, frivolity, and fashion." As she relates her own experiences in the "pre-March" [*Vormärz*] period (1840–48) and during the revolutionary struggles of 1848 and 1849, she returns time and again to "the necessity to extend education to women" (192), focusing on "the emancipation of woman, emancipation from the prejudices that until now have kept her fettered" (210). Meysenbug writes with an optimism about the future that attracted women of the next generation to her. Her engagement with women's issues even after the failed revolution convinced her that she had participated in a movement that would conclude in gender equality: "The thought of women on a course to complete freedom of their intellectual development, to economic independence, and to the possession of all civil rights had already been set in motion: this thought could not be extinguished" (287). There is probably no single book by a German woman of the 1848 generation that exercised a more palpable influence on the middle-class women's movement during the second half of the nineteenth century.

This direct and passionate advocacy for women's liberation was inspiring for the women studying in Zurich in the 1880s, but her engagement for a noble cause was also strongly validated by Nietzsche in the 1870s, when he became acquainted with Meysenbug and her writing. During the initial years of Nietzsche's friendship with Meysenbug, he does not appear to be interested at all in feminism or women's emancipation. But in letters, he indicates both a familiarity with, and approval of, her *Memoirs*. In 1869, Meysenbug had published her autobiographical account anonymously in French under the title *Mémoires d'une Idéaliste* and gave Nietzsche a copy of this book on a visit to Basel in 1872.[64] She explains that it is "truth without poetry," playing on the title of Goethe's celebrated autobiography *Poetry and Truth* [*Dichtung und Wahrheit*] (1811), and describes it modestly as bagatelles that should never have been published (4 September 1872, Nr. 358, KGB I 4.74). Writing to his closest friend, Carl von Gersdorff, at the beginning of October, Nietzsche calls the book "very instructive and touching" and advises him enthusiastically to read it (Nr. 258, KSB 4.58). When he finally responds to Meysenbug, he tells her that he identifies with the difficult circumstances she has encountered and overcome. She serves as his inspiration: "I think of you and it warms my heart that I have met you, revered madam, a lonesome champion for justice" (7 November 1872, Nr. 270, KSB 4.82). This sort of identification is repeated in April 1874, when Nietzsche writes of the good fortune that happens "when those involved in the struggle encourage each other" and "remind each other of their common beliefs" (Nr. 357, KSB 4.216). When the three-volume German edition of the *Memoirs* appeared in 1876, Nietzsche is even more enthusiastic. He tells his friend Erwin Rohde (1845–1898) that it is "a mirror for every dedicated person, into which one looks with shame as well as encouragement; I haven't read anything for a long time that stirred me up so much inside and that brought me nearer to health" (14 April 1876, Nr. 519, KSB 5.150). Writing to Meysenbug the same day, he is even more effusive: the day he read her memoirs was the most solemn Sunday of his life; he was filled with a mood of purity and love; Meysenbug is a much higher form of himself; he will henceforth measure himself on her example. How can a man live in the face of her book and not be unmanly? Nietzsche asks. "He must do everything that you did and not anything more" (Nr. 518, KSB 5.148). This enthusiastic response indicates the intimacy Nietzsche felt with Meysenbug, and his desire to emulate her actions and spirit are signs of the great respect he felt for her. At the same time, we have to wonder what Nietzsche understood about the causes that most moved his friend in her memoirs and how much Nietzsche supported them. Although he had not yet taken up his vehemently adverse stance toward socialism and the women's movement, neither is there any indication in his writings, letters, or notebooks from the early 1870s that he had any special interest in the issues that are most crucial for Meysenbug's autobiography. The only cause that they shared at this point was the Wagnerian cultural renaissance, a cause that does not play a role in the memoirs and that has little to do with the ardent advocacy for women's rights. And the only remark in their correspondence that possibly indicates a tension between the two friends regarding Nietzsche's views on women occurs in a letter from February 1887, where he imputes to her the statement that he is "even worse than Schopenhauer" (Nr. 809, KSB 8.35).[65] It is therefore difficult to understand exactly what Nietzsche found so admirable in this three-volume work, and why he emphasizes time and again the commonalities he shares with his motherly friend.

There is one additional incident that may strike us as odd today, knowing how Nietzsche expressed himself about women and women's rights in the 1880s. In relating her experiences after the revolution of 1848, Meysenbug tells of her engagement in an institution dedicated to the education of young women and the propagation of egalitarian instruction for male and female members of society. In 1850, she enrolled as a student in the High School for Women [*Hochschule für das weibliche Geschlecht*] in Hamburg, the first such school established on German soil. She also became a member of the staff, contributing to the liberal and, at times, radical nature of the undertaking. Although this institution was short-lived, disbanding after only two years, the notion of a different sort of educational institution, one that would promote gender equality and progressive thought, remained very much alive in Meysenbug. In the summer of 1876, when Nietzsche, his friend Paul Rée, and the student Albert Brenner (1856–1878) lived with Meysenbug in Sorrento, she reports that she conceived the plan of establishing a coeducational school that would constitute something of a continuation of the Hamburg School for Women:

> I received at the time a great many letters from women and girls whom I did not know, and who expressed their sympathy with me on account of my *Memoirs of an Idealist*, as, to my great pleasure and satisfaction, has continued to occur in the ensuing years. This fact nourished an idea that I had harbored and that I imparted to my companions, namely, to found a kind of mission house, in order to promote in young adults of both sexes the free development of a noble intellectual life, so that once they went out into the world again they would sow the seeds of a new and more spiritualized culture. The idea was received enthusiastically by the gentlemen; Nietzsche and Rée were immediately ready to contribute as teachers. I was convinced that I could attract many women pupils to whom I wanted to dedicate my special care in order to educate them to be the most noble representatives of the emancipation of women, so that they could help eliminate misunderstandings and distortions from this important and significant cultural work and lead it in a pure, dignified expansion to a fortuitous extension.[66]

It is difficult to reconcile this image of Nietzsche as an active and willing participant in a co-educational experiment designed to foster women's emancipation with the man who later found woman as a type to be a "dangerous, creeping, subterranean little beast of prey" (EH, Warum ich so gute Bücher schreibe 5, KSA 6.306). If Meysenbug is accurate in her account, this incident provides us with some insight into how drastically Nietzsche's views on women changed from the mid-1870s until the late 1880s, but also perhaps how the free spirits of *Human, All Too Human*, the book on which Nietzsche was working while he was in the "colony" in Sorrento,[67] were originally conceived as a concrete, pedagogical, and coeducational project and not as an abstract, philosophical scheme.

Not all women Nietzsche encountered were as solicitous of him as Meysenbug. Helene Druskowitz (1856–1918),[68] whom Nietzsche met in 1884 through Meta von Salis, was a precocious and ambitious individual who showed considerably less tolerance for Nietzsche's philosophical views than Meysenbug, and although we do not possess very much evidence about her reactions to Nietzsche's most misogynistic comments, we can conclude that she was less inclined to pardon his transgressions in that area too. Born in 1856 in Vienna, she was trained at the conservatory as a pianist, and completed her preparatory studies in 1873. Since women at that time were not admitted to higher educational institutions in Austria, she moved with her mother to Zurich, studied philosophy, archaeology, German literature, and modern languages, and earned a doctorate from the university at the age of twenty-two. She was only the second woman to receive a doctorate from the first section of the philosophical faculty and evidently the first Austrian woman to complete her doctoral studies. Her dissertation topic dealt with Lord Byron's satiric poem *Don Juan*. Like many of the women intellectuals of her time, Druskowitz became increasingly interested in the women's movement and increasingly impatient with a male world that denied women the equality they merited. Following her university studies, she held lectures in Vienna, Munich, Zurich, and Basel, then traveled to North Africa, France, Italy, and Spain before returning to Vienna. There she lived as a freelance writer, employing a variety of pseudonyms and producing plays, translations, and essays. By 1884, she had shifted her focus from the male literary world of England to its women authors, publishing a book on *Three English Women Writers*, the dramatist Joanna Baillie (1762–1851), the lyricist Elizabeth Barrett-Browning (1806–1861), and the novelist George Eliot (1819–1880). Nietzsche obviously learned of her existence by the summer of 1882, since he asks Franz Overbeck for her address (18 July 1882, Nr. 270, KSB 6.229). Over the next two years, it is likely that he met her personally in Zurich, and he was initially impressed with her precocious intellect and her numerous publications. Writing to his sister Elisabeth in October 1884, Nietzsche speaks of his long walks with his new friend "Helene Druscowicz": "of all the women I know she is the one who has by a wide margin studied my books most seriously." He recommends to her the book Druskowitz has written on three English writers and tells her she is now working on a book on Shelley and a translation of Swinburne. And he continues: "I believe she is a noble and honest creature, who will do my 'philosophy' no harm" (Nr. 549, KSB 6.548). In August 1885, he asks Köselitz to send her a copy of the fourth part of *Zarathustra*, which was privately printed, making her one of the privileged few to receive a copy of this book (Nr. 618, KSB 7.76); and at one point, he expresses the desire to have his works appear in the same publishing house as hers (to Franziska and Elisabeth Nietzsche, 4/5 November 1884, Nr. 552 KSB 6.552). Nietzsche respected Meysenbug and admired her courage and fortitude, but there is no other woman with whom he was acquainted whose intellect and achievement he esteems—for a time, at least—more than Druskowitz's.

The mutual admiration between the two volatile thinkers did not last very long. By the end of 1884, Druskowitz had already confided in a letter to the Swiss author Conrad Ferdinand Meyer (1825–1898) that her enthusiasm for Nietzsche's philosophy was only a "passion du moment," and that she considers his treatment of serious philosophical questions "completely superficial." She adds, referring to *Zarathustra*: "Nietzsche's prophet pose seems ridiculous to me."[69] Nietzsche appears to have known nothing of her change of heart, at least initially, since he asked Köselitz eight months later to forward a copy of *Zarathustra* to her Vienna address. We do not possess Druskowitz's letter to Nietzsche after she read the final part of his magnum opus, but he must have conceived it as an enormous insult and betrayal; this event precipitates an irreparable rupture in their short-lived relationship.[70] Only the draft of Nietzsche's response to Druskowitz survives, and in this missive he refers to the "honest, albeit not exactly kind and insightful, and not especially 'modest' letter" that she had written (middle of August 1885, Nr. 623, KSB 7.84). As Druskowitz moved closer to radical feminist and philosophical pursuits, she grew even less tolerant of Nietzsche's excesses. In a book titled *Modern Attempts at a Substitute for Religion*, she devotes an entire chapter to Nietzsche, since she conceives of *Zarathustra* as his endeavor "to create a new gospel" (45). In reviewing his previous writings, she criticizes his aphoristic work for not treating any problem thoroughly and for a lack of originality; she recognizes him only as a great stylist. *Zarathustra*, from which she quotes extensively, is characterized as a Darwinian text, and since it is predicated on dubious assumptions about the perfectability of the human being, it is based on an error.[71] Having learned of this attack on his philosophy, Nietzsche completely rejects his former friend, protesting emphatically to the Swiss poet Carl Spitteler (1845–1924) that "the little literature-goose Druscowicz [sic] is anything but my 'pupil'" (17 September 1887, Nr. 914, KSB 8.159). Nietzsche fell into insanity before the publication of Druskowitz's positive appraisal of Eugen Dühring,[72] a philosopher Nietzsche had come to despise in the 1880s. He would no doubt have considered this book a logical consequence of her apostasy. Approximately two years after Nietzsche's mental collapse, Druskowitz was herself forced into a psychiatric hospital in Dresden, and after she was moved to Vienna, she remained institutionalized until her death in 1918. But she continued with a wide range of literary activities, composing dramas and a variety of feminist writings, and even helping to found the women's reviews *The Holy Struggle* [*Der heilige Kampf*] and *The Call to Feud* [*Der Fehderuf*]. Among her literary remains is the polemical pamphlet *Pessimistic Cardinal Principles: A Vademecum for the Most Free Spirits*. Druskowitz was obviously referencing Nietzsche with the subtitle, although the body of the work has very little to do with Nietzschean philosophy. The fourth chapter of the book, "The Male as Logical and Moral Impossibility and Curse of the World," provides a good indicator of the tenor of the discussion. Here is a sample of her misandrist screed:

> With regard to his constitution, the male is unworthy of a spouse, a hindrance to marriage and not a binding spirit. He does not fit at all in the framework of a reasonable world. For he is too crude and deceitful, his thought is too full of gaps and digressions, his external ugliness is too striking, that he would be able to master life in a tactful manner. . . . The male is an intermediate stage between human being and animal; he is a monstrosity and as such cynically and ridiculously equipped so that in full reality he is neither one nor the other.[73]

Later in this chapter Druskowitz disparages Nietzsche's concept of the will to power as a patriarchal and pernicious notion, observing: "To the most infamous stupidities by which Teutonicism is enslaved belongs therefore the admiration for a certain Nietzsche, who flattered that evil principle in the most damnable and moronic fashion."[74] Druskowitz could not have been ignorant of Nietzsche's remarks about women in his later writings, and although she nowhere addresses directly his misogyny, it is likely that her familiarity with his attitude toward women played a role in her acerbic repudiation of him and his philosophy.

It is difficult to make complete sense of Nietzsche's attitude toward women in the 1870s and 1880s. As we shall see, his later written comments exhibit a vehement condemnation of the women's movement and any advocacy for equality in education and civil rights. Yet his circle of closest friends consisted of women who were intellectually ambitious and champions of liberation. Many of them had a university education and were among the first women in Europe to earn an advanced degree. Those who had no official academic credentials were likewise engaged with intellectual activities, often dealing with philosophy and literature at a high level. Meysenbug, whose experience with the Women's Question extended back into the 1840s, was Nietzsche's consistent supporter and widely considered the "mother" of the first wave of feminist thinking in German-speaking countries. Although there were few activists among his female acquaintances, and although several came from the elite and aristocratic stratum of society, most of these women expressed enthusiastic support for women's emancipation and equality of opportunity. Meysenbug had known Nietzsche the longest, and in the initial years of her relationship with him, we find very little in his writings that would have been directly offensive to women. But most of the emancipated women whom Nietzsche knew made his acquaintance after 1882, when his first virulent remarks about women in *Zarathustra* had already appeared in print. Few of these women directly challenged Nietzsche on his misogynist tendencies; there is some evidence that indicates they noticed his antifeminist remarks, but none took these statements seriously enough to cause a disruption in their relationship. Only Druskowitz attacked him publicly, and her disagreements had as much to do with questions of religion and epistemology as women's rights. In his personal interactions with these emancipated women, as well as with other women, we find Nietzsche always portrayed as courteous and considerate; there are no reports of him entering into arguments with women over their social status. Indeed, there are various indications that he encouraged their intellectual pursuits, and in his early correspondence with Meysenbug, he appears convinced that they share common goals, and that among these goals is equal educational opportunity for women. We do note that Nietzsche was not always completely forthright in his discussions with women, and that he occasionally wrote dismissively about his women friends in private. But generally we cannot fail to notice that many of his statements about women and women's issues contrast crassly with his own behavior toward the women he knew.

Men Writing on the Women's Question

With the rise of the Women's Question in nineteenth-century Europe, there appeared an extensive discourse about women's rights and the women's movement. While many who contributed to this discourse were women, there were also quite a few men who voiced opinions that were both more substantial and more reflective than Nietzsche's sporadic outbursts. The commentators on the topic of Nietzsche and women have largely ignored the not inconsiderable discourse on the subjection and the emancipation of women in the late nineteenth century, in particular the male contributions to this discourse. Indeed, there is no evidence that Nietzsche was particularly interested in the many writings women themselves produced on education, marriage, or their own subjection. The essays of men were more important for Nietzsche than women's works, and often we have the impression that Nietzsche is more concerned with a male audience than with women, and with refuting the arguments offered by men for the extension of women's rights. Of central importance for him was the most famous and forceful contemporary male advocate of women's rights: John Stuart Mill (1806–1873).

Mill's seminal text *The Subjection of Women* appeared in 1869, the year in which Nietzsche assumed his professorship at Basel, and it became a topic of discussion in Germany almost immediately thereafter. In promoting the equality of women and opposing what he recognized as an "almost universal opinion,"[75] Mill was also contradicting some of Nietzsche's most cherished convictions. Mill regards the sexes as equal in intellectual capacity and abilities, but unequal through an unfortunate, retrograde, but correctable social order. The reason that inequality arose is explained through the difference in physical strength, which has now ceased to be a persuasive ground for its perseverance. The reason that inequality is maintained is explained by the persistence of institutions and mentalities that must now be altered for the good of society as a whole. Mill rejects the contention—based on a simplistic view of biology—that the natural vocation of women is to be wives and mothers, and considers the marriage contract to be little more than the means by which slavery for half of humanity has been institutionalized. He also repudiates as unproven arguments based on other pseudoscientific principles, such as the size of the brain. In all fields of endeavor, Mill argues, women should be granted full and unequivocal equality: in commerce, in education, in professions. His is a plea of reason, as well as passion. He repeatedly emphasizes the disparity between women's subjection and the exigencies of the contemporary world: "The social subordination of women thus stands out as an isolated fact in modern social institutions; a solitary breach of what has become their fundamental law; a single relic of an old world of thought and practice exploded in everything else, but retained in the one thing of most universal interest."[76] This subjugation is not only untimely, but also amoral. Indeed, Mill claims at one point that "the moral regeneration of mankind will only really commence, when the most fundamental of the social relations is placed under the rule of equal justice."[77] Mill thus situates the Women's Question at the center of cultural, legal, political, social, and ethical concerns. Women's emancipation is a necessity for the continued progress of the human race.

Especially in his later writings, Nietzsche came to disagree with Mill on this point and on just about every other facet of his philosophical outlook. Although he never refers directly to *The Subjection of Women*, we know from his occasional remarks that his regard for the Englishman was low, particularly with respect to moral philosophy. Mill represents an idealized ethics of equality and sympathy that runs counter to what Nietzsche propounds. While there are few references to him in the 1870s, by the 1880s Nietzsche was certainly familiar with his work. In the winter of 1880–81, for example, he comments in his notebooks: "The 'love of humanity' with the help of a reasonable education—Stuart Mill, too funny for words" (Nachlass 1880–81, 8[46], KSA 9.393). In the late 1880s in his published work, Nietzsche considers Mill a "mediocre intellect" (JGB 253, KSA 5.196) or one of his "impossibilities": "John Stuart Mill: or offensive clarity" (GD, Streifzüge eines Unzeitgemässen 1, KSA 6.111). In his last unpublished notes from his final two sane years, Nietzsche refers to him dismissively as a "flathead" (Nachlass 1887, 9[55]; 1887–88, 11[148], KSA 12.362, 13.70). That Nietzsche was directly acquainted with Mill's text on women during the 1870s is unlikely; his knowledge of English was deficient, as we can see by the paucity of English books in his library. The English volumes we do find, such as the eugenicist Francis Galton's (1822–1911) *Inquiries into Human Faculty and Its Development* (1883), a gift from Joseph Paneth (1857–1890), were probably not read by Nietzsche, but translated for him by various acquaintances. It is almost certain, however, that he read Mill's essay in the German translation of the philosopher's collected writings. *The Subjection of Women* was rendered into German as *Ueber Frauenemancipation* [On the Emancipation of Women] in 1880. This change in title gives the essay a slightly different slant, emphasizing the struggle and future of the women's movement, rather than the reason for the movement itself. The translator of this important text was a young medical student from Vienna named Sigmund Freud (1856–1939), who, although more sympathetic to Mill's views on equality and morality, felt, like the reader of his translation, Friedrich Nietzsche, that women are very different from men, and that nature had destined them for a role in the social order that is defined by their biology. In Nietzsche's copy of Mill's essay, which can be examined in his library in Weimar, we find numerous marginal notations and underlinings, indicating that he read this work quite carefully. He was particularly interested in passages that claimed inequality was a moral depravity for the more favored as well as the lower classes, that advocated a just equality replace domination based on strength, and that downplayed the natural and putatively necessary subordination of women in society. It is possible that Nietzsche is referring obliquely to this essay in a note from 1884, where he comments that the "tone of disrespectfulness" is greatest in the age of "*suffrage universel*," adding: "Just read the philosophical cackling of George Sand or the woman John Stuart Mill" (Nachlass 1884, 25[337], KSA 11.100). His rejoinder to Mill—and his engagement with other unidentified interlocutors of the nineteenth century—is perfectly clear in his writings on the Women's Question from the 1880s.

Nietzsche was hardly alone among male German intellectuals in engaging Mill's arguments. Rather, as we can see from the large number of comments on women's issues during the late nineteenth century, he was part of a much larger discourse that is often forgotten today. Two of the many male scholars who entered into the ongoing dialogue on the Women's Question in a more direct and public fashion, and with whose writings Nietzsche had some familiarity, are Heinrich von Sybel (1870–1895) and Gustav Teichmüller (1832–1888).[78] The former, a noted historian and public figure in Nietzsche's time, delivered a lecture on the emancipation of women in 1870; the lecture was collected in a volume of occasional pieces and published in 1874.[79] He begins by stating that this general topic has aroused a great deal of attention in America, England, and Germany, and that although it comprises many different issues, emancipation is really a matter of equality before the law and is therefore a component of the general democratizing tendency of the times. While Sybel appears sympathetic to these tendencies, he simultaneously does not advocate, as Mill does, a universal notion of equality. His reasoning is familiar because, like most reflections on this issue through the ages, women's biological constitution is used to exclude them from full equality. By nature, women are destined to become mothers and are thus occupied for at least two decades of their lives with the necessary tasks of reproduction and motherhood. Everything else follows from this elementary fact. Although Sybel does not overtly oppose the integration of women into educational institutions, government, and business, he believes that such cases will be the exception, since women are both naturally disinclined to compete in these areas and disadvantaged when compared with men. Although girls have the same aptitude as boys, and can learn ancient languages with equal proficiency, nature dictates that their career trajectory should be in the home, and for this reason a different type of schooling is required. Finally, with regard to suffrage, Sybel argues that the married pair is one unified vote, and although he sees some justification for extending suffrage to single women and widows, who are apt to be more reasonable in their voting habits than, for example, stupid men, he asks whether it would not make more sense to take the vote away from stupid men rather than extending it to all unattached women. We have no way of knowing whether Nietzsche had any knowledge of this specific essay. We know he read some of Sybel's historical works in the mid-1880s, and he is mentioned along with Heinrich von Treitschke (1834–1896) in *Beyond Good and Evil* as an example of Prussian historiography (JGB 251, KSA 5.192). More important is that Sybel's position represents a typical stance on an issue that was debated publicly among Nietzsche's contemporaries: formally sympathetic to women's emancipation, it uses nature as an argument to counter Mill's impassioned plea for complete equality.

An alternative approach more favorable to women's rights can be found in Gustav Teichmüller's book *On Women's Emancipation* from 1877. Nietzsche knew Teichmüller personally. When he arrived in Basel in 1869, Teichmüller was one of the two philosophy professors at the Swiss institution. The chair he occupied was relatively new, having been established only in 1867; its first occupant was Wilhelm Dilthey (1833–1911), who left after a year for a chair in Berlin. Teichmüller did not last much longer: in 1871, he accepted a position at Dorpat (Tartu), and Nietzsche applied unsuccessfully to become his successor. Nietzsche's scheme was to secure a post for his close friend Erwin Rohde, who would replace him as Basel's classical philologist, but the plan fell through, probably because Nietzsche was clearly lacking credentials and publications in philosophy. Teichmüller, like Sybel, turns to the "burning question" of women's emancipation in the wake of Mill's essay. He criticizes the British philosopher for his lack of a scientific attitude toward the very questions he raises and endeavors to correct his errors by delineating quite precisely the concepts one needs to solve the Women's Question in a genuine philosophical manner. Teichmüller's text is pedantic and tedious, but in contrast to Sybel, Teichmüller ultimately concludes that we must reject the Aristotelian inequality of the sexes for a more Platonic and theoretical equality. He recognizes that on the biological level, men and women have different functions in the procreation of the species. But he declares that these functions entail merely the mechanical or materialist level of existence, and that society has an interest in the free and unhindered development of all its members, regardless of sex. He therefore maintains that all professions should be open to women, concluding from this that all educational institutions should be similarly accessible to any qualified candidate.[80] Nietzsche was certainly familiar with some of Teichmüller's philosophical writings. His book on Platonic dialogues is found in his library,[81] and it is quite evident that Nietzsche reflected on Teichmüller's volume on *The Real and the Apparent World* from 1882,[82] since this Kantian distinction becomes a favorite target for Nietzsche's criticism of traditional philosophy in the latter part of the decade.[83] We have no indication that he knew about Teichmüller's writings on the Women's Question, but what is important is that intellectuals from Nietzsche's circles treated these issues, that the Women's Question was part of an ongoing debate in the European public sphere, and that with his observations Nietzsche is commenting on and contributing to this ongoing and controversial conversation.

    Nietzsche was simultaneously making a contribution to the long philosophical tradition that reflected on the role of women in society. He was certainly familiar with this tradition from his classical studies, since, as we see in Teichmüller, the opinions of Plato and Aristotle were still important for his contemporaries. The newer philosophical tradition had continued to reflect on these matters, and one philosopher with whose writings Nietzsche was intimately acquainted had expressed very contentious views on this topic: Arthur Schopenhauer (1788–1860). While we are uncertain whether Nietzsche had any familiarity with the writings of Sybel or Teichmüller on women, it seems almost certain that in his early years, when he was a voracious reader of Schopenhauer, he had taken the opportunity to read the notorious section "On Women" in *Parerga and Paralipomena* (1851). In *On the Genealogy of Morals*, Nietzsche mentions that Schopenhauer treated sexuality and the "instrument" of sexuality, women, as enemies (GM, Dritte Abhandlung 7, KSA 5.349), making it likely that he still recalled Schopenhauer's essay in 1887. In his most offensive passages, Schopenhauer appears to advocate precisely the positions that Nietzsche would later assume. Continuing a long tradition of misogyny in philosophical reflection, he contends that women in general are inferior to men in all respects, from their physical stamina to their intelligence. In the human hierarchy he finds that they occupy a middle step between child and man, a contention, we will recall, that Helene Druskowitz neatly reversed. Women for Schopenhauer are unsuitable for great intellectual achievement; although they have a superior capacity for compassion, they possess a weak faculty of reason, "an instinctive craftiness and an ineradicable penchant for lying." For this reason, women are viewed as innate deceivers, unfit for anything that has to do with justice and truth. The only reason that men bother with them at all is because men's instinct has been bemused by sexual drives. Marriage is to be avoided as a foolish halving of rights and doubling of duties.[84] Although we may recall that Meysenbug accused Nietzsche of being "worse than Schopenhauer" (end of February 1887, Nr. 809, KSB 8.35), Schopenhauer is not really part of the conversation in which Nietzsche participates when he writes about women, despite similarities in views and temperament. Not only did Schopenhauer develop his ideas about women in a somewhat different climate, one in which there was no vital women's movement, but also his views do not appear to have exercised a significant influence on Nietzsche or on other writers dealing with women's issues in the 1870s and 1880s. With regard to Nietzsche, in his earliest writings, composed at a time when he was an avid reader of Schopenhauer, he hardly mentions the women's issue at all. In his aphoristic period, his views on women are substantially different in tone and emphasis; only after he has definitively rejected Schopenhauerian philosophy, during the 1880s, does he begin to write about women with a deprecatory rhetoric resembling Schopenhauer's. Nietzsche's comments on women thus certainly represent the continuation of a dominant misogynist tradition, but if we are going to understand his views, we must consider them chiefly a response to more immediate cultural, institutional, and personal contingencies.

Early Reflections on Women

In discussions of Nietzsche's views on the Women's Question, there is often a tendency to treat his works as a unity, to ignore the shifts in emphasis and changes in tone that we can detect over the years. While there are obvious continuities in his expressed opinions on women and their role in the social order, we must also be aware that Nietzsche was impacted at different points in his life by different experiences, and that the world around him, including the intellectual world he confronted in books, had a significant effect on how he conceived of women, their rights, and their emancipation in nineteenth-century Europe. At the start of his career, these issues are mostly absent from his writings. His initial focus on classical philology and Greek culture did not include extensive reflection on women: his scholarly texts do not include any reference to women, and his first book, *The Birth of Tragedy*, has only indirect references to the topic, for example, in the juxtaposition of Prometheus's Aryan, masculine defiance of the gods and Eve's Semitic, feminine disobedience to Jehova in the Garden of Eden (GT 9, KSA 1.69–70). One early note that discusses the role of women in Plato's *Republic* contains a few cryptic remarks, including the contention that women were "natural" in Greece, as demonstrated by the "great men" to whom they gave birth. Women are "the *night*" or "more accurately *sleep*"; they do nothing and are always the same, a "reversion to healing nature." A few comments follow that refer to woman as prophetess and the cause of evil, as in the Trojan War, giving the impression that Nietzsche was recounting various roles women could play in Greek thought (Nachlass 1870–71, 7[31–38], KSA 7.145–48). A more cohesive discussion of women in Greece occurs in *Human, All Too Human*, where Nietzsche titles an aphorism about classical Greek society "A Culture of Men" (MA 259, KSA 2.212–13). Nietzsche cites Pericles as an authoritative source for the Greek view of women: "They are at their best when men talk about them as little as possible." The homoerotic bond between older and younger men, the basis of Greek education, was much more important, and women were relegated to "child-begetting and sensual pleasure." Nietzsche appears to approve of the exclusion of women from public life and of their role in producing "handsome, powerful bodies in which the character of the father lived on as uninterruptedly as possible." The restriction on women kept Greek culture youthful for a long period of time since "in the Greek mothers the Greek genius again and again returned to nature." In his discussions of Greek civilization, Nietzsche implicitly recognizes the changing status of women in different historical periods; their exclusion from education and public life in antiquity contrasts with contemporary Europe. But Nietzsche appears to validate the role Greek society assigned to women as natural and necessary, and, as we shall see, he ultimately comes to evaluate women and the Women's Question in the context of an essentialism he suggests was determinant for Hellenic values.

The aphorism from *Human, All Too Human* on the masculine culture of Greek antiquity occurs just a few pages before Nietzsche's longest sustained commentary on women's issues in his aphoristic period (1878–82). When Nietzsche turned from classical studies to observations on contemporary life in his *Untimely Meditations*, he took up no issues related to women, but in his first work of the "middle period," he devotes an entire section to "Woman and Child." We have already seen that part of the intellectual context for these reflections was his scholarly preoccupation with ancient Greece, but we must add to that the influence of French moral philosophy, in particular François de La Rochefoucauld

(1613–1680). With regard to women, marriage, and children, Nietzsche places himself in the role of an observer of social behavior, as someone whose keen powers of perception allow him unusual psychological insight into the human condition. Most of his remarks in this section of his initial aphoristic volume and in subsequent works as well fall most conveniently under the rubric of "life wisdom," comments that are more observations on current social mores than ontological distinctions between the sexes or polemical comments on social movements. Many of the aphorisms from *Human, All Too Human* through *The Gay Science* were written in the context of his own unsuccessful search for a stable relationship with a woman and his own concerns about what it would mean to enter into matrimony. Some aphorisms are simply *bon mots* dealing with marriage and designed more for their display of wit than for philosophical insight. Under the title "Diverse Sighs," Nietzsche writes: "Some men have sighed over the abduction of their wives, most however over the fact that no one wanted to abduct them" (MA 388, KSA 2.267). In "Unity of Place and Action," an intentionally misplaced allusion to tragic theory, we read: "If married couples did not live together, good marriages would be more common" (MA 393, KSA 2.268). Other aphorisms may strike us as good advice and be completely non-offensive: "Marriage as a long conversation.—When entering into a marriage you ought to ask yourself: do you believe you are going to enjoy talking with this woman up into your old age? Everything else in marriage is transitory, but most of the time you are together will be devoted to conversation" (MA 406, KSA 2.270). Still other aphorisms distinguish men from women, but credit the latter with qualities that are unexpected from a traditional misogynist perspective. With regard to "female intellect," Nietzsche maintains that woman exhibit a "complete control and presence of mind and the utilization of every advantage" (MA 411, KSA 2.272). They possess more reason than men, who are characterized rather by temperament and passion. That in marriage men seek a woman of temperament, while women search for a man of superior reason, demonstrates only, according to Nietzsche, that they are both pursuing a partner that is the ideal of their own sex. Although Nietzsche retains the stereotype of the woman being more attached to persons than to things, thus explaining why women have a distorted relationship to politics and science, he adds in this rather conciliatory set of aphorisms: "Perhaps all this may change, but for the present that is how things are" (MA 416, KSA 2.274). This comment occurs in an aphorism titled "On the emancipation of women," and although it does not refer directly to the women's movement of his time, it does hold open the possibility of a different social and intellectual role for women in the future. On the other hand, Nietzsche expresses the conviction that the free spirits to which *Human, All Too Human* is dedicated will probably live without women (MA 426, KSA 2.279–80), indicating that he conceives of his free spirits as men, not women; but the general tenor of his remarks is playful and certainly devoid of the wholesale denigration of a Schopenhauer. Indeed, the statement so often reproduced by his feminist defenders, that the "perfect woman is a higher type of human being than the perfect man" (MA 377, KSA 2.265), opens the section on "Woman and Child" in Human, All Too Human.

This section also contains an aphorism that has been suggestive, particularly for interpreters who are psychoanalytically and biographically inclined. It deals with the influence of the mother on their sons' views regarding women: "*From the mother*—Everyone bears within him a picture of woman derived from his mother: it is this which determines whether, in his dealings with women, he respects them or despises them or is in general indifferent to them" (MA 380, KSA 2.265). It is worth noting that Nietzsche's upbringing was unusual in that after his father's death in 1849, he lived in a household consisting exclusively of women: his mother, his sister, his paternal grandmother, and his two maiden aunts on his father's side. His relationship with his sister and his mother was highly charged emotionally: while Nietzsche tried to break away from everything that the small-town morality of Naumburg represented, he was never quite able to escape the shadow of the middle class. The two women closest to him pampered him throughout much of his early life; from the correspondence we possess it is obvious that Nietzsche's career was the focal point for both women, and that they were willing to sacrifice their own comfort for his success. Nietzsche appears to have considered this attitude as normal as they did. But along with their devotion came an oppressive bondage, the resentment of which only occasionally breaks through to the surface. Nietzsche had more frequent conflicts with his sister—over Lou Salomé, over her marriage to Bernhard Förster, over her connections to anti-Semitism—but he always expressed loving feelings toward his mother in his letters and continued to correspond with her faithfully until his mental breakdown—after which she cared for him until her death. The remarks from *Ecce Homo* critics often cite are therefore odd, perhaps understandable regarding Elisabeth, but unusual with respect to his mother Franziska:

> When I look for my profoundest opposite, the incalculable pettiness of the instincts, I always find my mother and my sister—to be related to such canaille would be a blasphemy against my divinity. The treatment I have received from my mother and my sister, up to the present moment, fills me with inexpressible horror. . . . I confess that the deepest objection to the "Eternal Recurrence," my real idea from the abyss, is always my mother and sister. (EH, Warum ich so weise bin 3, KSA 6.268)[85]

Franziska was a devout Lutheran, and it is possible that as Nietzsche grew less tolerant of Christianity, he built up strong feelings of antipathy toward his mother. But there was really nothing unusual in Franziska's piety—she was, after all, the daughter and wife of Protestant pastors—and there is no indication of the "horror" Nietzsche professes to feel prior to this outburst. It is hard to imagine that these mixed emotions toward the women closest to him had no impact on his views of women and their role in his and any future social order. But it is also difficult to believe that Nietzsche's relationship to his mother, or to any of the women in his family, can be as determinant for his attitudes as aphorism 380 in *Human, All Too Human* would have us believe.

The witty aphoristic treatment of women in *Human, All Too Human* and various comments that suggest women's condition in a male-dominated society is subject to change and improvement are not the only views we find in his works prior to *Zarathustra*. We also encounter passages in Nietzsche's middle period that indicate a continuity with his apparent validation of women's subordinate position in the Greek world and the later writings that take up openly misogynist perspectives. In the section "Woman and Child," Nietzsche pays women the backhanded compliment that their shrewdness is demonstrated by the fact that "they have known how to get themselves fed." Through "subordination," they have secured for themselves "the preponderant advantage, even indeed the dominion." Their tending to children, Nietzsche speculates, may have been originally a ploy "for avoiding work as much as possible. And even now when they are genuinely occupied, for example, as housekeepers, they know how to make such a mind-confusing to-do about it that men usually overestimate the value of their activity tenfold" (MA 412, KSA 2.272–73). These remarks anticipate later passages in *Beyond Good and Evil*, where Nietzsche speaks more venomously of women's cunning in being "kept" (JGB 239, KSA 5.177). In another aphorism, Nietzsche asserts that women are not suited for scholarly activities, "for what could be rarer than a woman who really knew what science is?" (MA 416, KSA 2.274).[86] In a note from this period, Nietzsche states that he is disgusted at women's lack of a sense of justice (1877, 22[63], KSA 8.389–90). And in anticipation of Zarathustra's proclamation "The happiness of man is: I will. The happiness of woman is: he wills" (Za 1, Von alten und jungen Weiblein, KSA 4.85), Nietzsche observes: "Women want to serve and in that they discover their happiness; and the free spirit wants to be served and in that he discovers his happiness" (MA 432, KSA 2.282). In his aphoristic period, we also find the first versions of the association between women and Christianity. We will recall that poststructuralist interpretations often viewed this connection as a sign of ambivalence since women were being identified with truth.[87] In reality, the association is wholly negative, and the contention that truth *"becomes female"* and "becomes Christian" (GD, Wie die "wahre Welt" endlich zur Fabel wurde, KSA 6.80) reflects poorly on both women and Christianity. In *Dawn*, Nietzsche adds a third element: "There is something Oriental and something feminine in Christianity: it betrays itself in the idea: 'whom the lord loveth he chasteneth':[88] for in the Orient, the woman regards chastisements [*Züchtigungen*] and the strict seclusion of their person from the world as a sign of their husband's love, and complain if this sign is lacking" (M 74, KSA 3.72–73). In this passage, the stereotypical notion of the "Oriental" woman[89] dominated and locked away by her husband is linked with Christian masochistic tendencies. Already in the middle period, where women have a more respectable status in Nietzsche's writings, they are identified with characteristics and tendencies that contain the seeds of his later misogyny. Women are unintellectual and weak, unjust and cunning, lazy and subservient; and these judgments are accompanied by the tacit assumption that these descriptions accord with a feminine essence.

The Misogynistic Turn

Nonetheless, the aphorisms of Nietzsche's middle period often contain a neutral or favorable view of women that largely disappears in writings of the 1880s. The relatively complimentary remarks on women at the time of *Human, All Too Human*, in particular the fairly conciliatory observations on marriage, are quite different from the polemics we encounter in his later works. Several commentators have noted the marked change in Nietzsche's attitude toward women and the Women's Question from the middle period to the first book of *Zarathustra*,[90] where the notorious remark about the whip appears. Something seems to have altered Nietzsche's views, as well as his tone, toward the end of 1882, and it is not hard to discover reasons Nietzsche may have become less generous toward women at this precise moment in time. We could note his early aphorisms predate his largest disappointments with regard to women: not only his despair about not finding a matrimonial partner, but also, and more importantly, his disappointment with Lou Salomé and his partial estrangement from his sister. In his notebooks, we begin to find disparaging passages in the drafts for sections of *Zarathustra* as early as the summer of 1882, when Nietzsche still had not broken with Salomé and seems to have harbored hopes that the *ménage à trois* with Rée in Paris or Vienna would still happen. His altered views therefore do not seem to be solely the consequence of his disappointment in the break with Salomé, and we should also note that in his later works we still find occasional pieces of "life wisdom" about women similar to the remarks in his middle period.[91] From the writings published in 1883 until the end of his career, however, more often than not we find Nietzsche's opinions of women resembling in an alarming fashion the worst clichés from the misogynist cultural tradition of Europe. Aphorisms 231–39 in *Beyond Good and Evil* set the dominant tenor for much of the later work. Although, as recent poststructuralist commentary has reminded us, women are likened to truth in the preface to that work (JGB, Vorrede, KSA 5.11), they are dissociated from it in the body of the text: "But they [women] do not *want* truth—what do women care about truth! From the beginning, nothing has been more alien to women, more repellent, more inimical than truth—their great art is the lie, their highest concern appearance and beauty" (JGB 232, KSA 5.171). In this passage, the Schopenhauerian motif of women as innate deceivers and as shallow intellects reappears in Nietzsche's works, combined with observations evidently directed against and prompted by the agitation for education in the women's movement. The beginning of this aphorism makes clear that Nietzsche is responding to a contemporary plea for women's rights and equality, such as we have seen advocated by Mill and others: "Woman want to be autonomous, and to that end they have begun to enlighten men about 'women per se'—that is one of the worst signs of progress in Europe's overall *uglification*." In Nietzsche's view, if women really established "female scientific thinking," it would reveal only that women are "pedantic, superficial, carping, pettily presumptuous, pettily unbridled, and immodest" (JGB 232, KSA 5.170-71). Enlightenment and higher education, Nietzsche concludes, are clearly restricted to the domain of the masculine.

Further comments from *Beyond Good and Evil* indicate clearly that Nietzsche is responding to the ongoing discourse surrounding the European women's movement and its demands for justice and equality. In contrast to Schopenhauer, whose animosity arose from sources that had nothing to do with activist women, Nietzsche's reflections on the women's question, especially during the 1880s, are a direct retort to the demands of middle-class women—and to the women Nietzsche knew personally—for equality. Because relationships between men and women are characterized by "a most profound antagonism and the need for an eternal-hostile alertness," all talk of "equal rights, equal training, equal ambitions and obligations" is only a "*typical* sign of shallowness" (JGB 238, KSA 5.175). Indeed, the responsibility for such deplorable democratic tendencies lies ultimately with the men who have allowed women to feel justified in demanding any rights at all, and we must assume that Nietzsche has in mind not only Mill, but other, less noted proponents of women's emancipation such as Teichmüller. Since, in keeping with the "the democratic inclinations and basic taste," "the weaker sex" has been treated with such respect, women have "abused" the favorable situation by advancing further claims for equality (JGB 239, KSA 5.176). In the nineteenth century, women have lost all modesty, decorum, and fear of man. Nietzsche argues that women have gradually forfeited the advantages they formerly possessed, that the progress they have experienced in terms of formal rights and privileges has been purchased with a decline in their natural femininity. With the demise of military and aristocratic cultures, in which Nietzsche evidently believes women exercised considerable influence with appropriate feminine means, women have become little more than clerks. The women's emancipation movement is thus paradoxically held responsible for a worsening of the situation of women:

Ever since the French Revolution, women's influence in Europe has *decreased* to the same extent that their rights and ambitions have increased; and thus the "emancipation of women," in so far as women themselves (and not only shallow males) are demanding and encouraging it, turns out to be a curious symptom of increasing weakness and dullness in the most womanly instincts. There is *stupidity* in this movement, an almost masculine stupidity, which a truly womanly woman (who is always a clever woman) would have to be utterly ashamed of. (JGB 239, KSA 5.176)

The women's movement has been assisted in this "stupidity" by "idiotic woman-lovers and female-corrupters among scholarly asses of the male gender who are advising women to defeminize themselves in this way and to imitate all the stupidities that are infecting 'men' in Europe" (JGB 239, KSA 5.177). Nietzsche does not name any of these "idiotic friends" of the women's movement, but it is likely that he had in mind intellectuals like Mill or playwrights like Henrik Ibsen, who is taken to task in *Ecce Homo* for wanting to poison "naturalness" in sexual relations (EH, Warum ich so gute Bücher schreibe 5, KSA 6.307). Although Nietzsche never mentions specific individuals or organizations in *Beyond Good and Evil*, passages like these reveal that his remarks on the proper social role of women were developed in an antagonistic dialogue with the women's movement of his times and with men, like Mill, who legitimized philosophically the calls for change.

The model role for women that Nietzsche prefers appears to be one in which they depend on their "natural" cunning and sensuality to secure social influence. As Zarathustra had stated, women should be a "plaything" for men (Za 1, Von den alten und jungen Weiblein, KSA 4.85). In *Human, All Too Human*, as we have seen, Nietzsche had remarked that the "shrewdness of women" is demonstrated by the fact that "everywhere they have known how to get themselves fed, like drones in the beehive" (MA 412, KSA 2.272–73); and in *Beyond Good and Evil*, we read that they have learned how to get men to keep, protect, and indulge them "like delicate, strangely wild, and often pleasant domestic animals" (JGB 239, KSA.177). In this relationship to men, which they are now, out of ignorance and deception, sacrificing for equal rights, they were not only better served, but also potentially more powerful. Nietzsche appears to be propagating the image of an aristocratic or military culture in which women exert influence through manipulating males, in particular their husbands. Education of women is therefore a useless exercise, since what really counts is the will of the individual, not learning and erudition. "The most powerful and influential women in the world (not least Napoleon's mother) owed their power and superiority over men to their strength of will—and not to the schoolmasters!" (JGB 239, KSA 5.178). Thus if the man is particularly weak and his wife particularly willful, then she could attain a commandeering position over him and over others in a given social order. Nietzsche remains unconcerned with the plight and welfare of women as a group; his focus is solely the ability of a select few, the "highest specimens," to achieve greatness: in this case, women can strive through apposite, gender-specific means to exercise domination, but should not succumb to the erroneous path of imitating men to gain power. The worsening condition of women that Nietzsche detects in his age is thus really a worsening for only those "higher types" of women—the "sensible," "well-reared" women—who know how to use their wiles to their own advantage. The fate of women who associate with one of the "higher types" of men would perhaps be less fortunate, since she would then be subjected to the domination that only a few women enjoy. Nietzsche indicates that a "deep" man, "deep both in spirit and in desire, deep in a benevolence that is capable of rigor and harshness," regards women as "Orientals" do: "he has to conceive of woman as a possession, as securable property, as something predetermined for service and completed in it. He has to rely on the tremendous reason of Asia, on Asia's superior instincts, as the Greeks once did" (JGB 238, KSA 5.175). Nietzsche is never explicit about a hierarchy of women's roles in the social order he imagines, but from his comments it appears that his opposition to "emancipation" is fueled in part by an animus against the leveling of women to one liberated type and against the concomitant elimination of power for a properly feminine elite.

Nietzsche modifies his views on women and women's emancipation very little after *Beyond Good and Evil*—except for nuances and rhetoric. In the fifth book of *The Gay Science*, which was composed in 1887 and therefore belongs to his late writings,[92] he includes a section meant to deal with the divergent conceptions of love among men and women. In contrast to what we would expect from his earlier aphoristic writings, where the choice of a wife was deemed positive if one could converse with her into old age, his starting point is the assertion that equality or equal rights in the matter of love is neither possible nor desirable. In obvious opposition to the liberal and radical demands for equity in his era, Nietzsche posits ontologically fixed ideals of men and women and their respective expectations in love relations: "What woman means by love is clear enough: total devotion [*Hingabe*] (not mere surrender [*Hingebung*]) with soul and body, without any consideration or reserve, rather with shame and horror at the thought of a devotion that might be subject to special clauses or conditions. In this absence of conditions her love is a faith; woman has no other faith." Man desires precisely to secure this type of unconditional love from a woman and is "thus himself as far as can be from the presupposition of feminine love." Those men who themselves manifest unconditional devotion to a partner assume an alien characteristic: "A man who loves like a woman becomes a slave; a woman who loves like a woman becomes a more perfect woman." Nietzsche thus takes a social and historical relationship and ontologizes it, making it part of an inviolable human essence. In contrast to the advocacy for women's rights on the part of the women's movement and the women studying in Zurich with whom he had contact, Nietzsche can then argue that "a woman's passion" consists in the "unconditional renunciation of rights of her own" and in the expectation that the man will exhibit no similar renunciation. While real women in the nineteenth century were struggling to free themselves from their legal status as the property of their husbands and from legal restrictions that hindered them from inheriting property, Nietzsche maintains that "woman wants to be taken and accepted as a possession, wants to be absorbed into the concept of possession, possessed." In contrast to earlier reflections, the conceptions that Nietzsche now applies to women are not socially conditioned, but biologically fixed. And all attempts to evade biological destiny are doomed to failure: "I do not see how one can get around this natural opposition by means of social contracts or with the best will in the world to be just" (FW 363, KSA 3.610–12).[93] In keeping with tendencies found elsewhere in his later writings, biological essences are introduced to reinforce social hierarchies and to oppose emancipatory movements. While in *Human, All Too Human* Nietzsche could envision an equality between men and women, as well as a modification in the role of women over time, in his last sane years he dismisses this potential as a violation of unalterable physiological constraints.

Nietzsche's final and most abrasive remarks about the Women's Question occur in *Ecce Homo*. Immodestly declaring himself the "first psychologist of the eternal womanly"[94] and the love-object of all women, Nietzsche takes his parting shots at the feminist endeavor to introduce equality between the sexes. The women who do not love him are "the *abortive* women, the 'emancipated' who lack the stuff for children." Nietzsche employs the stereotypical defamation for women who resist men and demand equal rights: they are abnormal, not feminine, and unable to fulfill their biological destiny and procreate. Although he maintains that all women love him, he simultaneously demonstrates a deep contempt for the opposite sex: a woman is a "dangerous, creeping, subterranean little beast of prey"; women are more wicked than men; those who are good are aberrant; "goodness in a woman is already a form of degeneration." True to the biologism of his later years, Nietzsche attributes to the "beautiful soul" a Goethean ideal of woman in the novel *Wilhelm Meister* (1795–1796), a physiological disadvantage, and categorizes the struggle for equal rights as a "symptom of sickness." He reserves his most venomous remarks, however, for the notion of "emancipation of women." For Nietzsche, this ill-advised slogan

> is the instinctive hatred of the woman who has *turned out ill*, that is to say is incapable of bearing, for her who has turned out well—the struggle against "man" is always only means, subterfuge, tactic. When they *elevate*

themselves as "woman in herself," as "higher woman," as "idealist" woman, they want to lower the general level of rank of woman; no surer means for achieving that than high school education, trousers and the political rights of voting cattle. At bottom, the emancipated are the anarchists in the world of the "eternal womanly," the underprivileged whose deepest instinct is revenge. (EH, Warum ich so gute Bücher schreibe 5, KSA 6.305–7)

Amid this megalomaniacal raving of Nietzsche on the edge of sanity, we can still glimpse the central motifs of his position on the Women's Question: the rejection of equality in politics and education, the destruction of hierarchy in the leveling of women, the natural, biological superiority of men, and therefore the futility of social emancipation. Nietzsche's solution to the Women's Question, like his solution to other social questions, draws from a vision of hierarchical structures embedded in the more natural past and projected onto the future. With these statements, Nietzsche himself levels the subtleties and complexities that informed his views on women—in the philosophical, personal, and familial realm—as well as the more nuanced nature of his early writings. His final legacy, articulated in an absolute rejection of modern values, unfortunately lacks the sophistication and insight that have otherwise made his philosophy so fascinating for subsequent generations. In his writings of the 1880s, Nietzsche made it difficult for emancipated women of his time and ours to subscribe to his thought—although, as we have seen from feminist admirers in the early and late twentieth century, he evidently did not make it quite hard enough.

What can we learn about Nietzsche and his thought from his interaction with women and his writing on the Women's Question? Do we gain any insight into him as a person and as a thinker, or is the Women's Question, as Kaufmann suggested, marginal and largely irrelevant for those who have an interest in him? From the previous discussion we can reach several conclusions that are valuable for understanding Nietzsche and his responses to issues of his times. First, we have seen that Nietzsche expressed himself very differently in his personal interactions than he did in his published writings and notebooks. In the various memoirs and letters composed by women with whom he was in contact, he is uniformly depicted as a polite, solicitous, and respectful interlocutor, never angry or aggressive, rarely contradicting or disagreeing with his women friends. In his writings, he assumes an almost completely different personality, adopting the persona of a haughty, combative, intemperate polemicist. His style is at times witty and playful, but he does not hesitate to offend those who hold a different opinion or to denigrate individuals who fall short of his standards. With regard to his written work, we have noted a change in substance and tone from the writings of his middle, aphoristic period, to the publications beginning with *Zarathustra* and extending until the outbreak of insanity in 1889. The Women's Question does not play an important part in his "Wagnerian" years from 1872 until 1876, but starting with *Human, All Too Human*, we find remarks that are mostly observational, sometimes mildly antifeminist by even the standards of his era, but never venomous or rancorous. Only after 1882 does the tenor become vitriolic and malicious. A plausible reason for this change involves conflicts pertaining to his personal life, especially the events surrounding the demise in his relationship with Lou Salomé, but many sketches for misogynist passages in *Zarathustra* appear before Nietzsche's disappointment, and there are comments in even aphoristic works that anticipate some of his later positions. Instead of looking exclusively to the private realm for an explanation, therefore, we might consider again historical context. Nietzsche's hostile remarks about women were connected intimately with the movement for women's emancipation in his era. His deprecation of women is a response to their agitation for rights and privileges to which they are not entitled and which remove them further from the natural order that Nietzsche endorses. His violent rejection of the women's movement is part of his larger concern with a great variety of phenomena in contemporary society—with anti-Semitism, with ultranationalism, and with all socially redemptive movements and their advocates, who pose as "improvers of humankind."[95] In the 1880s, his campaign against "women," but especially against emancipated women, is one instance of his polemic against "the instinct of the herd, the timidity of the herd," and it is not coincidental that in his notebooks the idealists who embody herd-mentality "struggle for the 'emancipation of women'" (Nachlass 1887, 10[113], KSA 12.521). Indeed, when Nietzsche is sketching under the rubric "*the modern ideas as false*," he includes women's emancipation in a list that features "freedom," "equal rights," "humaneness," "race," "nation," "democracy," "progress," and "general education" (Nachlass 1888, 16[82], KSA 13.514). Women's emancipation and women in contemporary society became part of a complex nexus of movements and concepts in Nietzsche's thought of the 1880s that defined the ills of the modern world. His preoccupation with the Women's Question in these years is thus inseparable from his moral philosophy in *Beyond Good and Evil* and *On the Genealogy of Morals*, and his comments on women, as offensive as they may be, should be considered part of his ongoing dialogue with a social and political order that had continued to move in a direction antithetical to Nietzsche's most cherished values.

Chapter 5

The Colonial Question

Nietzsche and Colonial Discourse

It may come as a surprise that Nietzsche had any views on the growing German colonial movement of his times. If we search the voluminous secondary literature devoted to Nietzsche's life and philosophy, we find almost nothing related to remarks on colonies or colonialism. In most biographical studies of Nietzsche the topic is hardly mentioned,[1] and there is no entry for anything related to colonialism in either the *Nietzsche Handbook* or the *Nietzsche Lexicon*.[2] Nietzsche scholarship has hitherto taken seriously Nietzsche's own summary dictum about his thought, namely that it was untimely, and commentators have believed that he did not follow current events, and that he never followed matters of political interest in the newspaper. Especially in his last sane years, as we have seen, Nietzsche was disposed to admire individuals who were ignored in their own era, and when he states in *Ecce Homo* that some people are born posthumously (EH, KSA 6.298), he was undoubtedly thinking of himself.[3] When we examine these sorts of remarks today, we can think of Nietzsche as prophetic, but when he made them, he was more likely expressing his bitter disappointment that he had not attracted a readership, especially among the German public. Those who have followed Nietzsche's own self-assessment and deemed him a prophet for a later age have been too gullible in their assessment, and the fact remains that if we look closely at his works and thought, we can easily discern, as we have witnessed in previous chapters, that he was much more a citizen of his own era than he and his critics concede. Alongside the more abstract, "philosophical" comments in his writings, we find remarks on almost all the important social movements of his time, and as we shall see in Chapters 7 through 9, he also had a keen interest in the natural science of his age. Indeed, some of his "philosophical remarks" also have a dimension that is intertwined directly with occurrences during the Second Empire. In the previous chapter, we saw clearly that Nietzsche expressed controversial positions on the growing women's movement as it was spreading across Europe, and that he knew personally many women who were either leading figures in the quest for women's rights or among the first students at German-speaking universities in Switzerland. In Chapter 3, we examined some of his comments on socialism and workers at a time when industrialization had created a large proletariat, and Germany saw the emergence of a powerful socialist party representing the workers' interests. As we will see in the next chapter, he took an adversarial view toward the anti-Semitic movement that coalesced in Germany in 1880 and gained enormous popularity in many nationalist circles.[4] And the final three chapters will detail his involvement with topics in the biological and physical sciences. It would be an exaggeration, of course, for anyone to maintain that Nietzsche was well informed on these social issues, or had any expertise in natural science, and his knowledge about the colonial movement and the agitation for German colonies was surely not extensive. Most often he possessed only a partial view of a complex situation, and he was apt to draw conclusions from a paucity of information, his own "insights" into human psychology, and personal predilections frequently influenced by perceived allies or foes. His self-proclaimed untimeliness can be attributed to the fact that he sometimes took less popular positions, and to the fact that his views were so poorly disseminated in the German public sphere during his own lifetime. But it is simply inaccurate to believe that he was not reacting to movements, events, and discoveries that were themselves a very timely part of German and European life in the late nineteenth century, and if we are patient enough, we can delineate positions Nietzsche was assuming in relationship to these movements and events.

The colonial movement was one of the timely occurrences to which he responded. In the typical books and essays that appear today on German colonialism, scholars usually focus on a specific type of colonization related to geographical areas of the world that came under German domination. There is a great deal of material on the German procurement and governance of African and Pacific colonies starting in 1884, when Germany began to acquire Togoland, Cameroon, South West Africa, German East Africa, and New Guinea,[5] and ending in 1919, when it lost its tiny colonial empire. Most accounts dealing with the 1870s and 1880s focus on a number of limited topics. Especially important for most historians of Central Europe are the debates internal to Germany, the founding of various colonial societies that agitated for colonies, Bismarck's initial opposition, and his eventual change of heart. Other studies emphasize the men who themselves traveled to the colonies and made German imperialism a reality. Here the concern is the colonies themselves, rather than domestic policy, and the narratives frequently relate the African exploits of such men as Carl Peters (1856–1918), Adolf Lüderitz (1834–1886), or Gustav Nachtigal (1834–1885). Obviously, the campaigns—in domestic and foreign locations, both outside the government and within official circles—that ushered in the era of German colonial power reached their height during the years that Nietzsche was composing his major works, and they were significant for him at the very least as a background for his own feelings about the course of German global politics and its relationship to a problematic nationhood. He must have known about some of the more noted figures who were promoting colonial expansion, such as Heinrich von Treitschke (1834–1896), the German historian who was also a friend of Nietzsche's closest colleague at Basel, Franz Overbeck (1837–1905). There are no direct references to the various colonial societies or periodicals advocating colonial activity in his writings, but the general outlines of the discussions could hardly have escaped his notice entirely. And although the genocidal activities of the German government from 1904 to 1908 against the Herero and the Namaqua in Namibia, then German South West Africa, did not occur until well after Nietzsche's death,[6] racist views about Africans circulated freely in the German public sphere during the years Nietzsche wrote.

German Nationalism and Colonial Alternatives

But the colonial mentality hardly exhausts itself in this official story of German-national colonization. Just as important for Germany, however, and certainly more important for Nietzsche, were efforts on the part of small groups of Germans to colonize other regions of the globe, in particular in South America. The main way in which Nietzsche became involved in colonialist discourse was through one of these efforts at "emigration colonialization," undertaken by Bernhard Förster (1843–1889), who married Elisabeth Nietzsche (1846–1935) on 22 May 1885 (Richard Wagner's birthday)[7] and moved with her to Nueva Germania in Paraguay in February of the next year. Indeed, Förster and others of his ilk appear to have believed that the recently established German Empire was moving too slowly and too hesitantly toward colonialism in the widest sense of that word. In a work published in 1886, Förster emphasizes that he had broached the topic at an earlier date, but only in the mid-1880s did it become easier to speak of these matters in public.[8] He also stresses the un-German proclivities of the dominant political scene. Förster's remarks make us conscious that colonialism in general became an acceptable part of discourse in the German political public sphere only after 1880, and that many colonialists considered themselves, and not the recently established Second German Empire, to be the true bearers of Germanness. It is not hard to understand why he held such views. For Förster, the Germany of his time was too Jewish, too urban, and too materialist; his ideology, which is part of a larger reaction to the advent of modernity to which his brother-in-law—in a different manner—also objected, especially in his early years as a Wagnerian acolyte, is thus simultaneously conservative in many of its tenets and utopian in its tenor. In Förster's case, it combined many themes of Wagnerian derivation, such as vegetarianism, anti-Semitism, and anti-vivisectionism,[9] with a quasi-socialist longing for community, the rejection of private property as a modern cause of strife, and the reliance on productive, hard work as the primary source of prosperity and happiness.[10] Because the Germany of his time appeared no longer to advocate these positions, colonialists like Förster could not depend on the Fatherland as their only support. Important for him was not that the German government in Berlin controlled a colony, but that the colony be thoroughly German in its constitution. As Förster himself writes: "Whether colonies are founded in direct dependence on the German Empire or under foreign domination seems to me a matter of indifference: a colony that develops with vitality will know how to preserve its national and economic rights under a foreign flag, and a colonial land politically dependent on the motherland will, if it progresses with vigor, in any case come to the point where it frees itself and becomes independent."[11] Förster's need to escape Germany was therefore a peculiar type of self-exile, and it was unlike the self-exile of his brother-in-law Friedrich Nietzsche: Förster's was undertaken not so much as a rejection of German nationalism and the German nation as an affirmation of a more authentic nationalist spirit that could no longer be realized within the boundaries of the Second Reich.

Förster's perspective on colonization thus differs significantly from the efforts of Germany to obtain territory overseas in imitation of traditional colonial powers like England, France, or Spain. There was not complete agreement on the legitimacy of emigration colonies as a worthwhile goal of German policy. Indeed, some advocates of German national colonies expressed outright disdain for the type of "settlement colony" Förster attempts to justify in his writings and in his practice. Friedrich Lange (1852–1917),[12] an anti-Semitic journalist and disciple of Paul de Lagarde (1827–1891), is a case in point. Like Nietzsche, Lange was strongly opposed to the anti-Semitic movements of the early 1880s as too crude and ultimately inefficacious to bring about any real change, but, unlike Nietzsche, he retained a fiercely völkish and racist viewpoint in his promotion of "pure Germanness."[13] His views on colonies offer a stark contrast to those of Förster. As a founder of the Society for German Colonization in the mid-1880s, Lange had developed a keen interest in Germany's African colonies and contempt for other types of colonial ventures. Recalling activities in 1884, he reports in 1889 that he experienced fewer problems with the Boers, the descendants of Dutch farmers who had settled in southern Africa, than with individuals who were advocating dispensing with African colonies that would belong to Germany and instead investing energy and funds in South America, "where one of the republican governments had made land available with the condition that in a stipulated period of time a certain number of German emigrants would settle there."[14] Although it does not appear that Lange is referring in this passage to Förster's Nueva Germania, he is describing precisely the type of agreement that established the Paraguayan colony. The reason for Lange's opposition is simple. He claims to have understood that the establishment of a colony such as Förster's could be useful and pleasant for those participating, and portrays himself as merely a patient mediator in many of the controversies that surrounded the African enterprise. But he is uncompromising in opposing colonialist activities in South America and abandoning African colonies because it would mean sacrificing the "German-national character" of future colonies. Decisive for Lange and others involved in the early colonial movement was obviously German sovereignty, and although he and Förster both proceed from a hypernationalist sentiment when considering the colonial movement, they draw radically different conclusions from their Germanocentric premises.

Both Förster's colonial venture and the official colonialism of the Second Empire thus revolve around precisely the type of nationalist sentiment that Nietzsche had come to abhor, and his reaction and alternative to German colonialism has to be understood within the context of his antithetical sentiments toward the German chauvinism of his times. As we have seen in Chapter 2, in his youth Nietzsche had exhibited a definite proclivity for German nationalism. In correspondence from July of 1866, he wrote of his pride in the German army and of the honor he would have in sacrificing himself for the national cause; he subsequently supported a Liberal party candidate in an electoral campaign against a particularist rival, and when the war broke out with France, he requested permission from the University of Basel to enlist on the German side. But even at this point we detect signs that his nationalism was more of a response to pressures around him—including the encouragement of Richard and Cosima Wagner, both of whom were enthusiastic supporters of German nationalism and the war effort—than a genuine conviction on Nietzsche's part. More important for our present concerns, his flirtation with nationalism had no implications for colonization; during the 1860s and early 1870s, nationalism was purely a European, and even a Western European, phenomenon for Nietzsche. Gradually, as we have documented, Nietzsche's initial nationalist sentiments wane. Even in 1870, at the height of nationalist fervor in the Franco-Prussian War, Nietzsche was more concerned with a general European cultural renewal, led by Germany and Wagnerian opera, than with German political supremacy in Europe or the world. After the cessation of hostilities, when there was the initial possibility that Germany would obtain colonies as part of the peace treaty, Nietzsche uttered no opinion either pro or contra; his preoccupation at the time was the rumor that the Paris Commune had set fire to the Louvre, an occurrence he designated as an "earthquake of culture" (to Wilhelm Vischer-Bilfinger, 17 May 1871, Nr. 134, KSB 3.195). Part of his gradual, but decisive turn against all forms of German nationalism can be explained by Germany's failure to carry out the cultural mission he assigned to it; part is derived from his growing estrangement from Wagner and Wagner's political views;[15] and part is no doubt due to Nietzsche's disdain for the leveling that accompanies all politics and communal activities. But there is no evidence that colonial ventures play any role in his increasing distancing from the nationalism of his countrymen. Indeed, by the time the colonial movement had gained attention in the larger public sphere in Germany, Nietzsche was firmly entrenched in a strident antinationalism. This antinationalism manifested itself above all in an absolute negation of everything associated with Germany, as we saw at the end of Chapter 2. Remarks previously cited from *Ecce Homo* show the depth of his feelings about his former compatriots:

> It is even part of my ambition to count as the despiser of the German par excellence. I expressed my mistrust of the German character already at the age of twenty-six (third untimely essay)—the Germans are impossible for me. Whenever I picture to myself a type of man that goes against all my instincts it always turns into a German.... The Germans are canaille.... One lowers oneself by commerce with Germans.... If I subtract my commerce with a few artists, above all with Richard Wagner, I have experienced not a single good hour with Germans. (KSA 6.362)

We have seen that not all Nietzsche's comments on Germans and Germany emphasize this personal distaste. Often he takes a more principled stance, criticizing the narrowness of German chauvinism and smugness, the stupidities of racist Aryanism and Teutomania, or the depravity and ostentatiousness in the cultural sphere. But consistently from the mid-1870s Nietzsche rejected what he considered to be the dominant German ideology, which he associated with misguided nationalism, cultural philistinism, and petty party politics. Seldom does Nietzsche perceive colonization to be part of this ideological complex.

Förster, Nietzsche, and Wagner on Colonization

Nonetheless, Nietzsche's attitude toward German nationalism predisposed him against all varieties of colonialist mentality, which drew heavily on chauvinist tendencies of the times. With regard to Förster's particular project, however, his assessment was negatively overdetermined. Not only was Förster a fervent advocate of Aryan supremacy; not only was Förster a key figure in the rise of political anti-Semitism, which, as we shall see in the next chapter, Nietzsche despised; not only did Förster steal from him Elisabeth, his "beloved llama"; he was also associated with the Wagnerian cultural mission, which Nietzsche had come to reject. Indeed, Förster's first discussion of colonization for a wider audience appeared in the *Bayreuther Blätter* in 1883.[16] Published since 1878, this journal was more than an in-house publication celebrating Wagner and his cultural enterprise. Besides commentary on Wagner's music, and reports from the various Wagner Societies in Germany, Europe, and the world, the *Blätter* printed many articles and reviews that supported the ideologemes to which Wagner—and later the Wagnerians—was increasingly attracted in his final years. Antivivisection, for example, is a topic that recurs frequently in the journal, and in 1881 the *Blätter* even included a special supplement entitled "The Scientific Lack of Value of Vivisection in All of Its Variations," written by Richard Nagel. Also sprinkled in among the various essays on opera and performance are diverse items on a number of Wagnerian causes: calls for the support of the Boers in South Africa; articles and reviews on racial issues, including a series of essays summarizing Arthur de Gobineau's (1816–1882) *Inégalité des races humaines* (1852), penned by the editor of the journal, Hans von Wolzogen (1848–1938), as well as essays by and an obituary for Gobineau himself; commemorative historical essays on leading Germans such as Luther; excerpts from the writings of famous Germans, such as Goethe; reflections on the decline of the German language and suggestions to remedy this unfortunate state of affairs; criticisms of the educational system and recommendations for reforms; and discussions of the politics of Europe and Germany. Many of these topics were also of interest to Nietzsche, and we should remember that although he eventually rejected the nationalism and racism of the Wagnerians, he shared many of their political and social perspectives. In addition, Wagnerians remained throughout the 1870s and 1880s the circle with which the general public most closely identified Nietzsche.[17] Before his polemical writings against Wagner at the close of his sane life—*Nietzsche contra Wagner* (1888) and *The Case of Wagner* (1895)—many German readers must have presumed that Nietzsche's opinions on the composer were still adequately summarized in the overtly celebratory work *Richard Wagner in Bayreuth* from 1876. Thus although Nietzsche may have considered himself at odds with Wagner, and especially with Wagnerians, by the early 1880s, there still existed real as well as apparent connections with the ideology of the *Bayreuther Blätter*.

Förster's colonialist exhortation in the *Blätter* shows clearly why Nietzsche was initially unsympathetic to his enterprise. It begins with a rather contrived argument connecting Wagner with the question of colonization. Against recent comments by Eugen Dühring (1833–1921) and others who would reduce Wagner's importance to his musical compositions, Förster argues that Wagner's "reformatory spirit" [*reformatischer Geist*] enables him to express the "soul of the German people" in the form of music as well. "Wagner could become the unique artist, the purveyor of our hearts, he can become the reformer of his mistreated people above all because his being represents the most successful, the most fortunate, and generally the most valid incorporation of the type of the Aryan race."[18] Because colonization is in its essence a matter of preserving German culture, which is simultaneously a matter of the health and vitality of the *Volk*, Förster continues, Wagner's activity coincides with his own in proposing the establishment of German colonies. Supplementary to this nationalist and cultural justification for colonization, Förster also supplies an explanation that comes closer to material Nietzsche could validate. In what may be an argument drawn from his future brother-in-law's reflections on biology and the will to power, Förster contends that every organism, if it is vital and viable, exhibits the tendency toward the expansion, the enlargement, and the augmentation of its being. Arguing by analogy, the German people, if it is to remain vital, must seek to expand itself, enlarge itself, and augment itself through the founding of colonies. In Nietzsche's notebooks written at about the time of this essay, we find the following remark: "*The individual is an ovum.* Colony formation is the task for every individual" (Nachlass 1883–84, 24[36], KSA 10.664). And in a passage written a few years earlier, he notes: "A society must strive to become over-abundant [*überreich*] (over-population), in order to produce a new one (colonies), in order to divide into 2 self-sufficient beings. The means to give an organism duration *without* the goal of reproduction, destroy it, are unnatural—as are today's clever 'nations' of Europe" (Nachlass 1881, 11[134], KSA 9.491). In at least this one aspect Nietzsche's comments on colonies in his notebooks, albeit infrequent, thus exhibit a similar framework to Förster's. Although he rejects the notion of colonies as a necessity for preserving the national and racial superiority of Germany, he reasons, as Förster does, that colonization is a natural proclivity of groups, analogous to the biologically based reproduction of an organism.

Nietzsche does have other thoughts on colonies that precede his acquaintance with Förster's remarks in the *Bayreuther Blätter*, as well as the existence of German colonies in Africa and Asia. In the fall of 1881, we find the following cryptic remark in one of Nietzsche's notebooks: "Colonies—Corruption" (Nachlass 1881, 12[229], KSA 9.616). Because of the date of this notebook, Nietzsche could not have been referring to the actual corruption in existing colonies, such as the fraudulent dealings that occurred in Förster's Nueva Germania in the latter part of the decade. Nor does it appear that Nietzsche is thinking here of the widespread colonial corruption with regard to other nations in their colonial empires. His thoughts are more abstract and philosophical. Indeed, it is quite probable that he is not thinking of corruption in the usual sense of dishonesty on the part of those who exercise power. Rather, this note would appear to be the precursor of a thought developed a year later in *The Gay Science*. In a long aphorism titled "The signs of corruption," Nietzsche outlines the symptoms associated with societies that have fallen into corruption. These societies become more superstitious and lax; they refine their cruelties; and with the decay of morals, we detect the rise of individuals. Nietzsche refers specifically to Napoleon in this context, not as the conqueror of Europe, but as the paradigm for self-assertion and a nontraditional morality. Nietzsche summarizes by asserting: "times of corruption are those in which the apples fall from the tree. I mean the individuals, the seed-bearers of the future, the spiritual colonizers and shapers of new states and communities. Corruption is just a rude word for the *autumn* of a people" (FW 23, KSA 3.398). There is indeed a vague connection with actual thoughts of colonization, such as those that were contemplated and discussed publicly in the late 1870s and early 1880s, but Nietzsche places his observations in a biological and ethical framework that reflects his preoccupations in the writings of that period. In this particular aphorism, he is arguing that, just as a tree drops its fruit when it becomes overripe, thus disseminating its seed, so too a people, when it reaches a certain stage of development, the autumnal age, spreads itself in the world by establishing colonies. The colonial movement Nietzsche envisions is borne by individuals liberated from the constraints of morality and traditional religion, and considered "corrupt" for their deviation. This passage indicates that Nietzsche gave some thought to colonies and colonization prior to direct contact with Förster and his plans for a German settlement in Paraguay. It also points to perhaps his greatest difference from Förster and the colonial movement he encountered in Germany. Nietzsche's views here are already broader and not based on nationality; they encompass more general tendencies that he would later associate with European, not simply German developments, and suggest great political upheavals that would involve the domination of the entire globe.

In contrast to Nietzsche, Förster had a more restrictive, modest, nationalist, and racist view of colonization, and as a faithful disciple of Bayreuth and Wagner's teachings, he needed validation from the Meister for his undertaking. He must have recognized after he had completed his contribution on colonization in the *Bayreuther Blätter* that although Wagner was hardly focused on German settlements in his writings, he could be connected with advocacy for the colonial movement by more than just the vague notion of preserving German culture. In a self-advertisement of his book on the Laplata territory, which appeared in the *Bayreuther Blätter* in 1885,[19] Förster refers to a passage in a Wagner essay, "Religion and Art," from 1880, in which Wagner makes a more direct reference to the advantages of colonization, especially in more welcoming and agriculturally productive areas of the world like South America. At one point in his reflections, Wagner is discussing the benefits of vegetarian associations and criticizing the Old Testament, Jehova, and the Jewish religion for concealing the true original sin—consuming meat, not eating from the tree of knowledge, and preferring animal sacrifices to plants. Wagner claims that a vegetarian diet has a great impact on individuals and cites the success with hardened American criminals who suddenly become the "most gentle and most honest men" after they have been subjected to a diet of plants. Wagner continues by advancing the claim that the degenerate nature of the human race has been largely the consequence of its increasing distance from a natural diet. A portion of human beings—Wagner settles on about one-third as an estimate—are in this state of degeneration, and these people are the very ones who must be cured if humankind is going to experience "regeneration." Wagner then observes: "If one assumes that in Northern climates meat consumption is unavoidable, then what would prevent us from setting in motion a reasonably initiated mass migration of our peoples into other countries around the globe, since it is asserted about the South American peninsula that its enormous and uncontrolled productivity would be capable of feeding the present population from all parts of the world?" In this connection, Wagner also writes of the "richly fertile lands of South Africa," which are currently subject to the political actions of English trade interests, while the starving and impoverished people of Germany, who flee the country to secure a better existence, are unaided by those who are the ruling powers in the German state. He imagines the possibility of abandoning the northern climate zones entirely to the "hunters of wild boar and big game," who will slaughter the animals of the region unhindered by the hungry multitude, who have now emigrated. Comforting for him in this vision is not the mass slaughter of animals, but only the eventual cessation of meat consumption and the cultivated fields of the new, exclusively vegetarian societies in the southern hemisphere. Wagner adds that if the moneybags of our current civilization, a reference to capitalists and especially to wealthy Jews, raise a protest, then we would put them on their backs, like swine, and force them to view the heaven they have never seen and thereby silence them.[20] Förster, who sought faithfully to transform Wagner's fantasy into a reality, could thus easily identify his South American venture with the musings of the Meister in everything from the allegedly remarkable fertility of the soil in South America to the scorn for Jewish capitalists. Indeed, Förster's colony was conceived as a Wagnerian model, that is, as a vegetarian settlement that would repudiate the negative features of the northern hemisphere and its Jewified culture—although agricultural conditions soon forced the colonists to abandon the vegetarianism of Wagnerian ideology[21] and to content themselves with the establishment of a "true" German outpost in the center of Paraguay.

The remainder of Förster's justification for German colonization in his 1883 article is a confused concoction drawn from cultural criticism, racist prejudice, and the Protestant ethic. Förster detects two opposed phenomena in contemporary Germany. On the one hand, he finds the unmediated manifestation of the vital Aryan spirit: "nothing but healthy nature, normal pulsating life, unspoiled energy." On the other hand, he encounters—and describes in much more vivid detail—the symptoms of "sickness and degeneration" in German society. Citing evidence ranging from "'vivisecting' professors" and newspaper journalists to "'concerts' with the consumption of beer and tobacco" and "'balls' with the vilest pleasure music, to which fathers bring their adolescent daughters," Förster compiles a veritable catalogue of modernity's shortcomings in the eyes of a conservative, anti-Semitic, idealistic communitarian. In contrast to Nietzsche, however, who shared with his brother-in-law at least some of these criticisms of modern life, Förster's social analysis accords the highest honor to the farmers and workers, that hardworking, upstanding sector of the German population that is "fully healthy and completely unspoiled." At fault for Germany's deplorable decline are the upper classes, the educated, and the rich, who have become intellectually degenerate and have thus forgotten their task of being the true educators and leaders of the *Volk*. His conclusion is that European Germany cannot be saved from its de-Germanizing at the hands of Jews, journalists, band-leaders, and bureaucrats; the only hope for a revitalization of Germanness is for true Germans "to abandon the degenerate and forsaken fatherland in order to take up on another part of the planet's surface under more favorable climatic conditions with fresh resolve the undaunted journey to the ideals of the Aryan race."[22] Colonization is thus a necessity from a social perspective, but it is just as necessary if one considers the geopolitical position of Germany in Europe. Imperiled externally from the east by "the Russified and Tartarized Slavs" and from the west by "the Semiticized Latin races," Germans are left with no choice except colonization, which carries with it the hope that a German purity preserved in other parts of the world will have a salutary reciprocal impact on the Fatherland.

Förster summarizes his main arguments in a more concise form in a contribution to his essay collection, *Reminiscences of Parsifal* [*Parisfal-Nachklänge*], which likewise appeared in 1883. Like the *Bayreuther Blätter*, this book contains a sample of the topics and values most important to Wagnerians. The first four essays deal with cultural matters, mostly musical, but directly related to Wagner and his ideological predilections. A fifth essay opposes vivisection and promotes vegetarianism; a sixth relates to "the Social Question" in Germany, again with themes that are familiar to anyone who knows Wagner's opinions on contemporary Europe. The final essay deals with Förster's own hobbyhorse, colonization, and is significantly entitled "New Germanies." At this point, Nietzsche's future brother-in-law is envisioning more than one overseas colony, and from his analysis of the current situation we can easily understand why. There is only one hope for us, Förster maintains at the outset, describing the condition of Europe as one of precipitous and irreversible decline: "The old world is definitely becoming old; it carries the clearest symptoms of marasmus, of senile impotence, of beginning disintegration." Switching metaphors, Förster likens European culture to a rotting structure where a nail cannot be firmly secured; at fault are the so-called educated and cultured classes, the liberals, the humanists [*jene "humanen" Menschen*], "the voters, the newspaper readers, the products of our schools and taverns." In contrast to these agents of degeneration is the healthy kernel of German society, the working classes, the farmers, the craftsmen, the sailors, the blacksmiths; even some social democrats still remain acceptable, "although they have been largely poisoned through schnapps, newspapers, tobacco, and liberal slogans." There are some individuals in the educated classes who have not been completely ruined, but most have lost their ideals and elect "a little Jew or a lawyer or a professor" to represent them in "parliament" in their petty lawmaking and wordsmithery, "read lengthy newspapers, smoke tobacco, drink beer, use without necessity eyeglasses and walking canes, and gladly breathe the bad air of small rooms."[23] This desolate, false "German-Chinese society," which was once truly German, but has now fallen into the hands of lawyers, Jews, and mammon worshippers, can no longer be rescued. To preserve the integrity of race, to discover "a new form of Aryan culture," genuine Germans must emigrate and found "New Germanies," leaving behind the "Old Testament" and its adherents. Förster concludes that to recover truth, to probe the profundity of the human spirit, to discover the soul of animals, to research the mysteries of nature, to create art "in the manner of our race," he and his kind will have to abandon the "old 'Chinese' world," "the classical country of *Bildung*, lies, and corruption," and seek a new life in the southern hemisphere. Only in this fashion can a newborn and vital Germany overcome the tired and senile "Byzantium and China" that one is accustomed to calling Europe and acquire the freshness and strength for new life.[24]

Bernhard Förster's Colonial Project: Nueva Germania

Förster's selection of Paraguay as the site for his New Germany was based on arguments detailed in his article in the *Bayreuther Blätter* and in his subsequent monograph on German colonies. Searching the globe for an appropriate location for German settlements, Förster soon concluded that the northern hemisphere is already occupied and should therefore be ruled out. He recognizes that a large percentage of emigrants settle in the United States—six out of seven by his accounts—but he considers the United States too expensive and too threatening to his ideal of German purity. He grudgingly concedes that the United States, in spite of its mixed racial status, may be the harbinger of a new social order, but he believes that every gain for the United States is a loss for the German ideal: "Every time a German turns into a Yankee the totality of humanity suffers damage in richness."[25] The other possibilities in the northern hemisphere are in Eastern Europe, but in Russia there are too many Jews and nihilists, while in Austrian and Balkan territories there is a general decline. There are still some relatively unpopulated and felicitous spots left in Eastern Europe—he mentions Romania as well as areas around the Dnieper and Donau rivers—but in general the Germans face too much competition from the triumvirate of European and Asian racial powers: the Anglo-Saxon-Irish race, the Russo-Tartarian race, and the Mongolian race.[26] The southern hemisphere, by contrast, offers many attractive possibilities, from Australia and the Pacific islands to Madagascar and Africa. For us today, there is a certain irony in Förster's mentioning Madagascar, which was at times contemplated as a relocation point for Europe's Jewish population by ideologues in the Third Reich, as a possibility for a pure Aryan colony to escape a "Jewified" Europe. The most favorable location for German colonies, Förster concludes, however, lies in South America, in particular in the moderate regions in river valleys, and Förster singles out the area around the Amazon and the River Plate (Río de la Plata) as most conducive for German settlement. His historical and ethnographic convictions assist him in arguing for the exemplary nature of certain regions: "In general, I don't understand why the Aryans should not be able to learn to feel at home along the Amazon after they were able to establish themselves as heroes and thinkers and to develop a culture thousands of years ago in almost exactly the same climate on the Ganges."[27] Even before he himself visited South America, Förster did not rely solely on the Aryan heritage for his conclusions; he had obviously consulted several reports on South America written by German travelers and settlers before concluding that the La Plata region was most promising for his colonizing mission.

There is nothing in Nietzsche's writings or correspondence that indicates he had read Förster's essay in the *Bayreuther Blätter*, but it would be surprising if he did not take note of it in some way. Despite his break with Wagner and the Wagnerians, Nietzsche continued to be a paying member of the Wagner Society. On 28 October 1879, he wrote to Overbeck that he should continue to contribute the "small sum for the Bayreuth purposes"—Overbeck was the contact person for the Wagner Society in Basel in the late 1870s—but adds parenthetically that he has not read the *Blätter* since the fall of 1877 (Nr. 898, KSB 5.459). Since the first issues of the *Bayreuther Blätter* did not appear until 1878, either Nietzsche's memory failed him by a year or he was trying to impress on Overbeck his current distance from Wagner and the Wagnerians. On 3 September 1878, he wrote to Ernst Schmeitzner (1851–1895), his publisher and the original publisher of the *Blätter* in its initial year, that he had just read Wagner's polemic against him (Nr. 751, KSB 5.350). Nietzsche must have been referring to an essay Wagner penned in the August issue of the *Blätter* in which Wagner ridiculed certain professors for their eclectic manner of criticizing everything. It was quite obvious that Wagner was aiming at Nietzsche when he remarked that there are two kinds of critical individuals and two sorts of methods in epistemology; the first and obviously the less worthy in Wagner's view is associated with Voltaire, to whom Nietzsche had dedicated *Human, All Too Human*, and the "free spirits," which appeared in the subtitle to Nietzsche's first book of aphorisms.[28] A week later he asks Schmeitzner to discontinue sending him the *Blätter* on a monthly basis, but requests that he send him the issues for the entire year as a set. "Why should I feel duty bound to ingest a monthly dose of the annoying Wagnerian venom?" (Nr. 754, KSB 5.352). Whether Nietzsche was still glancing at the *Blätter* in 1883, when it had ceased to be published by Schmeitzner, or whether he took special interest in Förster's essay because of his sister's growing romantic involvement with him is not certain, but Nietzsche continued to receive and likely to read parts of the journal despite his alienation from Wagner. There are definite indications that he was familiar with *Parsifal-Nachklänge*, since he mentions to his sister in the draft of a letter that she can see how antithetical Förster is to everything he believes by looking at her husband's "Reminiscences of P[arsifal]" (December 1887, Nr. 968, KSB 8.218). We can be most confident that Nietzsche was acquainted with Förster's monograph about his exploration in South America, *Deutsche Colonien*. Nietzsche traveled to Germany in the autumn of 1885 in order to straighten out the difficulties he was having in disengaging himself from Schmeitzner, taking the opportunity to visit with his sister before her upcoming departure for the colony in Paraguay. At the time, the newlywed Elisabeth had been entrusted with overseeing the production of *Deutsche Colonien*, for which Förster could not find a publisher and therefore published himself in Naumburg, and Nietzsche evidently assisted in the redaction of the text. At the time of Nietzsche's arrival in Germany, Förster himself was traveling around the country trying to drum up support for the colonial enterprise and therefore delegated the project to his bride. Nietzsche mentions the volume several times in 1885 and 1886 (to Elisabeth Förster, 23 November 1885, Nr. 646, KSB 7.111; to Franziska Nietzsche, 10 December 1885, Nr. 652, KSB 7.124; and to Bernhard Förster, 11 April 1886, Nr. 685, KSB 7.172). We can be reasonably certain, therefore, that Nietzsche was well informed about Förster's motivation for colonization and his reasons for selecting Paraguay for settlement from written documents, as well as from conversations with both Förster and his sister.

The story of Förster's colonizing efforts has been told several times,[29] most recently by Ben Macintyre in his journalistic account, *Forgotten Fatherland*.[30] When Förster left Hamburg on 2 February 1883, he had a good idea of the areas of South America he would explore. Over the next two years, he traveled extensively in Argentina and Paraguay, and spent time working in San Bernardino, the first successful German colony in Paraguay, established in 1881. Particularly receptive to German efforts at colonization due to German neutrality in the War of the Triple Alliance in 1870—in which it had lost over one-half of the total population and three-quarters of the male population—Paraguay sought to attract German colonists in the 1870s and 1880s with the type of offer to which Lange referred in his newspaper article from 1889. Favorable impressions of Germans were enhanced by the activities of Colonel Heinrich von Morgenstern de Wisner, a Hungarian aristocrat and Austrian officer who had fought in the war on the side of Paraguay and later became Immigration Minister at the time Förster decided to found a colony.[31] After two years of exploration, Förster was able to return to Germany in March 1885, marry Nietzsche's sister, write his propaganda monograph for German settlement, and secure some support for his undertaking from E. Kürbitz, a banker in Naumburg, and Max Schubert (1840–1901), a factory owner in Chemnitz. Although he was less successful than he wanted to be or thought he would be in persuading German farmers and workers to follow him to the New World, he departed with his recent bride Elisabeth in February of 1886 for a continent from which he would not return. Convinced of the inherent appeal of colonial settlements in Paraguay, he entered into a shady financial deal that required him to attract 140 German families within a two-year period. When he was unable to accomplish his goal, he fell into deep depression and eventually took his own life; Elisabeth and some of the colonists covered up the suicide, obviously feeling that it would reflect poorly on the colony, which was still experiencing financial difficulties. Elisabeth returned to Germany in 1890, where she composed a spirited defense of her husband and Nueva Germania, but within a few years she too had abandoned the colonial venture for the more promising and ultimately more fruitful enterprise of promoting the works of her now insane brother, establishing an archive dedicated to his writings, composing a biography based on her personal knowledge of his life, and publishing an authoritative edition of his works and letters.

The unfolding of the events in Nueva Germania, as they were seen from the perspective of the Försters and other supporters of the colony, was a matter of continuing concern for the *Bayreuther Blätter*. It is possible that Nietzsche was acquainted with two articles about the colony published in 1888 shortly before he lapsed into insanity and that from these pieces he obtained a hint of the financial difficulties his sister and brother-in-law were confronting. The first is in the form of an open letter from Bernhard Förster to the editor of the *Bayreuther Blätter*, Hans von Wolzogen, which appeared in the October issue.[32] The pretext for the missive is an article Wolzogen wrote titled "Bayreuth Work" for the journal *Pionier*, in which Förster was lauded for being the only Wagnerian who translated the Meister's ideal into a practical activity.[33] Förster expresses appreciation that he is mentioned in the context of such eminent Wagnerians as Heinrich von Stein (1833–1896) and Carl Friedrich Glasenapp (1847–1915), the latter the editor of the Wagner encyclopedia (1891) and, together with von Stein, co-editor of the Wagner lexicon (1883). Förster emphasizes once again that his work is based "on R. Wagner's great and comprehensive reform ideas," and that "the immortal Meister" remains the inspiration and spiritual father for the community to which he is addressing his remarks. He proceeds to describe Nueva Germania as the first attempt to put German colonial thoughts into action and to declare it a completely successful undertaking. He provides details concerning the district [*Gau*] New Germany and the town of "Försterode," claiming "German fidelity and Christian love" permeate the entire venture. He cites further the many advantages for poor German workers in the new colony in comparison with "the old Fatherland": "We give him bread, while the liberal social democracy gives only a stone." At this point Förster turns to the real purpose of this open letter, which is a plea for funding so that impoverished workers can purchase land in the colony. "The poorest of the poor are perhaps not in a position to find their way to us, and here is the place where I wish to recommend to the well-intentioned and wealthy among the readers of this journal to follow the example of the Chemnitz Colonial Association." He requests that Wagner communities support Nueva Germania in a similar fashion to Chemnitz and to inquire about how to do so with the Chemnitz group. Although Förster closes by citing his desire to promote a "renewal of our aging and tired race" with "a community of German workers of healthy and strong bodies and free and devout mentality," and further claims that in this project his colonists are "the spiritual sons of R. Wagner," it is quite evident that the real purpose of this letter is to secure funding for Förster's colonial venture.

The second piece, written by Wolzogen for the December issue of the *Blätter*, is without any pretense a direct plea for monetary support of the endangered colony: its subtitle is "A Serious Appeal to Our Friends."[34] Like Förster, Wolzogen first justifies the colonial project by the claim that it was essential for Wagner and thus should be equally important for his loyal followers who subscribe to the journal. Writing to Heinrich von Stein, Wagner had commented on what measures "the German tribes" could take to avoid the "completely Semiticized" world of Europe and the threat of imminent degeneration, and in this context he points to the possibility of preserving their essence through "transplanting in new, virgin soil." Turning to Förster, the Meister's faithful acolyte, Wolzogen lauds him as the exemplary Wagnerian who has dared to survey previously unknown territory in Paraguay and encouraged his "afflicted German brothers" to follow him in establishing "a free and pure German essence" in the New World. Förster's book is a rich document about the colonial dreams of Germany, but, rather than summarizing its content, Wolzogen turns to his main theme: the survival of Nueva Germania. He advises his readers about the difficulties of founding a "pure German colony" with mostly "German settlers of no means" while simultaneously claiming that Förster's settlement has nonetheless demonstrated tremendous success in infusing "German loyalty into a foreign land." He continues: "The colony New Germany *lives*, it *can* live; the natural and moral conditions for its existence are present." Unfortunately, the practices and pitfalls of "oriental-European civilization" penetrate even into the primeval forest where New Germany is growing in freedom. "Even there without a foundation of capital the richest possibilities of German work cannot be secured and promoted; even there it cannot attain its full potential to escape finally the curse of the ring of the Nibelungs in free nature." Thus Wolzogen finds himself called upon to summon the "Bayreuther spirit" to support the colony with "Bayreuther capital" in a manner consonant with the memory of the "Bayreuther founder." Essential for Wolzogen, as it was for Förster and for Wagner, is that Nueva Germania is a genuinely

German undertaking, and Wolzogen even contrasts it with other colonial ventures that fall short of the patriotism benchmark. In an argument that recalls the conflict between emigration colonies and German-national colonies, Wolzogen adverts to East Africa and the recent campaign in Germany for supporting "an Egyptian officer," who is neither of German heritage nor employed by a German state, who has managed to get himself into a terrible situation and is being rescued by "un-German or formerly German capital." The claim is that 320,000 marks have already been raised for this "reversion to old German foggy idealism." Wolzogen is undoubtedly referring in this remark to the African explorer Mehmed Emin Pasha (1813–1881), who in the service of Egypt was named the governor of Equatoria in 1878. Cut off from an exit route by the Mahdi uprising in the early 1880s and without an army strong enough to secure free movement, Emin Pasha was eventually rescued by an expedition led by Henry Morton Stanley (1841–1904) in 1888. It seems, however, that German colonialists in the Fatherland competed with the English expedition and sought to organize a separate German expedition under the leadership of the colonialist Carl Peters to extricate Emin Pasha.[35] Wolzogen is referring to the money contributed toward the Germany expedition, but he is quite wrong in considering Emin Pasha an Egyptian. Emin Pasha was born Isaak Eduard Schnitzer in Oppeln, Silesia; originally Jewish, his mother had the family baptized Lutheran after her husband's death, and Schnitzer received the name Eduard Carl Oscar Theodor Schnitzer. In 1875 during his travels in the Middle East, he took the name Mehmed Emin; a decade later the Egyptians gave him the title of Pasha. It is possible, of course, that Wolzogen knew about Emin Pasha's Jewish heritage, and, as a fervent anti-Semite, did not consider him German despite his place of birth. But other Germans interested in the colonial enterprise obviously regarded Schnitzer under any name he had assumed as a compatriot, hence their endeavor to raise money to liberate him—and perhaps to annex the province he governed. Important for the Bayreuth faithful was only Wolzogen's argument that if Germans could raise so much money for an alleged Egyptian, they ought to contribute at least a third of that amount—he mentions specifically 100,000 marks—to save a colonialist who is truly of German extraction. Wolzogen closes his plea by reminding his readers that Christmas is celebrated in the middle of the summer in Paraguay, but that, since Christmas is fast approaching in Europe, Wagnerians should now do their Christian duty and help preserve "for us and our descendants" the new homeland Förster has created for the German people.

Nietzsche's sources of information about Förster's colony included various accounts from its supporters among the Wagnerians as well as its detractors, letters from his sister, and undoubtedly also some of the articles in the *Bayreuther Blätter*. If he did follow the progress of Nueva Germania in the Wagnerian journal, then Wolzogen's plea in the December issue was likely one of the last reports he encountered, since his breakdown occurred at the close of 1888 and the first days of 1889. The journal, however, continued to carry news from the colony through information supplied by individuals supportive of the Försters and their view of the unfolding events. In the fall of 1889, it reported on Förster's death, presenting it as a stroke [*Nervenschlag*] caused by the severe strains of running a colony, rather than the suicide that most scholars have long since concluded it was. The official obituary is framed with citations from Goethe to honor the recently deceased, who is regarded as possessing nearly divine qualities, and described as "good, noble, and true." "The most noble thought, the purest will, the highest courage, the most ardent loyalty, and the most steadfast belief" were united in him. His concern for Germany and for German values is applauded; he is deemed "one of the few vigorously striving and creative 'Bayreuther.'" Accompanying the Bayreuth obituary is one from fellow settlers who were faithful to him; this piece contains similar eulogistic features. In the same issue we also find a report written by Elisabeth Förster—she is not identified as Nietzsche's sister—obviously prior to her husband's death and titled "A Sunday in Nueva Germania." It recounts a typical day in the life of the colony, portraying the venture as completely successful, although not concealing that the colonists have to work hard to sustain themselves and that those who are less industrious and simply want to acquire land have a difficult time surviving. She also takes a swipe at detractors whose views have appeared in the German press, most notably Julius Klingbeil, who is depicted as part of the undesirable rabble that a colony unfortunately attracts. She makes a plea for monetary contributions—the colony was still not on financially sound footing, although Elisabeth does not give that impression—noting that they have managed to construct a school for the education of the children, but that they still have no functioning church or minister, although they have recently built a parish house. At one point, she advances the claim that Nueva Germania is the only "German community in far-away lands, which was recently established, but can justifiably call itself a German colony," and thus it alone fulfills the mission that the various colonial societies in Germany promote. It would receive its due if it were not "defamed, persecuted, unsupported by Germany, and treated as Cinderella in the Jewish press." In a further article in this issue, Santiago Schaerer (1834–1895), the General Commissioner for Emigration in Paraguay, rebuts the brochure composed by Julius Klingbeil, which was published in Germany and denigrated the colony and its management. Despite Nietzsche's close relationship to the founders of Nueva Germania, there are no allusions to him, his writings, or, after January 1889, his lapse into insanity. Nietzsche may have gained insight into the nature of the Försters' activities from the prominent place they occupied in the *Bayreuther Blätter*, but, after the publication of *The Case of Wagner*, the Wagnerians obviously did not want his name associated with their pet colonial project.

Nietzsche and Nueva Germania

Nietzsche's reaction to the colonial ventures of his sister and her husband was not as negative as one might anticipate considering his antipathy to the nationalism and anti-Semitism of his brother-in-law and the close connection between the colony and its Bayreuth supporters. We have already seen that a number of factors predisposed him against Förster and the colonialist mentality, but at times he also seemed intrigued by the idea, as well as the reality, of the Paraguayan settlement. While Förster was still on his exploratory travels in 1883, Nietzsche wrote to his mother and sister that he could empathize with Förster's unwillingness to continue living in Germany, but that he has found that there are still several favorable countries for discontent Germans left in Europe, and one need not leave the continent altogether. Above all, he had no enthusiasm for the Germanophilic and racist aspects of Förster's thinking (14 March 1885, Nr. 581, KSB 7.23).[36] What Förster and Nietzsche shared to some degree was a disdain for various manifestations of modernity that had begun to take hold suddenly and more forcefully in Germany, and if there is any overlap in their thought, it stems from their common dislike for specific symptoms of modern industrial societies. An additional factor in Nietzsche's thinking about a possible change of domicile was climate, a veritable obsession for him during the last decade of his sane life. His letters from the 1880s are replete with remarks about the percentage of sun and cloudiness, barometric readings, precipitation amounts, and atmospheric "electricity" in various locations he was considering for domiciles. In February 1883, shortly after Förster had left for South America, he wrote to Heinrich Köselitz that "the old Deluge-Europe [*Sündflut-Europa*] will kill me yet: but perhaps someone will help me and drag me to the highlands of Mexico" (Nr. 381, KSB 6.333). That the thought of emigration persevered with him is demonstrated by a letter to his sister from the following August in which he complains of the exceptionally poor weather, in particular the heavy cloud cover, which makes him "another person, morose, extremely malicious against myself, as well as against others." His solution to the problem is "still" [*immer noch*] "the valley of Oaxaca in Mexico, which has ca. 33 cloudy days in a year, the rest of the time day and night pure, cloudless Engadine weather, ca. 220!; while Sils has 80 pleasant days in a year. (the altitude is the same as here,[37] there is a Swiss colony, the costs are exceptionally inexpensive)" (Nr. 453, KSB 6.431). It is therefore not completely inconceivable that Nietzsche himself, in times of the great discomfort he attributed to the European climate, considered the possibility of emigration to Paraguay. In July 1885, a few months after Förster's return to Germany, he writes to Overbeck that he is concerned about many things: "to be sure also a few strange desires, especially concerning the New World in Paraguay. At a moment's notice Europe can become impossible for me; and think of it, perhaps there in that distant land there is a tree branch for a lost bird like me" (Nr. 609, SB 7: 61–62). It is impossible to ascertain with any certainty how serious Nietzsche actually was about moving to Paraguay, but if we take him at his own word he rejected any thoughts of emigration on chiefly climatological grounds:

> I have considered extensively the thought of colonization in Paraguay, not without the ulterior motive of whether I might not find for myself an asylum there. With regard to *this* prospect, I have come to an unconditional "no"; my climatic needs contradict. Otherwise, there is a great deal that is reasonable in the entire matter; Paraguay is a wonderful piece of earth for German farmers—and a Westphalian or Pomeranian can sail there in great confidence as long as he does not have exorbitant expectations. (to Franz Overbeck, 6 October 1885, Nr. 632, KSB 7.97)

These thoughts obviously echo the propaganda promulgated by Förster and his allies. In the same letter, Nietzsche also expresses concern that Paraguay might not be the right place for his sister and brother-in-law either, and that he, like his mother, is extremely apprehensive about the entire matter. But Nietzsche's initial reactions are quite favorable, and had Förster chosen a drier, sunnier climate for his New Germany, it is possible that the self-proclaimed "good European" would have become one more of the millions of Germans to leave the Fatherland for the New World in the second half of the nineteenth century.

Obviously, climate was not the only factor that dissuaded Nietzsche from joining his sister and her husband in Paraguay. In his correspondence, he cites several other reasons why he would be disinclined to participate in the colonial adventure in Nueva Germania. First and foremost, Nietzsche recognized that he would have difficulties existing in the ideological climate of his brother-in-law. He informed his mother that he had reached a *modus vivendi* with Förster, but added that it would be impossible for him to have closer connections with "such an agitator." Besides the ideological differences he harbored with Förster, we can imagine that an educated European like Nietzsche would not have felt very comfortable in a somewhat primitive settlement without a good library, with few books and difficult access to booksellers, and with severely diminished possibilities of intellectual engagement. He also recognized that class difference would make his presence in such a colony difficult. Förster had appropriately pitched Nueva Germania to farmers and workers, many of them impoverished and eager to get a new start in life, and it was obvious that only those who were willing to do manual labor would succeed under the conditions of colonial life. Nietzsche possessed enough self-awareness to realize that he could not survive well in this harsh environment, that he belonged to a different social stratum than the settlers Förster had attracted. He indicated as much to his mother: "For myself I am even too aristocratically minded to place myself legally and socially on the same level as 20 families of farmers: as he [Förster] has it in the program." Significantly, he recognized that others possess the qualities needed to thrive under these adverse circumstances: the individual with the strongest will and the most cleverness will gain the upper hand; German men of learning like himself are badly prepared in these two areas. He also objects to Förster's dogmatic vegetarianism, believing that carnivores make better colonizers: "A vegetarian diet like Dr. F[örster] proposes makes such people only more excitable and bad-mooded. Look at the meat-eating English: up to this point in time they have been the race that has been the best at founding colonies. A phlegmatic disposition and roast beef—up to now they were the recipe for such 'enterprises'" (end of May 1885, Nr. 604, KSB 7.54). Significant in this letter, however, are not the various reasons Nietzsche provides for not emigrating as much as the fact that he even considered moving to Paraguay. From the letters we possess from 1885 and the discussions in these letters, Nietzsche evidently took the proposition of emigration fairly seriously. Although the notion of Nietzsche living in the middle of a forest in Paraguay might appear ludicrous to us today, he gave it earnest consideration.

Although Nietzsche decided that he was not suited for overseas adventures, during the last four years of his sane life he began to pay increasing attention to colonial affairs in Paraguay. He did so to a large extent out of concern for his sister's well-being, and for one of the few times in his life we find him actively involved in the investigation of mundane nonacademic and nonphilosophical matters. In general, he appears to have pursued any information he could gather about colonies in the New World. Writing to his sister shortly after Förster's return from Paraguay, he mentions that former Italian colonists from South America to whom he had spoken in Rapallo and Santa Margherita have reported that they were able to acquire considerable wealth and were able to return to Genoa with substantial profits (5 July 1885, Nr. 611, KSB 7.64). On the other hand, he spoke with a Basel acquaintance in November 1885 about a failed Swiss colony that had settled in the La Plata region (Nr. 646, KSB 7.111), and was informed that the failure of such ventures was very likely owing to the mixing of nationalities (to Bernhard and Elisabeth Förster, 2 January 1886, Nr. 656, KSB 7.132); in both these instances Nietzsche, directing his comments at his sister prior to her departure, makes a case for her to remain in Europe, or even in Germany. In Nice, he attended lectures on South America held by a traveler who spent three and a half years abroad. And he evidently showed Förster's book to a pastor's wife in Nice, who related her experiences from a fifty-year stay in America. These various activities were directed no doubt at gathering information, but also in most cases at building an argument against settlement in South America. Once Förster and Nietzsche's sister had arrived in Paraguay, Nietzsche appears to have followed current events from South America closely, even reading newspapers to gather information on items potentially pertinent to the health of the colonial venture. He writes to Förster in April 1886 that the news of a revolution in Montevideo has made him concerned about the colony he wants to establish, and that he fears Argentina could simply absorb Paraguay (Nr. 685, KSB 7.172). In another newspaper report, he obviously read about the outbreak of a cholera epidemic in the region around Rosario and in Argentina (to Franziska Nietzsche, 2 December 1886, Nr. 782, KSB 7.293). What makes these passages in Nietzsche's letters unusual is his obvious pursuit of information relating to South America, and in particular to colonial activities in that part of the world. As far as we can tell, Nietzsche was a reluctant reader of newspapers and did not normally follow current events closely. Like Bernhard Förster, he often expressed his abhorrence for journalism and journalists, whom he believed were responsible for the destruction of genuine culture, as well as the deterioration of the German language. But in these years, out of concern for his sister and curiosity about the colonial enterprise in which she and her husband were involved, he turned to all sources at his disposal for information about the New World.

Nietzsche's interest in South American colonization and his attempt to assess the possibilities for the future failure or success of Förster's colony may have been motivated by more than simply an interest in his sister's welfare. Although most commentators have claimed that Nietzsche wisely rejected offers to invest in the colonial enterprise, it is not clear that he did so because of either the principled objections he harbored concerning Förster's views or his skepticism about the colony's prospects. The evidence is sketchy, but suggests other motives were also at play. Elisabeth must have approached her brother with an investment proposition while she and Förster were still in Germany, since Nietzsche wrote to his sister in Naumburg shortly before her departure:

> I just received your kind and amusing offer, and if it serves in any way to give your worthy husband a good opinion of the incorrigible European and anti-anti-Semite, your entirely inconsequential brother and loafer Fritz . . , then I will gladly follow in the footsteps of Miss Alwin[38] and beseech you in this regard to make me a South American property owner under the same conditions and stipulations: with the one variation that the plot of earth should not be called Friedrichsland or Friedrichshain . . . , but, to commemorate the name that I christened you—Llamaland. (7 February 1886, Nr. 669, KSB 7.147)

Elisabeth evidently tried to make good on this quasi-agreement when she wrote to her brother in September 1886 (Nr. 399, KGB III 4.205–13). She approached him with a concrete investment plan in land and cattle and informed him that he could keep the cattle himself or have Förster and herself integrate his stock into their herd, which will be branded "Eli." In total, she requests from him six thousand marks. She also proposes an alternative plan: she and her husband would be prepared to borrow the same sum of money at 8 percent interest. Two days later, Förster writes to "his dear brother-in-law Zarathustra" and includes a map of the area so that Nietzsche could see where his property would be (Nr. 400, KGB III 4.213–15). Even at this point, Nietzsche appears to have been at least mildly interested in such an investment. Writing to Overbeck in October, he informs him about the Försters' request for money and asks for advice (Nr. 769, KSB 7.272); his main concern is not the soundness of the investment, but any problems that might arise with regard to his pension from Basel. Nietzsche was dependent on pension money from three different funds in Basel.[39] None of the pensions were secure; each had to be extended or renewed, and one of the pensions had evidently been recently continued without any official renewal, which should have occurred in 1885. Because of the uncertainties surrounding his pensions, Overbeck informed his friend and colleague about his precarious financial situation and noted that his income could be reduced by one-third at any time (29 October 1886, Nr. 414, KGB III 4.233–34). Overbeck may have also harbored reservations about Nietzsche's sister and Förster and the soundness of their judgment—and certainly Elisabeth later came to have ill feelings toward him, fueled perhaps in part by his discouragement in this matter—but in any case, he strongly advised Nietzsche against investing in what he believed was a risky Paraguayan enterprise. Nietzsche then wrote to his sister, informing her that he had no desire to become a rancher in Paraguay, and that the precariousness of his Basel pension and the need to keep his money liquid prevented him from investing in their colonial scheme (3 November 1886, Nr. 773, KSB 7.278). At about the same time, he wrote to his mother that becoming a property owner in Paraguay might endanger his pension from Basel (13 November 1886, Nr. 774, KSB 7.280), a claim that overstates what Overbeck had written and may be the type of statement a son writes to his mother when he does not want to reveal to her the whole truth about his financial dealings and insecurities. Nietzsche's first opportunity for investment in the colonies thus never comes to fruition, not because of his wisdom or skepticism with regard to the success of the colonial enterprise, but because of Nietzsche's unusual financial situation and Overbeck's sage advice. At no time during this period does Nietzsche appear to doubt that Förster and his sister are capable of achieving their goals, at least the goals that have to do with the prosperity of the colony.

Shortly thereafter, Nietzsche would have another attempt to invest in the Försters' colony. At about the time that Nietzsche was considering whether he should be a partner in Llamaland, Förster was negotiating with Cirilio Solalinde (1832–1923), a Paraguayan landowner and financier, to obtain a home for Nueva

Germania. Förster eventually closed a three-way deal with Solalinde and the government of Paraguay by which the German colony obtained a tract of land north of Asunción called *campo cassaccia* for a ridiculously small down payment, but with the proviso that it had to attract 140 families within the next two years. In late November of 1886, Förster evidently put his signature to the agreement that eventually led to his own demise. In the next few months, however, buoyed by optimism and the prospects for enormous success, Elisabeth and her husband set about attracting emigrants and capital to their colony. She was able to secure money from her mother and various friends, as well as from Förster's family, and in this context she must have again written to her brother, requesting money.[40] We are fortunate to possess both the draft of Nietzsche's response and the letter that he actually sent, and the contrast between the two tells us a great deal about what Nietzsche repressed when dealing with his sister and the efforts he made to remain on good terms with her. In the draft, he is much less conciliatory toward her and more skeptical about the success of the colony. He upbraids her for participating in an anti-Semitic enterprise and states bluntly that if the colony succeeds, he will be content for her sake, but if it fails, he will be pleased at the demise of an anti-Semitic undertaking. He adds in the draft that he hopes Jews assume an increasingly greater position of power in Europe "so that they lose the characteristics (namely do not need them any more) on the basis of which they have succeeded thus far as an oppressed people" (5 June 1887, Nr. 854, KSB 8.82). His actual letter, sent on the same day, has a vastly different tone. He writes in a more measured fashion that he is entirely disinclined to give any money because his own position is too insecure and theirs is not yet secure enough. But he adds that on the suggestion of their mother he has made eight hundred thaler available to them that was tied up in the house in Naumburg.[41] As a postscript to the letter he sends his best wishes to Förster on the occasion of his land acquisition, adding the maxim "anyone who possesses, is also possessed" [*wer besitzt, ist auch besessen*], which carries the same pun in English as in German (Nr. 855, KSB 8.85). In her response, Elisabeth expresses disappointment that her brother "wants to remain a poor man," and slight annoyance that he could think she would advise him to invest in something that was less than a secure proposition. She presents the investment as a unique situation with a finite window of opportunity since "the colonists in our colony will increase the value of their land threefold and fourfold, but through their own personal efforts." To mollify her brother, she adds that he should be unconcerned about the future; she is confident of success and "what we have belongs to you as well" (12 September 1887, Nr. 472, KGB III 6.71–72). Elisabeth even makes good on this statement. In September of 1888 she informs "her dear Fritz" that she and Förster are giving him a piece of land; the price of one thousand marks they will consider paid by the sum she received from the sale of her furniture in Naumburg (Nr. 574, KGB III 6.296). The remainder of their correspondence contains no mention of investment.

We should not read too much into Nietzsche's refusal to invest in Nueva Germania, and in particular, we should be cautious about regarding it as a sign of antipathy between the two siblings. Commentators, especially since the end of World War II, have alleged that there existed an enmity between Nietzsche and his sister, and that Nietzsche harbored considerable resentment toward her because of her ideological leanings. But this allegation ignores much of the evidence we possess in correspondence that was actually exchanged between Friedrich and Elisabeth. There were moments of tension and even outright hostility that emerged in the 1880s, especially around the incident with Lou Salomé. And Nietzsche does not disguise his dislike for the views harbored by Bernhard Förster and other Wagnerians, and his sister's intellectual proximity to these views. It is also clear from the written record that Nietzsche suppressed some rather aggressive feelings toward both his sister as well as toward his mother. We certainly see evidence of this aggression in several draft letters to Elisabeth, but it is important to recognize that the actual letters usually assume a much different and more conciliatory tone. The same is true for remarks made in connection with *Ecce Homo*, which Nietzsche never included in the finished work and which he likely would have suppressed, just as he suppressed most negative sentiments toward his family in published writings and personal communication. We should remember that despite the occasionally strained relationship, Nietzsche continued to send his sister his published works, and to keep her informed about his activities and mutual friends. For her part, Elisabeth harbored genuinely positive feelings for her brother. Although some critics have claimed that in asking her brother to invest in Nueva Germania, Elisabeth was trying to wring money out of her poor brother for an enterprise she knew was risky, the evidence in letters does not support such a claim. Rather, Elisabeth continues throughout to respect her brother and his works, although she, like Förster, appears to believe that as an academic and philosopher, he was much removed from the practical life they had chosen. Elisabeth is generous in her praise of her brother—although it is legitimate to wonder how well she understood his writings—concerned with his health, and generally complimentary to him. In a letter written in January 1888, she comments enthusiastically about his latest musical composition, "Hymn to Life" [*Hymnus an das Leben*], and even suggests, possibly with some irony, that it could perhaps become the national anthem of Nueva Germania (Nr. 513, KGB III 6.146). Although she objects to Georg Brandes and his promotion of her brother's thought, quite probably because Brandes was a Jew, she nonetheless expresses delight—"I am extremely happy for you" [*Meinem Herzen thut es unendlich wohl*]—that through Brandes, Nietzsche is beginning to win the acclaim that he deserves. Elisabeth probably regretted that her brother did not choose to participate more directly in the colony, but the occasional tensions between the siblings should not be turned into an animosity that was not the dominant tone in their relationship.

The important question for us is what these refused investment opportunities tell us about Nietzsche's views of colonization. Do they reflect his own precarious financial situation or a distrust of the colonial enterprise? Are they evidence for a dislike of Förster's colony, or of colonizing efforts in general? Did his contact with Nueva Germania affect his views on politics and the geopolitical goals of Germany and Europe? These questions are difficult to answer with certainty. We know that Nietzsche disliked the nationalist, socialist, and anti-Semitic ideological aspects of Nueva Germania. He is most content with the colonial experiment when he believes Förster has abandoned his anti-Semitic activities, and most critical of him and his sister when he encounters their continued adherence to anti-Semitism. Despite these ideologically based objections to Förster's enterprise, Nietzsche remains surprisingly affirmative with regard to the colony. Supported by his sister's overly optimistic reports on the success of the undertaking, Nietzsche expresses admiration and a certain amount of pride in the colony in his letters. After reading Förster's book, he writes with apparent conviction that a good farmer and cattle breeder would have to be pleased with the prospects of the colony (to Elisabeth Förster, 23 November 1885, Nr. 646, KSB 7.111) and even makes a few favorable remarks about Förster himself, calling him a "not unsympathetic" person who has "something sincere and noble about his being" (to Franz Overbeck, 17 October 1885, Nr. 636, KSB 7.101). Once Förster closed his deal and acquired *campo cassaccia*, he writes to Malwida von Meysenbug, obviously repeating Elisabeth's propaganda that the colony has secured an enormous piece of land through a splendidly successful purchase, and that the colony will be larger than many German principalities and full of the most magnificent forests (end of February 1887, Nr. 809, KSB 8.34). He writes similarly to Overbeck, adding that the Paraguayan government has honored Förster, and that his sister is the center of Paraguayan high society. To impress Overbeck with how well things are going in the colony, he informs him that the newest arrivals are a German baker and butcher, as well as a German doctor (13 May 1887, Nr. 847, KSB 8.74). That Nietzsche was sincere in these letters is probable since they are addressed to two of his closest friends, from whom he had no reason to hide his genuine feelings. These missives immediately precede the letter in which he refuses to invest in the colony; it therefore seems likely that his refusal was not based entirely on skepticism about its success. In a letter to Overbeck from early 1888, Nietzsche continues to demonstrate his faith in Förster's colonial undertaking. He is impressed by the arrival of approximately one hundred colonists, and notes in particular that Nueva Germania was able to attract "Baron Malzahn" (Nr. 984, KSB 8.243).

Hermann von Maltzan (1843–1891), an aristocrat from Mecklenburg, was a naturalist and traveler in Africa who was instrumental in the creation of the German Colonial Association [*Kolonialverein*], which was involved in an earlier colony in Paraguay.[42] The elitist Nietzsche had commented disparagingly about Förster's enterprise because of the class of people it attracted, and the presence of someone like Maltzan, whom Nietzsche also mentions in a letter to Meysenbug (end of July 1888, Nr. 1078, KSB 8.379), obviously legitimated the colony in his eyes. Nietzsche also mentions to Overbeck that Förster's influence in Paraguay has reached such proportions that it is likely he will be considered a candidate for president. He adds that he and his brother-in-law have to make extraordinary efforts in order not to treat each other as enemies—Nietzsche was still smarting from the alleged cooptation of *Zarathustra* in the *Anti-Semitic Correspondence*[43]—but with regard to the affairs of the colony and the status of Förster, he appears to have only positive impressions.

We possess only two letters from Elisabeth to her brother from 1888, and since we know that the colony was experiencing great difficulties at this time, we have to assume that his continued favorable opinions about Nueva Germania stem largely from either direct reports or information flows that she controlled. In March of 1888, he tells Köselitz that his sister reports that eighty Germans and three Swiss are in the colony, and that so many have expressed an interest to come in the next months that they fear not being prepared to receive the onslaught (Nr. 1007, KSB 8.276).[44] To his mother, he writes in May that now the enterprise has proceeded so far that one ought to trust it: "even I am beginning to trust the thing" (Nr. 1039, KSB 8.321). And in June he informs Köselitz of a long passage in his sister's letter describing the ceremonious inauguration of Nueva Germania, adding: "The matter is really taking on a magnificent dimension" (Nr. 1045, KSB 8.332). Toward the end of the last year of his sane life, however, Nietzsche must have begun to suspect something was amiss, and he expresses serious doubts about the soundness of Förster's business dealings. Writing to his mother, who had obviously heard disturbing news about Paraguay from a Naumburg acquaintance, he concurs that they have no real information about the chief parameters of the contractual obligations to which Förster has agreed. He adds that one cannot found a colony without some capital, and that first attempts often fail, as he knows from Swiss acquaintances. His remark about the need for capital in a colonial undertaking may have stemmed from his reading of the articles we examined above in the *Bayreuther Blätter*. But he nonetheless tries to encourage his mother—and perhaps persuade himself—with the reasoning that no government would entrust such a large enterprise to someone without certain assurances. South Americans, he writes, "are very smart people. Stated clearly, if they exhibit trust, we ought to have a hundred times more" (Nr. 1114, SB 8.431). Eventually the disquieting news about the colony, which was circulating in private reports as well as in various periodicals, including, as we have seen, indirectly in the *Bayreuther Blätter*, convinced Nietzsche that the venture was experiencing serious difficulties. In one of his last letters to Overbeck from Christmas 1888, he remarks, "In Paraguay things are as bad as possible. The Germans who were lured over there are furious and demanding their money back—but there is none. Brutalities have occurred; I fear the worst" (Nr. 1210, KSB 8.549). Since Nietzsche opens this letter with the statement that "in two months I will be the first name on earth," it is difficult to know how conscious he was of the real situation in Paraguay, but it appears likely that prior to his breakdown and fall into insanity, he recognized the imminent collapse of Förster's project.

The Emergence of the Good European

Nietzsche's personal involvement with the colonial imagination has a "philosophical" counterpart in his writings. His actual contact with Nueva Germania through his sister was, as we have seen, marked by a detectable ambivalence: although Nietzsche did not disagree with colonization in principle, especially if it was conceived as a manifestation of the will to power, he objected to many principles on which this particular colony was founded and with the dominant nationalist ideology of the colonial movement. Nietzsche's own thinking about colonies, which was never very developed or delineated in any detail in his writings, is contained primarily in occasional remarks surrounding two slogans that became prominent in his oeuvre during the 1880s: the "good European" and "great politics." The first of these slogans appears earlier in Nietzsche's thought. In *Human, All Too Human*, we encounter the term "the good European" in an interesting reflection entitled "European man and the abolition of nations." In this aphorism, Nietzsche argues that the development toward a European union is an inevitable consequence of modernity. "Trade and industry, the post and the book-trade, the possession in common of all higher culture, rapid changing of home and scene, the nomadic life now lived by all who do not own land—these circumstances are necessarily bringing with them a weakening and finally an abolition of nations, at least the European: so that as a consequence of continual crossing a mixed race, that of European man, must come into being out of them." Working against this Europeanizing tendency are nationalism and national hostilities, which by comparison are artificial and benefit ruling dynasties, as well as "certain classes of business and society." Nietzsche continues: "once one has recognized this fact, one should not be afraid to proclaim oneself simply a *good European* and actively to work for the amalgamation of nations" (MA 475, KSA 2.309). Nietzsche's thought contains an apparent and unresolved contradiction: while he insists that trade and industry promote Europeanism, he claims simultaneously that business favors nationalism. More important than this contradiction is the context within which Nietzsche first develops the concept of a "good European." From its introduction here in the late 1870s, the good European was always conceived as the Nietzschean alternative to nationalism, and, as we have seen in Chapter 2, it had cultural and philosophical, as well as geopolitical, implications. Indeed, as Nietzsche's animosity toward nationalism, in particular German nationalism, becomes more virulent, his identification with Europeanism increases.

Although nationalism is the most precise antithesis for the Europeanism Nietzsche espouses, his anticipated European confederation should not be confused with anything resembling the postwar European community or the present European economic union.[45] The positive as well as the negative field of association for the "good European" makes it clear that Nietzsche's notion is antithetical to many of the democratic values that have in fact endured on the continent. Europeanism becomes another in a series of words that Nietzsche uses to express his disgust with democracy, religion, and Judeo-Christian morality. In a note from 1884, he writes that the good European is "against equality, against moral tartuffism, against Christianity and God" (Nachlass 1884, 25[524], KSA 11.150). In the preface to *Beyond Good and Evil*, good Europeans are opposed to Jesuits and democrats, as well as to Germans, and likened to "free spirits" (JGB, Vorrede, KSA 5.13) The European is synonymous with the "supra-national" (Nachlass 1884, 26[297], KSA 11.229), and Europeans are the "over-race" [*Über-Rasse*] (Nachlass 1884, 25[462], 11.136); Europeanism signals the overcoming of various epistemological, ethical, and political transgressions of the nineteenth century:

> Looking at nature as if it were proof of the goodness and governance of a god; interpreting history in honor of some divine reason, as a continual testimony of a moral world order and ultimate moral purposes; interpreting one's own experiences as pious people have long enough interpreted theirs, as if everything were providential, a hint, designed and ordained for the sake of the salvation of the soul—that is *all over* now, that has man's conscience *against* it, that is considered indecent and dishonest by every more refined conscience—mendaciousness, feminism, weakness, and cowardice. In this severity, if anywhere, we are *good* Europeans and heirs of Europe's longest and most courageous self-overcoming. (FW 357, KSA 3.600)

In this passage from an aphorism discussing the problem "What is German?", we find an unusual mixture of qualities possessed by the good European: antireligious and antiprovidential, the "Europeans of the day after tomorrow" (JGB 214, KSA 5.151) are also beyond ethics and opposed to modern social degenerations of modernity, such as democracy, socialism, and feminism. The "higher men" that

Nietzsche foresees emerging to dominate European affairs will be entrusted with revitalizing characteristics that persevere subterraneously. In various passages, Nietzsche suggests that Christianity and its attendant morality have temporarily negated some core of Europeanness. In contrast to the Greeks, in whom "morality thrived in the *ruling* castes" (Nachlass 1884, 25[163], KSA 11.56), in Europe the hypocrisy he associates with Christianity has emanated from the lower classes, from slaves and oppressed peoples. Occasionally in European history—for example, in the Renaissance or in such figures as Napoleon—we have witnessed a reemergence of the proper European spirit. For the most part, however, the good European, like his cousin the overman, is a project for the future,[46] a higher type of human being whom we must consciously create.[47]

The expansion of Nietzsche's reflections from German and European problems to global concerns occurs only in his writings of the 1880s. The bulk of Nietzsche's comments on Europeanism relate to issues that have little to do with world affairs: as an alternative to nationalism, it encompasses primarily cultural and philosophical concerns. But at times, especially during the 1880s, Nietzsche does reflect on Europe in the context of geopolitical considerations. As we might expect, most of his comments on colonies and on foreign affairs that pertain to colonization are penned after Nietzsche had become acquainted with Förster's project. But in at least one significant exception, Nietzsche's analysis and suggestions predate his acquaintance with Förster's thought and frame the problem in a way that may have actually influenced his future brother-in-law. In a unique passage from his pre-*Zarathustra* period, Nietzsche comments in *Dawn* on the miserable conditions of the working class in Europe, claiming that no ameliorative measures could turn this form of slavery into something desirable. We have already examined this passage in connection with the Social Question in Chapter 3, but Nietzsche's tentative solution to the Social Question has implications for his views on colonialism. We will recall that he suggests a remedy that was realized by millions of actual Germans during the late nineteenth century: emigration.

> The workers of Europe ought henceforth to declare themselves *as a class* a human impossibility and not, as usually happens, only a somewhat harsh and inappropriate social arrangement; they ought to inaugurate within the European beehive an age of a great swarming-out such as has never been seen before, and through this act of free emigration in the grand manner to protest against the machine, against capital, and against the choice now threatening them of being *compelled* to become either the slave of the state or the slave of a party of disruption. Let Europe be relieved of a fourth of its inhabitants! They and it will be all the better for it! Only in distant lands and in the undertakings of swarming trains of colonists will it really become clear how much reason and fairness, how much healthy mistrust,

mother Europe has embodied in her sons—sons who could no longer endure it with the dull old woman and were in danger of becoming as querulous, irritable and pleasure-seeking as she herself was. Outside of Europe Europe's virtues will accompany these workers on their wanderings; and that which at home began to degenerate into dangerous ill-humor and inclination for crime will, once abroad, acquire a wild beautiful naturalness and be called heroism. (M 206, KSA 3.184–85)

With the exception of the substitution of Europe for Germany, the sentiments here approximate the type of reasoning we find a few years later in Förster's essays and pamphlets. Nietzsche's compassion for the workers, his opposition to the German state and business, and his deprecation of the promise Europe holds for the downtrodden masses mimic much colonialist rhetoric during the Second Empire. Although one can hardly imagine that the lower classes to which Nietzsche refers are included in his notion of "good Europeans," they do appear to have inborn European characteristics Nietzsche hopes will thrive in foreign climes. He even suggests, as Förster does later, that colonization could have a salutary reciprocal impact on Europe. The benefit to Europe, however, would not necessarily result from the re-importation of the renewed health onto the continent, but rather the clearing of the air, the eradication of overpopulation, and the elimination of an overly reflective European habit. Nietzsche also suggests that to solve the problem of a depleted workforce, Europe could import Chinese, who will bring with them "the modes of life and thought suitable to industrious ants," and thus "contribute to the blood of restless and fretful Europe something of Asiatic calm and contemplativeness and—what is probably needed most—Asiatic *perseverance*" (M 206, KSA 3.185). In this suggestion, Nietzsche touches upon another aspect of the Europeanism he promotes in the 1880s: the inherent superiority of Europe and the inferiority of races living on other continents. He appears convinced that Europe, because of its supremacy over other nations, can simply attract or coerce a large mass of workers from Asia when they are needed.

In this early reflection on colonization and Europe, Nietzsche's focus is still ultimately Europe, which needs a type of bloodletting and transfusion in order to regain health. In later passages dealing with world affairs, most of which were composed after 1884 and thus after the actual beginnings of the German colonial empire, it is clear that Nietzsche's thoughts turn to a European subjugation of the world. Toward the middle of the decade, we find more frequent comments about European colonies. In his notebooks in the spring of 1884, he writes: "The way Europeans found colonies proves their predatory nature" (Nachlass 1884, 25[163], KSA 11.56); "Europeans betray themselves in the way in which they have colonized" (Nachlass 1884, 25[152], KSA 11.53); and "one can assess the character of Europeans according to their relationship to foreign countries, in colonization: extremely cruel" (Nachlass 1884, 25[177], KSA 11.61). Here we again encounter the suggestion that Christian ethics and moral platitudes are a veneer, that the European essence manifests itself only in unusual circumstances and outside of the continent, which has been too long subjected to the "civilizing" influence of Christianity and a morality of pity and compassion. Although these statements, taken out of context, could be employed to condemn European colonialism, Nietzsche is likely affirming the cruelty and aggressiveness of imperialism. We should note that the German term Nietzsche uses for "predatory nature" [*Raubtier-Natur*] appears in other Nietzschean contexts without any pejorative sense. In many writings from the 1880s, the beast of prey [*Raubtier*] is contrasted with the despised herd, the domesticated animal that human beings have become under the leveling influences of the Judeo-Christian heritage and a politics of democracy. We must evaluate similarly Nietzsche's identification of the good European with the criminal, which also often has a positive valence in Nietzsche's works.[48]

Other texts from the 1880s indicate that these colonialist criminals and predators are in fact the "good Europeans." Sometimes the European colonial project is justified in terms of a biological analogy. In the notebooks from 1888, Nietzsche claims:

> The right [*Recht*] to punishment (or to social self-defense) has in essence become the word "justice" [*Recht*] only through a misuse: a right is acquired through contracts—but self-protection and self-defense are not based on a contract. A people, at least, ought to consider with just as much justification its need for conquest, its craving for power, as a right, whether it be with weapons, with trade, commerce, and colonization—for example, a right to growth. A society that rejects war and conquest for all times and instinctively is in decline: it is ripe for democracy and shopkeeper regimes. (Nachlass 1888, 14[192], KSA 13.379)

In this passage, Nietzsche contrasts democracy and the shopkeeper mentality—a frequently used derogatory term in *Zarathustra*—with aggressive colonialism, interpreting European expansion as a natural right to self-preservation. In other remarks, Nietzsche uses a historical view to discuss the desired course for European domination of the world. In *The Gay Science*, under the general heading "Our faith that Europe will become more virile," Nietzsche praises Napoleon as a continuator of the Renaissance, a destroyer of nationalism, and an enemy of modern ideas; he is someone who "brought back again a whole slab of antiquity, perhaps even the decisive piece, the piece of granite. And who knows whether this slab of antiquity might not finally become master again over the national movement, and whether it must not become the heir and continuator of Napoleon in an affirmative sense; for what he wanted was one unified Europe, as is known—as mistress of the earth" (FW 362, KSA 3.610). Occasionally Nietzsche discusses the need for European hegemony over other nations in quasi-political terms. In a comment from *The Gay Science*, "we who are homeless," he refers to those people, like himself, who feel out of place in contemporary Europe. They are not liberal; they do not believe in progress or equal rights; they do not want to reestablish relationships from the past based on outmoded ideals.

> We simply do not consider it desirable that a realm of justice and concord should be established on earth (because it would certainly be the realm of the deepest leveling and *chinoiserie*); we are delighted with all who love, as we do, danger, war, and adventures, who refuse to compromise, to be captured, reconciled, and castrated; we count ourselves among conquerors; we think about the necessity for new orders, also for a new slavery—for every strengthening and enhancement of the human type also involves a new kind of enslavement. (FW 377, KSA 3.629)

These "children of the future" are later identified as "good Europeans," who, like the emigrants who "embark on the sea," share a common faith in the "European spirit."

Finally, in other rare passages, Nietzsche's thoughts include more specific references to geopolitical considerations. In two notebook entries written in the summer of 1885, Nietzsche looks past national wars and newly created empires to a much larger concern: the dominance of the earth by a united Europe. The first longer entry in which Nietzsche discusses this possibility was taken into the collection *The Will to Power* by Elisabeth as aphorism 957 in a section aptly titled "The Master of the Earth." Indeed, Nietzsche begins his reflection by posing the question that has presented itself "inexorably, hesitantly, terribly as fate": "how shall the earth as a whole be governed?" Not surprisingly Nietzsche turns to morality, one of his central concerns during the 1880s, observing that new "lawgiving moralities" are dependent on the appearance of "men of great creativity." In contemporary Europe, such men, however, "will be sought in vain today and probably for a long time to come." European morality, which has taken such a firm hold on the continent and the minds of its peoples, is the main barrier to the development of genuine creativity and a revision of a moral code that champions such values as "equal rights" and "sympathy with all that suffers." The new morality must be the antithesis of everything currently accepted as the moral norm in contemporary European society: "danger, severity, violence, danger in the street as well as in the heart, inequality of rights, concealment, stoicism, the art of experiment, devilry of all kinds" are necessary to promote the types of individuals

Nietzsche envisions. Only with such a reversal of moral values will Europe be prepared to train "a ruling caste—the future *masters of the earth*." Since these new values are diametrically opposed to everything that is currently acceptable, they must be taught initially in a surreptitious fashion, but Nietzsche makes it evident that gradually over the decades "a new kind of man," "a new master type and caste" will emerge, "in whom the duration of the necessary will and the necessary instinct will be guaranteed through many generations." These new European rulers of the world are likened to Nietzsche's "free spirits," insofar as they too will express discontent "with present-day man" and foster "the special rights of higher men . . . against the 'herd animal.'" Nietzsche further compares this new caste to similar structures in antiquity, which produced "strong and enterprising" individuals, a "more hegemonic morality," and had no use for democracy or Christianity (Nachlass 1885, 37[8], KSA 11.580–83). Nietzsche may also reference antiquity, because he is thinking of the imperial nature of Greek conquests under Alexander or, more likely, the conquests of the Roman Empire. There is no doubt from this section that, like their ancient models, the new men will not only reverse the pernicious European moral code, but also form a ruling class that will dominate the entire earth.

The next notebook entry is even clearer in its advocacy of European world dominance. Nietzsche begins by writing that he ignores wars between European nations, new "Reichs," and everything that stands in the foreground. His concern is with a united Europe that he is convinced will appear in the future. Citing the forerunners in this quest for unity, an unusual list that includes Napoleon, Goethe, Heine, Stendhal, Beethoven, Schopenhauer, and "perhaps" Richard Wagner,[49] Nietzsche claims that these individuals all anticipate a European mentality and were nationalistic only in their weaker moments. He sketches an economic situation that is already familiar to us. Commerce and trade, as well as monetary concerns, will compel the disintegration of national boundaries, as European nations pursue greater participation in world trade and commerce. But further measures will have to be undertaken when the stakes rise, and the issue goes beyond mercantile considerations:

> In order to enter into the struggle for the rule of the earth with a good chance of success—it is obvious against whom this struggle must be waged—Europe will probably need to reach a serious "understanding" with England; it needs England's colonies for that struggle just as much as today's Germany, to practice its new role as mediator and broker, needs Holland's colonies. No one really believes any longer that England itself is strong enough to continue to play out its old role for another fifty years; it is being destroyed by the impossibility of keeping the *homines novi* out of the government, and one must not have such a change of parties in order

that such protracted things———today one has to be a soldier first not to lose his credit as a merchant. Enough: in this, as in other things, the next century will be found in the footsteps of Napoleon, the first and most anticipatory man of modern times. (Nachlass 1885, 37[9], KSA 11.584)

Nietzsche's fragmentary vision, although confused and sketchy, is nonetheless clear about certain priorities. What is at stake for him is the domination of the earth by a ruling caste,[50] which will be European and bred to rule the globe, not national or simply economic in character, and it will by necessity have to proceed along the bellicose lines of a Napoleon in order to secure economic supremacy as well. These "good Europeans" of the future will have no recourse to a "public sphere" or parliaments (Nachlass 1885, 37[9], 11.584): casting off the veneer of civility enforced on Europe by the Christian ethics of brotherly love, they will rule by authoritarian means that may well entail conquest and subjugation of peoples. The notion of the good European in Nietzsche's writings is thus quite definitely an alternative to the nationalism of his time. But it simultaneously discloses a Eurocentric conviction that does not exclude the ruthless application of military force and economic exploitation in a vastly conceived colonial enterprise.[51]

The Task of Great Politics

The tasks Nietzsche sets for his "good Europeans" can be summed up in another Nietzschean concept: "great politics."[52] But we have to exercise caution when interpreting this notion in Nietzsche's works. Nietzsche appropriated the term "great politics" from the political sphere that existed in Germany during the Bismarck era, and frequently he employs it to refer to the foreign policies of the Second Empire, rather than to his own, more grandiose and speculative designs. As Peter Bergmann points out, the term in English may hide the associations that Nietzsche was trying to counter, as well as those he was trying to promote: "In German the term has a familiar, majestic ring, one rooted in the then fashionable conviction of the primacy of foreign policy, of a higher form of politics specifically addressing European and world power conflicts in contradistinction to a presumably lesser form of politics dealing with internal matters."[53] Looking back at the Wilhelmenian period in the 1920s, German historians published documents under the title "The Great Politics of the European Cabinets, 1871–1914" [*Die Grosse Politik der Europäischen Kabinette, 1817–1914*], and this usage captures the semantic field in which we should locate the term. The initial mention of "great politics" in Nietzsche's writings is thus informed by his own ambivalent relationship to the Second Empire and to the nation-state as a political entity. In *Human, All Too Human*, for example, the preoccupation with "great politics" diverts energy from other endeavors in which a people might engage. Nietzsche reasons that even worse than this sacrifice of time and energy is the loss of individualism that politicization brings with it: "There occurs a spectacle played out continually in a hundred thousand simultaneous acts: every efficient, industrious, intelligent, energetic man belonging to such a people lusting after political laurels is dominated by this lust and no longer belongs wholly to his own domain, as he formerly did." Nietzsche's objection to Bismarckian "great politics" is thus an extension of his objection to politics and nationalism in general. He closes this aphorism, entitled "Great Politics and What They Cost," by questioning whether the "inflorescence and pomp of the whole" is really worth the sacrifice, especially "if all the nobler, tenderer, more spiritual plants and growths in which its soil was previously so rich have to be sacrificed to this coarse and gaudy flower of the nation" (MA 481, KSA 2.315–16). In a more conciliatory and psychological view of "great politics" in *Dawn* ("On Great Politics"), Nietzsche claims that its central driving force is the "need for the feeling of power" [*das Bedürfniss des Machtgefühls*] in both rulers and subjects. Indeed, it is the coincidence of this need in sovereigns and the people that allows the realization of military actions. Once the masses are prepared to sacrifice "their life, their goods, their conscience, their virtues" for the intoxication that comes with victories on the battlefield and national hegemony over others, then the prince can instigate a conflict cloaking "his crimes in the good conscience of his people" (M 189, KSA 3.162). The rhetoric of the ruler is thus merely a reflection of feelings that already exist, and the morality he preaches is based on little more than what Nietzsche would later call the "will to power." Anticipating insights in his work on ethics and morality in the latter part of the 1880s, Nietzsche maintains that good and evil are relative and related to power differentials: possessing power, one calls oneself "good," while the people on whom one discharges one's power become "evil." In this aphorism Nietzsche therefore connects "great politics" with an ethical relativism and psychological imperative of the will, such as he would develop further in his later writings.

The psychologically nuanced and reflective considerations of "great politics" that we find in the aphoristic collections of Nietzsche's middle period cede to a more negatively charged association of "great politics" with the foreign policies of Bismarck's Germany. In *Beyond Good and Evil*, Nietzsche uses the notion inside quotation marks to indicate that it is a phrase belonging to someone else, contrasting it with his own concept of the good European. Nietzsche's usage in this book is familiar: although even some "good Europeans" will occasionally relapse into patriotic revelry, and some "sluggish, hesitating races" may need half a century to purge themselves of chauvinistic excess, Europeanism will eventually prevail. After this brief introduction to aphorism 241, Nietzsche continues by inventing a persona who "overhears" a conversation in which the vision of "great politics" is closely associated with Bismarckian objectives. The interlocutors, two old patriots, debate over whether a leader, quite obviously the Iron Chancellor, who could politicize a nation by depreciating its natural proclivities, undermining its conscience, narrowing its mentality, and nationalizing its taste, deserves the appellation great, strong, or mad. The debate becomes heated, and Nietzsche, rather than following the dispute, considers "in his happiness and apartness" how "soon a stronger one may become master of the strong" (JGB 241, KSA 5.180–82). In this aphorism, "great politics" is likened to the "superficializing of a people," a course obviously identified with the nationalism Nietzsche abhorred in the Second Empire.[54] In a later aphorism in the same work, this negative view of "great politics" is similarly associated with Bismarck's "blood-and-iron" politics and the German "infirmity of taste." The French, Nietzsche contends, despite a noticeable and unfortunate Germanization, remain the culturally superior people of Europe. One of the reasons for their superiority is their status as a synthesis of the northern and southern types. Germans, by contrast, are implicitly considered too northern and exhibit a colorless "gray-in-gray, from sunless conceptual-spectrism and from poverty of blood" (JGB 254, KSA 5.198–200). Their "great politics" at the moment are conceived as a remedy for the cultural sickness plaguing the nation; Nietzsche waits for the cure to take effect, but has no hope for improvement yet.[55] France thus exhibits an understanding for those "midlanders" who are neither southern nor northern, and who have relinquished their fatherland; in short, for the "good Europeans," who reject the nationalist narcotic of great politics.

Like most concepts that Nietzsche develops in his writings, "great politics" in this negative sense fits into a complex mosaic of terms and ideas. It refers not only to current events and to a particular psychological constellation, but also to a system of values and to a religious outlook. In his later work, when Nietzsche was most concerned with the development and mutual conditioning of morality and religion, great politics of the unfavorable, Bismarckian variety is located within the nexus of the Judeo-Christian heritage and an ethics of *ressentiment*. In *On the Genealogy of Morals*, Nietzsche sketches a history of the West in which Jewish vengeance and hatred, which are likened to the trunk of a tree, branch out eventually into a new love associated with Christ and Christianity. The function of Jesus of Nazareth in this scheme is to bring men into the proximity of the original Jewish ideals. The person who apparently opposed the reigning Jewish values is thus in reality their promoter. Nietzsche provides his reader with the following rhetorical question: "Was it not the secret black art of a truly *great* politics of vengeance, a far-sighted, subterranean, slowly working and carefully planned vengeance, that Israel had to deny its true instrument publicly and nail him to the cross like a moral enemy, so that 'the whole world' (namely, all the enemies of Israel) might naïvely swallow the bait?" (GM, Erste Abhandlung 8, KSA 5.269). Great politics is in this sense a politics of revenge, part of a Judeo-Christian value system that has come to dominate modern civilization and has furtively manifested itself in the nationalism and petty political attitudes of Bismarck's Germany. Because they are symptoms of a similarly detested European value system, Nietzsche can easily move back and forth from religious and ethical reflections to comments on the current political scene. Thus in *Twilight of the Idols*, Nietzsche embarks on a discussion of the "spiritualization of sensuality" and the emergence of Christian "love," but winds up speaking about the foreign policies of the Second Empire. Just as parties need other oppositional parties in order to achieve self-definition, so too Germany requires enemies, both external and internal, in order to assert itself. Great politics is tantamount to Judeo-Christian ethics translated into geopolitical terms: "A new creation in particular—the new *Reich*, for example—needs enemies more than friends: in opposition alone does it *feel* itself necessary, in opposition alone does it *become* necessary" (GD, Moral als Widernatur 3, KSA 6.84). The modernity that Nietzsche opposed with his good European appeared in many guises, and as the 1880s progressed, the "great politics" proclaimed by the newly unified Germany became for Nietzsche one of modernity's most loathsome manifestations.

At about the time that Germany was acquiring her first colonial possessions and Nietzsche was being introduced to colonization through his brother-in-law, we encounter the initial mention of an alternative type of "great politics." In the positive, Nietzschean sense, we find its first occurrence in the notes Nietzsche penned during the late spring and early summer of 1885, when he comments laconically: "Furthermore, the higher Europeans, precursors of *great politics*" (Nachlass 1885, 35[45], KSA 11.532). It is a bit difficult to tell what Nietzsche has in mind with his "great politics" at this point, but it is evident that the term is already closely associated with the elitist Europeanism he advocated throughout the 1880s and that we witnessed above in passages composed in 1885. In notes written a few months previously, possibly composed in connection with a plan for a continuation of his *Untimely Meditations*, Nietzsche lists five topics and an introduction that include many of his favorite themes of these years: "hierarchy of men," "knowledge as the will to power," "beyond good and evil," "the hidden artists," and "the hammer." The fourth topic he lists is "great politics" (Nachlass 1885, 34[188], KSA 11.484). In another note from 1885, he endows "great politics" with class distinctions and a direct geopolitical dimension: "The new philosopher can emerge only in connection with a ruling caste, as its highest spiritualization. Great politics, world hegemony up close; complete lack of principles for it" (Nachlass 1885, 35[17], KSA 11.533–34). This field of association continues to surround "great politics" in Nietzsche's writings and correspondence for the next three and a half years, although the term itself coexists in many texts with the negatively inflected, Bismarckian "great politics." In a sketch written in preparation for *Ecce Homo*, for example, Nietzsche expresses his absolute disgust for the "incitement to national and racial selfishness that now makes its claims under the name of 'great politics'" (Nachlass 1888–89, 25[6], KSA 13.640), while in the work itself he contrasts the politics he despises with his own version of "great politics": "The concept politics has then become completely absorbed into a war of spirits, all the power-structures of the old society have been blown into the air—they one and all reposed on the lie: there will be wars such as there have never yet been on earth. Only after me there will be *great politics* on earth" (EH, Warum ich ein Schicksal bin 1, KSA 6.366). Similarly, we find passages in notes from 1888 in which great politics is accused of devouring time that should be devoted to more worthwhile endeavors and of promoting a Teutonic patriotism (Nachlass 1888, 19[1], KSA 13.540), while in a letter to Georg Brandes (1842–1927) written a few months later, Nietzsche fantasizes about control of the world and the establishment of world peace; the elimination of races, nations, and estates; and the validation of the enormously long ladder of hierarchical relations between men and men. As a summary statement he adds: "There you have the first world-historical paper: Great Politics *par excellence*" (December 1888, Nr. 1170, KSB 8.502).

Although Nietzsche never entirely rids himself of the Bismarckian version of great politics, as the 1880s progress his own notion begins to predominate in his published texts, as well as his notebooks and correspondence. "Great politics" becomes one in a series of notions that encapsulates the final phase of Nietzschean thought. As such, it is closely related to other concepts of this period and serves as the shorthand for an antinationalist political standpoint that has world-historical, as well as global, compass. In a passage from his last notebook, composed in December of 1888, Nietzsche titles the first page "great politics" and explicates the term as follows:

> I bring war. *Not* between nation and nation: I have no word to express my contempt for the despicable interest-politics of European dynasties, which makes a principle, indeed nearly a duty out of the incitement to arrogant selfishness of peoples against each other. *Not* between classes. For we have no higher classes, therefore also no lower ones: what is today on top in society is condemned physiologically and moreover—what is proof of this—has become so impoverished in its spirit, so insecure, that it professes the *counterprinciple* of a higher type of man without scruples.
>
> I bring war directly at odds with all the absurd coincidences of nation, class, race, occupation, education, culture: a war as if between rising and falling, between the will to life and *vengeance* against life, between uprightness and deceitful mendacity. (Nachlass 1888–89, 25[1], KSA 13.637)

"Great politics" in the Nietzschean sense of the word is a political program that institutes his philosophical regime. It cancels nationalist and class-based conflicts, but eliminates neither domination nor differences, since it advocates a hierarchical order [*Rangordnung*] based on Nietzschean philosophical tenets. In other passages written shortly before the outbreak of insanity, "great politics" assumes a more ominous stance with regard to humanity. After two millennia of physiological absurdity, Nietzsche claims, the demise of instinctual contradictoriness had to come. Only during the past twenty years have all of the most important questions of nutrition, clothing, procreation, and health been handled with the proper rigor and seriousness (obviously by Nietzsche himself), and now it is time to proclaim an era of "great politics." Its first principle will be the primacy of physiology over all other matters. In keeping with Nietzsche's turn to biology in his later writings, he advocates the breeding of a higher form of humanity, and his wording slips into a rhetorical register that is familiar to us from racist eugenic experiments of the twentieth century. He demands "merciless severity against anything degenerate and parasitic on life—against anything that destroys, poisons, slanders, ruins . . . and that sees in the destruction of life the indication of a higher type of soul." At another point, he writes that great politics "puts a ruthless end to everything degenerate and parasitic" (Nachlass 1888–89, 25[1], KSA 13.638).[56] "Second principle: To create a party of life strong enough for *great* politics: *great* politics makes physiology the ruler of all other questions,—it will *discipline* humanity as a whole, it will measure the rank of the races, the peoples, the individuals according to the future . . . according to the promotion of life contained in them,—it mercilessly puts an end to everything that is degenerate and parasitic." In passages such as this one, composed while Nietzsche stood on the brink of insanity, his notion of "great politics" both falls short of and exceeds a colonialist imagination. Too laden with biological assumptions to be considered a direct reference to any specific venture in foreign policy, "great politics" nonetheless contains imperatives for global action and harbors implications for the entire human race.

Occasionally in his published works Nietzsche made the connection between "great politics" and the colonialist imagination more explicit. The *locus classicus* for this connection occurs appropriately in *Beyond Good and Evil*, where the struggle for world domination, for the hegemony of Europe over a vast colonial empire, a relevant topic whose actual outcome was perhaps the opposite of what Nietzsche predicted—if not economically, then at least politically—is viewed as an essential question for the nineteenth century. Nietzsche observes a "paralysis of will" spread unevenly across Europe. This "European disease" is most prevalent where civilization has prevailed longest: significantly, France, and not Germany, is deemed the worst of the infirm nations, while in Germany, especially northern Germany, and in England, Spain, and Corsica, Nietzsche finds that "the power to will and to persist" is somewhat stronger. Russia, "that immense middle empire where Europe as it were flows back to Asia," exhibits surprisingly the most strength in Nietzschean terms. It is difficult to determine precisely what is driving these evaluations, but it may be that the nations and regions Nietzsche deems strongest in terms of will are those that have been least affected by the civilizing practices of Judeo-Christian doctrine. Although Nietzsche foresees only an augmentation of sickness, with its attendant "parliamentary imbecility" and "the obligation of everyone to read his newspaper at breakfast," he has hopes that Russia will become such a danger that the European nations, in order to counter the Russian threat, will be compelled to band together and carry out their appointed task:

> to *acquire one will*, by means of a new caste ruling over Europe, a persistent, dreadful will of its own, that can set its aims thousands of years ahead; so that the long spun-out comedy of its petty-stateism, and its dynastic as well as its democratic many-willedness, might finally be brought to a close. The time for petty politics is past; the next century will bring the struggle for the dominion of the world—the *compulsion* to great politics. (JGB 208, KSA 5.140)

As this passage indicates, Nietzsche's negation of the virulent nationalism of his era does not mean that he opposed European domination of the earth. What he appears to oppose, instead, is that this domination has been accomplished under the auspices of nation-states ruled by political parties and informed by public debate. Consistent with the "beast-of-prey" morality that we encounter in his ethical writings, the "good European," practicing "great politics," will have the task of subjugating the entire earth.

Nietzsche's infrequent comments on colonialism cannot be separated from tenets that he developed elsewhere in his works. It is essential that we consider the will to power, biologism, and the transvaluation of values, as well as Nietzsche's heavy reliance on antinationalist, antistatist, antidemocratic thought, if we are going to understand his fragmentary and sporadic remarks on colonies and global politics. But it is also important to recognize that his views cannot be separated from the events of his epoch. No German could fail to notice the nationalism of the Second Empire and the building pressure for Germany to enter into the race for colonial possessions. No German could have ignored the mass exodus from German soil for a better life in the Americas and the propaganda for creating a new and better Germany on foreign territory. And no one living in Europe during the last quarter of the nineteenth century could be blind to the global political situation in which one continent had gradually gained supremacy over most of the remainder of the earth. Nietzsche's timeliness lies in his attentiveness to these tendencies of his era. With his sister and her husband, he was compelled to enter into a private and ongoing discussion about the possibilities and hazards of colonial life in Paraguay. Nietzsche's untimeliness—if we grant him this ascription—involves his unusual way of approaching the problems posed by foreign affairs and world politics. Eschewing the nationalist, mercantile, and utopian/idealist approach to colonization, he developed along the lines of his philosophical outlook a conceptual framework that entailed a geopolitical perspective. In the "good European," he found a term for a future elite that could overcome the nation-state, create a superior cultural life, and achieve domination of the world. With "great politics," he offered an alternative to parliamentary life and actual colonial fantasies, as well as a vague blueprint for global conquest on a grand scale. The visions Nietzsche harbored were certainly unrealistic for his own times, but their "untimeliness," their opposition to and negation of accepted norms of nineteenth-century European thought and realities, does not imply that they offered, or still offer, an acceptable alternative. As deleterious as actual developments have been for the third world, it is difficult to locate features of Nietzsche's "untimely" colonial imagination that would have mitigated the oppression and inequities still rampant in our own postcolonial reality.

Chapter 6

The Jewish Question

As we have seen in previous chapters, Nietzsche's positions are often misconstrued because commentators have failed to take into account the context in which he was writing. One of the areas in which Nietzsche has been most misunderstood because of a failure to consider the historical embeddedness of his views is in connection with the Jewish Question. The designation "Jewish Question" is imprecise, but it is used here to refer to a larger constellation of issues that encompass attitudes toward the anti-Semitic movement of Nietzsche's era, the sentiments, especially in the educated classes, toward Jews and Judaism, and the debates in Germany and Europe in the late nineteenth century about how to solve a perceived problem of a Jewish population living in countries where they were considered a foreign element. Previous commentators on these matters have often conflated these areas of concern, which need to be considered as part of a complex context in which Nietzsche was living and writing.[1] The predominant way of treating Nietzsche's views on Jews, Judaism, and anti-Semitism has been to lump them all together and to examine them through the lens of Nazi Germany, its racial policies, and the Holocaust.[2] It is quite obvious that in the era of National Socialism many philosophical commentators made an effort to assimilate Nietzsche to the ideology of the regime, as we see clearly in the works of Alfred Baeumler (1887–1968), Alfred Rosenberg (1893–1946), Heinrich Härtle (1909–1986), or Nietzsche's cousin, Richard Oehler (1878–1948).[3] But Nietzsche was not universally acclaimed in National Socialist circles. The many statements he made against Germany, some of which we examined in the last section of Chapter 2, and his polemics in the latter part of the 1880s against anti-Semitism disqualified him as a genuine forerunner of National Socialism in the eyes of many Nazis, and caused difficulties for those who wanted him integrated into the pantheon of the Third Reich. We could also note that prior to Hitler's assumption of power, Nietzsche had been appropriated by various and diverse groups; he was certainly not exclusively a right-wing philosopher during the first two decades of the twentieth century or during the Weimar Republic. Indeed, in his own time, although he initially appeared to some anti-Semites as a natural ally owing to his Wagnerian roots, his brother-in-law Bernhard Förster (1843–1889), a noted anti-Semitic agitator, and the considerable anti-Semitic activities of his publisher Ernst Schmeitzner (1851–1895), the anti-Semitic movement and press soon came to recognize that Nietzsche was unconditionally opposed to their cause.

Still, during the period 1933–45 the dominant view of Nietzsche was that he was a worthy precursor of National Socialist thought. Despite some dissenting opinions, we frequently find outside the German-speaking world a confirmation of the Nazi version of Nietzsche's views with regard to Jews and Judaism. Crane Brinton (1898–1968), an influential Harvard philosopher who wrote an important book on Nietzsche in 1941, accuses the philosopher of being a supporter of National Socialist ideology, claiming that "scattered through Nietzsche's work is a good deal of material suitable for anti-Semitic use" and that "most of the stock of professional anti-Semitism is represented in Nietzsche."[4] Only after the Second World War do we find philosophers in the United States and in Europe making a concerted effort to exculpate Nietzsche from any connection with National Socialism. Karl Schlechta (1904–1985) in Germany, Richard Roos (1923–1984) in France, and Walter Kaufmann (1921–1980) in the United States are a trio of thinkers from the 1940s and 1950s who wrote about Nietzsche and published editions of his writings, endeavoring to purge him of his Nazi associations. They rely in part on Nietzsche's own polemical remarks directed at the political anti-Semitism of the 1880s, but also blame his sister, Elisabeth Förster-Nietzsche (1846–1935), for manipulations and distortions that allegedly made her brother more easily integrated into Nazi ideology.[5] Their accounts of Nietzsche's relationship to the Jewish Question, however, are as inadequate as those produced by Nazi writers, since they too fail to understand Nietzsche's remarks on this topic as part of a historical context. Subsequent works have been similarly deficient in this regard.[6] Correction and differentiation are long overdue.[7]

Early Experiences with Jews and Judaism

One thing is certain: it would have been difficult for Nietzsche to avoid the Jewish Question, and we have already seen in previous chapters that his views on Jews and Judaism constitute important aspects of his thoughts on education, nationalism, and colonialism. Although during his life he had little sustained contact with individuals of Jewish heritage[8]—with the notable exception of Paul Rée (1849–1901)—various discourses about Jewry were so prevalent in the intellectual and popular circles Nietzsche frequented that he was almost compelled to enter into dialogue with them. As a boy growing up in the Saxon town of Röcken and the city of Naumburg, Nietzsche almost certainly had no direct exposure to actual Jews. Prussian Saxony, where Nietzsche spent all his pre-university years, had a mere 0.3 percent Jewish population at the outbreak of the 1848 revolution, and this proportion had not increased at all since the end of the Napoleonic Wars. Röcken was a tiny village; we do not have records of the town's population, but it is extremely unlikely that there were any Jewish inhabitants. Naumburg was by comparison a metropolis with a population of some 14,000, and the city did contain at one point a Jewish quarter, as indicated by street designations, houses dedicated for Jewish inhabitants, a synagogue, and a Jewish bath. Jews survived persecution threats in the wake of the Black Death, but were expelled in the late fifteenth century. Over the years, increases in commerce and a liberalization of regulations led to some Jewish presence, but the census of 1861 lists only nine Jewish families.[9] Jews were also depicted on the jube in the Naumburg Cathedral,[10] but Nietzsche mentions nothing about encountering Jews or about what he may have learned about Jews in his education in elementary school or as a pupil in the Cathedral *Gymnasium*. There is also no evidence that anti-Jewish attitudes were prevalent in Nietzsche's family; we find no obvious Judeophobia, for example, in the correspondence of his mother Franziska (1826–1897), and we have no reason to believe anti-Jewish thought was common in the Nietzsche household. The conclusion we are compelled to draw from the evidence that survives is that although it is unlikely that Nietzsche was not exposed to a cultural anti-Jewish sentiment that thrived in the narrow-minded, petty-bourgeois atmosphere he inhabited, little of this sentiment made a great impression on Nietzsche and even less found its way into Nietzsche's voluminous juvenilia. In Nietzsche's notebooks from the years 1854–1869, we encounter remarkably few references to Jews and Judaism and certainly very little that indicates he was attracted to Judeophobic views about contemporary or historical Jewry. There is a notable exception to this general rule, when in his notebooks from 1861 to 1862 we find him copying down the words to a popular song that contains the lyrics "Throw out Itzig the Jew, / Out of the temple, / The raven-black cantor house" (Nachlass 1861–1862, 11[36], KGW I 2.312–13). What significance this song had for the teenager is impossible to discern, but it stands virtually alone as an expression of anti-Jewish thought in his juvenilia.

His exposure to Jews and to anti-Jewish sentiments did not change appreciably throughout his years as a pupil at Pforta or his single year as a matriculant at the University of Bonn, if we judge by the written documents at our disposal. Nothing in Nietzsche's correspondence or coursework indicates any exposure to Jews or to writings we would classify as anti-Jewish. Bonn likely had some students of Jewish heritage[11]—earlier in the century both Heinrich Heine (1797–1856) and Karl Marx (1818–1883) were enrolled there for a time—and there was at least one known Jewish professor, the mathematician Rudolf Lipschitz (1832–1903). Bonn hired a Jewish classical philologist, Jacob Bernays (1824–1881), the year after Nietzsche left. Bernays was a student of one of the current classicists, Friedrich Ritschl (1806–1876), and he was hired to replace his mentor when the latter left for the University of Leipzig, where he directed Nietzsche's studies in the ancient world. Only when Nietzsche arrived in Leipzig, do we begin to detect the beginnings of anti-Jewish sentiments in his correspondence and presumably also in his view of the world. The city's history exhibits the normal vicissitudes with regard to Jews, having banned them at one point in the sixteenth century. But with the increase of trade and the establishment of annual fairs, Jews made their way back into the city, eventually securing permission to reside within municipal borders. Jewish traders brought economic prosperity to Leipzig, not least through the taxes they paid to conduct business in the city, but they also disrupted the normal life of some residents, especially students, some of whom were forced to relinquish their domiciles temporarily to house the itinerant traders. For the first time in his life, Nietzsche was exposed to a significant Jewish presence and to derogatory comments about Jewish habits and demeanor. In his academic studies, anti-Jewish remarks were much less likely, especially around his mentor Ritschl, who had married a woman of Jewish extraction, Sophie Guttentag. Indeed, from evidence in his correspondence, Nietzsche had a cordial and respectful relationship with Frau Ritschl, quite possibly the first "Jewess"[12] with whom he had ever been personally acquainted.

In Nietzsche's early Leipzig years, we begin to see Nietzsche's friends, both in the city and elsewhere in Germany, participating in a cultural banter that included frequent anti-Jewish comments. Wilhelm Pinder (1844–1928), whom we will recall was a fellow member of the club "Germania," writes from Berlin during the Austro-Prussian War about the common people in the city viewing publicly posted news reports pertaining to the latest official communications from the battlefield. Pinder places himself in the position of an observer of this activity: "Then one furtively observes the impression that the news makes on the gathered masses, rejoices when a Jew, who dares to cry out: 'but all that is not true' is properly treated with a beating" (9 July 1866, Nr. 127, KGB I 3.114). The casual nature of these remarks—Pinder further relates how he strolls down the main street, visits a café, and buries himself behind a wall of newspapers—indicates that neither he nor his reader should give a second thought to a Jew being roughed up for questioning the official war propaganda. Indeed, Pinder rejoices [*freut sich*] at the thought of the thrashing and exhibits no compassion or concern for the mistreated human being. Carl von Gersdorff (1844–1904), whom Nietzsche had met in Pforta, and who transferred to Leipzig the same term Nietzsche did, is more ideological in his considerations of Jews. Adopting a perspective that would become common in anti-Semitic writings of the early 1880s, he accuses Jews of promoting and then profiting from military hostilities with fraudulent financial maneuvers. Writing to Nietzsche from Görlitz at the end of March in 1866, just two and a half months before the outbreak of the Austro-Prussian War, he fulminates against alleged dishonest Jewish dealings: "Stock-market Jews mobilize army corps, although they know very well that we are still truly enjoying the deepest peace, and use contemptible deception to sell off low-priced securities: in short, it is a time of swindle in every sense of the word" (Nr. 115, KGB I 3.82–83). When Gersdorff travels to the Bavarian city Fürth, he invariably describes it with the epithet "Jew-city" (17 August 1866, Nr. 132, KGB I 3.136), referring no doubt to the long tradition of tolerance for Jews among the Christian population of the Bavarian municipality.[13] And when Gersdorff writes to Nietzsche in 1868 regarding Julius Frauenstädt (1813–1879), the Jewish editor of the works of Arthur Schopenhauer, he includes his uncle's comments, which claim Frauenstädt to be "a superficial, vain Jewish rascal whose chief concern is to obtain profit from the literary remains of the master" (12 August 1868, Nr. 283, KGB I 3.286). As far as we can tell, Nietzsche had never encountered these types of deprecatory remarks about Jews during the first two decades of his life, in particular from his closest friends and associates.

Nietzsche became a willing participant in this anti-Jewish banter, reacting in part to the perceived invasion of Leipzig by Jewish traders. We should recall that he was no longer a child or an impressionable teenager: when he matriculated at the Saxon university he was twenty-two years old. He was familiar with religious tolerance at the very least from his acquaintance with Lessing's *Nathan the Wise* (1779), as well as liberal commentaries on the play, and he knew and admired the Jewish wife of his professor. Nonetheless, when writing to his mother and sister about his experiences during the Leipzig fair, he emphasizes the unsavory impact of the Jewish tradespeople who descend on the city. He complains that he is unable to make progress on his work because of the disruption, and tries to relax by walking through the streets: "The food that you get in restaurants is hardly appetizing at present. Moreover, everywhere it is teeming with revolting, insipid apes and other merchants. So that I really long for the termination of this intermezzo. Finally, Gersdorff and I found a tavern where we didn't have to countenance oily butter and Jewish mugs [*Judenfratzen*], but where we are regularly the only customers" (22 April 1866, Nr. 502, KSB 2.125). Five days later he grouses in a similar vein to Hermann Mushacke (1845–1905) in Berlin: "Everywhere the food is very bad and just as expensive; in the theater *The African Woman*[14] is still playing; and everywhere you look there are Jews and associates of Jews [*Juden und Judengenossen*]" (Nr. 504, KSB 2.127–28). And writing again to his mother and sister on the final day of the fair in October of 1868, Nietzsche expresses relief that the turmoil is coming to an end and that he will soon be relieved of "the smell of fat and the numerous Jews" (Nr. 593, KSB 2.326). In these early letters, we may have the impression that Nietzsche's disparaging remarks about Jews are more thoughtless decoration than the expression of a deep-seated conviction. Jews have a traditional field of association in Nietzsche's mind; they are identified with merchants and money, with unsavory food, ugliness, and occasionally cleverness. The remarks and associations in Nietzsche's letters—and very likely in his casual conversations—are significant nonetheless. They do not show Nietzsche on the road to becoming a rabid anti-Jewish polemicist—which was the fate of several of his contemporaries—but they do indicate that in his early years he sought to blend in inconspicuously with a climate of anti-Jewish biases that flourished around him. Nietzsche never opposed anti-Jewish statements or sentiments coming from his friends, and he did not hesitate to employ them to spice up his own accounts of his travails in Leipzig during the fair season. His comments demonstrate that he succumbed to the easy path of parroting the prejudices of a noxious German Judeophobia. They also demonstrate that he harbored anti-Jewish views prior to his acquaintance with Richard Wagner (1813–1883). The notion that Wagner, a known Judeophobe, was principally responsible for infecting Nietzsche with a disdain for Jews and Judaism is false. The seeds of anti-Jewish bias were already implanted in the young Leipzig philologist by the time he met Wagner in November 1868. With regard to Jews and Judaism, Wagner's influence represents much more of continuity and intensification in ideology than a fundamental shift in beliefs.

Anti-Jewish Thought as a Wagnerian

In Wagner and his circle, Nietzsche encountered more vociferous and ideological discussions of Jews and Judaism. Although in the early 1870s, when Nietzsche was a member of Wagner's inner circle, the Meister had not yet become infatuated by the racial theories of Count Joseph Arthur Gobineau (1816–1882), the Wagner household was openly ill disposed toward Jews and actively embroiled in controversies about Wagner's anti-Jewish sentiments. Irritated by what he perceived to be an excessive Jewish influence on the musical world, Wagner had already composed a notorious anti-Jewish essay, "Judaism in Music," in 1850. The essay appeared anonymously in the *New Journal for Music* under the name K. Freigedank [K. Freethought] and was part of the ongoing debate about Jewish emancipation in the mid-nineteenth century. Despite advice from his consort and later wife Cosima (1837–1930), as well as from other friends, in 1869, Wagner decided to republish the essay as a brochure with a new and extensive addendum. The republication thus forms a bridge between anti-Jewish thought in German nationalist tendencies from the 1848 revolution and the growing anti-Jewish sentiment of the last three decades of the century, which would culminate in the appearance of political anti-Semitism in the early 1880s. At issue in the original core text from 1850 is the extent to which Jews can be considered Germans; its personal background, however, concerns slights perceived by Wagner on the part of what he regarded as the Jewish music establishment in the 1840s, in particular in Paris.

But the essay also includes, especially in its later rendition, several elements that were frequently repeated by anti-Semitic agitators of the Second Empire: the alleged Jewish control over finance and press, Jewish vindictiveness, and the dire necessity to eliminate Jewish influence one way or another for the salvation of the German people. *Judaism in Music* thus contains an admixture of motifs about Judaism that run through the entire second half of the century. The issue of Jewish emancipation is wrongly conceived according to Wagner: "The Jew is already more than emancipated: he rules, and will rule as long as money remains the power before which all our doings and our dealings lose their force." But it is not only the financial predominance of Jews that concerns Wagner; it is their racial qualities, which are "disagreeably foreign" not only to Germany, but also to all European nations they inhabit. Especially important for Wagner is Jewish speech, which is likened to "an insufferable, bewildering blabbering." If Jews are not able to speak properly, how could they contribute something worthwhile in song, Wagner reasons. Jewish music, which he identifies with prayers chanted in synagogues, evokes "the greatest revulsion of horror mingled with absurdity"; it is a "gurgle, yodel, and cackle, which defies sense and sound, and which no intentional caricature can distort more repugnantly than it presents itself here in complete, naïve seriousness." And no matter how Jews have tried to assimilate, Wagner claims, referring to Giacomo Meyerbeer (1791–1864) and Felix Mendelssohn-Bartholdy (1778–1862), these essential racial qualities prevent even the most accomplished among them from achieving any real virtuosity and eminence.[15] Indeed, in his addendum, Wagner, like Wilhelm Marr (1819–1904) a few years later in his infamous anti-Semitic pamphlet *The Victory of Judaism over Germanism*,[16] proceeds to claim a fundamental enmity between Germans and Jews, maintaining that in their current struggle the Jews are prevailing.[17] Like Marr's work, Wagner's is a clear call for the Germans to take control of their own destiny and reverse this deleterious trend in culture and society.

The publication of *Judaism in Music* occurred shortly before Nietzsche became a frequent visitor to the Wagner household, and he was exposed firsthand to the reaction it occasioned in the public sphere. The 1869 version of this Judeophobic diatribe provoked scores of published responses from both Jews and non-Jews and prompted disturbances in the performance of Wagner's operas in various cities. Nietzsche never comments directly on the essay, but from correspondence with Gersdorff in the early 1870s, we can conclude that he knew the essay, approved of its content, and urged his friend to read it as well (March 1870, Nr. 82, KGB II 2.164). The extent to which Nietzsche sympathized with Wagner's views on Jewish hegemony can be seen from the original version of his 1870 lecture "Socrates and Tragedy," a copy of which he dutifully sent to the Wagners. In this lecture, Nietzsche extends his views on Socratism, the rationalist principle responsible for the destruction of Greek tragedy, into contemporary times:

Should the Teuton have nothing else to place at the side of that vanished artwork of the past except the "grand opera," something akin to the ape appearing next to Hercules? This is the most serious question of our art: and anyone who, as a Teuton, does not understand the seriousness of this question, has fallen into the snares of the Socratism of our times, which, to be sure, is neither capable of producing martyrs, nor speaks the language of the wisest Hellene. This Socratism is the Jewish press: I'll say nothing more. (Drafts of ST, KGA III 5/1.670)[18]

The Wagners were disconcerted by Nietzsche's remarks, fearing that he was ruining his career. At first indirectly, then finally in blunt language, they advised their young acolyte to refrain from such frontal assaults on contemporary Jewry in the future. Cosima writes to Nietzsche about "stirring up a hornet's nest" and continues:

Do you really understand me? Don't mention the Jews, and especially not *en passant*; later, when you want to take up this gruesome fight, in the name of God, but not at the very outset, so that on your path you won't have all this confusion and upheaval. I hope you don't misunderstand me: you know that in the depths of my soul I agree with your utterance. But not now and not in this way. I see an army of misunderstandings that will whirl up around you. (5 February 1870, Nr. 72, KGB II 2.138–40)

Nietzsche understood and obeyed. He eliminated the offensive passage in his lecture, and in the entire period of his close association with the Wagnerian cultural mission, he never included a direct, derogatory reference to contemporary Jewry or Judaism in his published writings. He did not abandon his anti-Jewish sentiments, however, but rather concealed them, sometimes not very deeply, by employing an "anti-Semitic cultural code."[19]

Socratism continues to be the antithesis of Greek tragedy and all genuine cultural achievement in Nietzsche's first nonphilological work, *The Birth of Tragedy*, but it is associated with Jewry only to the extent that its modern manifestations are drawn from the arsenal of anti-Jewish ideology of the times. Socratic culture of the present, Nietzsche contends, thrives on the superficiality of the journalist, "the paper slave of the day," and in the "journalistic idiom" with its "frivolous elegance" (GT 20, KSA 1.130). It is the realm of the rationalist critic, which has now come to dominate the cultural arena to its detriment (GT 22, KSA 1.144). Above all, it is opposed to the Wagnerian renaissance and the true German spirit; therefore it must be eliminated if genuine cultural achievement is to prevail: "We think so highly of the pure and strong core of the German character that we dare to expect it to excise the foreign elements which have been forcibly implanted and consider that the German spirit may well be in the process of returning to itself" (GT 23, KSA 1.149). A tendency in modern German society that is optimistic, anti-artistic, rationalist, and critical; that partakes in journalism, the press, and newspapers; and that debases genuine German art, promotes entertainment, and fuels degeneration would surely suggest to an audience in 1872, especially a Wagnerian readership, that Socratism was a foreign and powerful force intimately related to Wagner's view of contemporary Jewry. Nietzsche is careful to follow the interdiction imposed on him by the Wagners in all matters related to the present, but he does allow himself to delve into the anti-Jewish spirit in discussing the ancient world. In section nine, he juxtaposes a "Jewish" and a "German" myth, the former being definitely inferior to the latter. Nietzsche associates the story of Prometheus "from the very beginning" with "the entire Aryan community of peoples and is evidence of their gift for the profound and the tragic." This Aryan interpretation of Prometheus is contrasted with another myth of defiance of divine power and suffering as the punishment for the transgression: "It may not be beyond the bound of probability that this myth contains precisely the same characteristic meaning for the Aryan character which the myth of the Fall possesses for the Semitic character," Nietzsche hypothesizes, "and that these two myths are related to one another like brother and sister" (GT 9, KSA 1.65–69). At the time, Nietzsche was postulating this contrast, the designations Aryan and Semitic were well established in European thought and identified with the Germanic and Jewish heritage.[20] He leaves no doubt which is nobler and preferable:

> The best and the highest blessing which humanity can receive is achieved through sacrilege, and its consequences must be accepted, namely the whole flood of suffering and troubles with which the insulted gods have no other choice but to afflict humanity as it strives nobly upward: a severe thought which, through the *dignity* ascribed to the sacrilege, stands in strange contrast to the Semitic myth of the Fall, in which curiosity, dissimulation, the susceptibility to be led astray, lasciviousness, in short, a series of eminently feminine feelings, are viewed as the origin of evil. (GT 9, KSA 1.69–70)

Prometheus commits an active, masculine offense; Eve a deceptive, feminine sin. At the origin of the two traditions are differing conceptions of the world, values, and meaningful actions. The Aryan/Dionysian/German heritage is heroic, masculine, and courageous; the Semitic/Socratic/Jewish paradigm is craven, feminine, and dissembling. Not coincidentally, these stereotypes accord well with the anti-Jewish rhetoric of Wagner and, later, of anti-Semitic agitation during the 1880s.

Wagner and the Wagnerians understood very well that Nietzsche's *Birth of Tragedy* was a contribution to the cultural mission, and that this mission involved two antithetical forces: those supporting Wagner, Germany, and the highest cultural achievement, and those opposing Wagner's ideals, which included first and foremost contemporary Jewry, as Wagner had detailed in *Judaism in Music*. The tendencies identified with this opposition may have manifested themselves with different designations in Nietzsche's work, but underneath the Apollonian-Dionysian synthesis and its destruction at the hands of Socratism in the fifth century BC was the distinction between Germany and Judaism that Wagner and, a few years later, Marr would identify. Accordingly, the Wagners are simultaneously overjoyed at the book's appearance and apprehensive at its fate and the ramifications for its author. As Cosima notes in her diary entry in early January 1872: "R. thinks of the people who at the moment set the tone in Germany and wonders what the fate of this book will be." In the middle of January, after they have received the deluxe editions, Cosima writes: "We consider how to prevent his [Nietzsche's] books being killed by silence."[21] Wagner contributes one of the only positive reviews of the book, and an enraged Cosima reminds Wagner's sister, Ottilie Brockhaus (1836–1903), that she should consider "that N. has jeopardized his whole career for the sake of her brother."[22] Nietzsche's Wagnerian friends, who likewise subscribed to a dichotomous view of the German culture wars, are more specific in naming the adversary to Tribschen and the Bayreuth plans for cultural renewal. We know that Nietzsche's book received no attention from any reputable classical scholar, with the exception of Ulrich von Wilamowitz-Moellendorff (1848–1931), who, like Nietzsche, was a former pupil at Pforta. Wilamowitz's reasons for writing the review appear to have been motivated by a cabal of sorts on the part of a young classicist envious of Nietzsche receiving the position in Basel.[23] But his pamphlet, parodying Wagner's "Music of the Future"[24] with its title *Philology of the Future!* [*Zukunftsphilologie!*] (1872), had a revealing reception from Nietzsche's closest friends. Gersdorff communicates his outrage:

> I have to express my regrets for the author, after I read it, not without agitation. I see this young individual, blessed with understanding and knowledge, on the easy path—no, already in the very middle of Berlin literary Jewry. I regret that a young man stemming from a good aristocratic family, who certainly devoted himself to scholarship out of a passion for knowledge, denying the advantages of his class, straying from the usual path of a young nobleman, and allowing himself to be carried along at such an early age by the current that dominates our present educational system. Dialectic à la Lessing,[25] the accumulation of learned materials, a lively language, apparent moral indignation toward your alleged ignorance

and deficient love of truth—that is entirely the customary tone of reviewers and critics, as it manifests itself in the feuilletons of political newspapers and scholarly journals. The hastiness, the obsessive focus on details, the petty faultfinding, abusing, quarreling, and despite all the application of discernment and knowledge, no view of the totality and its interconnections. (31 May 1872, Nr. 326, KGB II 4.9–10)

Gersdorff provides here a veritable inventory of traits associated with Jews by the academic Wagnerians: the use of dialectics, empty displays of learning, disingenuousness, journalistic language, critique, hastiness, quibbling. Writing two days later, Rohde is more succinct: "This is really a scandal in its most repulsive Jewish arrogance!" (Nr. 327, KGB II 4.11). Nietzsche gives credence to this theory of a Berlin plot inspired by Jewry when he responds to Rohde: "He [Wilamowitz] must be very immature—obviously someone has used, stimulated, and incited him—everything reeks of Berlin" (8 June 1872, Nr. 227, KSB 4.7). A week later he fulminates against the "boundlessly impudent tone of that Berlin youngster"[26] (Nr. 230, KSB 4.11), and to Ritschl he writes about eliciting a cry of rage from the Berliners (26 June 1872, Nr. 235, KSB 4.17).[27] In a letter to Gustav Krug, a childhood friend in Naumburg, he too makes the purported Jewish connection explicit: After punning on Wilamowitz's name,[28] he exclaims: "What a presumptuous-Jewish sickly fellow!" (24 July 1872, Nr. 242, KSB 4.30). That Wilamowitz had nothing to do with a Berlin-Jewish conspiracy is obvious enough to us today and may even have become clear to Nietzsche at some later point. Significant in this episode, however, is not the mistaken facts, but the understanding of the young academic Wagnerians—including Nietzsche himself—that *The Birth of Tragedy* was involved in a cultural war between urban, sophistic, journalistic Jews and noble, stalwart, superior Germans.

We find evidence of the "anti-Semitic cultural code" in other writings during Nietzsche's Wagnerian period. Derogatory remarks made about Meyerbeer and Mendelssohn; the rejection of Bertold Auerbach (1812–1882), a prominent Jewish author; repeated negative references to the press and journalism; and a general rejection of modernity are part of a tendency that contains a hidden anti-Jewish agenda. In at least two instances Nietzsche's non-reference to contemporary Jewry is so thinly disguised that the association is transparent. The first occurs in late 1872 in "Five Prefaces to Five Unwritten Books," a work he dedicated to Cosima and sent to her as a Christmas gift that year. In one of the books Nietzsche describes, "the Greek City-State," he includes a wholesale denigration of the "liberal-optimistic" worldview as un-German. An analysis of the contemporary state of affairs follows:

> I cannot help seeing in the prevailing international movements of the present day, and the simultaneous promulgation of universal suffrage, the

effects of the *fear of war* above everything else; yes, I behold behind these movements, as the really fearful, those truly international homeless money-hermits, who, with their natural deficiency of the state-instinct, have learned to abuse politics as a means of the stock exchange, and state and society as an apparatus for their own enrichment. Against the deviation of the state-tendency into a money-tendency, which should be feared from this side, the only remedy is war and once again war, in the emotions of which it at least becomes obvious that the state is not founded upon the fear of the war-demon, as a protective institution for egoistic individuals; but rather in love for fatherland and its monarch, it produces an ethical impulse, indicative of a much higher destiny. (CV 3, KSA 1.773–74)

The Jews are not named, but no one reading this text in 1872 could have failed to recognize the anti-Jewish sentiment contained in the criticism of the "international homeless money-hermits." The second illustration comes from another work drawn from Nietzsche's intimate connection with Wagner and the Wagnerian cause, the fourth *Untimely Meditation, Richard Wagner in Bayreuth* (1876). The text contains various motifs we could associate with the anti-Semitic cultural code, but in the sixth section Nietzsche makes a reference that is unmistakably related to the stereotype of Jewish financiers: "Previously people looked down with honest superiority upon those who traffic in money, even though they were in need of them; it was admitted that every society has to have its bowels. Now they are the dominant power in the soul of modern humanity, the group most coveted" (WB 6, KSA 1.462). Jews are the "bowels" of the social order, and their alleged domination in the present constitutes the "soul of modern humanity." Nietzsche employs in this passage thoughts that are drawn not only from Wagner's writings, but also from the contemporary and growing Judeophobic discourse of the Second Reich. He never mentions Jews or Jewry by name in his *laudatio* to Wagner, but Nietzsche demonstrates in this work and throughout his Wagnerian period an adherence to a program that parallels and augments the anti-Jewish animus of his friend and mentor.

The Post-Wagnerian Ambivalence Toward Jewry

Nietzsche's break with Wagner in the 1870s led to a change in his publicly expressed views on Jews and Jewry. We might surmise that his reason for severing relations with Wagner involved a rejection of the anti-Jewish sentiments of Wagner and Wagnerians, but it is difficult to discern any direct connection. In *Ecce Homo*, as we have seen in Chapter 2, Nietzsche provides one account of the reason for his alienation from Wagner and his cultural mission, and it has nothing to do with Wagner's Judeophobia. He emphasizes that Wagner had betrayed his own ideal at the 1876 opening of the Bayreuth opera house by pandering to a crowd of unmusical donors and wealthy supporters (EH, Kommentar, Warum ich so gute Bücher schreibe, KSA 14.489–90). Nietzsche's presentation of past events in his autobiography is notoriously fictional or exaggerated, so we have no reason to believe that his account accurately represents his reason for breaking from Wagner. It is conceivable that Nietzsche was disappointed in the scene he encountered in Bayreuth, but even if that were the case, it says very little about the subsequent modification in his views of Jews and contemporary Jewry. Other scholars have speculated that Nietzsche's move away from Wagner involves the latter's impropriety in discussing with Nietzsche's physician his sexual life, or at least what Wagner assumed it to be.[29] But the incident in question appears to have occurred at a date after Nietzsche had already distanced himself from the composer in his own mind. Nietzsche's account of the break in correspondence indicates that he was personally offended because Wagner had embraced Christianity in his opera *Parsifal*. Shortly after Wagner's death on 13 February 1883, he composed two letters, one to Franz Overbeck, the other to Malwida von Meysenbug (1816–1903), in which he writes of a "deadly insult" that he had suffered at Wagner's hands, adding to Overbeck that "it could have become terrible if he had lived longer" (Nr. 384, KSB 6.337). He appears to clarify the "insult" in the letter to Meysenbug when he writes about Wagner's "gradual retreat and creeping back into Christianity and to the church" (Nr. 382, KSB 6.335). Nietzsche asserts that he experienced this new religious fervor on Wagner's part as a personal affront or betrayal since he had paid homage for so many years to someone who then lapsed into Christian belief. But this account too is odd and does not comport well with the history of their relationship: Nietzsche must have been familiar with *Parsifal* well before its completion; Wagner had worked on it for over two decades and had mentioned its connection with Good Friday already in his autobiography, which Nietzsche proofread for him. Indeed, on Christmas day in 1869 Cosima records in her diary that she "read *Parzival* with Prof. Nietzsche," and adds: "renewed feelings of awe."[30] The Christian connection, which the devout ex-Catholic Cosima[31]—she converted to Protestantism before her marriage to Wagner—would have appreciated, thus could not have been a shock to Nietzsche in the mid-1870s. In Nietzsche's last published work, *Nietzsche contra Wagner* (1895), we find the suggestion that Wagner's anti-Semitism was a factor in his "breaking away from Wagner": "By the summer of 1876 during the time of the first *Festspiele*, I took leave of Wagner in my heart. I suffer no ambiguity; since Wagner had moved to Germany, he had condescended step by step to everything I despise—even to anti-Semitism." This fall into anti-Semitism is furthermore associated with his embrace of Christianity: "Richard Wagner, apparently most triumphant, but in truth a decaying and despairing decadent, suddenly sank down, helpless and broken, before the Christian cross" (NW, Wie ich von Wagner loskam 1, KSA 6.431–32). But the adherence to anti-Jewish views should have been even less of a surprise for Nietzsche than the putatively sudden espousal of Christianity. As we have already seen, Nietzsche was a firsthand witness to the republication and aftermath of *Judaism in Music*, and his correspondence with the Wagners about his own association of Jews and the press clearly demonstrates that he knew their feelings regarding contemporary Jewry. It is quite possible that Nietzsche's break with Wagner had multiple causes, and that the "Christianity" in his latest opera and the Bayreuth opening had something to do with it. Nietzsche may have come to object to Wagner's racism, his religious views, his jingoism, his vegetarianism, and any number of other positions he held, but the Meister's hostility toward Jews and Judaism could not have been something Nietzsche came to recognize only in the mid-1870s.

Nonetheless, a modification of Nietzsche's views on the Jewish Question in the years following his break with Wagner is unmistakable. It is an unusual change that has sometimes been erroneously considered a philo-Semitic turn. What we actually find is more complex. In many cases, Nietzsche retains the clichés about Jews he had employed in the late 1860s and the first half of the 1870s, but he alters the evaluation of these ascribed attributes as he becomes less invested in Wagner and the Wagnerian project. Thus the association of Jews with the press or with financial canniness remains very much alive in Nietzsche's thought until his lapse into insanity, but he deals with this central theme, usually associated with anti-Jewish invective, in a very different manner after 1878. As various remarks about Jews possessing financial aptitude indicate, he now situates this putatively Jewish attribute in a vastly altered framework. In the early 1870s under the influence of the rising tide of criticism regarding the Jewish role in the financial crisis of 1873, the so-called Founders' Crash [*Gründerkrach*], German Judeophobes accused European Jewry of undermining German prosperity through dishonest manipulation of markets and fraudulent business dealings. We have seen Gersdorff, Wagner, and Nietzsche himself anticipate these accusations in their letters and works, but the journalist Otto Glagau (1834–1892) penned the most celebrated attack on the Jewish world of finance beginning in 1874. Since his series of articles appeared in the popular journal *Die Gartenlaube* before they were collected in book form, Glagau's claims received wide exposure in Germany during the latter part of the decade.[32] Nietzsche, in the period postdating his *Untimely Meditations*, now makes the truly provocative and "untimely" suggestion that Jewish success in business partakes in the will to power, and that Jews are therefore preferred genetic material for a new European ruling class. In these years, Nietzsche also exhibits understanding and even some compassion for the Jewish plight in the diaspora, as well as for the discrimination and oppression they have borne for many centuries in German and European society. At the same time, we continue to find comments in his works and correspondence that are a continuation of his earlier anti-Jewish attitudes. Writing to his family from Marienbad, he notes that the resort is teeming with foreigners, adding parenthetically: "by the way three-quarters are Jews" (27 July 1880, Nr. 43, KSB 6.32). After meeting the spouse of his childhood friend, he comments to his mother about "Professor Deussen and his wife (somewhat Jewish)" (4 September 1887, Nr. 901, KSA 8.141).[33] He writes to Heinrich Köselitz (1854–1918) about "the rich Jew" Raphael Louis Bischoffsheim (1823–1906), an amateur astronomer who sponsored a conference in Nice, and remarks derisively: "Ecco! Jewish luxury in grand style!" (27 October 1887, Nr. 940, KSA 8.180). And he expresses his preference for a French translation of Dostoevsky over the German rendition of "the dreadful Jew Goldschmidt (with his synagogue rhythm)" (17 March 1887, Nr. 822, KSA 8.50).[34] It would be foolish not to recognize that Nietzsche modified significantly his evaluation of Jewry after his break with Wagner,[35] especially in what he wrote for public consumption, but it would also be mistaken to ignore the continuity in stereotyping and "cultural anti-Semitic" slurs from the mid-1860s through his last written documents.

The change in the depiction of Jewry can be detected most easily in his very first published work after his Wagnerian period, *Human, All Too Human*, which contains the first public mention of Jews since the episode with the Wagners in 1870. In this book of aphorisms, he is circumspect and differentiated in his discussion. In an early aphorism, he observes a difference between the Greeks' relationship to their gods and the Jewish view of their divinity: "The Greeks did not see the Homeric gods as set above them as masters, or themselves set beneath the gods as servants, as the Jews did" (MA 114, KSA 2.117), a relatively innocuous observation made in passing, unlike Nietzsche's comparison of the Semitic versus the Aryan myth in *The Birth of Tragedy*. In volume two, Nietzsche even speaks of the "Jewish-heroic impulse that created the whole Reformation movement" (VM 171, KSA 2.450), a striking contrast to the nationalist interpretation of Luther he had embraced in earlier writings. His most extensive discussion of Jews occurs in aphorism 475, entitled "European man and the abolition of nations." Nietzsche begins by reflecting on the current state of affairs in Europe, where an "artificial nationalism" is upheld for the benefit of a few princes and certain businessmen. National ties, he avers, are now under considerable strain owing to the expansion of trade and industry and, among other things, the "nomadic life now lived by all who do not own land." He therefore foresees "an abolition of nations" and the appearance of a "mixed race," presumably an amalgam of the various national strands, and the rise of the "good European," a post-Wagnerian notion, as we have seen in the previous chapter, that Nietzsche frequently opposes to the nationalist ideologies of his contemporaries. The Jews, as the prototypical nomads not possessing a homeland or real estate in the various European countries, are perfect allies for this post-national vision, and in a long aside Nietzsche deals with their history, their current status, and their potential contribution to a future Europe. Indeed, the Jewish Question exists only because of nation-states, "inasmuch as it is here that their energy and higher intelligence, their capital in will and spirit accumulated from generation to generation in a long school of suffering, must come to preponderate to a degree calculated to arouse envy and hatred." The result is that the Jews are scapegoated across Europe for anything that goes wrong.[36] Because of their virtues, the Jews will be an essential component in any future European race. Nietzsche recognizes that they possess "unpleasant, dangerous qualities," and that in the Jew "they may even be dangerous and repellent to an exceptional degree." Especially offensive is the "youthful stock-exchange Jew," whom Nietzsche calls perhaps "the most repulsive invention of the entire human race." But the positive characteristics outweigh the negative, and Nietzsche points to the fact that in their "grief-laden history" the Jews have produced "the noblest human being (Christ), the purest sage (Spinoza), the mightiest book and the most efficacious moral code in the world."[37] He goes on to credit Jewry with carrying the banner of enlightenment and of forging a firm connection with the ancient world: "it is thanks not least to their efforts that a more natural, rational and in any event unmythical elucidation of the world could at last again obtain victory and that the right of culture that now unites us with the enlightenment of Graeco-Roman antiquity remains unbroken." The passage as a whole is extraordinary in its praise of Jews: although Nietzsche does speak disparagingly about the clichéd notion of the "stock-exchange Jew," he reverses several other Judeophobic platitudes—the nomadic, landless Jew and the emphasis on intelligence—and expresses understanding for the plight of diaspora Jewry. Moreover, in most of Nietzsche's writings the Jews are viewed exclusively in opposition to the ancient world (as they are in the earlier passage in this book), especially to the Greeks. But in this work they are regarded as making "Europe's mission and history a *continuation of the Greek*" (MA 475, KSA 2.309–11). As Nietzsche's first extended public statement in which Jews are explicitly named, this passage represents an enormous modification of Wagnerian ideology, and was perhaps conceived intentionally as an affront to Wagner's views.

We find a similar differentiated attitude toward Jews in *Dawn* (1881). At one point Nietzsche writes of "Jewish importunity" (M 192, KSA 3.165), and in another passage he points to the hypocrisy of the phrase "love your enemies," "invented by the Jews, the best haters there have ever been" (M 377, KSA 3.246), which anticipates passages in *On the Genealogy of Morals* (1887). In a further aphorism, he deprecates the sincerity of Jewish philanthropy, claiming that the benefactor acts egotistically, satisfying "a need of his nature," and that when this need is strongest, he feels less for the object of his charity and often becomes "rough and, on occasion, offensive." He adds parenthetically the backhanded compliment: "This has been asserted of Jewish benefaction and charity, which, as is well known, is somewhat more effusive than that of other nations" (M 334, KSA 3.234–35). His protracted discussion of Jews in the aphorism entitled "Of the People of Israel," however, is a long litany of praise. Since Nietzsche's topic is the "destiny of the Jews of Europe" in the twentieth century, the title is a bit odd; it is meant to emphasize continuity between the ancient Hebrews and their modern descendants, a link that Nietzsche makes obvious at the beginning and close of his discussion. In some ways, the substance of this aphorism represents an intensification of *Human, All Too Human* 475. The Jews are at a crossroads, Nietzsche claims, just as they were in Egypt long ago: they can either "become the masters of Europe" or "lose Europe." They have undergone eighteen centuries of "schooling," which has forged in every one of them "extraordinary" "psychological and intellectual resources":

> Every Jew possesses in the history of his fathers and grandfathers a great fund of examples of the coldest self-possession and endurance in fearful situations, of the subtlest outwitting and exploitation of chance and misfortune; their courage beneath the cloak of miserable submission, their heroism in *spernere se sperni*, surpasses the virtues of all the saints. For two millennia an attempt was made to render them contemptible by treating them with contempt, and by barring to them the way to all honors and all that was honorable, and in exchange thrusting them all the deeper into dirty trades—and it is true that they did not grow cleaner in the process.

Nietzsche confesses an admiration for Jewish perseverance in the face of centuries of persecution and presents a defense of less desirable attributes they may have acquired because of their oppression. Despite their historical plight, they have retained a respect for the highest values; their marriage and family customs are laudable; and, perhaps most importantly, they have been able "to create for themselves a feeling of power and of eternal revenge out of the very occupations left to them." Yet they are also paragons of liberality, because they possess the "greatest experiences of human society." They are shrewd and intellectually supple; they have known how to avoid menial labor and still survived. Nietzsche interrupts his enumeration of virtues with a remark on Jewish deficiencies: "Their demeanor still reveals that their souls have never known chivalrous noble sentiments nor their bodies handsome armor: a certain importunity mingles with an often charming but almost always painful submissiveness." But he notes that since they will now unite with the aristocracy of Europe, they will soon shed these defects. In their present state, they know that they are not contemplating a mastery of Europe, but in the future, Europe "may fall into their hands like a ripe fruit." In the meantime, they will distinguish themselves throughout the continent and, on the basis of their onerous heritage, be the source of greatness: "And wither shall this assembled abundance of grand impressions, which for every Jewish family constitutes Jewish history, this abundance of passions, virtues, decisions, renunciations, struggles, victories of every kind—whither shall it stream out if not at last into great men and great works!" Then Jewry will be redeemed; it will have "transformed its vengeance into an eternal blessing for Europe"; and just as God rejoiced on the seventh day of his creation, "let us all, all of us, rejoice with him" (M 205, KSA 3.180–83). The notion of the Jews as masters of Europe was not original with Nietzsche, of course; it was the stock-in-trade of anti-Jewish thought and occupied a prominent place in the anti-Semitic movement of the early 1880s, at precisely the time Nietzsche composed *Dawn*. What was new for Nietzsche and antithetical to his former Wagnerian perspective was the celebration of Jewish hegemony. The solution to the Jewish Question is not assimilation—although there is some suggestion of intermarriage with the upper classes—or the gradual disappearance of Jewish vices in favor of their virtues. Rather, the dilemma of Jewish existence in a hostile Europe will be resolved by Jewish dominance over the continent.

A somewhat different perspective on a similar issue emerges in Nietzsche's notebooks from the summer of 1885, just four years after the publication of *Dawn*. Nietzsche asserts that if intellect, diligence, and aptitude were the sole criteria, Prussian Jews would have all governmental power in their hands. He adds "as they already have it in the pocket," employing the hackneyed notion of Jewish dominion owing to financial prowess. The stage is somewhat smaller in that Nietzsche is considering only Prussia, but the assertion that Jews have superior abilities and could easily obtain a hegemonic position parallels the passage in *Dawn*, and anticipates remarks in *Beyond Good and Evil*. The reason the Jews do not already control Europe, according to the earlier aphorism, has to do with their own unwillingness to claim it in a precipitous fashion. In his notebooks, Nietzsche cites less seemly reasons for Jewry being unable to ascend to a ruling role in Prussia. In rapid succession, Nietzsche maintains: Jews do not look you squarely in the eyes; they speak too quickly and clumsily; their anger is dishonest; they do not tolerate great quantities of food and cannot hold their liquor; their arms and feet do not give a noble impression; their hands quiver; "and even the manner in which a Jew mounts a horse (or a Jewish musician approaches a theme—'the Jewish leap'—) is not unobjectionable and allows us to understand that the Jews were never a *chivalric* race." He goes on to assert that Jews are uncertain in representing their own morality and concludes that the Jews of Prussia must be a debased and stunted type of Jew. Nietzsche does supply a reason for this pitiful state of Prussian Jewry: the "degeneration" of the Jew is the result of the wrong climate and of an association in Prussia with "unattractive and oppressed Slavs, Hungarians, and Germans." Jews in Portugal or the Jews of the Old Testament are very different and even exemplary in their behavior, and could even teach something to the Greeks. But what is remarkable in this aphorism is, in contrast to the published discussion of Jews, a very different kind of enumeration of Jewish character traits, all of which are unflattering and often drawn from the immense arsenal of European Judeophobia. Nietzsche continues his derogatory account of Jews by delineating two "dangers of the Jewish psyche": "(1) they try to gain a foothold in a parasitic manner," and "(2) they know how to adapt themselves, as the natural scientists say." These two Jewish tendencies have carved a "fateful rut" in the Jewish character. As a result, "even the most reputable wholesale merchant at the Jewish money market cannot resist, when the circumstances present themselves, reaching out with his fingers in a coldblooded fashion to gain petty and paltry defraudations that would make a Prussian financier blush" (Nachlass 1885, 36[42], KSA 11.568–69). Again we easily recognize that Nietzsche ascribes to Jews the very qualities that are frequently found in the writings of the worst German anti-Semites, but here the reversal or revaluation is absent. It is difficult to reconcile passages such as this one with Nietzsche's published comments on Jews. Not all of the published comments, as we have seen, are unambiguously positive, but in his longer discussions he portrays Jewry as a beneficial force for Europe's future, not as an inherently dishonest, fraudulent, degenerate blight on the contemporary world.

Nietzsche's aphoristic writings contain one additional long passage dealing with the Jewish Question of his time. It occurs in aphorism 251 in *Beyond Good and Evil*. He begins his discussion by noting the "becloudings of the German spirit," that is, the various nationalist tendencies to oppose the French, the Jews, and the Poles and to support the Wagnerian, the Teutonic, and the Prussian. In this context, he offers his only public apology for his own flirtations with this ideology in the 1870s: "May I be forgiven that I too, during a short, hazardous stay in a very infected area, did not remain entirely spared by the disease." He then presents an intriguing analysis of the Jewish situation in Germany. He has never met a German who was well disposed toward the Jews, and he therefore understands the existence of policies that restrict immigration. Nietzsche knew, of course, that prohibition on permission for Jews to enter Germany from the east was one of the central demands of the Anti-Semites' Petition from 1880–81, a document promulgated and supported by his future brother-in-law, Bernhard Förster, signed by over a quarter of a million persons, including Nietzsche's publisher Ernst Schmeitzner, and then presented to Bismarck, who refused any response. Nietzsche's explanation for the German reaction to Jews employs an extended alimentary metaphor: "That Germany has *more than enough* Jews, that German stomachs, German blood have found it difficult (and will continue to find it difficult) to deal with even this amount of 'Jew' (which the Italian, the Frenchman, the Englishman have dealt with, thanks to their stronger digestions): a general instinct states this in clear language, and one must listen to that instinct and act accordingly." In this passage Nietzsche may be referencing the mass deportation of Jews undertaken by the German foreign ministry in 1885.[38] Significant is that Nietzsche regards Germany and Germans from an external perspective; he does not identify himself with his birthplace, but he also seems to validate the German need to exclude Jews as crucial for the health of the nation. He continues with two sentences in quotation marks, and we have to presume they are something he is imputing to a German, and possibly even to an anti-Semite, responding to Jewish immigration: "'Do not allow any new Jews to enter! And bar especially those doors that face east (and also towards Austria)!'" This demand represents the instinct of a weaker people trying to fend off a stronger people; the Jews, Nietzsche tells his reader, are "without a doubt the strongest, toughest, and purest race living in Europe." They succeed because they employ specific virtues that are today considered vices; Nietzsche is probably thinking of the alleged financial acumen of Jews. As in the passage from *Dawn*, he claims that Jews could "gain the upper hand, could in fact quite literally rule over Europe," but he believes that it is clear "that they are *not* planning or working toward that end." Their desire is to be assimilated into Europe "to be established, legitimate, respected, somewhere at last, and to set an end to their nomadic life as 'wandering Jews.'" This assimilation should be encouraged, Nietzsche continues, but "with great caution, with selectivity, more or less as the English nobility does." And he concludes his thoughts on the contemporary Jewish situation in Germany with the vision of breeding the rulers of a new Europe from German Jewry and "the strongest types of the new German (an aristocratic officer from the March of Brandenburg, for example)" (JGB 251, KSA 5.192–95).

Nietzsche's attitude toward contemporary Jewry is again ambivalent in this passage. He certainly continues to recognize, as he did throughout the late 1880s, that Jewish financial abilities were a necessary element for a new ruling elite, and he rejects without reservation the ultranationalist political movements in Germany, including, as we shall see in more detail below, the various strands of anti-Semitism. But he also continues to reproduce stereotypes of German Jewry: they excel in matters of money; they have the potential to rule over other nations; they are nomads seeking to integrate themselves into "foreign" societies. There is a danger inherent in Jews, so they must be treated with care and assimilated on a selective basis: native populations should not accept every Jew. It is difficult to ascertain Nietzsche's feelings about eastern European Jewry from this aphorism—the comments about restrictions are put into the mouth of a hypothetical speaker—but a note he composed at the time he was writing *Beyond Good and Evil* is revealing in this regard. He refers in this draft aphorism, as he does in the published book, to the "imperative of the German instinct" against new Jewish immigration: "No more *new* Jews! And keep the gates to the East closed!" In the note, however, Nietzsche maintains that these imperatives ought to be the mantra of German Jews, not simply anti-Semitic petitioners. If Jews are going to achieve their objective, "integration into the German essence," and if they are going to acquire a "more German type of expression and gestures," then they should consider themselves advocates of "border-regulation." In this entry, Nietzsche propounds a theory whereby external behavior becomes internalized, where "appearance" becomes reality, and thus these outward forms of behavior will alter the Jewish psyche, making it more compatible with Germanness. Immigration is a hindrance to assimilation: The appointed task of the German Jews "should not be pushed back again and again into the realm of the insoluble by the horrible and despicable ugliness of the recently immigrated Polish and Russian, Hungarian and Galician Jews." This is the point, Nietzsche continues, "where Jews for their part must act and namely set limits." And he closes by observing that this is the single and last issue where Jewish and German interests overlap, and then admonishing the former: "but really, it is time, it is high time!" (Nachlass 1885, 41[14], KSA 11.688). The parallels between this note and aphorism 251 suggest it may have been originally part of Nietzsche's plan for the text, but it obviously did not find its way into the manuscript. That Nietzsche's derogatory view of Eastern European Jews was not an isolated instance, however, is demonstrated by a passage in *The Antichrist*, where he writes: "One would no more choose to associate with 'first Christians' than one would with Polish Jews: not that one would need to prove so much as a single point against them. . . . Neither of them smell very pleasant" (AC 46, KSA 6.223).[39] Nietzsche's celebration of the Jews of finance evidently did not extend to co-religionists from the shtetls of Eastern Europe.

Jewish Friends and Acquaintances

The ambivalence we find in Nietzsche's aphoristic writings can be detected in his relations with individuals of Jewish heritage during the 1870s and early 1880s as well. The best-known and longest lasting relationship during these years was with Paul Rée, a student of philosophy and law with an intense interest in natural sciences. Rée was not Jewish except by criteria that are applied by racist thinking. Prior to his birth his parents had converted to Protestantism shortly before their marriage in 1843. He thus had no connection with the Jewish religion or Judaism in his childhood, and from all the evidence we have in his writings, he was unconcerned with his parents' Jewish heritage. In an odd and anomalous remark, Lou Salomé (1861–1937) branded him a "self-hating Jew,"[40] but there is no substance behind this claim. Nietzsche first met Rée in 1873 through a mutual acquaintance, and the friendship between them was sealed when in 1875 Nietzsche discovered a copy of Rée's first book, *Psychological Observations*, and wrote to the author, who was at the time in Paris, praising the volume. Their admiration was mutual, and they decided to spend the summer of 1876 together in Sorrento at the villa of Malwida von Meysenbug working on their new book projects. Rée's Jewish background played no apparent role in this initial period; it is quite possible that Nietzsche did not even know about Rée's "Judaism" until he was informed about it by the Wagners, who vacationed in Sorrento in October at a hotel five minutes removed from Malwida's residence. At first Cosima made no revealing remarks in her diary, but on the last day of October, she wrote: "In the evening we are visited by Dr. Rée, whose cold and precise character does not appeal to us; on closer inspection we come to the conclusion that he must be an Israelite."[41] It is likely that the Wagners learned of Rée's Jewish heritage from Hans von Wolzogen (1848–1938), a trusted Wagnerian and fervent anti-Semite whom Wagner later appointed as editor of his house journal, the *Bayreuther Blätter*. Von Wolzogen had graduated from the Gymnasium Fridericianum in Schwerin one year ahead of Rée and knew him personally. According to Nietzsche's later accounts, Wagner warned Nietzsche about Rée at this time as well.[42] After the publication of *Human, All Too Human* in 1878, the Wagners, resorting to their dichotomous view of the world, blamed the Jewish influence of Rée for seducing Nietzsche into the opposing ideological camp. Cosima wrote the following explanation to a friend: "Many things came together to produce that deplorable book! Finally Israel intervened in the form of a Dr. Rée, very sleek, very cool, at the same time as being captivated by Nietzsche and dominated by him, though actually outwitting him: the relationship of Judea and Germania in miniature."[43] At this point, having already broken from Wagner internally, Nietzsche was unconcerned with Rée's heritage. Indeed, when Lou Salomé became their mutual acquaintance, the threesome planned to study together in Paris or Vienna.

How quickly more malicious anti-Jewish thoughts and language could emerge from Nietzsche is demonstrated by an incident that occurred shortly after he officially broke relations with Rée over Lou Salomé.[44] Angered and disgusted with what he assumed was Rée's suggestions of an impropriety on his part toward Lou, he wrote in July 1883 to Rée's brother Georg, who was managing the family estate in Stibbe. We have only the draft for the letter he sent, but if the final version resembled it, then it was highly inflammatory. Nietzsche first makes it clear that he is breaking all relations with his brother: "any further intercourse between him and me is *beneath me*." Then he blames Rée for the insults he and his sister have suffered from Lou, and he spares no words when he claims that "behind my back" Rée "dealt with me like a sneaking, slanderous, mendacious fellow." "Your brother," he continues, "brings shame to me, as well as to you and your honorable mother." He concludes by heaping abuse on Lou. In a letter Rée wrote to Nietzsche, he had called Lou "his destiny." Nietzsche comments: "*quel goût*! This scrawny, dirty, foul-smelling monkey with her false breasts—a destiny!" (Nr. 435, KSB 6.400–02). This unexpected, abusive, and scurrilous missive—or the variant he received—must have shocked Rée's brother. Georg Rée's return letter does not survive, but Nietzsche reports to Overbeck's wife Ida (1848–1933) that the brother's response to the "fulminating letter" was the threat of a lawsuit for libel. Nietzsche suggests strongly to Frau Overbeck that he countered by challenging him to a duel: "I threatened him with *something else*" (14 August 1883, Nr. 449, KSB 6.423).[45] Nothing comes of this angry exchange, and in August 1883, Nietzsche writes a letter to his sister containing four humorous poems summing up his experiences over the summer. It seems Nietzsche and Elisabeth were fond of inventing this sort of witty verse, which contained some Saxon dialect: in a letter to Köselitz in 1888 he includes a few new samples and informs his friend that he and his sister spent the time in transit from Rome to Genoa in the spring of 1883 creating such doggerel to amuse themselves on the journey (17 May 1888, Nr. 1035, KSB 8.316). The letter from August 1883 must be an attempt to recreate the mood from earlier in the year. The third poem is entitled "Libel Trial":

Vor strömendem Geblüte
Da förchtet sich der Jüde,
Es macht ihn mißvergnügt.
Viel lieber strömt er Gelder
An seine Rechtsanwälter
Bis *so*—"*die Ehre siegt.*" (Nr. 455, KSB 6.433)

[The Jew is fearful of flowing blood; it displeases him. He would much rather let his money flow to his lawyers until *in this way*—"*honor is victorious.*"]

We might take into consideration the audience for these anti-Jewish slurs, Nietzsche's sister Elisabeth, whom Nietzsche had introduced into Wagnerian circles, and who would later marry the anti-Semitic agitator Bernhard Förster. We might also take into account that while Nietzsche was composing these verses he was still distraught over the situation with Rée and Lou, and that this Judeophobic outburst reflects his troubled state of mind.[46] While it is undoubtedly true that Nietzsche remained upset at Rée and Lou in August of 1883, the fact that he resorts to a stereotype of Jews as cowardly, wealthy, and quarrelsome continues a prejudicial proclivity Nietzsche had exhibited prior to 1883 and that would continue to surface on occasion until his last sane year in 1888. Indeed, after this incident, Nietzsche for the first time refers to Rée as a Jew in his notebooks.[47] What this letter indicates is that even many years after his break with Wagner, Nietzsche still demonstrates ready access to the biases typical of many German Gentiles during the last decades of the nineteenth century. He is not virulently anti-Semitic, as were some of his contemporaries, and he did not reject association with Jews on principle, but in unpublished venues, he did associate them with features that reveal a biased perspective.

Nietzsche's relations with Viennese Jewish admirers also exhibit some abnormalities around the Jewish Question. Siegfried Lipiner (1856–1911), a member of the so-called Pernerstorfer circle, a group of mostly Jewish students studying at the University of Vienna,[48] contacted Nietzsche in 1876 and sent him a copy of his epic poem *Prometheus Unbound* (1876).[49] He sought personal contact with Nietzsche, traveling to Germany in 1877 to meet him, but he encountered instead Paul Rée and Erwin Rohde. Endeavoring to shield Nietzsche, who was in ill health, from disturbances, Rohde diverted Lipiner, but wrote to Nietzsche that Lipiner is "one of the most bandy-legged Jews I have ever seen." He mitigates by adding: "his vile Semitic face has certain not unsympathetic, shy and sensitive features," and continues with regard to *Prometheus Unbound*: "Please let me know soon [if you have received the book], and perhaps even make *pater patriae* Prometheus-Lipiner with a letter the happiest of all bandy-legged Jew-boys" (29 June 1877, Nr. 925, KGB II 6/1.595–96). Since Rohde also refused to disclose Nietzsche's current address, Lipiner traveled to Naumburg, where he met with Nietzsche's mother and finally obtained the information he desired, as well as a photograph of his object of admiration. Franziska Nietzsche reports the visit to her son, but unlike Rohde includes no comments on his Jewishness. It seems that Lipiner's book was lost in the mail, but he sends another, and upon reading it, Nietzsche is initially enthusiastic in his praise for Lipiner's talents. To his mother he writes of his "*indescribable* joy" in reading the poem, calling it a work of the "*first* order" and Lipiner a "*real* poet" (25 August 1877, Nr. 653, KSB 5.275). He writes in a similar vein to Rohde: "Just recently I experienced a truly sacred day through *Prometheus Unbound*: if the poet is not a veritable 'genius,' then I don't know anymore what one is: everything is wonderful, and for me it is as if I met in it my elevated and apotheosized self" (28 August 1877, Nr. 656, KSB 5.278). Nietzsche at first appears to ignore completely Lipiner's ethnicity. Indeed, he seems to be pleased that he has attracted Jewish followers in Vienna, perhaps because he had come to accept the Wagnerian contention that Jews had inordinate influence in cultural matters.

Nietzsche's enthusiasm for Lipiner cooled rather rapidly. The usual explanation given for his estrangement from his ardent disciple, whom he never met in person, is a difference in views on important matters of art and culture. Like other members of the Pernerstorfer circle, Lipiner was a pan-Germanist, and his initial interest in Nietzsche stemmed from his conviction that Nietzsche shared his values. We should recall that the Austrian Jews in the Nietzsche fan club knew only his early writings: *The Birth of Tragedy* and the *Untimely Meditations*. When they contacted Nietzsche with their letters of admiration and flattery in 1877 and 1878, they assumed that Nietzsche was still a German nationalist, that he supported a notion of *Bildung* that was meant to contribute to a recrudescence of the German spirit, and that he remained a loyal follower of Richard Wagner and his cultural mission. But Lipiner's Jewishness—or at least personality characteristics that Nietzsche associated with Jewry—also played a decisive role in his banishment from Nietzschean discipleship. Although Nietzsche began his relationship with Lipiner stating that he had great expectations of Jews (24 August 1877, Nr. 652, KSB 5.274), his remarks about Lipiner as a Jew become increasingly critical. In a letter to Reinhart von Seydlitz (1850–1931), Nietzsche calls him "shameless," because Lipiner was trying "to dispose over my life from a distance and to intervene in it through counsel and deed" (Nr. 721, KSB 5.327). Lipiner had obviously violated propriety—at least as conceived by Nietzsche—in seeking to persuade the philosopher to tend to his health by spending time with him in a vacation area in Austria (20 April 1878, Nr. 1057, KGB II 6/2.836–37).[50] Lipiner's putative pushiness and his deficiencies in decorum and social grace are features typically identified with Jews in Nietzsche's circles, and Seydlitz responds by first deflecting some of Lipiner's inappropriate behavior onto his own desire to convince Nietzsche to visit Austria, but then he continues by commenting: "You are right, it was a bit shameless, and you—and I—should remain separated from Lipiner by many miles in the future, and never have a constant telephone between you; for, like all Semites, he kills tender things." He goes on to compliment Lipiner for his candor, but qualifies, stating, "his book is the best thing about him." "To be sure, he must first seek out people who can tolerate his restless, shrieking goodness, his offensive frankness, his 'natural' tactlessness" (18 May 1878, Nr. 1069, KGB II 6/2.855). Nietzsche would appear to agree with the racial profiling Seydlitz has articulated, since he writes to his mother and sister that he is very concerned about Lipiner, and "does not confuse him with his Jewish characteristics, which he can't do anything about" (13 August 1878, Nr. 744, KSB 5.346–47). In later notebooks, when Nietzsche mentions Lipiner, it is usually in connection with negative traits associated with Jews. He criticizes him for obscurantism and sentimentality, and disqualifies him as a mere imitator of genuine art. Imitation is considered the "talent of the Jew," who is able to accommodate artistic production in a formal manner: "therefore actors, therefore poets like Heine and Lipiner" (Nachlass 1884, 25[282], KSA 11.84).[51] And in another passage, Nietzsche writes under the heading "Jew": "I emphasize with distinction Siegfried Lipiner, a Polish Jew, who understood how to imitate many forms of European lyric poetry in the most elegant fashion—'almost genuine,' as a goldsmith would say" (Nachlass 1885, 39[20], KSA 11.627).[52] These remarks reveal again that Nietzsche retained a good deal of his former bias about Jews. We might note here as well that Lipiner himself, like many in the Pernerstorfer circle, was not entirely free from what we would call today "cultural anti-Semitism,"[53] and that in the 1880s Nietzsche reports Lipiner converted to Protestantism and became an anti-Semite himself (to Franz Overbeck, 7 April 1884, Nr. 504, KSB 6.494).[54] Many commentators have regarded Nietzsche's association with Lipiner as a sign of absence from racial discrimination against Jews and Judaism, as proof that he had moved away from Wagner's allergic Judeophobia toward a position devoid of prejudice. The reality is clearly more complex, but at the very least, Nietzsche's relationship with Lipiner indicates that the philosopher harbored a profound ambivalence toward Jews, at times believing they were allies and promoters of his works, while on other occasions applying to them the platitudes common to anti-Semites of his own era.[55]

A third Jewish acquaintance was Josef Paneth (1857–1890), who, like Lipiner, was also a student in Vienna and a member of the Pernerstorfer circle. Unlike Lipiner, however, Paneth never converted and was concerned with the growing anti-Semitic movement in Europe. He became a natural scientist, studying physiology;[56] for a time he was employed in the laboratory of Ernst Wilhelm von Brücke (1819–1892), where Sigmund Freud (1856–1939) worked, and he was a close friend of the future father of psychoanalysis. He met Nietzsche during a three-month stay in Villefranche, while Nietzsche was residing in Nice, and during the first three months of 1884 he had regular conversations with Nietzsche, which we know about from his reports back to his fiancée in Vienna. Judaism and anti-Semitism, which had become a political movement since the beginning of the decade, were topics the two men discussed on occasion, and the overall impression we get from Paneth's summaries is that Nietzsche was not completely forthright when this subject was broached. When Paneth expressed his concern with anti-Semitism, Nietzsche maintained that he was resolutely against this virulently racist movement and that he was distressed that he had been associated in public with anti-Semites. Nietzsche was accurate in these contentions, but he also claimed that "from his youth onwards he held himself free from any prejudices regarding race and religion." Nietzsche gives Paneth the impression that he had never been involved with anti-Jewish thought at all, and that he was shocked when he learned the extent to which Wagner subscribed to racist views. He tells Paneth further that Christianity was mentioned only ironically when he was associated with the composer and indicates that Wagner's anti-Semitism is a later development.[57] Since we know that Nietzsche was often in the Wagner household when the repercussions from the republication of *Judaism in Music* were most intense, we have to conclude that these statements were disingenuous, and that Nietzsche was downplaying his own anti-Jewish convictions, remarks, and associations, quite possibly in order to please his interlocutor.[58] Taken as a whole, when we examine carefully the letters Paneth sent to his fiancée, we are apt to be suspicious of Nietzsche's motivation in pursuing contact with the Viennese scientist. Overbeck, who knew Nietzsche better than almost anyone else, supplies a rather cynical explanation: Paneth served, the Basler theologian claims, as a "helper in a time of emergency" in two respects: he assisted him in gaining "an orientation regarding his personal reputation with Viennese Jewry," and, since Paneth was a natural scientist and physiologist whom Nietzsche met at a time when he was extremely interested in these areas, he could provide him expert advice about matters of interest.[59]

In the area of science, Paneth was important for Nietzsche as a mediator of the writings of Francis Galton (1822–1911), Charles Darwin's (1809–1882) cousin and the father of eugenics. As we shall see in Chapter 9, this topic held an increasing fascination for Nietzsche as the decade progressed, and Paneth lent his interlocutor a copy of Galton's *Inquiries into Human Faculties and Its Development* (1883), which he eventually let him keep as a gift. The two men discussed various propositions related to eugenics in their wide-ranging discussions. Paneth recognized that Nietzsche's engagement with the natural sciences could not be separated from his views on morality, while he himself possessed a more traditional perspective on the role of science in human activity. Paneth objected to the Nietzschean notion of breeding "an improved human culture and race that he [Nietzsche] calls 'overmen,'" stating practical objections: that no one could rule over human beings the way a cattle breeder does over his cattle, and that the higher purpose is impossible to define.[60] In general, Nietzsche defended a eugenic program that Paneth rejects for its harsh and redemptive assumptions; in a role reversal, Paneth assumed the part of a traditional humanist, questioning Nietzsche's vision of social engineering to produce greatness. In this context, Nietzsche also must have broached a topic we have examined above concerning breeding as a solution to the Jewish Question. There is no question that Nietzsche did not advocate anything resembling the eugenics of National Socialism. As we have seen, Jews figure prominently in his eugenic calculations: assimilation of Jews by marriage is desirable not only to eliminate "negative" Jewish traits, but to reproduce favorable Jewish traits in a future ruling class. Paneth reports Nietzsche's thoughts on this matter: "His personal wish was that the Jews should enter into unions with the best and most noble families in all countries and in this way transmit their good qualities; all nations should really do that. And then, as the only and best refutation, the Jews should produce a number of great men; for the examples that one could cite up until now—Heine, Lassalle—were not pure enough."[61] The program Nietzsche is proposing for a solution to the Jewish Question is assimilation through marriage—a solution advocated by many others, including, for example, Schopenhauer—with an eye toward preserving the positive characteristics of the Jews, while integrating them into the upper classes of European society. We have seen Nietzsche suggest the pairing of the offspring of

Jewish bankers and military officers in *Beyond Good and Evil*, and similar suggestions surface on numerous occasions in notebook entries as well.[62] In essence, the qualities Nietzsche associates with Jews are still the same stereotypes drawn from the long tradition of anti-Jewish thought, but in his conversations with Paneth and his notes from the same period, he reverses their valuation, turning vices into virtues for his new ruling class. In particular, the claim of Jewish power or Jewry's potential to dominate and subject "native" populations is an important part of most anti-Semitic ideology in Germany in the last third of the century.[63] Once again, we find an underlying ambivalence in Nietzsche's dealings with contemporary Jewry: they continue to be considered a unified type endowed with fixed characteristics that anti-Semites of his era also identify, but Nietzsche, in his "transvaluation of values," supplies a positive assessment of these qualities—positive, at least from his perspective—considering them productive and serviceable for the type of hierarchical social order he envisions.

Anti-Semitic Associations

Nietzsche's solution to the Jewish Question through intermarriage and the resulting assimilation comes at a time when more radical suggestions had become part of the German political landscape. We have seen that Nietzsche's relationship to Jews and Judaism changed after his break with Wagner, but only in the 1880s do his views enter an implicit dialogue with a Judeophobic movement that went beyond the cultural prejudices of the Wagnerians and the scapegoating of Jewry for economic distress. This movement went by the name of anti-Semitism, and the designation has caused some confusion among proponents and opponents of anti-Jewish thought. Today the term has become synonymous with hostility and prejudice against the Jewish people, and it was used at times in this fashion in Nietzsche's era as well. But technically, anti-Semitism denotes an opposition to all Semitic peoples, not just Jews. Until anti-Semitism was invented in 1879, the word "Semitic" was in large part a notion of linguistic and ethnographic provenance. "Semitic" had become popular in the early nineteenth century as a category to classify specific groups of languages and only gradually in the course of the century did it become a description for a race of people. Important for this shift from historical linguistics to racist anthropology was Gobineau, whose *Essai sur l'inégalité des races humaines* (1852) [*Essay on the Inequality of the Human Races*] provided "scientific" legitimation for both the notion of "race" and the hypothesis that the "Aryan" race was opposed to and potentially corrupted by a "Semitic" race. According to such linguistic and ethnographic theories, then, not only Jews, but also Arabs were included under the category "Semitic," and "anti-Semitism," which was rarely encountered in this sense, would encompass an opposition to or prejudice against "Semites."[64]

Because of its pseudoscientific origin and academic trappings, the word "anti-Semitism" was adopted for use in the anti-Jewish political movement of the 1880s, but it has been questioned and rejected frequently as misleading or erroneous. In Nietzsche's time, Eugen Dühring (1833–1921), known today and referred to by Nietzsche as an anti-Semite, argued that anti-Semitism is an inaccurate designation: "It [the Jewish people] is a specific tribe, which has developed the characteristics of a race in the most marked opposition to other human beings, and not the entire Semitic race, which comes into question in our modern culture and society."[65] Bernhard Förster, the anti-Semitic agitator who married Nietzsche's sister in 1885, also rejects the term "Semitic" as a reference for Jews.[66] Even the National Socialists, seeking to distinguish between the Jews and the Arab nations they were courting, rejected the use of "anti-Semitism" as a false label, "since this movement directs itself against Jewry, the corrupters of all peoples, but not against the other peoples speaking Semitic languages, who have likewise been anti-Jewish since ancient times."[67] Nietzsche, like any good philologist, was apparently also uncomfortable with the equation of anti-Semitic and anti-Jewish. Even after the emergence of the political movement that went by this name, he employs the neologism "Misojuden" (literally, "Haters of Jew," from the Greek μῖσος, hatred, and the German word for Jews) to designate people he would later call "anti-Semitic."[68] Already at a very early stage in the second half of the nineteenth century, however, the word "Semitic" started to be associated with Jews in non-scholarly parlance, to the exclusion of other Semitic peoples, and it contained an implicit critique of "Jewish" modernity.[69] In a sense, by the late 1870s the appearance of the word "anti-Semitic," which would oppose "Jewish" modernity, was long overdue, despite its technical inaccuracy. A confluence of events around 1880 promoted the emergence of the term in the public sphere: the beginning of the anti-Jewish speeches of the Prussian court preacher Adolf Stöcker (1835–1909) in 1879; an article from 1879 composed by the noted historian Heinrich von Treitschke (1834–1896), "Our Views," which inaugurated a protracted debate known subsequently as the "Berlin Anti-Semitism Controversy";[70] and the publication of one of the seminal pamphlets in the incipient anti-Semitic movement, Wilhelm Marr's *The Victory of Judaism over Germanism Considered from a Non-Confessional Perspective*. Indeed, although Marr does not include the expression "anti-Semitism" or any derivatives in his anti-Jewish philippic, most scholars believe that the term originated in Marr's circles in connection with the foundation of the Anti-Semitic League and the announcement of the publication of an *Anti-Semitic Weekly*.[71] Once in the public domain, the word was quickly disseminated in the German-speaking world, and its usage then spread rapidly throughout the Western world.[72]

Nietzsche's relationship to political anti-Semitism, to which he was unequivocally opposed, does not tell us everything we need to know about his opinions on

Jews and Judaism. The two are obviously connected, but Nietzsche and many of his contemporaries regarded anti-Semitism as something different from mere anti-Jewish sentiments: for the 1880s, it has a specific referent in political agitation, especially in Berlin, and proposed a radical solution to the Jewish Question. Indeed, anti-Semitic groups in the German capital organized gangs that chased and harassed Jews, and destroyed Jewish property. In some of the provinces, racists set fire to synagogues.[73] The high point of these early outbursts of anti-Semitism occurred with the Anti-Semites' Petition that was submitted to Bismarck on 13 April 1881, and that requested, among other things, the prohibition of further Jewish emigration from Eastern Europe and the exclusion of Jews from official governmental positions; in short, a cancellation of the recently achieved Jewish emancipation throughout Germany. As we have seen, there were over a quarter of a million signatories to this petition,[74] the most prominent among them being Stöcker. Bernhard Förster, one of the chief organizers of this petition and a prominent voice in the new anti-Semitic movement, became well known to Nietzsche during the 1880s.[75] Nietzsche's repugnance for anti-Semitism was overdetermined; there were multiple reasons Nietzsche opposed the political anti-Semitic movement that had little to do with objections to hostility and prejudice toward Jewry. Although it is not entirely accurate when Nietzsche claims that anti-Semitism destroyed his relationship with Richard Wagner and his sister, and prevented him from acquiring "pecuniary independence, disciples, new friends, and influence" (to Franz Overbeck, 2 April 1884, Nr. 503, KSB 6.493), we should not discount the adverse impact anti-Semitism had on his personal life. One of the reasons that it affected him so greatly is his own acquiescence to anti-Jewish thought when he was associated with Wagner, and his own early admiration for writers who developed into important anti-Semitic thinkers. In the inner circle of Wagnerians, he became intimately acquainted with individuals who, following the lead of the Meister, themselves turned into advocates of anti-Semitic causes.[76] The *Bayreuther Blätter*, to which Nietzsche subscribed along with other members of the Wagner society, contained frequent racist articles, including excerpts from Gobineau. Marr was a member of the extended Wagner circle, as was Förster, whose colony of Nueva Germania in Paraguay, as we saw in Chapter 5, was designed to allow him and other anti-Semites to flee a "Jewified" Europe. We should not forget that Nietzsche was quite close to his sister, especially during the 1870s. Although their relationship was strained somewhat in the next decade, due at first to Nietzsche's involvement with Lou Salomé and then to Elisabeth's betrothal, it is obvious that he harbored strong feelings for his sister throughout his life, even after her marriage to Förster. Part of his reaction against anti-Semitism can be explained by the role he attributed to Elisabeth's anti-Semitic husband, who took his "beloved llama" away from him[77] and indoctrinated her in an ideology he disdained.[78] In this sense, anti-Semitism did, indeed, drive a wedge between Nietzsche and Wagner, as well as between Nietzsche and Wagnerians, including his sister and brother-in-law.

If we examine Nietzsche's readings during the early part of his career, we also find that he was positively inclined toward many writers who became anti-Semites. For example, he admired Treitschke's political tracts during the 1860s, and in Overbeck, who had known Treitschke well when the two studied together in Leipzig, he and Treitschke had a mutual close friend. Nietzsche was also an enthusiastic reader of Dühring's *The Value of Life* during the 1860s and read carefully many of his subsequent philosophical works.[79] In his early career at Basel, Nietzsche also knew and admired Johann Zöllner's (1834–1882) book *On the Nature of the Comets*; later Zöllner distinguished himself by being the sole academic to sign the notorious Anti-Semites' Petition.[80] Paul de Lagarde (1827–1891) was another future anti-Semite for whose writings Nietzsche expressed approval in the 1870s. Finally, Nietzsche's claim about anti-Semitism robbing him of financial independence, disciples, and influence has a grain of truth to it. Nietzsche's publisher, Ernst Schmeitzner, became heavily involved with anti-Semitic literature and organization, and Nietzsche frequently—and unfairly—blamed his lack of success as an author on Schmeitzner's neglect in promoting his writings. Anti-Semites and anti-Semitic thought thus surrounded Nietzsche during his years as a Wagnerian and, in some cases, well into the 1880s. That he himself did not undergo a transformation into an anti-Semite is certainly to his credit. But we should remember that his strong reaction against anti-Semitism as a political movement had a significant basis in perceived personal misfortune: in his mind, it had destroyed—or contributed to the destruction of—formerly solid relationships and was largely responsible for his isolation and relative lack of celebrity among his countrymen.

Nietzsche also had more general, ideological objections to anti-Semitism. Although we today commonly consider anti-Semitism, like other racist sentiments, to be part of a right-wing political profile, in the historical context in which it first appeared, it had many associations that we would consider odd in the twenty-first century. Within the circle of Wagnerian beliefs, for example, anti-Semitism was part of a palette of ideological convictions held by the Meister that included vegetarianism and anti-vivisectionism. In Nietzsche's own thought and writings, anti-Semitism was sometimes associated with the democratizing tendencies that he felt were leveling necessary hierarchies across Europe, as one of many "isms" that arise from *ressentiment*, including feminism and nationalism, which were likewise taking hold in contemporary Europe. In *Ecce Homo*, referring to the Wagner circle in Bayreuth, Nietzsche notes that anti-Semitism flourished in an atmosphere of narrow German virtues (EH, Warum ich so gute Bücher schreibe, Menschliches, Allzumenschliches 2, KSA 6.323–24), and, indeed, anti-Semitism is most frequently regarded as an ally of völkish, chauvinistic attitudes.

But anti-Semitism is also viewed as part of a political context that includes socialism and anarchism. In a letter to Overbeck in 1887, Nietzsche marvels at his popularity among "radical parties" and clarifies parenthetically: "socialists, nihilists, anti-Semites, Christian orthodoxy, Wagnerians" (24 March 1887, Nr. 820, KSB 8.48). In *On the Genealogy of Morals*, he observes that one can study rancor up close since it is a dominant trait in both anti-Semites and anarchists (GM, Zweite Abhandlung 11, KSA 5.309). Later in this work he reinforces this image when he calls Dühring an "apostle of revenge" and "the foremost moral bigmouth at the moment that exists, even among his own kind, the anti-Semites" (GM, Dritte Abhandlung 14, KSA 5.370), but he also considers Dühring the "most dreadful anarchist and calumniator" (to Franz Overbeck, December 1885, Nr. 649, KSB 7.117). And near the close of the *Genealogy*, he writes: "Nor do I like these most recent speculators in idealism, the anti-Semites, who, rolling their eyes in a Christian-Aryan-Philistine way, seek to rouse all the bovine elements of the people through an exasperating abuse of the cheapest means of agitation and moral attitudes" (GM, Dritte Abhandlung 26, KSA 5.407). What emerges from these passages is that Nietzsche opposed anti-Semitism not out of a belief in tolerance or equal civil rights for all people, or out of a particular respect for the Jews, the Jewish religion, or Jewish culture, but because he saw this movement as a further manifestation of an unhealthy moralism. Connected with anti-Semitism from Nietzsche's perspective was a quasi-socialist need to redeem the world through political activism. Writing to his publisher Schmeitzner, he comments that all movements, "your anti-Jewish movement included," lead to "anarchies and earthquakes," and he continues: "From a distance 'anti-Semitism' appears to be exactly like the struggle against the rich and the means previously employed to become rich" (2 April 1883, Nr. 399, KSB 6.356). This impression was no doubt reinforced by some of the anti-Semitic propaganda of his time. Dühring, we should recall, was widely known for his advocacy of socialism and is perhaps best remembered today because of Friedrich Engels's (1820–1895) polemic against him and his brand of socialism in 1878. Even Förster conceived of his colonial project in Paraguay as a German socialist venture. Nietzsche's response to and rejection of anti-Semitism, viewed from the perspective of the 1880s, is part and parcel of his assault on Christian ethics, narrow-minded nationalism, and redemptive socialism. It does not arise from philo-Semitic convictions and is unrelated to the liberalism we normally identify with attitudes opposed to racism and supportive of civil liberties in an egalitarian society.

This principled opposition to the various leveling phenomena in contemporary European society, as well as his personal irritations with the anti-Semitic movement, very probably accounts for Nietzsche's allergic reaction to the appearance of his name and work in the anti-Semitic press. In March 1887, Nietzsche evidently received copies of issues of the *Anti-Semitic Correspondence* from

Theodor Fritsch.[81] Fritsch, who later authored the extremely popular *Anti-Semitic Catechism*, which was subsequently renamed *The Handbook of Anti-Semitism*, went on to be one of the most influential voices of anti-Semitism until his death in 1933. In his letter to Nietzsche, which does not survive, he apparently took exception to some of the more positive evaluations of Jews in Nietzsche's works, although the very fact that he sent him the *Anti-Semitic Correspondence* indicates that he believed Nietzsche to be essentially an ally. If we consider Nietzsche's Wagnerian roots, his publisher, and his sister's husband, this assumption was not far-fetched in the least. Nietzsche, however, is dismissive in his response and defends his own views of the Jews. Although he confesses that he has no Jewish friends, he quickly adds that he also has no anti-Semitic friends either. His suggestion that Fritsch publish a "list of German scholars, artists, poets, writers, actors, and virtuosos of Jewish heritage" is meant as a critique of German culture rather than a dismissal of Jewish influence (23 March 1887, Nr. 819, KSB 8.45–46). Commenting to Overbeck about Fritsch's contact with him, he expresses bafflement that he has attracted so much attention in the "racial" parties, but at this point he appears more amused than angered at the "anti-Semitic interpretation" given to *Zarathustra* in the racist press (24 March 1887, Nr. 820, KSB 8.48). Evidently, after studying the *Anti-Semitic Correspondence* more closely, he was less sanguine, and he soon penned a second, more belligerent response to Fritsch:

> I hereby send back to you the three issues you sent me of your *Correspondence* periodical, thanking you for your trust, which allowed me to acquire an insight into the confused principles at the foundation of this strange movement. However, I would request that you no longer do me the honor of sending them to me;[82] for I fear that I will lose my patience. Believe me, this horrible desire on the part of annoying dilettantes to babble about the value of people and races, this deference to "authorities," who would be rejected by any more sober intellect (e.g. E. Dühring, R. Wagner, Ebrad, Wahrmund, P. de Lagarde[83]—who of these is the most unqualified, the most unjust in questions of morality and history?), this continuous and absurd falsification and appropriation of vague concepts, such as "Germanic," "Semitic," "Aryan," "Christian," "German"—all this could in the long run make me angry and rouse me out of the ironic beneficence with which I have up until now looked upon the virtuous velleities and Pharisaisms of contemporary Germans.
>
> Finally, what do you think that I experience when the name Zarathustra is uttered from the mouth of anti-Semites? (29 March 1887, Nr. 823, KSB 8.51)

Nietzsche was obviously displeased that his name had become associated with anti-Semitism, although it should be noted that at an earlier time he had expressed approval and enthusiasm for at least two of the men he rejects in 1887, namely Paul de Lagarde and Richard Wagner. We might also recall that Nietzsche himself had used several of the concepts he now derides ("Semitic" and "Aryan," for example) in early writings, and that he himself was hardly immune from generalizations about races and peoples, as we can see from the section "Peoples and Fatherlands" in *Beyond Good and Evil* (JGB 240–56, KSA 5.179–204). Nietzsche's response to Fritsch shows his extreme frustration with a situation from which he could not extricate himself. It was Nietzsche's fate to be associated with anti-Semitism from almost the inception of the movement, and while he was partially justified in his indignation at this association, anti-Semitic Nietzsche enthusiasts have been able to build on a not insubstantial Judeophobic foundation in Nietzsche's life and thought.

The personal dimension of Nietzsche's indignation at his unwanted anti-Semitic appropriation is evidenced in correspondence with and about his sister. In various letters Nietzsche writes of being abandoned by Elisabeth,[84] who is now among the anti-Semites, and of his ambivalence about the colony in Nueva Germania, which he would like to see succeed for his sister's welfare, but which he also hopes will fail because of what it represents.[85] His frustration with his sister's marriage to Förster comes to a head in particular in the draft version of a letter he composed in December 1887.[86] Upset with the fact that her husband, Bernhard Förster, had not given up his ties to the anti-Semitic movement,[87] Nietzsche writes that Förster's thought represents the very antithesis of everything he stands for. Nietzsche refers specifically to Förster's *Reminiscences of Parsifal* (1883), and he thus brings several elements into play: his dislike for Förster's Germanness and anti-Semitism, Wagner's putative turn to Christian ethics, and his own misuse by anti-Semitic agitators:

> When I read it [*Reminiscences of Parsifal*], the hair-raising idea occurred to me that you have understood nothing, nothing about my illness, and just as little about my most painful and most surprising experience—that the man whom I had most admired became disgustingly transformed and degenerate, what I have always despised most, in the swindle with moral and Christian ideals.—Now it has come to the point that I have to defend myself with hand and foot against the confusion of me with the anti-Semitic rabble; after my own sister, my earlier sister just as again Widemann[88] has given rise to this most unfortunate of all confusions. After I have read the name Zarathustra in the *Anti-Semitic Correspondence*, my patience is at its end. (Nr. 968, KSB 8.218)

Part of the incoherence of this letter is due to the fact that it was a draft, part, perhaps, that Nietzsche was venting his anger in written words. Nevertheless, it is a telling document for the place anti-Semitism occupied in Nietzsche's personal and intellectual life. He leaves no doubt that he rejects anti-Semitism in its entirety: he closes the paragraph with the exclamation: "I am now against your husband's party in a condition of self-defense. These accursed anti-Semitic-pusses should not interfere with my ideal!!" (Nr. 968, KSB 8.218–19). But from the various topics brought together in this draft, it is also obvious that anti-Semitism has more meaning for him than simply anti-Jewish prejudice. Anti-Semitism became something of an obsession for Nietzsche; in his last letters, in which insanity had already taken hold of him, he continues to fulminate against anti-Semites. To Franz Overbeck, he writes that he is "having all anti-Semites shot," and to Jacob Burckhardt, he comments, "Wilhelm, Bismarck, and all anti-Semites [have been] eliminated" (4 January 1889, Nr. 1249, KSB 8.575; and 6 January 1889, Nr. 1256, KSB 8.579). But his objections to anti-Semitism were always part of a complex that encompassed personal disappointments as well as intellectual convictions.

Nietzsche's frustration at being associated with anti-Semitism is understandable, but perhaps unrealistic. As we witnessed in his conversation with Paneth, he was uncomfortable with his earlier association with Wagner and sought to conceal his adherence to the anti-Jewish proclivities of the Wagnerian circle. Revealing for his discomfort is the response he gave to Paneth regarding his contribution to Schmeitzner's journal, the *International Monthly*. A series of Nietzsche's poems, "Idylls of Messina," appeared in the May 1882 issue, and Paneth asks the philosopher how he could become involved with an anti-Semitic publication. Nietzsche responded that the journal was not dedicated to anti-Semitism when he published in it; in fact, it was conceived "in an exactly opposite sense by those who wanted to be good Europeans," and both the journal and its publisher "became anti-Semitic only later."[89] Nietzsche's response denies that Schmeitzner was an anti-Semite in 1882 when the first issue of the *International Monthly* appeared, or, alternatively, that his anti-Semitism was not known to Nietzsche at that time. Although it is not possible to date precisely Schmeitzner's initial involvement with anti-Jewish politics, an indication of his racist sentiments is found as early as 1879 in a letter he wrote to Heinrich Köselitz.[90] At the very latest, Nietzsche learned of Schmeitzner's anti-Semitic activity when he saw a letter Overbeck had written to Köselitz in May 1880. Overbeck relates to Köselitz concerns about Schmeitzner's views and mentions specifically his involvement with an anti-Semitic journal.[91] A subsequent letter to Nietzsche also contains mention of the anti-Semitic journal Schmeitzner is publishing (Nr. 27, KGB III 2.71). To this news, Nietzsche reacts with disdain: "Schmeitzner's latest undertaking, about which you wrote, disgusts me; I'm indignant that he didn't say a word to me about it" (22 June 1880, Nr. 33, KSB 6.24). In June 1881, Nietzsche writes to Schmeitzner directly when he suspects that his publisher is no longer interested in his books: "I presume that you have secretly sworn to yourself that this will be the last piece of writing from me that you will publish. Really, I no longer fit in with your Wagner-Schopenhauer-Dühring-and-other-*party*-literature" (Nr. 117, KSB 6.93).[92] Nietzsche certainly knew about Schmeitzner's anti-Semitic activities long before he contributed his poetry to the journal.

Nor could Nietzsche have been entirely ignorant about the direction of the journal from its very inception. The editor, Paul Heinrich Widemann (1851–1928), like Schmeitzner a fervent anti-Semite, had studied under Nietzsche and was a friend of Heinrich Köselitz; it is not likely that Nietzsche was ignorant of his ideological leanings. The intellectual inspiration behind the journal, moreover, was Bruno Bauer (1809–1882),[93] who had a long history of Judeophobic writing to his credit, starting with his pamphlet on *The Jewish Question* in 1842, to which Karl Marx famously responded.[94] After the 1848 revolution, his anti-Jewish tendencies from the pre-March period became "a more prominent feature of his later thought."[95] While it is true that the most virulent anti-Semitic articles did not appear in the *Monthly* until the second half of 1882, and that the change in the subtitle of the journal to reflect its anti-Jewish emphasis did not occur until the second year of publication in 1883,[96] it is not credible that Nietzsche knew nothing of the racist foundation and direction of the undertaking. He had heard on numerous occasions that Schmeitzner was deeply involved in anti-Semitic publishing and political activity; he suspected the motivation for the journal was anti-Jewish; he knew that the editor of the journal, Paul Widemann, shared Schmeitzner's views on Jews and Jewry;[97] and the leading spiritual force behind the journal, Bruno Bauer, exhibited a long history of anti-Jewish thought dating back to the 1840s. Nietzsche would have had to ignore everything he knew about the men most intimately involved with the journal to believe that it was not a publication devoted to furthering anti-Semitic causes. His uneasiness at Paneth's queries about his participation in this enterprise is likely attributable in part to his recognition that he was to some degree complicit in his own anti-Semitic reputation and the problems it was causing him, both in his personal life and among his Viennese Jewish followers.

Anti-Semitism Versus Anti-Judaism

Between the two letters Nietzsche wrote to Fritsch in 1887, he sent a postcard to Köselitz that includes the short and dismissive statement we have already cited concerning the Dostoevsky translator, the "Jew Goldschmidt" and his "synagogue rhythms" (27 March 1887, Nr. 822, KSB 8.50). We have seen that Nietzsche continued to make such comments even after he broke with Wagner, but the timing of these letters is curious. How could Nietzsche include in such a casual fashion an anti-Jewish slur reminiscent of Wagner when three days before—and two days after—he wrote this remark, he was excoriating the anti-Semite Fritsch for his journal, his movement, and his ideological convictions? We have to suspect that the answer lies in the partial dissociation of anti-Semitism from anti-Jewish sentiments in Nietzsche's mind and, to a degree, also in the minds of his contemporaries. Obviously, Nietzsche recognized that anti-Semitic parties advocated measures against Jews, including the repudiation of legal emancipation and the introduction of restrictions that would eliminate Jewish influence in German society. At the same time, he did not consider anti-Semitism to be an ideology that exhausted itself in anti-Jewish thought, and although he had some favorable opinions about modern Jewry, he did not regard bias toward Jewry as incompatible with an aversion to anti-Semitism. For this reason, Nietzsche can even postulate that anti-Semites resemble Jews. In one of his late notebooks, Nietzsche differentiates between the two in a manner flattering to neither group: "What really separates a Jew from an anti-Semite: the Jew knows that he is lying when he lies: the anti-Semite does not know that he is always lying" (Nachlass 1888, 21[6], KSA 13.580). A bit later he defines the anti-Semite as "an envious, i.e. the most stupid Jew" (Nachlass 1888, 21[7], KSA 13.581). And in *On the Genealogy of Morals*, anti-Semitism appears as a modern manifestation of values originating in the Jewish priests. Nor, as we have observed, does an individual's adherence to anti-Semitism disqualify that individual from possessing positive characteristics and even from securing Nietzsche's admiration. In drafts intended for *The Case of Wagner*, Nietzsche speaks of the delightful and stimulating memories he has for Wagner and Cosima, and then comments: "Even for anti-Semites, for whom, as is known, I am not fond at all, I would have to acknowledge, according to my not inconsiderable experience, many favorable things: this does not hinder me from declaring a merciless war against anti-Semitism, rather it is the condition for it" (Nachlass 1888, 24[1.6], KSA 13.622–23). The opposition to anti-Semitism was something very different for Nietzsche than for us: it did not necessarily entail the elimination of bias against Jewry, nor was it a fatal character flaw in friends. For Nietzsche, as we have seen, his aversion to anti-Semitism has numerous dimensions, many of them personal: (1) He blames it for destroying his friendship with Wagner and Cosima. (2) He considers it a decisive factor in his estrangement from his sister. (3) It caused, in his mind, his publisher Schmeitzner to lose focus on his writings, which resulted in (4) a lack of financial security and independence, (5) an insufficient dissemination of his ideas to the general public in Germany, and (6) the absence of followers and disciples of sufficient quality and quantity. (7) It also threatened to destroy his reputation with the one circle of admirers he had secured over the years, the Viennese Jews at the university. There were also philosophical and ideological objections, the most important of which were its origins in *ressentiment* and its close connection with German patriotism and Christianity. In none of these considerations does hatred of Jews or prejudice against Jewry play a decisive role.

Nietzsche recognized the compatibility of opposition to anti-Semitism and espousal of anti-Jewish views in aphorism 251 of *Beyond Good and Evil*. After stating that he has not yet met a German favorably inclined toward the Jews, he draws a distinction between anti-Semitism and a more acceptable, less virulent anti-Jewish attitude: "and however unconditionally all careful and political people may repudiate real anti-Semitism [*Antisemiterei*], even this caution and politics is not directed against this class of feeling, but rather only against its dangerous immoderation, especially against the distasteful and ignominious expression of this immoderate feeling—we should not deceive ourselves about this" (JGB 251, KSA 5.193). Nietzsche is making a quite remarkable claim in this passage, one that is readily applicable to him and his circle of friends. Individuals who are cautious and conscious of the political realities of the time are against anti-Semitism, which Nietzsche ridicules further by calling it "*Antisemiterei*," clearly a derogative reference to this racist movement. At the same time, the "class of feeling" that gives rise to anti-Semitism is not really at issue, and those who are "cautious and political" do not reject anti-Semitism because they also renounce sentiments directed against Jews, but because the manner in which the anti-Semites conduct themselves is wholly distasteful to them. Anti-Semites and those who oppose anti-Semites share a common bond in their views on Jews and their effect in Germany, which appears to explain why Nietzsche claims to have met no German—anti-Semite or non-anti-Semite—who was well disposed toward Jews. Where they differ is in their solution to the Jewish Question. Anti-Semites are "immoderate" and "distasteful" in the means they choose toward their goal. Presumably the more refined strata of German society adopt other paths to achieve a similar objective. As we have seen, Nietzsche can very well be included in this latter group: he is virulently opposed to anti-Semitism, but he too has developed a solution to the Jewish Question that would eliminate the baleful characteristics of modern Jewry. In the remainder of the aphorism, Nietzsche juxtaposes the anti-Semitic perspective with its inherent dangers to his own. The anti-Semites, Nietzsche tells us, appear to want to force the Jews to assume dominance in Europe, a condition both Nietzsche and the anti-Semites should not welcome at the present time. The Jews themselves are strongly inclined toward assimilation, of which Nietzsche approves, and he states that they should be encouraged in this direction, since it represents "a softening of Jewish instincts," that is, German Jews are in the process of losing the traits they currently possess and becoming more suitable for the task of contributing to a ruling class for Europe. Because of their uncompromising and unreasonable political stance, Nietzsche makes the following ironic recommendation: "it might be useful and appropriate to banish the anti-Semitic loudmouths from the country" (JGB 251, KSA 5.194). With this suggestion, Nietzsche turns the tables on anti-Semites, who advocate expelling Jews from Germany, but he does so not necessarily because he repudiates their sentiments about modern Jewry, but because he disagrees with their "immoderate" method for solving the problem of Jewish presence on German soil. Nietzsche and the anti-Semites seek a resolution to the Jewish Question, but in aphorism 251, Nietzsche makes it clear that he opposes anti-Semites because their activities threaten to undermine more reasonable and realistic proposals, such as his own, for dealing with Jews.

Because today we tend to identify anti-Semitism, *tout court*, as prejudice against Jews, we may have difficulty appreciating the distinctions that Nietzsche was drawing. Without the historical context, we can easily believe that Nietzsche's rejection of anti-Semitism says everything we need to know about his relationship to Jews and Judaism. But it does not. Nor was Nietzsche alone in espousing anti-Jewish views while at the same time expressing the conviction that anti-Semitism was a crude way to reduce or eliminate the influence of modern Jewry and therefore must be rejected. We mentioned above a letter from 1880 that Overbeck had sent to Köselitz as evidence for Nietzsche's knowledge of his publisher's anti-Semitism. Overbeck expresses concern about Schmeitzner's publication of anti-Semitic materials—Schmeitzner also published some of Overbeck's works, adding to his concern—and while he is on the topic of anti-Semitism, which was a very recent German phenomenon at that point, he broaches a discussion of Jews with regard to this new political movement:

> Whatever grievances we have against the Jews, and whatever, as a rule, is repulsive about them: non-Jews as well as Germans can easily agree about this. But it seems to me that in today's whole public activity in Germany there is enough blindness, thoughtlessness, tactlessness, and narrow-mindedness, and that it would be increased even more by an agitation resting on the blindest instinct. It could be that Jews in Germany are a kind of state of emergency[98]—although in the torpor that has recently surfaced in our essence, I can't see how we could do without our Jews—but we would certainly not be thinking about resisting them *in this fashion* if the shoe didn't pinch us in an entirely different place.

Overbeck represents a position with regard to Jews in 1880 that is quite similar to what Nietzsche would describe six years later in *Beyond Good and Evil*. We can all agree on definite grievances against the Jews, as well as their repulsiveness, but we should not be dealing with the issue using the methods of the anti-Semites. He takes a neutral stance on the oft-cited anti-Semitic contention that the country is in a state of emergency owing to Jewish dominance of the press and the financial world, but recognizes wistfully that Jews are presently so ensconced in German affairs that they are indispensable. In any case, the sudden rise of anti-Semitism would not have been possible except for existing problems that have little to do with the Jewish presence or with an imagined Jewish dominance in Germany. Overbeck continues his reflections, referring to the National Liberals, the party with which Bismarck ruled Germany from 1871 to 1879, and its putative Jewish leanings. "Even if National Liberalism ever so loudly tells the Jew, now that he has provided his service, to leave, it will not be able to get rid of him, since I haven't really seen much else in it besides the Jew, and, to be sure, not the most pleasant sort. In short, I consider the attempts to improve our public circumstances from *that* side to be driving out demons by Beelzebub." While it is true that several important members of the National Liberal Party were Jewish, Overbeck's remark about them not being "the most pleasant sort" evidences a gratuitous, anti-Jewish sentiment. Despite this unfavorable view of Jews, he indicates that anti-Semitism approaches the issue in the wrong manner and that to embrace that position would only make a bad situation worse. Overbeck then refers specifically to the beginnings of the Berlin anti-Semitism controversy, which was instigated by his friend from his student years, Heinrich von Treitschke, the noted Prussian historian. Overbeck considers the legitimation of anti-Semitism by the Berlin academic to be wrong-headed and unseemly. "The endeavor of my friend Treitschke to turn a movement, whose sole effective rationale in the forms in which it has appeared hitherto has been admittedly base, into something wholesome through sanctimonious talk, and to give it the consecration of Christian Germanness—as if anyone, if it had to be, couldn't at present easily provide a shabby disguise for it—appears to me to be completely naïve." Overbeck, like Nietzsche, believed there was a problem with German Jewry and that Germans needed to find a solution to the Jewish Question, but he disapproves of anti-Semitic politics and is especially perturbed by their validation through otherwise respectable advocates. As we have seen, this letter was meant to be shown to Nietzsche, so it is appropriate that Overbeck concludes his remarks on Jews and anti-Semitism with the query: "What does Nietzsche say to this matter?"[99] The response appears in a letter Nietzsche wrote to Overbeck's wife, Ida, a few weeks later. Nietzsche asks her to thank his friend for the letter he has now seen and states that he is delighted to know that from such a distance there is such a harmony of sentiments: "For example, both of us do not need to waste another word with regard to our understanding of Jews and associates of Jews" (24 May 1880, Nr. 28, KSB 6.20).

The harmony that exists between Overbeck and Nietzsche with regard to the Jewish Question and anti-Semitism contains a cautionary lesson for today's readers not to evaluate matters of race and racial bias without the relevant historical context. Nietzsche and Overbeck both recoil from the crude excesses of political anti-Semitism, but they retain attitudes toward Jews we would categorize today as biased and perhaps even racist. The rejection of anti-Semitism entailed something quite different from an absence of anti-Jewish sentiments, and this distinction was obvious to writers of the late nineteenth century in a way that it is not to twentieth- and twenty-first-century commentators. In his recollections of Nietzsche, Overbeck returns to the same constellation of issues we have been examining and provides further confirmation for the necessity of historical contextualization. After discussing Nietzsche's relationship with Josef Paneth, Overbeck notes that although he and Nietzsche did not devote any special studies to Judaism, they came to appreciate the perseverance of the Jewish people in their native traditions; we may recall Nietzsche's respect for the "remarkableness of their tenacity" in his aphoristic writings. Overbeck then turns to the topic of anti-Semitism and draws a picture similar to the one contained in his letter to Köselitz:

> I believe that Nietzsche and I were very much in agreement in our thoughts with regard to anti-Semitism. Since fanaticism of any kind, nationalist hatred as well as religious hatred, was especially far from our thoughts—even though for different reasons that had to do with our divergent backgrounds—we had fundamentally no sympathy for anti-Semitism. Not that this closed attitude toward anti-Semitism made us so very different from other Europeans. This radically closed attitude was hardly anything other than what one would find in our contemporaries. In our era, almost everyone—at least every educated person—had a certain antipathy toward the Jews, so much so that in our circles the Jews themselves had this attitude. In our social milieu, this is inherent in practically everyone, only that almost everyone permits himself to express this antipathy in a great variety of nuances, while only a few conceal it completely, and not very many at all preach this antipathy out loud.

Overbeck continues by stating that he and Nietzsche did not pay much attention to anti-Semitism, considering it merely a passing sign of the times. However, he also comments that Nietzsche's writings exhibit a noticeable dose of "anti-Semitism" (Overbeck uses quotation marks here)[100] or at least only a slight love of Semites (by which he obviously means Jews), and that he suffered a great deal of personal frustration at the hands of anti-Semites. He wishes Nietzsche would have been spared all dealings with both Jews and anti-Semites since he recognizes from his last notebooks and letters how much these matters weighed on his thoughts. "Nietzsche was a heartfelt adversary of anti-Semitism," Overbeck states in summary, but he adds the caveat: "as he experienced it." Nonetheless, Overbeck comments that "when he spoke honestly, his remarks about Jews in his writings were much sharper than those of the anti-Semites themselves. His anti-Christianity was chiefly founded on anti-Semitism."[101] What Overbeck is observing in his friend is important for clarifying the historical specificity of Nietzsche's position toward the Jewish Question. An opponent of anti-Semitism, which he conceived in his time as a political, vulgar racist movement, Nietzsche, like many of his contemporaries, could still harbor significant anti-Jewish sentiments and propound theories that could easily be judged a contribution to anti-Semitic thought by even a sympathetic readership.

The Genealogy of Jewish Slave Morality

In the last sane years of his life, Nietzsche expanded his observations on Jewry to include discussions involving the history of religion. His preoccupation with the Jewish tradition involved two interrelated themes that are of central importance for his thought in 1887 and 1888: the history of morals and the rise of Christianity. He had been interested in these topics for quite a few years, but what changed in the latter half of the 1880s was Nietzsche's hypothesis that there existed a strong continuity between Jewish values in the centuries prior to the birth of Jesus and the teachings that were ultimately incorporated into the official Christian faith. He was assisted in developing this hypothesis by various sources, most of which are never mentioned in his published writings. In his Basler years, we have to assume that Nietzsche learned a great deal from his closest friend on the faculty, Franz Overbeck, who was a specialist in early Christian theology. In the early 1870s, Nietzsche was also impressed by the theological writings of Paul de Lagarde (1827–1891), whose negative evaluation of the apostle Paul anticipates Nietzsche's later assessment.[102] In the 1880s, we find Nietzsche reflecting critically on the writings of Ernest Renan (1823–1892), one of the foremost French intellectuals of his era and a noted writer on the Christian tradition.[103] Perhaps most important for Nietzsche's thought in the 1880s, however, was Julius Wellhausen (1844–1918), a distinguished Old Testament scholar with great expertise in the history of Judaism.[104] As Nietzsche focused his writing more on the connection between the history of morality and the rise of Christianity, we encounter with increasing frequency the mention of Jews and Judaism. His published books and notes from the 1880s, especially from 1887 and 1888, contain an abundance of references to Jews, many of them alluding to historical Jewry and speculation on Jewish history during the time of the prophets. It is sometimes difficult to know precisely what period of Jewish history Nietzsche means when he is making claims about Jews and their morality, since he rarely includes dates or historical markers. From his sources and occasional allusions, however, we can assume that he was primarily concerned with the transition from the ancient Israelites, who possessed a nationalist God Yahweh, to the phase of Judaism in which their divinity became universal in character and morality enters strongly into religious practices and laws. Although Nietzsche's last writings have become notorious for their attacks on Christianity, Judaism and its history emerge in these years as a central and perhaps even more pivotal concern.[105]

Judaism plays a prominent role in the initial essay in *On the Genealogy of Morals*. In the first six sections, Nietzsche outlines two opposed value systems, one aristocratic, based on the notions of "good" and "bad," the other a slave or herd morality associated with the antithesis "good" and "evil." In describing the transition from the more original noble morality to slave morality, Nietzsche introduces the figure of the priest, who betrays his fellow nobles and gains power by propagating a value system based on *ressentiment*. But Nietzsche interrupts this account in section seven, and the Jews are suddenly thrust into this semihistorical narrative. They represent "the most important example" of the morals that overturn aristocratic values: "Nothing that anyone else has perpetrated against the 'noble,' the 'powerful,' the 'masters,' the 'rulers' merits discussion in comparison with the deeds of the Jews—the Jews, that priestly people who ultimately knew no other way of exacting satisfaction from their enemies and conquerors than through a radical transvaluation of their values, through an art of *the most intelligent revenge*" (GM, Erste Abhandlung 7, KSA 5.267). In this initial mention of the Jews, there are three features worth noting. First, they are portrayed as aggressively opposing the value system that has subjugated them; Jews are directly antithetical to "aristocratic" social orders that Nietzsche has previously identified with the "master race," with "Aryans," and with blond and fair-haired peoples. This juxtaposition, even if Nietzsche did not intend it to be read as a concession toward anti-Semitic doctrines, resembles the opposition between Jews and Germans that was so prominent in racist propaganda from Gobineau to Richard Wagner and Wilhelm Marr. Second, Jews are identified closely with intelligence; they extract revenge on their despised enemies through their mental prowess. Nietzsche is employing one of the favorite stereotypes of Jews in the modern world as clever and conniving, as well as seeking to gain advantage over an unsuspecting Gentile population through manipulation rather than direct confrontation. Third, Nietzsche changes completely the dynamics that he had established before the introduction of the Jews. While the priests were part of the noble order that gradually usurps dominance from the aristocratic "warriors," the Jews are a people or race that is itself "priestly." We are not dealing here with "Jewish priests"; the phrase appears nowhere in the *Genealogy* or in any of Nietzsche's notes for this text. Rather, the essence of Judaism is "priestly." He continues in this passage from section seven with uncomplimentary remarks about Jews and their reversal of noble values:

This was only as befitted a priestly people, the people of the most downtrodden priestly vindictiveness. It has been the Jews who have, with terrifying consistency, dared to undertake the reversal of the aristocratic value equation (good = noble = powerful = beautiful = happy = blessed) and have held on to it tenaciously by the teeth of the most unfathomable hatred (the hatred of the powerless). It is they who have declared: "The miserable alone are the good; the poor, the powerless, the low alone are the good. The suffering, the deprived, the sick, the ugly are the only pious ones, the only blessed, for them alone is there salvation. You, on the other hand, the noble and the powerful, you are for all eternity the evil, the cruel, the lascivious, the insatiable, the godless ones. You will be without salvation, accursed and damned to all eternity." (GM, Erste Abhandlung 7, KSA 5.267)

Nietzsche's disdain for Christianity in his late writings has led many commentators to believe that his remarks are not infused with Judeophobia because his "real" target lies elsewhere. But this conclusion is odd because Christians are not the originator of the fundamental and deleterious transvaluation; they are merely the vehicle that propagates "Jewish values" in the centuries following the establishment of the church. Without Jews, there would be no Christians. Nietzsche's anti-Christian sentiments can be understood more accurately as a continuation of anti-Jewish stereotypes and tropes. Indeed, it is not the Christians who undertook "the monstrous initiative, disastrous beyond all bounds," but the Jews, who have issued, as it were, "the most fundamental of all declarations of war" (GM, Erste Abhandlung 7, KSA 5.267–68). And Nietzsche reminds us proudly that he had revealed Jewish responsibility for the demise of aristocratic values in a previous publication, adverting to aphorism 195 in *Beyond Good and Evil*, where he had written "that with the Jews the slave revolt in morals begins" (JGB 195, KSA 5,117). This revolt has a history of two millennia, Nietzsche informs us, and the reason today we have lost sight of it is because it has been "victorious" (GM, Erste Abhandlung 7, KSA 5.268). Nietzsche, the opponent of political anti-Semitism in his own era, infuses his text with a motif from his adversaries by proclaiming, as Wagner had done in his "Judaism and Music" and Marr had claimed in his *Victory of Judaism over Germanism*, the ultimate victory of Jewry over peoples closely resembling Germans.

Section eight continues Nietzsche's discussion of the "slave-revolt" in morals as an instrument for Jewish domination that employs Christianity as a vehicle. Although the transition from Judaism to Christianity and Christianity's spread across Europe over the centuries are the most momentous events in the advent of slave morality, Nietzsche makes it apparent that its origins lie in the Jewish heritage: "from the trunk of that tree of revenge and hatred, Jewish hatred—the deepest and most sublime hatred, that is, the kind of hatred that creates ideals and changes the meaning of values, a hatred the like of which has never been on earth—from this tree grew forth something equally incomparable, *a new love*, the deepest and most sublime of all the kinds of love—and from what other trunk could it have grown?" (GM, Erste Abhandlung 8, KSA 5.268). The emergence of Christian love is a late fruit from a tree that is fundamentally Jewish. Thus at the origin of doctrines that purport to be opposed to Judaism are Jewish values. While much of the Christian tradition had sought to differentiate itself from its Jewish roots by claiming to reverse Jewish values, Nietzsche is at pains to associate the two religions, while always giving primacy and ultimate responsibility to Judaism. Nietzsche's discussion therefore contradicts the Christian anti-Semitism of his era, which was based on a strict antagonism between Christianity and Judaism. But he does so only by implicating Jews and Judaism for the degeneracy and mediocrity of the modern world at a more profound level. Nietzsche anticipates the objection that would emanate from Christian advocates:

> But let no one think that it [the new love] somehow grew up as the genuine negation of that thirst for revenge, as the antithesis of Jewish hatred! No, the opposite is the case! Love grew forth from this hatred, as its crown, as its triumphant crown, spreading itself ever wider in the purest brightness and fullness of the sun, as a crown that pursued in the lofted realm of light the goals of hatred—victory, spoils, seduction—driven there by the same impulse with which the roots of that hatred sank down ever further and more lasciviously into everything deep and evil. (GM, Erste Abhandlung 8, KSA 5.268)

Christian values are derivative. Jesus Christ, who embodies the doctrine of love and promises redemption and salvation, represents "the most sinister and irresistible form of the very same temptation, the indirect temptation to accept those self-same *Jewish* values and new versions of the ideal" (GM, Erste Abhandlung 8, KSA 5.268–69). Christ is not the rebel against the Jewish establishment, the divinity who announces a new religious order, but the continuator of an essentially Jewish moral regime, the secret agent, as it were, of Judaism in the Roman world. Appearances and tradition are deceptive about Christ's role in the ancient world, since they have obscured the role Jewry plays in this historical drama:

> Has Israel not reached the ultimate goal of its sublime vindictiveness through the detour of this very "redeemer," who appeared to oppose and announce the dissolution of Israel? Is it not characteristic of the secret

black art of a truly *great* policy of revenge, of a far-sighted, subterranean revenge which unfolds itself slowly and thinks ahead, that Israel itself was obliged to deny the very instrument of this revenge as a mortal enemy and crucify him before the whole world, so that the "whole world," all the opponents of Israel, might unthinkingly bite on just this very bait? And, on the other hand, would it be possible, with the most refined ingenuity, to devise a *more dangerous* bait? (GM, Erste Abhandlung 8, KSA 5.269)

Far from undermining Judaism and redressing its shortcomings, Christianity represents a means to further the cause of "Israel" with activities and persons designed to mislead observers and interpreters. "Israel" employs Christ for its own ends, deceiving the world into believing that he opposes his Jewish persecutors. The advent of Christ and of the Christian Church is in reality an invention of Jewish interests bent on extracting revenge on enemies and ultimately conquering the world under the repressive and life-negating regime of slave morality. It is a dangerous gambit because of the enigma involving a God dying a gruesome death for the sake of humankind, out of love for his fellow human beings. But it is under this sign, Nietzsche writes, alluding to Constantine's "in hoc signo vinces" [in this sign you will conquer], that Jewry celebrates its victory; in this radical reinterpretation of Christian iconography, the cross symbolizes not Christianity and the passion of Christ, but "Israel's revenge and transvaluation of all values" (GM, Erste Abhandlung 8, KSA 5.269), its defeat of all noble ideals.

We can now understand better Nietzsche's dissatisfaction with the anti-Semitic political movements of his own era and what Overbeck meant when he maintained that his anti-Christianity was based on anti-Semitism. In Nietzsche's much larger framework, anti-Semites of the 1880s were petty and crude ideologues; they partake of the same *ressentiment* against the Jews that ultimately derives from Jewish values. Anti-Semites are similar to early Christians or to Luther in the Reformation: in opposing Jews, they remain caught up in moral valuations that are essentially Jewish. In the *Genealogy*, Nietzsche makes the case that these instances of opposition are in reality a ploy designed by Jews to secure their supremacy. Anti-Semites are therefore not opposed to Jews; they are tools of the Jewish spirit that has become pervasive in nineteenth-century Europe. For this reason, Nietzsche can equate Jews and anti-Semites, noting only that the former know when they are lying, while the latter, being dupes of the former, are ignorant of their actual status in propagating and reinforcing Jewish values (Nachlass 1888, 21[6], KSA 13.580). Anti-Semites despise modern Jews for their wealth and for their influence over politics and culture. They disdain, in short, the very qualities that demonstrate to Nietzsche that diaspora Jewry embodies the will to power. Nietzsche did not want to strip Jews of the qualities that had made them successful in the modern world; instead he wanted to have these traits bred into a European race that would exercise hegemony over the entire world. Presumably this hegemony would entail something other than the domination he associates with the current European state of affairs, which is still under the authority of Jewish values of *ressentiment* and life-negating morality. The anti-Semites, therefore, fail to grasp the real power that the Jews represent in world history, as well as the tremendous potential that they harbor in the contemporary world for overcoming the social order of mediocrity and degeneration. In the first essay of the *Genealogy*, Nietzsche was thus more consistently and unrelentingly anti-Jewish than his anti-Semitic adversaries. Rhetorically and substantively Nietzsche makes it clear that the introduction of "good and evil" has been detrimental to everything of genuine worth. He ultimately postulates an anti-Jewish historical trajectory that resembles anti-Semitic propaganda, but on a grander scale: Jewry displaces and defeats noble morality, associated with Aryans and fair-haired races, substituting for it life-negating and degenerate valuations, and, through deception or direct confrontation, manages well into the nineteenth century to retain its hegemony over the peoples it has conquered.

Jewish History in *The Antichrist*

Nietzsche's readings in Jewish history and early Christianity in the second half of the 1880s did not produce any remarkable change in his attitude toward Jewry during the last year of his sane life. The Jewish presence in *The Antichrist* contains some nuances that Nietzsche derives from Wellhausen and others, but in essence, he reinforces the tendencies found in the *Genealogy*. Sections 24 through 28 contain the main material pertaining to Jewish history and its foundational position for the development of Christianity. To this point in the text, Nietzsche had been exploring the reasons for decadence and anti-naturalness in modern life. Christianity is marked as the chief cause of the miserable state of humankind in contemporary Europe, but section 24 makes clear for the reader, as in the *Genealogy*, that Christianity is only the derivative of a more original "Jewish instinct"; indeed, Christianity "is *not* a counter-movement against the Jewish instinct, it is actually its logical consequence, one further conclusion of its fear-inspiring logic."[106] He continues with a discussion that contains apparent—or perhaps reluctant—admiration for ancient Jewry: they were faced, Nietzsche claims, with an existential crisis, threatened with extinction, and chose the only viable means for survival. The price that the Jews paid for their survival was extremely detrimental for them and for the modern world. It entailed "the radical *falsification* of all nature, all naturalness, all reality, the entire inner world as well as the outer. They defined themselves *counter* to all those conditions under which a nation was previously able to live, was *permitted* to live; they made of themselves an antithesis to *natural* conditions—they inverted religion, religious worship, morality, history, psychology one after the other in an irreparable way into the *contradiction of their natural values*" (AC 24, KSA 6.191–92). Almost all of these claims have their source in Wellhausen. The notion that Jews chose survival "at any price" may have multiple origins in literature familiar to Nietzsche, but it is noteworthy that the indestructible nature of Jewry, its perseverance in the face of extreme hardships and hostility, is also an integral part of anti-Semitic discourse about Jewry in the 1880s.[107] The departure from norms associated with national religious practices was emphasized in both Renan and Wellhausen, and Nietzsche had broached this topic already in section 16, where gods may either be "national" and an embodiment of the will to power, or else a sign of impotence, in which case they metamorphose into "good" gods (AC 16, KSA 6.183). The notion of a transformation of values in opposition to nature and naturalness is directly derived from passages in Wellhausen, but Wellhausen appears to mean something quite different when he speaks of "nature": the departure from nature for him implies a shift from what is natural for the relationship between a people and their divinity,[108] while for Nietzsche this transformation in the godhead is clearly connected with a perversion of natural life, as embodied in its instincts and urges. Nietzsche is primarily concerned with the introduction of life-negating values and a degenerate system of morality when he introduces the concept of a god who inverts nature; Wellhausen's focus is the "natural" or traditional or customary religious circumstances of ancient peoples.

There is a further twist in Nietzsche's narrative of ancient Judaism, remarkable because it appears in none of his known sources, but revealing for his attitude toward Jews and the connection with anti-Jewish thought of his own era. In the *Genealogy*, the Jews as a people were considered responsible for the introduction of slave morality; Christianity was merely a continuation or tool of original Jewish impulses, and Nietzsche repeats this theme in *The Antichrist* in calling the Christian Church "only a copy" of Jewish values "in unutterably vaster proportions"; Nietzsche does not make it clear whether the "vaster proportions" of which he speaks pertain to the extent of the violation of naturalness or simply to the larger reach of the Christian religion in comparison with the essentially local influence of Judaism. He leaves no doubt, however, that this revaluation makes the Jews "the most *fateful* nation in world history." Indeed, their impact has been so pervasive that today's Christians do not even recognize they are participating in an original Jewish transvaluation when they "feel anti-Jewish." Nietzsche himself makes reference to his thesis from the *Genealogy* and cites again the antithetical value systems of "*noble* morality" and "*ressentiment* morality." But in the *Genealogy*, we have the impression that the Jews embraced the value system they introduced, propagating it with sincerity and conviction. In *The Antichrist*, Jews are likewise considered the proponents of slave morality, but they employ it deviously in the service of self-preservation. Nietzsche appears to compliment Jewry when he calls the Jewish nation "a nation of the toughest vital energy." But when faced with "impossible circumstances," the Jews channel this vital energy into a herd morality to which they themselves do not subscribe. The Jews, in short, are duplicitous in opposing master morality; they act out of "the profoundest shrewdness in self-preservation." Jewry endorses "*décadence* instincts," but it does so "*not* as being dominated by them but because it divined in them a power by means of which one can prevail *against* 'the world.'" In *The Antichrist*, the slave morality of the *Genealogy* becomes just another mechanism by which Jews ensure their own survival and their dominance over the rest of humankind: "The Jews are the counterparts of all *décadents*: they have been compelled to *act as decadents* to the point of illusion, they have known, with a *non plus ultra* of histrionic genius, how to place themselves at the head of all *décadence* movements (—as the Christianity of Paul—) so as to make of them something stronger than any party *affirmative* of life" (AC 24, KSA 6.192–93). *Décadence* is for them "only a *means*" to attain and maintain power, whether it be through Judaism or its "imitator" Christianity. To secure their own survival and enhance their power, Jewry has perverted all noble values and set humankind on the path toward sickness. The strength of Judaism, its "vital energy," as well as the "shrewdness" of the Jewish people, translates into enslavement in a morality of *ressentiment* and self-abnegation for the entire Christianized world.

This passage is quite remarkable. Although it has frequently been regarded as a validation of Jewry, or at most, a condemnation of only a specific period of Jewish history—the post-exilic years in which the religion was transformed from a national into a universal religion—it is actually quite consonant with a larger anti-Jewish sentiment that is foundational for Nietzsche's later thought.

1. Nietzsche's primary target in this work is undoubtedly Christianity: the very title of the book, which can mean both "the Antichrist" and "the anti-Christian," clearly identifies the adversary in Nietzsche's polemic, as does the subtitle: "A Curse on Christianity." But Nietzsche consistently reminds his reader that Christianity, as the religion of the sick, the feeble, and the ill-constituted, is the continuation and copy of an original Jewish impulse or instinct.[109] Perhaps the most important individual in the early Christian era and the author of over half the books of the New Testament, the apostle Paul, is frequently considered a Jew by Nietzsche; his advocacy for Jesus as the son of God and his conversion from Judaism to Christianity are unimportant for Nietzsche, since Paul, more than Jesus himself, represents the continuity between the Jewish anti-natural tradition and its widespread dissemination in Christianity. Nietzsche's association between Paul and

the Jews can be found early in the 1880s, for example, in *The Gay Science*, where they are contrasted with the Greeks in their consideration of passions (FW 3, 189, KSA 3.488–89), and it continues through Nietzsche's final works, where, as in the passage just cited, the Jews are regarded as the driving force behind "Paul's Christianity."[110] In *The Antichrist*, Paul is described as "Chandala hatred against Rome, against 'the world,' become flesh and genius, the Jew, the *eternal* Jew *par excellence*" (AC 58, KSA 6.246). The Christian religion may be the current enemy of everything Nietzsche deems noble and worthwhile, but it is ultimately the bearer of a more original and pernicious Jewish tendency.[111] As Overbeck correctly noted in his discussion of Nietzsche's "anti-Semitism," his anti-Christian attitude is based on anti-Jewish thought.

2. In the language that Nietzsche employs in section 24 to characterize the Jews and Judaism, he resorts to notions that closely resemble the stereotypical character traits associated with Jews by the anti-Semitic movement of his era. The Jews are a people seeking to preserve themselves at any price: they are not concerned with the welfare of their adopted nations or with the fate of humankind, but only with their own egotistical interests. They are physically inferior and unable to survive on the basis of somatic attributes, but they use their overdeveloped mental acuity, their cleverness and shrewdness, to devise a path for their own salvation. Their plan is inherently dishonest; they are hypocritical and do not believe the values that they espouse and promote among an innocent and gullible populace. They are therefore a paradigm for deceit and duplicity in their dealings with others. If we comb the anti-Semitic tracts and periodicals written during the early 1880s, these features would fit in seamlessly with those of European Judeophobes, although Nietzsche may not always consider them defects. While he shows admiration for Jewish tenacity and recognizes the historical dilemma the Jewish nation faced, his description of Jewish actions and attributes is frequently proximate to the anti-Semites he disdains.

3. This passage confirms and intensifies anti-Jewish sentiments we have identified in earlier utterances. In his years as a Wagnerian acolyte, Nietzsche had learned about the tremendous power that Jewry wielded. In this passage, he recognizes that this power derives not just from their positions in the journalistic, financial, and cultural sphere, but from their more pervasive and malevolent propagation of the will to power as life-negation, which ultimately forms the foundation for their hegemony in contemporary Europe. His explanation of the domination achieved by the Jewish instinct also reaffirms his opposition to the anti-Semitism of his era. As he

makes clear in section 24 and later in section 55 (AC 55, KSA 6.238), the anti-Semites have adopted Jewish values. Their hatred for the Jews is narrow and petty: it takes superficial features, such as Jewish finance, and misses the real power Jewish interests exercise: the power stemming from the reversal of noble values. Anti-Semitism occupies a space within Jewish values; Nietzsche's anti-Judaism is more encompassing and contains more far-reaching implications for humankind.

The continuation of the discussion of Jewish history in sections 25 through 27 indicates how Nietzsche, using Wellhausen as a source, biased his presentation of the scholarly material to emphasize considerations consonant with his own sentiments about Jewry. His description of the "*denaturalizing* of natural values" draws heavily on passages from Wellhausen. Israel's relationship to its divinity during the period of the Kingdom was "*correct*" and natural: it follows the logic of national self-affirmation. Even the "anarchy within" and "the Assyrians from without" did not alter the values associated with the Kingdom. But when God could no longer supply his people with the required assistance, his nature changed: "One altered the conception of him: at this price one retained him. Yaweh the God of 'justice'—*no longer* at one with Israel, an expression of national self-confidence: now only a God bound by conditions." The new priestly regime introduces sin as the cause of misfortune and develops an anti-natural (in Nietzsche's sense of the word) system of values: "*Morality* no longer the expression of the conditions under which a nation lives and grows, no longer a nation's deepest instinct of life, but become abstract, become the antithesis of life" (AC 25, KSA 6.193–94). Thus Nietzsche summarizes Wellhausen in section 25, simplifying a more complex narration of the interplay of prophets and priests, and emphasizing more than his source the role of morality as a life-negating force, which was but a marginal concern for Wellhausen. Returning to his selective recapitulation of Wellhausen in section 26, Nietzsche provides a version of Wellhausen's philological hypothesis concerning the composition of the Old Testament. Wellhausen was part of a nineteenth-century tradition of historical biblical criticism that disputed the authorship and unity of the Old Testament. Although he was not the originator of the contention that various authors composed different sections of the Old Testament, he became the most important authority for the "Grafian" or "developmental" hypothesis.[112] An important aspect of this hypothesis is that several sections of the Old Testament were written later and projected backward, lending these sections the appearance that they had been part of a more original Judaism. While Wellhausen provides an explanation for this procedure that considers historical circumstances, Nietzsche's "translation" of Wellhausen contains the direct accusation of the falsification and rewriting of history to serve the interests of a priestly regime. Nietzsche follows the general framework of the developmental hypothesis, but distorts the careful historical account provided by Wellhausen in order to portray Judaism of the postexilic period as manipulative and dishonest. For Nietzsche, the notion of later authorship becomes the "most shameful act of historical falsification," which propagates "the *lie* of a 'moral world-order'" "with cold-blooded cynicism." Responsible for this situation is the priest, "a parasitic kind of human being who prospers only at the expense of every healthy form of life": "every natural custom, every natural institution . . . , every requirement presented by the instinct for life, in short, everything valuable *in itself*, becomes utterly valueless, *inimical* to value through the parasitism of the priest" (AC 26, KSA 6.194–97). While the change from a "natural" religion to one focused on morality can be found in Wellhausen, the sole ascription of this change to the "priest" and the enormity of the violation of historical fact are Nietzschean elaborations. Particularly troubling is Nietzsche's repeated accusation of priestly "parasitism," found nowhere in his source; the notion of the Jew as a parasite is a recurring motif in anti-Semitic literature of the era. The initial passages in section 27 also exhibit anti-Jewish sentiments, here in connection with the advent of Christianity. Nietzsche emphasizes that Christianity could arise only "on a soil *falsified* in this way, where all nature, all natural value, all *reality* had the profoundest instincts of the ruling class against it." Wellhausen admitted some continuity between Christianity and Judaism, but in Nietzsche's presentation the former is merely an intensification of the latter. It negates "the last remaining form of reality, the 'holy people,' the 'chosen people,' the *Jewish* reality itself," but it does so paradoxically "*once more*" in accord with the "Jewish instinct," the "priestly instinct" (AC 27, KSA 6.197). Wellhausen's text serves as the basis for these remarks, in particular Nietzsche's contention that "Christianity *negates* the Church"—by which he means "the Jewish Church"—but the scholar's careful exposition contrasts sharply with the philosopher's polemical tirade. Wellhausen was the most important source for Nietzsche's expanded remarks on Jewish history in *The Antichrist*, but everywhere the appropriation injects into the historiographical account a heavy dose of anti-Jewish sentiment.

The Antichrist contains Nietzsche's final extended thoughts on the Jewish Question in the form of historical reflections on the Jewish people at a time of transition to the Christian era. The account allows Nietzsche to incorporate and summarize almost twenty years of opinions on Jews and Judaism. We have seen that since Nietzsche's student days in Leipzig, he had harbored and expressed views on Jewry and the Jewish religion that contain clichéd notions common among his peers. Nietzsche never relinquished stereotypical attitudes about Jews, although at various points in his development, he did ascribe to these stereotypes a valuation that was opposed to that of more traditional Judeophobes. In his discipleship to Wagner, he had learned about the power of the Jews, and attributed to them a unity of action and purpose. He retained these views, which were originally expressed as fears when they threatened the Wagnerian cultural mission, but later, as an anti-Wagnerian, became a vision of Jewish domination or Jewish assimilation into a ruling caste. In his writings, we can detect two essential dimensions to the Jewish Question that appear to be incompatible. Jews are regarded as powerful, as a pure race, as a people whose knowledge of money makes them suitable for authority and breeding. In this sense, they partake of the will to power. But they are also considered increasingly in the 1880s the originators of a slave morality that has contributed to the degeneration and mediocrity of European society. In this regard, they are responsible for the destruction of everything natural and any prospect of genuine cultural achievement. Nietzsche's exposition of Jewish history in *The Antichrist* allowed him to reconcile these two apparently antagonistic depictions of Jewry. By claiming Jews used slave morality deceptively for their own interests, Nietzsche is able to present Jewry as deleterious to Europe and simultaneously as a hope for Europe's future. Slave morality becomes merely a ploy for power; indeed, it becomes another form of the will to power, as Nietzsche makes clear in his later writings. But it is a form that can be eliminated in a new self-assertiveness when Jews no longer need to exercise deception in order to wield authority, when they are assimilated members of a new European ruling class. At the same time, *The Antichrist* enables Nietzsche to sharpen his differences with the political anti-Semitic movement, which unwittingly partakes in Jewish morality, and to present his own, more encompassing vision of potential Jewish power, as well as the broader Jewish threat to Europe— paradoxically in the guise of Christianity. In *The Antichrist*, Nietzsche has worked out as well as he could the various contradictions and paradoxes that, during a period of two decades, confronted him as the Jewish Question. In the final analysis, Nietzsche never participated in the crude anti-Semitism of his time, and he consistently rejected anti-Semitism, as he understood it. But he also adopted, retained, developed, and sometimes inverted a great many strands of anti-Jewish thought in dialogue with issues related to contemporary Jewry, Jewish history, and the appropriate place of Jews in modern society.

Chapter 7

The Evolution Question

The Overman and *Zarathustra*

The word "overman" [*Übermensch*], translated originally as "superman," is probably the most widely disseminated concept in Nietzsche's writings among the general public. It has been commonly regarded as an enhanced form of human being, but in its immediate historical context, it was understood as a contribution to evolutionary thinking. George Bernard Shaw's play *Man and Superman* (1903) provides evidence for this contention. Nietzsche's "post-Darwinian" philosophy is given practical expression in "the Revolutionist's Handbook," which accompanies the play and suggests, among other reforms, the establishment of a "State Department of Evolution."[1] The second theoretical underpinning to Shaw's drama of social reform—aside from Nietzsche's superman—is Henri Bergson's notion of creative evolution, and the play itself became a demonstration of Shaw's idea of a life force, a primeval impulse in all organic life that determines the relationship between the sexes and the choice of a partner. The life force, responsible for the creation of a superman, clearly belongs to the biological realm; it propels our species forward to new evolutionary heights. This type of favorable reception of the "superman" did not last very long, however. Nietzsche's philosophy as a whole, and the concept of "superman" along with it, fell into disrepute, at least outside of Germany, in the wake of Germany's aggression in the two world wars of the twentieth century. The Aryanization of the notion by the National Socialists after 1933 squeezed Nietzsche's thought inappropriately into the narrow strictures of racist ideology: the Teutonic race of supermen was supposed to assume hegemony on earth over the various types of *Untermenschen* [inferior peoples], which included Jews, Slavs, and non-Europeans around the globe. It is interesting to note that the word "Untermenschen," which the Nazis used frequently to refer to inferior races, occurs but once in Nietzsche's writings (FW 143, KSA 3.490), and it is clear that he is referring to mythologically subaltern figures rather than to lesser human races. There is thus no justification in his works for the racist uses employed during the Third Reich.

After the war, however, Nazi associations with "Übermensch" persisted, and the alteration in the translation of *Übermensch* from "superman" to "overman," proposed by Walter Kaufmann, was obviously meant to reinstate the original German meaning of the term and more precisely render it into English, by eliminating both its megalomaniacal implications and its comic-book associations.[2] Besides literal accuracy to the German and avoidance of the accrued negative connotations, the now accepted translation has the virtue of situating the "overman" more appositely in the text in which it first appears: *Thus Spoke Zarathustra* (1883–85). Indeed, the term occurs only a handful of times outside of this four-part work, and most of the other occurrences refer back in some way to the original context. In the framework of this text, "overman" resonates not only with the "last man" and the "higher man,"[3] but also with two contrasting prefixes that are conspicuous in the metaphorical economy of Nietzsche's magnum opus. The word has a rather obvious relationship with several other terms that occur more frequently in this text, in particular, "overcoming" [*Überwindung*] and "passing over" [*übergehen*]. It also contrasts with a series of words that are constructed with the prefix "under" [*unter*], and that are therefore opposed to words containing "over." The meaning field within which the "overman" operates is thus overdetermined in *Zarathustra*. Although the notion of "overcoming" is frequently implied elsewhere in Nietzsche's oeuvre, nowhere is it as prevalent and as consciously emphasized as in *Zarathustra*.

If the "overman" is characterized best by the notion of "overcoming," then the attentive reader will understandably want to pose the question: What does he overcome? The answer is "man" as he exists in his present state. Nietzsche's first mention of the "overman" in *Zarathustra* makes it clear that the overman results from an overcoming of man. Descending from his mountain retreat, Zarathustra, Nietzsche's prophetic persona in the text, declares to the townspeople assembled in the marketplace expecting to witness the show of a tightrope walker: "*I teach you the overman.* Man is something that shall be overcome. What have you done to overcome him?" Like many of Zarathustra's pronouncements, this one is riddled with ambiguity. The nature of the overcoming is multifaceted, as we can ascertain by the variety of interpretations the overman has enjoyed over the past three quarters of a century. But the various ethical and ontological dimensions of this notion should not obscure the obvious biological implications, which come into clearer focus in Zarathustra's very next utterance:

> All beings so far have created something beyond themselves; and do you want to be the ebb of this great flood and even go back to the beasts rather than overcome man?
>
> What is the ape to man? A laughing-stock or a painful embarrassment. And man shall be just that for the overman: a laughingstock or a painful embarrassment.

You have made your way from worm to man, and much in you is still worm. Once you were apes, and even now, too, man is more ape than any ape. (Za, Zarathustra's Vorrede 3, KSA 4.14)

The evolutionary message is clear, especially in the context of the late nineteenth century. Evolution itself is considered metaphorically as a great flood, rushing forward and creating something always beyond what it is at present, a movement that will not, or at least should not, cease with the current state of affairs. The transition from ape to man, the commonplace and most controversial hypothesis associated with evolution from its first appearance early in the nineteenth century and a notion identified explicitly with Darwin's views, is cited as an analogy for the future development from man to overman. Furthermore, the entire course of evolution, captured in abbreviated form as the progression from the invertebrate worm to our nearest mammalian ancestors to *Homo sapiens*, is presented to a reader who could hardly avoid association with recent findings and debates in evolutionary theory. Zarathustra's point is that man, as man currently is constituted, should not be considered the pinnacle of the development of the species; humankind, like other species, can and must be surpassed or overcome, and Zarathustra's designation for this future, unknown, and higher species is appropriately designated as the "overman."

In the earliest writings on Nietzsche, the evolutionary implications of this passage and other remarks in Nietzsche's writings appeared obvious.[4] But as twentieth-century scholarship on Nietzsche developed, commentators shied away from drawing the obvious connection with evolutionary biology, and three factors have been most important in their reluctance to integrate a biological or evolutionary dimension into their interpretations. Perhaps the most significant of these factors is Nietzsche's own exegetical remarks on the overman found in the section "Why I write such good books" in *Ecce Homo*. Commenting on his introduction of the concept of an overman, Nietzsche disparages any connection with Darwinism. After stating that the word was employed to designate a higher type of man in contrast to "modern" men or to "good" men, Nietzsche criticizes those who have understood it as an ideal or as a type of moral imperative: "a word, which in the mouth of Zarathustra—the destroyer of morality—becomes a very thoughtful word, has almost everywhere been understood with complete naiveté in the sense of those very values whose antithesis makes its appearance in the figure of Zarathustra: that is to say as an 'idealist' type of higher species of man, half 'saint,' half 'genius' " (EH, Warum ich so gute Bücher schreibe 1, KSA 6.300). In this passage, Nietzsche is objecting to a moralistic and idealist distortion of his work: the overman does not embody a perfected sense of values such as one would find in a saint; nor does he represent an ideal to which humanity should aspire. The overman is not a variant on the perfectibility of humankind that was so popular during the Enlightenment. The teachings of Zarathustra explicitly oppose precisely the moral valuation, as well as the hero worship, contained in such an interpretation.[5] But Nietzsche continues: "Other learned cattle caused me on its account to be suspected of Darwinism." With this comment Nietzsche appears to object to exactly the interpretive framework suggested by the passage cited above in the Prologue to *Zarathustra*, in which he first adumbrates his notion of the overman. The contradiction is solved, however, when we understand correctly that for Nietzsche, and for most of Nietzsche's contemporaries, Darwin's notion of evolution was not the sole way to conceive of the development of the species. As we shall see, Nietzsche, like many of the scientists and philosophers engaged with biological thought in the late nineteenth century, consistently distinguishes between Darwin's theory and other competing models for evolutionary change. Indeed, what Darwin himself advocated was sometimes not very clear to his nineteenth-century audience or to scientists who received and propagated alternatives to his theory, and we find a broad range of interpretations of his thought—especially its philosophical implications—among both prominent peers and popularizers. Nietzsche's notion of the "overman," while in his view not borrowed from or exemplary of Darwinism, nonetheless partakes in the general framework of evolutionary reflection during the late nineteenth century. While it was not derivative from Darwin's theoretical framework and in some senses was opposed to it, we might more accurately view the overman—in part at least—as Nietzsche's response to the problems raised by Darwin and his European followers, as Nietzsche's contribution to the ongoing discussions on evolution among his contemporaries.

In this passage in *Ecce Homo*, Nietzsche was also relating a frustration that is often expressed in his late works. Earlier in the very same section in which he accuses others of suspecting him of Darwinism, he writes in a megalomaniacal fashion that in the future "institutions will be needed in which people live and teach as I understand living and teaching: perhaps even chairs for the interpretation of Zarathustra will be established." In this passage and on several other occasions in his last sane years, Nietzsche expresses the concern that his writings have not been interpreted carefully enough,[6] that commentators have been too hasty to assimilate his ideas to writings of his contemporaries and have thereby ignored the unique qualities of his thought. Although he expects to be misinterpreted since there are no "ears *and hands* for *my* truths already today," he does not want to be confused with other writers of his era: "I still do not want to be taken for what I am not" (EH, Warum ich so gute Bücher schreibe 1, KSA 6.298). That he emphasizes a particular objection to the confusion between his thought and Darwin's is understandable from the reactions to his philosophy during his lifetime. From his earliest writings to his last reviewed works, we find mention of his intellectual derivation from the English naturalist and his views on evolution. In the controversy surrounding the scholarly status of *The Birth of Tragedy*, a reviewer, commenting on the polemics of Wilamowitz-Möllendorff, writes that Nietzsche is "Darwinism and materialism translated into the realm of music," that "the primeval pain of the primeval unity" is "Darwin's primeval cell," and that his delight in the destruction of the individual is "the developism [*Developismus*] of the protoplasm *in infinitum*, the cessation of the autonomous personality and species!"[7] Nietzsche cites this passage verbatim in letters to his two best friends at the time, Erwin Rohde (1845–1898) and Carl von Gersdorff (1844–1904), but at this point he appears to be amused by the preposterous nature of these contentions (Nr. 296, 21 February 1873, KSB 4.125; and Nr. 301, 5 April 1873, KSB 4.139–40). These types of associations continued, however, and in a late review of *On the Genealogy of Morals*, which Nietzsche read and mentioned in a letter to Heinrich Köselitz (Nr. 1007, 21 March 1888, KSB 8.276), he encountered the following assertion about his theory of values: "It is essentially Darwin's theory of evolution from lower to higher organisms, which, like many other endeavors in our time, also forms the basis of Nietzsche's."[8] In the passage cited above from *Ecce Homo*, Nietzsche is quite possibly reacting against the confusion of his project with Darwin's, which he could trace from his first book to his publications in his final years. Indeed, the inclusion of anti-Darwin and anti-Darwinism remarks and aphorisms in his published works and notebooks in 1888 may be attributed in part to the persistence of this association and Nietzsche's desire to clarify his own views on evolution as different from those of the renowned English naturalist.

A second reason for avoiding the connection with evolutionary biology has to do with subsequent discussions of the overman in *Zarathustra* itself and other writings, including Nietzsche's voluminous notebooks. The actual number of clarifying remarks is rather limited; like most of Nietzsche's most celebrated concepts, there is no systematic exposition of meaning, no extended explanation of import. Although a centerpiece in the "Prologue," the overman is hardly mentioned in the body of the work and never explicated in other subsequent references. In the "Prologue," however, he is associated consistently with a rejection of otherworldly values and with an affirmation of the body and the material world. Zarathustra cries out to the uncomprehending townspeople: "The overman is the meaning of the earth. Let your will say: the overman *shall be* the meaning of the earth! I beseech you, my brothers remain faithful to the earth, and do not believe those who speak to you of otherworldly hopes!" (Za, Vorrede 3, KSA 4.14). This passage connects the overman vaguely with the notions of eternal recurrence and *amor fati*: the townspeople are called upon to embrace what must come, to will destiny. Shortly thereafter, Zarathustra contrasts the body and the soul; in rather typical Nietzschean fashion, the traditional valorization of mind over matter, soul over body, thought over flesh, is reversed:

Once the soul looked contemptuously upon the body, and then this contempt was the highest: she wanted the body meager, ghastly, and starved. Thus she hoped to escape it and the earth.

Oh, this soul herself was still meager, ghastly, and starved: and cruelty was the lust of this soul.

But you, too, my brothers, tell me: what does your body proclaim of your soul? Is not your soul poverty and filth and wretched contentment? (Za, Vorrede 3, KSA 4.14)

The correction to centuries of abuse of the body for the sake of untenable ethical restrictions is one of the cornerstones of Nietzsche's teaching; its result, in part, is the proclamation of the overman. He is the great sea that can receive the "polluted sea" that is currently man, absorbing it, cleansing it, and enveloping it. The overman is thus characterized by his ties to this world, to material reality, and with a rejection of previous ethical systems and religious ideals. He is called overman at least in part because he has overcome the values that have hitherto been constitutive of the human species. Commentators could easily interpret this further clarification of the overman as something quite different from his introduction as the product of evolution, although, as we shall see, Nietzsche does not necessarily conceive morality and values to be topics that fall outside evolutionary change. Indeed, the separation of the physiological sphere from the sphere of human habits, customs, and conventions is consistently disputed in Nietzsche's late writings.

A final reason that much Nietzsche scholarship, at least during the twentieth century, was reticent to connect the overman with evolutionary theory and, indeed, ignored to a large extent Nietzsche's active engagement with the biological thought of his times has to do with an unfortunate turn in his reception history. As we have seen, Nietzsche's philosophy was drawn into the orbit of nationalist and racist political programs during two world wars, and subsequent commentators, seeking to divorce it from these connections, tended to remove it entirely from its historical context. Typical and most influential in this regard was the work of Martin Heidegger (1889–1976), who denied Nietzsche's connections with biology in the latter half of the nineteenth century and categorized him more abstractly as a philosophical mind dealing with ontology and metaphysics. Because Heidegger was confronted directly with the distorted biologism of the National Socialists during the 1930s and 1940s, he was compelled to address the issue in his writings, and his statements are unequivocal—and not entirely accurate. Nietzsche only "appears to speak and think biologically," Heidegger contends. The privileged position he accords to "life" has nothing to do with "the phenomena of life in plants and animals." When Nietzsche writes of a "beast of prey," Heidegger continues, "he is not thinking biologically. Rather, he grounds this apparently merely biological worldview *metaphysically*."⁹ In his lengthy discussion of the overman, Heidegger carefully avoids citation or discussion of the most obvious evolutionary passage cited at the start of this chapter, since he is concerned to defend Nietzsche against the vulgar racist views with which he was associated by cruder Nazi proponents, and which usually contained a heavy reliance on biological or even eugenic associations. The downside to this understandable effort to dissociate Nietzsche from vulgar biologism is that Nietzsche's views are removed from their connections with science and scientists of his era and situated exclusively in the ethereal realm of more recondite concerns: "Just as Nietzsche's thought of will to power was ontological rather than biological, even more was his racial thought metaphysical rather than biological in meaning."¹⁰ While Heidegger perhaps served Nietzsche scholarship well in separating him from National Socialist ideology, he almost certainly underestimated Nietzsche's considerable interest in natural scientific developments of his own times. Nietzsche's own defense against Darwinist misinterpretation and Shaw's play are testimony to the proximity of Nietzsche's overman to evolutionary trends. That subsequent philosophical commentary often chose, like Heidegger, to minimize a body of thought that was demonstrably important for Nietzsche himself demonstrates perhaps both the power of certain central philosophical thinkers for the interpretation of Nietzsche's thought and the unwillingness of subsequent exegetes to engage with Nietzsche on his own terms. Although it would be foolish to believe that evolution is the only element contributing to the notion of the overman, and that contemporary speculation in natural science is the only context for Nietzsche's writings, it is impossible to understand Nietzsche's worldview fully without some knowledge of the discourses that surrounded him and with which he was in dialogue.

Thus there may be many significant and intricate connections between the overman and Nietzsche's ethical and ontological reflections, especially as they would manifest themselves in the mid- and late 1880s, but at the same time there is no reason to think that ethical, religious, and metaphysical commentary exhausts the meaning of the concept, and that the overman is not—at least in part—a response to evolutionary biology. Indeed, Nietzsche's characterization of man as a tightrope or a bridge in *Zarathustra* (Za, Vorrede 4, KSA 4.16) is not simply an expression of man's "ontological predicament," as Walter Kaufmann (1921–1980), following the mid-twentieth-century rejection of biologism, asserts,¹¹ but also an image that reinforces the evolutionary associations found in the initial discussion of this figure. The townspeople, having taken the "over" in overman too literally, interrupt Zarathustra's proclamation wrongly and request that the tightrope walker, whose appearance was the reason for the gathering in the marketplace, begin his performance. In their simple-minded fashion, they believe that the overman is someone who literally will appear above them.

Zarathustra, however, is quick to re-metaphorize the reality of the tightrope walker into a symbol relating to the overman: "Man is a rope, tied between beast and overman—a rope over an abyss." And further: "What is great in man is that he is a bridge and not an end: what can be loved in man is that he is an *overture* [*Übergang*] and a *going under* [*Untergang*]" (Za, Vorrede 4, KSA 4.16–17). In the litany of what Zarathustra loves, which follows this citation, Zarathustra embraces all those who, like himself, serve as preparatory for the overman: "Behold, I am a herald of the lightning and a heavy drop from the cloud; but this lightning is called overman" (KSA 4.18). What Zarathustra evokes here with different imagery is the transitory nature of the human being. In serving as a transition (*Übergang*) to the overman, it simultaneously rushes toward its own demise (*Untergang*). It is rather simple to translate this thought into an evolutionary understanding of the development of humankind: The human species, Nietzsche is hypothesizing, is not the final stage in evolutionary history, and certainly not the most advanced stage, but an intermediate form that will itself cede to a higher order of being. As in the initial passages, the imagery suggests a proximity to evolution, at least as it was popularly conceived in the nineteenth century. It may not accord precisely with Darwinism as we understand it today, but it most certainly partakes in the widespread notion that species develop and change, that some transitory forms become extinct, and that other, "higher" forms of life emerge and persevere.

Although many critics have continued to shy away from a discussion of the overman in its evolutionary context, we have already noted at the outset of this study that in the last two decades we find a welcome return of scholarship to dealing with the relationship of Nietzsche's thought to the evolutionary biology of his times.[12] Since the late 1980s, but particularly after the turn of the millennium, several books and significant portions of books, as well as at least a dozen essays, have examined Nietzsche's relationship to some aspect of evolution, in particular the theory of Charles Darwin (1809–1882).[13] These studies have not, however, produced anything resembling a consensus on Nietzsche's views. Many recognize Nietzsche's implicit and extensive conversation with his contemporaries. Gregory Moore, who has perhaps the best command of the material among recent commentators, writes in his introduction to *Nietzsche, Biology and Metaphor*: "Nietzsche's thought is so deeply rooted in the issues, fears and values of the nineteenth century, that it is unthinkable outside of this context."[14] But many other studies revert inadvertently to the familiar structure of Nietzsche as a great thinker who is most adequately understood in relationship to other great thinkers. In the area of evolutionary theory, this other thinker would be Charles Darwin, and we encounter attempts to reconcile Nietzsche's philosophy with the thought of the English naturalist, as well as resolute declarations of Nietzsche's opposition to Darwinian theory. The extremes of these debates do not bring us very far in understanding Nietzsche's writings since we are often called upon to make assumptions about Nietzsche's intentions that are unsupported by textual evidence in order to cast him as a "New Darwinian" or an "Anti-Darwinian." The focus on Darwin, supplemented occasionally with references to other biological theorists of Nietzsche's time, is understandable since Darwin's theory of evolution obviously emerged from the nineteenth century as the hypothesis with the greatest degree of scientific validity. But there are several reasons that pitting these two "great men" against each other, or viewing them as compatible with each other, distorts Nietzsche's intellectual path and conclusions:

1. As far as we can determine, Nietzsche had no direct contact with Darwin's writings, neither with his *On the Origin of Species* (1859) nor his *Descent of Man* (1871). It appears that Nietzsche's proficiency in English would not have allowed him to read either text easily in the original, but there is no evidence of the English versions or German translations in his library, and no remarks in any correspondence that would lead us to believe that he had ordered anything by Darwin from a book dealer. If Nietzsche read any words that Darwin wrote, in English or in translation, then they were almost certainly citations in secondary sources.
2. Nietzsche's knowledge of Darwin was thus purely secondhand, and since the sources Nietzsche used were not completely consistent about Darwin's theory and its philosophical implications, it would be difficult to describe with any precision what it would mean for Nietzsche to understand or follow Darwin.[15] Nietzsche certainly formed a view of Darwin, but that view was not necessarily drawn from his exposure to Darwin's writings or even from the secondary sources that mediated his thought to him.[16]
3. What Darwin advocated may be clear enough to us today, since his theoretical position has been refined and made more precise by subsequent writers and developments, but in retrospect, in his own writings he was not consistently "Darwinian." As we know, he did not exclude the possibility of the inheritance of acquired characteristics, a feature associated with Jean-Baptiste Lamarck (1744–1829) and usually regarded as inconsistent with natural selection, and he adopted, or at least expressed at times, "social Darwinist" positions that appear to be incompatible with his own scientific observations.

The almost exclusive focus on Nietzsche's relationship to Darwin and Darwinism fails to capture the richness of his dialogue with evolutionary theory in the second half of the nineteenth century and narrows the focus on what is a much wider field of influence and interest. It is impossible to ignore Darwin, since he was a recognized authority in evolutionary theory in his times, and since, as we have seen, Nietzsche references him and his work directly on several occasions. But to obtain an accurate feeling for what Nietzsche understood as evolution and what implications could be drawn from it, we have to widen our circle to include the actual and most likely points of contact Nietzsche had with biological evolution during his mature life.

Early Contact with Evolutionary Theory

We will thus come to recognize that part of the problem in our identifying Nietzsche's overman as a response to evolutionary theory is that our knowledge of evolution is apt to diverge significantly from what Nietzsche and his contemporaries understood by the term. That the species developed gradually over a long period of time was a quite common view among scientists even before Nietzsche began attending university in 1864,[17] but the publication of Darwin's *On the Origin of Species* in 1859 moved the discourse from academically inclined circles of naturalists and biologists into the purview of a wider public. There is no question that Nietzsche became acquainted with the name Darwin and the general outlines of evolution while he was still a teenager, and quite possibly before he enrolled at Bonn to study theology.[18] At the very latest in the mid-1860s, he would have encountered an extensive discussion of evolutionary biology in the chapter "Darwinism and Teleology" from Friedrich Albert Lange's (1828–1875) *History of Materialism* (1866).[19] That Nietzsche read and appreciated Lange, not only the first edition, which he read in his early twenties, but also the later, revised editions of his popular book, has been long established in Nietzsche scholarship.[20] The best indication of Nietzsche's esteem for Lange comes from his correspondence with his closest friend at the time, Carl von Gersdorff (1844–1904). Already in August 1866, Nietzsche lauds Lange, somewhat misleadingly in connection with their mutual admiration of Schopenhauer, whose views differed substantially from Lange's on several essential matters (Nr. 517, KSB 2.159–60). Nietzsche repeats his encomium for Lange on 16 February 1868, noting, among other things, that Lange's book is an excellent source for a sound knowledge of "Darwinist theories": "If you have the desire to instruct yourself completely in the materialist movement of our times, in the natural sciences with their Darwinist theories, their cosmic systems, their animated camera obscura, etc., and at the same time in ethical materialism, in the Manchester theory, etc., then I can recommend to you nothing more excellent than The History of Materialism by Friedr. Alb. Lange (Iserlohn 1866), a book that gives infinitely more than its title promises, and that one will reread and consult again and again as a true treasure-house" (Nr. 562, KSB 2.257). The formulation here is significant: although Darwin had several ideas about evolution, one usually refers to his views as a single unified theory or hypothesis. Nietzsche appears to have selected the plural not to signal the multivalence of Darwin's thought, but rather, in keeping with the practice of a popularized view of Darwin, to refer to evolutionary theories in general. At this point in his development, Darwin stands for evolution in general, and his main source is Lange's discussion.

The title of the chapter in which Darwin figures most prominently indicates that Lange is just as interested in the philosophical implications of Darwin's thought as he is in the scientific value. In Lange's estimation, Darwin has effectively refuted the various teleological views of nature, from those associated with ancient philosophy, such as Plato and Aristotle, to Christian theology and natural philosophy indebted to religious ideas. Like many of his contemporaries, Lange's judgment about the scientific merits of Darwin's views is somewhat equivocal: while he has undoubtedly made a great advance on previous worldviews in natural philosophy, Lange asserts, his contentions are based on hypotheses that have yet to be demonstrated. Lange therefore calls for experiments to confirm what Darwin has conjectured.[21] He also intimates that Darwin's solution to the mechanism for evolution, which was the central issue troubling members of the scientific community who objected to Darwin's work, is only partially valid. Citing other prominent biologists critical of Darwin, Lange obviously believes that natural selection, which he views as an outgrowth of Darwin's preoccupation with artificial breeding, must be supplemented by internal mechanisms in order to account for the fecundity of species development.[22] In general, Lange emphasizes the struggle for existence as the centerpiece of the Darwinian hypothesis, and we can imagine that Nietzsche was fascinated by an extended citation from *Origin of Species* in which Darwin writes about how one species of birds lives from insects and seeds, and how birds of prey and other animals in turn devour these birds.[23] While the image of nature as indifferent and essentially predatory would have ramifications for Nietzsche's later ethical speculations, he was obviously less enamored with the emphasis Darwin, in Lange's presentation, places on utility as the primary determinant for the survival of a feature or a type. But Nietzsche must have come away from Lange with a slightly confused picture of Darwin's views, as well as an exposure to various opposing positions. At one point, Lange ascribes to Darwin the "proven principle concerning the acquisition of inherited characteristics,"[24] a notion that Darwin does not exclude, but that today and even in the nineteenth century was associated more appropriately with the French naturalist Jean-Baptiste Lamarck, who wrote a half century before Darwin's magnum opus appeared. Indeed, Lange remains at times mysteriously vague about Darwin's achievement, calling Darwinism "in the widest sense of the word" merely "the teaching of a strictly scientific and conceptual evolution."[25] Just as Nietzsche's pluralization of Darwin's theory may indicate that he understands it as the designation for a generic evolutionary model, so too Lange's discussion, although it delineates—and criticizes—some ideas specific to Darwin, ultimately identifies his thought with evolution *tout court*.

Subsequent to his reading of Lange, Nietzsche is also apt to have learned to distinguish Darwin's views from those of other competing models when he came into contact in Basel with Ludwig Rütimeyer (1825–1895). A wide-ranging scientist with interests in geology, paleontology, zoology, and biology, Rütimeyer was appointed professor of comparative anatomy and zoology at the University of Basel in 1855. He was especially interested in his local Swiss environment, and many of his writings are dedicated to the natural surroundings in his native land. Rütimeyer was also a well-respected professor at Basel; in 1865, he became rector of the university, and he remained active in the institution until 1894.[26] Nietzsche mentions him infrequently in his correspondence but in a complimentary manner, referring twice in a letter to Gersdorff to Rütimeyer's writings on Switzerland (Nr. 443, 8 May 1875, KSB 5.39). Indeed, the only book by Rütimeyer in Nietzsche's library was a volume from 1854 on *The Changes in the Animal World in Switzerland Since the Presence of Man*.[27] His only significant mention in a notebook passage occurs in the early 1880s, and it indicates the respect Nietzsche harbored for his former colleague several years after he had resigned from the university. Nietzsche is reflecting on the fact that in Switzerland, "German qualities" have developed more purely and richly than in Germany, and in this connection he asks rhetorically what German could compare with Gottfried Keller (1819–1890) in literature, with Arnold Böcklin (1827–1901) in painting, and with Jacob Burckhardt (1818–1897) in historical scholarship. In the natural sciences, Rütimeyer is judged far superior to his German counterpart: "Does the great fame of the natural scientist Häckel detract from the even greater worthiness of praise due to *Rütimeyer*?" (Nachlass 1881, 11[249], KSA 9.536). Significant here is that Nietzsche compares Rütimeyer with Ernst Haeckel (1834–1919), who was known, perhaps not entirely correctly, as the chief representative of orthodox Darwinism in Germany. Although Nietzsche cites in his only other mention of Rütimeyer in his notebooks the two works on Swiss topics he had mentioned to Gersdorff (Nachlass 1875, 4[2], KSA 8.39), he obviously considered him not only a foremost naturalist dealing with local Swiss topics, but also a rival of the most noted evolutionary thinker in the German-speaking world.

Nietzsche had good reason to do so. Like many university professors in the biological sciences, Rütimeyer was preoccupied with Darwin's thought after the publication of *On the Origin of Species* and responded to its main outlines in print. Although we cannot be sure whether Nietzsche read any of Rütimeyer's objections to Darwin, we can surmise that the recently appointed classical philologist knew of Rütimeyer's writings either from the author himself or from general discussions among colleagues in Basel. Rütimeyer was especially able to comment on Darwin since his broad research interests, especially in areas like geology and paleontology, touched on issues that were at the center of controversy about evolution.[28] Like Lange, Rütimeyer accepted large portions of Darwin's theory, but was unable to agree with his most original and controversial hypothesis: that the sole explanation for the advancement of the species involves natural selection. Rütimeyer was hardly alone in this reservation about natural selection as the mechanism by which species evolve. The pervasiveness of this ambivalent response to Darwinism in the first two decades after the publication of *Origin of Species* is indicated in the summary evaluation of Emil du Bois-Reymond (1818–1896), the influential secretary of the Prussian Academy of Sciences. In a speech before the Academy in 1876, he comments on the general perception of Darwin's teachings for his contemporaries: "Darwin's real accomplishment is to have established the theory of evolution. The theory of natural selection, on the other hand, is considered at best an ingenious, cleverly presented idea that has no significance in reality."[29] Ernst Mayr (1904–2005), perhaps the leading evolutionary biologist of the twentieth century, observes: "The majority of the biologists who accepted the theory of evolution after 1859 simultaneously rejected Darwin's proposed explanatory mechanism, natural selection."[30]

Rütimeyer was among those who contributed to Darwin's equivocal reputation, and in order to expose the weakness of natural selection, he examines, in two lectures delivered at Basel shortly before Nietzsche's arrival and published in pamphlet form in 1868, just one year before Nietzsche assumed his position, perhaps the most controversial evolutionary claim among Nietzsche's contemporaries: the development of the human being from the apes. Among Rütimeyer's observations are the fact that humans are similar to apes in their muscle formation, but not in the nature of their brains; that the human species is a unity, while the apes represent several species; and that there are essentially two types of apes, those with long skulls and those with short skulls. He concludes that the human being developed in two strands: the Africans are descended from the long-skulled gorillas, while Asians and Europeans have the short-sculled orangutan as ancestors. The mechanism by which the evolution from ape to man was achieved, however, cannot be natural selection, Rütimeyer asserts. He reasons that selection is responsible for the perfection of the various species of apes. In order for apes to be more efficient apes and therefore to improve their odds in the contest for survival, they need to increase the size of their teeth and muscles. The distinction between apes and humans, however, lies in an increased brain capacity, which contradicts, according to Rütimeyer, the direction of maximally efficient ape evolution. Indeed, Rütimeyer contends that the improvement of muscles and teeth is accomplished at the expense of greater brain capacity. For this reason, Darwin's notion of natural selection cannot adequately account for the most important evolutionary jumps:

> The struggle for existence, in which one has come to believe the greatest impulse for evolution lies, and which would be capable of assisting creatures to ascend from a lower to ever higher steps of organization, is not

able to raise the orangutan to the height of the human being. Rather, we must consider it the force that holds it back and hinders the forward movement. It is able to achieve perfection, but only perfection of the somatic or, here, of the animal attributes of a creature, the muscle power, the weapons of all species; and all this is done at the expense of the proficiency of the brain.[31]

Thus, although no one should doubt the validity of Darwin's theory with respect to somatic developments within a species, it posits an insufficient mechanism for elucidating the transformation of one species into another. Rütimeyer has difficulties explaining the significant leap from apes to human beings, and he mentions in a rather cursory fashion an internal impulse toward consciousness. Nietzsche is not apt to have been very impressed by some of the more conservative implications of Rütimeyer's thoughts, since in some regards he appears to reinstitute creationism through the back door with his cursory mention of inherent directionality, but he certainly would have been attracted to other aspects of his thought, in particular the notion of an internal dimension to the "struggle for survival." But perhaps more important for his outlook in these early years Rütimeyer was among those naturalists who opened his eyes to the possibility of evolutionary alternatives by suggesting a mechanism that made changes in evolution intelligible without resorting to chance occurrences and the struggle for existence associated with natural selection.

As important as a scientist like Rütimeyer was for Nietzsche's introduction to the breadth of evolutionary thought, in the history of biology, he was a rather minor figure whose ideas on Darwin were derivative of other scientists'. In order to understand the discourse in which Nietzsche was engaged, we must look past Rütimeyer to the writings of more eminent figures whom Nietzsche likely knew, perhaps through Rütimeyer's and Lange's mediation. Rütimeyer's lectures outlining the transition from ape to man were dedicated to one of these figures, the noted embryologist and natural historian Karl Ernst von Baer (1792–1876), whose writings Rütimeyer also mentions in his necrology for Darwin as a necessary supplement to the Englishman's work.[32] Nietzsche refers to Baer only once in his published books, in aphorism 265 from the first part of *Human, All Too Human*, but not in connection with Darwin or evolution: Baer is cited instead for his support of the racist notion that Europeans can be distinguished from Asians because the former are able to support their beliefs with reasons, while the latter are not (MA 265, KSA 2.220). But Nietzsche's sister Elisabeth reports not only that Rütimeyer was essential for her brother's knowledge of evolutionary theory, but also that he was acquainted with the writings of Baer.[33] It is not unlikely that Nietzsche knew Baer's views on evolution, either through Rütimeyer or through other sources—he is also cited in a footnote in Lange—since Baer was a renowned scientist with a

European reputation. Born in the German Baltic region in 1792, he studied in Dorpat (Tartu) and then in Vienna under Ignaz Döllinger (1799–1890), a student of Friedrich Schelling (1775–1854). He received his first university post in Königsberg, but in 1834, he was appointed to the Academy of Science in St. Petersburg, where he remained until he returned as a professor to Dorpat in 1867.[34] Testimony to his European prestige comes from none other than Darwin himself, whose historical sketch at the beginning of On the Origin of Species solicits support from Baer, "towards whom all zoologists feel so profound a respect," for his conviction "that forms now perfectly distinct have descended from a single parent-form."[35]

Darwin's remarks notwithstanding, Baer found considerable cause to disagree with his English colleague. Indeed, Baer was one of the few scientists of the older generation to respond in detail to Darwin's challenge.[36] He reacted variously and somewhat contentiously, but his most extensive criticisms appeared in 1876 in a longer work devoted solely to Darwin's theory. Baer admits that natural selection possesses limited validity; indeed, he himself had suggested as much several decades before Darwin published his treatise, and for this reason, Baer laments that he has been accused of both Darwinism and anti-Darwinism.[37] But he does not believe that the variety and extent of species can be explained in their entirety from transformations accomplished via natural selection. Baer lists five questions for Darwinian theory, all of which are fairly typical for the objections raised by his contemporaries. First, with regard to the creation of the first organism, from which all other organisms then develop, Baer asks why it must occur only once? Second, if one species gradually transforms itself into another, why do we not find a wealth of transitional stages in existence? Third, if there are deviations in one generation, why would they not revert to the norm when they procreate with the nondeviant population? Fourth, how can Darwin explain the relative stability of species? According to his view, shouldn't a chaos of unstable organisms be the normal state of affairs? And finally, why do we find no historical verification for transitional stages either in the fossil record or in other evidence, such as mummies? Although this type of discussion, which filled the scientific literature about Darwin in the decades following the publication of Origin of Species, was perhaps of less interest to Nietzsche than the philosophical implications found in Lange's exposition and the extension of evolutionary theory into the realm of ethics by social Darwinists, he was certainly not unaffected by these objections. His main interest in evolution and in Darwin's contribution to it involved human beings and their behavior, but, as we shall see, in his notebooks from the 1880s he occasionally mused about matters pertaining to other organisms, their appearance, and their development. Above all, however, the dissent in the scientific literature served to cast doubt on Darwin's daring hypothesis of natural selection and to reinforce in his mind the possibility of alternative mechanisms for advancement or development within species and from one species to another.

Baer's own solution to what he conceived as Darwin's dilemma was derived from an analogy to the discipline he knew best: embryology. Just as organs in an embryo are transformed in various stages on their way to a final goal, so too, Baer reasoned, the species develop with a direction and a purpose. He does not use the standard philosophical term purposefulness [*Zweckmäßigkeit*] in his account, however, preferring the more unusual term goal-directedness [*Zielstrebigkeit*] to describe the mechanism by which organisms strive to achieve a more perfected or final form—although, as Du Bois-Reymond points out, they are really the same.[38] Indeed, Baer contends further that even Darwin's hypothesis of natural selection cannot avoid the notion of goal-directedness since it includes both hereditability [*Erblichkeit*] and adaptation [*Anpassung*]. Hereditability, writes Baer, "is nothing other than the tendency or goal-directedness to repeat the life process of the parents, to be sure, under conditions and with means that the maternal body has given to begin with, but that later create the new individual out of its environment" (280). Adaptation is clearly goal-directed since it is "nothing but the endeavor to use existing conditions for the maintenance of life" (436). Thus Baer maneuvers Darwin into implicitly validating his concept of goal-directedness, which is allegedly more encompassing than the Englishman's limited hypothesis for the development of species. Although the reintroduction of purpose and goal into nature appears retrograde and was anathema to Nietzsche's philosophy, in particular in the 1880s, Nietzsche could certainly agree with the manner in which Baer refutes Darwin. In Baer's view, Darwin asserts "that every purposeful manifestation arises only on account of the survival of the fittest and not because of an inner necessity, which appears as a thought or a will of nature that accomplishes it. We are of the opposite opinion" (433). The suggestion that one could rely on a ubiquitous will to account for species variation rather than the mechanistically conceived process of adaptation and selection would be prominently reflected in Nietzsche's late philosophy, just as Baer's assertion that the goal of human development has not yet been attained (463) found a possible Nietzschean variant in the postulate of the overman.

From the reflections on Darwin contained in Lange, Rütimeyer, and Baer, we can see that evolution was not only a matter of central importance for Nietzsche's contemporaries, but also of considerable confusion, in particular about matters that had philosophical ramifications. The amount of teleology in Darwin's hypothesis, for example, seems to have been an issue of considerable uncertainty in the 1860s and 1870s among German writers. While most commentators, like Lange, believed that Darwinism refutes a teleological worldview, since this theory leaves evolution up to chance occurrence, other scientists did not agree. Baer, as we saw, regards Darwin as sneaking in some sort of teleological principle through the back door with his notions of hereditability and adaptation. Even more direct in this assertion is Rudolf Albert Kölliker (1817–1905), a native son of Zürich who taught for over five decades at the University of Würzburg and was perhaps the foremost histologist of his time.[39] In a lecture delivered at Würzburg in 1864, Kölliker accuses Darwin of advocating a teleological model for evolutionary change. Kölliker obviously believed that Darwin had posited an internal proclivity of organisms to produce useful variations that would then be the object for natural selection.[40] Kölliker would later correct his misconception, but in 1864 he finds himself advocating with Darwin—or with his misinterpretation of Darwin—a notion of evolution proceeding according to "heterogeneous creation." Like other biologists we have discussed, he disputes the ubiquity of natural selection, propounding instead a "greater developmental scheme," which seems to proceed by leaps from one species to another. He indicates that under unusual circumstances the egg or germ of one species can produce another, different species.[41] Kölliker also touches briefly on the issue of the apes as man's ancestors, and, unlike Rütimeyer and Baer, the latter of whom devoted a large section of his treatise on Darwin to this topic, he is not disinclined to admit this lineage, especially if one looks at the chimpanzees, the gorillas, and the orangutans, on the one side, and at the bushmen and other not-so-developed humans on the other side.[42] What is important for our considerations is not whether Nietzsche was specifically acquainted with Kölliker's writings, or whether his objections to Darwinism are supported by scientific evidence. It is immaterial for us at this point whether Darwin's theory is teleological or not,[43] or whether human descent from apes was universally accepted by Nietzsche's contemporaries. Rather, what is significant if we are going to appreciate Nietzsche's place in these discussions is the disparity of views on Darwin's *Origin of Species* in the writings of respected scientists with whose thought Nietzsche was likely acquainted, and the recognition that on issues concerning the philosophical implications of Darwinism there was likewise scant consensus among Nietzsche's contemporaries.

Darwinism in Strauß and Hartmann

Nietzsche's initial introduction to evolutionary theory and especially to the thought of Charles Darwin was, for a young intellectual with deficient scientific training, apt to have been puzzling and contradictory. If the scientists working in the field not only objected to specific aspects of Darwin's theory, but also could not agree on the substance and implications of his writings, it would have been impossible for Nietzsche, who was anyway acquainted with Darwin solely from secondhand accounts, to come to an accurate understanding of the hypotheses propounded by the English naturalist. To the extent that he understood Darwinism in the 1870s, he considered it true, as he confirmed in his notebooks (Nachlass 1872–73, 19[132], KSA 7.461), although his most thorough dialogue with contemporary trends in evolutionary biology would not occur until the 1880s, when the overman and the will to power constitute his "contribution" to this conversation. Indeed, throughout Nietzsche's lifetime it is difficult to know what he understands when he uses the word "Darwinism," that is, whether he is referring specifically to the theoretical work of Darwin as opposed to rival theories of evolutionary biology, or whether the term refers in general to a theory of evolution that encompasses Darwin and various other scientists who are in substantial agreement with him, or, finally, whether it encompasses the scientific theory of evolution as well as its philosophical and social implications. As we have already seen, at times Nietzsche appears to use "Darwinism" as a synonym for evolution, and it remains uncertain whether he conceives of the "truth" of Darwin in the hypothesis of natural selection or the more general notion that species evolve over time. Nietzsche, however, did have occasion to confront what at least one contemporary considered to be Darwinism in the 1870s, when, in his first *Untimely Meditation*, he inveighed against David Friedrich Strauß (1808–1874) and his recently published book of reflections, *The Old Faith and the New* (1872). The attack was overdetermined. To a certain degree, as we observed earlier, it was something of an assignment given to Nietzsche by Richard Wagner to exact revenge on a rival. Strauß had publicly defended Franz Lachner (1803–1890), the Munich court conductor who had opposed Wagner when he correctly perceived that Wagner was to replace him as Ludwig II's (1845–1886) favorite. Wagner intervened in print, composing three barbed sonnets, which, however, did not enjoy any public acclaim. In Wagner's mind, the score remained unsettled, and he therefore chose as his instrument of vengeance the young philology professor whom he had befriended a few years earlier and who, like most of Wagner's mesmerized entourage, was eager to comply with the wishes of the charismatic Meister. Nietzsche diligently set out to accommodate Wagner, and the last section of his work *David Strauß, the Confessor and the Writer*, which takes Strauß to task for stylistic and linguistic infelicities, is even modeled on Wagner's earlier critique of the theater director Eduard Devrient (1801–1877) from 1869.[44]

But Nietzsche was also unfavorably inclined toward Strauß because he represented in his mind the satiated middle-class philistine who championed German cultural achievement after the victory in the Franco-Prussian War. At this point, Nietzsche probably still considered the victory a great accomplishment, but he certainly did not equate military conquest with cultural superiority. Nietzsche is especially critical of Strauß's views on art and culture, but an important part of Strauß's intellectual profile was also a firm belief in the scientific discoveries of recent years and in the ineluctable progress of knowledge in natural science. It was in this context that Darwin became an issue in Nietzsche's writings, and for the first time in Nietzsche's polemic against Strauß, we observe that he has attached an ideological valence to Darwinism. In viewing Darwin in this fashion, he was actually quite timely. Although Darwin's writings and evolution may be largely devoid of political implications for most intellectuals in the twenty-first century, in the early 1870s, forces on the left of the political spectrum were already appropriating Darwin as a political ally. Part of Darwin's attractiveness for left and liberal groups resulted no doubt from the antireligious implications of evolutionary theory, although Nietzsche in no way identified with reactionary objections that sought to discredit Darwin through reliance on the Bible and religious dogma. What troubled him about Darwinism—as distinguished from evolution—was its association with tendencies he believed were inimical to German cultural greatness. Darwin's influence was particularly evident in the popular realm, which was the arena that Strauß entered with the publication of his book and that Nietzsche repeatedly criticized. As Alfred Kelly has remarked, "German popular Darwinism was a continuation of the old eighteenth-century Enlightenment tradition. German Darwinism sought to crush superstition, to inform, to liberate, and, indirectly, to democratize. In a more narrow sense, popular Darwinism may profitably be viewed as a cultural extension of the radical democratic spirit of 1848."[45] That Darwin's thought "became entangled with the theories of the Social Democrats"[46] certainly proved a deterrent to a positive assessment for Nietzsche, who, as we have already seen, was staunchly antisocialist even in the early 1870s. Indeed, the popular association of Darwinism and socialism was so ensconced in the minds of many Germans that Rudolf Virchow, the renowned pathologist and liberal activist, even blamed the Paris Commune on Darwin.[47]

Strauß was not a socialist,[48] however, and from his previous writings one might have suspected a certain affinity between his views and Nietzsche's. Strauß's most famous book, *The Life of Jesus* from 1835, questioned the biblical accounts of Jesus and argued for a distinction between the mythical trappings in the Gospels and the historical figure. A work of the left-Hegelian school, it was a pivotal text for the movement away from religious orthodoxy and toward atheism. But both *The Life of Jesus* and *The Old Faith and the New*, which were separated by almost half a century, exuded a Hegelian faith in progress and enlightenment that Nietzsche, especially under the influence of Schopenhauer and Wagner, found difficult to stomach. Strauß's main themes in *The Old Faith and the New* are theological and progressive. The old faith of his title refers to the obsolete convictions of religion, while the new faith, which is in formation and embraced by a growing "we," includes a skeptical attitude toward religious dogma, a validation of secular cultural traditions in literature and music, and a belief in the accumulation of natural scientific knowledge. In connection with this latter concern, Darwin is lauded as "one of the greatest benefactors of the human race" (181). Although Strauß notes in his first mention of the English naturalist that he was unable to conceive of a beginning of organic life on earth without resorting to the non-naturalist notion of a "miracle" (173), the chief reason for his admiration for Darwin is that his explanation of the development of species destroyed religious convictions and "eliminated the miracle from observations of the world" (216). When we consider Strauß's explication of Darwin's achievement, we must keep in mind the type of book the German theologian was writing. *The Old Faith and the New* was a text that was conscious of being a popular account of many things in the modern world, from the theological debates of the past century to the literary and musical life of contemporary Germany and the latest developments in the natural sciences. The book subsequently appeared in a more affordable popular edition [*Volks-Ausgabe*], and it went through seventeen editions in approximately three decades. The discussion of evolution in general and Darwin in particular occupied a large part of the third chapter, "How do we understand the world?," which is a testament to Darwin's importance for intellectual life in the last third of the nineteenth century. But Strauß, unlike Rütimeyer, Baer, or Kölliker, was not a scientist himself and was seeking only to mediate to the larger public during the Second Empire the most important developments of which they should be aware. We therefore find Strauß patiently explaining the important issue of the transition from an inorganic world to the first one-celled organism, criticizing the older metaphysical notion of a "power of life," and advocating a completely naturalist origin of organic life on earth. He argues that organic life is essentially an extension of inorganic matter; materialism and the mechanistic universe are firmly entrenched in his discussion since for him "life is only a special and, to be sure, the most complicated sort of mechanics" (175). Similarly, it is important for Strauß to deal with the older naturalist traditions in which species were considered fixed and unchangeable. Georges Cuvier (1769–1832) and Louis Agassiz (1807–1873) are mentioned specifically as advocates of fixed species, which presented no challenge to creationism as the explanation for the variety of species. Strauß recognizes that evolutionary theory has been subjected to ridicule because of its contention that human beings are descended from monkeys, and although he admits that the theory is still incomplete, leaving many important items unexplained, it has a validity that cannot be ignored. The service it has performed is not only one of placing the development of species on firm scientific ground, but also, and more important for Strauß, ridding us of the dependence on miracles, metaphysics, and superstition.

Strauß leaves no doubt that Darwin's chief achievement is that he has explained the origin of life and its subsequent development in a thoroughly scientific fashion. Before proceeding to discuss the English naturalist, however, Strauß cites his most important predecessors for a German audience. Jean-Baptiste Lamarck is credited with destabilizing the notion of a fixed array of species, but he could provide no real explanation for evolutionary change; Strauß obviously regards the hypothesis concerning the inheritance of acquired characteristics as unsatisfactory. Besides Lamarck, Strauß cites perhaps the two most famous thinkers in the German tradition, Johann Wolfgang Goethe (1749–1832) and Immanuel Kant (1724–1804), as precursors to Darwin and promoters of early evolutionary thinking. The former is cited for his discovery of the intermaxillary bone in human beings, which helped demonstrate our relations to higher primates, and his work on the metamorphosis of plants. Kant's remarks about the similarities in form among various species and a footnote relating to the fact that human infants cry at birth, while they could not have done so in the wild without endangering others, are seen as a recognition that his thought is compatible with insights from evolution.[49] Strauß recognizes, however, that the most important piece of the evolutionary puzzle—the mechanism by which species evolve—was Darwin's greatest achievement. Proceeding from artificial selection, with which he was familiar as a breeder of pigeons, Darwin posited the celebrated notion of a "struggle for existence," whereby stronger organisms survive, while weaker ones perish, and over generations varieties evolve into separate species. In an effort to make the process by which new species appear more plausible to his readers, Strauß notes that Darwin's theory of natural selection is analogous to occurrences in the business world or among doctors, where competition not only leads to improvement of a business or a physician, but also to an increase in specializations, that is, to businesses or physicians who are a different "species" from the parent from which they evolve (178–93). Strauß also comments about the importance of physical separation for the development of new species, but argues that nature provides numerous possibilities in its rivers and mountain ranges to account for the isolation of a new type. Strauß even provides a defense of human descent from apes and speculates about the origins of humanity in Africa. Unlike other commentary on evolution with which Nietzsche is likely to have had contact, Strauß supplies a straightforward explanation that embraces both natural selection and the place of *Homo sapiens* in the primate lineage.

From the perspective of the 1870s, Strauß would therefore have been judged a doctrinaire Darwinist, since he validates all aspects of the Englishman's theory and does not cite any of the misgivings that were frequently discussed in the scientific literature. Although at some points he calls evolution the "Lamarckian-Darwinian theory" (187), he clearly believes that Darwin has provided the essential scientific, as well as philosophical grounding for the origin and development of species. Despite Nietzsche's acquaintance with works that disagreed with portions of Darwin's propositions, he has very little to say about Strauß's presentation of the science of evolution. More interesting and potentially attractive for Nietzsche are some religious and ethical ramifications of Darwinism that Strauß briefly explores. Consonant with his critique of the Judeo-Christian tradition is Strauß's historical perspective on how we came to accept our separation from the animal kingdom. The ancient world and Asian religions think differently about our place among the species, as evidenced by the doctrine of reincarnation. In these traditions, we participate in a unity with the animal kingdom. Our conception of the human being altered drastically with later Western religious thought:

"The advent of Judaism, which was inimical to natural divinities, and dualistic Christianity dug a chasm between man and animal" (205). In his writings of the 1880s, Nietzsche would repeatedly broach similar themes, accusing the Judeo-Christian tradition of denying our natural instincts and thus falsifying our essence. Likewise, Strauß's comments on Darwinian ethics resonate with later Nietzschean pronouncements. Writing of the incipient forms of conscience in higher animals such as horses and dogs, Strauß speculates on the origin of similar moral compulsion in human beings: "If we are not entirely unjustified in tracing conscience in dogs back to the stick, we can also inquire whether the situation is very different with coarser men?" (208). Nietzsche's affirmative answer to this implicit query is explicated at length in the second essay of *On the Genealogy of Morals*.

The affinities between many of Nietzsche's religious views and Strauß's, and the fact that an attack on Strauß, despised since the 1830s by the orthodox establishment because of his freethinking, could potentially identify Nietzsche with a camp he himself opposed meant that the strategy for attacking him was selective and complex. Most of Nietzsche's polemic focuses on cultural issues, which Strauß deals with in the final sections of his book, and Nietzsche is able to portray his adversary as a smug, tasteless Babbitt, unable to fathom the profundity of genuine artistic achievement. Nietzsche's ire is also aroused because Strauß was not appropriately respectful of Arthur Schopenhauer, whose work constituted a strong philosophical bond between Nietzsche and Wagner.[50] A third prong of Nietzsche's offensive deals with ethical issues, and in this connection, Strauß's failure to derive an ethics consistent with his advocacy of Darwinism is a target for ridicule. Nietzsche refers derisively to Strauß covering "himself with the shaggy coat of our ape-genealogists" and to his claim that Darwin is humankind's greatest benefactor. In his critique, Nietzsche does not consider the remarks Strauß includes in his discussion of Darwin. Rather, he looks at the next chapter in Strauß's book, "How do we order our lives?," in which Strauß deals more directly with ethics and the development of morality in human society. Strauß does not mention Darwin in his discussion, but he describes what we might consider the optimistic Darwinian view on ethics.[51] Human societies that develop strong moral principles of cooperation and altruism have an advantage over those that remain "immoral." Nietzsche, by contrast, insists that Darwinism validates a Hobbesian "*bellum omnium contra omnes* and the privileged right of the strong," and that Strauß's unwillingness to adduce this moral code from his scientific worldview demonstrates both his lack of courage and his furtive adherence to the "old faith" he maintains he has discarded.

> To be sure, this moral code would have had to have been born of an inwardly undaunted sensibility, like that of Hobbes, and born of a love of

truth utterly different from one that always only explodes in angry invectives against priests, miracles, and the "world-historical humbug" of the resurrection. For the same philistine who takes the side of all such invective would take sides against a genuine Darwinian ethic that was consistently carried through. (DS 7, KSA 1.194–95)

Especially problematic for Nietzsche is Strauß's claim that "all moral activity is the self-determination of the individual according to the idea of the species."[52] This claim appears to make assumptions about moral qualities that are inherent in human beings. But we know that *Homo sapiens* has undergone a long period of development and that qualities we may prefer today are not "natural" to humankind. If Strauß had been a consistent Darwinian, Nietzsche argues, he should be able to explain "the phenomena of human kindness, compassion, love, and self-denial, whose existence one simply cannot deny" (DS 7, KSA 1.195), with evolutionary premises. In essence, Strauß has forgotten Darwin's most fundamental principle when he divorces human beings from their natural existence and insists they must obey an inherent, moral imperative connected to their essence as a species.

> How can this be innate to human beings when, according to Darwin, the human being is wholly a creature of nature and has evolved to the heights of humanity by adhering to a completely different set of laws; namely, by no other means than by constantly forgetting that other similar creatures possess the same rights, by feeling himself to be the stronger and gradually bringing about the demise of other specimens displaying a weaker constitution. (DS 7, KSA 1.196)

Nietzsche is convinced that a consistent Darwinian ethics entails differences and competition—between species and among individuals within species—while Strauß, in order to advance a notion of inherent moral goodness common to all human beings, relies on harmonious and idealized qualities associated with, or even drawn from, the very religious traditions he rejects.

Nietzsche presents a valid and pertinent argument. If Darwin situates the human species in the animal world and claims that we are the highest stage of evolution based on natural features, rather than some spiritual or moral superiority, then his theory implicitly calls into question the ethical standards of not only the Christian tradition, but also the idealist philosophical heritage. From this perspective, Strauß's rejection of Christianity is halfhearted and lacks the courage of its failing conviction. Nietzsche assumes the pose in this passage of the more consistent Darwinian. There are several counterarguments to Nietzsche's extrapolation of moral indifference from evolutionary thought, and he himself a few years later supplied one response to his own early immoralist interpretation. In a note from the mid-1870s with the rubric "On Darwinism" and in *Human, All Too Human* (aphorism 224), he hypothesizes that heightened social spirit and sympathetic attitudes in human beings result in a hardier, more stable tribe, and that those tribes containing the most devoted individuals survived best. Practical mores develop to which the members of the tribe must submit. Nietzsche recognizes the dangers of this arrangement since he believes that all progress comes from the outcasts or rebels, whom he would later designate provocatively as "criminals" [*Verbrecher*], but from these reflections we can see that he is able to understand how community moral values can arise within an evolutionary framework (MA 224, KSA 2.187; Nachlass 1875, 12[22], 8.257). Perhaps more germane is the fact that the issues Nietzsche raises with regard to a Darwinist morality were hardly foreign to discussions in his own era. Rütimeyer, for example, while disagreeing with the hypothesis of natural selection, envisions an evolution beyond the current version of the human species that will result in a "birth of goodness" that will pave the way for progress to the beautiful and the true.[53] Thus even those scientists more skeptical toward Darwin could imagine that the essence of human evolution lies precisely in the ability of human beings to reflect upon their own actions and thus to raise themselves above the pure necessities of the animal world. In *David Strauß*, Nietzsche's remarks give us a fair indication of the way he would eventually extend evolutionary theory for his own thought, and at this point he appears to validate Darwin and claim that Strauß has only appropriated a watered-down version in harmony with conventional ethical values. Already at this time, however, we find a hint of the shortcomings Nietzsche would later associate with Darwinism as a worldview: not only did it contribute to the atmosphere of progress and optimism in European society, it also provided a rather unsatisfactory mechanism for promoting the cultural renaissance of great individuals, which was Nietzsche's educational and cultural project in his Wagnerian period and his biological project in the 1880s. That Nietzsche is at least ambivalent about Darwinism is perhaps best indicated by the derogatory reference to "ape-genealogists" and by his ridicule of Strauß for considering Darwin "humankind's greatest benefactor."

In the 1870s, Nietzsche was able to find limited value in Darwin's notion of a struggle for existence: Nietzsche appears to suggest that if we appropriately extrapolate from Darwin's theory, then we can obtain insights into ethics and values. In comparison to Strauß and the left-liberal optimists of the new Second Empire, Darwin's worldview has at least the potential for a productive appropriation. A case similar to Strauß's arose in the mid-1870s in connection with Eduard von Hartmann (1842–1906), whom Nietzsche likewise considered too Hegelian and too smug, and whose views are judged inferior to Darwin's. We encountered Hartmann in Chapter 1 in connection with historical knowledge and education.

Almost unknown today, in 1869 Hartmann, who had obtained a doctorate in 1867 from the University of Rostock, became a minor celebrity in Germany with the publication of his *Philosophy of the Unconscious*, which relied heavily on the philosophy of Schopenhauer. Nietzsche appears at first to have been ambivalent about Hartmann's accomplishment, but at some point after the summer of 1872 he decided that Hartmann had to be publicly censured in much the same way as Strauß.[54] There is some irony in Nietzsche's turn against Hartmann directly after his ridicule of Strauß, since Strauß had himself criticized the philosopher of the unconscious for introducing an absolute entity that controls the "world process," and thus he does not advance beyond religion in his views on natural history.[55] For Nietzsche, Hartmann is an understandable target for condemnation. Although Hartmann was more reverent toward Schopenhauer, Nietzsche evidently took offense at the Hegelian twist he gave to pessimism, and the concomitant affirmation of the present state of affairs and blind faith in future progress. Nietzsche was especially critical of Hartmann's teleological notion of a world process and his contention that humankind is advancing toward an unconscious goal. In short, despite their common interest in Schopenhauer—or perhaps because of Hartmann's attempt to cover his philosophy in the mantle of Schopenhauer—Hartmann, like Strauß, came to represent for Nietzsche the self-satisfied, naively optimistic worldview of the Bismarck era.[56] Constitutive for this worldview was an appreciation of evolution, especially the Darwinism version, and in his celebrated work, Hartmann cites Darwin with admiration and approval, although it is evident that he, like many contemporaries, believed his hypothesis of natural selection needed to be supplemented with other explanations.[57] Indeed, in 1872, Hartmann anonymously critiqued his own book from the standpoint of physiology and evolutionary theory, even accusing himself of composing important sections of his earlier work without the knowledge of Darwin.[58]

Nietzsche's public polemical remarks against Hartmann occur in the penultimate section of *On the Advantage and Disadvantage of History for Life* (1874); in these passages, there is no mention of Hartmann's Darwinian connection. In an early note written in preparation for this text, however, Nietzsche comments on a section of Hartmann's work in which the philosopher of the unconscious argues that the world cannot have an infinite duration. Nietzsche begins by writing: "*World* process!! It's only a question of the paltry tricks of the human earth fleas!" After citing Hartmann, who asserts that the world has a definite beginning and is proceeding toward a definite goal, thus directly contradicting Nietzsche's later postulate of eternal recurrence as well as any common notion of evolution, he continues: "One gladly escapes this Hartmannian world process to the Democritic maze of atoms and to the Darwinian teaching of the survival of the fittest among the countless combinations. At least there is here still a place for great individuals, even if they are only spewed out by chance" (Nachlass 1873, 29[52],

KSA 7.649). With this reference to "great individuals," Nietzsche may be recalling a remark he read in Lange, who cites the following passage from a recent review of evolutionary theory: "Instead of a purposive albeit miraculously effective, extraworldly causality, it is preferable to posit the *possibility* of fortunate chance occurrences, and one finds consolation in the progressive development from a fortunate chance occurrence for the fact that everything in the world is ultimately meaningless and without purpose, and that the beautiful and the good lie not at the beginning, but only at the end, or at least only appear in the progression of events."[59] Compared with Hartmann, whose evolutionary world process implies a leveling of cultural achievement and a homogenized collective, similar to Strauß's "we" of the new faith, Nietzsche's Darwin at least offers the hope that greatness will be the fortuitous product of random combinations. Nietzsche's concern with this very issue is evident in the section in which he derides Hartmann in his *Untimely Meditation*. In a clear rejection of the "world process" and its final goal, Nietzsche counters: "No, the goal of humankind cannot possibly be found in its end stage, but only in its highest specimens" (HL 9, KSA 1.317). As long as Nietzsche believed that Darwin offered a theoretical foundation for these "higher specimens," his thought was preferred to that of Hartmann or Strauß, whose appropriation of the Englishman's views deflected from the genuine potential of evolution and the only legitimate goal for humankind.[60] Only when Nietzsche revisited Darwin and evolutionary theory in the 1880s, however, was his suspicion confirmed that Darwin's thought, loudly championed by the liberals and socialists of his time, was an inappropriate, or at least incomplete, explanation for the evolutionary change he could validate.

Alternatives to Darwin 1: Wilhelm Roux

Nietzsche's negative opinions about Darwinism, although not about some version of evolution, are evidenced shortly after his polemics against Strauß and Hartmann. His readings as well as the general climate had by that time convinced him that Darwin's scientific model—or what he understood as Darwin's model—was of diminished validity and that it needed to be supplemented by other mechanisms and principles or replaced by a different approach altogether. In his skepticism about Darwin, Nietzsche was hardly an untimely meditator. Peter Bowler has argued that anti-Darwin evolution theories gained ascendancy in the decades before and after 1900, and that in the 1870s and 1880s many scientists believed that Darwinism was in decline. Bowler does not mean the retrograde theological objections to Darwin, which were prevalent among certain adherents to religious orthodoxy, but had no real impact on the scientific and scholarly discussions of the times and did not affect Nietzsche in the least. Among the alternatives to Darwin that were most popular in Nietzsche's lifetime were

Lamarckism, which proposed the inheritance of acquired characteristics, or some variant on Lamarckism; orthogenesis, which argued a single evolutionary path determined within the organism; and mutation theory, which hypothesized that evolution proceeded by the sudden appearance of significantly new forms.[61] Bowler's categorization needs to be augmented by the many theorists, a few of whom we have already examined, who advanced a combination of these theories, or who granted partial validity to Darwin's hypothesis of natural selection, but believed that another guiding principle provided a more cogent explanation. Although it is impossible to ascertain precisely which writings actually persuaded Nietzsche that Darwin was in error, he obviously drew from a larger discussion of these issues among scientists, philosophers, and other intellectuals. As evidenced by Strauß and Hartmann, there were multiple works of general philosophy produced during the 1870s and 1880s that make some reference to evolution and to Darwin in particular,[62] and Nietzsche was certainly no exception.

While his animadversions of Strauß's timidity with regard to evolution could have been understood as partisanship for Darwin, Nietzsche left little doubt in aphorism 224, "Ennoblement through degeneration," in *Human, All Too Human* that he felt Darwin offered only one, and not the most likely, evolutionary alternative. We have already examined part of this aphorism since it provided a potential explanation for the preference for an ethics of cooperation that would be in harmony with Darwinism. Nietzsche speculates that the stable tribe evolves only through the appearance of "unfettered, uncertain, and morally weaker individuals" who undertake new ventures. Although many perish and have no impact whatsoever, occasionally these "weak" individuals effect change in the strong and stable community. Nietzsche's formulaic version of this process is "the strongest natures *preserve* the type, the weaker help it to *evolve*." Within individuals, we observe the same mechanism: a degeneration or mutation will produce a certain compensatory advantage. Nietzsche concludes that the "struggle for existence," the most popular slogan in the popularized German reception of Darwinism,[63] is only one possible perspective, although in the note that formed the basis for this aphorism, he is more dismissive of Darwin's notion.[64] More important as an explanation for progress is "the augmentation of the stabilizing force through the union of minds in belief and communal feeling" combined with "the possibility of the attainment of higher goals through the occurrence of degenerate natures and, as a consequence of them, partial weakenings and injurings of the stabilizing force" (MA 224, KSA 2.187). It is not clear precisely what Nietzsche is proposing as a counterargument to natural selection at this point, but he appears to speculate that there is an internal struggle to overcome a weakness, deficiency, or degeneration. In his notebooks, however, Nietzsche leaves no doubt that his alternative explanation is vastly superior to Darwinism, which is branded a "philosophy for butcher's helpers" (Nachlass 1875, 12[22], KSA 8.257), a sentiment that prefigures Nietzsche's deprecatory remarks about Darwin in the 1880s. Nietzsche would move decidedly away from this holistic, community-oriented interpretation of evolution after 1880, and by the second half of the 1880s, he would publicly call the struggle for existence an "incomprehensible, one-sided theory" (FW 349, KSA 3.585);[65] but already by the mid-1870s, he, like numerous contemporaries, had determined that Darwinism alone was insufficient to explain evolution and contained erroneous presuppositions.

Nietzsche's early readings in the sciences, as well as his contact with biology and biologists while he was employed at Basel, supplied him with sufficient arguments against Darwin in the 1870s. His decisive turn against Darwinism, however, appears to have been precipitated by increased attention to the natural sciences in the 1880s. We have noted that Nietzsche's initial intellectual concerns in the 1870s were mostly nonscientific, revolving around a number of cultural and academic issues: classical philology, Wagnerian opera, education, and at least a superficial enthusiasm for Schopenhauer. He had occasionally read works in the natural sciences in his Wagnerian period, and he had been introduced to scientific topics in various philosophical works, such as Lange's *History of Materialism*, but his preoccupation with biology, physiology, and physics is more pronounced after 1880. With regard to evolution, three books were particularly important for him: Wilhelm Roux's *The Struggle of the Parts in the Organism* (1881), William Henry Rolph's *Biological Problems as well as an Attempt to Develop a Rational Ethic* (1884), and Carl von Nägeli's *A Mechanical-Physiological Theory of Organic Evolution* (1884).[66] Each of these works is found in Nietzsche's library and contains considerable evidence of careful reading in marginal notation and underlinings. Appearing in the first half of the 1880s, they were all critical of Darwin's thought in different ways and therefore offered Nietzsche fresh perspectives on what Darwinism lacks and how he might conceive of evolution as a process that did not entail natural selection as the sole mechanism for the development of species. Nietzsche must have read other biologists in these years as well; among his notes we find a single reference to Karl Semper (Nachlass 1880, 4[95], KSA 9.123), an anatomist who coexisted on somewhat uneasy terms with his colleague Kölliker at the University of Würzburg, and we know that Nietzsche's library contains his important two-volume work *The Natural Conditions of Existence as They Affect Animal Life* from 1880.[67] Semper, although a partial advocate of natural selection, was championed by neo-Lamarckians,[68] and some scholars have argued that Nietzsche himself was attracted to Lamarckian theory.[69] More significant is that Nietzsche evidences scant interest in the considerable Darwin school in Germany. Ernst Haeckel is mentioned only a handful of times, usually in a dismissive fashion;[70] Emil Du Bois-Reymond figures only in connection with his preference for Lessing over Goethe with regard to the German language (SE 6, KSA 1.390). From his readings and his remarks on selected scientists, we can conclude that particularly in the 1880s, Nietzsche simply found Darwin's critics more fruitful for his thoughts about evolution than Darwinists, a hypothesis confirmed to some degree by his reading of Roux, Rolph, and Nägeli.

Roux was the youngest of the three (1850–1924), and the volume that was influential for Nietzsche was a very early work that contains only indications of the theory of developmental mechanics [*Entwicklungsmechanik*] for which Roux would later become famous. A student of Haeckel in his native city of Jena before continuing his studies in Strasbourg and Berlin, Roux was fascinated by the Darwinian notion of struggle and investigated in his later work the mechanical process of ontogenetic development. He was the founder of experimental embryology, and subsequent researchers appreciated his methods even if his conclusions about evolution soon became obsolete. These early reflections were precisely what interested Nietzsche, however. Like many biologists, Roux granted partial validity to the Darwinian hypothesis of natural selection. At the same time, Darwin and Alfred Russel Wallace (1823–1913), the co-discoverer of natural selection, could supply, in his view, no explanation for functional adaptation involving the ability of an organism to adjust directly to its environment under certain new conditions. Roux postulates that variability can already be located in embryonic development, and if one wishes to avoid positing a new type of teleological principle that accounts for successful adaptation, then one should consider an internal self-regulation that involves internal struggles. Rather than modify Darwin's notion of a struggle for existence by propounding, as Baer had done, an inherent mechanism that is goal-oriented, Roux extends the struggle to the individual parts of the organism. The organism does not develop harmoniously, but by means of internal conflict that prepares it best for its environment. The inequality of the parts sets up the basis for internal competition that ensues and is the basis for the struggle.[71] Roux envisions the struggle occurring on all levels, beginning with competition within cells, where molecules compete for nourishment and space, to a cellular rivalry and conflict at the level of tissues, to a struggle among organs. On each level, external stimulation plays a role in deciding the victor in the competition, and the result is a strengthening of the organism as a whole for its exoteric struggles. Roux thus establishes two sets of struggles for existence: an internal competition among various parts at all levels of organic life, and, drawn from the Darwin-Wallace hypothesis, a macro-struggle of organisms among other organisms that results in natural selection of the fittest varieties, thus affirming the success of the internal process.

Nietzsche was not the only reader who found Roux fascinating. Roux evidently sent a copy of his book to Darwin himself, who lauded the volume as the "most important book on Evolution, which has appeared for some time."[72] What interested Nietzsche, however, was less the affirmation of celebrated naturalists than the fact that Roux provided a foundation for his own intuition that the external struggle for existence and the survival of the fittest did not give a complete and adequate account of the evolutionary process. Nietzsche evidently read Roux's book several times, once shortly after its appearance, and at least once again in 1883 or 1884, and in both cases we find that his notebooks contain significant references and commentary. His first impressions give us an indication of how he worked with—and against—his scientific sources. In a note from 1881 he writes: "Now one has again discovered the struggle everywhere and talks about the struggle of cells, tissues, organs, organisms. But one *can* find again in them all the affects of which we are conscious—finally, when this has occurred, we turn the matter around and say: what really occurs by the arousal of human affects are those physiological movements, and the affects (struggles, etc.) are just intellectual interpretations, where the intellect doesn't know anything, but pretends to know everything" (Nachlass 1881, 11[128], KSA 9.487). Nietzsche takes Roux as a starting point for a reflection on topics with which Roux was not centrally concerned: the role of emotions and their physiological basis, as well as the difficulties of describing any of these activities in anything but a symbolic language.[73] By contrast, in his notes from the period 1883–84, he appears to be more interested in Roux's remarks with regard to mechanistic and teleological explanations.[74] But Roux's central importance for Nietzsche in the 1880s was his role as a biologist whose book called into question the preeminence of Darwin for evolutionary thought. Thus we find in the period 1886–87, long after his initial acquaintance with Roux, that Nietzsche recalls the struggle of the parts as a counterweight to the model of natural selection:

> —the individual itself as a struggle of the parts (for food, space, etc.): his development dependent on *conquest, prevailing* of individual parts, on the *wasting away*, the "becoming-an-organ" of other parts
> —The influence of "external circumstances" is ridiculously *overestimated* in Darwin; the most essential thing in the life process is precisely the tremendous formative power, which works internally, which *takes advantage of* and *exploits* the "external circumstances" (Nachlass 1886–1887, 7[25], KSA 12.304)

In this note, one of several from his last conscious years entitled "Against Darwinism," Nietzsche employs Roux's notion of an internal dynamics to call into question the emphasis on utility he had come to associate with Darwin and English theorists in general. The use of an organ does not explain its appearance, Nietzsche argues; in fact, the very notion of "use" is incoherent, since something that extends individual existence can be detrimental to its strength and splendor, while a deficiency can be "useful" in acting as a stimulant to other organs. What counts,

Nietzsche suggests, extending Roux's notion of inner struggles, are not measurements of utility, which are inevitably inconclusive, but something internal and forceful, something Nietzsche came to name in his later writings "will to power."

Alternatives to Darwin 2: William Rolph

Nietzsche entered into an equally productive dialogue with Rolph's work. In contrast to Roux and Nägeli, Rolph (1847–1883) was not a preeminent researcher in his field. Born in 1847, he had attended universities in Berlin and Leipzig and published his initial scientific study in 1876. Soon thereafter, he developed a severe respiratory disease, and despite attempts to return to his profession, he succumbed to his illness just prior to his thirty-sixth birthday. Before his death, however, he completed *Biological Problems*, the monograph Nietzsche owned and carefully read, and was even able to revise the first six chapters for a second edition. Most of this monograph is devoted to a critique of Herbert Spencer's (1820–1903) book *Data of Ethics* (1879), a work that endeavored to develop a theory of morality from evolutionary principles. Rolph evidently associated Darwin and Spencer very closely, as did Nietzsche at times (JGB 253, KSA 5.196), and believed, as he reported to the editor of his posthumously published second edition, that he was able to refute incontestably their theory.[75] Although he spends considerable time disparaging Spencer's derivation of altruism, a topic that also interested Nietzsche in his reflections on morality, his objections to the more narrowly defined scientific theory of Darwinism are also outlined in some detail. Like Roux, Rolph did not believe Darwin accounted adequately for what occurs inside the organism, and he begins his critique by positing a principle of insatiability operative in both organic and inorganic life. Organisms do not merely try to satisfy themselves in a climate of scarcity, which he assumes is Darwin's claim, but to increase their consumption in an almost constant fashion. On the basis of this internal drive, Rolph comes to radically different conclusions with regard to the evolutionary process. Organisms do not produce varieties, Rolph maintains, because of insufficient food or space, but rather under conditions of prosperity and abundance. Although Rolph admits that under advanced conditions of culture, natural selection, a theory founded on scarcity and competition for scarce resources, may obtain, in more primitive situations the principle of insatiability provides a more adequate explanation for the growth, augmentation, perfection, and individual development of organisms. "Thus increased intake is not the result of growth, perfection etc., but rather growth and perfection are the result of intake that is more or less dependent on the will of the creature."[76] The struggle for self-preservation is really a struggle for acquiring a surplus, and the struggle for existence is essentially one of aggression, which becomes defensive only under specific conditions. Evolutionary development from prosperity is the rule: Darwin's scenario of scarcity and competition is the exception.

In Nietzsche's notebooks, we find only one reference that includes Rolph's name, and it is fairly dismissive. He writes of a "German half-Englishman" who demolished Spencer's *Data of Ethics*, that "union of *bêtise* and Darwinism," and continues: "Aside from the polemics, there is nothing to praise in this book, and what is in essence offensive here just as in the book that he opposes is the desire of insignificant men to express their views in areas where only a select type of men of knowledge and experience can speak without immodesty" (Nachlass 1885, 35[34], KSA 11.525–36).[77] Despite this note, we find that Rolph's thoughts on evolution appear rather prominently in several of Nietzsche's writings and in many of his notes.[78] Two illustrations should suffice to show Nietzsche's active appropriation of Rolph. When Rolph adduces reasons for his hypothesis that periods of prosperity are responsible for the formation of varieties, he remarks: "We have sufficient and abundant evidence of the fact that domesticated species, which therefore are protected, cared for, and fed, and which are removed entirely from a competitive struggle, vary enormously and produce the most marvelous monstrosities."[79] In aphorism 262 from *Beyond Good and Evil*, Nietzsche reproduces a very similar version of this thought: "A *species* comes into being, a type grows strong and fixed, by struggling for a long time with essentially similar *unfavorable* conditions. Conversely, as we know from the experiences of stockbreeders, a species that is given over-abundant nourishment and extra protection and care generally shows an immediate and very pronounced tendency to variations in type, and is rich in marvels and monstrosities (and monstrous vices, too)" (JGB 262, 5.214). In this passage, Nietzsche has grafted together an apparently Darwinian explanation for the origin and stability of a species with the Rolphian notion of variety production. Indeed, Nietzsche was evidently most attentive to Rolph's contention that within the framework of his prosperity thesis, the struggle for self-preservation is less important than the struggle for surplus acquisition.[80] In several notes from the latter half of the 1880s, Nietzsche shows his fascination with Rolph's rethinking of the relationship between self-preservation and self-expansion. Accordingly, he opens aphorism 349 in *The Gay Science* with the following observation: "The wish to preserve oneself is the symptom of a condition of distress, of a limitation of the really fundamental instinct of life which aims at *the expansion of power*" (FW 349, KSA 3.585). Clearly Nietzsche's notion of the will to power corresponds closely to Rolph's contention of an internal drive for surplus accumulation and growth, although Nietzsche's notion, as we shall see in the next chapter, also has a relationship to cosmological theory. In *Beyond Good and Evil*, Nietzsche again relates, as Rolph does, the instinct for self-preservation and an insatiable impulse for expansion: "A living being wants above all to *release* its strength; life itself is the will to power, and self-preservation is only one of its indirect and most frequent *consequences*" (JGB 13, KSA 5.27). The process of Nietzsche's appropriation is rather typical for his writings: he reconfigures as a hierarchy what he found in Rolph as an opposition. Self-preservation does obtain, but only insofar as it derives from the more encompassing principle of the will to power. In general, Nietzsche's scientific readings are not simply source material for his writings, but opportunities for dialogue and further development.

Despite the derogatory assessment of Rolph in his notebook entry from 1885, Nietzsche also found in his book a welcome and critical discussion of perhaps the most celebrated English evolutionary theorist of his day, Herbert Spencer. Indeed, Spencer used "evolution" much more extensively than Darwin and applied it to all aspects of existence. He was also responsible for the phrase "survival of the fittest," which was taken by many intellectuals in the nineteenth century—including Nietzsche—as a shorthand for Darwinism, although Darwin's insights into biology and Spencer's differed significantly. Unlike Darwin, whose works Nietzsche never read in the original, Spencer was represented in Nietzsche's library with three volumes, and each shows some evidence of the German philosopher's reading. He had purchased the two-volume German translation of *The Study of Sociology* (1873) in 1875, and although there are some indications he read this introductory work, it left no impressions in his notebooks at the time or in later years. Much more interesting for Nietzsche was the German version of *The Data of Ethics*, which he acquired in 1880, a year after the original was published, read with obvious interest, as evidenced by numerous underlinings and marginal notes,[81] and discussed in a series of notebook entries in 1880 and then in later years. There is little doubt that Nietzsche associated Spencer with evolutionary biology, but it is uncertain how closely he believed Spencer's theory resembled Darwin's. From his early remarks directed against Strauß, it appears that Nietzsche considered the natural extension of Darwinism into the field of ethics would be a Hobbesian struggle among individuals, something he certainly did not find affirmed in Spencer. But in *Beyond Good and Evil*, Nietzsche includes under "mediocre Englishmen" Darwin, John Stuart Mill, and Spencer (JGB 253, KSA 5.196), and his references to the "shopkeeper" mentality and narrowness of English intellectuals appears to apply to both Spencer and the celebrated English naturalist. In the introduction to *On the Genealogy of Morals*, he comments on Paul Rée (1849–1901) that he had read Darwin so that in his writings "the Darwinian beast civilly extends a hand to the morally meek and mild, the ultra-modern soul who has learnt 'not to bite' " (GM, Vorrede 7, KSA 5). And in later notes that we will examine below under the title of "anti-Darwin,"[82] Nietzsche refers to the "Darwin school" in ways that indicate he is thinking as much of Spencer as of Darwin himself.[83] It appears that as Nietzsche moved into the latter part of the 1880s he came to identify Spencer with Darwin, or at least Darwin's "school" with the "English" version of evolutionary theory.

Spencer and Nietzsche both proceeded from common presuppositions about the biological nature of ethical life. But their conclusions were radically different. The Englishman assumes that there is progress in "conduct," and that this progress is in natural accord with evolutionary development. "Greater organic evolution," he writes, "is accompanied by more evolved conduct," so that if we trace behavior from the lowest forms of organic existence up through the animal world and then from the most "primitive" classes of the human species through to the most modern and advanced, we will find a smooth progression. Ethics itself involves conduct, but only the conduct associated with the most advanced forms, humankind in its various stages, culminates in cooperative social orders: "Ethics has for its subject-matter, that form which universal conduct assumes during the last stages of its evolution. We have also concluded that these last stages in the evolution of conduct are those displayed by the highest type of being, when he is forced, by increase of numbers, to live more and more in presence of his fellows."[84] Spencer's ethical theory thus seeks to define good and bad in relationship to the development of species, but in particular with regard to humankind as these terms relate to three aspects of human existence: the welfare of self, the welfare of offspring, and the welfare of fellow human beings. The first of these aspects refers us to self-preservation, the second to the continuance of the species, the final one to a social order that will eventually evolve into a harmonious unity of conduct and associated actions. In the fully evolved stage of humankind, goodness will thus be attributed to conduct that "aids the sick in re-acquiring normal vitality, assists the unfortunate to recover the means of maintaining themselves, defends those who are threatened with harm in person, property, or reputation, and aids whatever promises to improve the living of all his fellows." Badness will then refer to conduct that promotes the contrary effects (24–25). Spencer proceeds to examine evolution in conduct from various perspectives that emphasize different criteria. From the physical view, for example, coherence in conduct increases as we go through the species from the lowest levels to humankind, and among humankind from the "savages" to the more civilized societies. When viewed from a biological perspective, Spencer finds an increase in the balance of functions through the evolutionary process. And in terms of psychology, he detects an increased control of more primitive feelings by more complex, "compound and representative" processes, culminating in the development of conscience in the most evolved social orders. Viewed from the perspective of society, Spencer approaches a utilitarian conclusion, where "ethics becomes nothing else than a definite account of the forms of conduct that are fitted to the associated state, in such wise that the lives of each and all may be the greatest possible, alike in length and breadth" (133).[85] In *The Data of Ethics*, all dimensions of conduct in the organic world fit neatly into a progressive evolutionary schema. Humankind, which represents, as it does for Nietzsche, the species that has not achieved the final stage on its evolutionary path, will inevitably reach "the naturally-revealed end towards which the Power manifested throughout Evolution works" (171).

Spencer's teleologically informed views on evolutionary ethics attracted Nietzsche's criticism and ridicule in remarks from the early 1880s through to his last published writings and notebooks. A further issue that would interest Nietzsche was Spencer's discussion of egoism and altruism, which is contained in the second half of his treatise. In his initial treatment of the topic in the eleventh chapter, "Egoism versus Altruism," the Englishman explores positions that come closest to Nietzsche's observations on the topic. "Ethics," he begins, "has to recognize the truth, recognized in unethical thought, that egoism comes before altruism." If those that are better adapted and leave better adapted offspring advance the species, while those who are "ill-adapted" are disadvantaged in the struggle for existence, then it would seem to follow that those who tend to themselves first are preferred, while assisting those who are unable to sustain themselves would do a disservice to humankind as a species. "Any arrangements which in a considerable degree prevent superiority from profiting by the rewards of superiority, or shield inferiority from the evils it entails . . . are arrangements diametrically opposed to the progress of organization and the reaching of a higher life." Although this conclusion may not be pleasing to us from an ethical perspective, it would appear to be valid "under its biological aspect" (187, 189). In the next chapter, however, Spencer presents the opposing argument, asserting from the outset that "from the dawn of life, altruism has been no less essential than egoism." To demonstrate this proposition, Spencer has recourse to the somewhat dubious notions of "automatic altruism" or "unconscious altruism." In single-celled organisms, for example, the division into two new organisms destroys the original or parent; in higher organisms, parents sacrifice parts of themselves or their nourishment to nurture their offspring. This self-sacrifice, which Spencer understands as a primitive type of altruism, "is no less primordial than self-preservation" (201, 203). In the social setting of human beings, Spencer first refers to the "negative altruism" that curbs egoistic impulses to prevent aggression. He reasons that "each profits egoistically from the growth of an altruism which leads each to aid in preventing or diminishing others' violence." Indeed, Spencer argues further that in order for individuals to pursue their own interests in an egoistic fashion, they require the introduction of justice, which can only be established in the application of altruism in a social order. Moreover, assisting others less fortunate benefits each member of society not only egoistically by reducing such things as the cost of commodities produced or taxes paid, but also through psychological mechanisms: "The sensitiveness to purely personal enjoyments is maintained at a higher pitch by those who minister to the enjoyment of others, than it is by those who devote themselves wholly to personal enjoyments." And, similarly without much proof or argumentation, Spencer asserts that "the range of aesthetic gratifications is wider for the altruistic nature than for the egoistic nature" (211, 213, 214). Egoism thus depends to a considerable extent on altruism according to Spencer's argument, and in the final discussion of this topic he seeks to reconcile the two seemingly opposing and equally basic tendencies. As time progresses and the need for altruistic conduct diminishes, "postponements of self to others in large ways will become very infrequent," although opportunities for altruistic behavior will not disappear in the course of daily life. While in our current state of affairs, altruism is understood as self-sacrifice, and self-sacrifice is not pleasurable, this situation will change as we increasingly gain pleasure from the pleasures we produce through our conduct. Ultimately, "altruism will be the achievement of gratification through sympathy with those gratifications of others which are mainly produced by their activities of all kinds successfully carried on—sympathetic gratification which costs the receiver nothing, but is a gratis addition to his egoistic gratification." At this point, the opposition between egoism and altruism will vanish: the individual will no longer have to choose "between self-regarding impulses and other-regarding impulses"; "the motive of action will not consciously be the attainment of altruistic pleasure; but the idea present will be the securing of others' pleasure"; and "the highest altruism" will be the kind that "ministers not to the egoistic satisfactions of others only, but also to their altruistic satisfactions" (255–56). In the utopian world that Spencer envisions, the antagonism that appeared to inform ethical and unethical behavior will no longer obtain.

In Nietzsche's initial reading of Spencer's *The Data of Ethics*, he criticizes him for his imputation of purpose and use into morality and for the projected goal orientation in his discussion of evolutionary ethics, as well as his exclusion of "bad" conduct from human activity. "These extollers of purposefulness in natural selection (like Spencer) believe they know what the favorable conditions of evolution are! and they don't include evil in it! And what would man be without fear, envy, possessiveness!" (Nachlass 1881, 11[43], KSA 9.457). Or: "It is not true that good and bad are the collection of experience about purposeful and purposeless. All evil drives are just as much purposeful and species-preserving as good ones!" (Nachlass 1880, 6[456], KSA 9.316). In the middle of the decade, he makes a similar observation: "That purposefulness of means has increased in the entire history of organisms (as Spencer asserts) is an English-superficial judgment" (Nachlass 1885, 40[4], KSA 11.630). What changes in Nietzsche's evaluation of Spencer's arguments about the progressive nature of ethics, paralleling a "progress" in evolution, is only the degree of ridicule. In his later works and writings, Nietzsche repeatedly dismissed the Englishman as a representative of a "shopkeeper" mentality (Nachlass 1887, 9[44], KSA 12.357; 10[118], KSA

12.525; 1888, 15[115], KSA 13.475) or a "décadent" (GD, Streifzüge eines Unzeitgemässen 38, KSA 6.139). In a notebook entry from his last sane year, he cites two sentences from Spencer and characterizes them as "*Inscriptions over a modern insane asylum*" (Nachlass 1888, 14[48], KSA 13.242). Spencer's evolutionary ethics and the assumption of ineluctable progress with its idealist underpinnings become part of the decadent worldview in modern times that Nietzsche rejects and seeks to overcome. His remarks against Spencer's discussion of egoism and altruism are equally harsh. He notes in more patient commentary that Spencer's characterization of altruism is inconsistent with any theory of drives or instincts, that it is "completely false" to regard instinctual behavior, such as care for young or the act of reproduction, as the expression of an altruistic drive (Nachlass 1880, 6[137], KSA 9.231). His confusion comes from a projection of his own desires for innate altruism onto purportedly scientific thinking (Nachlass 1880–81, 8[35], KSA 9.390).[86] And in Nietzsche's later writings, the reconciliation of egoism and altruism with which Spencer concludes his reflections in *The Data of Ethics* is viewed not only as a product of fantasy, but also as undesirable, even disgusting: "a human race that adopts as its ultimate perspective such a Spencerian perspective would strike us as deserving of contempt, of annihilation" (FW 373, KSA 3.625). The late notebooks ridicule the subsumption of instinctive activities under altruistic behavior with the sarcastic remark that in England the passing of urine already belongs to altruistic activities (Nachlass 1884, 26[303], KSA 11.231; 1885, 35[34], 524). Nietzsche certainly agrees with Spencer about the biological nature of ethics, and he also underscores with the overman the unfinished evolution of the human species. But for Nietzsche, morality is not connected with goal-directed behavior, and certainly not with the progress of humankind toward a future in which altruism and egoism are reconciled under the banner of the greatest happiness for everyone. Instead, it appears to consist of human explanations for actions that occur anyway, of our conscious, and therefore erroneous, reflection on what is resolved at a physiological level by the struggle of instincts with each other. Nietzsche's remarks on Spencer, first in 1880, then just prior to the composition of his works on morality from the mid-1880s, and finally in his last notebooks and writings provide considerable insight into his thinking about ethics. To some extent, we can regard *On the Genealogy of Morals* as a detailed response to Spencer and to what Nietzsche came to believe was a specifically English mode of thought about ethics and its relationship to evolution.[87]

In Rolph's *Biological Problems*, Nietzsche found his views on Spencer confirmed by someone involved in evolutionary thought and natural science. Rolph's book contains many different criticisms of Spencer's moral theory, scattered in various chapters. His main objections reinforce remarks Nietzsche made in his notebooks, and occasionally, without mentioning Spencer by name, in his published works. Like Nietzsche, Rolph observes that Spencer departs from a Darwinist foundation in his ethical reflections, ignoring the basic notion of a struggle for existence and the destruction of animal and vegetable species by species that succeed in their own preservation.[88] The Anglo-German scientist advocates a Hobbesian perspective that very much resembles what we encountered in Nietzsche's commentary on Strauß. Cooperation among men is not the result of utility; the first impulses of men who come upon each other are enmity resulting in open struggle. Social life must be forced on humankind; "war" is the natural condition of humans when they come into contact with one another (196–97).[89] Rolph also detects and detests the teleological aspects of Spencer's theory and its inherent idealism:

> Spencer's theory is eminently idealist, and it cannot do without a good dose of hidden teleology. Obviously proceeding from the assumption that whatever is natural cannot be immoral, he seeks to present normal and moral as synonymous, an endeavor that has been already tried many times. And to this he adds the further assertion that the normal and only the normal can bring pleasure. Of course, he admits that this is the case only for an ideal situation that has not yet been achieved, but which—and that is a further sign of his idealist optimism—can be and will be achieved. (52)[90]

Similar to Nietzsche, Rolph mocks Spencer's naïveté in matters of morality, stating that the perfect harmony he projects as the end point of evolution has about as much justification as a prediction that death and birth will cease (52). His ethics consists of an unconscious, but fundamental teleological core that amounts to little more than his own "subjective optimism" (221). Rolph shares Nietzsche's disdain for Spencer's discussion of egoism and altruism, noting that the latter notion confounds instinctual and willful impulses, and that to make sense it must be associated with consciousness (37–38, 184). Rolph goes even further in approximating Nietzsche's views when he writes that "the fundamental principle of animal life is eminently egoistic and recognizes no other law than that of the individual person, and the law that grants power"—a remark next to which Nietzsche comments "very good" in the margins (183). Indeed, Rolph suggests, much as Nietzsche does, that Spencer validates the mediocre or the "normal" and fails to recognize that most important in the evolutionary process are an "increase of life, not a preservation of life, struggle for preference, not for existence," not merely "the acquisition of the necessities of life and nourishment," but "richness, power, and influence" (222–23). Rolph, in short, suggests something resembling the will to power as a corrective to an ethical theory based on an optimistic interpretation of the survival of the fittest and the preservation of the species.

Nietzsche's similarity with Rolph in his critique of Spencer and in his general evaluation of evolution and "evolutionary ethics" is apparent. Nietzsche's appreciation of Rolph's views is likewise obvious: in his library the copy of *Biological Problems* contains numerous marginal remarks, most of them exclamation marks or words indicating that Nietzsche concurs with Rolph's assessment. The uncharitable comments in his 1885 notebook entry pertaining to Rolph are thus odd and may reflect only Rolph's more pedestrian approach to Spencer and ethical theory, rather than any fundamental difference of opinion.

Alternatives to Darwin 3: Carl von Nägeli

Nietzsche's relationship with Carl von Nägeli's (1817–1891) *A Mechanical-Physiological Theory of Organic Evolution* is of a slightly different nature. The author of this treatise was one of the foremost botanists of the nineteenth century, and his book, in contrast to the works Nietzsche read by Roux and Rolph, was his final large publication, not the initial offering of a neophyte. It was a genuinely scientific study, containing a fair amount of detailed materials, rather than an abstract combination of evolution and speculative philosophy. What is rather remarkable is that, from the copy we find in Nietzsche's library, which has marginal markings throughout, we have to conclude that Nietzsche studied it rather carefully and in its entirety. Nietzsche may have been acquainted with Nägeli, at least by name, from his earlier writings; he is mentioned in Lange and occupied a prominent place in several other works in Nietzsche's possession.[91] Nägeli himself was an old-school scientist. Born in 1817, he gave up his medical studies to pursue his passion for science, and along the way he was influenced by Lorenz Oken (1779–1851), perhaps the most important biologist of the idealist tradition in Germany, and by Hegel, whose school of thought he personally experienced in Berlin in the 1840s. Thus Nägeli's ideas were shaped both by Romantic currents in natural philosophy and by the notion of an inherently progressive development of spirit or mind [*Geist*], both of which were intellectual tendencies in the first half of the century; and although he contributed a great deal to the understanding of cell formation and plant physiology, his theoretical outlook, even in his later years, was informed by these vitalistic and teleological associations from this earlier period. In the history of biology, Nägeli is unfortunately known best today for his discouragement of Gregor Mendel (1822–1884). Nägeli was the only distinguished scientist with whom Mendel was in contact, and he received from the Austrian monk a pioneering paper on plant hybrids. But Nägeli could not reconcile the conclusions in this paper with his own theoretical model, and he therefore dismissed Mendel's hybrid ratios and demonstration of complete reversion as a matter of merely empirical significance, rather than a theoretical breakthrough.[92]

Nägeli therefore has the unique distinction in the history of biology of disregarding the achievements of both Mendel and Darwin. With respect to evolution, Nägeli, like so many of the scientists read by Nietzsche, did not dismiss Darwin entirely, but rather felt that the adaptation model of natural selection offered only a partial answer to the secrets of species change and development. Already in 1865, Nägeli had pointed out that Darwin's work was unable to account for nonadaptive characters, and Darwin himself conceded that this shortcoming was a major lacuna in his theory.[93] In his monograph from 1884, he devotes a long chapter to the failings of Darwinism; in it, we encounter some of the usual litany of complaints about natural selection that we witnessed in Rütimeyer, Baer, and Kölliker.[94] In general, Nägeli is convinced that Darwin does not really provide a sufficient explanation for evolution, and much of the preceding and subsequent discussion is devoted to a clarification of his own outlook. Over the years, he had developed a vocabulary and a concomitant theory that accounted for hereditary mechanisms and evolutionary change. His concept of micelles posited the existence of cellular building blocks in regular crystalline form; stimuli had the possibility of changing the composition of the micelles and effecting modifications or variations since some micelles could always be found in the idioplasma, which was conceived as the basic unit of hereditary transmission. Idioplasma is a solid material, in contrast to the half liquid material in the rest of the cell, and since it is located throughout the body, Nägeli could adapt a Lamarckian model to account for changes caused by repeated exposure to environmental stimuli. A stimulus does not actually lead to an immediate change in the organism, but rather, if sufficiently strong or of sufficient duration, to a modification of the idioplasma; eventually, in a future generation, the idioplasma generates an alternation in an observable, external characteristic. Overseeing this process of change is a perfecting impulse [*Vervollkommnungstrieb*] that resides in the idioplasma and that determines the direction of the organic development. Since Nägeli believed in spontaneous generation, he could posit many different inherent goals for the idioplasma, and conjectured that the more complex organisms—since the tendency of the perfecting impulse was toward complexity—were in fact older in terms of idioplasma than simple organisms, which are at the beginning of their idioplasmic journey. Nägeli thus discounted adaptation as a significant force in evolutionary development; change occurs primarily through the perfecting impulse, which slowly but surely alters the configuration of the idioplasmic system, or through external influences, which alter the configuration in a specific direction.[95]

The detailed account of micelles and idioplasma must have been daunting reading for Nietzsche. In his writings, there are no references to the former concept and only a single mention of the latter term, in which its use is somewhat idiosyncratic. In a notebook entry, he writes that "the same leveling and ordering power that reigns in the idioplasma, also reigns in the assimilation of the external world" (Nachlass 1885–86, 2[92], KSA 12.106–7). In this statement, Nietzsche employs Nägeli's notion to explain why perception is always mediate and never the result of a pure "impression." Our sensory apparatus is the result of an evolutionary history that produces conformity through the idioplasma, which represents the accumulated past in us. Nietzsche appears to have been more attentive to the hypothesis of a perfecting impulse, and he comments at one point, apparently correcting Nägeli, that perfections involve not only greater complexity, but also greater power (Nachlass 1885–1886, 2[76], KSA 12.96). He recognizes that Nägeli's notion harkens back to a Romantic conception of the world, and he lists "perfecting" along with "nature," "progress," and "Darwinism" as possible remnants of a Christian worldview that still inheres in modern times (Nachlass 1887, 10[7], KSA 12.457).[96] In general, Nägeli's work, despite its affinities with historical explanations from the early part of the century, confirmed for Nietzsche what he had read in almost all the anti-Darwinians he had pursued since his earliest preoccupation with evolutionary theory: Darwin relies too exclusively on external factors, and while stimuli do have an effect on an organism's behavior, the mechanism of natural selection may not be adequate to account for the changes that really matter. Nietzsche was not able to subscribe to a quasi-Hegelian perfecting drive that impels evolution forward to new and higher levels of complexity. But he was able to appreciate the argument that the motive forces behind changes in the species are not simply adaptation and selection. For him, as for Nägeli, it must involve something internal, more vital, and capable of producing results that culminate in salutary modifications and advances.

It seems evident that Nietzsche's notion of the will to power, whatever else it may entail, is meant to be the vital force in organic life and is therefore an important part of Nietzsche's answer to the various internal mechanisms he encountered in the numerous anti-Darwinists he read. Indeed, in one of his several anti-Darwin reflections in his later years, he maintains that the Darwinians have deceived themselves, and he touts the will to power as "the ultimate ground and character of all change" (Nachlass 1888, 14[123], 13.303). Under this same heading he returns to a theme that quite possibly stems from his reading of Nägeli. "That the highest organisms have developed themselves from the lower ones is hitherto proven by no instance" (Nachlass 1888, 14[123], KSA13.304). Nietzsche is here disputing a fundamental principle of Darwinian evolution: the progression from lower forms of life to more complex and therefore "higher" forms. That he is not disagreeing merely with the notion that the so-called higher forms are really "higher" is shown by a remark in another anti-Darwin passage a few pages later. After claiming that natural or "unconscious" selection has never occurred and repeating anti-Darwinian platitudes such as the nonexistence of transitional forms, he comments: "The primitive beings are supposed to be the precursors of the present ones. But a look at the fauna and flora of the Tertiary period permits us only to think as if about a yet unexplored land, where there are types that do not exist anywhere else and are related to each other and even those that exist elsewhere" (Nachlass 1888, 14[133], KSA 13.316). This passage is somewhat confusing, because fragmentary, but it does suggest that Nietzsche at times doubted a linear and a progressive notion of evolution and toyed with some variation of spontaneous generation suggested by Nägeli. In a later thought in the same passage, he appears to confirm his adherence to the eminent botanist: "The entire animal and plant world does not develop itself from the lower ones to the higher ones.... Rather everything at once and next to one another and in disorder and in competition" (Nachlass 1888, 14[133], KSA 13.316–17).[97] These contentions apparently contradict the implications of the overman as an evolutionary stage in the development from worm to ape to man. But what Nietzsche is really opposing in this passage is the notion that evolution proceeds according to a linear mechanism involving variation and the survival of the fittest. There is no contradiction between believing that simpler (lower) species preceded more complex (higher) species, but that new species can arise even after more complex species have appeared, as Nägeli suggests. Nietzsche's conception of the course of evolution is nonlinear, and to his understanding therefore anti-Darwinian, but it does not necessarily contradict the tenet that man was once an ape, and that man will become "overman." In Nägeli's terms, the overman may be the last stage of an old idioplasma that started as worm and progressed through ape and man on its way to perfection. But what Nietzsche appears to be opposing most vehemently in this lengthy anti-Darwin note is the notion of progress, especially as it regards man. As we shall see more clearly in Chapter 9, in his later years, Nietzsche subscribed to a view of the degeneration of man, as appeared evident to him in modern society. Man flatters himself by thinking that he is superior to the animal world, but he is really a regression, not an advance. Thus he insists that "the human being as species does not represent an advance in comparison to any other animal." Even in the animal world, the "richest and most complex forms" more easily perish, while the "lower forms" seem to have a better knack for persevering. In human societies, the "higher types," the "fortunate cases of development," are at a disadvantage in the struggle for survival; the genius is "the most sublime machine that exists," but for that very reason "the most fragile" (Nachlass 1888, 14[133], KSA 13.316).

The Anti-Darwinist

For the most part, Nietzsche is less concerned about the evolutionary sequence from worm to ape and from ape to man, that is, about the formation of ascending species as a scientific theory, than he is about the implications of evolution for humankind. In almost every one of his later remarks about Darwin, Darwinism, the struggle for existence, and selection, Nietzsche concerns himself with the species Darwin mentions but a single time in his *Origin of Species*: *Homo sapiens*. Having witnessed the conversation into which Nietzsche entered when he broached the topic of evolution in the post-*Zarathustra* period, and having seen the way in which this topic was broached in his last notebooks, we are in a better position to understand the central passage on Darwin in his published writings. It occurs in *Twilight of the Idols* (1888), and it is appropriately and simply titled "Anti-Darwin":

> As regards the celebrated "struggle for *life*," it seems to me for the present to have been rather asserted than proved. It does occur, but as the exception; the general aspect of life is *not* hunger and distress, but rather wealth, luxury, even absurd prodigality—where there is a struggle it is a struggle for *power*. . . . One should not mistake Malthus for nature.—Supposing, however, that this struggle exists—and it does indeed occur—its outcome is the reverse of that desired by the school of Darwin, of that which one *ought* perhaps to desire with them: namely, the defeat of the stronger, the more privileged, the more fortunate exceptions. Species do *not* grow more perfect: the weaker dominate the stronger again and again—the reason being they are the great majority, and they are also *cleverer*. . . . Darwin forgot the mind (that is English!): *the weak possess more mind*. . . . To acquire mind one must need mind—one loses it when one no longer needs it. He who possesses strength divests himself of mind (—"let it depart!" they think today in Germany, "—the *Reich* will still be ours." . . .) One will see that under mind I include foresight, patience, dissimulation, great self-control, and all that is mimicry (this last includes a great part of what is called virtue). (GD, Streifzüge eines Unzeitgemässen 14, KSA 6.120–21)

We find several themes that are familiar from Nietzsche's readings in, and dialogues with, anti-Darwinian evolutionary theorists. The disbelief in the centrality of a struggle for existence is a common conviction among those who posit alternatives to natural selection. The focus on abundance and prosperity as the motor for evolution, rather than deprivation and competition, is recognizable as Rolph's central hypothesis.[98] The opposition of strength and mind is a topic that Nietzsche found in discussions of evolution from ape to man in Rütimeyer and Baer. And the debate about perfectibility and teleology with regard to a species was a focal point for several of Nietzsche's sources, including Lange, Baer, Kölliker, Roux, and Nägeli.

There are two aspects of this passage that still require comment, however. The first is Nietzsche's strange attribution of Darwin's shortcomings to his being English. National prejudices were more common in the nineteenth century, even among the educated (and, indeed, in certain circles up to the present day), and although they rarely found their way into serious scholarly or scientific works, they were not entirely absent from Nietzsche's readings. Rolph, for example, also ascribes in part Darwin's theory of natural selection to his uncritical reception of his countryman Malthus,[99] and Eugen Dühring, whose works, as we have seen, Nietzsche read in the 1870s and 1880s, writes of a "specific English obtuseness" and "English prudery" inherent to Darwinism.[100] Although we may be tempted to dismiss these explanations as nonserious, from remarks in other writings in almost all phases of his life it appears that Nietzsche consistently regarded such factors as heritage, climate, and even diet as constitutive for intellectual positions. As we have seen previously, in the initial sections of *Beyond Good and Evil* he writes that every great philosophy is "the personal confession of its author, a kind of unintended and unwitting memoir" (JGB 6, KSA 5.19), and scattered throughout his writings are statements attributing moral and philosophical beliefs to personal—both social and somatic—and environmental circumstances. With regard to Darwin and English theorists in general, Nietzsche frequently comments that social origin and homeland have a determinative influence on their thought. The mundane views about life among English natural scientists, Nietzsche argues in apparent good faith, can be explained by their humble origins: "their ancestors were poor and undistinguished people who knew the difficulties of survival only too well at firsthand." England, because of a perceived overpopulation, contributes to an incorrect interpretation of evolutionary change by fostering the notion of privation and scarcity: "The whole of English Darwinism breathes something like the musty air of English overpopulation, like the smell of the distress and crowding of small people" (FW 349, KSA 3.585). And in the opening section of the first essay in *On the Genealogy of Morals*, Nietzsche writes of the "English psychologists," suggesting strongly that there is something in the nationality of these commentators on morality that prejudices their views.[101] Indeed, he claims that they are the "enigma," that "*they themselves are interesting*," or at least as interesting as the historical problem they are unable to solve (GM, Erste Abhandlung 1, KSA 5.257). We should be skeptical of the ad hominem arguments Nietzsche makes with regard to Darwin, but there is no indication that he did not consider these arguments to possess a level of seriousness that we would not accord them today.

The second and more important aspect of Nietzsche's "anti-Darwin" passage is his suggestion of a negative course of evolution. We have already noted that Nietzsche associated Darwin with progress, and to a certain extent, he had done so since his polemic against Strauß in 1873. But by the middle of the 1880s, as we have seen from his notebooks, Nietzsche was entertaining the notion that evolution does not mean the development of higher forms, and that therefore the survival of the fittest does not coincide with the survival of the most noble or most beautiful, and certainly not of the most preferable. We will recall also that in the late 1870s Nietzsche had expressed the view that stronger and weaker types worked together toward an improvement of the species. The stronger type, by which Nietzsche at that point meant those who had adapted best to their environment, provided stability for the community, while the weaker types, a designation for any individual that fell outside the social norm, have the potential for moving the species forward. The weaker types were either a variety that could prevail by selection or a deficiency that compelled the community to defense and overcoming of a threat. By the 1880s this symbiotic relationship had become an absolute antagonism. Moreover, Nietzsche reverses his categorization of weak and strong. The weaker types, who in human society survive owing to spirit or mind, come to dominate the stronger individuals, who are now cast as the outsiders. Indeed, this view, which contributes to Nietzsche's thoughts on decadence during the last years of his conscious life, becomes a veritable obsession for him. Repeatedly he maintains that if there is a struggle for existence, then it is not the strongest, the most beautiful, and the most genial who prevail, but the most base and common. For this reason, the species as a whole is not headed for perfection, as several non-Darwinists contended and as Darwin, in Nietzsche's view, suggests, but for mediocrity based on the lowest common denominator:

> What has surprised me most in surveying the great fate of mankind is that always what appears to my eyes is the opposite of what Darwin and Darwin's school today see or *want to* see: selection in favor of the stronger, the fitter, the progress of the species. Precisely the opposite is quite obvious: the cancellation of fortunate exceptions, the uselessness of more highly developed types, the unavoidable hegemony of the mediocre, even the less-than-mediocre types. (Nachlass 1888, 14[123], KSA 13.303)
>
> With the struggle for existence one counts on the death of the weakest beings and the survival of the most robust and most gifted; as a consequence, one imagines a *continuous growth of perfection for the species*. We have assured ourselves, in contrast, that in the struggle for life, chance benefits the weak as well as it does the strong, that cunning often supplements strength with an advantage, that the *fruitfulness* of the species stands in a remarkable rapport with the *chances for destruction*. (Nachlass 1888, 14[133], KSA 13.315)

In passages like these, Nietzsche, assuming the role of inverse social evolutionist, presents us with the identical paradox that we find in his ethical writings: noble values are subjugated to slave morality, the strong succumb to the weak, those who are fittest to survive are not the best or most desirable individuals.

We can resolve the paradoxical situation that Nietzsche describes if we consider that the strong and the genial in Nietzsche's terms are not necessarily the best suited to the exigencies of life. The weak are associated with intelligence and spirit, which enable them to overcome their natural weakness and to prevail against those who are presumably physically stronger or more genial. The "strongest and happiest are weak" (Nachlass 1888, 14[123], KSA 13.303), Nietzsche insists paradoxically, especially when these exceptional human beings have to confront the great masses with their herd instincts. In his last reflections, Nietzsche's chief difficulty with Darwinism is therefore that it does not account adequately for the very phenomena that he detects in the Europe of his own time: the decline in greatness, the destruction of genuine culture, the disappearance of exceptional figures that he calls the highest specimens or the fortunate exceptions. If the fittest have indeed prevailed, if the struggle for life has resulted in a victory for the masses, in short, if Darwin's theory has accurately predicted the dubious "progress" of Nietzsche's contemporary Europe, then Darwinism must be considered simply a biologistic apology for the decadence of the nineteenth century. "The error of Darwin's school has become a problem for me: how can one be so blind, so that precisely *here* one sees falsely? . . . That the *species* represents progress is the most unreasonable assertion in the world" (Nachlass 1888, 14[123], KSA 13.303). Nietzsche's anti-Darwinism is firmly rooted in his conviction that the mediocrity and leveling he witnessed around him are not progress and do not represent the survival of anything but the average and contemptuous—and in his hope that this mediocrity and leveling can be overcome.

The instrument that he introduced in the early 1880s to embody this overcoming was the overman; the principle operative in living beings is not natural selection, but the will to power. These notions, never fully explicated in his writings, constitute something of his evolutionary alternative, his contribution to a biologistic theory of development that would lead to something nobler and more elite than the herd that comprises nineteenth-century reality. His differences with Darwinism are thus not to be understood as a dispute about the possibility of evolution, but about the direction and goal of evolution. In this regard, his views are more radical and proactive than the biologists whom he read and from whom he learned. His belief is that the "human being as a species is not progressing. Higher types are certainly achieved, but they do not survive. The level of the species is not raised" (Nachlass 1888, 14[133], KSA 13.316). Simultaneously, he holds that the present "domestication" of the human being, the adaptation of the human being to exigencies of his contemporary society, is not a development that cannot be reversed. Beneath the surface of the tame, moral, and religious creature that populates Europe is the " 'wild' man," the genuine "return to nature" (Nachlass 1888, 14[133], KSA 13.317). Because the natural course of evolution appears to favor leveling and disadvantage geniality, Nietzsche's strategy advocates a conscious intrusion into the natural process, a willed evolution toward a higher type of human being. In a late section in his notebooks entitled "The Overman," which is the only extensive treatment of this topic outside of *Zarathustra*, Nietzsche clarifies as follows:

> I do not ask what will supersede man: rather what kind of man of higher value should be chosen, willed, *bred*. . . .
>
> Humankind does *not* represent a development to something better; or something higher; in the sense in which it is believed today: the European of the 19th century is, in his value, far inferior to the European of the Renaissance; progression in time is simply not with any necessity a raising, an increasing, a strengthening. . . .
>
> in another sense, there is a continuous *success* of individual cases in the most different places on earth and from the most various cultures; these cases indeed *represent a higher type*: something that is an "overman" in relationship to the totality of humanity. Such fortunate exceptions of great success were always possible and will perhaps always be possible. (Nachlass 1887–88, 11[413], KSA 13.191)

Whatever else it may represent philosophically, the "willed overman" in Nietzsche's thought is thus an essential element of Nietzsche's contribution to his ongoing conversation with the evolutionary biology of his times. He represents the overcoming of all that is wrong—in Nietzsche's view—with nineteenth-century society and is at once an advance over the current state of humankind and a remedy for the dubious project that evolutionary theory postulates. It is somewhat unclear how the overman will come into being, whether through the internal activity of the ubiquitous will to power or via a conscious plan among Nietzschean disciples and breeders. But Nietzsche does not appear content to entrust the appearance of the overman to the natural, evolutionary processes that have thus far achieved only mediocrity in the human race. In this sense, his thought goes beyond evolution, often involving the social engineering that is the topic to be examined in greater detail in the final chapter of this book.

Chapter 8

The Cosmological Question

The Importance of Eternal Recurrence

Along with the overman, the highlight of *Zarathustra* for most philosophical interpretations of Nietzsche's writings is the teaching of eternal recurrence, explicated most fully in the third of the four books that compose that work. Although Nietzsche presents the hypothesis of the infinite repetition of all things and events as a revelation of the early 1880s, specifically a revelation that occurred in August 1881 at his Swiss summer retreat in the Engadine, the outlines of such a conjecture concerning cosmological repetition can be traced back to his early writings. At the very least, we find an anticipation of it in the second *Untimely Meditation*, *On the Advantage and Disadvantage of History for Life* (1874), when Nietzsche poses the hypothetical question concerning how one might respond to the prospects of living or reliving the last ten or twenty years of one's life. We have seen in Chapter 1 that in *Advantage and Disadvantage*, Nietzsche was primarily concerned with various modes of historical thought, in particular in relation to the educational system and the culture of the new German Reich. In that connection, he notes that both the historical and the superhistorical would answer the question in the same manner, but for different reasons. The former answers "no," because he is a historical optimist who believes in progress: taking a look at the past, placing himself in the historical process, he optimistically looks forward to a more pleasant future. The paradox of the position taken by the historical man is clearly stated: "They [the historical men] do not know how unhistorically they think and act despite all their history, and how even their concern with historiography does not serve pure knowledge but life" (HL 1, KSA 1.255). Since by Nietzsche's definition, action is connected with a suspension of the historical, those who feel that they are spurred on to action by the past and by their optimistic vision of the future—indeed, those who act decisively in any fashion—are really unhistorical and thus implicitly repudiate the very knowledge that caused them to take action. The superhistorical men answer "no" to the same question because from their vantage point, situated above the historical process—that is, removed from the historical continuum, yet conscious of it ("as a cognitive being")—there is no distinction between past and present: "the past and the present is one and the same, that is, typically alike in all manifold variety and, as omnipresence of imperishable types, a static structure of unchanged value and eternally the same meaning" (HL 1, KSA 1.256). Thus, since the next ten or twenty years will bring nothing different from the past ten or twenty, there is no reason to relive them. Although the query posed in this early text is not identical with the "revelation" of eternal recurrence, it obviously confronts the reader with many of the same ethical considerations so prominently raised in the 1880s.

In his text from 1874, Nietzsche never answers the question for the unhistorical man, and in the penultimate aphorism in *The Gay Science* (ß341) from 1882, entitled "The Greatest Weight," he may be responding to what was omitted in his earlier text.[1] We noted when we examined the essay on history that Nietzsche exhibited a clear predilection for the unhistorical, and his affirmation of eternal recurrence is perhaps the continuation of what remained unsaid in the early 1870s, since we can surmise that the unhistorical man alone would answer the posed query in the affirmative. Like the celebrated aphorism dealing with the death of God (ß125), which is contained in the third section of *The Gay Science*, "The Greatest Weight" is also formulated as a narrative, although it is less developed than the account of the madman who announces God's death in the marketplace. Complicating any interpretation of Nietzsche's thought is that the proclamation of eternal recurrence is presented as a hypothetical:

> What, if some day or night a demon were to steal after you into your loneliest loneliness and say to you: "This life as you now live it and have lived it, you will have to live once more and innumerable times more; and there will be nothing new in it, but every pain and every joy and every thought and sigh and everything unutterably small or great in your life will have to return to you, all in the same succession and sequence—even this spider and this moonlight between the trees, and even this moment and I myself. The eternal hourglass of existence is turned upside down again and again, and you with it, speck of dust!"

Nietzsche gives two alternative reactions to the hypothesis of eternal recurrence: the first is a reaction of extreme despair, involving gnashing of teeth and the cursing of the demon who has announced this terrible fate. This inappropriate response suggests that the person who would react in this fashion exhibits an inability to accept his fate, and his response is tantamount to a rejection of his own existence. The second reaction is an affirmation of the divinity of such a grand thought, and it is obviously preferable. In Nietzsche's view, the hypothesis of eternal recurrence—or, more accurately, the acceptance of this hypothesis—

has the power to transform the individual because it places the heaviest weight on human action. It can potentially lead to a radically different self-understanding, for one would have to be well disposed toward oneself in order to *"crave nothing more fervently than this ultimate eternal confirmation and seal"* (FW 341, KSA 3.570). In terms of personal behavior and action, the stakes that Nietzsche sets are extremely high; eternal recurrence has ramifications for the core of our very being.

In *The Gay Science*, Nietzsche's introduction of the notion of "eternal recurrence" can hardly be considered the direct positing of a hypothesis, or even the disclosure of a revelation. It is phrased rhetorically as a hypothetical question, and therefore represents an intermediary stage between its appearance in the second *Untimely Meditation* and its completely developed form in *Zarathustra*. It occurs in the later work in the second section of volume three, which bears the title "On the Vision and the Riddle." At this point in the loose narrative of the book, Zarathustra is aboard a ship, and after two days' silence he deigns to speak to his comrades, relating to them a riddle. He tells of walking upward on a rocky path, when his devil, half dwarf and half mole, dripped lead into his ear. The lead is the statement that what goes up must come down. "O Zarathustra, far indeed have you thrown the stone, but it will fall back on yourself," says the "spirit of gravity" [*Geist der Schwere*] (Za III, Vom Gesicht und Räthsel 2, KSA 4.197–98). After the dwarf falls silent, and silence reigns for a long time, Zarathustra finally bursts out his reply, more or less a challenge to his interlocutor: "Dwarf! It is you or I!" And he continues: "But I am the stronger of us two: you do not know my abysmal thought. That you could not bear!" The thought Zarathustra hides within him is the hypothesis of eternal recurrence. He relates it to the dwarf (and hence to the reader) as a parable:

> Behold this gateway, dwarf! . . . It has two faces. Two paths meet here; no one has yet followed either to its end.
>
> This long lane stretches back for an eternity. And the long lane out there, that is another eternity.
>
> They contradict each other, these paths; they offend each other face to face; and it is here at this gateway that they come together. The name of the gateway is inscribed above "Moment."
>
> But whoever would follow one of them, on and on, farther and farther—do you believe, dwarf, that these paths contradict each other eternally? (Za III, Vom Gesicht und Räthsel 2, KSA 4.199–200)

The dwarf tries to interpret this parable in a simple fashion, claiming that all truth is crooked and time is circular. But Zarathustra rejects this simplistic interpretation, believing that his own thoughts are more profound and more momentous:

"Behold," I continued, "this moment! From this gateway, Moment, a long, eternal lane leads *backward*: behind us lies an eternity.

Must not whatever *can* walk have walked on this lane before? Must not whatever *can* happen have happened, have been done, have passed by before?

And if everything has been there before—what do you think, dwarf, of this moment? Must not this gateway too have been there before?

And are not all things knotted together so firmly that this moment draws after it *all* that is to come? *Therefore*—itself too?

For whatever *can* walk—in this long lane *out there* too, it *must walk* once more.

And this low spider, which crawls in the moonlight, and this moonlight itself, and I and you in the gateway, whispering together, whispering of eternal things—must not all of us have been there before?

And return and walk in that other lane, out there, before us, in this long dreadful lane—must we not eternally return?" (Za III, Vom Gesicht und Räthsel 2, KSA 4.200)

No commentary accompanies this discussion of eternal return. In *Zarathustra* there is no exploration of the ramifications of eternal recurrence for our lives, no reference to a correct and an incorrect manner of dealing with this hypothesis. The text continues with the tale of the black snake in the throat of the young shepherd. But this portion of the parabolic narration relates less to the doctrine of eternal recurrence than to Zarathustra as the possessor of the doctrine.

No matter how we as readers may evaluate the postulation of eternal recurrence, it is clear that Nietzsche was fascinated by it and, at times, obsessed with it. Unusual about eternal recurrence, but consistent with many other concepts in Nietzsche's philosophy, is that he provides no detailed exposition of it. Over the past century, the coherence in this concept has been supplied by one or another philosopher interpreting Nietzsche, which perhaps accounts for the frequent disputes among exegetes. These two passages in Nietzsche's published writings are the only ones where eternal recurrence is treated in any sort of detail, and both are curious—if we compare them with the philosophical tradition—because they avoid the typical language of philosophical exposition. The passage from *The Gay Science* consists of a series of unanswered questions, while the excerpt from *Zarathustra* is part of a narrative within a narrative, recalled by the eponymous hero of the book. Although in his writings recurrence is expressed less as a certainty than as a thought experiment or hypothesis, it appears Nietzsche came to consider it a plausible account that, as we shall see, even accorded well with scientific evidence. Certainly Nietzsche believed that its implications were enormous. In his notebooks from the 1880s, we find frequent reference to the doctrine and its importance for humanity. It is tantamount to a new enlightenment, and in 1883 Nietzsche comments that "the teaching of eternal recurrence is the *turning point in history*" (Nachlass 1883, 16[49], KSA 10.515). Other notebook entries indicate that Nietzsche believed the Greeks knew about recurrence, but sought to conceal or disguise this knowledge in a shroud of mystery. Eternal recurrence emerges in his later thought as the quintessential Dionysian myth, and, accordingly, in *Twilight of the Idols*, Nietzsche declares himself to be "the last disciple of the philosopher Dionysus,—I, the teacher of eternal recurrence" (GD, Was ich den Alten verdanke 5, KSA 6.160). The brevity of Nietzsche's comments, especially in works other than *Zarathustra*, is deceptive; the doctrine was so central to his thinking that he frequently sketched the idea of composing an entire work on "Eternal Recurrence"—although we should remember that his notebooks are filled with prospective projects that never came to fruition. One sketch has the general title "Eternal Recurrence" with the following sections: "The New Sincere Ones" (*Die neuen Wahrhaftigen*), "Beyond Good and Evil," "The Hidden Artists," "The Self-Overcoming of Man," and "The Hammer and the Great Midday" (Nachlass 1884, 27[82], KSA 11.296) Another sketch has a narrative voice proclaiming Nietzsche—or perhaps a figure representing his views—as "the teacher of eternal recurrence. That is: I teach that all things recur eternally and you with them—, and that you have been here already countless times and all things with you; I teach that there is a great, long, enormous year of becoming, that, when it has run its course, ends like an hourglass again and again reversed: so that all these years are the same in the smallest and largest things" (Nachlass 1884, 25[7], KSA 11.10). Many of these book projects are found in notebooks from 1884 at the time of the writing and publishing of the third part of *Zarathustra*. But Nietzsche obviously regarded this topic as important right until the end of his sane existence. We find the prospective title "Eternal Recurrence: Zarathustra's Dances and Processions by Friedrich Nietzsche" as the penultimate entry in a notebook from the summer of 1888 (Nachlass 1888, 20[167], KSA 13.577), just months before the outbreak of insanity. Indeed, the seriousness with which Nietzsche treated his project of eternal recurrence is indicated by his inclusion of the title "Eternal Recurrence" as a forthcoming book, along with "The Will to Power" and "Songs of Prince Vogelfrei," on the title page of *On the Genealogy of Morals*. Although it is mentioned infrequently in published texts, from the emphasis it receives in the notebooks and its prominence when it is discussed, it is very likely that Nietzsche considered eternal recurrence to be an important revelation and a major part of his philosophy.

Ancient and Contemporary Discourses of Recurrence

While it is relatively easy to determine that Nietzsche considered "eternal recurrence" a pivotal doctrine, it is somewhat less certain what he actually meant by it.

Because it is never discussed at length and appears infrequently in published writings, it retains a certain amount of ambiguity that has generated a great deal of divergent critical commentary. Bernd Magnus calls it his most difficult, his most obscure, and his most controversial teaching.[2] It has been viewed as a mystical hypothesis akin to a new religion, a contradictory postulate marked by inconsistencies and confusions, and a piece of dogmatic metaphysics that nevertheless can reveal an existential truth. It does not appear to have been taken very seriously by critics until the 1930s, when Martin Heidegger (1889–1976) made it a central theme in his lectures on Nietzsche, and Heidegger's student, Karl Löwith (1897–1973), from his Italian exile wrote a book dedicated to the topic.[3] For Heidegger eternal recurrence formed an inherent unity with the notions of will to power and the transvaluation of values, but he ultimately regards it as one more indication of Nietzsche's fundamental inability to escape the Western tradition of metaphysics. Löwith views eternal recurrence from the perspective of Nietzsche's diagnosis of the nineteenth century as an age of nihilism; recurrence, along with the will to power, is Nietzsche's answer to man's predicament in a world stripped of its divine origins. Both Heidegger's and Löwith's concern with recurrence were relatively unknown until after the war: Heidegger's lectures were collected and appeared only in 1961, while Löwith's book, published in Berlin in 1935, was not widely distributed because of political considerations in the Third Reich. The views of Heidegger and Löwith mark, however, a turning point in the discussion of the formerly neglected doctrine of eternal recurrence. Once it was taken seriously as a philosophical notion, eternal recurrence became increasingly regarded as a postulate that has ontological, ethical, or metaphysical dimensions, and it has remained a centerpiece for exegetically accomplished critics ever since. As we have already seen, Nietzsche's own discussions in his published writings are suggestive for philosophical interpretation: he repeatedly affirms that the belief in his doctrine will significantly alter our way of understanding ourselves in relationship to the world, to other human beings, and to our ultimate purpose on earth.

At the same time, it is obvious that eternal recurrence contains implications for a possible Nietzschean cosmology, and that it is not devoid of connections with natural science. Indeed, several early Nietzsche scholars who considered this doctrine emphasized its relationship to theories of the physical universe developed during the nineteenth century. The growing tendency in the twentieth century for "genuine" philosophical interpretations to exclude mundane considerations contained in findings of the natural sciences has led to a virtual divorce between Nietzsche's context, which was informed primarily by discoveries and theories of the physical universe, and Nietzsche's putative value for philosophy, which ignores or even deprecates as inessential anything but existential, ontological, or ethical concerns. We should not forget that Nietzsche's readings in the very years he posited eternal recurrence consisted of many books written by scientists, or by philosophers who drew on the natural sciences for their philosophical outlook. Once again we find that Heidegger contributed enormously to the neglect of the natural sciences in Nietzsche studies by establishing rigid parameters for valid philosophical discussions. In the previous chapter we saw that he sought to exclude recent discoveries in biology and evolution from interpretations of Nietzsche, and he considers the physical sciences of similar, nugatory worth. Objecting tacitly to a 1936 article by Oskar Becker (1889–1964), which dealt with the scientific dimensions of Nietzsche's doctrine of eternal recurrence,[4] Heidegger seeks to clarify the "evidentiary procedure" pertaining to the "natural sciences."[5] He asks rhetorically: "What is 'scientific' about it?" and responds laconically: "nothing at all."[6] He argues that investigations of natural scientists may employ terms that are similar to the notions found in Nietzsche's discussions (force/energy, space, motion, time, becoming), but that science and genuine philosophy remain separated by an insuperable barrier. The natural sciences can employ concepts, but they are unable to ask what these concepts really mean, since the natural sciences have no access to fundamental questions concerning their own status or the status of the terms they use. "To ask what a science is, is *to ask a question* that is no longer a *scientific* question," Heidegger reasons; the realm in which such essential matters are raised is the realm of philosophy.[7] A science can become philosophical only by approximating thinking appropriate to philosophy, or by searching back to its origins, which lead it to foundational concerns. This dismissal of the importance of natural science for Nietzsche dominated scholarly commentary until the last decade of the twentieth century, when some scholars again began to recognize that Nietzsche, as we have seen repeatedly in this study, was responding less to the great philosophical tradition than to more worldly issues and theories raised in writings of his contemporaries.

The inference from Heidegger's argument is clear. Nietzsche cannot have been dealing with the natural sciences since his type of inquiry is fundamental, rather than empirical or related specifically to one of the specialized branches of scientific inquiry. Thus Heidegger can state unequivocally: "Nietzsche did not stray into the natural sciences. Rather, the natural science that was contemporary to him drifted dubiously into a dubious philosophy."[8] In making this claim, Heidegger is thinking either unhistorically or too categorically. While it is certainly true that several natural scientists in Nietzsche's time included philosophical speculation concerning the matters they were investigating, there is nothing unusual about these speculations, and they should not be demeaned as violations of some sacred and self-proclaimed boundary: scientific and philosophical thinking are inseparably linked in the Western tradition, and Heidegger must have been aware of their intimate connection in the long history of thought. By relegating all philosophical understanding to a level that is more fundamental than anything conceived by natural science, Heidegger separates two realms that most philosophers in the nineteenth century—and certainly in previous centuries—would have regarded as mutually reinforcing. Certainly Nietzsche's frequent concerns with his need to acquire more complete knowledge in the sciences, and his awareness of his deficiencies in physics, chemistry, and biology, speak more for the importance of science in Nietzsche's own mind than Heidegger's imputation of his purity as a "philosopher" separated from all considerations in natural science. Heidegger concludes his argument by stating that since Nietzsche did not restrict his comments to issues pertaining to the sciences, his writings are not really dealing with science at all. He cites a note written in preparation for the composition of Zarathustra: "everything has returned; Sirius and the spider and your thoughts during this past hour and this very thought of yours, that everything recurs" (Nachlass 1881, 11[206], KSA 9.524), and comments decisively with a final question: "Since when are 'thoughts' and 'hours' objects of physics or biology?"[9] It is difficult to treat this comment seriously as an argument. Heidegger, convinced that Nietzsche is preoccupied with "the totality of beings" in much the same way that he himself was, reduces his references to the rich array of scientific thought in his published writings and notebooks to a parochial project that ignores Nietzsche's actual practices and concerns. Heidegger's exclusion of science from any place in Nietzsche's intellectual universe is absolute, and it has been followed, to the detriment of an understanding of Nietzsche's real concerns, by many subsequent and prominent interpreters. But Heidegger finalizes his divorce proceedings only by starting with a preconceived, dogmatic notion of what Nietzsche must actually be doing and then by disregarding what Nietzsche himself considered of utmost importance for his writing and development. It would be foolish to reduce Nietzsche's remarks on eternal recurrence to their relationship to the natural sciences of his times; recurrence was not a scientific postulate and was certainly not meant to be solely a contribution to the scientific speculation about the universe in the nineteenth century. But it would be equally foolish to insist that Nietzsche's preoccupation with eternal recurrence had nothing to do with the scientific knowledge of the nineteenth century, that it did not draw on scientific theories, and that it was not formulated in conversation with scientists and scientifically inclined philosophers writing in his era.

If we examine the written evidence, we find that Nietzsche was familiar with notions of eternal recurrence before he came to realize in the early 1880s that there was a scientific discourse that possibly underscores its importance. Commentators have frequently noted that in the ancient world Nietzsche would have encountered several sources for his revealed doctrine, and Nietzsche's growing disapprobation of Christianity, which promulgates an eschatological worldview, and with notions of progress in lay discourse and German idealism in the nineteenth century made recurrence an attractive alternative. Heraclitus, whose name appears in Nietzsche's earliest writings from the 1870s, is certainly a likely nonscientific influence on his thought, although in the sixth century BC, it is not at all clear that we can separate the cosmological reflections of Heraclitus from natural scientific speculation of his day. His claim that the world has no beginning, but has always existed, and his emphasis on becoming and change bring him into proximity of Nietzsche's later doctrine. Indeed, in a retrospective discussion of *The Birth of Tragedy* in *Ecce Homo*, Nietzsche concedes that Zarathustra's important revelation "*could*" have been formulated by Heraclitus, but he places special emphasis on the hypothetical and counterfactual nature of his statement. Portraying himself as the first philosopher of tragic wisdom, Nietzsche excludes pre-Socratic influences and affirms only an affinity of concern. Similarly, Nietzsche downplays the effect Stoic philosophers had on his thought, especially their pantheistic materialism, by admitting only that they inherited their major ideas from Heraclitus, and that their philosophy "shows traces" of eternal recurrence (EH, Warum ich so gute Bücher schreibe, Die Geburt der Tragödie 3, KSA 6.312–13). Mihailo Djurić has asked with some justification why Nietzsche never mentions the Pythagoreans in this context, since in *On the Advantage and Disadvantage of History for Life*, he ascribes to them something very similar to recurrence: "Fundamentally what was possible once could only be possible a second time if the Pythagoreans were right in believing that with the same conjunction of the heavenly bodies the same events had to be repeated on earth down to the minutest detail" (HL 2, KSA 1.261).[10] In a note from the 1870s, Nietzsche connects Pythagoras and the Pythagoreans with recurrence [*Wiederkehr*] (Nachlass 1872–73, 19[134], KSA 7.462; 1873, 29[108], KSA 681), but neither of these references appears to have had a significant impact on Nietzsche at the time, and he certainly never includes any of the philosophers or philosophical schools of antiquity as decisive for his later formulation of eternal recurrence. From the non-Western world, Nietzsche could have encountered several doctrines that resonate with his notion of eternal recurrence.[11] Outside of the aforementioned nod toward Heraclitus and the Stoics, however, Nietzsche admits no other forerunners for his revelatory thought.

Scholars of nineteenth-century thought, however, would have no difficulty pointing to illustrious predecessors who articulated ideas nearly identical to Nietzsche's eternal recurrence. At around the time of Nietzsche's death, Henri Lichtenberger (1864–1941) had already noted that recurrence was a topic found in the writings of Heinrich Heine (1797–1856).[12] Specifically, Lichtenberger pointed to a passage composed in the year 1826 or 1827 and included among fragmentary remains connected with Heine's *Journey from Munich to Genoa* (1828), the first piece in his third volume of his *Travel Pictures*, although the motifs in the passage are more reminiscent of an earlier *Travel Picture, Ideas: The Book of Le Grand* (1826). This passage did not find its way into the final edition of either work and was published only after Heine's death in 1869 in a book edited by Adolf Strodtmann (1829–1879), Heine's first biographer and editor, entitled *Last Poems and Thoughts of H. Heine*. Although Elisabeth Förster-Nietzsche (1846–1935) claimed that Nietzsche had this book in his possession, it was not recorded in Max Oehler's (1875–1946) inventory of Nietzsche's library from 1942, but it is included in the latest, and most authoritative, compilation of books he owned.[13] It is quite possible that Nietzsche read and admired this passage if he was indeed in possession of the volume. There is sufficient evidence that Nietzsche, like most intellectuals of the nineteenth century, was acquainted with Heine's writings, and we have indications that he knew some of his works very early on. In a few notebook entries from the 1870s, he speaks of him in rather derogatory terms, calling him a *farceur* (Nachlass 1873, 27[29], KSA 7.595; 1876, 15[10], 8.281), connecting him with Edward von Hartmann as an unwitting self-ironist (Nachlass 1873, 29[67], KSA 7.659), and coupling him with Hegel as a corrupter of the German language (Nachlass 1873, 27[38], KSA 7.598). These notes, however, were composed while Nietzsche was still under the influence of nationalist sentiments and Wagnerian tutelage, so that he was preconditioned to malign Heine, the Jew[14] who had resided in Paris and who was frequently contrasted with the "genuine" representative of the German spirit, Johann Wolfgang von Goethe (1749–1832). In his later writings, Nietzsche changes his attitude completely with regard to Heine. By 1880, he credits him with having "something pure" about him (Nachlass 1880, 7[40], KSA 9.326); in *Beyond Good and Evil* and *Ecce Homo*, Nietzsche praises his lyrics (JGB 254, KSA 5.198; EH, Warum ich so klug bin 4, KSA 6.286), and in several published passages, he refers to him in an extremely complimentary fashion as one of the first true Europeans (JGB 256, KSA 5.202; GD, Was den Deutschen abgeht 4, KSA 6.107; GD, Streifzüge eines Unzeitgemässen 21, KSA 6.125); in *Ecce Homo*, Nietzsche even identifies Heine as his stylistic equal: "It will one day be said that Heine and I have been by far the first artists of the German language" (EH, Warum ich so klug bin 4, KSA 6.286). At no point in his published writings or his notebooks, however, does Nietzsche mention Heine in connection with eternal recurrence or any related matter.

Regardless of whether or not Nietzsche read Heine's passage on recurrence, its existence is indicative for the unexceptional nature of Nietzsche's later revelation. Nietzsche may have claimed a special status for his vision in 1881, but he shared his thought with many writers of the nineteenth century, not to mention classical antiquity. The context of Heine's remarks is one of his many poses as a lover of a deceased woman. In this passage, his poetic persona is the knight of the falling star, mourning for his lost love Maria and recalling a time when he observed her hand playing the piano. As he watches, he comments: "I died, I lived, and died again, eternities rushed past me," and, after scolding her for her coldness toward him, she responds: "Pardon me, I was very naughty." Heine comments as follows:

> What I have told you here, dear reader, is not even from yesterday or the day before yesterday; that is a primeval story, and millennia, many thousand millennia will roll by before it receives a conclusion, a good conclusion. For time is infinite. But the things in time are finite; they can be dispersed in the smallest particles, but these particles, the atoms, have their determinate number, and determinate is also the number of configurations that God himself built from them. No matter how much time goes by, according to the eternal combinatory laws governing this eternal play of repetition, all configurations that once existed again appear, and meet, attract, repulse, kiss, and corrupt each other again, as they did before. And so it will happen, that again a man will be born, just like me, and a woman will be born, just like Maria, only the man's brain may contain a bit less foolishness than mine does now—and they will meet in a better country, and observe each other for a long time, and the woman will extend her hand to the man and say with a tender voice: "Pardon me, I was very naughty."[15]

Unlike Nietzsche, Heine obviously treats recurrence playfully, not as a terrifying and momentous revelation; the repetition that he imagines revolves, as it frequently does in his early writings, around an unhappy love affair whose anguish he is compelled to experience throughout eternity. The thought of all things occurring again is integrated into Heine's arsenal of romantic motifs, and it is likely that Heine, like many of his contemporaries, was influenced in his thinking about recurrence by discoveries in Sanskrit philosophy by Friedrich Schlegel (1772–1829). But it is also quite probable that Heine, like Nietzsche a half century later, was affected by the scientific thought of his day. In particular, his reference to atomic structure and the circular path of all natural occurrences is reminiscent of the materialist Baron d'Holbach's (1723–1789) *System of Nature* from 1770, a work with which Heine was very likely familiar.[16] Quite obviously Heine did not experience recurrence and its implications as a great weight or an iron law—he even hopes in contradictory fashion for a favorable conclusion to the story after many thousand millennia, as well as a bit less foolishness attached to his own person—but the formulation in this passage resembles closely that of his later admirer, captivated by a very similar notion in the Engadine region of Switzerland in 1881.

Heine and Nietzsche were hardly unique in their enthusiasm for the hypothesis of recurrence. In 1872 the socialist activist and elected president of the Paris Commune, Auguste Blanqui (1805–1881), published a similar thought in a text entitled *L'éternité par les astres* [*Eternity Through the Stars*]. Arrested in March of 1871 for his participation in the uprising, he composed his work in prison, including in it his conviction that what he was doing was part of a cycle that would be repeated into eternity: "What I am writing in this moment in a prison cell in the fort of Taureau, I have written and will write for all eternity on a table, with a pen, in these clothes, under these circumstances exactly the same. . . . The universe repeats itself without end and prances in place. Eternity plays imperturbably and infinitely the same images."[17] Blanqui's inspiration for his version of eternal recurrence is more openly scientific than Heine's. In particular he focuses his discussion on two major scientific achievements: spectral analysis, which establishes a finite number of elements that make up the entire universe, and the cosmology of Pierre-Simon de Laplace (1749–1827), whose writings on comets and on the nebular origins of the universe merited special attention. But Blanqui would also have been able to draw on other, more recent developments in science for support, for example, from discoveries in thermodynamics that demonstrated the conservation of energy. In essence, his notion of eternal recurrence involves the assumption of infinite time combined with a constant, never diminishing, never increasing amount of material. On the level of the cosmos, the problem he confronts is how to explain the disappearance and reappearance of heavenly bodies. The stars, he reasons, are only ephemeral phenomena; they will eventually die out. However, if they do not re-illuminate, then the universe is condemned to perpetual darkness. He conjectures, therefore, a "counter-shock" that will recharge the stars and restore them to their former intensity.[18] Blanqui thus, like Nietzsche, seeks to explain "eternal recurrence" on a cosmological scale; his theory of the entire universe posits the extinguishing of stars, their collapse and reinvigoration, and, in adaptation of Laplace's nebular hypothesis, the appearance again of numerous solar systems as the result of the contracting and cooling of large, flattened, and slowly rotating clouds of incandescent gas.

If Blanqui had simply proposed that the universe will recur again exactly as it now exists, his theory would be identical to Nietzsche's, merely anticipating it by a decade.[19] Blanqui, however, speculated further than mere recurrence. Positing that space is infinite, he reasons that the hundred elements must be configured in a great number of different combinations in different stellar-planetary systems, but that the number, as large as it may be, is still finite. Moreover, nature, he claims, has a definite uniformity; it is not infinitely creative and original in each case. In the various stellar systems that form, one must be able to observe specific regularities, determined by the finite number of elements and the immutable laws of gravitation. The similarity in the formation of stars means for Blanqui a fraternal similarity in the constitution of solar systems, which approaches identity. Blanqui conceives of each solar system as distinct and proceeding at its own pace. Thus he can postulate that at every instant there are a myriad of systems that are reviving, dying, and beginning to form planets. At that same instant, however, there will also be a myriad of solar systems that are identical to each other. For that reason, he argues that at every moment there are duplicates of our own world, exact replicas that develop from a nebular mass identical to the one that formed our solar system. In these systems, we would find copies of the people, animals, objects, and events on our earth. In each of these simultaneously existing worlds, Blanqui believes that the course of events is not determined, only the final outcome, which is the inevitable death of the globe. Thus there will be duplicate situations that then diverge from ours, and series of occurrences that duplicate the same exact course that they follow in our world. "Our earth, just as the other celestial bodies, is the *repetition* of a *primordial* combination that always reproduces itself in the same way, and that exists simultaneously in billions of identical exemplars."[20] The implications for each individual human being are evident: "Each human being possesses in the expanse an endless number of doubles who live his life, absolutely as he himself lives it. He is infinite and eternal in the body of others himself, not only of his actual age, but of all his ages. At every moment, he has simultaneously billions of twins who are born, and others who die, others whose ages are spread out from second to second from his birth right to his death."[21] Blanqui goes beyond the hypothesis of mere recurrence by drawing consequences from the finite number of elements, the infinite time and space in which these elements exist, the necessary similarities in the formation of solar systems, and the finite combinations in which elements can be arranged. Not only does everything repeat infinitely; every possible combination of elements, and therefore everything that has ever happened or will happen occurs somewhere in the universe, indeed, in numerous places, at every moment. Blanqui thus hypothesizes a more literal notion of eternal *occurrence*, not simply the repetition of the same occurrences in one continuous cycle.

A further illustration that demonstrates the widespread speculation on eternal recurrence by Nietzsche's contemporaries is supplied in an early work of Gustav Le Bon (1841–1931). Today Le Bon is remembered primarily for his book *The Psychology of the Crowd* (1895), and if Sigmund Freud (1856–1939) had not made extensive reference to this study in his *Mass Psychology and Ego Analysis* (1921), it too would very likely not have survived the test of time. In his own era, however, Le Bon had considerable renown, even if his views were somewhat controversial. Hailed as "one of the foremost men of science in Europe"[22] in his *New York Times* obituary in 1931, he was something of a polymath, publishing in a wide range of fields over a career that spanned more than half a century. Equally versed in the physical, the biological, and the social sciences, he wrote presciently of nuclear energy in the first decade of the twentieth century; he discussed in various works the advance, but also the inherent deficiencies, in socialism; and he explored the lineage and development of humankind in their biological and social formations. In one of his earlier writings from 1881, the two-volume *L'homme et les sociétés: leur origines et leur histoire* [*Man and Societies: Their Origins and Their History*], Le Bon devoted himself to an exploration of how the human being emerges from an animal state and then sketches a social and cultural history of human society. Controversial among his conclusions is the biological determinism that he ascribes to development: each generation is able to add something to what it has inherited, but its additions are minimal when compared with the weight of its ancestors. These conclusions, derived from the evolutionary discourse of his times, very likely influenced his socio-political views on the impossibility of a radical restructuring of society, the inherent inequality of races, which will lead inevitably to the demise of inferior types, and the augmentation of distinctions between higher and lower classes within a given society. In some regards, Le Bon occupied the position of an "untimely meditator" in expressing convictions that offended the more widespread liberalism and progressivism in Western Europe.

Significant for the context of eternal recurrence is that Le Bon, at the very close of his lengthy treatise on human and social development, includes ruminations that disclose his views on cosmology. There are few general laws applicable to all peoples, Le Bon muses, but one can be certain that everything living, whether it be a society or a planet, will go through a cycle of birth, growth, decline, and death. Astronomers have already described the demise of the earth as a gradual cooling process that will leave the surface desolated and without any form of life. But Le Bon, like Blanqui in the previous decade, calls on three principles that are very similar to his countryman's to ground a theory of recurrence: infinite time, which he takes as a fact that needs no further proof; a finite number of elements; and a hypothesis that the solar system will regenerate itself through either a cosmic shock or some other method of rejuvenation. Eventually Le Bon believes that a new nebula will form and by means of a series of evolutions similar to what has taken place in the past, a new world will appear, which will in turn develop, decline, and die. The world will be similar to or exactly like our own world because it contains the identical elements:

> If the same elements from each world serve in the reconstruction of others after its destruction, it is easy to understand that the same combinations, that is, the same worlds inhabited by the same beings will have to repeat themselves many times. The possible combinations that a given number of atoms are able to form are limited, while time is not; all forms possible from development have been necessarily realized for a long time, and we are only able to repeat the combinations that have already been attained.
> ... Like Sisyphus always rolling the same rock, we repeat interminably the same task without ever being able to put an end to it.[23]

At about the same time that Nietzsche was experiencing his revelation about eternal recurrence in the Swiss mountains in August 1881, Le Bon was publishing a coda to his cultural history of humankind, which contains essentially the same doctrine.

Early Reflections and Encounters with Recurrence

Le Bon's discussion of recurrence is included as a brief codicil at the close of an enormously ambitious text. It indicates, however, like Heine's and Blanqui's reflections on this issue, that the ancient cosmological notion of a repetition of all things had nineteenth-century versions based in developments in the natural sciences. Recent scientific advances likewise reinforced Nietzsche's early acquaintance with recurrence in his classical studies. In Nietzsche's case, however, and in contrast to both Le Bon and Blanqui, the cosmogony associated with the Kant-Laplace hypothesis and the establishment of a finite number of elements in the universe did not appear to have a significant impact on his thinking. Indeed, there is but a single reference to "Laplace-Kant" in Nietzsche's notebooks, and it is clear that Nietzsche is ill-disposed toward this theory—he writes "Against Laplace-Kant"—since he appears to believe that it conflicts with his notion of the incessant struggle between atoms for supremacy, which may result in an aggregation or a disaggregation of atoms—although Nietzsche hastens to add that he is against the absolute concept "atom." The note is short and cryptic, but directly prior to mentioning Laplace-Kant, he writes that force or energy is continual (Nachlass 1885, 43[2], KSA 11.701). The atomic aggregation and disaggregation he postulates and the ubiquitous continuity of force would appear to relate to the will to power, and thus he dismisses the Laplace-Kant nebular hypothesis as a theory that is not broad enough to encompass the real, underlying reasons for the formation of solar systems. More attractive in general for Nietzsche, as we shall see in more detail in a later section, are theories that deal abstractly with force or energy,[24] and we find in Nietzsche's notebooks, especially from the 1880s, that the recently developed theories concerning the conservation of energy were of primary importance in his discussions of recurrence. Known today as the first law of thermodynamics, the proposition that energy could not be lost or created was first formulated in the middle of the century. Although James Prescott Joule (1818–1889) is usually credited with the authorship of this principle, in Germany it was widely associated with Julius Robert Mayer (1814–1878), a physicist whose writings Nietzsche read at the instigation of his friend Heinrich Köselitz in the early 1880s.[25]

It is likely, however, that Nietzsche's acquaintance with Mayer's theories, which occurred when he was formulating his hypothesis of eternal recurrence, was mediated secondhand in the 1860s and 1870s by Friedrich Albert Lange's (1828–1875) *History of Materialism*, which was the chief source for Nietzsche's scientific knowledge, especially in the early period of his creative activity. In the second edition of his work, Lange mentions Mayer as the discoverer of the equivalence of heat,[26] although he does not introduce Mayer for his cosmological speculations about the origins and potential regeneration of the universe in the section in which he discusses the conservation of energy. In general, Lange is less interested in the first law of thermodynamics than in matter in its relationship to force, perhaps because, as a historian of materialism, he is more focused on discussions of the materialist tradition of the nineteenth century. Thus Ludwig Büchner (1824–1899), whose book *Force and Matter* (1855) was immensely important for the materialist tradition in the middle of the century, and who is discussed extensively in Lange's work, sought to establish the indestructability of matter, which is likened to the noumenal realm, while force or energy is something observable or detectable and similar to the phenomenal. Or, as Lange expresses it, "in our contemporary natural sciences everywhere matter is the unknown, while force is known. If one wanted to say instead of force 'property of the material,' then one would have to be careful of circular reasoning." In his extended discussion of matter and force,[27] Lange is less interested in the conservation of energy (which he calls force) than in the dispute between dogmatic materialists and those who believe that matter and force cannot be conceived apart from each other. Thus he concedes that dogmatic materialist philosophers have exhibited a reluctance to adopt the theory,[28] but includes a long citation from a pamphlet by Hermann von Helmholtz (1821–1894), "On the Conservation of Energy," in which the author argues that

> the ideas of matter and force, as applied to nature, *can never be separated*. Pure matter would be indifferent to the rest of nature, because it could never determine any change in nature or in our sense organs; pure force would be something that must *be*, and yet again not *be, because we call the existent thing matter*. It is just as inaccurate to try and explain matter as something real, and force as a mere notion to which nothing real corresponds; both are rather abstractions from the real, formed in exactly the same way. We can perceive matter only through its forces, never in itself.[29]

Lange's own position on this controversy is equivocal, and he winds up concluding that with regard to the nature of matter and force, we may have reached the "limit of natural knowledge."[30] As we know, Nietzsche was on a very different path, rejecting dogmatic materialism and its mechanistic explanations and moving toward a notion of pure force or energy or, as he comes to formulate it in his later writings, "will to power." Lange thus provides some insight for Nietzsche into the first law of thermodynamics and to controversies about force and matter, but ultimately his work on materialism was more useful for its information than for its solution to problems that Nietzsche confronted in the 1880s.

We can be certain, however, that Nietzsche took an interest in the conservation of energy, which became a central scientific pillar supporting eternal recurrence, even before it figured in his revelation of 1881 and in subsequent references in his notebooks. In 1874, Balfour Stewart (1828–1887), a professor of natural history at Owens College in Manchester, dedicated a book to *The Conservation of Energy*, and a German version appeared in the Brockhaus publishing house the following year.[31] Stewart's activity in Manchester very likely brought him into contact with Joule, a scientist whose wealth allowed him to work from his home in Manchester, but who maintained close ties to Owens College. In 1847 Joule's lecture in the reading room of St. Anne's Church in Manchester announced the theory of the conservation of energy and the mechanical equivalence of heat, so that Manchester was something of the center of thought on the first law of thermodynamics when Stewart arrived in 1870. Stewart's book is not a research monograph, but rather a summary of developments and therefore just the sort of work Nietzsche required to keep himself current with recent trends in this area of scientific endeavor. In the summer of 1875, Nietzsche obviously obtained the translation of Stewart's book, and his copy is found today in his library in Weimar. There are no marginal comments in this monograph, although it is very possible that he read the book in its entirety. We do find extensive passages that he excerpted for his notebooks, but these occur only in the first chapter, which deals with the definition of energy and work (Nachlass 1875, 9[2], KSA 8.181–85). Even from these few notebook entries, however, the implications about the conservation of energy are clearly drawn: for every action there is an equal reaction, equal in terms of the energy lost and gained. Nietzsche does not incorporate in his published writings in the mid-1870s any indication of his interests in the physical sciences; at the time he read Stewart he was busy preparing his fourth *Untimely Meditation* on *Richard Wagner in Bayreuth*. Cultural regeneration was still clearly his main focus. But his early enthusiasm for Lange and his preoccupation with Stewart demonstrate that even before he articulated his doctrine of eternal recurrence, he had sufficient acquaintance with a portion of the natural scientific evidence that would later bolster his claims.

Perhaps just as important for Nietzsche in the years prior to his revelation were the philosophical implications that others drew from recent theories in physics and cosmology. In Arthur Schopenhauer's (1788–1860) *World as Will and Representation* (1819, 1844, 1859), he had already encountered a brief philosophical aside that suggested something like recurrence. At the beginning of his fourth book, Schopenhauer contrasts historical knowledge, which deals with the "whence, whither, and why of the world," with a more fundamental and penetrating knowledge of the inner nature of the world that questions the "what" alone. The former type of knowledge is far from genuine philosophy, he asserts, noting that such historical philosophizing inevitably furnishes either a cosmogony that has various guises or else "a system of emanations, a doctrine of diminutions, or finally, when driven in despair over the fruitless attempts of those paths to the last path, it furnishes, conversely, a doctrine of a constant becoming, springing up, arising, coming to light out of darkness, out of the obscure ground, primary ground, groundlessness, or some other drivel of this kind." Schopenhauer ridicules these historical attempts, it appears, because they misconstrue the temporal aspect and connect time with the things-in-themselves; they therefore ignore Kant's fundamental insight into the separation of a phenomenal from a noumenal world, and deal only with the realm of representations or appearance. Schopenhauer himself does not develop his thoughts into a larger consideration of the nature of the universe, as Nietzsche did, but his dismissal of such attempts suggests that he might have arrived at something akin to recurrence if he had: "All this [historical philosophizing] is most briefly disposed of by remarking that a whole eternity, in other words an endless time, has already elapsed up to the present moment, and therefore everything that can or should become must have become already."[32] The assertion that everything that can happen has already happened is certainly not equivalent to the doctrine that everything happens again and has already happened before, but the extension of Schopenhauer's thought, which is based on temporal infinity and an apparent finitude of possible events, could easily lead to a hypothesis proximate to eternal recurrence. What is important, however, is not whether Schopenhauer or any other individual Nietzsche read anticipates precisely his theory of eternal recurrence, but merely that the constituent elements of Nietzsche's revelation, at least those drawn from the realm of the physical sciences, as well as the exposition of a hypothesis of eternal recurrence, are suggested in various and very different types of speculations during the course of the nineteenth century.

Although Nietzsche in his early years is overtly a proponent of Schopenhauer's thought, and at the very least an admirer of him as a person (as evidenced in the third *Untimely Meditation*), he also encountered reflections on cosmology in the authors he openly opposed. David Strauß (1808–1874), for example, Nietzsche's target in the first *Meditation*, includes an extended discussion of scientific theories in *The Old Faith and the New* (1872). In Lange's second edition, which Nietzsche quite possibly read after its appearance in the mid-1870s, he devotes several pages to Strauß as a materialist philosopher and includes a summary of his thoughts on cosmogony. Nietzsche's initial acquaintance with Strauß was quite obviously not mediated by Lange, however,[33] and although Nietzsche deals mostly with Strauß's cultural observations in his attack in his first *Untimely Meditation*, he could have found in Strauß a potential ally for his speculations on scientific advances. Strauß proceeds from the Kant-Laplace hypothesis in his text and includes mention of the constitution of planets and their orbits. But after dealing briefly with Kant's thoughts on the Milky Way, he turns to the "unexpected discovery" of Gustav Kirchhoff

(1824–1887), who applied spectral analysis to achieve results not accessible through a mere telescope. Kirchhoff demonstrated with the spectroscope he invented that in the universe there exist not only completed stars, like our sun, but also stars that are just coming into existence. The implications for cosmology are significant in Strauß's view: "If we then remember those stars that were not noticed or hardly noticed before, but that raise themselves to stars of the first or second order through a sudden flare and then after a shorter or longer time again disappear, then it suggests that we consider here worlds that are collapsing into each other and that head towards a new formation through a combustion process."[34] Strauß is suggesting in this passage something we have encountered previously: the emergence of new solar systems from the collapse of stars, and thus the eternal nature of the cosmos. Significant in this perspective is the insistence on a cyclical process and the denial of any ultimate purpose or goal in the universe. Indeed, on the basis of the scientific evidence, Strauß imagines a time when the earth will no longer be inhabitable,[35] and although he does not mention the recurrence of the same, his thoughts on the emergence of new stars and planets suggest a possible pattern of repetition. Strauß did not anticipate Nietzsche's eternal recurrence, but it is interesting to note that philosophical speculation in this era, whether lauded or condemned by Nietzsche, often included cosmological thought and quite frequently suggested a repetitive process in the cosmos.

Nietzsche's most productive moments often occur when he reacts *ex negativo* to the ideas of others. Although Strauß's perspective may exhibit similarities to his with regard to general cosmological principles, the writings of the adversary of the second *Untimely Meditation* may have been more fruitful because he could assume a principled adversarial stance. In the work of Eduard von Hartmann (1842–1906), in particular in his *Philosophy of the Unconscious* (1869), Nietzsche encountered and commented on a philosopher who avoids contemporary scientific evidence and therefore disregards any thought of recurrence. Hartmann's position is perhaps surprising since he presents himself as a disciple of Schopenhauer. But his Schopenhauerian roots do not extend to his mentor's cosmogony, and Nietzsche comments satirically on an important passage in Hartmann's popular text that discusses the telos of the world process. The framework for Nietzsche's thought in this *Meditation* is, as we have seen in Chapter 1, the educational system and in particular the deleterious effects of historical thought on German *Bildung*. However, Nietzsche's objections to the progressive nature of the world process and to a linear development of human beings toward a pre-established goal possess implications for recurrence that perhaps become obvious to him only in hindsight. After affirming that the goal of humanity does not lie in a preordained process and end, but rather in the production of genius, the "highest specimens" of the race, he cites Hartmann at length, interspersing his own sardonic exclamations in the text:

"As little as it would be compatible with the concept of development to ascribe an infinite past duration to the world process because in that case every conceivable development would already have to have occurred, and this is definitely not the case (oh you scoundrel!), just as little can we concede an infinite future duration of the process; each would invalidate the concept of a development toward a goal (oh more of a scoundrel!), and would equate the world process with the Danaides' futile attempts to draw water. The complete victory of the logical over the illogical (oh scoundrel of scoundrels!), however, must coincide with the temporal end of the world process, with judgment day." (HL 9, KSA 1.317–18)[36]

Nietzsche has much to contest in this passage. Not only does he find these thoughts typical for the mindless historical optimism of the Second Reich, but he also disagrees with the notion of an end to history or finds absurd the notion of the victory of logic over illogic. But what Nietzsche could detect in Hartmann's negative example as well was that teleological perspectives entail an adherence to a religious conception of the universe, in particular one drawn from the Judeo-Christian tradition. If our world has a goal toward which it is proceeding, then it also has a definite moment of creation from which it has developed. Nietzsche's later notion of a boundless span of time is thus, in the context of his critique of religion, a counter to a Judeo-Christian conception of genesis and afterlife, but it also contradicts atheistic variants that deny the divinity, but retain the temporal pattern, such as those inherent in various versions of German idealist philosophy. Hartmann of course could have been referring to an equally anti-religious view: the finitude of our world does not necessarily imply that the universe is finite, or that an infinite amount of time has not passed before our world came into existence; nor does it mean that an infinite amount of time might not pass after we have reached the end of our development. Hartmann refers only to the world process having a temporal duration, a definite beginning and end, not to the cosmos. The manner in which Hartmann phrases his thought, however, resonates negatively with Nietzsche's later formulations of eternal recurrence. The certainty with which he asserts that it is not the case that every conceivable development has already occurred would be rebuffed by Nietzsche with the contention that, precisely because time stretches infinitely backward, everything must have already happened. Even if Hartmann manages to avoid postulating a divinely authorized order, his thought contains the language of an account of the universe that runs counter to Nietzsche's later formulations of the doctrine of eternal recurrence. And Nietzsche notes his differences with this account through his insertions in the passage cited above.

Eternal Recurrence and Thermodynamics

At the outset of this chapter, we noted that Nietzsche presents his hypothesis of eternal recurrence as a sudden revelation that occurred in August 1881. He presents this view in retrospect in *Ecce Homo*, when he begins his reflections on the composition of *Zarathustra*:

> I shall now tell the story of Zarathustra. The basic conception of the work, the *idea of eternal recurrence*, the highest formula of affirmation that can possibly be attained—belongs to August of the year 1881: it was jotted down on a piece of paper with the inscription "6000 feet beyond man and time." I was that day walking through the woods beside the lake of Silvaplana; I stopped beside a mighty pyramidal block of stone that reared itself up not far from Surlei. Then this idea came to me. (Za, Warum ich so gute Bücher schreibe, Also sprach Zarathustra 1, KSA 6.335)

Several aspects of this passage are odd. In the first place, eternal recurrence, as we have seen, did not appear first in *Zarathustra*, but in aphorism 341 of *The Gay Science*, in a place of considerable prominence as the penultimate aphorism in the original four-part work. The last aphorism in the book is an introduction to the figure of Zarathustra, and the phrasing and content of this aphorism are repeated in the first part of "Zarathustra's Prologue" the next year. Nietzsche claims in *Ecce Homo* that "the basic conception" of *Zarathustra* revolves around eternal recurrence, but the passage in which it is discussed comes in the second section of the third book, hardly a place of prominence for something that Nietzsche later considers foundational. It is easier to formulate an argument that the fourth book of *The Gay Science* was conceived around eternal recurrence, since the initial aphorism in that section contains the notion of *amor fati*, which has an obvious relationship to the questions asked about the acceptance of recurrence in the aphorism (FW 276, KSA 3.521). We could also note that we find no entry in Nietzsche's notebooks that bears the inscription "6000 feet beyond man and time." We do find a note on the "recurrence of the same," which contains the remark "the beginning of August 1881 in Sils-Maria, 6000 feet above the sea and much higher over all human things" (Nachlass 1881, 11[141], KSA 9.494). But Nietzsche repeats the phrase "6000 feet above" in other remarks in his notebooks as an obvious reference to how removed and superior he is to other places on earth, for example, Bayreuth (EH, Warum ich so weise bin 4, KSA 6.270); or in reference to his distance from and above Germany and the German reading public (Nachlass 1888, 19[1], KSA 13.540; 19[7], 543). Finally, if we examine Nietzsche's correspondence from August 1881, we encounter no references to eternal recurrence and nothing that contains the specific mention of Lake Silvaplana or the village of Surlej. Most of the matters he includes are rather mundane, relating to books and drugs he wants procured, his fascination with acquiring a typewriter to relieve his eyes, or the weather "6000 feet higher than Genoa" (to Franziska Nietzsche, 24 August 1881, Nr. 142, KSB 6.120). The only possible reference to eternal recurrence comes in a letter to Köselitz, in which he writes of "thoughts, the likes of which I have never seen" and "the tears of rejoicing" he has shed as well as the singing and nonsense he spoke on his recent walks. But there is no specific mention of recurrence, and the letter continues with thoughts on the lack of encouragement he receives from Germans, including Jacob Burckhardt (1818–1897), the ideal climate of Oaxaca in Mexico, and the attitude he has to take toward his publisher Ernst Schmeitzner (1851–1895). We are certainly accustomed to Nietzsche's exaggeration and stylization of past events in *Ecce Homo*, but in dealing with what he considers his most important philosophical thought and the foundation of his most important work, he presents his readers with a fiction that bears little resemblance to any reality we can reconstruct from the other documents we possess.

The story the documents tell is rather different. If we examine Nietzsche's notebook entries from the summer and fall of 1881, we can more easily conclude that at the origin of his hypothesis about eternal recurrence lies a preoccupation with theories of natural science in the nineteenth century, in particular the first two principles of thermodynamics. Or, perhaps more accurately, we find that Nietzsche's "revelation" and his first public utterances about eternal recurrence are accompanied by various remarks that reflect Nietzsche's understanding of the first and second laws of thermodynamics.[37] In his notebooks beginning with 1881, we begin to witness Nietzsche reflecting not only on the implications of a finite amount of energy that cannot be created or reduced, but also on the consequences of the second law of thermodynamics, which deals with entropy and states of equilibrium in a confined system. These two principles were part of larger considerations in the nineteenth century regarding heat transfer: at the time, the German phrase for these notions was "the mechanical theory of heat" [*die mechanische Wärmetheorie*], although the notion of thermodynamics, which would later have an equivalent in the German "Thermodynamik," was introduced in English in the latter part of the century. The earliest considerations of thermodynamics stem from the first decades of the nineteenth century, Sadi Carnot (1796–1832) having first articulated the second law of thermodynamics in 1824, but the first two principles, which were the major focus for Nietzsche in the 1880s, became popular scientific knowledge only in the second half of the century.[38] The clear enunciation of these principles was accomplished in Germany by Rudolf Julius Clausius (1822–1888), a German mathematician and physicist, in 1850, and Clausius published a book on the topic in 1864, revised and expanded in a second edition in 1876.[39]

At about the same time in England, William Thomson (1824–1907), better known as Lord Kelvin, similarly published on the first two principles of the transfer of heat and mechanical energy. Although Nietzsche never mentions Clausius in published writings or notebooks—nor did he own his books—as we have seen, he does make reference to Julius Robert Mayer, one of the key theorists dealing with these topics in the 1870s, and in a late note we also find Nietzsche referring to Thomson. It is not surprising to learn that Nietzsche's first mention of Mayer comes in notebook entries composed from the spring to the autumn of 1881, at the time of his "revelation" on recurrence. It is also not surprising to find that one of the books that Nietzsche asked Overbeck to procure for him in August 1881 (Nr. 139, KSB 6.117) was a short treatise by Otto Caspari (1841–1917) on "The Thomson Hypothesis,"[40] a pamphlet that is found in Nietzsche's library. Obviously, neither Mayer nor Thomson is the "source" for Nietzsche's hypothesis of eternal recurrence in *The Gay Science* or *Thus Spoke Zarathustra*; we have already noted that the notion is anticipated in the second *Untimely Meditation* and that Nietzsche was acquainted with various versions of recurrence from antiquity and modern times. Rather, the theories dealing with the transfer of energy, as they were formulated in the nineteenth century, provide a scientific legitimation for Nietzsche's own endeavors to articulate laws that reign in the universe. Quite obviously these same scientific theories do not include the philosophical implications Nietzsche assigned to recurrence, and we should exercise care in distinguishing scientific support and philosophical importance. As with the overman and evolutionary biology, however, Nietzsche's eternal recurrence participates in an ongoing discourse, reflecting at times an agreement with scientific sources named and unacknowledged, as well as Nietzsche's own contribution to this conversation.

Nietzsche's acquaintance with theories of heat transfer and questions of energy occurs well before his reading of—or about—Mayer in 1881. We have already seen that in the mid-1870s Nietzsche evidences an early interest in Stewart's book, whose subject, the conservation of energy, subsequently became known as the first law of thermodynamics. It is quite possible that he gained knowledge of some aspects of thermodynamics even as a student, but his chief source for scientific developments in his university years was Lange's *History of Materialism*. The 1866 edition of this work, however, contains very little on thermodynamics: the conservation of energy is mentioned only in passing, and Lange devotes just a single sentence to James Prescott Joule's (1818–1889) experiments with "the mechanical equivalence of heat."[41] The second edition, as we have seen above, makes up for this lacuna in scientific knowledge. In this work, Nietzsche had the opportunity to read about the theories of both Mayer and Clausius and learn about the first two laws or principles of thermodynamics in more detail.[42] The first law accords rather well with Nietzsche's doctrine, since in positing the conservation of energy, it suggests, at least to Nietzsche, that there are a large, but finite number of states or configurations [*Lagen*] of energy in the universe. Indeed, Nietzsche writes at one point: "The proposition of the conservation of energy demands *eternal recurrence*" (Nachlass 1886–87, 5[54], KSA 12.205). Lange's discussion does not suggest this conclusion, and we have already noted its equivocation on the duality of matter and energy. The second law of thermodynamics, however, which postulates that energy achieves a state of equilibrium inside closed systems, appears to contradict Nietzsche's hypothesis, and this topic is taken up in more detail and with suggestive comments in Lange's book. If a state of equilibrium were in fact reached, then all things would not recur since we would reach a condition of absolute stasis. It is therefore not insignificant how Lange's discussion deals with the second law of thermodynamics, in particular with the related notion of entropy, which is roughly a measure of the degree of disorderedness of energy in a given system.

> With the equilibrium of temperature in any system, the possibility of further alterations cease, as well as every type of life. The content of alteration, or the entropy, according to Clausius, has reached its maximum. However, whether these consequences, based on valid mathematical principles, can really be applied to the universe in the strictest sense of the word depends essentially on the conception that one has about the infinite nature of the universe, and with this one reaches a point that is of transcendent nature. Nothing prevents us, to be sure, from multiplying arbitrarily such static world systems in our minds, from conceiving them as attracted to one another from infinite distances, and from believing then that out of their collision the play of the cosmogony, as if in a magnified scale, begins anew. Nothing, as I said, prevents us from such an assumption—except the question whether we have a right to presuppose the infinite nature of the world systems as an existing reality just because we cannot imagine an end to creation.[43]

Like many nineteenth-century scientists, Lange is concerned that the sun will eventually lose its ability to provide heat, and, when that occurs, life will necessarily cease, at least on earth. The phenomenon he describes is "heat death," which occasioned a lively debate in the nineteenth century and which was a concern, as we shall see, to which Nietzsche obviously felt impelled to respond quite often in his notebooks. Lange continues, however, by speculating that nothing prevents us from imagining that there are many such systems that come to equilibrium, but that then are subject to the laws of attraction, and that the ensuing collision could allow the play of cosmogony to be renewed.[44] Lange may have drawn this hypothesis of an eternal death and revitalization of cosmic systems from the correspondence between Friedrich Ueberweg (1826–1871) and Heinrich Czolbe (1819–1873), which he cites in his penultimate chapter: Ueberweg contends that the starting point for the Kant-Laplace hypothesis is only a relative beginning, and that the collapse of earlier worlds is repeated infinitely.[45] Noteworthy in this passage is therefore that Lange not only hypothesizes the notion of eternal recurrence, bringing it into association with the laws of thermodynamics, but also provides some indication of what scientific assumptions are needed to sustain such a hypothesis. Unlike Nietzsche, as we shall see, Lange appears to stress the potential harmony between recurrence and the second law of thermodynamics. The contradiction to eternal recurrence would be overcome if we assume, as Lange suggests, a macro perspective, and continue to regard equilibrium and entropy as valid principles on a micro level. If we are correct in assuming that Nietzsche read this edition of Lange's book with care, then it is obvious that he encountered in at least the second and later editions discussions that were suggestive for his hypothesis that everything recurs.[46]

Until the early 1880s, however, the principles of thermodynamics that Nietzsche encountered in Lange or in Stewart's book or elsewhere left little obvious imprint on his thought; the allusion to recurrence in *On the Advantage and Disadvantage of History for Life* is formulated without any obvious scientific foundation and is truly a thought experiment. In 1881, the stakes for recurrence change, and perhaps the greatest difference between Nietzsche's hypothesis and those of earlier writers we have examined—besides the monumentality Nietzsche attaches to it—is its reliance on a foundation in the natural sciences that excludes Kant-Laplace. Whether he collected and began utilizing the elementary lessons in science from earlier readings, or whether new intellectual encounters imparted to him the insights he felt necessary for a scientifically grounded theory of recurrence, we do find him just after the start of the new decade intensely interested in engaging in a dialogue with recent developments in scientific literature. At this point, we might want to inquire more generally about Nietzsche's abilities to understand the material he confronted in the various books and articles he read. Unlike the evolutionary theories we examined in the previous chapter, the work on thermodynamics was more detailed and more mathematical, and thus not easily understood by individuals without a proficiency in mathematics and natural science. From Nietzsche's education, we know that the study of natural science was not his primary focus, neither as a *Gymnasium* student at Pforta, nor at the University in Bonn or Leipzig. At Pforta, he had very few hours in physics, for example, in comparison to the amount of time devoted to ancient languages. Indeed, Nietzsche was said to have been a rather poor student in mathematics, and, as we saw in the first chapter of this book, his sister Elisabeth related the anecdote about her brother's Greek professor, Wilhelm Corssen (1820–1875), reprimanding the mathematics teacher who dared to threaten the graduation of the talented student just because he did not perform well in his subject area.[47] The disciplines he studied at Bonn do not include anything in the natural sciences, and his training at Leipzig was almost exclusively in classical philology. We suspect that Nietzsche felt this deficiency in his training at various periods in his life. Prior to receiving his appointment in Basel in 1869, he had planned to travel to Paris with Erwin Rohde (1845–1898) to devote himself to the study of natural sciences.[48] In the early 1880s, Lichtenberger asserts that Nietzsche intended to cease writing for ten years at about the time of his discovery of eternal recurrence in order to study natural sciences in Vienna or Paris and secure a scientific foundation for his hypothesis.[49] Lichtenberger appears to have obtained this information from Lou Salomé's (1861–1937) book on Nietzsche[50]—a source that is not completely reliable—but it is obvious from his correspondence that Nietzsche, Paul Rée (1849–1901), and Salomé did have plans to travel to Vienna to continue their studies,[51] an undertaking that collapsed when Rée and Salomé left for Berlin, abandoning and embittering Nietzsche. From these incidents and from the type of books Nietzsche frequently ordered, it appears certain that Nietzsche aspired to more knowledge of the natural sciences of his era, but it is also clear that he, unlike other philosophers, was ill prepared—at the very least mathematically—to comprehend the scientific literature pertaining to such topics as thermodynamics. This failing, however, did not prevent Nietzsche from entering the ongoing conversation on thermodynamics and heat death with philosophical speculation, although it may have been the reason that his reflections on these topics are confined to his notebooks, while his treatment of recurrence in his published writings contains more hypothetical and literary contours.

In his earliest notebooks on thermodynamics and eternal recurrence, we obtain the impression of someone in serious dialogue with recent scientific developments. The first entry we encounter begins with a simple statement of the first law of thermodynamics: "The world of forces suffers no diminution." Nietzsche reasons *ex negativo*: if there were a loss of force or energy in the world of forces, that is, if the principle of conservation of energy were not true, then we would witness a gradual enervation in the world and eventually a complete cessation of activity: "otherwise it [the world] would become weak in a finite amount of time and perish." Having established that forces do not diminish, Nietzsche advances the claim that forces do not cease to act, that they never come to rest; again Nietzsche argues from the negative case, since if a cessation of forces were possible, we would have already reached that point. He does not state the necessary condition for this conclusion, which is that time must be infinite, since if it were finite and the world had a beginning, it could also have an end. Infinite time is nonetheless an assumption Nietzsche must be making, and he states it explicitly elsewhere: "The world of forces suffers no stoppage: for otherwise it would have been attained, and the clock of being would stand still." Nietzsche's third contention about the world of forces follows from his second statement and maintains that forces will not reach equilibrium, and in this claim he is taking direct exception to the second law of thermodynamics, in which the notion of equilibrium plays a central part. Nietzsche does not provide an explanation, however, or an argument to support his claim, just a rephrasing of the original proposition: "The world of forces therefore will never come to equilibrium; it never has a moment of rest; its force and its movement are the same for every period of time." In the last part of this statement, Nietzsche may have been referring back to the first law of thermodynamics, since he posits that force will always remain the same. But he also includes movement in this claim, and the conservation of the same amount of movement is not the result of any proposition in thermodynamics. After the articulation of these three propositions, Nietzsche believes he is prepared to draw his conclusion: the hypothesis of eternal recurrence.

> Whatever state this world could have attained, it must have already attained it; and not once, but countless times. Thus this moment: it was already there once and many times and will return as well, all forces distributed as they are now; and it is the same for the moment that gave birth to this one and with the one that is the child of the present one. Man! Your entire life will be like an hourglass always turned upside down and running again and again—a great minute of time in between until all conditions out of which you came into existence in the cycle of the world again come together.

Significant in this version of eternal recurrence is the initial emphasis on the attainment of all possible states: Nietzsche's claim is that any state that could have been attained must have already been attained. Unstated, but assumed in this argument is that a state of equilibrium is impossible; thus not all states or constellations of forces are attainable. Nietzsche suggests strongly in continuing that there is a specific pattern that repeats itself, that the moments of existence are bound together in an unbroken and unbreakable chain that repeats throughout eternity. He completes this first entry on thermodynamics and recurrence with reflections that relate more specifically to the individual experience: "And then you will find every pain and every pleasure and every friend and enemy and every hope and every error and every blade of grass and every snatch of sunlight, the entire connectivity of all things." Unlike other thinkers who have considered recurrence, Nietzsche is concerned that the ramifications are not simply cosmological, but also existential. It is important for us to understand that we are caught up in this grander scheme of repetition: "This ring, in which you are a speck, sparkles again and again." He completes the passage with an indirect reflection on the advent of the hypothesis and its importance for humankind: "And in this ring of human existence there is always an hour when first one, then many, then all of the most powerful thoughts emerge, the thought of the eternal recurrence of all things—it is at all times for humankind the midday hour" (Nachlass 1881, 11[148], KSA 9.498). Unusual about this first entry is that it combines, as most entries do not, claims based on Nietzsche's dialogue with thermodynamics with metaphorical and existential reflections. As we have seen, only the latter survive in his published writings on eternal recurrence.

In other entries from 1881, Nietzsche demonstrates that he has familiarity with alternative hypotheses about eternal recurrence that proceed from similar assumptions, but arrive at conclusions that are vastly different and in some cases clearly retrograde. Nietzsche writes, for example, that the modern alternative to a belief in God is the belief in a universal organism that controls the functioning of the cosmos. If we proceed from the assumption of a finite amount of matter and infinite time, we can avoid the conclusion of eternal recurrence, which seems to rely on a rather mechanical process of repetition, by conceiving of the universe as an organism that can alter the course of events and the constellation of forces. But recourse to the organic is distasteful to Nietzsche. It amounts to little more than a "personification of nature." Where did Nietzsche find this proposition of the universe as organism? He suggests his source when he refers to the "furtive polytheism in the monads that together form the universal organism [*All-Organism*].[52] Be careful! Monads that know how to prevent certain possible mechanical consequences like the equilibrium of forces! What a fantasy!" (Nachlass 1881, 11[201], KSA 9.522). The reference to monads leads us to believe Nietzsche is referring to Leibniz and perhaps to his nineteenth-century disciples. We cannot be certain that Nietzsche is referencing a specific text in this passage, but in Caspari's pamphlet on Thomson's hypothesis, which, we will recall, Nietzsche requested Overbeck purchase for him, Caspari writes about Leibniz's endeavor to escape Cartesian mechanistic perspectives and to posit "the universe as an organism." He continues: "in the reference to the reconceptualization of the purely mechanical view of the world of substances into an organic view lies the focal point of the philosophy of this significant thinker."[53] Ultimately, Caspari solves the problems raised by the second law of thermodynamics by rejecting the mechanistic views of Descartes and embracing the notion of "organic distribution" derived from Leibniz. Equilibrium is a local phenomenon; on a cosmic level, forces continue to exhibit movement and never fall into stasis.[54] Nietzsche's implicit response to Caspari and the alternative he deduces from Leibniz is that this postulate is just as much a *deus ex machina* as Descartes's was. "If the universe could become an organism," he writes, "it would have become one. We have to think of it in its entirety as removed as possible from the organic" (Nachlass 1881, 11[201], KSA 9.522). We cannot determine with absolute certainty that Nietzsche read this pamphlet. But we can ascertain that Nietzsche was conversant with alternatives to eternal recurrence posed by other philosophers who dealt with thermodynamics, such as the alternative contained in Caspari's essay. And, furthermore, we can see that eternal recurrence is regarded not only as a conclusion drawn in part from the first principle of thermodynamics, as well as an argument against the second principle, but also as an alternative to theistic foundations of cosmology and the attempt of modern philosophers to retain what Nietzsche considered theistic principles in a concealed fashion.

These initial entries from 1881 are significant because they present arguments for eternal recurrence based on Nietzsche's understanding of the physical universe, but also because they explore various uncertainties that Nietzsche harbors. In a few of the passages, we encounter repeated and insistent questions that Nietzsche appears to be posing for himself, as well as possible answers to these questions. Thus one entry begins with a familiar argument against equilibrium—"if equilibrium of force had ever been attained, then it would still persist: therefore it never happened"—but it then continues by approaching thorny issues that would contradict recurrence. First Nietzsche repeats the argument we saw above. The current condition must have occurred countless times in the past and will occur countless times in the future, as well as all the conditions that lead up to it and follow from it. But Nietzsche then poses the question of whether all conditions are possible in an infinite amount of time, given a finite quantity of energy. By the logic of his own argument—namely, that a condition of equilibrium cannot have been achieved and will never happen—he is compelled to deny that all possible conditions occur. Since he can conceive of equilibrium, Nietzsche has to admit that although it is conceivable, it must be excluded as one of the possible constellations of forces. But what about the possibility that nothing identical occurs, that we have ever new conditions that never repeat? Nietzsche could have examined this thought by citing mathematical examples, but he appears to be focused on dismissing this possibility, rather than demonstrating that it could be true. Simple reflection will tell us, however, that the occurrence of a finite number of elements existing in an infinite, nonrepeating sequence is not only possible, but also a known and accepted mathematical fact. For pi is just such a case. Nietzsche responds to his own query about the possible nonrecurrence of the same in a different fashion: "That nothing the same recurs could not be explained by chance, but only by some intentionality present within the existence of force: for assuming an enormous mass of cases, the chance attainment of the same throw is more probable than the absolute never-sameness [*die absolute Nie-Gleichheit*]." The second half of this sentence, which makes the attainment of the same only "more probable," and not certain, contradicts previous passages in which Nietzsche claims that all constellations of forces recur in identical fashion and in identical sequence. But the first half of the sentence states that chance cannot be used as an explanation for the nonrecurrence of the same, suggesting that the only explanation for nonrecurrence would be some sort of intentionality in the essence of force itself. Although Nietzsche does not offer an argument against intentionality, it cannot be the reason for nonrecurrence since it would presuppose precisely what Nietzsche disallows in the previous passage we examined: a God or God-equivalent, a Leibnizian universal organism or monad that would be able to alter the inevitable sequence of events and prevent repetition of the same from occurring.

We see in these notebook entries that some doubt creeps into Nietzsche's thought about the conclusions he draws, although he appears to be more secure about his accuracy in presenting the scientific evidence that leads to these conclusions. Perhaps his largest area of uncertainty regarding recurrence involves the last term in his hypothesis: "the same." How identical are the conditions or constellations that recur? In one note Nietzsche begins, as is customary, by relating the scientific evidence as he understands it.

> The total amount of force [*All-Kraft*] is *limited*, not "infinite." Let us beware of such conceptual excesses! Consequently, the number of constellations [*Lagen*], combinations, changes, and developments of this force is tremendously great and practically "*immeasurable,*" but in any case finite and not infinite. But the time through which this total force works is infinite, that is, force is eternally the same and eternally active:—up to this moment an eternity has already passed, that is, all possible developments must have already occurred. That means that all possible developments must *have taken place* already. *Consequently*, the present development is a repetition, and thus also that which gave rise to it, and that which arises from it, and so backward and forward again! Insofar as the totality of energy constellations [*die Gesammtlage aller Kräfte*] always recurs, everything has happened innumerable times.

To this point, the passage reiterates what we have seen before as the scientific basis for eternal recurrence, based primarily on the conservation of energy and infinite time. But Nietzsche follows these sentences with a skeptical attitude toward the precise nature of the repetition. Do we really have a recurrence of states that are exactly the same, that are identical?

> Whether, *aside from this*, something the same occurs is entirely unprovable. It appears that the totality of states forms anew the *properties* in the smallest details, so that two different states of totality can produce nothing that is the same, for example, *two leaves*? I have my doubts: it would presuppose that they have an absolutely identical origin, and for that we would have to *assume* that something identical has existed *back into all eternity* despite all modifications in the totality of states and the creating

of new properties—an impossible assumption! (Nachlass 1881, 11[202] KSA 9.523)

Nietzsche is not entirely clear in this passage, but he seems to harbor reservations about the possibility of the exact identity of states or constellations of energy. Just as two leaves that appear to be identical will have minute differences, so too the slightly different constellations of energy will produce something similar, but not the same. He explores these doubts in greater detail in a lengthy passage that consists almost entirely of questions. He begins as follows: "Isn't the existence of *some sort of* divergence and not complete circularity in the world around us already a sufficient *counter-proof* against an identical circularity of everything that exists?" Nietzsche proceeds to mention in brief and somewhat cryptic fashion different possibilities for the introduction of variability in the circular process. At one point he assumes a uniform "energy of contraction" in all "force centers" and asks how even the smallest divergence could result. The notion of a "force center" appears to be inherited from Lange, who introduced the term in his discussions of the controversy between materialists and dynamists. In Lange, the term appears to be a concession to the latter theorists and a critique of philosophers who subscribe to atomist theories, but, unlike Nietzsche, Lange does not want to completely eliminate the material from consideration.[55] In Nietzsche's notebook entry, his introduction of "force centers" compels him to postulate the possibility of coexisting identical worlds and not just the recurrence of one identical world, a postulate that recalls Blanqui's reflections from the previous decade. Nietzsche also speculates that force perhaps does not operate by uniform principles and so can produce different states or even produce something arbitrary (Nachlass 1881, 11[311], KSA 9.560–61). He does not resolve the issue of observed variability and recurrence—the passage ends with a question, not a resolution to his queries—but the doubts expressed in this notebook entry do not recur in his published writings, where, as we have seen, an identical recurrence down to blades of grass is postulated, or in his later notebook entries. Whether and how Nietzsche resolved these issues is not evident from his writings; we can only observe that he must have overcome them after his initial reflections in 1881.

After the initial flurry of reflections that preceded his "revelation," Nietzsche continues to mention eternal recurrence throughout the decade, but rarely in connection with the laws of thermodynamics. As already remarked, it appears frequently in his notes in titles of prospective books or in section headers for books, but Nietzsche apparently did not feel the need to explore again its relationship to contemporary theories of natural science. We have already examined the inclusion of eternal recurrence in *The Gay Science* and *Zarathustra*, and the passages we cited contain the most extensive treatment of the hypothesis in his published writings. Almost all other remarks about recurrence are incidental by comparison, or refer the reader back to the more substantial discussions, as we have seen in *Ecce Homo*. In Nietzsche's notebooks, there is one longer entry from 1888 (Nachlass 1888, 14[188], KSA 13.374–76) that takes up the issue of recurrence as part of his "New-World Conception," which is as close as Nietzsche comes to outlining important dimensions of his response to the question of cosmology in nineteenth-century Europe. The entry contains five points. The first states a Nietzschean, philosophical variant on the first principle of thermodynamics, claiming that the world is neither becoming nor perishing, that it has no beginning and no ending. His second point dismisses the hypothesis of a created world as belonging to theological superstition. In his third point, which appears under the rubric "eternal recurrence," he turns to the question of infinite time, asserting that prior to this moment and after this moment there is no stoppage of time, but also no regression or progression. This moment, in other words, represents, as Nietzsche writes metaphorically, both "the head" and "the tail." The fourth point recapitulates well-rehearsed territory concerning the second law of thermodynamics and Nietzsche's objection to the hypothesis of heat death. He begins, however, by recounting his own history with eternal recurrence: "I came across this thought [eternal recurrence] in earlier thinkers: every time it was limited by some additional second thoughts (—mostly theological, in favor of a *creator spiritus*)." But he then turns to the familiar objection to the hypothesis of equilibrium: "If the world could really reach stasis, dry up, die out, become *nothing*, or if it could reach a state of equilibrium, or if it in general really had some kind of a goal that would include in itself duration, invariability, the once-and-for-all (in short, metaphysically stated, if becoming could flow into being or into nothing), then it should have reached this state already. But it has not reached this state." Having cited his opposition to the creationism of earlier notions of recurrence, he then turns to his disagreement with "mechanism," by which he means atomistic materialism. "This is our only certainty, which we have in our hands, to serve as a corrective against the great mass of possible world-hypotheses. If, for example, mechanism [*der Mechanismus*] cannot escape the consequence of a final state, which Thomson deduced from it, then mechanism is thereby *refuted*." We will recall that Nietzsche purchased and read Caspari's pamphlet on Thomson, in which he too argued against heat death, although in a fashion different from Nietzsche. In this fourth point, Nietzsche clearly rejects the materialism of mid-nineteenth-century Germany represented by philosophers like Büchner, and we shall see shortly that his differences have ramifications for another important hypothesis in his cosmology. Finally, in his fifth point, Nietzsche returns to the notion of force centers, but without questioning recurrence of the same.

> If the world *can* be conceived as a definite quantity of force and as a definite number of force centers—and every other conception remains

indefinite and consequentially *useless*—then it follows that it has gone through a calculable number of combinations in the great dice game of its existence. In an infinite time span every possible combination would be attained at some point, more than that, it would have been attained an infinite number of times. And since between every "combination" and its next "recurrence" all combinations that are still possible at all must have occurred, and every one of these combinations determines the entire sequence of combinations in the same series, so we can prove with this a cycle of absolutely identical series: the world as a cycle that repeats itself already infinitely often and that plays its game *ad infinitum*.

Noteworthy in this final entry concerning the scientific foundations of eternal recurrence is the absence of any doubt concerning the repetition of an identical sequence of events, of "the same." Nietzsche asserts that each sequence in the unending cycle is "absolutely identical," without deviation or qualification, and that since every combination determines the next one, there must be identical sequences. In his own mind, it appears he had resolved the issues that troubled him in 1881, and that provided the basis for the "revelation" that occurred in the Swiss mountains in August of that year.

The Force of the Will to Power

Like his hypothesis of eternal recurrence of the same, Nietzsche's notion of the "will to power" is a phenomenon of the 1880s. There is one isolated reference to the will to power in a note composed in the latter half of the 1870s, but its use in this passage relates to the personality trait of ambition, and the notebook entry resembles the type of topics Nietzsche broached in his early collections of aphorisms (Nachlass 1876–77, 23[63], KSA 8.425). Unlike eternal recurrence, the will to power ascends slowly into a place of prominence in Nietzsche's vocabulary and thought. The "revelation" that Nietzsche associates with eternal recurrence occurs in August 1881, and the hypothesis was incorporated in prominent places in his next major writings, *The Gay Science* and *Thus Spoke Zarathustra*. We find some mention of the will to power in notebook entries from the early 1880s, but an early passage from the new decade gives an indication that Nietzsche had not fully worked out its significance. He refers to a monk, who takes the oath of poverty, chastity, and obedience, as an individual who has renounced the "will to power" and exists in a world where power does not lead to happiness (Nachlass 1880–81, 9[14], KSA 9.412–13). A few years later, in aphorism 51 of *Beyond Good and Evil*, Nietzsche would regard this type of abnegation as a manifestation of the will to power (JGB 51, KSA 5.71). The will to power does not occur in the first four books of *The Gay Science*, but it receives some attention in *Zarathustra*, almost exclusively in the second book in the section "From Self-Overcoming." It is included as one of Zarathustra's teachings and contrasted, as it will be so often in the 1880s, with the will to truth, the will to life, and the will to existence (Za II, Von der Selbst-Ueberwindung, KSA 4.146–49). But in the years prior to 1885, and in contrast to eternal recurrence, it rarely surfaces as part of Nietzsche's cosmology. It is almost always connected with humankind and with what seems most important to human beings, which is then revealed to be not as essential as the will to power. Only in the notebooks written in the middle of the decade and in the writings of the last three years of his sane life do we find the will to power as a notion that extends beyond human and biological existence, referring to matters that define the workings of the cosmos.[56] Nietzsche extends it to the entire organic world, for example, as the "cardinal drive in an organic being"—"life itself is will to power" (JGB 13, KSA 5.27)—and in a note from 1885 also to the inorganic: "the will to power also directs the inorganic world" (Nachlass 1885, 34[247], KSA 11.504). The frequent sketches for book titles and chapter headings under the rubric "will to power" indicate how dear the notion was to Nietzsche, and although scholars have upbraided his sister Elisabeth for putting together a posthumous volume under that title from notebook entries in the 1880s, the centrality of the concept in the second half of the decade makes it understandable that she would have thought Nietzsche had planned and would have authorized such an undertaking. In the writings after *Beyond Good and Evil*, it appears somewhat less frequently, although it continues to occupy a prominent place in notebook entries from 1886 to 1888. But what is most evident is that Nietzsche never supplies an extended explanation for the term. The longest and most suggestive discussion occurs in the second section of *Beyond Good and Evil* in aphorism 36 and, like the introduction of eternal recurrence, it is couched in the language of hypotheticals (JGB 36, KSA 5.54–55). No doubt this dearth of elucidation on Nietzsche's part has contributed to the large number of interpretations and the excessive attention the will to power has received in subsequent criticism. Like eternal recurrence, the will to power has far more sustained and cogent explications in scholarship than in any of the published or unpublished writings of Nietzsche himself.

Most commentators have focused their exegetical skills on the implications of will to power for humanity, especially in the areas of epistemology, ethics, and ontology. We saw in the previous chapter that it has connections with the biological sciences and the discourse on evolution. Our concerns in this chapter, however, will be restricted to the cosmological dimensions of this notion, and our first observation is that the will to power plays an important role for the cogency of eternal recurrence. As we have seen, in Nietzsche's discussions of recurrence, he frequently has recourse to the repetition of identical states or configurations, and most often these recurring states are formulated in terms of constellations of force or energy. The question of the nature of the universe is thus centrally important for his hypothesis of eternal recurrence, and in the penultimate decade of the nineteenth century he was confronted with three main alternatives in the scientific and philosophical literature. The first, from the early years of the century, was a Romantic natural philosophy that incorporated mind or consciousness in some fashion into natural phenomena. Nietzsche may have flirted with some aspects of German idealism in his youth, but by the 1880s, this direction appeared to him not only outdated, but also essentially wrong. Nietzsche treats Schelling, who was the author of the most noted contribution to Romantic natural philosophy, in a dismissive fashion in his notebooks. Grouped together with Fichte, Hegel, Feuerbach, and Strauß, he remarks that they all "stink of theology and church fathers" (KSA 11.262). Rejecting idealism as a falsification and associating Schelling—not altogether fairly—with a group of philosophers that regard subjectivity and consciousness as the highest values, Nietzsche never considers Romantic natural philosophy to be consonant with his concerns.[57]

The second alternative arose in mid-century and was identified with materialism; Nietzsche was familiar with the history of the main representatives of this movement from his readings in Lange's history. Perhaps the most noted of the materialist philosophers, Ludwig Büchner, gives a good indication of the composition of the universe in the title of his most noted work, *Force and Matter*.[58] The materialists generally favored a dualism consisting of dead matter being animated by force under predictable laws, while conceding at the same time that matter is unthinkable without force and vice versa. Nietzsche often refers to this sort of materialism in his writings with the term mechanism [*Mechanismus*]. Although he was attracted to materialism as a corrective to idealism in his earlier notebooks and writings, by the 1880s, he finds mechanism as ill conceived as idealism. In an entry from 1888, for example, he writes that in order to uphold mechanism, we must subscribe to two fictions: "a concept of motion (taken from our language of the senses) and a concept of atoms = unity (stemming from our physical 'experience'): it thus has both the bias of the senses and the psychological bias as its presupposition" (KSA 1888, 14[79], 13.259). With regard to recurrence, Nietzsche associates this materialist direction in philosophy with Thomson and the theory of heat death. Materialism or mechanism cannot be attractive to Nietzsche because it would validate his understanding of the second law of thermodynamics and ultimately lead to an absolute equilibrium in the universe.[59] His reasoning appears to be that either the "dead matter" of the materialists would desist from any motion as energy dissipates into heat, or the entire system would need a *deus ex machina* to invigorate it when it approaches equilibrium. But Nietzsche also comes to believe that mechanism, which theorizes about "matter, atoms, pressure and thrust, gravity" as if they were "facts in themselves," is guilty of building a philosophical system out of reified, psychic fictions (Nachlass 1888, 14[82], KSA 13.262).

Nietzsche found a theory of the composition of the universe that was better suited to his hypothesis of eternal recurrence in dynamism, which was becoming increasingly popular as an alternative to materialism in the second half of the nineteenth century. As we shall see in a moment, Nietzsche was particularly attracted to philosophers dealing with natural science who evidenced two features: (1) they either rejected entirely the notion of atoms, matter, and substance, relying instead on a notion of force or energy; or else they severely diminished the role of substance in their descriptions of the universe; and (2) they subscribed to monistic views or at least proposed theories that could be easily reconciled with monism.[60] In several of the books Nietzsche read, the philosophical origins of a dualistic mechanism or materialism versus a monistic dynamism were traced back to Descartes, whose mind-body distinction supplied the theoretical underpinnings for the worldview informing nineteenth-century materialism, and to Leibniz, Descartes's philosophical adversary in the seventeenth century, whose monadology postulates elementary and eternal particles, obeying their own laws as the ultimate composition of the universe. That Leibniz's monads possess no mass and occupy no space, and that they are likened to force centers, made Leibniz the philosophical father of monistic dynamism as an alternative to the materialist directions that Lange described and that had attained a great currency in mid-century. Indeed, several authors Nietzsche read and appreciated refer directly to Leibniz as their intellectual predecessor. Nietzsche himself mentions Leibniz in only a few places, mostly disparagingly, not for his views of the physical world, but rather for his theologically informed assertion that we are living in the best of all possible worlds. For this reason, Leibniz and Kant are considered "the two greatest drags on the intellectual integrity of Europe" (EH, Warum ich so gute Bücher schreibe, Der Fall Wagner 2, KSA 6.360). And we have already seen above that Nietzsche harbored suspicions about employing monads as "organisms" to solve the problem of heat death. Indeed, unlike the monistic dynamists he consulted, Nietzsche appears to have consistently regarded monads as simply a variant on atoms and thus did not recognize Leibniz's philosophy as a possible alternative to the crude materialism he too opposed.[61]

Nevertheless, it is easy to understand how a theory of force or energy that is the sole source of activity in the universe was suggestive for Nietzsche as he developed his notion of will to power conceived as a cosmic entity. And it is understandable how this conception of the composition of the universe is consonant with eternal recurrence. Nietzsche consistently refers to the repetition in terms of constellations of force or force centers or force totality [All-Kraft], and although he never refers to will to power in these passages, he does appear to conceive of will to power as a variant on the force or energy involved in recurrence. In a note referring to how Christianity tries to break those who are strong, for example, he places will to power in apposition to force (Nachlass 1887–88, 11[55], KSA 13.28); in *Beyond Good and Evil* he writes: "A living being wants above all else to *release* its strength [*Kraft*]; life itself is the will to power" (JGB 13, KSA 5.27); and in a notebook entry we find the following: "The will to power in every force-combination [*Kraft-Combination*], *defending itself against what is stronger, rushing at what is weaker, is more correct*" (Nachlass 1885, 36[21], KSA 11.560).[62] Will to power cannot be simply equated with force or energy as they are used by natural scientists, since it implies activism, the desire for expansion, the externalization of an inner strength. Thus Nietzsche explains in one note: "The victorious concept 'force,' with which our physicists have created God and the world, needs a supplement: it must be accorded an internal world that I designate 'will to power,' i.e., an insatiable demand for the demonstration of power, or utilization, exercise of power, as creative drive etc." (Nachlass 1885, 36[31], KSA 11.563). But it still seems clear that the force that Nietzsche requires to realize recurrence, the energy that exists in various constellations, producing identical sequences of repeating events, resembles several of Nietzsche's formulations of the will to power. The essence of the world, Nietzsche affirms, is will to power (JGB 186, KSA 5.107), or as Nietzsche claims in one of his notes: "*This world is the will to power—and nothing else. And you yourselves are also this will to power—and nothing else!*" (Nachlass 1885, 28[12], KSA 11.611). Like force or energy, which constitute the universe in their sequential combinations, will to power is everything that there is in the world. And like force in his discussions of recurrence, the will to power, which involves expansion and continuous activity, excludes heat death, alleviates the need for a *deus ex machina*—whether conceived as an organism or a divinity—and ensures the dynamism required for eternal recurrence of the same.

Nietzsche sought to bolster the cosmological dimension of the will to power with the natural science of his era, and, as we shall see in a moment, he consulted a number of sources in the early 1880s that supported a dynamic view of force in opposition to the materialism of mid-century. He was already predisposed toward these views from his readings in the 1870s. As we have seen, Lange referees various positions in the materialism-dynamism controversy and indicates that the scientific consensus is moving away from a reliance on matter [*Stoff*] and toward hypotheses that focus on force [*Kraft*]: After his review of recent atomic theories, he writes that "progress in science has brought us to the point that more and more forces are assuming the place of matter, and that the continuing precision of observation has dissolved matter for me into more and more forces."[63] During the past few decades, however, a scholarly consensus has been building that during his years in Basel, the dominant influence for Nietzsche regarding matter and force was the Dalmatian mathematician and astronomer Ruggiero Giuseppe Boscovich (1711–1787).⁶⁴ From lending records at the University of Basel library, we know for certain that Nietzsche borrowed Boscovich's *Theory of Natural Philosophy* [*Philosophiae naturalis theoria*] (1758) in March 1873 and on two occasions in 1874,⁶⁵ but how Nietzsche came upon this seminal work of the Jesuit scientist and what the exact nature of its influence was are rather less certain. Several scholars have assumed that Nietzsche learned of Boscovich from Lange's book, and that the brief discussion of Boscovich in Lange led Nietzsche to Gustav Theodor Fechner's (1801–1887) treatise *On the Physical and Philosophical Doctrine of Atoms* (1855¹, 1864²), which was referenced in a footnote in Lange, and which contains a slightly longer discussion of Boscovich, as well as, in an appendix, excerpts from the *Theory of Natural Philosophy*.⁶⁶ But the chronology is faulty in this assumption, since in 1873, when he borrowed Boscovich's book from the university library, Nietzsche had read only the first edition of Lange from 1866; the second volume of the second edition, which contains the reference to Boscovich, as well as the footnote citing Fechner, was not published until 1875, by which time Nietzsche had long since returned Boscovich's work to the library. Moreover, there is no reference to Fechner in Nietzsche's writings or correspondence and thus no evidence at all that Nietzsche was familiar with this source.⁶⁷ Recently, several scholars have also assumed that a passage in Nietzsche's notebooks from 1873, now known as the "Time Atomism Fragment," was composed under the direct influence of Boscovich, and at least one scholar has claimed that Nietzsche's concepts of eternal recurrence and the will to power, as well as hundreds of passages in his notebooks, are all directly related to his reading of the *Theory of Natural Philosophy*, which he is alleged to have read again in the 1880s. The problem with these contentions is that there is little supporting evidence. There is no copy of Boscovich's magnum opus in Nietzsche's library, making it unlikely that Nietzsche read this work again after 1874, and the conceptual apparatus he developed in the 1880s, as we have seen above and will continue to see below, has resonances with many other works that were part of a larger intellectual conversation about the nature of the cosmos. Even in the 1870s, there were several other works, including the writings of various philosophers of antiquity, that could have inspired, or at least contributed to, the cryptic reflections on "time atomism" in the 1873 notebooks. Significantly, nowhere in these reflections does Nietzsche mention Boscovich by name.⁶⁸

In his published writings, his notebooks, and his correspondence, we do find that Nietzsche praises Boscovich and considers him a pioneering figure who contributed immensely to his own worldview. But the contribution he made, or at least what Nietzsche invariably mentions when he speaks of him, is his advocacy of the dynamic alternative to materialism, his substitution of force for matter as the essence of the universe.⁶⁹ The sole reference to Boscovich in a published text occurs in *Beyond Good and Evil*:

> As regards materialistic atomism, hardly anything has even been so well refuted; in all Europe there is probably no scholar so unschooled as to want to credit it with serious meaning, apart from a handy everyday usefulness (that is, as a stylistic abbreviation). This we owe primarily to the Pole Boscovich, who along with the Pole Copernicus achieved the greatest victory yet in opposing the appearance of things. For while Copernicus convinced us to believe contrary to our senses that the earth does *not* stand still, Boscovich taught us to renounce the last thing that "still stood" about the earth, the belief in "substance," in "matter," in the bit of earth, the particle, the atom: no one on earth has ever won a greater triumph over the senses. (JGB 12, KSA 5.26)

Nietzsche was mistaken about Boscovich's nationality, but his admiration is nonetheless evident. Most important for Nietzsche is that the Jesuit scholar taught us that our senses are not a reliable guide to the composition of reality. Just as we perceive the sun moving around the earth, so too we encounter objects apparently with solidity and mass, and thus conclude that these objects consist of components that are equally solid. Genuine science therefore has the potential to correct commonsense misunderstandings about the world in which we live. What is noteworthy for us as well is not only that Boscovich is credited with this discovery, but also that Nietzsche maintains that the materialistic atomism that it negated is no longer a viable theory and has few adherents in contemporary Europe. In a notebook entry from the early 1880s, at a time when Nietzsche was developing his cosmology, Boscovich is regarded—with Copernicus—as the "opponent of ocular appearance" and as the annihilator of "matter-superstition" (Nachlass 1881, 15[21], KSA 9.463). In notebooks written in preparation for *Beyond Good and Evil*, he is simply associated with an absence of matter (Nachlass 1884, 26[302], KSA 11.231) and with the "dynamic view of the world" (Nachlass 1884, 26[410], KSA 11.261). In reviewing his own "philosophical genealogy," Nietzsche identifies himself with an anti-teleological perspective and with mechanism, insofar as it entails the consideration of moral and aesthetic questions as physiological, chemical, and ultimately mechanistic. But he adds that he rejects the theory of matter and considers Boscovich a great turning point in this regard (Nachlass 1884, 26[432], KSA 11.266). Similarly, Nietzsche writes in two letters to Köselitz in the early 1880s that Boscovich refuted the notion of mass (20 March 1882, Nr. 213, KSB 6.183) and that he had mathematically demonstrated that the assumption that atoms contain mass was not a useful hypothesis for scientific research (August 1883, Nr. 460, KSB 6.442).[70] Nietzsche recruits Boscovich exclusively for dynamism and for his conception of a universe in which there are only forces of different magnitudes contending with each other in constellations that inevitably recur.

The question we might want to ask is why Boscovich, whose book Nietzsche had not read since the first half of the 1870s, suddenly becomes important for Nietzsche in the years 1881–86. The answer is not necessarily that Nietzsche again read Boscovich—where would he have obtained a copy of his *Theory of Natural Philosophy*, and why would he make no mention of it in his notes or correspondence?—or that his preoccupation with him was continuous from 1873 until the early 1880s—we find no direct evidence that Nietzsche was thinking about Boscovich in the intervening period. Much more likely is that as Nietzsche began to occupy himself with cosmological hypotheses and their scientific foundations, he discovered a series of writers who had developed models that reinforced dynamism or even mentioned Boscovich as a predecessor to their own concerns. One such individual was Johannes Gustav Vogt (1843–1920), a young professor of philosophy at the University of Leipzig who published a volume titled *Force: A Real Monistic Perspective* in 1878. Vogt's book, the first volume of a two-part project that was never completed, was one of the books Nietzsche requested from Overbeck in August 1881 (Nr. 139, KSB 6.117). Most frequently Vogt's book has been regarded as a contribution to or at least a verification of eternal recurrence.[71] Vogt does refer at the outset of his lengthy treatise to the world as the mirror "of an eternal world process, a *cyclical process*," and he insists later that "the grounding of the cyclical process is . . . the first and highest task of a genuine mechanism." He goes on to make the familiar argument against a "limit condition," such as would result from the second law of thermodynamics, stating that it would have long since been attained; thus he, like Nietzsche, questions the consistency of scientists like Clausius, who posit entropy, but are not genuine mechanists since they cannot explain why heat death has not already arrived.[72] But it does not appear that Vogt validates a recurrence of the same,[73] as Nietzsche does, and, in any case, his book could not have reached Nietzsche prior to his "revelation" and to the various notes on recurrence in August 1881. It seems likely, however, that Vogt did contribute to Nietzsche's thought on the cosmological possibilities for the will to power. Like Boscovich and Lange, Vogt tends to reject matter, at the very least noting that we can never get to the essence of matter empirically. He points out that although substances appear to be solid, they are all subject to gasification, so that the notion of solidity is not something in which we can place any faith. He rejects the dualism associated with mid-century materialism as well as an external force, usually of divine nature, and postulates, as the title of his volume so aptly implies, that force is the sole substance of the universe and, moreover, that all forces are reducible to one particular force, that of contraction or compression [*Verdichtung*]. "We negate the material and allow this completely superfluous, hypothetical notion that originates exclusively in naïve realism to be absorbed into a pure concept of force."[74] What makes Vogt even more interesting for Nietzsche is his conception of force as active and dynamic.⁷⁵ Nietzsche's concept of the will to power developed over a number of years, and Nietzsche does not mention its cosmological dimension until the mid-1880s. But it would be difficult to ignore the affinity between active centers of force as a monistic explanation for the entire universe, which is Vogt's hypothesis, and later formulations of the will to power in Nietzsche's texts and notebooks.

Nietzsche likely had learned about Vogt's monograph from Otto Caspari, a professor of philosophy at the University of Heidelberg, who had reviewed Vogt's book and included the piece in a collection of essays and reviews that Nietzsche read intensively in the early 1880s. Caspari was also one of the chief editors of *Kosmos*, a journal that Nietzsche read avidly, and that contributed immensely to his knowledge of contemporary science. The subtitle of *Kosmos* is "Journal for a Unified Worldview on the Basis of Evolutionary Theory," indicating a great deal about its general direction and the convictions of the editorial staff. Highlighted on the first page of the initial issue is the claim that the journal is published in connection with Charles Darwin (1809–1882) and his most celebrated German disciple, Ernst Haeckel (1834–1919). The first essay, written by Caspari, carries the title "Philosophy in Union with Scientific Research," and the collection from which Nietzsche originally read about Vogt, *The Interconnection of Things* (1881), uses this essay as an introduction, emphasizing a "new reunification of philosophy and scientific research."⁷⁶ The copy of this book in Nietzsche's library contains extensive marginal notes and underlinings, most of them in the sections of the book that deal with Darwinism and evolutionary theory, psychology, and ethics. Indeed, Nietzsche's reliance on Caspari for his views of science, especially the biological sciences and their human implications, has been underemphasized in scholarship.

Our concerns in this chapter, however, are the connection between cosmology and the will to power, and how Caspari mediated and reinforced a dynamic alternative to materialism. From the outset he takes aim at materialism, which conceives of the cosmos as a "dead block"; unable to explain the nature of matter, it eventually devolves into mysticism. Like Vogt and Nietzsche, Caspari attributes the attraction of materialism to our perception and consciousness of the world, not to the nature of matter itself. The alternative to a universe of matter is a universe of force, but Caspari is careful to differentiate and not simply embrace all theories that prefer the monism of force to the duality of matter and force. There are false conceptions of force, for example, in the notion of a primeval force, which Caspari calls a pseudo conception of force that acts as a *deus ex machina* in avoiding a state of equilibrium. We have seen that Nietzsche shares this disdain for explanations that are external and contain theological remnants. Caspari reviews briefly various notions of force from antiquity to the present day, claiming that genuine notions of force are relational, not absolute. He maintains that a genuine philosopher, learning from Lange and other neo-Kantians, will be an adherent of "*critical* empiricism," and from this rational foundation will comprehend the "interconnection of things" in the cosmos: "If empiricism and the facts teach him to comprehend the cosmos as a system of forces and their *relations*, then further consequences of a transparent doctrine of force will compel him not to regard this system as dominated by some sort of absolute (as a mystical pseudo force), but rather he will see himself compelled to regard this very force-system as a constitutionalism of members related to one another, united through the condition of natural laws."[77] Caspari is thus in substantial agreement with Vogt and therefore also supportive of Nietzsche's cosmological variant of the will to power. Although Caspari objects to Vogt's reliance on contraction as conceding too much to mechanism, he too advocates a monism of dynamic force as foundational for the universe.

Nietzsche's search for external support for his cosmological presumptions led him to read less eminent writers of the nineteenth century as well. While Vogt and Caspari were both on the faculty of first-class institutions and involved with important projects at the boundaries of science and philosophy, Nietzsche also consulted thinkers who today are obscure, although relevant for his own cosmological speculations. One of them was Otto Schmitz-Dumont (1835–1897), who was not associated with any academic institution, although he had studied philosophy and natural science at the University of Bonn and worked subsequently as a mining engineer. His occupation took him from the Rhineland to Hungary and finally to North America, where he was employed in various occupations in Mexico, Texas, and other parts of the continent. After developing a rational system of viticulture in southern California, he returned to Germany in 1871, settling in Dresden, where he renewed his interest in academic pursuits.[78] Two of his writings, *The Mathematical Elements of Epistemology* (1878) and *The Unity of Natural Forces* (1881),[79] found their way into Nietzsche's hands, and the latter work, which evidences significant markings from an inquisitive reader, appears to have been important for Nietzsche as he was contemplating the notion of the will to power.

Like Vogt and Caspari, Schmitz-Dumont argues against a dualism of matter and force since this dualistic model leads to irreconcilable inconsistencies. Recognizing that matter amounts to nothing, representing merely "the hole into which metal must be poured in order to produce a canon,"[80] he contends further that the postulate of a single, unifying force is superior to the hypothesis of many forces. Examining various types of force—gravitation, electricity, magnetism, among others—in his search for a primeval force [*Urkraft*], he reflects on forces of attraction and repulsion. If attraction were the force to which every other variety is reducible, however, the world would have long ended as a single mass, since all matter would have come together. In arriving at this conclusion, Schmitz-Dumont, like Nietzsche, postulates an infinite amount of time. He therefore selects repulsive force, which acts inversely with the square of distance ($-1/r^2$), as the answer to the unity of natural forces, and most of his book is devoted to demonstrating how other forces can be expressed in terms of repulsion: "I want to show . . . that all physical forces can be derived from this one law in the sense that every particle of physics that acts according to another law can be dissolved into an atomic grouping of a definite arrangement whose elements obey that one law." The theme of his book is thus clearly summarized in one claim: "Our hypothesis reads as follows: There exists nothing else besides force centers [*Kraftzentren*] of equal intensity in various conditions of motion, which, repelling each other, act upon each other inversely to the square of distance."[81] Schmitz-Dumont is obviously an atomic dynamist, much like the other writers Nietzsche read in the early 1880s, and he even cites Boscovich in a positive fashion,[82] disagreeing only with the Jesuit mathematician's failure to isolate a single force to which all other forces are reducible. His dynamic monism undoubtedly appealed to Nietzsche, although it is quite evident Nietzsche never adopted the repulsive force as the basis of all force centers. At one point, Schmitz-Dumont refers to the primeval force of nature that he is seeking and adds: "In order to cause no confusion in the common use of the word 'force,' this primeval force should be given another name."[83] He does not suggest what this other name might be, but one reader of this book might have been thinking that, with sufficient modifications, this singular dynamic force in the universe might bear the designation "will to power."

The connection between the will to power and dynamic forces in the universe is made more explicit in Maximilian Drossbach's (1810–1884) *On the Apparent and Real Causes of Occurrences in the World* (1884), a study Nietzsche also read in the mid-1880s. Like Schmitz-Dumont, Drossbach was what we would call today an independent scholar, unaffiliated with any institution of higher education. He was a textile manufacturer whose only celebrity besides his connection with Nietzsche was an essay he composed in 1849 on reincarnation and his subsequent sponsorship of a contest for an essay on the topic in 1851, activities that have accorded him modest celebrity in anthroposophical circles.[84] Unlike the works of Vogt and Schmitz-Dumont, Drossbach's book is not primarily concerned with force or with the alternatives of mechanistic dualism and dynamic monism. His focus is instead the way in which we understand causality and necessity in the world, topics that also occupied Nietzsche's thought throughout the 1880s. Starting with observations on Hume and Kant, Drossbach observes that the former ultimately grounds causality in habit, while the latter has recourse to synthetic judgments. Neither philosopher, therefore, is able to prove causality in the things themselves, and even in the phenomenal world, they do not succeed in showing anything except change over time, not cause and effect.[85] His conclusion is that causality exists only as a result of our own subjective perspective on nature and is not based on nature itself: "Accordingly, we place causality, as well as regularity and order, into the phenomena which we call nature, and we would not be able to find them in it if we had not previously placed them there."⁸⁶

As interesting as these considerations might be for Nietzsche's own reflections on causality and necessity in his late writings, more important for our concerns in the present chapter is that Drossbach, while discussing sensations, has recourse to a notion of effective forces [*wirkende Kräfte*] interacting with our sense organs. For this theory he, like other dynamists of his times, cites Leibniz as his philosophical source:

> It is entirely correct when Leibniz says: the self-sufficient force is the truly substantial entity; the concept of substance is inseparable from, and really in a strict sense identical with, the concept of energy, force, activity, activity *through itself*, self-activity. The active force [*Die thätige Kraft*], Leibniz says, has a drive in it; therefore it passes over into action through itself without needing something else additional to it, like the removal of an external resistance, so that the action must occur, if nothing hinders it. The substance of things lies in their power to act. (19)

Drossbach explains further that if we observe two billiard balls, one impacting the other, we should conceive of their interaction not in terms of cause and effect, but in terms of reciprocal forces. "All processes in the world are reciprocal processes of causes, and all are connected through reciprocity, that is, through the relationship of *cause* and *cause*" (22). Every being in the world is for him "an original, self-sufficient force-substance. No being is caused by another, every one affects with its force the other, none is early, none later, they affect each other, but they do not cause each other. As strongly as I am influenced by the other, just as strongly do I influence the other. Effect and counter-effect are always equal" (23). In a marginal note to the hypothesis of reciprocal action, Nietzsche translates Drossbach into his own terminology: "Instead of reciprocal action I say *struggle for hegemony.*" Things happen in the world not because of cause-and-effect relations or out of some sort of mechanical necessity, but because of the unfolding of the forces that each entity possesses. For Drossbach, then, matter does not have any real existence; it represents "only the fictions of our imagination"; forces, by contrast, "are the things that really exist and are perceived sensually" (43). His reflections on causality thus lead him to a position familiar to us and to Nietzsche: opposed to the dualism of matter and force and advocating force as the explanation for everything in the universe. Drossbach's depiction of forces as active and unfolding, however, contains notions that are even more suggestive for Nietzsche and that confirm for him his key philosophical insight. "Force strives to expand," Drossbach writes, "force that has not yet expanded is striving, the expanded force is deed." And, in a reformulation of this basic thought, he asserts: "Entities do not move because—from where one does not know—they are pushed or driven, but because they strive to expand themselves. One only has the correct concept of force when one recognizes it as the striving toward expansion" (43–45). In the margins on this page, Nietzsche comments: "I say will to power." Nietzsche had developed the notion of will to power prior to the publication of Drossbach's book. But, as we have seen, Nietzsche's insertion of will to power into his cosmological speculations occurs only in the middle of the decade, at the time he was occupied with reading Drossbach. His encounter with Drossbach's book may not have precipitated this expansion of the will to power into the realm of cosmology, but it certainly provided at least a welcome confirmation that others were validating a dynamic monism that could account for the entire universe and that could supply the element necessary for the hypothesis of the eternal recurrence of the same.

Nietzsche's readings supporting a dynamic, monistic notion of force—and these readings included the works we have briefly reviewed by Caspari, Vogt, Schmitz-Dumont, and Drossbach—form the background for his expansion of the will to power into a cosmological concept. In doing so, he entered into a dialogue with contemporaries, some of whom were scientists and others of whom were philosophers with keen interests in the implications of contemporary physics for a conception of the universe. Nietzsche's contribution to this dialogue was thus timely: many late nineteenth-century thinkers were contemplating similar issues, and what Nietzsche concluded about the constitution of the universe resembles various hypotheses he found in writings that opposed mid-nineteenth-century materialism. To some degree, Nietzsche's reflections in the area of cosmology partake in the neo-Kantianism of the latter part of the century[87] and voice implicitly a preference for Leibniz's monadic solution over the rationalism of Descartes. We have already noted that Nietzsche rarely supplies much detail or explanation to this cosmological dimension of the will to power, neither in his published writings nor in his notebooks. The most notable exception in his books is aphorism 36 of *Beyond Good and Evil*, where we can see the nature of Nietzsche's contribution and his dialogue with contemporaries most clearly. He begins with an assumption and a question: if nothing else is really "given" except our desires and passions, can we not try to explain whether what is given suffices to explain our entire understanding of the world, including the mechanical or materialist world? We understand that Nietzsche is proposing in this sentence an alternative to the materialism of a Ludwig Büchner or a Jacob Moleschott (1822–1893) based on a variant of force: force as it manifests itself in our desires and passions, or even in our thinking, which is in reality, Nietzsche informs us, only a relation of drives to one another. We are on a familiar path, seeking a solution to the dualistic proposition of matter and force in a dynamic monism, which becomes a recurring theme in this aphorism. Nietzsche eliminates the subjective idealist alternative—he dismisses anything deriving from Berkeley or Schopenhauer, which would place primacy in human subjectivity—and advocates for something more fundamental in the world of affects. In exploring alternatives, he mentions various organic functions—self-regulation, assimilation, nourishment, excretion, metabolism—all of which he reconceives as a relation of various drives or forces. Alimentation, for example, involves at least the instinct connected to self-preservation opposed by the force of something being consumed that resists becoming incorporated into the alimentation process; it is not a matter of cause and effect (hunger causing eating; digestion as the result of ingestion), but of the reciprocal processes of forces Drossbach describes in connection with billiard balls. In this example from the organic sphere, we can see that Nietzsche does not want to deal with somatic processes necessary for our survival, but instead with activities involved in these processes that are regarded purely as forces that interact with each other. Nietzsche, however, also does not want to conceive these processes as the combination of many different and distinct kinds of forces/drives/instincts/desires/passions; instead, he maintains that the reduction of the apparent multiplicity of forces to a single force is "commanded by the conscience of *method*." In this reduction to a single source of explanation, which posits no more than the ultimate ability to convert all forms of energy or force into a single, unitary, basic force, we will recognize the commonality between Nietzsche's undertaking and what we have briefly examined in Vogt, Schmitz-Dumont, and Drossbach. If we can account for everything in terms of one concept, such as the will, then we will have discovered the ultimate "cause" of the world and the universe, and we will have simultaneously solved the issue of causality (in a manner very similar to Drossbach's solution). Nietzsche states his hypothesis succinctly: "wherever 'effects' are recognized, will is operating on will—and that all mechanical occurrences, insofar as a force is active in them, are force of will [*Willens-Kraft*], effects of will [*Willens-Wirkung*]." Nietzsche appears to be more comfortable expressing his hypothesis in the organic realm, even in the realm of humankind, and throughout his writings the will to power is most often mentioned in connection with organic life in general and human life in particular. But in this aphorism, he obviously also wants to extend his insights beyond the desires and internal workings of human beings into a realm of the inorganic world where mechanism reigns, and where we need not account for the complex play of forces that involve human activity. If we can explain all our instinctual life in terms of one form of will, which Nietzsche proposes to call "the will to power," then he claims we are justified in expanding this insight into the arena where "*all* effective force" [*wirkende Kraft*], which was the term Drossbach introduced, could be defined "unequivocally as *will to power*." Nietzsche's hypothesis of the will to power is tantamount to "the world seen from the inside"—that is, from the perspective of the effective force that explains "all occurrences in the world," as Drossbach states it, and we can conceive of the cosmos then, in all its complexity, as " 'will to power' and nothing else" (JGB 36, KSA 5.54–55). In this brief aphorism, Nietzsche has condensed many of the hypotheses he encountered in his readings from the early part of the decade and arrived at an alternative, at least in name, to the various propositions of other writers of his time, who were similarly concerned with force or energy as the single element in the cosmos. The will to power as the single explanation for all occurrences in the organic and inorganic realms derives in large measure from Nietzsche's preoccupation with theories of dynamic monism and constitutes his original contribution to the Cosmological Question as it existed in the last third of the century.

―

It can easily be argued that Nietzsche never developed a cosmology, or that his thoughts on cosmology were fragmented and incomplete. The notions he entertained and the hypotheses he offered can be considered too disconnected and underdeveloped to constitute a genuine theory of the universe. In advancing this claim, however, we would be simply observing again that Nietzsche was not a philosopher who elucidated his concepts with extensive exposition. Nietzsche may not have possessed a detailed cosmology, but he did definitely interact with the cosmological speculation of his era. Two notions that have attracted considerable attention in the secondary literature on Nietzsche's philosophy, the eternal recurrence of the same and the will to power, have most often been regarded separately from his scientific concerns. While there is no doubt that these notions can be mined for their ethical, ontological, and metaphysical implications, there should also be no question that they were also responses to developments in the natural sciences of his era, as well as to philosophical reflections connected with these developments, and that they reflect an effort on Nietzsche's part to enter into a conversation with both the scientific speculation about the cosmos and the philosophical commentary that incorporated this speculation. What has deterred many earlier commentators from exploring the rich literature in science and philosophy with which Nietzsche was familiar, and to which he was contributing, stems in part from the antiscientific proclivities of the commentators themselves. Often concerned with constructing a viable philosophy out of the fragmentary and diffuse comments in Nietzsche's published and unpublished writings, these commentators have either ignored the connections with the late nineteenth century discourse on cosmology, or regarded Nietzsche as responding to a more familiar and venerable philosophical tradition, one that Nietzsche often knew mostly secondhand through contemporary texts. Nietzsche assists in this kind of interpretation by covering well his actual dialogic partners and thus downplaying the discourses that form the context for his thought. In Nietzsche's published writings, we find no specific references to the laws of thermodynamics when he brings up eternal recurrence; all of these discussions occur in notebook entries or in personal correspondence. If we possessed none of his notebooks, we might suspect that his grand hypotheses relate only to the philosophy of antiquity and to nonscientific concerns. We could always establish that Nietzsche shared the notion of an infinite repetition of all occurrences with many other thinkers, both in his era and prior to the nineteenth century. But without the notebooks it would be difficult to ascertain what sort of theoretical developments concerned him most. Similarly, the names of most authors Nietzsche read who embraced a dynamic monism of force are absent from published writings and in large part even from his notebooks and letters. The names Vogt and Caspari appear only a handful of times; Schmitz-Dumont and Drossbach are entirely absent from his writings. Yet we can be certain not only that Nietzsche read works of these authors, but also that he was inspired by their insights and often found confirmation of his own developing thoughts on cosmology in their works. Even if we believe that eternal recurrence and the will to power possess implications that are far more important for conventional philosophical subfields than they are for our understanding of the universe, if we want to appreciate the genesis and implications of these hypotheses, the issues with which Nietzsche was struggling, and their timely nature, then we must examine, as we have done in the course of this chapter, the context of the Cosmological Question in which they emerged.

Chapter 9

The Eugenics Question

The Shift from Culture to Biology

Until now, we have seen that Nietzsche's preoccupation with writings dealing with natural science is intimately linked with his conceptual, philosophical universe. Many of the central notions in his works were developed in an ongoing conversation with theories in the physical or biological sciences, and his notes and works make frequent reference to contemporary research and publications. In this ongoing and pervasive dialogue, Nietzsche was not trying to contribute to knowledge in the natural sciences, but rather seeking to support his observations about the world and to confirm intuitions he harbored about the way in which humanity had developed with evidence from contemporary scientific theories. Nietzsche's ultimate purpose was not to increase knowledge of science or to validate science, but to develop philosophical insights about human beings and the universe they inhabit; his intercourse with science therefore always has philosophical ramifications that exceed purely scientific dimensions. But like many of his contemporaries, Nietzsche was not immune from believing that applying science or scientific principles to problems in the world could bring novel solutions and cure many of the social ills that he observed around him. As we have witnessed in his observations on social issues, for Nietzsche the problems in nineteenth-century Europe, in particular in Germany, were manifold and manifest. In the cultural realm, as evidenced in the first four chapters, Nietzsche believed he detected a severe decline in excellence that extended over many different areas of German and European life. Although he had hoped for a renaissance in European societies with the music dramas of Richard Wagner (1813–1883), he was soon disappointed in these hopes, and his outlook for a genuine cultural revival became bleaker as time progressed. In the social and political world, Nietzsche observed a regression that led in his later work to speculation on decadence and nihilism involving more than simply an aesthetic and artistic level, since Nietzsche increasingly came to understand that these levels could not be separated from psychology and physiology. Nietzsche was particularly troubled by democratizing tendencies in European countries, which extended suffrage to the working class and encouraged such "leveling" movements as socialism and women's emancipation; for him these trends in European nations were symptoms of a decay in the social fabric and a hindrance to the production of greatness and the propagation of genius, which remained definite goals for him even after his Wagnerian period ended. The widespread adherence to moral and religious value systems, especially those associated with the pernicious Judeo-Christian tradition, are increasingly portrayed in Nietzsche's writings as enervating manifestations in the evolution of the human species that only demonstrate unequivocally the ineluctable decline of the modern world. By the time we reach the 1880s, and certainly by the middle of that decade, Nietzsche was convinced of a palpable and pervasive dissolution in all areas of human endeavor.

In the 1880s, however, Nietzsche increasingly came to embrace biological explanations for, and remedies to, the wayward tendencies he had identified throughout his mature life. We have seen that in his earliest years, Nietzsche focused on education and culture as solutions for social ills, but by the 1880s, he had lost faith in the aesthetic and pedagogical models that occupied so much of his attention in the early 1870s. As he turned away from educational imperatives, he became increasingly fascinated by biology and more convinced of the seminal role that heredity plays in determining human behavior. In his later works, we therefore find Nietzsche influenced by, and contributing to, an ongoing discourse that involves evolution, heredity, degeneration, and eugenics. His metaphors, but also his thought, become increasingly infused with biological vocabulary. Indeed, it is fair to say that, from *Zarathustra* onward, when he becomes an adherent of philosophical naturalism,[1] he conceives of no essential difference between the biological, the physiological, the psychological, and the ethical in his speculations. Some of his early interests continued to play a role in his thought, but their value changes, and his perspective on them shifts perceptively. Richard Wagner, for example, who had earned Nietzsche's unquestioned admiration during his earliest writings, and who assumed the more ambivalent role of "the artist" in many of the texts in Nietzsche's middle period, becomes in the later works a paradigmatic case for illness and decadence in contemporary art. While in *The Birth of Tragedy* his music was regarded as the exception to a mediocrity that had enveloped contemporary culture, by the late 1880s, it was conceived as a symptom for the decline of European artistry. Critics have often been too ready to dismiss Nietzsche's various remarks about physiology and biology in connection with Wagner and art in general as merely figurative. But for the mature Nietzsche, there was no easy separation between the metaphorical register and the phenomena he was describing in terms of physiology. Nietzsche's description of Wagner's "sickness" is not an indirect way to criticize his music, as was Johann Wolfgang Goethe's

(1749–1832) reference to romanticism as "sick" and classicism as "healthy" in his conversations with Johann Peter Eckermann (1792–1854).[2] For Nietzsche in the 1880s, the biological and the cultural spheres are not distinct realms of human endeavor; thus apparent metaphors shed their function as figures and establish real connections. Much of Nietzsche scholarship has failed to recognize the nonfigurative dimension of his arguments. One consequence of this failure has been the persistent neglect of the natural sciences as important for an understanding of Nietzsche. But a more important result is that scholars have sometimes ignored or distorted the unusual and insistent claims that he is actually advancing.

These claims may strike us as unusual today, or they may be conceived as inappropriate for a philosopher, but they were part of an immense discourse that flourished in Europe and with which Nietzsche was familiar and fascinated. The notion of a decline in human affairs or in cultural achievements was certainly nothing unusual for the nineteenth century, and Nietzsche could readily point to predecessors in the ancient world who decried the demise of cherished artistic ideals and accomplishments. In the seventeenth and eighteenth centuries, intellectuals debated about progress in conflicts centered on the ancients and the moderns; in these discussions, although progress in some areas was conceded to advances in science or economic activity, in the aesthetic realm, the ancients were usually regarded as superior, as an ideal that could not be emulated or attained by a modern culture. For much of the Grecophilic tradition that reigned in Germany from Johann Winckelmann (1717–1768) through Heinrich Schliemann (1822–1890), Greek art represented a pinnacle of human achievement that could never be reached again. Friedrich Schiller's (1759–1805) reflections on these issues ascribed a naïveté to the Greeks that was inaccessible to contemporaries, identified as sentimental. Goethe admired the ancients as the bearers of artistic excellence unknown in his own times. G. W. F. Hegel (1770–1831) maintained that Greek sculpture was the erstwhile manifestation of the world spirit, succeeded in the Christian and the modern era by religion and philosophy, respectively. But he made it clear in his renowned thesis concerning the "end of art" that human endeavors in the aesthetic realm would never regain their central importance for the development of mind or spirit. In none of these earlier pronouncements about cultural decline, however, was there any indication that it was connected with a biological degeneration or a mechanism of heredity that has been generally deleterious to the human race. What is new for Nietzsche and for the late nineteenth century is that the discourse of cultural decline became associated with medicine and biology, and that the remedy for this situation, identified increasingly with the newly discovered science of eugenics, became an alternative to social, cultural, and educational models of an earlier era. Schiller's utopian projection of an ethical and cultural paradise in his *Aesthetic Education* (1794) could no longer be achieved by a resolute pedagogy and by models of artistic excellence, since the problem, now redefined as degeneracy and identified with large portions of the population, was hardwired in humankind.

The Discourse of Degeneration

Thus degeneration became the watchword for the pessimistically inclined intellectual establishment during Nietzsche's era. Although Georges-Louis Leclerc, Comte de Buffon (1707–1788), had first used the word as a scientific term to indicate the reversion of a species to its original type, the *locus classicus* for the term as a biological and medical concept occurs in Bénédict-Augustin Morel's (1809–1873) book *Traité des dégénérescences de l'espèce humaine* [*A Treatise on the Degeneration of the Human Species*], published in 1857. Morel's interest in cretinism, which he studied in the 1850s and initially felt was treatable with certain hygienic measures, led him eventually to his theory of degeneration, when he recognized that there were certain types of abnormalities that were apparently not susceptible to cures.[3] Cretinism plays no central role in the 1857 treatise, but it is an example of the more general phenomenon of degeneration that Morel detects in European society. As a devout Christian who understood the Bible literally, Morel postulates that the creation produced a perfect primitive being in the image of the divinity. It is no wonder, then, that European man of the nineteenth century appears to Morel as a morbid deviation from this original type.[4] Morel exhibits an extremely wide understanding of degeneration and its causes; indeed, anything that causes a human being to fall short of the proposed norm is labeled degenerate. Heredity can be one of the causes, but Morel, like many contemporaries in the nineteenth century, also finds alcoholic degeneration in connection with "the depravation of a moral sense, the violation of the laws of hygiene, the exigencies of certain habits of education."[5] Modern society is also at fault since industrial life entails demoralization and a general decline in social conditions that result in the appearance of degenerative human beings. Indeed, in his lengthy descriptions, Morel points primarily to environmental agents as the source of contemporary degeneration, eschewing hereditary origins.[6] Although degeneration is ubiquitous in modern societies, Morel focuses much of his treatise on intoxicants, primarily alcohol and drugs, as well as various types of malnourishment. Morel, of course, is concerned mostly with how to combat degeneration, and while he believes that some forms are incurable,[7] he recommends moral instruction, direct treatment of the most acute causes and symptoms, and prophylactic regimes involving physical and mental hygiene to arrest degeneration and introduce "regeneration."[8] Moreover, Morel hypothesizes that from the perspective of the species, degeneracy frequently takes care of itself: the effects of degeneration become so severe in successive generations that the ability to reproduce is impaired and the particular type of degeneracy is not passed on to any offspring.⁹ Despite the therapeutic and optimistic tenor of Morel's discussion, and despite his environmentalist proclivities, his book surveyed a phenomenon that in the succeeding decades was more often viewed as a biologically based, hereditary threat unsusceptible to customary medical procedures and moral persuasion.

Part of the reason that degeneration was increasingly viewed as less susceptible to individual therapeutic correction was its connection to evolution. Morel's treatise appeared two years prior to Charles Darwin's (1809–1882) *On the Origin of Species*, which altered the tenor of the discussion on degeneration and the urgency in seeking solutions to the putative downward spiral of the human race. Darwin did not focus on human beings in his initial explanation of evolutionary theory; he turned to the subject only twelve years later in *The Descent of Man* (1871), but the implications for human beings, even in his earlier, epoch-making volume, were obvious and immediately seen by many commentators. The discourse on degeneration had always contained references to heredity, which had long been recognized as a factor in disease, somatic abnormalities, and other characteristics, both physical and mental. Although the mechanism of inheritance would remain unknown throughout the nineteenth century, everyone recognized that ancestry was a powerful determinate of human traits. When evolutionary theory was mixed with commonplace notions of heredity and the observations of general degeneration, especially among the masses, the stakes changed radically. Although Darwin's theory can be understood as negating teleological notions of human development, such as those that gained acceptance during the Enlightenment in the hope for the perfectibility of the human species, the slogan "the survival of the fittest," introduced by Herbert Spencer (1820–1903) and associated with evolution, which Spencer also popularized as a term, suggested that the most viable specimens of a given species thrive and continue to propagate, while those that are unfit are gradually eliminated. For most animal and plant classifications, this notion presented no great problem for philosophically minded observers; to some extent it could even be harmonized with the more traditional notion of perfectibility. A difficulty entered only in the consideration of human affairs (and perhaps in the affairs of other species in which human beings intervened). Increasingly, intellectuals suspected that civilization somehow interferes with natural selection, canceling or distorting the direction of evolution and producing results that might be contrary to "Nature's plan." And, of course, if civilization interferes with natural selection, human beings could also make a conscious decision not to interfere and thus restore Nature to her rightful place, or, alternatively, human beings could intervene differently, as they had for centuries in domesticating and breeding other species through artificial selection, producing results that would be beneficial to society and civilization as a whole.

English Optimism About Evolution

In the second half of the nineteenth century, there were two radically different conclusions reached by individuals who reflected on how civilization affected evolutionary trends. The optimistic conclusion, associated to a degree with Darwin, Alfred Russel Wallace (1823–1913), and some of their followers, observed progress over the past generations of human endeavor, and projected a continued improvement of the human race into the future. For these scientists, degeneration may still occur under special circumstances, but it is outweighed by a propensity toward a general betterment of the human condition. In the fifth chapter of *The Descent of Man*, Darwin touches on these issues when he discusses whether natural selection is favorable to an improvement of the intellectual and moral qualities of humankind. His conclusion is not unequivocal, but it is generally favorable. On a global level, he detects only progress. Intellectually inferior peoples have died out and ceded their place in the annals of history to those who are intellectually superior. "It is, therefore, highly probable that with mankind the intellectual faculties have been mainly and gradually perfected through natural selection," he concludes from his brief survey.[10] Similarly, morality is on the increase in the aggregate. Darwin assumes that "primeval man" was influenced by praise and blame of his fellow men, and that the qualities we associate with a moral individual—he lists patriotism, fidelity, obedience, courage, and sympathy—give groups or tribes possessing this morality an advantage over others. "At all times throughout the world tribes have supplanted other tribes; and as morality is one important element in their success, the standard of morality and the number of well-endowed men will thus everywhere tend to rise and increase" (137–37). Within civilized nations, however, the effects of natural selection are more ambiguous. While among "savages" men who are weak or mentally deficient will be subjected to elimination, in civilization they are protected by laws, medicine, and charity, and allowed to procreate. Darwin recognizes that "this must be highly injurious to the race of man" and that such practices will ultimately lead to "the degeneration of a domestic race" (138–39). Similarly, current practices in conscription into the army and the conduct of warfare, which reduces the proportion of able-bodied and sound men compared to those who are less able, will result in a decline in the fitness of humankind as a whole. We can take some consolation in the fact that the most inferior members of society do not marry and reproduce at high rates, Darwin observes, but he seems uncertain whether this factor offsets his other concerns. With regard to intellectual qualities, he is likewise equivocal (141). He is more confident that the morally depraved are less advantaged in civilized societies since the worst specimens are subjected to imprisonment and execution, while the melancholic and the insane are confined or take their own lives. Other categories—the violent and quarrelsome, the restless, and the intemperate—seem variously disadvantaged in reproduction; profligate women bear few children, while profligate men rarely marry. Like his cousin, Francis Galton (1822–1911), he is concerned that the "superior class" seems to prefer later marriage and therefore produces fewer total children than the "very poor and reckless." But Darwin suggests that this tendency may be countered by the fact that the poorest classes lead more often an urban existence in which the death rate is higher. He reasons further that checks such as city life may not prevent the proliferation of inferior men, and that we should remember that the history of the world has many examples of civilizations that fell; he cautions that "progress is no invariable rule" (142–45). But in general, Darwin is not convinced that degeneration can be detected in human affairs, and he is not inclined to believe that it is so prevalent and dominant that we should expect devolutionary consequences. Rather than take such a "pitiably low view of human nature," he prefers to believe that "progress has been much more general than retrogression; that man has risen, though by slow and interrupted steps, from a lowly condition to the highest standard as yet attained by him in knowledge, morals and religion" (151). For Darwin, natural selection appears to be in harmony with progress in human affairs, and even in civilized, modern nations, where societies may be judged to have interfered with the course of nature, he does not believe that degeneration is an overriding concern.

Wallace, the co-discoverer of natural selection, propounds a similarly optimistic account of human progress, making a slightly different sort of argument. At a meeting of the Anthropological Society of London in 1864, Wallace maintained that on the level of physical form and structure, humankind has removed itself from the effects of natural selection, while on the level of mental and moral abilities it has not. He reasons that in all human societies, the sickly and less robust members have been protected and nourished; natural selection therefore no longer holds sway over the somatic features of these societies since "defective" individuals who would not remain alive or otherwise be prevented from engaging in procreative activity in the wild survive and reproduce in civilized environments.[11] As physical characteristics decline in importance for natural selection in human groups, moral and mental qualities gain a prominence that determines which group, tribe, or race will thrive, and which will be driven into extinction. Wallace argues that from the time of the appearance of what we would today recognize as human societies' nonphysical qualities assumed the most important role in the "survival of the fittest."

> Capacity for acting in concert, for protection and for the acquisition of food and shelter; sympathy, which leads all in turn to assist each other; the sense of right, which checks depredations upon our fellows; the decrease

of the combative and destructive propensities; self-restraint in present appetites; and that intelligent foresight which prepares for the future, are all qualities that from their earliest appearance must have been for the benefit of each community, and would, therefore, have become the subjects of "natural selection."[12]

Humankind is both inside and outside nature; it has conquered nature insofar as it no longer allows the physically weak and deformed to perish, but it adheres to natural selection in that groups that evidence highly developed moral and mental faculties are favored. In this schema, there is no room for degeneration as part of evolutionary theory: although selection for physical features is diminished, Wallace apparently detects no diminution in the physical form and structure of individuals not subject to competition, while he sees tremendous advantages and progress in mental and moral qualities. That such arguments harmonized well with British imperialist designs is evident, and Wallace declares at one point the natural superiority of Europeans over native populations in various places on the globe. Nietzsche, as we have seen in Chapter 5, harbored similar convictions about European superiority. Internationally, natural selection functions just as we would expect in displacing indigenous peoples with their imperialist conquerors, since the latter are both more physically able and more advanced in moral and mental attributes.[13]

Wallace even concludes his observations with a quasi-utopian reflection that highlights the optimistic conclusions he draws from evolution and his skepticism toward degeneration. Human beings are in the process, it seems, of separating themselves from natural selection; they not only are the dominant species on earth, but also are forming "in some degree a new and distinct order of being."[14] Wallace foresees continuous improvement in the development of intellectual capabilities and moral qualities, the eventual displacement of lower and less viable races by more advanced races, and eventually a state in which human beings are optimally adapted to both nature and society.

> Each one will then work out his own happiness in relation to that of his fellows; perfect freedom of action will be maintained, since the well balanced moral faculties will never permit any one to transgress on the equal freedom of others; restrictive laws will not be wanted, for each man will be guided by the best of laws; a thorough appreciation of the rights, and a perfect sympathy with the feelings, of all about him; compulsory government will have died away as unnecessary (for every man will know how to govern himself), and will be replaced by voluntary associations for all beneficial public purposes; the passions and animal propensities will be restrained within those limits which most conduce to happiness; and

> mankind will have at length discovered that it was only required of them to develop the capacities of their higher nature, in order to convert this earth, which had so long been the theatre of their unbridled passions, and the scene of unimaginable misery, into as bright a paradise as ever haunted the dreams of seer or poet.[15]

This utopian projection, derived from humankind's unusual position both within and outside the order of nature, is the consequence of an optimistic application of natural selection. For Wallace, as for Darwin, progress is the inevitable consequence of evolution, and the ubiquitous degeneration observed by contemporaries like Morel appears to be but a minor hindrance on a path toward the perfectibility of human relations.

It is easy to understand why this extrapolation of evolution by advocates of natural selection was anathema to Nietzsche. Although Nietzsche, like Wallace, also projected a "new and distinct order of being" when he postulated the "overman" in *Zarathustra*, he does not conceive of his new race as a perfection of intellectual and ethical qualities of contemporary Europeans. To some degree, Nietzsche's understanding and rejection of Darwinism is a consequence of the optimistic conclusions drawn by Darwin, Wallace, and Herbert Spencer, although, as we shall see in a moment, Spencer on occasion indicates that degeneration is a dangerous development in European nations. Nietzsche saw in the evolution promulgated by the "Darwin school" an attempt to justify and perpetuate the values and convictions of a smug, middle-class Britain. While his own remarks on colonialism indicate that he may not have been averse to the imperialism and overt racism in the writings of Darwin and his adherents, he most certainly found their propagation of a utilitarian morality objectionable, as well as their naïve faith in human perfectibility. Questionable also for Nietzsche is the reliance on intellectual and moral qualities as those most susceptible to development and most important for the evaluation of human progress. Nietzsche's more elitist, more vitalist, anti-dualist, and anti-egalitarian proclivities are at odds with what he perceived as the consequences of Darwinian theory and its hypothesis of natural selection. Indeed, Nietzsche's frequent invectives against the English in his later works are largely related to his disdain for the banal optimism attributed to Darwin and the school he associated with the English naturalist. In *Beyond Good and Evil*, for example, he identifies the British with mediocrity and commonness, but also with Christian morality. He mentions Darwin specifically, making the backhand compliment that he was adept at ascertaining common little facts, which at the same time meant that his abilities—and the abilities of those that follow him—for genuine philosophical reflection are completely lacking (JGB 253, KSA 5.196–98). As he writes in his notebooks in 1884: "The goal that the English see makes *every* higher being *laugh*. It is not desirable: *many happy people of low rank* is almost a repulsive thought" (Nachlass 1884, 26[234], KSA 11.210). Or as Nietzsche writes in his "Anti-Darwin" aphorism in *Twilight of the Idols*, "species do *not* grow more perfect: the weaker dominate the strong again and again—the reason being they are the great majority, and they are also *cleverer*. . . . Darwin forgot the mind (—that is English!): *the weak possess more mind*" (GD, Streifzüge eines Unzeitgemässen 14, KSA 6.120–21). Whether or not Nietzsche possessed firsthand familiarity with the writings of Darwin and Wallace cited above, his objections take aim at precisely the progressive outlook they deduce from natural selection. In a notebook entry from his last sane year, Nietzsche also refers obliquely to the optimistic, moralistic evolutionary discourse he associated with Darwin. Asserting that "they" (it is unclear to whom he is referring) ignore and even detest the body, he envisions a revaluation of natural values "until ultimately a pale, sickly, idiotic-fanatical being is conceived as perfection, as 'English,' as transfiguration, as higher human being" (Nachlass 1888, 14[96], KSA 13.273). As we saw in Chapter 7, for Nietzsche the "English" are philosophically unschooled thinkers who blithely ignore degeneration and seek to project their own mediocre existence into the future, maintaining their projection is based on the latest scientific evidence. Their understanding of the implications of evolution is deficient because, unlike Nietzsche, they fail to appreciate the genuine origins and ramifications of contemporary values and to recognize the precarious, decadent state of affairs in modern European societies.

Evolution and Degeneration

Not all English adherents to evolution were so oblivious to phenomena Nietzsche deemed manifest. Indeed, one of the most convincing claims concerning degeneration was composed by E. Ray Lankester (1847–1929), a professor at Exeter College in Oxford and an obvious enthusiast for Darwin's account of evolution. He observes, however, that the course of evolution for a given species is not absolutely determined by the principle of natural selection. Lankester maintains that there are three alternatives when an organism is reacting to its environment: An organism can maintain the status quo when it is in balance with its environment; it can develop toward more complexity, which Lankester terms "elaboration"; or it can diminish its complexity in response to the natural world and degenerate. Most of Lankester's discussion involves lower plants and animals. He is especially fascinated by the ascidian or sea squirt, since in his view these creatures present a clear instance of degeneration: they are descendants of higher animals with more elaborate structures and have evolved in a direction that has resulted in a simpler organism.[16] After discussing various illustrations of degeneration in lower forms of organic life, he turns briefly to the human being. He observes first the obvious fact that civilizations, once great and powerful, decline, and although he rejects the doctrine that "savage races of mankind" are descendants of "higher and civilised races," he does contend that degeneration is a very large part of "the explanation of the condition of the most barbarous races."[17] Turning to the "white races of Europe," he notes the widespread perception that they have progressed significantly over their ancestors and that they will continue to advance into the foreseeable future. But he considers these commonplace notions illusory, suggesting our fate may not be so different from many species that evidence decline in the evolutionary process:

> As compared with the immediate forefathers of our civilisation—the ancient Greeks—we do not appear to have improved so far as our bodily structure is concerned, nor assuredly so far as some of our mental capacities are concerned. Our powers of perceiving and expressing beauty of form have certainly *not* increased since the days of the Parthenon and Aphrodite of Melos. In matters of reason, in the development of the intellect, we may seriously inquire how the case stands. Does the reason of the average man of civilised Europe stand out clearly as an evidence of progress when compared with that of the men of bygone ages? Are all the inventions and figments of human superstition and folly, the self-inflicted torturing of the mind, the reiterated substitution of wrong for right, and of falsehood for truth, which disfigure our modern civilisation—are these evidences of progress?[18]

The advantage we possess over the ascidians is only that we are thinking beings and able to contemplate our situation, and if there is any consolation for the human species, it is that through science and its application we may be able to obviate the degeneration that other organisms cannot avoid.[19] For Lankester, however, a decline in human affairs is apparent in Europe of the nineteenth century, and despite the fact that most of the items he cites as evidence for decline might be more easily ascribed to conservative taste than to devolution, he, like other scientists of his era, regarded the regression of civilization to be the consequence of a biological process.

One of the most eloquent and persuasive arguments for degeneration, however, predates Lankester's essay by a dozen years and came in response to the aforementioned lecture by Wallace. It was also very likely a reference point for Darwin's discussion in *The Descent of Man*. An anonymous contribution to *Fraser's Magazine* in 1868, it begins by extolling the validity of Darwin's theory of natural selection. After citing a lengthy passage from Wallace concerning the dualistic effects of evolution on the human race, it states its disagreement with Wallace's claims. While the author acknowledges that superior races have an evolutionary advantage over "savage tribes," it disputes resolutely any optimistic projection for civilized societies:

> Our thesis is this: that the indisputable effect of the state of social progress and culture we have reached, or our high civilisation, in a word, is to counteract and suspend the operation of that righteous and salutary law of "natural selection" in virtue of which the best specimens of the race—the strongest, the finest, the worthiest—are those which survive, surmount, become paramount, and take precedence; succeed and triumph in the struggle for existence, become the especial progenitors of future generations, continue the species, and propagate an ever improving and perfecting type of humanity.[20]

The author's reasoning is familiar and derived to a certain extent from Wallace himself; it also bears a strong resemblance to arguments that would be repeated in European discourses on degeneration and eugenics for the next three-quarters of a century. Artificial laws, the author argues, have taken the place of natural laws, so that society protects individuals who would otherwise perish. Survival and advantage in civilization are often confirmed upon "those emasculated by luxury and those damaged by want, those rendered reckless by squalid poverty, and those whose physical and mental energies have been sapped, and whose *morale* has been grievously impaired, by long indulgence and forestalled desires."[21] The author thus contends that the laws and practices of current civilization favor both extremes in society, the profligate and superfluous upper classes, injured by "indulgence and excess," and the demoralized poor, characterized by privation and want. Especially disconcerting are marriage practices in contemporary society, since members of the solid middle class abstain from familial life until they have secured a sound financial basis, while classes less worthy of reproduction appear to have no inhibitions about procreating even if they lack the means to support their offspring. Everything in civilized countries appears to conspire against an improvement of humankind; once selection is no longer natural, degeneration is the ineluctable consequence.

With the spread of evolutionary thought, we thus encounter an optimistic and a pessimistic interpretation of human development. Technically, Darwinism would predict only that natural selection would produce human beings more suited to the environment in which they live and reserve judgment on whether adaptive changes represent an improvement or a decline in the species. In practice, however, it was difficult to avoid taking sides either for or against progress in *Homo sapiens*. It is noteworthy that even commentators who belonged to the optimistic camp conceded that civilization calls into question the full and pervasive mechanism of natural selection. Evolution and degeneration could coexist without any difficulty. As we have seen, Darwin and Wallace, who are generally convinced that moral and mental faculties are progressing, note the possibility of degeneration, and, indeed, the discourse surrounding degeneration appears to gain in strength as we proceed toward the last decades of the nineteenth century. A not unbiased observer, Eugene Talbot (1847–1924), who published a veritable compendium of degeneracy, its proponents, and its manifestations in 1898, wrote that "with the close of the year 1883 the degeneracy doctrine may be regarded as having practically been accepted in biology, in anthropology, in sociology, in criminology, in psychiatry, and general pathology."[22] We do not have to search far for confirmation of this claim. In France, for example, the psychologist Théodule-Armand Ribot (1839–1916) makes several references to degeneration in his celebrated study *Heredity*. In his understanding, evolution includes both a progressive and a regressive tendency, and it is perfectly possible to observe a movement toward a lower form that is degraded both physically and morally.[23] Heredity plays an essential role, since just as it makes progress possible in the ascendancy of a species, it also regulates and confirms its decline. "When the sum of vitality and of aptitudes begins to fail, decay commences. This process of decay may at first be of no moment, but heredity transmits it to the next generation, from that to the following one, and so on till the period of utter extinction, if no external cause interferes to stay the decay."[24] Ribot also observes the atavism of savage instincts within civilization, and in what we might consider an agreement with Nietzsche's views on colonialism, he advocates against their elimination, since they are needed to tame otherwise uncivilized lands. In the German realm, we could cite Eduard Reich (1839–1919), who discusses the dual nature of civilization: on the one hand, it protects us from deleterious illnesses through increased hygiene and nourishment, but it can also contribute to degeneration that damages the ability to procreate and threatens the race. A decline in physical well-being is accompanied by a demise in morality, so that an increase in criminality goes hand in hand with the diminution of fertility and life expectancy.[25] In England, even Herbert Spencer, whom, as we have seen in Chapter 7, Nietzsche associates with an altruistic and superficial English morality, raises the specter of the pernicious effects of civilization for progressive evolution. Like the author of the essay in *Fraser's Magazine*, he reasons that honest and upstanding individuals wait to marry and have children, while less desirable moral social strata have no compunction about procreating without the necessary resources to raise a family. We are thus breeding the race from the improvident and dissolute, rather than from the prudent and respectable sectors of society. Yet after centuries of allowing this process to persist, we are astonished at its results:

> If men who, for a score of generations, had by preference bred from their worst-tempered horses and their least-sagacious dogs, were then to wonder because their horses were vicious and their dogs stupid, we should

think the absurdity of their policy paralleled only by the absurdity of their astonishment; but human beings instead of inferior animals being in question, no absurdity is seen either in the policy or in the astonishment.[26]

The discourse on degeneration thus came in many forms, was popular in many different academic disciplines, and was propagated by diverse individuals in many countries. As it spread across Europe in the late nineteenth century, gaining momentum from practitioners of medicine and from the growing acceptance of evolution, it supplemented ongoing sentiments about decline that were originally conceived outside of the biological realm, lending these sentiments on occasion a scientific grounding or veneer. The way in which degeneration was discussed also suggested, as we shall see, possible avenues for action.

Nietzsche on Degeneration

We have already seen that Nietzsche was predisposed toward acknowledging decadence and degeneration by various discourses in the cultural and aesthetic realms, and by his generally critical attitude toward European society, in particular German developments following unification in the 1870s. Most commentators agree that he was introduced to the notion of decadence when he read the essay on Charles Baudelaire (1821–1867) in Charles Bourget's (1852–1935) *Essais de psychologie contemporaine* [*Essays in Contemporary Psychology*] in 1883. But the actual word does not receive prominence in his writings until much later in the decade, even though we can ascertain that he must have read Bourget's work shortly after its publication.[27] Degeneration has a slightly different history in his writings. In its German form, *Entartung*, it is a term that Nietzsche used rather liberally throughout his life; the Germanized form of the French term "dégénérescence" [*Degenerescenz*] appears only in Nietzsche's last published works and in notebooks from 1888. The general tendency that emerges from tracking key concepts connected with degeneration in Nietzsche's writings is that he used the notion, in particular for cultural phenomena, throughout his life, but that only in the 1880s, and notably during the final years of his sane life, did the physiological and evolutionary dimensions of degeneration assume a prominent place in his thought. The biological aspect was perhaps not completely absent even in his earliest discussions,[28] but as Nietzsche's scientific interests and knowledge expanded, and as he began to examine decadence as the cultural manifestation of a deeper physiological decline in Europe, the discourses in which he was implicitly engaging changed from predominantly cultural and aesthetic criticism to scientifically influenced philosophical speculation. There were any number of texts he could have read during this period that would have reinforced his predilection for understanding the cultural decline he observed in Germany and Europe in scientific terms. It is certain that in the year or so before his mental collapse, he read and appreciated the works of Charles Féré (1852–1907). Féré's influence through *Sensation et mouvement* [*Sensation and Movement*] (1887) and *Dégénérescence et criminalité* [*Degeneration and Criminality*] (1888) is well documented in the literature focusing on Nietzsche and physiology.[29] But it is obvious from published works and especially from notebooks of the early 1880s that Nietzsche was enveloped at a much earlier date with the discourse of degeneration and its various manifestations in European culture. An approximate timeline for Nietzsche and the discourse of degeneration would probably discern three stages: an initial preoccupation with the symptoms of decline as they pertain to European culture in his earliest writings and throughout much of the 1870s, the growth of a scientific foundation for a more generalized conception of decline starting in the early 1880s, and finally a focus on decadence and degeneration as fully developed notions in the final year or two before his mental breakdown.

It is perhaps easiest to observe this change in perspective if we examine Nietzsche's reinterpretation of *The Birth of Tragedy* in his preface from 1886. This "Attempt at a Self-Criticism" amounts to an endeavor to recast the main themes of the early text in terms of the topoi and perspectives he had developed in the intervening decade and a half, in particular his scientific studies. In the original work, Nietzsche had associated the Dionysian with music, madness, intoxication, oblivion, and humankind prior to individuation. These associations are largely in accord with the mythological tradition from which Nietzsche drew; in 1872, there was no discussion of a natural scientific dimension to the Dionysian or a biological basis for it in physiology. It was understood as an aesthetic principle opposed to the Apollonian mask of appearances. But in introducing the Dionysian to his readership in the mid-1880s—Nietzsche shows little interest in the Apollonian half of the duality and rarely mentions it after *The Birth of Tragedy*—he brings in a scientific and quasi-medical aspect completely absent in the work itself: "And what then is the meaning in physiological terms of that madness from which tragic and comic art grew, the Dionysian madness? What? Is madness perhaps not necessarily a symptom of degeneration, of decline, of a culture in its final stages? Are there perhaps—a question for psychiatrists—such things as *healthy* neuroses?" (GT, Versuch einer Selbstkritik 4, KSA 1.16). What had become obvious to Nietzsche from his readings in the 1880s was that madness was a sign of degeneration; in texts from Morel to Talbot, various types of deficiencies in mental development were viewed as somatically based abnormalities, some of which had heredity components. The romantically inspired glorification of madness found in *The Birth of Tragedy* was therefore suddenly at odds with the rudimentary biological knowledge Nietzsche has acquired in the interim.[30] The correction from 1886 therefore reinterprets madness as part of a complex of degeneration and psychiatry, but raises the rhetorical question of whether there is a variety of madness that stands outside this tradition. The point Nietzsche wants to drive home in his preface is that there is an inverse relationship between madness and optimism: the Greeks embraced a pessimistic worldview at their pinnacle and succumbed to the shallow optimism of reason and utilitarian thinking when they were in decline. This thesis exists uneasily beside the perspectives Nietzsche acquired in the 1880s, since he subscribed largely to the tenets of degeneration proposed by contemporaries. His solution was in part to make accepted symptoms of degeneration, such as madness, criminality, and sickness, the way in which the overman/outsider/advocate of new values appears to a contemporary degenerate society: "All signs of overmanliness [*des Übermenschlichen*] appear as sickness or insanity in men" (Nachlass 1882–83, 5[1], KSA 10.217).[31] The most unusual aspect of Nietzsche's discourse of degeneration is thus that he simultaneously embraces the physiological and medical notion of degeneration, but often assigns the accepted symptoms of degeneration to the anticipated overcoming of decline, or at least to those individuals who fall outside the norms of the degenerating societies of his own era. The result is a frequently confusing doubling of terms: madness is sometimes part of degenerate culture, for example, when it is associated with Judeo-Christian morality, and sometimes a sign of how contemporary degenerate human beings misunderstand and categorize the truly free spirits and philosophers of the future.

A second unusual dimension of Nietzsche's intervention in the discourse of degeneration is his questioning of cause and effect. In writings throughout the 1880s, the confusion of cause and effect in demotic, as well as philosophical discourse, was a frequent and multifaceted theme, and we have seen in the previous chapter that Nietzsche's reading of Drossbach exposed him to an alternative way of thinking about causality. In *Beyond Good and Evil* and *On the Genealogy of Morals,* Nietzsche points out how grammar seduces us to identify a sovereign subject that has control over actions, stipulating the former as cause and the latter as effect. In connection with degeneration, Nietzsche takes exception to the commonsense claim that decline is the result of sickness, increases in criminality, political agitation, a regression in standards of morality, or other unpleasant phenomena of societies in a downward spiral. In a note from the 1880s, he writes that his first principle is that what "one has formerly seen as *causes of degeneration* are its *effects*" and then presents a list of phenomena that are typical for the contemporary discourse on degeneration: vice, sickness, sterility, crime, libertinage, as well as its antithesis celibacy, enervation of the will, pessimism, anarchism, and a host of other phenomena ranging from skepticism to nihilism (Nachlass 1888, 14[74], KSA 13.255). Nietzsche posits the primacy of physiological decline, attributing to other phenomena a secondary, derivative, or coincidental status. In the section of *Twilight of the Idols* entitled "The Four Great Errors," he elaborates on the confusion of cause and effect in analyzing degeneration. Morality and religion have it backwards: long life and health do not result from a virtuous existence; rather the slowing down of the metabolism leads to a long and prosperous life. On the other hand, one does not prosper because of a healthy way of living. Cornarism, the philosophy of long life contained in the popular book by the sixteenth-century "centenarian" Luigi Cornaro (1484–1566), *Discorsi sulla vita sobria* [*Discourses on a Sober Life*] (1550–1562), which recommends a restricted caloric intake for increased longevity, fails to recognize that the consumption of smaller amounts of food is the consequence, not the cause of a more profound physiological change. The usual analysis of decline is similarly confused:

> The Church and morality say: "A race, a people perishes through vice and luxury." My *restored* reason says: when a people is perishing, degenerating physiologically, vice and luxury (that is to say the necessity for stronger and stronger and more and more frequent stimulants, such as every exhausted nature is acquainted with) *follow* therefrom. A young man grows prematurely pale and faded. His friends say: this and that illness is to blame. I say: *that* he became ill, *that* he failed to resist the illness, was already the consequence of an impoverished life, a hereditary exhaustion. (GD, Die vier grossen Irrthümer 2, KSA 6.89–90)

If we reason with Nietzsche that the symptoms of decline are manifestations of a primary physiological condition, then we can understand why he does not, like Morel, advocate therapy and hygiene as remedies for degeneration. Treatments and the "relief" they might bring are themselves signs of an already declining life; they do not cure the source, but merely continue, and sometimes facilitate or precipitate, the decline. Solutions must address instead the realm of degenerating physiology, the hereditary exhaustion that underlies the symptoms.

A third peculiarity in Nietzsche's conception of degeneration is its unusual relationship to both Christianity and to the moral system Nietzsche associates with the Judeo-Christian heritage. Most theorists of degeneration assume an ambivalent position with regard to religion and morality. On the one hand, they identify the increase in moral turpitude, such as one finds among the criminal element in a given society, with degenerative effects. Degeneration occurs when there is a breakdown in social mores and order, and when institutions, like the church, formerly foundational, begin to crumble. Thus the decline in religious observance and moral attitudes may be regarded as a symptom of degeneration. On the other hand, as we have seen especially among writers sensitive to heredity and evolution, observers of degeneration recognize that a devout Christian implementation of charity and compassion may unwittingly lead to a prolongation and propagation of degenerative individuals, thus contributing to the demise of a nation or race. In this case, degeneration is the direct result of Christian praxis and its attendant moral doctrines. Nietzsche is unequivocal on this topic: "The Christian movement is a degenerative movement of all types of deteriorating and excluded elements; it does not express the decline of a race; it is from the very beginning an aggregate formation of illness structures pressed together and seeking each other.... It is therefore not national, not determined by race; it appeals to the disinherited everywhere" (Nachlass 1888, 14[91], KSA 13.267–68). Since Christianity and its moral value system is part of decadence, Nietzsche does not view an increase in atheism or the turn away from Judeo-Christian morality as part of a decline. He does believe, however, that atheism as such and adherence to secularized ethical tenets do not necessarily represent an overcoming of, or opposition to, decadence. Much of his work published in the last three years of his life details why current tendencies in European society, although apparently antireligious and secular, are really covert continuations of the Judeo-Christian tradition in modified or disguised form. Perhaps the main reason that the apparently secularized nineteenth century is still degenerative is that religion and morality are not independent from the biological devolution of European nations. Indeed, as Nietzsche makes clear on a number of occasions, "moral degeneration cannot be thought separately from physiological: the former is merely a symptom complex of the latter; one is necessarily bad in the same way that one is necessarily sick." Nietzsche continues by observing that moral categories are grounded in a physiological reality: "Bad: the word expresses a certain *inability* connected physiologically with the type of degeneration, e.g., weakness of will, ... the powerlessness to control the reaction to a stimulus, to control oneself; the absence of freedom in the face of any kind of suggestion by the will of another. Vice is no cause; vice is a *consequence*" (Nachlass 1888, 14[113], KSA 13.290). Christianity is likewise not an autonomous religious movement that then produces an effect in the nations or among the peoples who adhere to it. Christianity or any religion is not the cause of decadence and illness; its appearance confirms only that the given nation, race, or people adopting Christianity was already in decline. It is ultimately the symptom of a much larger phenomenon of degeneration that has a primarily physiological dimension and various moral, religious, and cultural manifestations.

Much of the writing in Nietzsche's final years was devoted to describing the effects of degeneration and decadence in contemporary society. Although, as we have seen, his emphases make his observations and analysis particularly provocative, many remarks in his published and unpublished writings are consonant with the dominant discourse on degeneration during his times. Like most of his contemporaries who speculated about degeneration, Nietzsche believes that progress is not inherent in human activities just because time passes. As he writes in *The Antichrist*: "Mankind does *not* represent a development of the better or the stronger or the higher in the way that is believed today.... The European of today is of far less value than the European of the Renaissance; onward development is not by *any* means, by any necessity the same thing as elevation, advance, strengthening" (AC 4, KSA 6.171). In his notebooks, he observes phenomena that are prevalent in the discourse of degeneration: increases in sickness, such as anemia, hysteria, diabetes, and dystrophy; socially deviant behavior, such as prostitution and theft; the appearance of neuroses and psychoses; a recrudescence of criminality; a general weakening of the will and the proclivity for avoiding struggle; more frequent murder and suicide; and a general pessimism and an attraction for items that are deleterious to health and hasten further degeneration.[32] Nietzsche is particularly interested in alcohol and its connections with degeneration, an extremely timely observation. Alcohol is one of the main foci in many nineteenth-century discussions of degeneration: Morel devotes considerable attention to the effects of alcohol on both those who consume it and on subsequent generations, and in many medical circles, its prohibition was frequently regarded as a key to fending off degeneration and the reacquisition of health and vitality.[33] Perhaps owing to his own obsession with diet and nutrition, Nietzsche frequently focused on alcohol and its detrimental impact. Although some of his remarks are obviously humorous, they are too frequent in his works and notes to be disregarded as mere moments of levity. In *On the Genealogy of Morals*, for example, Nietzsche mentions the "poisoning of Europe with alcohol" as the only noxious agent that competes with "the ascetic ideal and its cult of sublime morality" in the disastrous decline of the continent (GM, Dritte Abhandlung 21, KSA 5.392), while in *Twilight of the Idols*, he refers to Christianity and alcohol as the "two great European narcotics." He continues in the latter work, referring to the pernicious effect of beer consumption on the German intellect and particularly on the academic youth, and contending that beer is the root cause of "the degeneration of our first German free-thinker, the *shrewd* David Strauß" (GD, Was den Deutschen abgeht 2, KSA 5.104). And in *The Antichrist*, the absence of German nobility in the history of higher culture is attributed to Christianity and alcohol, "the two *great* means of corruption" (AC 60, KSA 6.250). Nietzsche had adopted this anti-alcohol attitude in the early 1880s before biological degeneration and decadence became a central theme in his writings. In one note, he calls for a temperance movement in Germany, since alcohol is responsible for an increase in criminality and suicide (Nachlass 1880, 6[208], KSA 9.252), and in another, he writes that alcohol brings one back to a stage of culture that has been overcome (Nachlass 1881, 12[71], KSA 9.588).[34] At various points, Nietzsche also touches on other issues prominent in discourses of degeneration, for example, the effects of the mixing of races on the health or decline of a nation (GM, Dritte Abhandlung 17, KSA 5.378), or the role of atavism in heredity (EH, Warum ich so weise bin 3, KSA 6.268). Finally, Nietzsche evidences direct knowledge of trends in criminology, associated with the school of Cesare Lombroso (1835–1909), that connects outer appearance with criminal propensities. In his discussion of Socrates in *Twilight of the Idols*, he notes that ugliness "appears as a development in *decline*. Anthropologists among criminologists tell us the typical criminal is ugly: *monstrum in fronte, monstrum in animo*" (GD, Das Problem des Sokrates 3, KSA 6.68–69). Indeed, in his writings of the 1880s, particularly in the last two years of his sane life, Nietzsche discusses in his published works and notebooks almost all the central topics found in contemporary writings on degeneration. While his original contributions to this discourse are found in his observations on morality and Christianity, and perhaps his remarks on ascetic ideals, he was obviously familiar with a wide range of writings on this topic and participated in a much wider discussion on degeneration as a minatory phenomenon of late nineteenth-century Europe.

Eugenic Remedies for Degeneration

In the writings of nineteenth-century observers who detected degeneration in European society, there were several types of actions proposed to halt or reverse the decline. As we have already seen, the initial medical discourse on degeneration, as represented by Morel, recommended various therapeutic and hygienic measures to combat degeneracy and its symptoms in the population. Those writers who discuss degeneration in the context of heredity and evolutionary biology, however, often arrived at different, more radical, and more unsettling conclusions. The anonymous author of the essay in *Fraser's Magazine*, for example, suggests that a truly enlightened society should not need to undertake any remedial actions to correct for the absence of natural selection; sagacious leaders and wise individuals in all ranks of the social order should need no prodding to agree upon the restoration of nature to its rightful place in human endeavors. His description of what would result if this counterfactual state of affairs existed is revealing:

> The sick, the tainted, and the maimed, would be too sensible and too unselfish to dream of marrying and handing down to their children the curse of diseased or feeble frames;—or if they were not self-controlled, the state would exercise a salutary but unrelenting paternal despotism, and supply the deficiency by vigilant and timely prohibition. A republic is *conceivable* in which paupers should be forbidden to propagate; in which all candidates for the proud and solemn privilege of continuing an untainted and perfecting race should be subjected to a pass or a competitive examination, and those only should be suffered to transmit their names and families to future generations who had a pure, vigorous and well-developed constitution to transmit;—so that paternity should be the right and function exclusively of the *élite* of the nation, and humanity be thus

enabled to march on securely and without drawback to its ultimate possibilities of progress.³⁵

The vision conjured by the author is a race of perfect human beings, geniuses and saints, creative artists and intellectual prodigies. The reason that humanity has not already achieved this blessed state and, indeed, has not even begun to proceed along the road toward it, is that the wisdom and foresight necessary for its attainment has existed thus far only in isolated individuals. Far from proceeding toward this ideal, which, after all, amounts only to the reinstitution of natural selection in the social order, we are unfortunately fostering tendencies that move humankind in the opposite direction. The author mentions three trends specifically: the increase of individual liberties; the refusal to allow the poor, the incapable, and the diseased to perish; and the growth of democracy, which enables the unenlightened and the most ignorant to control governmental policies and priorities. Enlightenment, by which the author means awareness of the eugenic solution he propounds, is being defeated by the forces of deterioration; the failure to act in the name of rationality threatens to maintain humanity on its current downward path.

Many of the thoughts expressed by the anonymous author of "On the Failure of 'Natural Selection'" would have resonated with Nietzsche, and we find similar sentiments scattered throughout his writings. We have no evidence that he was familiar with this particular essay, and we can speculate that his poor knowledge of English would probably not have permitted him to read this article easily even if he had encountered it. We can be more certain of two things. The first is that Nietzsche was attracted to the solution to degeneration that eugenics provided. As we shall see, throughout his writings of the 1880s, and in particular in the last years of sanity, are remarks that draw on and contribute to the growing discourse in eugenics. Second, we can ascertain that Nietzsche was acquainted with writings in which the authors proposed eugenic utopias and eugenic solutions to degeneration in the nineteenth century. Certainly Nietzsche must have been familiar in the first instance with ancient reflections on this topic. Although Nietzsche often expresses unfavorable views of Plato, he must have taken notice of the sections in the *Republic* that deal with breeding. In the fifth book of that dialogue, Socrates maintains that the lawmakers will be responsible for arranging marriages, and to achieve the most beneficial results for the state, these unions should be based on a positive eugenics. Socrates's reasoning proceeds from animal husbandry, according to which animals are bred according to the best stock in order to produce the heartiest progeny. The same principles ought to hold true for human procreation except that the arrangement of partners will have to be accomplished by dissimulation so that there is no dissension among the people. Although Plato deals mostly with positive eugenics, he leaves no doubt that it must be paired with negative eugenics if the perfect republic is to be created and maintained: "The offspring of the good, I suppose, they will take to the pen or crèche, to certain nurses who live apart in a quarter of the city, but the offspring of the inferior, and any of those of the other sort who are born defective, they will properly dispose of in secret, so that no one will know what has become of them."[36] Those who produce offspring outside of the official sanctions of the state, whether because they are outside the prescribed age limits for procreation or because a woman has begotten a child with a man not sanctioned by the republic, must dispose of their offspring if they have not already prevented the birth by other means. The notion of disposing of offspring unfit for the social order would have also been familiar to Nietzsche from Plutarch's "Life of Lycurgus," which relates the eugenic practices of Sparta. The elders of the tribe held the ultimate authority over the offspring of all men and women, and decided on life and death according to the health of the infant:

> [I]f they found it stout and well made, they gave order for its rearing, and allotted to it one of the nine thousand shares of land above mentioned for its maintenance, but, if they found it puny and ill-shaped, ordered it to be taken to what was called the Apothetae, a sort of chasm under Taygetus; as thinking it neither for the good of the child itself, nor for the public interest, that it should be brought up, if it did not, from the very outset, appear made to be healthy and vigorous.[37]

The putative Spartan method for enhancing the stock of their city was well known to Nietzsche and his contemporaries, and although Nietzsche mentions the Spartans only sparingly and in several cases disparagingly, he surely was acquainted with Plutarch's text. In the "Five Prefaces to Five Unwritten Books," where Nietzsche comments on both Sparta and Plato's *Republic* (3.2: 258), he mentions that Sparta aimed at creating military genius (CV 3, Der griechische Staat, KSA 1.775), but in these early writings, he is more focused on the promotion of aesthetic and cultural excellence as part of the Wagnerian movement than on eugenic solutions to a degenerative society.

Nietzsche had ample opportunity to become acquainted with eugenics in readings of his contemporaries. Ernst Haeckel (1834–1919), the most celebrated adherent to Darwinism in the German-speaking world, even provides some illustrations of what he calls "artificial selection" in his *History of Creation* (1868; 4th ed. 1873). Although Haeckel, like Wallace and Darwin, ultimately subscribes to an optimistic view of evolution, maintaining that the species progresses in intellectual, nonsomatic characteristics over time, he cites several societies that endeavored to control reproduction in order to remove their fate from chance variations in nature. His first example is the "Red Indians of North America," who, he claims, owe their bodily strength to selection among newborn children. Those that are weak or sickly are immediately killed, so that the race is engineered to contain only superior specimens. Like most writers dealing with these issues in the nineteenth century, he cites the case familiar to Nietzsche and most educated Europeans, the Spartan attempt to produce a stronger military through selection of the hardiest offspring. Turning to contemporary society, he bemoans the fact that "military selection" removes the fitter and stronger young men from society, leaving the infirm, weak, and useless to thrive and reproduce. "Medical selection" has a similar effect, allowing those with chronic illnesses to survive long enough to produce offspring who will be similarly inclined toward infirmity. Haeckel recognizes that the sentiments in nineteenth-century Europe are opposed to eugenic measures, but he points out the hypocrisy of permitting the finest and fittest youth to be killed in wars without protest from those who would oppose disposing of "miserable, crippled children." He cites likewise the hypocrisy in the liberal opposition to capital punishment, which removes criminals from human society who presumably should not be permitted to procreate. His reasoning is that "capital punishment for incorrigible and degraded criminals is not only just, but also a benefit to the better portion of mankind; the same benefit is done by destroying luxuriant weeds, for the prosperity of a well cultivated garden." Haeckel, like most of his contemporaries, considers criminality to be a quality that is not only inherent in individuals, but also inheritable. The elimination of criminals thus constitutes "an advantageous artificial process of selection" that prevents "injurious qualities" from being passed down from one generation to the next.[38] Although Haeckel retains faith in natural selection to improve the human race, since the evolving feature of our species is mind, not body, his discussion of the societal benefits of artificial selection shows that he had some sympathy for eugenic intervention as well.

Despite Haeckel's prominence in Germany during the last decades of the nineteenth century, Nietzsche refers to him only a handful of times and, as we have noted in Chapter 7, almost invariably in a pejorative fashion. We have already seen that he compares him unfavorably to Ludwig Rütimeyer (1825–1895), but in other notes he also regards him as a narrow specialist unqualified to make pronouncements on larger issues and as an ally of David Strauß (1808–1874) in his evolutionary optimism.[39] No books by Haeckel are found in Nietzsche's library, although there is some evidence that he was familiar with his *History of Creation*, in which he could have read his remarks on artificial selection.[40] Nietzsche's own comments on eugenics more likely enter into a direct dialogue with French sources. Although Nietzsche did not possess Théodule Ribot's book on *Heredity*, he must have known something of its contents from other volumes in his library.[41] As we have already seen, Ribot contributed to the discourse on degeneration. A prominent psychologist who taught at the Sorbonne during the 1880s, Ribot was familiar with psychological theories in Germany, having composed a history of German psychology in 1876. In his earlier work on heredity, he had already broached the notion of controlled selection in order to improve the human race. Observing that a stratum of "unintelligent savagery" in some areas is overlaid by civilization, he asks whether we might not use other means to eliminate undesirable traits: "Can we, by means of selection and heredity, increase in a race the sum of its intelligence and morality?"[42] He quite sensibly opposes consanguine unions, since heredity studies have shown that they multiply the chances of unwelcome characteristics. Instead, he prefers a crossing of families to strengthen the stock of the race, "selecting a pair out of two different families, both possessed in a high degree of the particular quality, talent or tendency, which it is desired to transmit to the progeny in increased proportion." He appears to regret that arrangements of this sort have never been tried systematically, and only in medieval times under aristocratic regimes. For he has no doubt that "if this selection were carried out methodically, it would lead to good results for the improvement of the human race."[43] Ribot's positive eugenics finds its complement in the negative eugenics of Féré, whom Nietzsche certainly read. In chapters in both *Sensation et mouvement* and *Dégénérescence et criminalité* entitled "the harmful" [*les nuisibles*], Féré bemoans the lack of actions and laws undertaken to remove the pernicious effects of those individuals "who have nothing to give in exchange for what they receive."[44] Society has a right to protect itself against the criminals and decadents, to diminish as much as possible the numbers of "harmful" individuals, and to make sure that they do not have a deleterious impact on the future of the human race. We must go beyond merely decreasing their influence on the social order, however: "It is not only in limiting as much as possible the action of the harmful by the rigidity of law that could moderate the progress of their degeneration, it is above all in opposing their ability to reproduce." Féré regrets the absence of laws that would prevent marriages among degenerate individuals, although he does recognize the difficulty of determining precisely what degree of degeneration should disqualify someone from procreation. Rejecting unions between the healthy and the harmful as detrimental for the latter and infective for the former, he concludes in a Nietzschean fashion: "It is necessary that the weak perish; such is the inevitable law."[45] Only through this apparently inhumane regime can we hope to protect the species and secure favorable conditions for further development.

We know that Nietzsche came across eugenic remarks in various books he read, but it is not entirely clear how much he drew upon the founder of eugenic theory, Francis Galton, the polymath cousin of Charles Darwin. A number of years ago it was established that Nietzsche's library contains a single issue of the

Atlantic Monthly from 1883 in which Henry W. Holland (1844–1909) reviews Galton's *Inquiries into Human Faculty and Its Development*,[46] published earlier in the same year, and it has been suggested that Nietzsche had the essay translated for him orally by an English acquaintance.[47] A subsequent study has claimed that Nietzsche's firsthand knowledge of Galton's book went well beyond the review, and that there are indications in his writings that he had studied four chapters from *Inquiries* intensely.[48] There is no evidence that Nietzsche was familiar with anything else that Galton wrote. He is not mentioned in his published works or in his notebooks, even where he may be citing or paraphrasing from *Inquiries*. He cites Galton in a quotation that has not been verified in a letter to Franz Overbeck in July 1888 (Nr. 1056, KSB 8.347), and in a letter to August Strindberg composed shortly before the outbreak of his insanity, he refers to Galton, placing in parentheses after his name "('the hereditary genius')" (Nr. 1176, KSB 7.508).[49] In this piece of correspondence, Nietzsche is discussing the hereditary criminal, and he comments that the criminal is without a doubt a "décadent" and even an "idiot." But using the material gathered by Galton in *Inquiries*, Nietzsche concludes that the criminal is indicative of an individual who is too strong for a certain social stratum. Resa von Schirnhofer (1855–1948) also reports that Nietzsche showed her his copy of Galton's *Inquiries* in 1884, and that he proceeded to clarify for her the issues involved in the book, as well as the results Galton achieved in the area of heredity and evolution, in part extending Darwin's theory and in part contradicting it.[50] It is probable that the copy Nietzsche possessed at that time had formerly belonged to Joseph Paneth (1857–1890), the Viennese physiologist whom we encountered in Chapter 6. Paneth, we will recall, like Sigmund Freud (1856–1939), had worked in the laboratory of Ernst von Brücke (1819–1892), and he was affiliated with a group of Viennese Jewish students who admired Nietzsche very much. Paneth was also favorably inclined toward Galton, and there are indications that he first lent his copy of Galton's *Inquiries* to Nietzsche, and when the latter indicated a few months later that he had not finished it, Paneth gave it to him as a memento of their relationship. The copy of *Inquiries* in Nietzsche's library, one of the few items in English, has Paneth's name on the title page.[51] Owing to his poor knowledge of English, Nietzsche would probably have had to engage someone to assist him with reading the book, and it is likely that his deficiencies in English were the reason that he was unable to return the borrowed volume to Paneth in a timely fashion. From the evidence we possess, therefore, we can conclude with some degree of certainty that Nietzsche was acquainted with the outlines of Galton's thought, and that he displayed to his closest friends his interest in the founder of eugenics. There is no evidence that Nietzsche knew any writings of Galton beyond *Inquiries*, although the reference to "hereditary genius" does suggest he knew about the existence of Galton's book with that title, which appeared in 1869.[52]

Nietzsche gives us no indication that he was familiar with Galton's remarkable career as a scientist, which involved subjects as disparate as exploration in Africa, meteorology, fingerprinting, statistics, and studies in the hereditary characteristics of various plant and animal species.[53] Although Galton was known for several areas of scientific research in the nineteenth century, Nietzsche's focus was eugenics, a word coined by Galton in 1881, but which Nietzsche never used. Galton's reputation and language may have outstripped his scientific ambitions, but it is impossible to ignore his seminal contributions to various fields, including his work on the study of heredity. Indeed, he is responsible for the meaning we currently attach to the word "heredity" (previously "inheritance" occupied this meaning field), as well as the distinction between "nurture" and "nature," which occupies one of the chapters in *Inquiries*. It was undoubtedly his scientific rigor that Paneth admired, since he did not otherwise share a eugenicist viewpoint, in particular, one that involved the elimination of groups unfit for breeding. In the English society of his times, Galton's work can be situated politically as a reaction to the liberalism of a John Stuart Mill (1806–1873) or a Jeremy Bentham (1748–1832), and as supportive of the cultural conservative direction represented by Matthew Arnold (1822–1888) or John Ruskin (1819–1900). In some ways, Nietzsche occupied an analogous political position in Germany of his day, since he opposed the democratic tendencies of his epoch, but clung to many of the elitist perspectives that were associated with the conservative establishment. Galton's views were also part of an anti-religious tendency, and Nietzsche could easily identify with him in this area as well. Implicit in Galton's discussions of human heredity is the absence of the traditional deity; if biology explains physical and mental characteristics, then God's role in the constitution of the human soul is effectively eliminated. The partial overlap in worldviews would not have attracted Nietzsche so much, however, if Galton had not discussed themes that piqued Nietzsche's interest. To a certain extent, Galton touched on two related topics that attracted Nietzsche's attention. In *Hereditary Genius* (1869), he demonstrated that exceptional artistic and intellectual abilities run in families, thus suggesting that social engineering might be efficacious in promoting the type of greatness Nietzsche had advocated so strongly as a Wagnerian and continued to promote after his break with the Meister. And in *Inquiries*, he showed at various points that the social order was threatened with degeneracy, that there are commonalities among various types of degenerate individuals, and that eugenics offers a scientifically grounded method for improving humankind by eliminating degenerates and promoting healthy and vital individuals. Above all, as Holland notes in his review in the *Atlantic Monthly*, Galton "brings ethics almost within the circle of the physical sciences,"[54] a notion that was especially suggestive for a philosopher like Nietzsche, who was increasingly convinced that the moral realm could not be separated from the biological.

The Aristocracy of the Spirit

Other books in Nietzsche's library give us further indication of his interest in eugenics as a solution to problems he confronted in German and European society. One illustration stands out in particular among the items he must have consulted. It is an anonymous pamphlet with no indication of publication date entitled *The Aristocracy of the Spirit as a Solution to the Social Question* [*Die Aristokratie des Geistes als Lösung der sozialen Frage*]. Research has discovered that it was authored by the journalist and Protestant minister Erdmann Gottreich Christaller (1857–1922)[55] and appeared in 1885; the first half of the book evidences Nietzsche's characteristic underlinings and marginal marks, including several "NB" notations (*Nota Bene*). It is easy to see why Nietzsche might have been interested in this work, since the author ponders a predicament that had often bothered Nietzsche: in modern societies, the fittest do not often have positions of dominance and seem not to survive best. Those who are wealthy have a better chance of survival, and they pass their advantages down to their offspring through favorable laws of inheritance, but wealthy individuals are not necessarily the "fittest" and their survival and offspring are not necessarily the most beneficial for the further propagation of the human species. The author concedes that we should not conceive of fitness in terms of physical strength. Like many of the writers reflecting on the evolution of the human being, he notes that we have advanced past the stage where physical strength and other somatic features determine survival, as it still does among animals or even in earlier epochs of human existence. The attributes that have become more essential in modern societies are intelligence and superior morality. Unfortunately, they are also not indicative of progress in evolution, since in many instances individuals with lower intellect do better, while individuals with a high degree of egoism, rather than more refined moral qualities, seem to be preferred. Like so many theorists of degeneration, the author is observing that natural selection has failed to improve the species, because advanced civilizations have interfered with its operation. There is something terribly wrong in the distribution of goods in modern society: "The consequence of this avoidance of selection is that a large part of the best circumstances in life are wasted on unworthy individuals, whose personal quality worsens the species. By contrast, a portion of the personally excellent individuals languishes more or less under the bad circumstances that fall to them."[56] The author's book is dedicated to analyzing what precisely is wrong with our current social order and then to proposing a solution to the ills of society in a eugenic utopia.

Like many writers dealing with degeneracy and the possible solution to degeneracy, Christaller divides human characteristics into several groupings—physical, intellectual, and moral—and analyzes them separately. His guiding principle, however, is that if we are to improve the species, we must eliminate the falsely compassionate and myopically humanitarian principles that currently shape our attitudes toward individual human beings. The dominating mores in modern European societies are responsible for the preservation of many individuals who are unfit for life. If we wish to improve humankind, we have to be ready to discard our false, counterproductive notions of moral actions and attitudes, and adopt a completely different posture: "That humanity as a whole is damaged by this humane avoidance of the most ruthless selection (which is on the contrary perhaps the most considerate for the species), and that humanity is thereby hindered in its progress is plain and evident" (20–21). In the realm of physical deficiencies, whether they are deformities or susceptibility to illness, we are simply placing the species at risk by failing to take any action. Indeed, not only do we do nothing to eliminate the unfit from our midst, by prolonging their existence, we also permit them to procreate and pass on their physical weaknesses to the next generation. It is obvious that "the consequence of this artificial preservation of the sick and the weak is a habitual worsening, that is, reduced physical adaptability of the species type, at first by means of procreation" (27). The social disadvantages of permitting the diseased to exist in our midst are multiple. Not only do they propagate and produce more infirmity in the communities they inhabit, they also may infect other, robust members of society, thus diminishing the overall health. Their continued existence creates more work for everyone else, since their inability to shoulder their share of the social burden means that others have to do more, and since society feels obliged to establish institutions and other means to deal with their illnesses. The author suggests that providing fewer ameliorations, rather than increased care, would be preferable, since allowing a body with an inferior constitution to exist or even thrive weakens the natural and inherent drive toward improvement. The inference is that by tending to the weak and the sick, we unwittingly promote weakness and sickness. The entire situation of deteriorating corporal fitness is destined to worsen unless we intervene more decisively; at the moment, we are doing nothing to halt the "physical debilitation of the species as a result of deficient purging through selection" (31), and are in fact promoting it through perverse and shortsighted policies and perspectives. Although physical prowess is no longer the determinate evolutionary feature of the human species, our refusal to take action reduces the happiness and pleasure of humankind, and has a deleterious effect on intelligence as well.

 In turning to our intellectual capabilities, the author notes a similar degeneration, but with slightly different consequences. Revealing for the consistently biological vantage point of *The Aristocracy of the Spirit* is the way in which intelligence is defined in strictly evolutionary terms: "the capacity of adaptation by means of the brain." Indeed, the need for intelligence is something the author explains biologically as a mechanism arising from animal needs: "All thought and all knowledge [*Wissenschaft*] are originally only the endeavor to grasp the relationships among things in order to avoid pain and to increase pleasure" (31). The development of the sciences is explained as an exponential increase in brain development departing from this primitive state: gradually humankind in its evolution became increasingly complex and varied in its scientific procedures, eventually reaching the heights of advanced mathematical abstraction. The question that poses itself in the nineteenth century, however, is whether the human species can continue on the evolutionary path of increasing scientific knowledge as a boon to humankind. Like most theorists of degeneration, the author harbors doubts about the direction in which we are heading. For one thing, he bemoans the fact that not everyone who can contribute is given the opportunity. Although today we might identify advocates of eugenics in general as racially biased or as furtive promoters of an already advantaged class, Christaller actually scorns the upper classes and looks frequently toward the working class, the underprivileged, and the disadvantaged as a source of future progress in a more rational order. In a sense, he is strictly egalitarian, in that he advocates favoring individuals from all social strata as long as they exhibit the requisite mental capabilities. Like Thomas Gray (1716–1771) in his "Elegy Written in a Country Churchyard" (1751), he wonders openly how many great minds have gone untrained and have therefore not been able to assist the species in its progress because of the unequal distribution of wealth and its pernicious consequences for the poor. In our present societies, those who possess great wealth have ready access to education, but those educational opportunities may be squandered, and there are likely many talented persons who are deprived of any chance to enhance their standing. The wealthy, if they are not able to acquire intelligence through education, can sustain their status by renting intelligence in others, but these actions contribute nothing to advancing the intelligence or welfare of the species as a whole. Human societies have simply failed to develop institutions that consistently promote intelligent individuals, by not providing equal opportunity to everyone based on ability. In the realm of negative eugenics, we have not sought to eliminate individuals unable to perform intellectually at a satisfactory level: "For intelligence too the human species has only weak vestiges of mechanisms for removing unsatisfactory individuals" (39). Christaller is not simply a conservative or reactionary defending existing privilege: he supports the notion that any individual, no matter how rich or poor, may possess superior abilities if given the proper opportunity. Nonetheless, he is ruthless in his pursuit of biological selection to improve the race. We are cruel to our fellow human beings, especially those without abilities in the lower class, but we are not consequential enough when it really matters: "With regard to those who have no possessions, the natural course of events is interrupted by humaneness exactly at that moment and place where it would start to become better for the deficient and superfluous individual, namely at the point of the individual's disappearance. Humaneness allows individuals to deteriorate, but not to perish easily, even if they want to" (40).⁵⁷ The "stupid" [*die Dummen*] among the underprivileged classes, he argues, are in a practical sense not a real danger to the social order since their influence is so minimal; they are more likely to be a threat in terms of physical or moral degeneration. In terms of intelligence, the chief threat emanates from the upper echelons of society. In general, however, the maxim to which the author subscribes is that anyone not contributing to the higher development of humankind is wasting resources that should be devoted to potential contributors and therefore detracting from the progress of the species as a whole.

Before offering his eugenic solution to the Social Question, the author proceeds to examine a variety of phenomena that are in some regard consequences of our collective failure to institute selection. The manifestations of our blatant neglect for the welfare of the species are found in numerous areas of our social existence, and Christaller does not hesitate to catalogue our deficiencies. Ultimately responsible for our general predicament is the gross imbalance between mediocre individuals, who proliferate and disdain genuine free thinkers, and more worthy persons, who feel compelled to hide their talents in order to avoid the contempt and castigations of the majority. Like Nietzsche in *On the Genealogy of Morals*, Christaller employs the term "people of the herd" [*Herdenmenschen*] for the masses he despises (43). The dominance of mediocrity discourages the elimination of pernicious social customs and habits, for example, the wearing of certain types of clothing, which should be reasonable, but because of fashion often is not. Other examples of what he considers detrimental provides an insight into how ubiquitous he believes the problems are: he cites the giving of tips and the dutiful subservience toward women as social conventions that should be—and will be—jettisoned in a more reasonable social arrangement. Like Nietzsche, the anonymous author of this work holds governmental structures and activities in low repute. Because of the failure to apply biological selection, the electorate is ill suited to choose the most capable leaders and officials, and the abuse of power and influence leads to representatives who are neither effective nor intelligent executives and legislators. Indeed, the root cause of revolutions is our refusal to apply selection rigorously, since eventually the depravity of the government becomes manifest, even to the multitudes, and they seek remedies outside of normal electoral procedures. Art and science suffer as well under our laissez-faire attitude toward procreation. "The oft lamented low level of literature and art derives ultimately from the deficient nature of selection, which allows under certain circumstances the intellectually inferior and the most mediocre people to become dominant and to thrust their way to the top" (53). Further evidence for our depraved social order is "the barbaric custom of applause, especially at musical concerts," which indicates the lack of real appreciation for creative accomplishment and performative virtuosity (54). Moreover, Christaller detects the pervasiveness of false, limited, and unclear thinking, in part the consequence of the spread of substandard linguistic practices, such as the use of incorrect compound words and defective syntax; he observes a negative impact on scholarship and science; and in the realm of behavior, the decline is all too evident despite general efforts to inculcate morals into those who need them most. Worst of all, our neglect of breeding can only intensify the already ubiquitous social deterioration: "Since now those individuals whose development is arrested at a morally lower level, or even worse, are able to procreate, they contribute activities that endanger the community and degrade the character pool passed downward in human affairs from one generation to the next" (68). No matter where he turns, Christaller finds degeneration and decline with scant initiative or insight into amelioration or reversal. Ultimately, however, he remains confident that human beings, applying reason and becoming sufficiently enlightened, will eventually undertake measures to ensure that the best individuals will be placed in positions of authority, while those who are unfit, incompetent, and dysfunctional will be rendered harmless.

The first step in Christaller's remedy for society's ills is a proposed division of individuals into different groupings with distinct characteristics. He suggests this strategy in part because the most expedient alternative, which would involve an overall improvement of society through the elimination of imperfect individuals, would be impossible given the pervasive moral codes, and in part because social divisions of various sorts exist and have existed previously in different historical periods. Classes came into being when the human species increased production enough to allow some individuals to enjoy leisure; in the past, however, these class distinctions did not necessarily maximize the potential of humankind, and they were never groupings that were both permanent and reasonable. The slaves in ancient society were frequently better trained and more highly proficient than their masters, so that the master-slave distinction was arbitrary and eventually collapsed. Feudal society in the Middle Ages made a greater step toward a meaningful separation by developing a consciousness of nobility, but the aristocracy allowed other social classes to develop areas of human endeavor that really matter—knowledge and intellectual affairs—and it thereby contributed to its own demise. Since the French Revolution and the introduction of bourgeois regimes in European nations, society has been divided into two main classes, but the middle class, which currently exercises hegemony, is characterized by its halfhearted ideological stance toward its subjects. On the one hand, it manifests "class egotism," a consciousness of itself as the ruling class, and the determination to extend its domination beyond the economic sphere. On the other hand, it has embraced from the very outset of its existence an ideal of equality and humanity, inherited from Christianity, that was necessary to justify its hegemonic aspirations. This class "never understood the either-or: either decisive equality, in which case its institutions are unjust, or decisive domination, in which case they are foolish" (111). The contradiction at the heart of bourgeois ideology indicates that the class structure of modern society is untenable, and the author is convinced that only the introduction of an "aristocracy of spirit" can provide a reasonable and stable social order. The two main classes in contemporary Europe will embrace this new aristocracy because they will recognize the obvious deficiencies in the current arrangement and the equally evident advantages of the new order: "It is the aim of this work to demonstrate the deficiency, or even the absurdity of the current distribution of favors and to show that it is expedient and necessary to grant to the common consciousness of more noble individuals, to ideal humanity, the dominion over everything, and to feel a commonality with the remaining bipeds only secondarily" (124). The ruling class will eventually recognize the bankruptcy of the current social order and prefer the establishment of an aristocracy of spirit to a regression to other forms of class rule: it is the "most agreeable thought" (129) for the bourgeoisie. In the working class, the author believes that the leaders of the Social Democratic Party, as well as the most intelligent portion of its followers, will opt for an aristocracy of spirit as a means to achieve their own ideals of progress in human affairs. Future society will thus consist of a new aristocracy drawn from former members of various social strata and a subaltern class made up of the residual, inferior individuals.

More provocative and intricate are the author's remarks about the future subaltern class, which he divides into two types: the stupid and the bad. The stupid must be made harmless for their own sake and for the sake of the rest of society; the bad have "to die on the counter-will of society like sparrows perishing in winter owing to cold weather." By contrast, the author envisions no class of the weak and infirm. Whenever such deficiencies appear, in whatever class, the individuals will be subject to a eugenic regime: "Physical qualities will form no special class; those with terminal or hereditary illness have to refrain from procreation, or be restrained." Some may heal naturally, in which case no further measures will be necessary. In general, the principles for running the future society are simple and in accord with a tripartite division: "Selection of the best people; weakening of the stupid people; and elimination of the bad people" (135). Christaller envisions that these divisions will also entail physical separation; members of the ruling class will associate solely with each other in order to heighten the pleasure they derive from life and to reduce the risk of infection from inferiors. The aristocracy of spirit will enlist the most intelligent and most capable leaders, and rapidly assume absolute authority over the rest of humankind. They will procreate among each other and in time learn that any of their class born with physical or mental defects must be eliminated for the good of the entire race. They will become true believers in, and enforcers of, the science of eugenics. The stupid, by contrast, will have to be subdued and indoctrinated. Citing the lessons drawn from his reading of Karl Marx's (1818–1883) *Capital* (1867),[58] Christaller admonishes the future ruling class to deal with its inferiors in a different fashion than the currently dominant capitalists. Cruelty and oppressive exploitation are counterproductive. Members of the subaltern group will have to be segregated and restrained, but they must be given economic security and be educated in such a fashion that they know and accept their place in the social order. The formula the author uses is "education to modesty," and he, like Nietzsche in *On the Genealogy of Morals*, uses the Chinese as the paradigm for a subservient class in which a monotonous sameness prevails. Like Nietzsche at times, the author advocates religious training for the masses as consolation and education to obedience.[59] The bad individuals, the final class in this utopian projection, present a more difficult problem, since their influence must be eliminated entirely if the species is going to thrive. Accordingly, the author suggests that they be lured away and forced to congregate in places where they can have their own separate social order, complete with bordellos, taverns, gambling casinos, dancing halls, and foul literature. They can be encouraged to inhabit their own territories by a concerted effort to isolate them socially and economically, and by increasing punishments and eliminating outlets for their desired transgressions in the new aristocratic society. They will be enticed to their new homes by the attraction of a "paradise of vices" (155). The author also envisions a penal system for the criminal class that will restrict freedom entirely; only a change in character will be cause for parole; any recidivism will entail incarceration for life.

Nietzschean Eugenics

To what extent Nietzsche agreed with the eugenic recommendations and other strange assessments in this text is difficult to ascertain. In his writings, correspondence, and notebooks he makes no direct reference to Christaller's pamphlet, and the phrase "aristocracy of spirit" occurs only once in a notebook from the mid-1880s when Nietzsche refers to it as the "favorite slogan of the Jews" (Nachlass 1885, 35[76], KSA 11.543). On the other hand, we should recall from previous chapters that Nietzsche certainly favored an "aristocracy" in the form of a ruling caste. In Chapter 5, we saw that part of his advocacy of Europeanness entailed an elite that would exert domination over the globe, and that he frequently referred to Jews as part of a future "aristocracy of the spirit" owing to their proficiency in dealing with money matters. With regard to his copy of Christaller's pamphlet, we should note that he makes fairly frequent marginal marks and underlinings up to page 73 (about halfway to the end of the text) and frequently writes "NB" beside passages, presumably because they sparked particular interest in him. He never resorts to the sort of derogatory marginalia we find repeatedly in other books, where he writes "ass" [*Esel*] or "blockhead" [*Rindvieh*] to indicate his displeasure with auctorial claims. Although some of what Christaller includes in his discussion will strike us today as crude or silly, Nietzsche may well have taken a different view on some of the main arguments. Like Christaller, Nietzsche too conceived of degeneration as an issue that pervaded all areas of social life, and included physical and mental dimensions. As we have seen from many of Nietzsche's notebook entries, he also detected symptoms of degeneracy in various manifestations in nineteenth-century life, and although he never cites the giving of tips or applauding performance as signs of cultural decline, he certainly believed that degeneration could be associated with a wide range of phenomena in the political, social, and artistic realms. Unlike some eugenic proponents, Christaller does not promulgate an overt racial or classist bias in his arguments for social engineering; his proposed aristocracy of the spirit would likely include individuals from various ethnic groups, as well as meritorious members from any social stratum. Nietzsche, as we have seen, expresses similar views when he includes Jews as an essential part of a prospective ruling caste for Europe, and in general, he, like Christaller, exhibits no predilection for predetermining a future "aristocracy" or the "overman" based on current position in the social hierarchy. Both Christaller and Nietzsche thus advocate a "rank order" [*Rangordnung*] as necessary and beneficial for the future development of the human species, but they do not want to transfer present privileged roles or purely racial distinctions into a future society.

Although Nietzsche's analysis of degeneration resembles those of many advocates of eugenics, and although there is no question that he was familiar, or even sympathetic, with eugenic solutions, there exists no consensus in Nietzsche scholarship with regard to his views on social engineering. Indeed, in most recent critical accounts, the topic is almost completely absent despite its frequent mention in Nietzsche's later notebooks and writings. Certainly most National Socialist commentators, as well as many of Nietzsche's detractors during the first half of the twentieth century, felt that he was a proponent of social engineering, but liberal interpreters and Nietzsche scholars of the postwar era recommend reading Nietzsche's statements on breeding and the eradication of undesirables as metaphorical or hyperbolic rhetoric. If we consider only the published writings, we may be inclined toward the latter view. In most works, Nietzsche's remarks on topics like racial hygiene, procreation to improve the species, and the elimination of "inferior" types tend to be more circumspect and ambiguous, although frequently they strongly echo the biological vocabulary of eugenics. In *Zarathustra*, for example, the title figure preaches to his "brothers" about the need for a "*new nobility*" "to be the adversary of all rabble," and informs them that they "shall become procreators and cultivators [*Züchter*] and sowers of the future" (Za III, Von alten und neuen Tafeln 11–12, KSA 4.254). Considering the generally symbolic tone of this text, these remarks may not strike us as a reference to eugenic tasks, but we should not ignore completely the reference to breeding a new nobility and its similarity to Christaller's proposal. We read in *Beyond Good and Evil*, in an aphorism we have examined in connection with the Jewish Question, that the "European problem" can be approached by "the rearing [or breeding] [*Züchtung*] of a new ruling caste for Europe" (JGB 251, KSA 5.195). In *Twilight of the Idols*, he speaks disparagingly of the "improvement" of humankind through "*taming*" and "*breeding*" [*Züchtung*] (GD, Die "Verbesserer" der Menschheit 2, KSA 6.99). His argument in this passage is that the enforcement of a certain type of morality, whether accomplished by domestication or prohibitions on procreation, has led to an inferior human being. However, in *The Antichrist*, Nietzsche writes a bit more ominously—and in a more overtly biologistic framework—about the conscious creation of a higher type of human being: "The problem I thus pose is not what ought to succeed mankind in the sequence of the species (the human being is a *conclusion*), but what type of man shall be bred [*züchten*], shall be willed, for being higher in value, worthier of life, more certain of a future" (AC 3, KSA 6.170). What makes these passages ambivalent in their relationship to eugenics is the German word "züchten" and its various derivatives. Although it can be translated as "breeding" and has a primary meaning associated with the transformation of a species through procreative activity, it is also used frequently to refer to strict and coercive training, a disciplinary upbringing that falls on the side of nurture rather than nature. The various translations—"to rear," "to educate," "to procreate," as well as "to breed"—give an indication that the term is open to interpretive renderings and can therefore be employed to reinforce the "gentle" Nietzschean view that he was less interested in eugenics than in an educational project involving self-discipline, creativity, and increased intellectual achievement.[60]

One thing seems certain. If Nietzsche was promoting eugenic views in his published writings, these views are only one part of a mosaic of recurring themes revolving around religion, morality, and social stratification. In *Beyond Good and Evil*, for example, Nietzsche suggests breeding as an antidote to a perceived degeneration of the human being. It is clear that Nietzsche is drawing heavily on the biologically influenced language we have encountered in European literature on degeneration and eugenic solutions to degeneration. He writes of a person "with the rare vision to see the general danger that 'man' himself is *degenerating*," and continues by connecting this degeneration to a randomness that "has thus far been at play in determining the future of mankind." This rare individual "grasps everything that *mankind could be bred to be* if all its energies and endeavors were gathered together and heightened" (JGB 203, KSA 5.127). If we consider the context of these remarks, namely, nineteenth-century debates on Darwinism and evolutionary alternatives, Nietzsche's arguments appear to disdain the randomness associated with free procreation and natural selection in the population, favoring instead controlled procreation associated with eugenic alternatives, for example, Haeckel's "artificial selection." It is interesting to note that this randomness, the fact that the future of humankind is left to the chance practices of individuals rather than regulated by some higher authority for the benefit of creating and maintaining a "ruling caste," is in Nietzsche's mind a chief contributing factor to the demise of aristocratic and hierarchical value systems and the concomitant influx of mediocrity and its attendant social movements. "The *overall degeneration of man*, right down to what socialist fools and flatheads call their 'man of the future' (their ideal); this degeneration and diminution of man into a perfect herd animal (or as they call it, man in a 'free society'); this bestialization of man into a dwarf animal with equal rights and claims is *possible*, no doubt about that!" (JGB 203, KSA 5.127–28). The biological notion of degeneration is here connected, as it is in the texts of other writers, to various adverse social phenomena. In the case of Nietzsche's contemporaries, however, adverse degenerative phenomena were usually associated with the breakdown of the status quo and involved deviations from normalcy, such as mental illness or criminality. For Nietzsche, by contrast, degeneration also—perhaps primarily—entails ideologies of equality such as socialism, as well as their implementation, all of which were part of a widespread discussion in the 1880s, as we saw in Chapter 3. In closing this passage, Nietzsche does not explicitly call for a eugenic solution to the social problems he recognizes. In a typically ambiguous ending to both this aphorism and the fifth section of *Beyond Good and Evil*, he merely notes the disgust with which some people may confront this possibility, but also the alternative of "a new *task*" (JGB 203, KSA 5.128), one that will presumably counter both the degenerative effects and the randomness that has allowed them to persist.

Remarks from other passages in *Beyond Good and Evil*, and in other writings of his last sane years, give an indication that Nietzsche believed that moral codes were inextricably bound up with the maintenance of a social order precisely because they proscribed certain types of marital unions and promoted others. These societies from the past advanced a definitive class hierarchy, and hence often a superiority of cultural attainment, by enforcing measures that in Nietzsche's contemporary world would be associated with eugenics. Solutions that in the late nineteenth century would be regarded as biological were in former times instinctively enforced by social mores. In aphorism 262, after speaking of stock breeders and their experience with overabundant nourishment,[61] Nietzsche turns to two illustrations of past human societies that produced extended excellence in the cultural realm because they propagated themselves according to strict regulation of procreation:

> Now let us consider an aristocratic community, such as the ancient Greek *polis*, say, or Venice, as an organization whose voluntary or involuntary purpose is to *breed*; there are people coexisting in it, relying on one

another, who want to further their species, chiefly because they *must* further it or run some sort of terrible risk of extermination. In such a case, good will, excess, and protection, those conditions that favor variation are missing; the species needs to remain a species, something that by virtue of its very harshness, symmetry, and simplicity of form, can be furthered and in general endure throughout all its continual struggles with its neighbors or with oppressed peoples who threaten rebellion or revolt. (JGB 262, KSA 5.214–15)

These two exemplary societies are cited primarily because both exhibit social codes of conduct and behavior that serve to perpetuate a stratified status quo. Moreover, it is clear from Nietzsche's mention of stock breeders that he is thinking primarily of the biological implications of social conventions, and that, if we desire to establish and maintain excellence, he advocates external controls on reproduction for the overall benefit of a society, or even for the species. Virtues in this sort of social order are defined as those qualities that maintain or further the hierarchical structure; these virtues are enforced by various means, including education and legal structures, but also "in disposing of its women," and "in its marital customs" (JGB 262, KSA 5.215). At a certain point, however, when prosperity or the absence of external enemies allows for more luxury, the strict moral code becomes more lax; at that point "variation" and "deviance" ensue. The result is described by Nietzsche in terms redolent of the nineteenth-century discourse involving biological decline: "degeneration and monstrosity is suddenly on the scene in all its greatest fullness and splendor," and the final result is the mediocrity that Nietzsche detects everywhere in contemporary Europe (JGB 262, KSA 5.216–17). From this discussion, we can easily infer that the introduction or reintroduction of a positive eugenics, one that promotes the breeding of an elite ruling caste, is consonant with Nietzsche's solution to moral and social decline in the nineteenth century.

Indeed, Nietzsche's attraction to societies based on severe restrictions on marriage is evident in his enthusiasm for other, non-European social orders based on codes of rigid ethics and on inflexible standards for marriage and procreation. In the last year of his sane life, Nietzsche was fascinated by the *Traditions of Manu*, traditionally one of the most authoritative books of the Hindu code in ancient India, and he was especially interested in the hierarchy that this social code reinforced. Nietzsche's discussion of chandalas, whom he associated at times with Jews, has implications for his stance with regard to anti-Semitism,[62] but he was undeniably attracted to this Sanskrit text because it introduces strict regulations for the reproduction of a social structure. In *Twilight of the Idols*, Manu is hailed as "the most grandiose example" of "the *breeding* [*Züchtung*] of a definite race and species" (GD, Die "Verbesserer" der Menschheit 3, KSA 6.100). This breeding has the function of maintaining a social hierarchy, which Nietzsche considers tantamount to a *"natural order"* (AC 57, KSA 6.242). Nietzsche does not adopt this natural order found in the caste system of *Manu* when he discusses a somewhat different *"order of castes*, the supreme, dominating law." Rather than the four castes described in *Manu*, Nietzsche sketches a tripartite schema in his own terminology, but based on divergent physiological tendencies originating in nature: "the predominantly spiritual type, the predominantly muscular and temperamental type, and the third type distinguished neither in the one nor the other, the mediocre type—the last as the great majority, the first as the élite" (AC 57, KSA 6.242). Each of these castes is fixed and possesses its own rules, its own hygiene, and its own methods for achieving perfection. Admission to the caste is determined not by training or education, but by nature, and one cannot choose to belong to another caste. The ultimate purpose of the strict definition and the propagation of three distinct classes is to preserve society and to make possible "higher and the highest types" (AC 57, KSA 6.243). Nietzsche does not explicitly delineate how these types would have to be maintained, but his emphasis on nature and on segregation and hierarchy provides a good indication that the kind of marital restrictions found in *Manu* (or Venice or the Greek *polis*) must be adopted if a social order is to persevere and achieve its ultimate goals. Nietzsche's extremely derogatory evaluation of chandalas, who are the product of violations of prohibitions on procreation between castes, supplies further evidence that Nietzsche was attracted to expressions of positive eugenics in order to establish and maintain "natural" social orders, and to prevent the degeneration that necessarily accompanies the interbreeding of one caste with another.[63]

Perhaps the most vitriolic and offensive eugenic comments in Nietzsche's published writings involve negative selection—the elimination of individuals who are deemed unworthy of life. In many instances these comments involve Christianity, which Nietzsche believes responsible for protecting and promoting individuals who do not contribute to the progress of the species. At the beginning of *The Antichrist*, for example, Nietzsche broaches a discussion of eugenics not by asking "what ought to succeed mankind in the sequence of the species," since the human being is "a *conclusion*," but by inquiring about "what type of human being one ought to *breed*, ought to *will*, as more valuable, more worthy of life, more certain of the future." Nietzsche focuses at first in this passage on positive eugenics: he claims that valuable types have hitherto been only chance occurrences, but have never been consciously planned. On the contrary, "out of fear the reverse type has been willed, bred, *achieved*: the domestic animal, the herd animal, the sick animal man—the Christian" (AC 3, KSA 6.170). He soon turns to negative eugenics, however, as part of his harangue against Christian ethics. He had already formulated a negative eugenic invective in the previous section: "The weak and the ill-constituted should perish: first principle of our love of humankind. And one should help them to do so" (AC 2, KSA 6.170). But the purpose of this work is to disclose Christianity as a barrier to this eugenic program. Accordingly, he claims that not only has the Christian religion "waged a *war to the death* against this *higher* type of man," it has also nurtured and preserved human beings whose existence has contributed to the degeneration of nineteenth-century Europe: "Christianity has taken the side of everything weak, base, ill-constituted, it has made an idea out of *opposition* to the preservative instincts of strong life; it has depraved the reason even of the intellectually strongest natures by teaching man to feel the supreme values of intellectuality as sinful, as misleading, as *temptations*" (AC 3, KSA 6.171). The ethics of Christianity, which advocate compassion for less fortunate members of society, is decried as a violation of the natural order and an impediment to progress in the species. Nietzsche's objection to a morality based on pity became a dominant theme in his late writings, whether it is identified with Schopenhauer's philosophy or with the implications of Wagner's opera *Parsifal* (1878), and in these publications a morality of pity or compassion is inextricably bound to notions of evolution, degeneration, and eugenics: "Pity on the whole thwarts the law of evolution, which is the law of *selection*. It preserves what is ripe for destruction; it defends life's disinherited and condemned; through the abundance of the ill-constituted of all kinds which it *retains* in life, it gives life itself a gloomy and questionable aspect" (AC 3, KSA 6.172). The identical thoughts are found in *Beyond Good and Evil*, where Nietzsche castigates "*absolute* religions" for their "indulgent and supportive" treatment of humanity's "*surplus* of failed cases": "*absolute* religions are among the main reasons that the species 'human' has been stuck on a lower rung of development—they have preserved too much of what *ought to perish*" (JGB 62, KSA 5.81–82). It is difficult to understand these passages outside of the discourses associated with eugenic thought. Nietzsche adopts both the analysis and the language of eugenics; he suggests a positive eugenics based on a rigidly controlled caste system; and he advocates that European society eliminate the moral and religious impediments to allowing those individuals "ill suited for life" to perish, or even to enforcing their elimination.

In his notebook entries, especially those composed during the latter half of the 1880s, Nietzsche's preoccupation with ideas related to eugenics is even more pronounced and prevalent. Already in the early 1870s, before he became acquainted firsthand with the writings of Galton or the pamphlet on the *Aristocracy of Spirit*, he had composed numerous passages in which he recognizes that experiments with human reproduction have the potential to produce a more genial social order and to eliminate those constitutionally unable to contribute to the progress he envisions. As early as the mid-1870s, in refereeing thoughts from Eugen Dühring's (1833–1921) *Value of Life* (1865), Nietzsche wrote about the implications of Darwinian natural selection for human beings, commenting that if humankind proceeded conscientiously, it could achieve an improvement of the species (Nachlass 1875, 9[1], KSA 8.161). In these early years, he was often circumspect about intervention into natural processes, indicating that improvement can occur if we simply allow nature to take its course. In one note, he speculates accordingly about the "future in a few centuries. Economy of the earth; letting the bad races die off, breeding of better ones; one language. Entirely new conditions for human beings, even for a higher being?" (Nachlass 1876, 19[79], KSA 8.349). But in notes from the early 1880s, he expresses discontent with the arbitrariness of natural selection and impatience with the ponderousness with which the "natural process of breeding" proceeds, proposing instead that *"whole parts of the earth"* be devoted to *"conscious experiments"*: "Why shouldn't we be able to accomplish with human beings what the Chinese have learned to do with trees—that it carries roses on one side and pears on the other? This natural process of the breeding of human beings, e.g., which until now has been carried out excruciatingly slowly and clumsily, could be taken in hand by human beings" (Nachlass 1881, 11[276], KSA 10.547–48). Nietzsche recognizes at an early date that the conscious production of an improved species through "artificial selection" would entail not only the breeding of individuals who would be the finest and most creative specimens, but also the elimination of individuals unable to contribute to a healthy, reinvigorated social order. At one point in his notes, he discusses expanding the notion of crippled to include all manner of deformity since all "habits and strengths" are transmitted through heredity and unalterable. "With respect to this sort, the rest of humanity has the same right that it does with respect to the crippled and the monsters: it can destroy them, in order to prevent the propagation by the ill-formed who are left behind; e.g., the *murderer* is a deformed person" (Nachlass 1877, 23[59], KSA 8.424). Nietzsche favors experiments with human beings that are analogous to interventions into various species of plants and animals, and whose aim is the improvement of the quality of the species or the production of specific characteristics. Even in these early years, the goal for *Homo sapiens* is a better individual, as defined by Nietzsche's own standards of geniality and greatness, and the elimination of categories of human beings who are deemed unworthy of life. Although he couches his thoughts quite often in categories that are moral or religious, we can confirm that eugenic solutions were part of his thought as early as the mid-1870s and became more frequently expressed as he moved into the next decade.

    Nietzsche must have recognized that the eugenically perfected species of which he dreamed would not be attainable without strict regulations, and his pronouncements about breeding are therefore often accompanied by references to specific social rules and measures to accomplish the intended goals. Above all, his reflections in his notebooks focus on marriage, sexual desire, and procreation. Nietzsche understood that sexual pleasure could not be legislated or regulated out of existence; abstinence was not a realistic regulatory mechanism for him. At the same time and in accord with the aim of "ennobling" the species, he frequently expresses the view that marriage should not be left to chance, and that greatness can only be achieved with the restriction of procreation to those who would produce appropriate offspring. The following remarks penned in 1880 provide us with the full scope of his concerns:

> The satisfaction of desire should not lead to a practice by which the race suffers, that is, where there is no selection anymore and everyone can pair off with everyone else and produce children. The *extinction* of many kinds of people is just as *desirable* as their reproduction. . . . Only marriages 1) for the purpose of higher evolution 2) in order to leave behind the fruits of such humanity.—For all others concubinage suffices, with the prevention of conception.—We must make an end to this silly frivolity. These geese should not marry. Marriage should become more infrequent. Just walk through the big cities and ask yourself whether these people should procreate. Let them go to their whores. Prostitution [is] not sentimental. It should not be a sacrifice that is given to the ladies or the Jewish moneybag—rather for the improvement of the race. And moreover, one should not judge this sacrifice falsely: the whores are honest and do what they like to do and do not ruin a man with the "bond of marriage"—this strangulation. (Nachlass 1880, 5[38], KSA 9.189)

As we have seen previously in his remarks on ancient Greece, Renaissance Italy, and select non-Western, hierarchically ordered social arrangements, marriage was very much on his mind when he considered how older societies maintained and regulated themselves. Nietzsche recognizes that with regard to the older social orders, in which nobility reigned, marriage had the purpose of "*breeding* a race" of rulers (Nachlass 1886, 4[6], KSA 11.179). The deficiency with modern societies is that marriage has degenerated into a free-for-all in which the advancement of the species and the preservation of an appropriate hierarchy are no longer paramount. Reflecting on older aristocratic traditions, Nietzsche concludes that they need to be reintroduced to contemporary Europe:

> How have noble races preserved themselves so well, in all epochs? By not insisting that the young man seek sexual satisfaction in marriage and as a consequence he allows himself to be advised that he should *not* let himself be swept away into a marriage on account of *amour passion* or *amour physique*. First the young men who married were *experienced* in matters of love; and furthermore they had to think about representation, etc., in short, more about their race than themselves. I am in favor of breeding

again moral aristocracies and granting some freedom outside of marriage. (Nachlass 1880, 4[81], KSA 9.120)

In this passage, Nietzsche's thoughts go beyond affection for old social orders or a romantic vision of aristocracy and nobility. He was most certainly not an anachronistic advocate of feudalism, and he was openly critical of many aspects of the upper classes, including the aristocracy of his own era. Rather, his argument is that earlier aristocratic societies developed models for self-perpetuation, but also mechanisms for potential improvement of the social order that could be accomplished in his times through an altered, more reasonable, and more purposeful attitude toward procreation and sexual mores.

The creation of a new aristocracy might be a worthy goal if it were solely aimed at promoting greatness, but Nietzsche recognizes that a new social order demands placing restrictions on marriages and controlling the sexual practices of the rest of society. Further reflections on these matters are topics he discussed in other notebook entries throughout the 1880s. We have already seen a hint of Nietzsche's views on prostitution, but he makes them more explicit in other comments. It seems most important for him that sexual desires, especially those of the lower classes, be satisfied outside of wedlock: "sexual satisfaction should never be the aim of marriage.—The working class needs good whore houses,—Temporary marriages" (Nachlass 1881, 11[82], KSA 9.472). We also encounter remarks concerning restrictions on marriage, since according to Nietzsche it should be considered not a right of individuals, but something supervised by a higher authority, which should be concerned primarily with qualifications for parenthood. Since Nietzsche believed that the modern state is not interested in promoting excellence or quality, it has not concerned itself with matters of breeding and would not qualify as the higher authority that should make these important decisions. Maintaining that "the state is not necessary any longer," Nietzsche advocates a practical solution for procreation: "Individual outstanding men should have the opportunity to impregnate many women; and individual women, who exhibit specially favorable conditions, should not be bound by the coincidence of one man. Marriage must be taken more seriously!" (Nachlass 1881, 11[79], KSA 9.508–9). In one passage, Nietzsche even supplies fairly precise bureaucratic policies and constraints to ensure that marriages will be appropriately arranged for the benefit of an improved social order. Under the rubric "*On the Future of Marriage*," we encounter the following set of regulations and recommendations:

> *An extra taxation* on inheritance, etc. also an extra taxation on military service for bachelors from a specific age onward and continuing (inside the community)

> *Advantages* of every kind for fathers who put numerous boys in the world: under some circumstances a majority of votes
>
> a *physician's certificate* before every marriage and signed by the community leaders: in which several specific questions about the engaged couple and the physicians must be answered ("family history"—
>
> as a remedy to *prostitution* (or its ennoblement): term marriages, legalized (for years, months, days), with guarantees for the children
>
> every marriage accountable to and recommended by a specific number of reliable men in the community: as a communal affair (Nachlass 1888, 16[35], KSA 13.495)

Nietzsche had obviously devoted time and effort to thinking about the institution of marriage, both historically and in the contemporary world, within the framework of a socially engineered order. What remains unclear in Nietzsche's sketchy outlines about marriage and procreation is who would be responsible for developing and enforcing such bureaucratic regulations since the state, as we have seen, has no interest in the "breeding of human beings" for "better quality," but only for "masses" (Nachlass 1881, 11[79], KSA 9.508). What is apparent, however, is that Nietzsche, like many of his contemporaries, including Galton and others attracted to eugenics, conceived of social mechanisms as an indispensable aid to addressing the problems caused by degeneracy, which was ultimately regarded as a matter of physiology. While it is sometimes difficult from his fragmentary notes to understand with precision all his ideas on this topic, and to know which ones he seriously advocated and which were merely "thought experiments," Nietzsche's notebooks, taken together with his published writings, provide overwhelming evidence of the extent to which he was intellectually engaged with manipulating society through the institution of marriage for eugenic ends.

Nietzsche considered restrictions on matrimony to be essential, of course, because of the relationship between marriage and procreation. We have already seen that at some points he imagines the pairing of couples based on the presumed excellence of their attributes, and that in these instances marriage may not even be important or necessary; procreation is what matters. Nietzsche also writes that the permission to produce a child ought to be considered an honor or a distinction accorded to designated individuals, and encouragement is especially important since "the higher spirits are not very eager in erotic things." Positive eugenic procedures to encourage high-quality progeny are a staple of nineteenth-century ideas about social engineering, and in Nietzsche's thought they are then often coupled with discussions of negative eugenic measures, as they are in this entry. While society ought to promote procreation in distinguished individuals, means ought to be implemented to prevent procreation in other cases; otherwise, "the *low minded* will gain the upper hand." Those who are from the subaltern strata—Nietzsche mentions specifically the ill and the criminals—should be considered ineligible for producing offspring (Nachlass 1881, 14[16], KSA 9.627). Similar remarks can be found in his notebooks throughout the 1880s, and they become more frequent as the decade progresses. In the spring of 1888, for example, we find him demanding that procreation for certain groups of people—the chronically ill and the neurasthenic (basically those who have suffered a nervous breakdown)—be considered a crime. Nietzsche means "crime" quite literally, since he states that social dishonor and disdain do not suffice: "one ought to proceed against such crimes with the severest of all fines, under certain circumstances with the loss of 'freedom,' with quarantine, regardless of class, social stature and culture. To bring a child into the world, in which one does not have a right to be oneself, is worse than taking a life" (Nachlass 1888, 15[3], KSA 402). Nietzsche's reasoning is perfectly consonant with eugenic theorists of his epoch: if we permit the "ill-constituted," "weak," and "diseased" to procreate, we will contribute to a further deterioration of the species. Nietzsche's illustration of an individual suffering from luetic infection contains its own irony, since after his collapse into insanity, he himself was diagnosed with syphilis. "The syphilitic who produces a child starts an entire chain of failed life; he creates a pretext against life; he is a pessimist of the deed; through him the value of life is really diminished indefinitely" (Nachlass 1888, 15[3], KSA 402). The identical thoughts resurface in an entry that became aphorism 734 of the *Will to Power*, where Nietzsche is even more incisive in his demands for social intervention.

> After all, society has a *duty* here: few more pressing and fundamental demands can be made upon it. Society, as the great trustee of life, is responsible to life itself for every miscarried life—it also has to pay for such lives: consequently it ought to prevent them. In numerous cases, society ought to prevent procreation: to this end, it may hold in readiness, without regard to descent, rank, or spirit, the most rigorous means of restraint, deprivation of freedom, in certain circumstances castration.— The Biblical prohibition "thou shalt not kill!" is a piece of naïveté compared with the seriousness of the prohibition of life to decadents: "thou shalt not procreate!"—Life itself recognizes no solidarity, no "equal rights," between the healthy and the degenerate parts of an organism: one must excise the latter—or the whole will perish.—*Sympathy* for decadents, *equal rights* for the ill-constituted—that would be the profoundest immorality, that would be *anti nature* itself as morality![64] (Nachlass 1888, 23[1], KSA 13.599–600)

The reflection on the sixth commandment recurs in other passages, where Nietzsche again contrasts the prohibition on killing and the interdiction on procreation, as well as labeling the commandment naïve and "immoral" for protecting life that should not be preserved (Nachlass 1888, 22[23], KSA 13.594). Nietzsche recognizes in these various comments that the improvement of the species must be promoted not only by encouraging marriages that will result in healthy and superior offspring, and perhaps even genius, but also by restricting in the most severe fashion the proliferation of children who are a burden on an already degenerate social order.

As offensive as Nietzsche's eugenic remarks may be for us today, we should recall that they were made in the context of growing European reflections on degeneration, evolution, and biological solutions to social issues. Although the more sustained and pernicious eugenic writings in Germany did not appear until well after Nietzsche's lapse into insanity,[65] there was already a significant literature that either advocated directly social engineering for the improvement of the species or that included comments on eugenics in the course of discussions of related issues. Nietzsche's were thus timely remarks, and they differ from the sentiments expressed by other writers only in the occasional severity of formulation. It is not unimportant to emphasize again, however, that unlike later writers in Germany, Nietzsche does not consider race an essential component of his eugenic vision. While we can find passages in his writings from the very earliest years until the last notes that have racist implications, his discussions of controlled marriages and sanctions on procreation are never directed against any particular race; nor do they promote any notion of racial purity. Occasionally, we find him using race to refer to the human race, bemoaning the degeneration of the species; at other times, he uses race as a sign of excellence, for example, when he mentions that the Greeks bred for "race" (Nachlass 1882, 21[3], KSA 9.683). In other instances, however, Nietzsche writes about the decline of the "European race" (JGB 62, KSA 5.82), or about the necessity to breed a new, ruling race. Nations are sometimes identified as races as well, and occasionally in this context Nietzsche makes comments about the mixing of races. But these various usages of race never involve a eugenic intervention in favor of one race and against another. The notion of the natural superiority of the Nordic or Aryan "race," which should be promoted by eugenic or other means at the expense of inferior races, such as the Semitic, is foreign to Nietzsche's thought. It is also worth mentioning that the type of eugenic thoughts entertained by Nietzsche were not strictly the province of the right wing or radical conservatives in his own era. Social democrats partook in eugenic speculation and sometimes supported experiments that were meant to improve the stock of a given nation. In England, George Bernhard Shaw was an ardent proponent of social engineering, often bemoaning the pernicious consequences of promiscuous breeding in his own country.[66] These caveats to Nietzsche's discussions of eugenics are not meant to excuse them or to diminish their offensiveness. They do help us understand Nietzsche's interest in eugenic topics and the nature of the dialogue into which he implicitly entered. Nietzsche, like many of his contemporaries, was concerned about a perceived decline in human excellence in the European societies he knew. Solutions he had touted in earlier years, involving the Wagnerian renaissance of culture, pedagogical reform, and aesthetic imperatives, were gradually discarded as inefficacious. Like many of his contemporaries, Nietzsche began to regard the decline ultimately in terms of biology. In adopting breeding in the biological sense of the word as a means to control the future and destiny of humankind, Nietzsche joined with many intellectuals in nineteenth-century Europe seeking a remedy for a social order threatened by degeneracy and skeptical that natural selection without any human intervention would produce the desired improvement in the species.

Concluding Remarks

In this study of Nietzsche's "timely meditations," we have examined his participation in nine different discourses that were important during his lifetime. Each of these chapters formed something resembling a separate account of issues and Nietzsche's response to them, and could be read therefore without knowledge of the other chapters. Nietzsche did not consider these topics, however, distinct from one another; for him they were related and part of a larger complex. At various points in the preceding chapters, we have noticed obvious connections between discourses, as Nietzsche understood them. We have seen, for example, that his involvement with Wagner and the Wagnerian movement had a profound impact on his views on nationalism, as well as his relationship to the "Jewish Question" and aspects of colonialism; the "German Question" and German Jewry were intimately connected for Wagner and remained linked for Nietzsche even after his break with the Meister. We saw that in his later years, he associated anti-Semitism with the same type of chauvinism he encountered earlier in his life, so that a belief in a German essence and hostility toward Jews and Judaism went hand-in-hand. Colonial discourse was an outgrowth of nationalism as well, and on occasion, as we saw with Förster's Paraguayan settlement of Nueva Germania, a reaction to an imagined Jewish hegemony in Germany or even Europe. Similarly, there are connections in Nietzsche's mind between socialism and the women's movement, since both partake of the egalitarian tendencies of the nineteenth century. Ultimately, they both stem from the same false and unnatural assumptions about human psychology, and Nietzsche savages both in the harshest fashion in his late writings. In the 1880s, we also cannot distinguish clearly between these social movements and a biological realm that Nietzsche associates with the unfortunate survival of those "unfit for life." The psychological and the physiological, as well as the values that accompany the degeneration of the nineteenth century, are not clearly distinguished because Nietzsche believes they are part of one downward spiral toward nihilism. Eugenic solutions begin to become more prominent in Nietzsche's writings, not only as a remedy for the degeneracy he detects all around him, but also for the Jewish Question, and the new ruling caste that will result from the positive eugenic recommendations in Nietzsche's discussions will also have implications for the shape of colonial domination of the globe. Thus the clean separation between topics suggested by distinct chapter rubrics belies the interconnectedness in Nietzsche's understanding of the issues. Indeed, one of the most compelling aspects of his thought is that he denies the division between a realm of the body and material reality, on one side, and an area of psychic activity, where consciousness and intellect reign. Although the chapters in this study can be read as separate essays, the reader gains a better understanding of the way in which Nietzsche conceived of the world if they are all comprehended as part of an interrelated totality.

Nietzsche makes it difficult to consider his views as coherent and consistent positions in the separate realms defined by the chapters, as well as integrated parts of a more comprehensive totality or vision. His style and temperament did not allow him to build arguments in a systematic fashion, and the reader will not fail to have noticed that in order to construct a unified view of any social or scientific question, we had to examine passages from various works and mine his notebooks and correspondence for unpublished remarks on the various topics. In contrast to a philosopher like John Stuart Mill, Nietzsche did not write a treatise on women's issues of the nineteenth century or on their "subjection" and the need for equality between the sexes; nor did he author an essay about socialism and the working class. The absence of an essay or treatise does not mean that Nietzsche did not harbor definite opinions on these matters. But we can discern his overarching—and sometimes evolving—views only by gathering and pasting together comments from various published and unpublished sources, and by then supplying connections among Nietzsche's comments to form something more comprehensive. This procedure is really no different from the way in which scholars have treated his philosophy since intensive commentary began in the early twentieth century. We have noted in the course of our observations that Nietzsche did not commit himself to a fully developed exposition of even his most celebrated concepts, such as the overman, the eternal return of the same, or the will to power. Subsequent to his death, interpretations of these notions and other central issues in his writings were accomplished by the same means we have employed to explore his views on the German Question or colonialism or eugenics. In one instance, in the initial chapter, we could rely on a more substantive text, the unpublished lecture series on education, but in all other cases we had to proceed as Nietzsche enthusiasts have done for many decades: with careful attention to multiple texts and contexts. Part of Nietzsche's attraction for critics has probably been the openness of his works to various readings, which results often from the fragmentary nature of his views and the extensive use of aphorisms. That his writings have remained vital for so many years and have been seen to influence and engender so many different intellectual and philosophical movements is no doubt connected with his style and the somewhat diffuse nature of his argumentation. If we want to establish what Nietzsche was really advocating, it is therefore of the utmost importance—and more so than for other philosophers—for us to pay careful attention to all utterances about a theme and to understand, as we have been at pains to do throughout this book, how his thought is in communication with contemporary discourses. To recognize what a writer is saying, it is important to know the events and ideas to which he is responding. Otherwise, commentary runs the risk of ignoring the sense of a statement and reading into it a meaning that it could not possess.

In constructing the chapters for this study, I selected major social, political, and scientific discourses of the late nineteenth century. These discourses were not the only ones to which Nietzsche was responding, however, and it would have been possible to expand the number of chapters with additional materials. We saw in the introduction, for example, that in the 1880s Nietzsche was interested in comparative legal studies, and in general he was attracted at various points in his life to what we would consider anthropological reflections. There is also a psychological discourse in the nineteenth century in which Nietzsche was engaged.[1] Although he demonstrates no intimate knowledge of Wilhelm Wundt and Hermann von Helmholtz, two of the pioneering figures in German psychological research in the nineteenth century, he was certainly attracted to more philosophically inclined French psychologists who produced works that addressed issues concerning the maladies of the will and psychological degeneration in contemporary society. Nietzsche mentions, for example, Théodule Ribot's (1839–1916) journal *Revue philosophique* [*Philosophical Review*] in a very positive manner in letters from 1877 (to Paul Rée, August 1877, Nr. 643, KSB 5.266; to Malwida von Meysenbug, 4 August 1877, Nr. 644, KSB 5.268); Ribot wrote on Schopenhauer, but he was also the author of *Les Maladies de la volonté* [*Maladies of the Will*] (1882) and numerous articles and books that touch on Nietzsche's interests in the 1880s. We have already mentioned Nietzsche's relationship to Charles Féré in Chapter 9, and we know from Nietzsche's library that he read his *Dégénérescence et criminalité* [*Degeneration and Criminality*] (1888) very closely. Some of the connections with psychology have already been examined in considerable detail, especially the influence of Féré,[2] but certainly a more thorough exploration of Nietzsche and French psychology could easily be pursued. It would also be possible to situate Nietzsche in the many philosophical discourses in which he was participating. In this area, we would need more studies that recognize that the conversations he entered were largely with contemporaries and only secondarily with the greatest names in the philosophical tradition.[3] But I am confident that the various "Questions" I chose for the preceding chapters include some of the most important discourses for the nineteenth century, especially during the decades of the 1870s and 1880s, and that Nietzsche's responses and contributions to them demonstrate how timely he really was in his writings.

There will undoubtedly be some readers, especially those of a more traditional philosophical bent, who will wonder whether situating Nietzsche in the discourses of his era adds significantly to an understanding of his philosophy. The response to this implied query depends very much on what we consider to be Nietzsche's philosophy. Proponents of analytic or linguistic philosophy, who have been attracted to Nietzsche's writings in growing numbers over the past few decades, have usually not regarded the type of context on which this study is based to be of great value in determining what Nietzsche is propounding. Likewise, as we have seen in previous chapters, philosophers focused on existential and ontological issues have declared themselves uninterested in the discourses contemporary to Nietzsche and how he might be participating in them. Despite their differences, these directions in philosophy prefer to concentrate on the works themselves and the concepts and words contained in them, and to exclude historical material as unimportant or extraneous to the task of the philosopher. Their work is made especially difficult by Nietzsche since, as we have noted several times, he does not offer whole and cohesive presentations for many of his most important concepts.[4] These philosophical commentators are thus left to stitch together coherent arguments from various fragmentary remarks, a process that sometimes leads to quite strained interpretations. In some cases, we suspect that we are learning more about the exegete than about Nietzsche; Heidegger's Nietzsche, for example, tells us more about Heidegger than about the nineteenth-century philosopher he purports to analyze. There are three reasons, however, that the contextual approach that the present study advocates contributes essentially to the objective of understanding Nietzsche's thought. The first is simply that Nietzsche throughout his lifetime included discussions of historical issues in both his published and unpublished writings. Nietzsche delivered a series of lectures on the educational system in Germany; he remarked in various works on "Peoples and Fatherlands"—for example, in *Beyond Good and Evil* (JGB 240-56, KSA 5.179–204); he includes a section on "Woman and Children" in *Human, All Too Human* (MA 377–437, KSA 3.265–84); he composed several aphorisms dealing with the Jewish Question; he included comments on the working class, on capitalists, and on socialism in many writings; he wrote aphorisms on Darwin and many others that relate to evolutionary theory; he framed his hypothesis of eternal recurrence in terms that allude directly to thermodynamics. Concerns with contemporary issues and specifically with the nine questions identified in the preceding chapters are found in published texts and unpublished notebook entries throughout his lifetime. Nietzsche obviously considered them part of his "philosophy," and so should we. Second, as we have seen repeatedly in previous chapters, Nietzsche consulted books and essays related to "nonphilosophical" topics and used them in his writings. He read tracts on educational reform, on socialism, and on political affairs; he consulted books on biology and the physical nature of the universe; he read on issues relating to women and the colonial movement. Nietzsche did not consider these readings and his commentary on them to be something apart from his philosophy, and neither should we. Finally, Nietzsche's own "philosophy" on what constitutes and determines "philosophy" includes considerations beyond the philosophical text itself. We have already seen that in *Beyond Good and Evil* he wrote that he had come to understand "what every great philosophy to date has been: the personal confession of its author, a kind of unintended and unwitting memoir" (JGB 6, KSA 5.19). The events impacting philosophers, their physical constitution, and the conditions in which they live are inseparable from the philosophy itself. Nietzsche argues that there is no thought that is pure and abstracted from the concrete circumstances of life. If Nietzsche claims that personal and historical context are inseparable from philosophical claims, perhaps we, as interpreters of Nietzsche, should apply this lesson and pay more attention to these factors in analyzing his own philosophy.

A second issue that might arise from the presentations in previous chapters is the liberal use of evidence from Nietzsche's unpublished notebooks and from his correspondence. There are some commentators who regard only those works authorized by Nietzsche as legitimate in considerations of his philosophy; notebook entries and remarks in letters, as well as conversations reported by other individuals, are considered material that may not express what Nietzsche really meant to say. This view makes sense on one level: we can be relatively certain that Nietzsche allowed only his convictions to be published, while the thoughts contained in his notebooks and correspondence may represent experimental pronouncements or immediate responses that would not survive the moment in which they were penned. One can even argue that the very fact that a notebook passage did not make it into a published piece of writing indicates that Nietzsche did not feel it captured his genuine beliefs. But there are many good reasons that consulting materials in notebooks and correspondence may afford us insights into Nietzsche's thought that we would otherwise miss. First, for some periods of Nietzsche's life, we have no knowledge of what he was thinking or what he considered important except for unpublished writings. Nietzsche's first published work other than items he wrote as a classical philologist, *The Birth of Tragedy*, did not appear until he was in his late twenties; if we want any access to his nonphilological activities for the first half of his life, we are compelled to seek it in notebooks and letters. Any account that emphasizes the development of his views from his student years must consider these materials as a primary source. Second, while it may be true that notebook entries remained unpublished because Nietzsche rejected them, we cannot exclude the possibility that Nietzsche is more forthright and bold when he is writing for himself, and more circumspect in his published works. The largest collection of unauthorized notebook entries published after Nietzsche's death was *The Will to Power*, which was compiled by his sister, Elisabeth Förster-Nietzsche. But if we examine this work carefully, we find very little that is not contained in one form or another in his published writings, and although we may rightfully object to the arrangement of the aphorisms, very little strikes Nietzsche aficionados as something foreign to his way of thinking. A few entries may be thought experiments that Nietzsche rejected, and portions of his notebooks are obviously notes taken from books he is reading; not everything can be ascribed directly to Nietzsche. But there is no reason to believe that most of what he included in his notebooks is something he would repudiate; in many cases, it appears to be the formulation rather than the thought that was deemed unfit for publication. Indeed, in many instances, notebook entries supply the thought process behind the eventual published aphorism. Third, rejecting unpublished writings and accepting only what is in print is not as tidy a solution as it appears to be. We would then have to decide what to do with the three works published after Nietzsche's mental breakdown: *The Antichrist*, *Nietzsche contra Wagner*, and *Ecce Homo*. Nietzsche never gave his final approval to these volumes—and from his mental state toward the close of 1888, it is difficult to know whether a sane Nietzsche was editing and approving what he had written—and we know from previous writings that Nietzsche frequently undertook revisions in the final moments. But we would also have reservations about early writings. *The Birth of Tragedy* may have represented Nietzsche's convictions when he composed it in the early 1870s, but much of what he advocated from these years was quite obviously no longer part of his thought by the 1880s. In this case and in other cases, it is difficult to claim that the restriction to published writings provides us with more reliable access to "Nietzsche's philosophy" than the consideration of unpublished notes. The solution I have favored in this study is the judicious use of all materials. Notebook entries and remarks in letters also have a context, and we can often estimate their value by considering carefully the topics Nietzsche is exploring. In the case of correspondence, it is important to take into account the addressee and Nietzsche's relationship to that individual, as well as the circumstances of the letter. The key to using unpublished material is to exercise caution and, as with published works, pay attention to the discourse in which the utterance participates.

Finally, some readers might question what the results of this study tell us about Nietzsche and whether the conclusions we reached about him should change our views. In the course of investigating his relationships to various questions of his era, we have confirmed that he consulted many contemporary sources. We have also seen that when he includes ideas from these sources in his own writings or when he adapts thoughts of others, he rarely credits the books he consulted. For example, he was a consistent reader of philosophers who argue for monistic dynamism, but we know more about Nietzsche's reactions to these readings from marginalia and markings in Nietzsche's library than from any direct references in his works. In light of his unacknowledged borrowings, should we be less inclined to consider him a great thinker? And with regard to the purity of his concerns, are his insights into philosophical concepts and concerns tarnished by regarding him as an individual involved with contemporary issues in society and science, and in readings he does not cite? We have also drawn some conclusions about his social views that do not accord well with the values we typically embrace in the twenty-first century. He advocated an elitist and undemocratic educational system, rejecting the precepts of liberal education and equal opportunity. He expressed disdain at times for the working class and rejected parliamentary procedures and the democratic movements of his day. He exhibited misogynist tendencies, in particular after 1882, and pillories men and women who promote equality among the sexes. He retained at least an undercurrent of anti-Jewish thought even as he rejected the anti-Semitic political tendencies of the 1880s, and in his last years of sanity he accused Jewry of introducing a degenerate slave morality. And he embraced eugenic solutions to social ills, based not on race or ethnicity, but on dubious categories of fitness and the ability to promote the dystopic, hierarchical type of society he sanctioned. We may therefore be confronted with the questions: Do some of these more offensive positions on matters that are of great importance today damage his reputation as a critical thinker? Should Nietzsche be considered worthwhile reading for our times? There are a variety of responses to these sorts of concerns depending on individual predilection and interests. But let me attempt to provide some perspective on these questions that is consonant with the principles informing this study. With regard to Nietzsche's originality and his greatness as a thinker, we should consider that no philosophers or writers exist outside their time—or ahead of their times—and that even the desire to appear "untimely" may itself be a timely feature. Nietzsche entered into preexisting and developing discourses of the late nineteenth century, but his participation in these discourses usually entailed a unique intervention, and certainly one that was stylistically original. In responding as he did, he was no different from other philosophers and writers we deem worthy of attention. With regard to Nietzsche's somewhat unsettling views on social phenomena, we should consider that he shares many of his perspectives with contemporaries, and that his sentiments were often expressed in a daring and forceful fashion, but that they were in many instances not as virulent and abhorrent as many others among his peers. If we consider his views critically, we may conclude with ample justification that in various areas he was not always and in all regards the great thinker we once assumed he was, but a sober reflection on what he advocated should allow us to assess more accurately his place in any number of traditions. The purpose of this study has not been to denigrate or champion Nietzsche, but to understand some of the social and scientific confrontations that informed his thought. This book will have had a salutary effect if it assists us in viewing Nietzsche as someone who, like all great intellectuals throughout history, was intensely engaged with the discourses of his times.

Notes

Introduction

1. The word *unzeitgemäss*, which I here translate as untimely, has been rendered also as "unfashionable" and "out of season." It also contains the connotation of antimodern, or at least not modern, and thus partakes to some degree in the conservative critique of modernity.

2. The first four books of *The Gay Science* were published in 1882. The fifth book, from which this aphorism comes, was added in 1887.

3. Curt Paul Janz, *Die Briefe Friedrich Nietzsches: Textprobleme und ihre Bedeutung für Biographie und Doxographie* (Zurich: Editio Academica, 1972), 48.

4. A few of the most impressive books in this trend toward situating Nietzsche in his readings and in his times are Thomas H. Brobjer, *Nietzsche's Philosophical Context: An Intellectual Biography* (Urbana: University of Illinois Press, 2008); Hugo Drochon, *Nietzsche's Great Politics* (Princeton, NJ: Princeton University Press, 2016); Christian J. Emden, *Friedrich Nietzsche and the Politics of History* (Cambridge: Cambridge University Press, 2008), and *Nietzsche's Naturalism: Philosophy and the Life Sciences in the Nineteenth Century* (Cambridge: Cambridge University Press, 2014); Gregory Moore, *Nietzsche, Biology and Metaphor* (Cambridge: Cambridge University Press, 2002); Gregory Moore and Thomas H. Brobjer, eds., *Nietzsche and Science* (Aldershot: Ashgate, 2004); and Robin Small, *Nietzsche in Context* (Aldershot: Ashgate, 2001).

5. Léon Dumont, *Vergnügen und Schmerz: Zur Lehre von den Gefühlen* (Leipzig: Brockhaus, 1876); Harald Höffding, *Psychologie in Umrissen auf Grundlage der Erfahrung* (Leipzig: O. R. Reisland, 1887); William Edward Hartpole Lecky, *History of European Morals: From Augustus to Charlemagne*, 2 vols. (New York: D. Appleton, 1895; orig. 1877) (Nietzsche read the 1879 translation from the first English edition published in Leipzig and Heidelberg, *Sittengeschichte Europas von Augustus bis auf Karl den Großen*); and *History of the Rise and Influence of the Spirit of Rationalism in Europe*, 2 vols. (London: Longmans, Green and Co., 1904) (Nietzsche read the German translation from 1873 published in Leipzig, *Geschichte des Ursprungs und Einflusses der Aufklärung in Europa*); James Sully, *Pessimism: A History and a Criticism* (London: Henry S. King & Co., 1877) (Nietzsche read a French translation, *Le pessimisme [histoire et critique]*, published in Paris in 1882); Afrikan Spir, *Denken und Wirklichkeit: Versuch einer Erneuerung der kritischen Philosophie*, vol. 1, *Das Unbedingte*, 2nd ed. (Leipzig: J. G. Findel, 1877); Otto Liebmann, *Zur Analysis der Wirklichkeit: Eine Erörterung der Grundprobleme der Philosophie* (Straßburg: Trübner, 1880); and W. H. Rolph, *Biologische Probleme zugleich als Versuch zur Entwicklung einer rationellen Ethik* (Leipzig: Wilhelm Engelmann, 1884). All of these books evidenced heavy use in Nietzsche's library on the basis of marginal notes and underlinings.

6. See Anthony K. Jensen, *An Interpretation of Nietzsche's On the Uses and Disadvantage of History for Life* (New York: Routledge, 2016): "Nietzsche was a dialogical thinker in the sense that a great deal of what he wrote involves a sort of intellectual conversation with his colleagues and with his reading. But just as reconstructing a conversation having overheard only one of the interlocutors would be a poor substitute for listening to both, so is the scholarly representation of Nietzsche's arguments often unduly handicapped by ignoring the views of those with and against whom he was writing" (xv).

7. Even this image is probably unoriginal with Nietzsche, since it was evidently contained in the philosophy of Arthur Schopenhauer.

8. See Jensen: "Nietzsche often leaves his conversation partners unacknowledged, and often his partner's views have been mostly forgotten" (*An Interpretation*, xv).

9. Kohler is referring to an early Roman legal code from 450 BC.

10. Josef Kohler, *Das Recht als Kulturerscheinung: Einleitung in die vergleichende Rechtswissenschaft* (Würzburg: Stahel, 1885), 17–18. The Latin citation, taken from the sixth paragraph of the third tablet, may be rendered as: "If they take more or less, let that be no crime."

11. It appears Nietzsche cites the Latin incorrectly, when he wrote "ne" instead of "se."

12. In this passage, Nietzsche is berating philosophers for relying on fixed concepts, rather than seeing concepts as evolving over time and as human creations. He is asserting the notion of becoming over being. But he also makes it clear that philosophers ignore the senses and the body. In this sense he critiques philosophical procedures that depend on fixed concepts and the purity of thought.

13. The foremost authority on Nietzsche's readings and reading habits is Thomas H. Brobjer, whose essays and books over the past few decades have provided innumerable insights into the context for Nietzsche's thought. In *Nietzsche's Philosophical Context*, he writes, for example, that Nietzsche's "firsthand knowledge of Kant appears to have been slight" (36) and that he "never read Spinoza" (77). He concludes that Eugen Dühring's *Cursus der Philosophie als streng wissenschaftlicher Weltauschauung und Lebensgestaltung* was "clearly one of the most important philosophical works that Nietzsche thoroughly examined and entered into dialogue with" (68) and that Dühring's *Kritische Geschichte der Philosophie von ihren Anfängen bis zur Gegenwart* was "one of the major sources for Nietzsche's knowledge of the history of philosophy and its major representatives, such as Bacon, Locke, Hobbes, Descartes, Spinoza, and Comte" (69). There were many other works Nietzsche read carefully that supplied him with knowledge about the modern philosophical tradition, but there is little evidence that he himself bothered to study the major figures firsthand.

14. Even in the 1930s, Karl Jaspers, in *Nietzsche: An Introduction to the Understanding of His Philosophical Activity*, trans. Charles F. Wallraff and Frederick J. Schmitz (Chicago: Henry Regnery, 1965) (original German from 1935), noted that we "know which books he borrowed from the Basel library between the years 1869 and 1879." Jaspers also remarks: "He has weekly lists of new books sent to him," and observes: "Especially conspicuous is the large number of books dealing with natural science and ethnography, as though he wished to make up for having neglected factual knowledge while studying philology" (31).

15. Although the fourth estate commonly refers to the media in the United States, in nineteenth-century Germany it was the common designation for the proletariat. The first three estates were the aristocracy, the clerics, and the peasantry (sometimes also the bourgeoisie), respectively.

Chapter 1. The Education Question

1. See Curt Paul Janz, *Friedrich Nietzsche: Biographie*, 2nd rev. ed., vol. 1 (Munich: Hanser, 1993), 533–34.

2. Cosima did not marry Wagner until 25 August 1870, but she had lived with him for several years prior to their marriage and given birth to three children with him before the wedding. When Nietzsche met Wagner in 1868, Cosima was still married to the conductor Hans von Bülow (1830–1894).

3. "My 'Admonition' was *not* accepted in Bayreuth" (to Elisabeth Nietzsche, 14 November 1873, Nr. 327, KSB 4.178). Although we have no letter from Bayreuth rejecting Nietzsche's "Admonition," we would have to agree with the response of Nietzsche's friends Rohde and Gersdorff. The former gently notes that Nietzsche's text was intended less for those who have to be convinced than for those who are already true believers in the Wagnerian cause; the latter points out that at the very least something has to be said about donations, about where to send them, and about why they are needed (from Erwin Rohde, 29 October 1873, Nr. 473, KGB II 4.331–33, and from Carl von Gersdorff, 1 November 1873, Nr. 475, KGB II 4.334–35).

4. For a sober and realistic view of the Nietzsche-Wagner relationship, see Joachim Köhler, *Nietzsche and Wagner: A Lesson in Subjugation*, trans. Ronald Taylor (New Haven: Yale University Press, 1998).

5. The "Self-Presentation of the State School in Pforte" states that its mission was to prepare "a definite number of young people of evangelical faith . . . for an advanced scientific career or for the profession of scholar" (298). See Reiner Bohley, "Über die Landesschule zur Pforte: Materialien aus der Schulzeit Nietzsches," *Nietzsche-Studien* 5 (1976): 298–320.

6. See E. M. Butler, *The Tyranny of Greece over Germany: A Study of the Influence Exercised by Greek Art and Poetry over the Great German Writers of the Eighteenth, Nineteenth and Twentieth Centuries* (Cambridge: Cambridge University Press, 1935).

7. Although Nietzsche continued to identify himself as a German—except when he was feigning Polish ancestry—he was never a German citizen, having given up his Prussian citizenship when he accepted his appointment at Basel. For the rest of his life, he was a citizen of no nation.

8. Nietzsche makes it clear that the "our" in the title refers to German and not Swiss or European institutions of higher education (BA, Einleitung, KSA 1.644).

9. The exact dates of the lectures were 16 January, 6 and 27 February, and 5 and 23 March.

10. Nietzsche planned a sixth and perhaps even a seventh lecture, but never produced them.

11. Nietzsche wrote on 28 January 1872 to Rohde in Kiel: "I am currently holding here lectures 'on the future of our educational institution' and have created a 'sensation' and here and there aroused much enthusiasm" (Nr. 192, KSB 3.279). In a letter to his publisher, Ernst Wilhelm Fritzsch, on 22 March 1872, he estimates his audience at three hundred for each of his "six" lectures. Since he delivered only five lectures, his assessment of attendance may also be an exaggeration (Nr. 204, KSB 3.300). Jacob Burckhardt, however, agreed that Nietzsche's lectures had aroused much interest, as he states in a letter to Arnold von Salis on 21 April 1872. See Janz, *Nietzsche*, 1:447. Rudolf Eucken remarked on the lectures: "In the winter of 1871–72, he gave his lectures on the reform of education, which attracted a great deal of attention and enthusiastic support." In *Conversations with Nietzsche: A Life in the Words of His Contemporaries*, ed. Sander L. Gilman (New York: Oxford University Press, 1987), 40.

12. He offers this volume to Fritzsch, whose usual fare was music scores and writings on music, but the project never comes to fruition (22 March 1872, Nr. 204, KSB 3.300).

13. Lionel Gossmann, *Basel in the Age of Burckhardt: A Study in Unseasonable Ideas* (Chicago: University of Chicago Press, 2000), 423.

14. I will continue to use the German terms for these institutions since there are no real English equivalents. The *Gymnasium* of the nineteenth century was a secondary school that prepared students for university study; its curriculum was usually based on classical studies. The *Realschule*, as we shall see later, was a flourishing institution of secondary education to train students for more practical occupations; its curriculum sometimes contained Latin, but was more focused on the natural sciences and modern languages.

15. Eduard von Hartmann, *Zur Reform des höheren Schulwesens* (Berlin: Carl Dunker, 1875).

16. See Schiller, "Reform des Gymnasium," *Encyklopädie des gesamten Erziehungs- und Unterrichtswesens*, ed. K. A. Schmid, 2nd ed. (Leipzig: Fues, 1885), 948.

17. Heinrich von Treitschke, *Die Zukunft des Gymnasiums* (Leipzig: S. Hirzel, 1890); the remarks in this short book originally appeared in the *Preussische Jahrbücher* in 1883.

18. R[udolf] Eucken, *Der Kampf um das Gymnasium: Gesichtspunkte und Anregungen* (Stuttgart: Cotta, 1891). It is interesting to note that Eucken, born in 1846, was also appointed at Basel when he was twenty-four years old, like Nietzsche. Previous scholarship has perhaps made too much of how unusual Nietzsche's appointment was at such a young age. Basel, in fact, was known for appointing young and promising professors, many of whom later moved on to more prestigious German universities. See Janz, *Nietzsche*, 1:285–86.

19. Nietzsche obviously believed at the time of their delivery that his lectures would be published at some point. The second of the "Five Prefaces to Five Unwritten Books," which he presented to Cosima Wagner as a Christmas gift in 1872, is "On the Future of our Educational Institutions," but at a later point it seems he gave up on the idea of publishing the lectures. The "Preface," however, does contain the same type of remarks on tables and hourly study plans found in the preface to the lectures (BA, Vorrede, KSA 1.761–63).

20. That this scene is contrived should be obvious. In the first place, Nietzsche mentions an informal organization to which he belonged, and his description matches Germania, a group from his Naumburg years, rather than the Burschenschaft Franconia he joined in Bonn. Second, he was never in Bonn on a late summer day, since he went there only in the autumn of 1864. Finally, it is extremely unlikely that Nietzsche was ever involved regularly in shooting pistols; neither his disposition nor his eyesight would have permitted this type of activity.

21. Thomas H. Brobjer, "Nietzsche's Education at the Naumburg Domgymnasium, 1855–1858," *Nietzsche-Studien* 28 (1999): 302–22.

22. See Thomas H. Brobjer, "Why Did Nietzsche Receive a Scholarship to Study at Schulpforta?" *Nietzsche-Studien* 30 (2001): 322–28. Brobjer points out that Nietzsche's mother Franziska had the offer to send Nietzsche to another boarding school, the "Waisenhaus" in Halle, when he began attending the *Domgymnasium*. On Nietzsche's maternal side, the Oehlers had a tradition of going to Halle, which was reputed to be the best *Gymnasium* for the training of future pastors. But Franziska refused to send her son away at this earlier date. See Reiner Bohley, "Nietzsches christliche Erziehung," *Nietzsche-Studien* 16 (1987): 164–96; here 193–94.

23. See Bohley, "Über die Landesschule zur Pforte," 298–320.

24. Elisabeth Förster-Nietzsche, *Der junge Nietzsche* (Leipzig: Kröner, 1912), 129.

25. Hans Gutzwiller, "Friedrich Nietzsches Lehrtätigkeit am Basler Pädagogium, 1869–1876," *Basler Zeitschrift für Geschichte und Altertumskunde* 50 (1951): 147–224.

26. See Johannes Stroux, *Nietzsches Professor in Basel* (Jena: Fromann, 1925), 35.

27. *Nachträge (Stand Ende 1986) und Register zu Friedrich Nietzsches Sämtlichen Briefen* (Berlin: de Gruyter, 1987), 12–13; Gutzwiller, "Friedrich Nietzsches Lehrtätigkeit," 184–85.

28. Gutzwiller, "Friedrich Nietzsches Lehrtätigkeit," 170–71.

29. The most recent translation of these lectures also renders "Bildungsanstalten" as "educational institutions." Friedrich Nietzsche, *Anti-Education: On the Future of Our Educational Institutions*, trans. Damion Searls, ed. Paul Reitter and Chad Wellmon (New York: New York Review of Books, 2016).

30. It is not entirely clear what Nietzsche means when he refers to the foundations of the educational system. He may be referencing the Humboldtian ideal, but he gives no definitive indication that he is thinking of the ideals of the great German educational reformer.

31. Marjorie Lamberti, *State, Society, and the Elementary School in Imperial Germany* (New York: Oxford University Press, 1989), 13–21.

32. Although Nietzsche emphasizes the economic aspect in his lectures, in his notebook he makes reference to the expansion of *Bildung* as a means to improve the intelligence of civil servants, and attributes this tendency to "Hegelian influence" (Nachlass 1870–72, 8[57], KSA 7.243). Nietzsche does allude later to the education of civil servants and soldiers as an instrumental aim of the state in providing education when he is discussing his second explanation for expanding education: the fear of religious oppression (BA 1, KSA 1.669), and then again in his third lecture (BA 3, KSA 1.707–8). In his notebooks, the association of the educational system and the civil service as part of the economic complex is more evident.

33. Lamberti, *State, Society, and the Elementary School*, 40–87.

34. See E. J. Passant, *A Short History of Germany, 1815–1945* (Cambridge: Cambridge University Press, 1969), 88–89; and Dietrich Orlow, *A History of Modern Germany: 1871 to Present* (Englewood Cliffs, NJ: Prentice Hall, 1995), 43–45.

35. The emphasis placed on genius could have emanated or been reinforced by many other sources, for example, Ralph Waldo Emerson, who asserts in his essay "Self-Reliance": "The great genius returns to essential man." Ralph Waldo Emerson, *Essays: First and Second Series* (New York: Vintage, 1990), 50.

36. Arthur Schopenhauer, *Züricher Ausgabe: Werke in zehn Bänden* (Zurich: Diogenes, 1977), 9:79.

37. Schopenhauer, *Züricher Ausgabe*, 4:453, 457–58.

38. Schopenhauer, *Züricher Ausgabe*, 9:94.

39. I feel justified in using only the masculine pronouns since Schopenhauer states categorically that although women [*Weiber*] can have significant talent, they cannot possess genius because they remain always subjective. Schopenhauer, *Züricher Ausgabe*, 4:464.

40. For some revealing statistics, see Hartmut Titze, *Die Politisierung der Erziehung: Untersuchungen über die soziale und politische Funktion der Erziehung von der Aufklärung bis zum Hochkapitalismus* (Frankfurt: Athenäum, 1973), 197–218.

41. Nietzsche remarks on the Paris Commune in a letter to Wilhelm Vischer-Bilfinger on 27 May 1871 and in a letter to Carl von Gersdorff on 21 June 1871. See KSB 3.195 and 203–5.

42. Nietzsche was hardly unique in noticing this increase in specialization. See, for example, Treitschke, *Die Zukunft des Gymnasiums*, 12–15.

43. Again, Nietzsche was not alone in these views, especially among conservative thinkers; his remarks align well with comments on the press and newspapers made in 1883 by Treitschke, *Die Zukunft des Gymnasiums*, 8–11.

44. For example, in Nachlass 1869, 1[8], KSA 7.13.

45. See, for example, Wagner's essay "Modern," originally published in 1878 in the *Bayreuther Blätter*. Richard Wagner, *Sämtliche Schriften und Dichtungen* (Leipzig: Breitkopf & Härtel, 1912–14), 10:54–60. See also Domenico Losurdo, *Nietzsche der aristokratische Rebell* (Berlin: Argument, 2012), 137.

46. I treat this episode in more detail in chapter 3 of *Nietzsche's Jewish Problem: Between Anti-Semitism and Anti-Judaism* (Princeton, NJ: Princeton University Press, 2016), 49–88.

47. August Beger, *Die Idee des Realgymnasiums für Freunde und Beförderer höherer und zeitgemäßer Jungendbildung* (Leipzig: Hinrichsche Buchhandlung, 1845), VI–VII.

48. Treitschke, *Die Zukunft des Gymnasiums*, 21–22.

49. Rudolf Eucken in *Der Kampf um das Gymnasium* was also concerned with a renewal of classical learning, but he refrains from attacks on practical education and focuses on making antiquity relevant for the new generation of pupils.

50. Treitschke, *Die Zukunft des Gymnasiums*, 64.

51. See Jörg Schneider, "Nietzsches Basler Vorträge 'Über die Zukunft unserer Bildungsanstalten' im Lichte seiner Lektüre pädagogischer Schriften," *Nietzsche-Studien* 21 (1992): 308–25.

52. Nietzsche was hardly alone in noting deficiencies in German instruction. See, for example, the anonymous pamphlet *Über nationale Erziehung* (Leipzig: Teubner, 1872), 73.

53. Nietzsche mentions in this connection the writers Karl Gutzkow and Berthold Auerbach. Auerbach is censured for his German in a number of places, including in the first *Untimely Meditation*, where his every phrase is considered "un-German, awkward, and false" (DS 11, KSA 1.222). In his notebooks, Nietzsche states plainly: "Auerbach can neither tell a story nor think; he only pretends that he can. He is in his element when he can swim in an insipid, gossipy pool of emotions; but we don't like to be in his element" (Nachlass 1874, 37[4], KSA 7.830). It is probably not a coincidence that Nietzsche's chief representative of "un-German" style and language was Jewish and also disliked by the Wagners. Gutzkow, who is best known for his role as a Young German in the 1830s, was often considered a foreign element in German letters because of the risqué themes he selected and his aggressive journalism. Although he was not Jewish, some critics mistook him for Jewish because of these tendencies.

54. Tycho Mommsen, "Sechszehn Thesen zur Frage über die Gymnasialreform," *Preussische Jahrbücher* 34 (1874): 149–84.

55. In preparation for his lectures, Nietzsche had read *Fr. Aug. Wolf in seinem Verhältnisse zum Schulwesen und Pädagogik* by J. F. J. Arnoldt (Braunschweig: Schwetschke und Sohn, 1862) and was obviously impressed by Wolf's engagement for secondary education and in particular his advocacy for German instruction. See Torsten Schmidt-Millard, "Nietzsches Basler Vorträge 'Über die Zukunft unserer Bildungsanstalten': Die Aporie der Bildungstheorie des 'Genius' und ihre Überwindung in den 'Unzeitgemäßen Betrachtungen'" (Diss. University of Köln, 1982), p. 64.

56. Meyerbeer, born Jacob Liebmann Beer, was a German Jew who had great success in Paris with his opera *Robert le diable*. Originally a supporter of Wagner, the two became bitter enemies, and much

of what Wagner deprecates as "Jewish" in music belongs to Meyerbeer. Nietzsche is again playing with anti-Semitic allusions that would have been evident to his audience.

57. See Stroux, *Nietzsches Professur in Basel.*

58. See Nietzsche's autobiographical summary of his first two years in Leipzig, "Rückblick auf meine zwei Leipziger Jahre: 17 Oktober 1865–10 August 1867" (KGW, I 4.506–31, esp. 511–12).

59. See Richard Meister, "Nietzsches Lehrtätigkeit in Basel 1869–1879," *Anzeiger der österreichischen Akademie der Wissenschaften, philosophisch-historische Klasse* 84 (1947): 103–21; and Curt Paul Janz, "Friedrich Nietzsches akademische Lehrtätigkeit in Basel 1869–1879," *Nietzsche-Studien* 3 (1974): 192–203.

60. For a later and very possibly derivative criticism of "academic freedom" and a plea for the university to consist of leaders and followers, see Martin Heidegger, "The Self-Assertion of the German University: Address, Delivered on the Solemn Assumption of the Rectorate of the University Freiburg," *Review of Metaphysics* 38.3 (1985): 470–80. Heidegger delivered the speech originally on 27 May 1933, shortly after his appointment as rector of the university and barely four months after Hitler and the National Socialists had assumed power in Germany.

61. There is a definite tension in Nietzsche regarding the Humboldtian ideal of *Bildung* he appears otherwise to embrace. In these passages, Nietzsche is more narrowly nationalistic. But in essence, he still validates the notion of self-formation, as he had earlier, and he maintains something close to this ideal throughout his life.

62. Although Hartmann is mentioned specifically only in the ninth section, his attempt to mix the views of Schopenhauer with Hegel's historical outlook is surely one of the driving forces behind the entire essay.

63. Literally "time of the founders."

64. There is some evidence in Nietzsche's notebooks that the third term in each of these triads was added at a later point. See Nachlass 1873, 29[90], KSA 7.672. In this entry, the first Roman numeral contains only "historical—unhistorical"; the second Roman numeral contains "monumental—antiquarian." For a discussion of the textual history, see Anthony K. Jensen, *An Interpretation of Nietzsche's* On the Uses and Disadvantage of History for Life (New York: Routledge, 2016), especially 10–30.

65. Nietzsche will exhibit a greater appreciation for historical knowledge in his post-Wagnerian writings, in particular in his *On the Genealogy of Morals* (1887), where history is essential for understanding how we have become what we are as nineteenth-century beings.

66. Nietzsche's notebooks make it evident that his original plan was to write an essay on truth, and that only gradually did he move toward the topic of history and historical education.

67. See, for example, Kant's "Idea for a Universal History from a Cosmopolitan Point of View," in *Kant on History*, ed. Lewis White Beck (Upper Saddle River, NJ: Prentice Hall, 2001), 11–26.

68. As in his *Philosophy of History*; see G. W. F. Hegel, *Introduction to the Philosophy of History* (Indianapolis: Hackett, 1988).

69. For a comprehensive view of Nietzsche's relationship to history, historicism, and historical scholarship, see Christian J. Emden, *Friedrich Nietzsche and the Politics of History* (Cambridge: Cambridge University Press, 2008).

70. Emden, *Friedrich Nietzsche*, 106.

71. Nietzsche was not alone in noting Hartmann's connection with Hegel's philosophy. Shortly before he composed the second *Untimely Meditation*, he had read Julius Bahnsen's *Philosophie der Geschichte* (1872), which advanced similar claims. See Emden, *Friedrich Nietzsche*, 48–49.

72. See Arthur Schopenhauer, *Handschriftlicher Nachlaß*, ed. Eduard Grisebach, vol. 4, *Neue Paralipomena* (Leipzig: Reclam, 1893), 290 (§ 517).

73. For a fuller account of Nietzsche's relation to Hartmann, see Anthony K. Jensen, "The Rogue of All Rogues: Nietzsche's Presentation of Eduard von Hartmann's *Philosophie des Unbewussten* and Hartmann's Response to Nietzsche," *Journal of Nietzsche Studies* 32 (2006): 41–61.

74. Nietzsche's decision not to publish his lectures may well have been the result of this change in perspective. We should also note that the latest translation of Nietzsche's lectures bears the title "Anti-Education," although his real anti-educational position only becomes apparent in the last three of his *Untimely Meditations*.

75. David E. Cartwright, *Schopenhauer: A Biography* (Cambridge: Cambridge University Press, 2010), 362–65.

Chapter 2. The German Question

1. The phrase "of the German Nation" [*deutscher Nation*] was used intermittently starting in the late fifteenth century.
2. Peter Alter, *The German Question and Europe: A History* (New York: Oxford University Press, 2000), 14–34.
3. The "large German" format would have included Austria.
4. See Sigrid Nieberle, 'Und Gott im Himmel Lieder singt': Zur prekären Rezeption von Ernst Moritz Arndts Des Deutschen Vaterland," in *Ernst Moritz Arndt (1769–1860): Deutscher Nationalismus—Europa—transatlantische Perspektiven*, ed. Walter Erhart and Arne Koch (Tübingen: Niemeyer, 2007), 121–36.
5. Daniel Blue, "What Was Nietzsche's Nationality," *Journal of Nietzsche Studies* 33 (2007): 73–82.
6. See Johannes Stroux, *Nietzsches Professur in Basel* (Jena: Fromann, 1925), 35–36.
7. Eduard His, "Friedrich Nietzsches Heimatlosigkeit," *Basler Zeitschrift für Geschichte und Altertumskunde* 40 (1941): 159–86; here 164–65.
8. Nietzsche's most extensive note on his Polish origins occurs in Nachlass 1882, 21[2], KSA 9.681–82. His remarks on Poland and its history have been traced to Ernst von der Brüggen's *Polens Auflösung* (1878) by Daniel Devreese and Benjamin Biebuyck in " 'Il Placco': Überlegungen zu Nietzsches polnischer Legende im Lichte einer neuen Quelle: Ernst von der Brüggens Polens Auflösung," *Nietzsche-Studien* 35 (2006): 263–70.
9. Elisabeth Förster-Nietzsche, *Das Leben Friedrich Nietzsche's* (Leipzig: Naumann, 1895), 1:12.
10. The most thorough investigation of the Polish issue is found in Hans von Müller, "Nietzsches Vorfahren," *Nietzsche-Studien* 31 (2002): 253–75.
11. See Peter Bergmann, "Nietzsche, Friedrich III and the Missing Generation in German History," *Nietzsche-Studien* 17 (1988): 195–217.
12. Nietzsche's earlier listing makes it evident that he was the sole submitter of material since June of 1862 (Nachlass 1862, 13[28], KGW I 2.482–83). The fate of the club and Nietzsche's actions in precipitating its demise are described in David Blue's *The Making of Friedrich Nietzsche: The Quest for Identity, 1844–1869* (Cambridge: Cambridge University Press, 2016), especially 153 and 163.
13. "Der Weltenorgel Machtakkord": A line that defies translation. "Akkord" can mean a musical chord or a compact or agreement. The line suggests "the agreement of world powers," but also "a powerful chord sounded from the organ of the worlds."
14. In the Colli-Montinari critical edition that is cited for all references to Nietzsche's writings, the last line of this stanza has been omitted, presumably inadvertently. It can be found, however, in an earlier edition, BAW 2.107: "Des Geistes auserkorne Recken!"
15. Heinrich Heine, *Historisch-kritische Gesamtausgabe der Werke*, ed. Manfred Windfuhr (Hamburg: Hoffmann und Campe, 1985), 4:123–30.
16. See Christian J. Emden, *Friedrich Nietzsche and the Politics of History* (Cambridge: Cambridge University Press, 2008), 21–22. "The political remarks in Nietzsche's correspondence of the mid-1860s suggest that, in the period between 1858 and 1868, Nietzsche held essentially conventional political views that corresponded entirely to the conservative program of national liberalism in Germany" (39). See also Henning Ottmann, *Philosophie und Politik bei Nietzsche*, 2nd ed. (Berlin: de Gruyter, 1999), 11–16.
17. Heinrich von Treitschke, *Die Zukunft der norddeutschen Mittelstaaten* (Berlin: Reimer, 1866).
18. For an account of this electoral campaign, see Peter Bergmann, *Nietzsche, "the Last Antipolitical German"* (Bloomington: Indiana University Press, 1987), 48–49.
19. See, for example, his letter to Gersdorff at the end of November (Nr. 554, KSB 2.241).

20. See Richard J. Bazillion, *Modernizing Germany: Karl Biedermann's Career in the Kingdom of Saxony, 1835–1901* (New York: Lange, 1990).

21. Ottmann suggests this interpretation of Nietzsche's shift in *Philosophie und Politik bei Nietzsche*, 16–18.

22. Richard Wagner, "Was ist deutsch?" *Sämtliche Schriften und Dichtungen* (Leipzig: Breitkopf & Härtl, 1911), 10:36–53.

23. Cosima Wagner, *Diaries*, vol. 1, *1869–1877*, trans. Geoffrey Skelton (New York: Harcourt Brace Jovanovich, 1978), 246.

24. See Curt Paul Janz, *Friedrich Nietzsche: Biographie*, 2nd rev. ed. (Munich: Hanser, 1993), 1:375; and Ronald Hayman, *Nietzsche: A Critical Life* (New York: Penguin, 1980), 127. Nietzsche's letters to Mosengel do not survive, and we have only one letter that Mosengel wrote to Nietzsche (26 October 1870, Nr. 127, KGB II 2.256–58). Mosengel also served as a medical orderly, and he cared for Nietzsche when he fell ill. They appear to have become instant friends in 1870, but there is no evidence that their friendship survived the war.

25. Elisabeth Förster-Nietzsche, *Das Leben Friedrich Nietzsche's* (Leipzig: Naumann, 1897), 2.1: 32. As many commentators have noted, Elisabeth's reports are not always trustworthy. She claims that her brother had already handed in the request for a leave to Vischer before his conversation with her and his extended conversations with Mosengel. If this were the case, it would weaken her implicit claim that she had something to do with Nietzsche's decision. But the letter to Vischer is dated 8 August, after his return to Basel. The version of the letter Elisabeth includes in her biography (32–33), however, is slightly different from the letter Vischer received, and she indicates she is citing a draft. It is possible that she is quoting from a draft in her possession, and that she had no knowledge of the official letter when she was writing her biography. The draft would then have been the basis for the letter sent on 8 August. It is therefore impossible to ascertain with absolute certainty when Nietzsche decided to request a leave of absence, and when he first drafted the letter to Vischer requesting the leave. But if he were so profoundly affected by a desire to serve in the Franco-Prussian War, his sentiments in letters composed immediately after the declaration of war, and his actions in leaving Basel for a vacation and visit to Tribschen indicate that the decision to reenlist was not spontaneous and most likely developed only with some reflection over the next few weeks.

26. See, for example, Cosima's letter to Nietzsche from 16 July 1870, in which she writes of the "outrageousness of French arrogance" and adds: "I hope that all of Germany recognizes that the King of Prussia could not and should not have acted differently, and now go with Prussia; perhaps then German unity will be achieved, the hegemony of the Parisian mode will be broken forever, the *chignons* in flight, the olive tree will rise from the abyss on which Bayreuth's castle lies" (Nr. 115, KGB II 2.232–33).

27. See, for example, her letter to Nietzsche on 9 August 1870, in which she writes that she understands his decision, but does not approve of it. It is not 1813, she reminds her friend. We have a fully trained army and well-organized medical support. He will only be in the way. She advises him that money is needed more than volunteer service, and that his talents are more usefully applied outside the military (Nr. 118, KGB II 2.237–38).

28. He relates the same events to Gersdorff on 20 October (Nr. 103, KSB 3.147–49).

29. Rohde is especially concerned: "Blood and again blood, and want and misery pile up daily; when will it finally end!" (11 December 1870, Nr. 138, KGB II 2.280).

30. M. S. Silk and J. P. Stern in *Nietzsche on Tragedy* (Cambridge: Cambridge University Press, 1981) give a complete description of the sources and the development of the *Birth of Tragedy* and comment as follows on Wagner's influence: "Wagner's role in the genesis of *BT* has not hitherto been accurately defined. It was twofold: first, the material of the book had a Wagnerian stimulus behind it and a discernible 'Wagnerian connection'; and secondly, the decision to write a whole book on the basis of that material was prompted by Wagner's personal advocacy" (40).

31. Cosima's birthday was 24 December. In her diary entry from 26 December 1870, Cosima reports that Richard read aloud from the manuscript. Cosima comments: "the depth and excellence of his survey, conveyed with a very concentrated brevity, is quite remarkable; we follow his thoughts with

the greatest and liveliest interest. My greatest pleasure is in seeing how R.'s ideas can be extended in this field" (312–13). It is thus quite obvious to Cosima that Richard had greatly influenced Nietzsche in his thought.

32. When this publisher, Wilhelm Engelmann, did not respond quickly enough to Nietzsche's submission—quite possibly because he had expected a work of genuine philology and did not know what to reply—Nietzsche demanded the manuscript returned. He eventually published his first non-philological work with Wagner's publisher, Ernst Fritzsch, after changing the title from "Music and Tragedy" to "The Birth of Tragedy out of the Spirit of Music." See William H. Schaberg, *The Nietzsche Canon: A Publication History and Bibliography* (Chicago: University of Chicago Press, 1995), 19–28.

33. Schaberg, *Nietzsche Canon*, 21–22.

34. The foreword was written on 22 February; the war did not conclude until 10 May.

35. Richard Wagner, *Beethoven* (Leipzig: Schmeitzner, 1870), 28.

36. Nietzsche's book was almost completely ignored by the academic world. Rohde was bullied into writing a favorable review out of friendship, and when Ulrich von Wilamowitz-Möllendorf wrote a sharp criticism of it, Rohde and Wagner defended Nietzsche in print.

37. Friedrich Nietzsche, *Nachträge (Stand Ende 1986) und Register zu Friedrich Nietzsches Sämtlichen Briefen* (Berlin: de Gruyter, 1987), 11.

38. See Cosima Wagner's *Diaries*, 1:247.

39. Wagner, *Beethoven*, 2.

40. Wagner, *Beethoven*, 26.

41. Wagner, *Beethoven*, 68.

42. Heinrich von Treitschke, "Unsere Ansichten," in *Der "Berliner Antisemitismusstreit 1870–1881": Eine Kontroverse um die Zugehörigkeit der deutschen Juden zur Nation*, ed. Karsten Krieger (Munich: Saur, 2004), 6–16; here 14–15.

43. See Curt Paul Janz, "Die 'tödliche Beleidigung': Ein Beitrag zur Wagner-Entfremdung Nietzsches," *Nietzsche-Studien* 4 (1975): 263–78; Sander L. Gilman, "Otto Eiser and Nietzsche's Illness: A Hitherto Unpublished Text," *Nietzsche-Studien* 38 (2009): 396–409; Janz, *Friedrich Nietzsche*, 1:785–90; Joachim Köhler, *Nietzsche and Wagner: A Lesson in Subjugation* (New Haven: Yale University Press, 1998), 139–57.

44. For a more complete treatment of this topic, see my book on *Nietzsche's Jewish Problem*, 89–96. Most likely the "deadly insult" to which Nietzsche refers is Wagner's embrace of Christianity, but it seems unlikely that there was only one reason Nietzsche and Wagner distanced themselves from each other.

45. Richard Wagner, "Was ist deutsch?," *Gesammelte Schriften und Dichtungen* (Leipzig: Fritzsch, 1898), 10:36–53.

46. On occasion, Schopenhauer is placed back in the category of German, particularly in association with Wagner.

47. Nietzsche here alludes to a popular comic epic of the time, *Der Trompeter von Säckingen* [The Trumpeter of Säckingen] (1853) by Joseph Victor von Scheffel (1826–1886); he may also be thinking of the opera with the same name by Viktor Nessler (1841–1890), whose first performance occurred in 1884.

48. Paul de Lagarde, *Deutsche Schriften*, vol. 1, *Schriften für das deutsche Volk* (Munich: Lehmann, 1940), 68. The unusual word "Judaine" appears in Nietzsche's notebooks (Nachlass 1887–88, 11[384], KSA 13.182), as well as in *The Antichrist* (AC 56, KSA 6.240), which indicates that Nietzsche had likely read Lagarde and borrowed the notion from him.

49. Paul de Lagarde, *Deutsche Schriften*, 1:114. Both essays are in this volume. Only the second essay was found in Nietzsche's library. See Giuliano Campioni et al., ed., *Nietzsches persönliche Bibliothek* (Berlin: de Gruyter, 2003), 337. Nietzsche evidently acquired the book in January 1876.

50. *Conversations with Nietzsche*, ed. Sander L. Gilman (New York: Oxford University Press, 1987), 76–83.

51. Winfried Schüler, *Der Bayreuther Kreis von seiner Entstehung bis zum Ausgang der wilhelminischen Ära* (Münster: Aschendorff, 1971), 6.

52. See Bergmann, *Nietzsche*, 1–8.
53. Just as Wagner was frequently the referent for "the artist."
54. Drafts of letters to Kaiser Wilhelm II and Bismarck, declaring his enmity, can be found in KSB 8.503–4 (Nr. 1171–73).
55. For a detailed consideration of Nietzsche's views on Bismarck, see Theodor Schieder, "Nietzsche und Bismarck," *Historische Zeitschrift* 196.2 (1963): 320–42.
56. See Janz, *Friedrich Nietzsche*, 3:212–13.
57. Carl Albrecht Bernoulli, *Franz Overbeck und Friedrich Nietzsche: Eine Freundschaft* (Jena: Eugen Diederich, 1908), 1:135–37.
58. There is some speculation that Eduard Mushacke (1873+), the father of one of Nietzsche's university friends, Hermann Mushacke (1845–1905), may have introduced him to Stirner's writings. See my *Nietzsche's Jewish Problem*, 39–40.
59. This phrase was applied to Nietzsche's thought by the Danish scholar Georg Brandes in a letter he wrote to him late in 1887. Brandes, who had evidently read *Beyond Good and Evil*, *On the Genealogy of Morals*, and *Human, All Too Human*, was effusive in his praise: "A new and original spirit wafts to me from your books. I do not fully understand what I have read; I do not always know what you want. But many things concur with my own thoughts and sympathies, the disregard for the ascetic ideal and the deep antipathy to democratic mediocrity, your aristocratic radicalism" (Nr. 500, KGB III 6.120). Nietzsche, obviously flattered, replies that Brandes is among a select few who have appreciated his works; he names Jacob Burckhardt (1818–1897), Hans von Bülow (1830–1894), Hippolyte Taine (1828–1893), and Gottfried Keller (1819–1890) among those living who are appreciative readers, and among those who have passed away, Bruno Bauer (1809–1882) and Richard Wagner. The letter is obviously intended to impress Brandes with the exclusive circle to which he now belongs. He continues his flattery by writing the following: "The expression 'aristocratic radicalism,' which you used, is very good. If you will allow me to say so, it is the most intelligent phrase that I have ever read about myself" (2 December 1887, Nr. 960, KSB 8.205–7). That the phrase has only vague political significance is obvious.
60. In *Human, All Too Human*, Nietzsche makes it clear that by "Europe" he means not only the geographical Europe, "the little peninsula of Asia," but also America, "the daughter-land of our culture" (WS 215, KSA 2.650).
61. The term usually refers to the initial two decades of the Second Empire, from 1871 to 1890.
62. For example, in a letter to Köselitz he writes that a Danish newspaper has reported "that a cycle of public lectures 'om den tüzke Filosof Friedrich Nietzsche' were held at the university in Copenhagen.... Consider my Leipzig friends at the university and how many miles away they are from the thought of lecturing on me" (20 April 1888, Nr. 1022, KSB 8.298).
63. Nietzsche, obviously still thrilled about the news from Denmark, brags to Knortz about Brandes's lectures and lauds his own *Zarathustra* as "the most profound work that exists in the German language" (21 June 1888, Nr. 1050, KSB 8.339–41).
64. See Andreas Rupschus, "Nietzsche und sein Problem mit den Deutschen," *Nietzsche-Studien* 40 (2011): 72–105; esp. 74.
65. Nietzsche's understanding of the Italian Renaissance was no doubt influenced by his reading of Jacob Burckhardt's *The Civilization of the Renaissance* (1869). For a detailed exploration of this topic, see Martin A. Ruehl, *The Italian Renaissance in the German Historical Imagination, 1860–1930* (Cambridge: Cambridge University Press, 2015), 58–104.
66. Nietzsche writes that they are all mere "Schleiermacher," which is the name of the famous philosopher, but which literally means "veil makers."
67. See Daniel W. Conway, "Nietzsche's Germano-mania," *Nietzsche and the German Tradition*, ed. Nicholas Martin (Bern: Lang, 2003), 1–37.

Chapter 3. The Social Question

1. Karl Marx, "Manifest der Kommunistischen Partei," *Marx Engels Werke*, vol. 4 (Berlin: Dietz Verlag, 1990), 459–93; here 492.

2. Conservatives and most National Liberals supported this law.

3. Max Hödel (1857–1878), the first assassin, had been expelled from the party prior to his assassination attempt; the second assassin, Karl Eduard Nobiling (1848–1878), was never associated with the party.

4. Although the German usually refers to "law" in the singular, most English translations cite this legislation as the "Socialist Laws." The official German law refers to the "Gesetz gegen die gemeingefährlichen Bestrebungen der Sozialdemokratie," the "law against the public danger of social democratic endeavors." I refer to Socialist Laws in this chapter to conform to common practice.

5. This was the name the party assumed after the convention in Gotha in 1875.

6. We should recall, however, that both Wagner and Malwida von Meysenbug had radical connections from their past lives, and that Nietzsche would not have been completely unexposed to left-wing thought from these personal connections.

7. The most authoritative discussions of Nietzsche's library and his readings are contained in the work of Thomas Brobjer. Relevant for this chapter is his essay "Nietzsche's Knowledge, Reading, and Critique of Political Economy," *Journal of Nietzsche Studies*, no. 18 (1999): 56–70; and his article "Nietzsche's Knowledge of Marx and Marxism," *Nietzsche-Studien* 31 (2002): 298–313.

8. As we shall see in Chapter 5, Nietzsche did have a passing interest in August Bebel's work, *Die Frau und der Sozialismus*. But it is an exception, and Nietzsche's interest in it appears to have had very little to do with the author's leadership of the Social Democratic Workers' Party.

9. See Brobjer, "Nietzsche's Knowledge of Marx and Marxism," 302.

10. Nietzsche had the third printing of Lange's book (Winterthur: Bleuler-Hauscher und Comp., 1875) and the seventh printing of Schäffle (Gotha: F. A. Perthes, 1879). Neither writer would be considered a socialist.

11. Nietzsche had in his library the following edition of this popular book: *Der alte und der neue Glaube* (Leipzig: S. Hirzel, 1872), 272–77, 278–81.

12. Nietzsche's decision to transfer from Bonn to Leipzig appears to have occurred prior to Ritschl's, although it is possible that Nietzsche had learned about Ritschl's desire to leave Bonn for Leipzig from Ritschl.

13. See Katherine Roper, "Friedrich Spielhagen (24 February 1829–25 February 1911)," in *Dictionary of Literary Biography*, vol. 129, *Nineteenth Century German Writers, 1841–1900*, ed. James Hardin and Siegfried Mews (Detroit: Gale, 1993), 348–60; and Jeffrey L. Sammons, "Friedrich Spielhagen: The Demon of Theory and the Decline of Reputation," in *A Companion to German Realism, 1848–1900*, ed. Todd Kontje (Rochester, NY: Camden House, 2002), 133–57.

14. Friedrich Spielhagen, *In Reih' und Glied* (Leipzig: L. Staackmann, 1890), 1:312–13, 425, 508. The novel originally appeared in 1867.

15. This work appeared in 1864. The title refers to Franz Hermann Schulze-Delitzsch (1808–1883), a noted liberal in the Prussian parliament who also enjoyed some popularity with the working class. In contrast to Lassalle, whose views on economy were closer to those of Marx and Engels, Schulze-Delitzsch advocated the organization of cooperative banks in which workers would save money and in this fashion improve their condition. He is known today as the founder of the credit union. Bastiat refers to Claude Frédéric Bastiat (1801–1850), a liberal French economist influential for Schulze-Delitzsch. Julian refers to the liberal journalist Julian Schmidt (1818–1886), against whom Lassalle had written a polemical piece in 1862.

16. Almost as a sop to his friend, Gersdorff then writes that the Lassalle-Gutmann connection is "of far less significance" than the tragic renunciations of the heroes and heroines, "which even in the first volume reminds one of the Meister, to whom we owe so much" (KGB I 3.230).

17. Spielhagen, *In Reih' und Glied*, 1:508–9.

18. Spielhagen, *In Reih' und Glied*, 2:177.

19. Spielhagen, *In Reih' und Glied*, 2:488.

20. *Geschichte der sozial-politischen Parteien in Deutschland* (Freiburg: Herder'sche Verlagsbuchhandlung, 1867). Parenthetical citations in this paragraph are from Joerg's book.

21. As far as we can document Nietzsche's reading, he never did read the work Gersdorff had suggested and never read anything by Lassalle. See Peter Bergmann, *Nietzsche, "the Last Antipolitical German"* (Bloomington: Indiana University Press, 1987), 53.

22. See Domenico Losurdo, *Nietzsche, der aristokratische Rebell: Intellektuelle Biographie und kritische Bilanz*, vol. 1, *Die Kritik der Revolution von den jüdischen Propheten bis zum Sozialismus*, trans. and ed. Jan Rehmann (Berlin: Argument, 2012), 404. At this point in his development, however, Nietzsche was still sympathetic with the National Liberal position, against which Joerg's criticism is directed. In some ways, Joerg anticipates Nietzsche's drift toward conservative thinking after 1870, when he evidences disappointment with the results of German unification. See Urs Marti, *"Der grosse Pöbel- und Sklavenaufstand": Nietzsches Auseinandersetzung mit Revolution und Demokratie* (Stuttgart: Metzler, 1993), 96–103.

23. See Brobjer, "Nietzsche's Knowledge, Reading, and Critique of Political Economy."

24. The passage on which Nietzsche draws in Joerg is on pages 107–8.

25. Nietzsche was in Naumburg doing military service at the time of this police action.

26. Cosima Wagner, *Diaries, 1869–1877* (New York: Harcourt Brace Jovanovich, 1978), 1:369.

27. The Wagnerian framework pits Wagner's genuine art against "Romanic"-Jewish art. In the letter to Gersdorff, Nietzsche writes of "French-Jewish leveling and 'elegance'" (21 June 1871, Nr. 140, KSB 3.203). There is another side to Wagner's relationship to revolution, however, which might have mitigated his reaction to the Commune. He had known Bakunin in the revolutionary years 1848–49 and participated to a degree in the campaign against reactionary forces at that time. Indeed, in her diary entry, Cosima writes about her conversation with Nietzsche: "Spoke of Bakunin—whether he was among the arsonists" (1:369). And a few days later Cosima writes to Nietzsche: "I confess that I am now terribly disgusted by the continued murders. A good friend, member of the Commune, has now been shot as well" (2 June 1871, Nr. 191, KGB II 2.382). It is possible that Nietzsche's refusal to place sole blame on the fourth estate is a consequence of Wagner's earlier relationship to revolutionary activity and revolutionaries.

28. For a more detailed exposition of Nietzsche's relations to the Paris Commune, see Marc Sautet, *Nietzsche et la Commune* (Paris: Editions Le Sycomore, 1981); and Urs Marti, *"Der grosse Pöbel- und Sklavenaufstand,"* 143–45.

29. Nietzsche claims that this notion is "one of the strongest pieces of knowledge of my great predecessor" and states that others were too "soft" to understand or state it (Nachlass 1870–71, 7[79], KSA 7.156).

30. Nietzsche's thoughts about the necessity of freedom in labor accord with the notions developed at an earlier date by Karl Marx; Nietzsche draws a wholly different conclusion, however, insisting on the necessity of "slavery," while Marx advocates freedom from wage labor as a solution to the Social Question.

31. In some places I have modified slightly R. J. Hollingdale's translation of the section "The labour question" from *Twilight of the Idols*. In Nietzsche's last series of notebooks from late 1887 to 1888, the draft of this section carries the title "Modern Unclarity" [*Die moderne Unklarheit*]. See Friedrich Nietzsche, *Twilight of the Idols/The Anti-Christ* (London: Penguin, 1968), here p. 106.

32. Franz Mehring, "IX [Friedrich Nietzsche]," *Gesammelte Schriften*, vol. 11, *Aufsätze zur deutschen Literatur von Hebbel bis Schweichel* (Berlin: Dietz Verlag, 1961), 210–21; here 219. This volume contains articles Mehring wrote for the socialist journal *Die neue Zeit* in the late nineteenth and early twentieth centuries.

33. Parenthetical references refer to page numbers from Georg Lukács, *Die Zerstörung der Vernunft*, vol. 2, *Irrationalismus und Imperialismus* (Darmstadt: Luchterhand, 1974). The book was originally published in Aufbau Verlag in Berlin in 1954. The explanatory subtitle to the book is "The Path of Irrationalism from Schelling to Hitler."

34. Vladimir Ilyich Lenin, "Imperialism, the Highest Stage of Capitalism," *Collected Works*, vol. 22 (Moscow: Progress Publishers, 1964), 187–304.

35. Karl Marx, "Manifest der Kommunistischen Partei," 465. George J. Stack, "Marx and Nietzsche: A Point of Affinity," *Modern Schoolman* 60 (1983): 247–63, hypothesizes that the "reason why

Nietzsche seems to picture his age in what appear to be Marxian terms is that he has absorbed some of the language and concepts of Marx from his study of Lange" (251).

36. See Paul Lawrence Rose, *Wagner: Race and Revolution* (New Haven, CT: Yale University Press, 1992); and Marc A. Weiner, *Richard Wagner and the Anti-Semitic Imagination* (Lincoln: University of Nebraska Press, 1995).

37. For example, in a notebook from 1873, where Nietzsche mentions by name Spielhagen's novel *In Rank and File*: "It should no longer be the age of harmonious personality, but of 'work in common.' But that means only: men, *before* they are finished, are used in the factory. But you will be convinced that in a short period of time scholarship will be similarly ruined, as men are in this factory work" (Nachlass 1873 29[57], KSA 7.652). We see that factory work diverts individuals from genuine development, just as industriousness in work does.

38. Urs Marti (178) suggests that Nietzsche's remarks on "machine culture" may have been inspired by sections of Jules Michelet's study *Le Peuple*, a German translation of which under the title *Das Volk* (Mannheim: H. Hoff, 1846) is found in Nietzsche's library.

39. Stack, "Marx and Nietzsche," asserts that while he was writing *Human, All Too Human,* "Nietzsche was very definitely under the influence of socialistic ideals even if he never embraced socialism as a panacea for the troubles of Europe" (256).

40. In August 1885, Nietzsche requests from his friend Heinrich Köselitz a copy of Bebel's *Woman and Socialism* (Nr. 624, KSB 7.86–87). I discuss this episode in Chapter 5 of this book.

41. It is chapter five, titled "Capital and Labor" (212–62). Friedrich Albert Lange, *Die Arbeiterfrage: Ihre Bedeutung für Gegenwart und Zukunft*, 3rd ed. (Winterthur: Bleuler-Hauscher und Comp., 1875). Nietzsche could have encountered discussions of Marx's theories from a number of sources. Thomas Brobjer gives a detailed account of his potential acquaintance with Marx in "Nietzsche's Knowledge of Marx and Marxism." But the impression Marx made was very slight if we consider that his name appears nowhere in Nietzsche's notebooks, published writings, or correspondence, and that his accounts of socialism do not appear to engage the central concerns of Marx's writings.

42. John Stuart Mill, *Collected Works*, vol. 12 (Leipzig: Fues's Verlag, 1880). The entire volume evidences page markings that indicate Nietzsche's engagement with the three texts.

43. *Die Quintessenz des Socialismus*, 7th ed. (Gotha: F. A. Perthes, 1879). The pamphlet evidently contains a stamp with the name "Dr. Bernhard Förster" on the title page, so it is likely that the book belonged to Nietzsche's brother-in-law and was somehow later incorporated into Nietzsche's library, or that Förster lent or gave him the book at one point. This popular text went through its twenty-fifth edition in 1920.

44. See Peter Bünger, *Nietzsche als Kritiker des Sozialismus* (Aachen: Shaker, 1997). Bünger notes that Mehring was in Leipzig at the same time that Nietzsche studied there. He doesn't note, however, that Mehring, like Nietzsche, studied classical philology at the University of Leipzig—as well as history—in the years 1866–68, and that he was not a socialist at this time. Mehring was a liberal journalist for many years before he became radicalized. He joined the SPD only in 1891.

45. There is a historical irony in Nietzsche's fear of activities imputed to the International, since that fissiparous organization was in a state of dissolution, precipitated by the struggle between a "Marxist" and an anarchist faction, as well as the resolution passed in 1872, supported by the former and opposed by the latter, to relocate the headquarters of the International in New York City.

46. Cosima Wagner, *Diaries, 1869–1877*, 1:693. Cosima's entry from 30 October contains the following strange comments: "In the afternoon a meeting in the street with Prof. Nietzsche. He, completely outlawed, tells us unbelievable things: that the International is reckoning him as one of their own, encouraged in that direction by a writer in *Die Grenzboten*, whose article, entitled 'Herr Nietzsche and German Culture,' exceeds all bounds and actually denounces our friend!" (692). Nietzsche was obviously upset at the virtual boycott of his classes because of *The Birth of Tragedy*. Why he believes he is being associated with socialism is more difficult to ascertain. The article in *Die Grenzboten* criticizes Nietzsche's first *Untimely Meditation* on David Strauß, especially Nietzsche's disparaging remarks about the newly established Second Reich. The author, who remains anonymous with the initials B.F., writes at one point about "Nietzsche's international sphere of culture" (327), but this

reference has little to do with socialism. The author has been variously identified; there is a suspicion it may have been composed by Bernhard Förster, Nietzsche's later brother-in-law, but there are also several other possibilities. See "Herr Friedrich Nietzsche und die deutsche Cultur," in *Rezensionen und Reaktionen zu Nietzsches Werken, 1872–1889*, ed. Hauke Reich (Berlin: de Gruyter, 2013), 322–28. Cosima's report indicates how distraught Nietzsche was that his name was associated with socialism, which represented for him a destructive element in European culture.

47. Curt Paul Janz, *Friedrich Nietzsche: Biographie*, 3 vols. (Munich: Hanser, 1978), 1:548.

48. See Carl Albrecht Bernoulli, *Franz Overbeck und Friedrich Nietzsche: Eine Freundschaft*, 2 vols. (Jena: Eugen Diederichs, 1908), 1:115–18, 269–70.

49. In this confusing letter, she appears to have had mixed feelings about meeting Nietzsche, who has pleased her, but also hurt her. Bergmann (*Nietzsche*, 87) believes that Nielsen persisted in associating the Dionysian with revolution, but there is no indication in the documents that this interpretation is accurate.

50. William H. Schaberg, *The Nietzsche Canon: A Publication History and Bibliography* (Chicago: University of Chicago Press, 1995), 39. Nietzsche's sister relates that she met Nielsen in Basel as she was exiting Nietzsche's apartment, and that her brother told her that Nielsen had related to him that the publisher Fritzsch was in severe financial difficulty, and that an "international society"—she does not mention it as the socialist international or the International Workingmen's Association (1864–76)—had an interest in buying Fritzsch out. She indicated that they wanted to continue publishing Nietzsche, but that their goal was to ruin Wagner, who was in the process of trying to finance Bayreuth and was also in financial difficulties. The story told by Förster-Nietzsche is odd, as is the entire affair. In her version, Nielsen is not a part of a socialist conspiracy, but someone warning Nietzsche about it, or at least relating that the "international society" retains an interest in his writings. See Elisabeth Förster-Nietzsche, *Wagner und Nietzsche zur Zeit ihrer Freundschaft* (Munich: Georg Müller, 1915), 164–65. In Nietzsche's letter to Gersdorff, however, he indicates Nielsen's involvement with the international society, and Cosima understood Nielsen also as someone acting to take over Fritzsch's business, presumably in the service of the "international society." We do know that Fritzsch was in financial difficulty, and we can also easily see that Nietzsche was paranoid about a socialist plot to ruin the Wagnerian movement. But the exact contours of this episode remain hazy. The most extensive biographical account of Nielsen I have seen is contained in Carl Albrecht Bernoulli's *Franz Overbeck und Friedrich Nietzsche: Eine Freundschaft* (Jena: Eugen Diederichs, 1908), 1:115–18, but in this account there is just the mention that in Italy she was interned as a revolutionary and an associate of Mazzini (117). There is no mention of her acting on behalf on the International with regard to Wagner or his publisher.

51. The notion of the "withering away" of the state is most explicit in Friedrich Engels's diatribe against Eugen Dühring: *Herrn Eugen Dührings Umwälzung der Wissenschaft*. This text appeared first in the journal *Vorwärts* in 1877–78 and then in book form in 1878. The phrase about the state "withering away" (German: *absterben*) may be found in Karl Marx and Friedrich Engels, *Werke* (*MEW*), vol. 20 (Berlin: Dietz Verlag, 1962), 262.

52. Lange cites a work on wages by Lujo Brentano (1844–1931), a noted economist then teaching at the University of Breslau. Brentano had concluded that workers should be engaged more in producing essential commodities rather than non-essentials. Lange then writes: "In fact, here is the key to the entire Social Question and at the same time the proof it is essentially identical with the Workers' Question." He goes on to state that the only non-revolutionary solution can be attained when the wealth differentials in society are reduced. "But this is the same thing as the reduction of work for luxury goods and the refined enjoyment of the few, and the increase of work for the measured beautification and amusement of life for all." Lange, *Die Arbeiterfrage*, 190–91.

Chapter 4. The Women's Question

1. This interpretation accords well with a famous photograph taken in May 1882, shortly before the composition of *Zarathustra*. In it, we find Paul Rée and Nietzsche harnessed to a cart in which Lou

Salomé is sitting; she is holding a whip in a raised right arm, as if she were about to strike the two men. The idea for this strange arrangement of persons and props was evidently Nietzsche's.

2. Ellen Kennedy, "Nietzsche: Women as Untermensch," in *Women in Western Political Philosophy: Kant to Nietzsche*, ed. Ellen Kennedy and Susan Mendus (New York: St. Martin's Press, 1987), 179–201; here 196–98.

3. See Barbara Helm, "Combating Misogyny?: Responses to Nietzsche by Turn-of-the-Century German Feminists," *Journal of Nietzsche Studies* 27 (2004): 64–84.

4. The reference here is to Nietzsche's discussion of women in aphorisms 231–39 in *Beyond Good and Evil*, specifically here to JGB 232, KSA 5.170.

5. The correct spelling is Malwida von Meysenbug (1816–1903).

6. Hedwig Dohm, *Die Antifeministen: Ein Buch der Verteidigung* (Berlin: Dümmler, 1902), 20–33. These remarks on Nietzsche from 1902 are a reworking of an earlier article, "Nietzsche und die Frauen," *Die Zukunft* 6.25 (24 December 1898): 534–43.

7. Helene Stöcker, *Die Liebe und die Frauen*, 2nd rev. ed. (Minden: Bruns, 1908), 2–3. The first edition appeared in 1906. The book consists of essays that had appeared over the past decade in various periodicals.

8. The title of this first section is "Our Revaluation of Values" [*Unsere Umwertung der Werte*]. The original essay appeared in *Magazin für Literatur* in 1897.

9. Nietzsche uses the phrase "religion of joy" only once. It appears in a notebook from the end of 1880 where he is comparing Judaism, "the religion of terror," with Greek religion, "the religion of joy," although it is also viewed occasionally as a "religion of envy" (Nachlass 1880, 7[175], KSA 9.353).

10. Citations are taken from the initial section in Stöcker, *Die Liebe und die Frauen*, 5–18.

11. Nietzsche was aware of the uproar his remark about the whip had caused. In a letter to his sister from early July 1885 he comments: "By the way, I am considered in circles of women students the 'bad dog' [*böses Tier*]—it seems that a certain allusion to an instrument that makes noise and cracks has had a nearly enchanting effect!" (Nr. 611, KSB 7.65).

12. Citations in this paragraph are taken from the section "Nietzsches Frauenfeindschaft," 71–80. The original essay from which these remarks were drawn appeared in 1901 in *Zukunft*.

13. Helene Stoecker, "The Newer Ethics," *Mother Earth* 2 (March 1907): 17–23.

14. Walter Kaufmann, *Nietzsche: Philosopher, Psychologist, Antichrist*, 4th ed. (Princeton, NJ: Princeton University Press, 1974), 84.

15. Jacques Derrida, *Spurs: Nietzsche's Styles/Éperons: Les Styles de Nietzsche*, trans. Barbara Harlow (Chicago: University of Chicago Press, 1979).

16. Luce Irigaray, *Marine Lover of Friedrich Nietzsche*, trans. Gillian C. Gill (New York: Columbia University Press, 1990); French edition: *Amante marine: de Friedrich Nietzsche* (Paris: Éditions de Minuit, 1980).

17. Sarah Kofman, *Nietzsche et la scène philosophique* (Paris: Union générale d'éditions, 1979).

18. See Duncan Large's chapter on Kofman in *Interpreting Nietzsche: Reception and Influence*, ed. Ashley Woodward (London: Continuum, 2011), 116–30.

19. Paul Patton, ed., *Nietzsche, Feminism and Political Theory* (London: Routledge, 1993); Peter J. Burgard, ed., *Nietzsche and the Feminine* (Charlottesville: University Press of Virginia, 1994); Kelly Oliver and Marilyn Pearsall, eds., *Feminist Interpretations of Friedrich Nietzsche* (University Park: Pennsylvania State University Press, 1998); Diane Elam, *Feminism and Deconstruction* (London: Routledge, 1994); and Kelly Oliver, *Womanizing Nietzsche: Philosophy's Relation to the "Feminine"* (London: Routledge, 1995).

20. Kofman argues a similar position, claiming that his remarks against women are a mark of ambivalence and even "symptomatic of a deep love for women, who had abandoned him, when they might have served him as a lightning rod." Sarah Kofman, "Baubô: Theological Perversion and Fetishism," *Feminist Interpretations of Friedrich Nietzsche*, 21–49; here 47.

21. See, for example, Kelly Oliver, "Woman as Truth in Nietzsche's Writing," in Oliver, *Feminist Interpretations of Friedrich Nietzsche*, 66–80: "Truth is as ambiguous in Nietzsche's writings as woman" (66), and "Nietzsche has the same love-hate relationship to woman which he has to truth" (67).

22. Derrida, *Spurs*, 57, 53, 64–65.

23. Peter J. Burgard, "Introduction: Figures of Excess," *Nietzsche and the Feminine*, 4, 11, 14.

24. Tamsin Lorraine, "Nietzsche and Feminism: Transvaluing Women in *Thus Spoke Zarathustra*," in Oliver, *Feminist Interpretations of Nietzsche*, 119–29; here 120, 126.

25. I have cited from the article by Lynne Tirrell, "Sexual Dualism and Women's Self-Creation: On the Advantages and Disadvantages of Reading Nietzsche for Feminists," in Oliver, *Feminist Interpretations of Friedrich Nietzsche*, 200–201.

26. Summing up the appeal of Nietzsche's writings for philosophical feminism of the late twentieth century, Keith Ansell-Pearson writes: "The consensus which seems to be emerging at the present moment in time is that the most fertile aspect of his writings for the formulation of a radical philosophy lies, not in their overt pronouncements (on women, for example), but rather in their 'style'(s), in their attempt to communicate a philosophy of the body, in their disclosure of the metaphoricity of philosophical discourse, and in the exemplary way in which they are seen to deconstruct the logocentric bias of western thought and reason" (28–29). "Nietzsche, Woman and Political Theory," in Patton, *Nietzsche, Feminism and Political Theory*, 27–48.

27. Derrida, *Spurs*, 97.

28. Irigaray, *Marine Lover*, 79.

29. Bianca Theisen, "Rhythms of Oblivion," *Nietzsche and the Feminine*, 82–103; here 83.

30. Janet Lungstrum, "Nietzsche Writing Woman / Woman Writing Nietzsche," *Nietzsche and the Feminine*, 135–57; here 136.

31. As we have seen in Chapter 2, the term was first applied to Nietzsche by the Danish intellectual Georg Brandes.

32. For an account of Otto-Peters's development, see Ruth-Ellen Boetcher Joeres, *Die Anfänge der deutschen Frauenbewegung: Louise Otto-Peters* (Frankfurt: Fischer, 1983).

33. Rosemarie Nave-Herz, *Die Geschichte der Frauenbewegung in Deutschland* (Hannover: Niedersächsische Landeszentrale für politische Bildung, 1997), 15.

34. Information about this conference and the contributions of several participants can be found in P. A. Korn, ed., *Die erste deutsche Frauen-Conferenz in Leipzig: Erste Versammlung den 15. Oktober 1865* (Leipzig: Julius Werner, 1865). See also Christine Susanne Rabe, *Gleichwertigkeit von Mann und Frau: Die Krause-Schule und die bürgerliche Frauenbewegung* (Cologne: Böhlau, 2006), 31–33.

35. Louise Otto-Peters delivered much the same message in her book *Das Recht der Frauen auf Erwerb: Blicke auf das Frauenleben der Gegenwart* (Hamburg: Hoffmann und Campe, 1866).

36. Daniel Blue speculates that Nietzsche may have been acquainted with the elder Mushacke from the latter's visits to see his son in Bonn. See *The Making of Friedrich Nietzsche: The Quest for Identity, 1844–1866* (Cambridge: Cambridge University Press, 2016), 202.

37. See Tanja-Carina Riedel, *Gleiches Recht für Frau und Mann: Die bürgerliche Frauenbewegung und die Enstehung des BGB* (Cologne: Böhlau, 2008), 22–23.

38. See Lorenne M. G. Clark and Lynda Lange, eds., *The Sexism of Social and Political Theory: Women and Reproduction from Plato to Nietzsche* (Toronto: University of Toronto Press, 1979).

39. Richard J. Evans, *The Feminist Movement in Germany, 1894–1933* (London: Sage, 1976), 24.

40. We should not overlook Dühring's influence in some socialist circles, however. Although he opposed both parties that eventually merged to form the Socialist Workers' Party of Germany, he gained a following in the late 1870s. But his attacks on Engels, Engels's attacks on him, and his increasingly public anti-Semitic positions led to a loss of influence in the 1880s, when the SAPD was officially proscribed from public life during the Socialist Laws (1878–90). Nietzsche had known Dühring's writings since the 1860s, when he was impressed by *Der Wert des Lebens* (1865), and he read his philosophical works of the 1870s with interest before turning resolutely against him in the 1880s.

41. The 1879 edition of this book carries the title *Die Frau und der Sozialismus*, but the revised edition from 1883, which was likely the one Köselitz possessed and Nietzsche knew, had the title *Die Frau in der Vergangenheit, Gegenwart und Zukunft*. Later editions evidently reverted to the more popular title.

42. Nietzsche could evidently not recall Blackwell's name and refers to her as "an English woman (Elisab...)," but Köselitz figured out what his friend wanted.

43. August Bebel, *Die Frau in der Vergangenheit, Gegenwart und Zukunft* (Hottingen-Zürich: Schweizerische Volksbuchhandlung, 1883), 38. Bebel also cites her later in the book on the topic of prostitution (83). These citations from Blackwell do not appear in the 1879 edition. During the period of the Socialist Laws, the book was outlawed in Germany, which accounts for its publication in Switzerland.

44. Evans, *Feminist Movement in Germany*, 26.

45. When the college opened in 1833, it stated its willingness to matriculate not only women, but also men and women of all races in order to prepare them for appropriate positions in the workforce. In its initial years, Oberlin designed a Ladies' Department, which was evidently known as the "female appendage." The educational enterprise was separate, but hardly equal, since woman were asked to cook, sew, and wash for the men students; Mondays were without instruction in the Ladies' Department so that women could tend to their womanly duties vis-à-vis "the leading sex." In 1837, however, women students, discontent with their segregated status, applied for and were granted admission to men's courses, and in 1841 Oberlin graduated three women who had completed the formerly all-male course of instruction. See Elizabeth Seymour Eschbach, *The Higher Education of Women in England and America, 1865–1920* (New York: Garland, 1993), 43–44.

46. Evans, *Feminist Movement in Germany*, 20.

47. Curt Paul Janz, *Friedrich Nietzsche: Biographie*, 3 vols., 2nd rev. ed. (Munich: Carl Hanser, 1993), 1:624–25.

48. Janz, *Nietzsche*, 2:110–15.

49. See Christine Johanson, *Women's Struggle for Higher Education in Russia, 1855–1900* (Kingston: McGill-Queen's University Press, 1987); Thomas Neville Bonner, *To the Ends of the Earth: Women's Search for Education in Medicine* (Cambridge, MA: Harvard University Press, 1992); Marianna Muravyeva, "Russian Women in European Universities, 1864–1900," in *Women, Education, and Agency, 1600–2000*, ed. Jean Spence, Sarah Jane Aiston, and Maureen M. Meikle (New York: Routledge, 2009), 83–104; Ruth A. Dudgeon, "Higher Education for Women in Nineteenth- and Early Twentieth-Century Russia," in *Encyclopedia of Russian Women's Movements*, ed. Norma C. Noonan and Carol R. Nechemias (Westport, CT: Greenwood Press, 2001), 30–32.

50. The most sober and well-documented accounts are in Janz, *Nietzsche*, 2:119–58; and Robin Small, *Nietzsche and Rée: A Star Friendship* (Oxford: Oxford University Press, 2005), 130–53. A different sort of account is found in Elisabeth Förster-Nietzsche, *Friedrich Nietzsche und die Frauen seiner Zeit* (Munich: Beck, 1935), 111–14; Elisabeth, whose dislike for Lou is obvious, sees Lou as an unscrupulous opportunist who tried to gain intimacy with her brother.

51. See Carol Diethe, *Nietzsche's Women: Beyond the Whip* (Berlin: de Gruyter, 1996), 59.

52. Nietzsche may have also been slightly dishonest in his conversations with Schirnhofer. She reports, for example, that he repeatedly spoke of his Polish ancestry, claiming that Nietzsche derives from the Polish Niezki, which is a complete fabrication that Nietzsche must have recognized as such (252). He also reported to her as fact that Wagner's stepfather, Ludwig Geyer, was his real father and that therefore Wagner had Jewish blood. She continues by noting that although Nietzsche never spoke to her in a derogatory fashion about Jews, she could detect it in this instance (256). Hans Lohberger, "Friedrich Nietzsche und Resa von Schirnhofer," *Zeitschrift für philosophische Forschung* 22.2 and 3 (1968): 248–60; 441–58.

53. Lohberger, "Friedrich Nietzsche und Resa von Schirnhofer," 255.

54. "Llama" was his pet name for his sister.

55. Förster-Nietzsche, *Friedrich Nietzsche und die Frauen seiner Zeit*, 8–10.

56. [Emily Fynn] Silex, "Quelques souvenirs sur Frédéric Nietzsche," *Bibliothèque universelle et revue suisse* 52 (1908): 340–53; 545–558; here 345–46. "On a aussi faussement accuse notre philosophe de haine et de mépris pour l'élément féminin! Tout au contraire, il avait une admiration sincère pour les capacités de la femme; pour son cœur, son intelligence, sa force de volonté et d'abnégation. La sincère amitié de Nietzsche pour diverse femmes distinguées, la déférence qu'il témoignait à toute

femme quelle qu'elle fût, jeune ou vieille, belle ou laide, intelligente ou non, prouvent surabondamment que Nietzsche ne méprisait pas la femme."

57. Cited from Sander L. Gilman, ed., *Conversations with Nietzsche: A Life in the Words of His Contemporaries* (Oxford: Oxford University Press, 1987), 68.

58. In his private correspondence, however, Nietzsche is sometimes less than gentlemanly. For example, in a letter to Malwida von Meysenbug he also makes a gratuitously negative reference to Schirnhofer's physical appearance, stating that "I cannot stand ugliness around me any more" (1 September 1884, Nr. 528, KSB 6.523).

59. Meta von Salis-Marschlins, *Philosoph und Edelmensch: Ein Beitrag zur Charakteristik Friedrich Nietzsche's* (Leipzig: Naumann, 1897).

60. What makes this remark even more reprehensible is that it is likely that Nietzsche encouraged her to seek permission to study with Burckhardt. On this occasion, Burckhardt evidently voted on the side of the petitioner, but the vote failed anyway.

61. In the second instance, Nietzsche is reporting to his sister about his activities in Sils-Maria: "Fräulein von Salis has been at Sils for six weeks recovering from the stresses of her doctoral promotion; she has a sick little friend with her, the daughter of Professor Kym, and I summoned enough of my humanity to put up with these examples of womanhood [*Weiblichkeiten*], who are in essence unedifying, albeit otherwise respectable."

62. After her father died, she inherited a considerable fortune. She used her inheritance at one point to support the publication of Nietzsche's writings, since he no longer had a publisher (Meta von Salis to Nietzsche, October/November 1888, Nr. 597, KGB III 6.343; and to Heinrich Köselitz, December 9, 1888, Nr. 1181, KSB 8. 514). She also purchased Villa Silberblick in Weimar for Elisabeth as a home for the insane Nietzsche and the Nietzsche archives.

63. Citations in this paragraph are taken from the first volume of the three-volume third edition of *Memoiren einer Idealistin* (Leipzig: Albert Unflad, 1881).

64. As the subtitle to the French edition indicates—"(entre deux révolutions.) 1830–1848"—this first version of the *mémoires* is an abbreviated account that would be expanded in the German version to cover her life until 1861.

65. In this letter, Nietzsche is speaking of Helene Druskowitz's polemic against him, and the fact that he deserves the opposition of women. The notion that he is worse than Schopenhauer refers to his notorious views on women, which will be discussed below.

66. Malwida von Meysenbug, *Der Lebensabend einer Idealistin: Nachtrag zu den "Memoiren einer Idealistin"* (Berlin: Schuster & Loeffler, 1906), 57–58.

67. Von Meysenbug referred to the Sorrento experience frequently as a "colony" in later years and often sought to recreate it—to no avail.

68. Her name is spelled variously; it appears as Druscowicz, and on at least one of her publications the editor makes her "von Druskowitz." In Nietzsche's first reference to her in his letters, he calls her "Truschkowitz" (to Franz Overbeck, 18 July 1882, Nr. 270, KSB 6.229).

69. Helene Druskowitz writing to Conrad Ferdinand Meyer on 22 December 1884, cited in Richard Frank Krummel, *Nietzsche und der deutsche Geist*, vol. 1, 2nd ed. (Berlin: de Gruyter, 1998), 111.

70. Nietzsche writes to Köselitz: "Sending the 4th part of Zarath[ustra] to mademoiselle Druscowicz was a stupidity on my part." He goes on to say that Druskowitz believes she was only to read the book and is returning it to Köselitz's address, which Nietzsche has sent to her (21 August 1885, Nr. 624, KSB 7.86).

71. Helene von Druskowitz, *Moderne Vesuche eines Religionsersatzes: Ein philosophischer Essay* (Heidelberg: Georg Weiß, 1886), 45–59.

72. Helene von Druskowitz, *Eugen Dühring: Eine Studie zu seiner Würdigung* (Heidelberg: Georg Weiß, 1889).

73. Helene von Druskowitz, *Pessimistische Kardinalsätze: Ein Vademekum für die freiesten Geister* (Vezseny, Hungary: Ngiyaw, 2012), 18–19; originally (Wittenberg: Geister Herrosé Zimsen Verlag, 1905).

74. Druskowitz, *Pessimistische Kardinalsätze*, 34–35.

75. John Stuart Mill, "The Subjection of Women," in Mary Wollstonecraft and John Stuart Mill, *A Vindication of the Rights of Woman/The Subjection of Women* (London: J. M. Dent & Sons: 1985), 220.

76. Mill, "The Subjection of Women," 237.

77. Mill, "The Subjection of Women," 311.

78. We will recall that Nietzsche attended Sybel's lectures while he was a student at Bonn; Teichmüller was for a short time a fellow faculty member at Basel.

79. Heinrich von Sybel, "Ueber die Emancipation der Frauen," *Vorträge und Aufsätze* (Berlin: A. Hofmann & Co., 1874), 57–79.

80. Gustav Teichmüller, *Ueber die Frauenemancipation* (Dorpat: C. Mattiesen, 1877).

81. Gustav Teichmüller, *Ueber die Reihenfolge der Platonischen Dialoge* (Leipzig: Köhler, 1879).

82. Gustav Teichmüller, *Die wirkliche und die scheinbare Welt: Neue Grundlage der Metaphysik* (Breslau: Koebner, 1882).

83. It is quite possible that Nietzsche borrowed this volume from Franz Overbeck, since he mentions he is returning two books by Teichmüller to his friend in a communication from November 1885 (Nr. 645, KSB 7.109).

84. See Arthur Schopenhauer, *Werke in zehn Bänden*, Züricher Ausgabe, ed. Arthur Hübscher (Zurich: Diogenes, 1977), 10:667–81 ("Ueber die Weiber," ß362–71). In this section we also find suggestions for legalized prostitution that come very close to Nietzsche's suggestions, and that are proposed for similar reasons.

85. This passage appears in the German and English editions of *Ecce Homo*, but it is not at all certain that Nietzsche would have authorized it if he had not had a mental breakdown. It is unusual for Nietzsche to include public criticism of his family in a published work. He was careful to avoid incendiary statements about his family in his writings, and he rarely included anything even in letters that would upset his mother. We should recall that Nietzsche did not authorize the final edition of *Ecce Homo*, and if he had not fallen into insanity, this autobiographical text may have looked quite different.

86. *Wissenschaft* is often translated as "science," but Nietzsche clearly means by this any kind of scholarly activity, not activity restricted to the natural sciences.

87. Derrida, *Spurs*, 97.

88. Hebrews 12:6.

89. The "Orient" for Nietzsche and the nineteenth century, of course, referred to the Middle East, not to the Far East.

90. The most recent discussion of this issue is found in Julian Young's contribution "Nietzsche and Women" in *The Oxford Handbook of Nietzsche*, ed. Ken Gemes and John Richardson (Oxford: Oxford University Press, 2013), 46–62.

91. For example, in section 4, "Epigrams and Interludes," in *Beyond Good and Evil*: "Men and women have the same emotions, but at a different tempo: that is why men and women never cease to misunderstand one another" (BGE 85, KSA 5. 89).

92. The first four books appeared in 1882 and belong therefore to Nietzsche's middle period prior to *Zarathustra*.

93. Nietzsche adds that it may be desirable "not to remind oneself constantly how harsh, terrible, enigmatic, and immoral this antagonism is," but he evidently believes that the traits about which he writes are so firmly implanted in the human being that they cannot be altered.

94. The "Eternal-Feminine" (*Ewig-Weibliche*), translated by Hollingdale as the "eternal-womanly," refers to the final lines of Goethe's *Faust*.

95. The "improvers of humankind" is a section from *Twilight of the Idols* (GD, Die "Verbesserer" der Menschheit, KSA 6.98–102).

Chapter 5. The Colonial Question

1. It is taken up in the most thorough of Nietzsche's biographies by Curt Paul Janz, *Nietzsche: Biographie*, 2nd rev. ed., 3 vols. (Munich: Hanser, 1993), in volume 2, 415–21 *et passim*.

2. Henning Ottmann, ed., *Nietzsche Handbuch: Leben—Werk—Wirkung* (Stuttgart: Metzler, 2000); and Christian Niemeyer, ed., *Nietzsche-Lexikon*, 2nd ed. (Darmstadt: Wissenschaftliche Buchgesellschaft, 2011).

3. He also includes this remark in the preface to *The Antichrist* (KSA 6.167), and in a letter written to Carl Fuchs shortly before the composition of *Ecce Homo*, he remarks: "Some are born posthumously" ["Einige werden posthum geboren"] (26 August 1888, Nr. 1096, KSB 8.403).

4. See also Robert C. Holub, *Nietzsche's Jewish Problem: Between Anti-Semitism and Anti-Judaism* (Princeton, NJ: Princeton University Press, 2016).

5. In 1897 Germany acquired Kiaochow; in 1899 Samoa.

6. See Jürgen Zimmerer and Joachim Zeller, eds., *Genocide in German South-West Africa: The Colonial War of 1904–1908 and Its Aftermath*, trans. Edward Neather (Exeter: Merlin Press, 2008).

7. The significance of this day for the wedding did not escape Nietzsche, who wrote to Franz Overbeck on 7 May 1885: "My sister will be married on the 22nd of May; you understand the date" ["Den 22. Mai ist die Hochzeit meiner Schwester, Du verstehst das Datum"] (7.46). Nietzsche had been estranged from Wagner and the Wagnerians—at least in his own mind—since the inauguration of Bayreuth in 1876.

8. Bernhard Förster, *Deutsche Colonien in dem oberen Laplata-Gebiete mit besonderer Berücksichtigung von Paraguay: Ergebnisse eingehender Prüfungen, praktischer Arbeiten und Reisen, 1883–1885* (Naumburg: Selbstverlag, 1886), 1.

9. See, for example, Förster's article opposing vivisection titled "Die Frage der Vivisektion im Deutschen Reichstage," *Bayreuther Blätter* 5 (1882): 90–96. His brother Paul continued this opposition while Bernhard was in Paraguay with "Die Bewegung wider die Vivisektion," *Bayreuther Blätter* 9 (1886): 125–34.

10. See, for example, Förster's review of Constantin Frantz's book *Zur Reform des Steuerwesens* in *Bayreuther Blätter* 5 (1882): 315–17. Förster praises the call for a progressive income tax and writes: "We demand a higher taxation of the stock market, every form of luxury and in general all mobile property not only in the interest of our financial economy, but above all because of important *ethical* and *socio-political* considerations. Even if those taxes bring in very little for the state, the impoverished proletariat should have and retain the consciousness that justice reigns supreme in the state, that the rulers are an entity not only for the bankers, the privileged, and the 'educated,' but in the spirit of the Evangelium of love also harbor sentiments for the poor and the oppressed" (316).

11. Förster, *Colonien*, 8.

12. Not to be confused with the philosopher Friedrich Albert Lange (1828–1875), whose book on the history of materialism Nietzsche admired and frequently consulted.

13. "Pure Germanness" is the title of a book that collects many of Lange's journalistic pieces from the last three decades of the nineteenth century and first years of the twentieth. Friedrich Lange, *Reines Deutschtum: Grundzüge einer nationalen Weltanschauung*, 5th ed. (Berlin: Alexander Duncker, 1904). In an article titled "Gobineau and Nietzsche" from 11 November 1900, Lange criticizes Nietzsche for his aristocratism because it is not based on nations and race (248–58).

14. Friedrich Lange, "Kolonialpolitische Erinnerungen: Vergebliche Arbeit? (14. Sept. 1889)," in *Reines Deutschtum*, 261–86; here 263. This article contains updates from 1893 and 2004 as well, in which Lange is increasingly pessimistic about the colonial enterprise because of its lack of support in Germany and in the German parliament.

15. The connection between Wagner and manifestations of German nationalism is evidenced in the following passage from Nietzsche's notebooks, written at a time when Nietzsche, making notes for *Richard Wagner in Bayreuth*, was still apologetic about Wagner's nationalist proclivities: "There are elements in Wagner that appear to be *reactionary*: the medieval-Christian, the relations to princes, the Buddhist, the miraculous. From these things he may have gained adherents. They are his *means* of *expression*, the language that is still understood, but has a new content. These things are artificial in the artist, and should not be taken dogmatically. *German nationalism* belongs to this. He seeks analogies for things in future occurrences in the past; thus it seems to him that the German quality of Luther,

Beethoven and himself, the German quality and its great princes, can serve as a guarantee that something analogous to that which he considers necessary for the future, was once in existence. Courage, loyalty, simplicity, goodness, sacrifice, as he placed all of this in the splendid symbolism of his 'Imperial March'—that is his Germanness. He is seeking the *contribution* that Germans can make to future culture" (Nachlass 1875, 11[4], KSA 8.190–91). In the 1880s, he appears to associate German nationalism less with Wagner than with Wagnerians: "The R[ichard] W[agner] who is today revered in Germany, and who is revered with all the boastful trash of the worst sort of German jingoism: that R[ichard] W[agner] I do not know and really I have the suspicion that he never existed: that is a figment of the imagination" (Nachlass 1885, 34[227], KSA 11.497). At other times, however, Nietzsche contends that Wagner himself adopted an unflattering chauvinism at the end of his life: "What was most foreign to me was the Germanomania and quasi-religiosity of his last years" (Nachlass 1886, 2[34], KSA 12.81).

16. Bernhard Förster, "Ein Deutschland der Zukunft," *Bayreuther Blätter* 6 (1883): 44–56.

17. Nietzsche himself was often conscious of, and dismayed by, his association with Wagner and the Wagnerians. Writing to Overbeck in December 1885, he remarks that *Zarathustra* sold poorly and that the few hundred volumes that were sold were purchased by Wagnerians and anti-Semites (Nr. 649, KSB 7.118). In a letter from the following year he comments as follows: "It is wonderful how faithfully these Wagner adherents still cling to me; I think they know that still today as much as in the past I believe in the ideal that Wagner believed—what does it matter that I stumbled across the many human, all-too-human things that R[ichard] W[agner] had placed in the path of even his ideal?" (27 October 1886, Nr. 769, KSB 7.273).

18. Förster, "Ein Deutschland," 11–15.

19. Bernhard Förster, "Deutsche Gemeinden im Laplata-Gebiete: Selbstanzeige meines Buches," *Bayreuther Blätter* 8 (1885): 325–26.

20. Richard Wagner, "Religion und Kunst," *Bayreuther Blätter* 3 (1880): 269–300; here 291–93.

21. In her report from early 1889, Elisabeth Förster notes that because they have frequent visitors, they cannot be consistent in their vegetarianism. But from her description of the abundant livestock in the colony, it appears that the vegetarian principles of Wagner ceded quickly to the reality of life in the forests of Paraguay. See Elisabeth Förster, "Ein Sonntag in Nueva-Germania," *Bayreuther Blätter* 12 (1889): 285–98; in particular 291. She does insist at another point, however, that vegetarians can do well in the colony and asserts that a vegetarian diet kept her and her husband from illness that others suffered, but she also notes that meat prices are very inexpensive and that many carnivorous settlers experience no problems with illness (292).

22. Förster, "Ein Deutschland," 48.

23. Disparaging Germans for drinking beer or alcohol and for reading newspapers is something found in many comments by Nietzsche—during and after his Wagnerian years.

24. Bernhard Förster, "Neu-Germanien," *Parsifal-Nachklänge: Allerhand Gedanken über deutsche Cultur, Wissenschaft, Kunst, Gesellschaft* (Leipzig: Theodor Fritsch, 1883), 87–90.

25. Förster, *Colonien*, 6.

26. Förster, "Ein Deutschland," 50.

27. Förster, "Ein Deutschland," 51.

28. Richard Wagner, "Publikum und Popularität," *Bayreuther Blätter* 1 (1878): 213–22; here 220.

29. Ernst Podach, *Gestalten um Nietzsche* (Weimar: Lichtenstein, 1932), 139–76; H. F. Peters, *Zarathustra's Sister: The Case of Elisabeth and Friedrich Nietzsche* (New York: Crown, 1977), 85–125; Janz, *Nietzsche*, vol. 2, 415–21 et passim.

30. Ben Macintyre, *Forgotten Fatherland: The Search for Elisabeth Nietzsche* (New York: Farrar, Straus & Giroux, 1992). This readable account is unfortunately lacking in scholarly rigor and accuracy to detail.

31. Joseph Winfield Fretz, *Immigrant Group Settlements in Paraguay: A Study in the Sociology of Colonization* (North Newton, KS: Bethel College, 1962), 36–38; and Macintyre, *Forgotten Fatherland*, 8–10.

32. Bernhard Förster, "Offener Brief an den Freiherrn Hans Paul v. Wolzogen in Bayreuth," *Bayreuther Blätter* 11 (1888): 357–60.

33. A version of this essay is available as "Bayreuther Arbeit: Ein Schlusswort (1888)" in *Wagneriana: Gesammelte Aufsätze über R. Wagner's Werke, vom Ring bis zum Gral: Eine Gedenkgabe für alte und neue Festspielgäste zum Jahre 1888* (Leipzig: E. Freund, 1888), 252–63.

34. Hans Paul Freiherr von Wolzogen, "Neu-Deutschland in Paraguay: Ein ernster Aufruf an die Unserigen," *Bayreuther Blätter* 11 (1888): 438–39.

35. See Wilfried Westphal, *Geschichte der deutschen Kolonien* (Munich: Bertelsmann, 1984), 126–29. Westphal puts the amount of money raised at 400,000 marks (129).

36. Nietzsche also mentions in this letter that he does not believe Förster will return to Paraguay. He obviously misjudged the determination of his future brother-in-law, or was indulging in wishful thinking.

37. He is writing from Sils.

38. The housekeeper of Nietzsche's mother.

39. Janz, *Nietzsche*, vol. 3, 181–85.

40. We have Nietzsche's response, but not Elisabeth's letter requesting money.

41. From the correspondence it is not entirely clear to whom this money belonged. It appears that Nietzsche had freed up some part of Elisabeth's share in the house, since in her response to her brother she expresses disappointment that he has not seen fit to invest.

42. See Mary Evelyn Townsend, *Origins of Modern German Colonialism, 1871–1885* (Diss. Columbia University 1921), 138–45.

43. Nietzsche states that he is now being criticized with abandon in the same periodical, a turn of events that is a hundred times more pleasing to him than the cooptation of his writings (3 February 1888, Nr. 984, KSB 8.243). We will have a chance to look at this incident more carefully in the next chapter.

44. The fragment of Elisabeth's letter of 14 January 1888 does not contain any such information.

45. Nietzsche as a precursor of the European Union would seem to be the premise of the discussion in "Was ist aus Nietzsches Ideal des 'guten Europäers' geworden?: Impulsreferat Carlo Gentili: 'Der "gute Europäer" als neue Idee des Menschen nach der Säkularisierung des Christentums,'" *Nietzsche-Studien* 43 (2014): 106–17.

46. Nietzsche makes it clear that the reemergence of good Europeans involves an overcoming of nationalism in *Beyond Good and Evil*: "Indeed, I could imagine that even within our quick-moving Europe, some dull, sluggish races might need half-centuries to overcome these atavistic attacks of fatherlandism and attachment to the soil, and return to reason, that is to say to being 'good Europeans'" (JGB 241, KSA 5.180–81).

47. Many of Nietzsche's notes on Europeanism occur at the time he was composing *Zarathustra*, yet there is no mention of the good European in that work. Evidently, Nietzsche made a conscious decision to eliminate all temporal or geographical specificities from his parabolic work. But his notebooks evidence at least one instance in which the "good European" was associated with the "higher men." In the winter of 1884–85 we read: "It occurred to the good European: 'And though there are swamps and melancholy on earth, and entire seas of mud, whoever has light feet, like Zarathustra, runs even over mud, quickly as on swept ice.'" (Nachlass 1884–85, 32[13], 11.412).

In the fourth book of *Zarathustra*, this passage is incorporated without any mention of the good European in the seventeenth part of the section "On the Higher Man":

17.

All good things approach their goal crookedly. Like cats, they arch their backs, they purr inwardly over their approaching happiness: all good things laugh.

A man's stride betrays whether he has found his own way: behold me walking! But whoever approaches his goal dances. And verily, I have not become a statue: I do not yet stand there, stiff, stupid, stony, a column; I love to run swiftly. And though there are swamps and thick melancholy on earth, whoever has light feet runs even over mud and dances as on swept ice. (Za 4, Vom höheren Menschen 17, KSA 4.365–66)

48. For example, in notes made in preparation for the fourth part of *Zarathustra*, Nietzsche wrote: "the good European 'I have committed all crimes. I love the most dangerous thoughts and the most dangerous women'" (Nachlass 1884–85, 29[51], KSA 11.348). Beginning in the late 1870s, the criminal becomes synonymous with the original thinker, the destroyer of accepted norms, or the creative man in much of Nietzsche's writings; the fact that a person is called a "criminal" is society's method of concealing and canceling this originality and iconoclasm. "It has been concealed that in the criminal there is evidence of a great deal of courage and originality of intellect, independence" (Nachlass 1880, 4[108], KSA 9.127). Or in *Zarathustra*, where Nietzsche makes the etymological connection between breaking [*Brechen*] and committing a crime or breaking laws [*Verbrechen*]: "Behold the good and the just! Whom do they hate most? The man who breaks their tables of values, the breaker, the lawbreaker; yet he is the creator" (Za 1, Zarathustra's Vorrede 9, 4.26).

49. Nietzsche produces in various places several lists of "good Europeans" or anticipators of Europeanism, but these names are not surprising considering Nietzsche's views on them in other writings. In a letter to Georg Brandes, he establishes a somewhat different group of contemporary "good Europeans," which includes Jacob Burckhardt, Hans von Bülow, Hippolyte Taine, Gottfried Keller, Bruno Bauer, and Richard Wagner, but he was limited in his selection because he is boasting to Brandes that these "good Europeans" are his readers (2 December 1887, Nr. 960, KSB 8.205).

50. The notion of a caste bred to rule the world is mentioned in other notebook passages besides the one discussed above, for example: "The task is to form a *ruling caste* with the most expansive souls, capable of the most diverse tasks of ruling the earth" [Die Aufgabe ist, eine *herrschende Kaste* zu bilden, mit den umfänglichsten Seelen, fähig für die verschiedensten Aufgaben der Erdregierung]" (Nachlass 1884, 25[221], KSA 11.72). In another note he declares: "The hegemony over the earth as a means of producing a higher type" (Nachlass 1884, 25[211], KSA 11.69), thus reversing his usual sequence of events, which views the production of a higher type of individual as the prerequisite for the rule of the earth. In a third note, he states: "I am writing for a species of human being that is not yet present: for the 'rulers of the earth'" (Nachlass 1884, 25[137], KSA 11.50). He then cites a passage from Plato's "Theages," a dialogue attributed to the philosopher, but of doubtful authenticity, that appears to affirm something like a will to power in each of us: "Each of us would like to be the master, if possible of all men, best would be to be god" (Theages 125e–126a).

51. There are some variants on these views in other notes. For example, in 1884 Nietzsche wrote about "the rule over the earth" as a "first question." At that point he identified it with the Anglo-Saxons and thought the Germans did not understand how to exert domination. He also hypothesized that the ascendancy of France signaled that Europe had been reduced to a cultural center. He did urge Russian dominance over Europe and Asia, stating that it must "colonize and win China and India" (Nachlass 1884, 25[112], KSA 11.41–42).

52. The most extensive discussion of "Great Politics" comes in a recent book, Hugo Drochon's *Nietzsche's Great Politics* (Princeton, NJ: Princeton University Press, 2016).

53. Peter Bergmann, *Nietzsche "the Last Antipolitical German"* (Bloomington: Indiana University Press, 1987), 162.

54. "The two old men had obviously become heated by yelling their 'truths' at one another in this fashion. But I, happy to be above and beyond them, reflected on how quickly a strong man will find a stronger master, and also that spiritual shallowness in one people is balanced out by greater depth in another" (JGB 241, KSA 5.182).

55. "Their temperament, periodically inclining towards and away from the South, occasionally bubbling over with Provençal and Ligurian blood, protects them from the horrible northern grey-on-grey, the sunless world of spectral concepts and anemia: our *German* aesthetic disease, against whose excesses people today are unequivocal in prescribing blood and iron, that is to say 'great politics' (submitting to a dangerous cure that has taught me to wait and wait, but not as yet to hope)" (JGB 254, KSA 5.200). A similar contention regarding the function of "great politics" in covering for a lack of

culture is found in *Twilight of the Idols*: "Our culture suffers from nothing *more* than it suffers from the superabundance of presumptuous journeymen and fragments of humanity; our universities are, *against* their will, the actual forcing-houses for this kind of spiritual instinct-atrophy. And all Europe already has an idea of this—great politics deceives no one.... Germany counts more and more as Europe's *flatland*." "If one makes a reckoning, it is obvious not only that German culture is declining, the sufficient reason for it is obvious too. After all, no one can spend more than he has—that is true of individuals, it is also true of nations. If one spends oneself on power, great politics, economic affairs, world commerce, parliamentary institutions, military interests—if one expends in *this* direction the quantum of reason, seriousness, will, self-overcoming that one is, then there will be a shortage in the other direction" (GD, Was den Deutschen abgeht 3–4, KSA 6.105–6).

56. The language of these passages cannot help but remind us of National Socialist phraseology: "First principle: great politics will make physiology the ruler over all other questions. It will create a power strong enough to breed humanity as a whole and something higher, with merciless severity against the degenerate and parasitic in life, against anything that ruins, poisons, slanders, destroys... and in the annihilation of life sees the sign of a higher type of soul" (Nachlass 1888–89, 25[1], KSA 13.638).

Chapter 6. The Jewish Question

1. Perhaps the most differentiated previous study of these questions was one of the first: Richard Maximilian Lonsbach's *Friedrich Nietzsche und die Juden: Ein Versuch* (Stockholm: Bermann-Fischer Verlag, 1939). This study was republished after the Second World War (Bonn: Bouvier, 1985) with a transcript of Lonsbach's radio speech "War Nietzsche ein Wegbereiter des Dritten Reiches?" Lonsbach turns out to be a pseudonym for Richard Maximilian Cahen, a German-Jewish lawyer and writer of creative literature who left Germany in the 1930s but returned to Cologne in 1948.

2. We should note here, however, that the issue of Nietzsche's views on Jews, Judaism, and anti-Semitism did not arouse much interest until after the Nazis' ascent to power. Certainly there is little evidence that the many intellectuals and writers, both Jewish and non-Jewish, who were attracted to Nietzsche in the early twentieth century considered this topic especially important.

3. Alfred Baeumler, *Nietzsche der Philosoph und Politiker* (Leipzig: Reclam, 1931), and "Nietzsche und der Nationalsozialismus," in *Studien zur deutschen Geistesgeschichte* (Berlin: Junker und Dünnhaupt, 1937), 281–94; Alfred Rosenberg, *Friedrich Nietzsche* (Munich: Zentralverlag der NSDAP, 1944); Heinrich Härtle, *Nietzsche und der Nationalsozialismus* (Munich: Zentralverlag der NSDAP, 1937); Richard Oehler, *Friedrich Nietzsche und die deutsche Zukunft* (Leipzig: Armanen, 1935). Richard's brother Max (1875–1946) worked in the Nietzsche archives and assumed the directorship after the death of Elisabeth Förster-Nietzsche in 1935. Their father, Oskar Ulrich Oehler (1838–1901), was the brother of Nietzsche's mother, Franziska Nietzsche.

4. Crane Brinton, *Nietzsche* (Cambridge, MA: Harvard University Press, 1941), 215.

5. See my essay "The Elisabeth Legend or Sibling Scapegoating: The Cleansing of Friedrich Nietzsche and the Sullying of His Sister," in *Nietzsche: Godfather of Fascism? On the Uses and Abuses of Philosophy*, ed. Jacob Golomb and Robert S. Wistrich (Princeton, NJ: Princeton University Press, 2002), 215–34.

6. A more differentiated essay on the topic is Peter Heller's "Nietzsche and the Jews," in *Nietzsche heute: Die Rezeption seines Werks nach 1968*, ed. Sigrid Bauschinger et al. (Stuttgart: Francke, 1988), 149–60. Heller brings in much relevant material, but he too falls short on historical differentiation when he calls Schopenhauer and Wagner "belligerent anti-Semites" and finds that the younger Nietzsche was not "an active proponent of anti-Semitism" (151). Much more important are two books by Thomas Mittmann: *Friedrich Nietzsche: Judengegner und Antisemitenfeind* (Erfurt: Sutton, 2001) and *Vom "Günstling" zum "Urfeind" der Juden: Die antisemitische Nietzsche-Rezeption in Deutschland bis zum Ende des Nationalsozialismus* (Würzburg: Königshausen und Neumann, 2006).

7. In my monograph *Nietzsche's Jewish Problem: Between Anti-Semitism and Anti-Judaism* (Princeton, NJ: Princeton University Press, 2016), I give an account of Nietzsche's reception as an anti-Semite and the endeavor to cleanse him of these associations in the postwar era (1–30). I also

provide in the rest of the book a more accurate and detailed analysis of Nietzsche's relationship to the Jewish Question.

8. Nietzsche was in correspondence with Siegfried Lipiner and in conversation with Joseph Paneth, both of whom we will deal with later in this chapter, and, toward the end of his life, he exchanged letters with Georg Brandes. Perhaps these correspondents and occasional casual acquaintances account for Nietzsche's remark that "between 1876–86, I owe to Jews and Jewesses almost all my pleasant moments" (Nachlass 1888, 24[3], KSA 13.619).

9. See Mittmann, *Vom "Günstling" zum "Urfeind" der Juden*, 25.

10. See Martin Onnasch, "Naumburg," *Wegweiser durch das jüdische Sachsen-Anhalt* (Potsdam: Verlag für Berlin-Brandenburg, 1998), 142–49; and Jacqueline E. Jung, "The Passion, the Jews, and the Crisis of the Individual on the Naumburg West Choir Screen," in *Beyond the Yellow Badge: Anti-Judaism and Antisemitism in Medieval and Early Modern Visual Culture*, ed. Mitchell Merback (Leiden: Brill, 2008), 145–77.

11. There were 41 Jewish students from an overall 1,177 students enrolled in 1886–87. See "Universities," in *The Jewish Encyclopedia*, ed. Isidore Singer, vol. 12 (New York: Funk & Wagnalls, 1901–6), 379.

12. Sophie Ritschl was the daughter of a Jewish doctor, but, like many Jews of her era and class, she was baptized and thus a "Jewess" only by heritage, not by religious affiliation.

13. At the beginning of the nineteenth century, every fourth citizen of Fürth was Jewish, and Jews enjoyed rights of citizenship in Fürth that they possessed nowhere else in Germany.

14. The last opera of Giacomo Meyerbeer.

15. Richard Wagner, *Das Judenthum in der Musik* (Leipzig: J. J. Weber, 1869), 9–32.

16. W. Marr, *Der Sieg des Judenthums über das Germanenthum* (Bern: Rudolph Costenoble, 1879).

17. Wagner, *Das Judenthum in der Musik*, 52–54.

18. I am citing here from the version that must have been close to what Nietzsche actually delivered in his lecture on 1 February 1870. The original version of the lecture, which Nietzsche must have sent to the Wagners, is not included in the *Studienausgabe*.

19. See Shulamith Volkov, "Antisemitismus als kultureller Code," in *Antisemitismus als kultureller Code* (Munich: Beck, 1990), 13–36.

20. Léon Poliakov, *The Aryan Myth: A History of Racist and Nationalistic Ideas in Europe* (New York: Barnes and Noble, 1996), 255.

21. Cosima Wagner, *Diaries*, vol. 1: *1869–1877* (New York: Harcourt Brace Jovanovich, 1978), 445–46; 450.

22. Cosima Wagner, *Diaries*, 1:681. Cosima is reacting to Ottilie's frivolous talk about how poorly Nietzsche's book was received in academic circles.

23. The conspiracy was probably related to the Bonn "battle of philologists" [*Philologenstreit*], a conflict that originated in the animosity between Nietzsche's dissertation director, Friedrich Ritschl, and his colleague Otto Jahn. The details of the academic politics that form a background to the Nietzsche-Wilamowitz controversy are explicated best in William Musgrave Calder III, "The Wilamowitz-Nietzsche Struggle: New Documents and a Reappraisal," *Nietzsche-Studien* 121 (1983): 214–54.

24. Wagner's enemies used the term "Music of the Future" [*Zukunftsmusik*] to ridicule him.

25. Lessing is referenced not only as an Enlightenment thinker and rationalist, but also as the author of two plays on religious tolerance of Jews, the most noted of which was *Nathan the Wise* (1779).

26. Wilamowitz was the son of a Prussian Junker born in the province of Posen. Like Nietzsche, he started his studies in Bonn, where he, unlike Nietzsche, had the opportunity to take seminars from Jacob Bernays. He transferred to Berlin to complete his studies and returned to the city after serving in the Franco-Prussian War.

27. Berlin was associated with Jews for many reasons by the Wagnerians, but we should also recall Nietzsche's initial visit to the city and his encounter with Eduard Mushacke, which I discuss in *Nietzsche's Jewish Problem*, 39–40.

28. He calls him "Wilamo-Wisch" (literally, "Wilamo Rag") and "Wilam Ohne witz" (literally, "Wilam Without Wit").

29. In the summer of 1877, Nietzsche met a Frankfurt physician named Otto Eiser, who took great interest in his health, which had deteriorated so severely that he took leave from his teaching duties at Basel. He visited Frankfurt in October 1877 and was examined by Eiser for eye problems and headaches. Eiser believed the illness originated in the nerve centers of the eyes and prescribed a prohibition on reading and writing for several years, avoidance of light stimulation by wearing blue sunglasses, and abstention from all somatic and psychic exertion. When Wagner learned Eiser was treating Nietzsche, he expressed concern and did not hesitate to offer his own diagnosis to Eiser: "In judging Nietzsche's condition, for a long time I have carried around the memory of identical and very similar experiences, which I have observed in other young men of great intellectual abilities. I have seen similar symptoms have ruinous results and found out very definitely that they were the consequences of onanism." See Curt Paul Janz, "Die 'tödliche Beleidigung': Ein Beitrag zur Wagner-Entfremdung Nietzsches," *Nietzsche-Studien* 4 (1975): 263–78. Janz quotes from Wagner's letter on pp. 270–71.

30. Cosima Wagner, *Diaries*, 1:176. What they read was likely a draft of the 1865 sketch of the opera.

31. See Pamela Andre, "Christ and Wagner: The Religion of Cosima," *Journal of Religious History* 14 (1987): 419–31. "The Church was not a strong force in Cosima's life but religion was. It was naturally closely connected with her ideas of sin and repentance, and traditional religious beliefs were the rationale for her idea of suffering. The penance of atonement which she imposed on herself came from her own sense of religious conviction and not from observance of an externally imposed sanction such as that of church or creed. She did not adhere closely to traditional patterns of religious observance nor was she a regular churchgoer. She held with tradition in such matters as praying and instructing her children, but not without personal modifications" (427). We might note here that Cosima's religious convictions, which were quite strong, apparently presented no problem for Nietzsche.

32. Otto Glagau, *Der Börsen- und Gründungs-Schwindel in Deutschland*, 2 vols. (Leipzig: Frohberg, 1876–77).

33. Paul Deussen (1845–1919) was married to Marie Volkmar (1863–1914), the daughter of Jewish parents. Her father, Leopold Moritz Levy (1817–1864), had converted in 1837 and taken the name Volkmar. See Heiner Feldhoff, *Nietzsches Freund: Die Lebensgeschichte Paul Deussen* (Cologne: Böhlau, 2009), 127.

34. The reference here is very likely to Wilhelm Goldschmidt's (1841–1922) translation of Dostoevsky stories, *Erzählungen von F[edor] M[ichajlovic] Dostojewskij* (Leipzig: Reclam, 1886). There is an echo of Wagner's remarks on Jews and language from *Judaism in Music* in Nietzsche's comment.

35. Mittmann in *Friedrich Nietzsche: Judengegner und Antisemitenfeind* argues unconvincingly that Nietzsche's views remained the same after his break with Wagner.

36. Nietzsche could very well be thinking about the assaults on Jews resulting from the economic difficulties in Europe in the 1870s.

37. Nietzsche would have harsher words for the Jewish moral code in his writings of the second half of the 1880s. Indeed, as we see in the citation from *Dawn* in the next paragraph, his disdain for the slave morality of the Jews was already evident early in the decade.

38. Mittmann, *Friedrich Nietzsche*, 61–62.

39. Jacques Le Rider, "Les intellectuels juifs viennois et Nietzsche: Autour de Sigmund Freud," *De Sils-Maria à Jérusalem: Nietzsche et le judaïsme: Les intellectuels juifs et Nietzsche* (Paris: Les Éditions du Cerf, 1991), 181–200, advances the claim (186) that Nietzsche's reference to Polish Jews in *The Antichrist* is an allusion to Lipiner.

40. Cited in the supplementary materials to Lou Andreas-Salomé, *Lebensrückblick: Grundriß einiger Lebenserinnerungen* (Zurich: Mas Niehans, 1951), 301. It is noteworthy that her description of Rée in the actual memoir does not even mention his Jewish heritage. She does write that he was a "melancholic" and a "pessimist" who overcame these traits of his youth and became a "confident, cheerful man," and that therefore his "neurotic substratum remained for me undiscovered" (113). How she finally discovered the key to Rée, and why she assumed he was a self-hating Jew, are certainly not

evident from her portrayal of him in her memoirs proper. On the basis of Salomé's statement and some faulty biographical research, Theodor Lessing in *Der jüdische Selbsthaß* [Jewish Self-Hatred] (Berlin: Jüdischer Verlag, 1930), 55–79, considered Rée a prime illustration of a self-hating Jew.

41. Cosima Wagner, *Diaries*, 1:930 and 931.

42. In the draft of a letter to Rée from July 1883, Nietzsche writes: "R[ichard] W[agner] once warned me about you and said: 'one day he will treat you badly; he has nothing good in mind for you'" (Nr. 434, KSB 6.399).

43. Cited in KSA 15.83–84.

44. What actually occurred among the main actors in this drama will probably never be known exactly. We can say with certainty only that the plan for Rée, Lou, and Nietzsche to spend an extended period of time together in Paris or Vienna never happened, and that Nietzsche was left alone, while Rée and Lou were for a time together in Berlin. We know that Nietzsche had exceedingly bitter feelings toward Lou and then toward Rée. What role Elisabeth Nietzsche played is not entirely clear, although it is evident that she did everything possible to prevent the proposed *ménage à trois*. The best account in English can be found in chapters 8 and 9 of Robin Small's book, *Nietzsche and Rée: A Star Friendship* (Oxford: Clarendon Press, 2005), 130–62. For a documentation of this triangular relationship, see *Friedrich Nietzsche Paul Rée Lou von Salomé: Die Dokumente ihrer Begegnung* (Frankfurt: Insel Verlag, 1970).

45. In his draft for the letter to Paul Rée, Nietzsche writes: "How I would treat a man who speaks this way about me to my sister, there can be no doubt. I am a soldier and will always be one; I understand how to use a weapon" (beginning of December 1882, Nr. 339, KSB 6.285). Nietzsche had engaged in a duel as a student in Bonn and received the obligatory scar to prove his manliness.

46. Small in *Nietzsche and Rée* uses this line of argument for Nietzsche's "loss of self-control" (150).

47. In Nachlass 1885, 35[34], KSA 11.524–25, and Nachlass 1886–1887, 5[5], KSA 12.186.

48. For a comprehensive history of the Pernerstorfer circle, see William J. McGrath, *Dionysian Art and Populist Politics in Austria* (New Haven, CT: Yale University Press, 1974).

49. The Prometheus figure appeared on the cover of Nietzsche's *Birth of Tragedy*, so the title of this epic poem already pays tribute to the philosopher Lipiner so admired.

50. Lipiner also wanted him to consult with physicians in Vienna, especially Josef Breuer, who played such a significant role in the development of psychoanalysis by developing the "talking cure."

51. The notion that Heine was an insincere copier of authentic verse and its attendant emotional states is a frequent claim in the anti-Semitic disqualification of him in the late nineteenth century.

52. Nietzsche may have been thinking of Lipiner when he wrote in *The Antichrist*: "One would no more choose to associate with 'first Christians' than one would with Polish Jews: not that one would need to prove so much as a single point against them.... Neither of them smell very pleasant" (AC 46, KSA 6.223).

53. See Aldo Venturelli, "Nietzsche in der Berggasse 19: Über die erste Nietzsche-Rezeption in Wien," *Nietzsche-Studien* 13 (1984): 448–80; here 453.

54. Lipiner had converted to Protestantism in 1881. Nietzsche heard about Lipiner from Joseph Paneth. See Richard Frank Krummel, "Dokumentation: Josef Paneth über seine Begegnung mit Nietzsche in der Zarathustra-Zeit," *Nietzsche-Studien* 17 (1988): 478–95; here 480. See also Venturelli, "Nietzsche in der Berggasse 19," 475.

55. Müller-Buck includes a good overview of Lipiner's relationship with Nietzsche, including some of his correspondence with Köselitz and Malwida, as well as a brief account of his life after his dealings with Nietzsche, when he was the director of the Library of the Austrian Imperial Council, the translator of Adam Michiewicz, and a close friend of Gustav Mahler. Renate Müller-Buck, "'Ach dass doch alle Schranken zwischen uns fielen': Siegfried Lipiner und der Nietzsche-Kult in Wien," in *Friedrich Nietzsche: Rezeption und Kultus*, ed. Sandro Barbera et al. (Pisa: Edizioni EETS, 2004), 33–75.

56. In scientific circles, he is still known today for his description of "Paneth cells," which are found in the epithelium of the small intestine.

57. Krummel, "Dokumentation," 492–93.

58. Nietzsche also made other dubious assertions to Paneth—about his Polish heritage and about his exclusive readership, claiming that his "silent community" included Gottfried Keller and Jacob Burckhardt, which was at best an exaggeration. Krummel, "Dokumentation," 490. Nietzsche frequently tried to impress a correspondent with a list of famous readers, who in reality were just persons to whom he sent his writings. For example, in a letter to Hippolyte Taine, he confesses he is a hermit who doesn't care about readers or being read—which is not at all true—and then cites Wagner, Bruno Bauer, Burckhardt, and Keller as readers who are "very devoted" to him (4 July 1887, Nr. 872, KSB 8.107).

59. Franz Overbeck, *Erinnerungen an Friedrich Nietzsche* (Berlin: Berenberg, 2011), 77.

60. Krummel, "Dokumentation," 490–91.

61. Krummel, "Dokumentation," 484. It might seem odd that Nietzsche would mention Ferdinand Lassalle, the socialist and political activist, in such a positive fashion, although, as we have seen in Chapter 3, Nietzsche had expressed reluctant admiration for him in his early years. Also Schmeitzner, hardly a promoter of a Jewish socialist, had published part of Lassalle's correspondence with Sophie Solutzeff.

62. In the spring of 1885, he includes Jews as a necessary component of a German ruling elite: "The Germans should breed a ruling caste: I confess that the Jews possess inherent abilities that are essential ingredients for a race conducting world politics. The sense for money must be learned, inherited, and a thousand times inherited" (Nachlass 1885, 34[111], KSA 11.457). During the summer of 1885, he returns to this topic. After citing Jews as "the oldest and purest race" and as "actors," he turns to the "problem of the amalgamation of the European aristocracy or rather of the Prussian Junker with Jewesses." This passage may relate to a thought directly preceding it: that "the future of German culture depends on the sons of Prussian officers" (Nachlass 1885, 36[43, 44], KSA 11.569). What Nietzsche apparently projects as desirable for Germany and Europe is a pairing of Prussian military with Jewish women to produce a new class of superior individuals. The former have the discipline necessary for a ruling class; the latter possess quick intelligence and financial acumen. In a note from the previous year reflecting on the potential greatness of the German Reich, he writes similarly of the intertwining of the German and the Slavish races, but adds: "we also need the cleverest people with money, the Jews, without question, in order to have dominance over the earth" (Nachlass 1884, 26[335], KSA 11.238).

63. See Robert Nola, "Nietzsche as Anti-Semitic Jewish Conspiracy Theorist," *Croatian Journal of Philosophy* 3.7 (2003): 35–62, especially 44–45.

64. Paul Lawrence Rose, in "Renan versus Gobineau: Semitism and Antisemitism, Ancient Races and Modern Liberal Nations," *History of European Ideas* 39.4 (2013): 528–40, points out that the noted Jewish scholar Moritz Steinschneider used the term "anti-Semitism" in 1860, but at that point he was responding to the writings of Ernest Renan, which had nothing to do with the Judeophobic political movement that would emerge in Germany around 1880: "Steinschneider's charge of 'anti-Semitic prejudices' referred to Renan's prejudice concerning the historical and intellectual superiority of Aryan religion and 'race' over their Semitic counterparts, rather than to any anti-Jewish position as such, that is 'antisemitism' as it became known in the 1870s in Germany" (533).

65. Cited in Christoph Cobet, *Der Wortschatz des Antisemitismus in der Bismarckzeit* (Munich: Fink, 1973), 140. Dühring, like Nietzsche, evidently later gave up on his objection to the word and used it rather liberally.

66. Bernhard Förster, *Das Verhältnis des modernen Judenthums zur deutschen Kunst* (Berlin: Schulze, 1881), 11.

67. Cited in Alex Bein, *Die Judenfrage: Biographie eines Weltproblems* (Stuttgart: Deutsche Verlags-Anstalt, 1980), 2:168. In 1935, the Propaganda Ministry of the Third Reich advised its press organs to avoid the use of "anti-Semitic" and employ "anti-Jewish" in its stead. See Thomas Nipperdey and Reinhard Rürup, "Antisemitismus," in *Geschichtliche Grundbegriffe: Historisches Lexikon zur politisch-sozialen Sprache in Deutschland*, ed. Otto Brunner et al. (Stuttgart: Klett, 1972), 129–53; here 151.

68. The term "Misojuden" appears in his notebooks in the fall of 1881, shortly after the term "anti-Semitism" had become popular. See Nachlass 1881, 12[116] and 15[43], KSA 9.597 and 649.

69. In *Anti-Semitism: A Historical Encyclopedia of Prejudice and Persecution*, 2 vols. (Santa Barbara, CA: ABC-CLIO, 2005), Richard Levy writes: "Although there are those who claim that the term initially had a fairly neutral connotation, this was no longer the case by midcentury, when it had come to signify a body of uniformly negative traits supposedly clinging to Jews" (1:24). Most commentators have failed to regard Nietzsche's use of the term in *The Birth of Tragedy* as part of his anti-Jewish sentiments in his Wagnerian period.

70. Walter Boehlich, ed., *Der Berliner Antisemitismusstreit* (Frankfurt: Insel, 1965); and Karsten Krieger, ed., *Der "Berliner Antisemitismusstreit" 1879–1881: Eine Kontroverse um die Zugehörigkeit der deutschen Juden zur Nation* (Munich: Saur, 2004).

71. Moshe Zimmermann, *Wilhelm Marr: The Patriarch of Anti-Semitism* (New York: Oxford University Press, 1986), 90–95.

72. See Nipperdey and Rürup, "Antisemitismus," 129–53; and Georges Roux, *Ancient Iraq* (London: Penguin, 1992), 123–35.

73. See Léon Poliakov, *The History of Anti-Semitism*, trans. George Klim (New York: Vanguard Press, 1985), 4:19–20.

74. Actually, estimates vary from one source to another. The lowest number I have seen is 225,000 (Bein, *Die Judenfrage*, 2:168); the largest number is 270,000, in Jens Glüsing, "Das Erbe von Nueva Germania," *Der Spiegel* 47.28 (12 July 1993): 136.

75. As we saw in Chapter 5, Förster, a former high school teacher removed from the profession after involvement in anti-Semitic roughhousing, married Nietzsche's sister Elisabeth in 1885.

76. Massimo Ferrari Zumbini, *Die Wurzlen des Bösen: Gründerjahre des Antisemitismus: Von der Bismarckzeit zu Hitler* (Frankfurt: Klostermann, 2003), notes that because of his early connection with Wagner and his circles, Nietzsche was "one of the most knowledgeable individuals about the emerging organized Anti-Semitism" (425).

77. "Llama" was Nietzsche's pet name for his sister.

78. We should not forget, however, that Nietzsche introduced Elisabeth into the circle of Wagnerians when he was a true believer, and that his letters to her from his early student years contained anti-Jewish sentiments that we have cited previously.

79. See Aldo Venturelli, "Asketismus und Wille zur Macht: Nietzsches Auseinandersetzung mit Eugen Dühring," *Nietzsche Studien* 15 (1986): 107–39.

80. See Dieter B. Herrmann, *Karl Friedrich Zöllner* (Leipzig: Teubner, 1982); and Robin Small, "Nietzsche, Zöllner, and the Fourth Dimension," *Archiv für Geschichte der Philosophie* 76 (1994): 278–301. There is no evidence that Nietzsche knew Zöllner personally, either as a student at Leipzig or at any time thereafter. Nietzsche's familiarity with this petition is evidenced in aphorism 251 from *Beyond Good and Evil*.

81. The *Anti-Semitic Correspondence* began publication in 1885, and considering the average duration of anti-Semitic journals was very brief, under its various names, editors, and publishers, it was one of the longest-running Judeophobic periodicals in Germany, ceasing publication in 1924. It was originally conceived as an internal party forum to discuss anti-Semitic politics, as the second part of its title indicated: "Discussion Room for Internal Party Affairs." The cover page also emphasized that the journal should be disseminated only among reliable "party comrades," and the third issue boldly features the word "Discretion" to reinforce this message. Eventually, however, the journal became available to the general public, a decision evidently aimed at promulgating anti-Semitic doctrine to a larger segment of the general population. In its initial year, it appeared every other month, but by 1887 it was a monthly, and by the following year it was published every two weeks. The contributors consisted of a familiar list of known anti-Semitic writers from the late nineteenth century. Fritsch wrote many of the pieces himself, using either his own name or one of several pseudonyms, and in the first issues its express purpose as a forum was taken very seriously, many of its contributions coming in the form of letters (some of which were perhaps not real letters) from anti-Semites around Germany. Wilhelm Marr wrote for the journal, as did Paul Förster, Bernhard's brother. Bernhard Förster was something of an honored contributor: his name appears in the very first issue, announcing his upcoming report on his two-year trip to the La Plata River region of South America and heralding him as the

originator of the Anti-Semites' Petition from 1880 to 1881. There is a repeated attempt to educate the readership on the most important writings of anti-Semites, and several of these listings contain names very familiar to Nietzsche: Wagner, Bruno Bauer, and Eugen Dühring. There was also a veritable obsession with impressing the readership about the nature of its supporters and soliciting new ones: one issue includes information on the status and occupation of the subscribers, which included five princes, forty-three dukes, sixty-two professors, and 156 members of the military. In another issue, the editor asks for addresses of potential new subscribers by name: included are the eminent physiologist Emil du Bois-Reymond and the popular philosopher Eduard von Hartmann. It is quite possible that Fritsch contacted Nietzsche in the context of an ongoing drive to increase subscriptions to the journal. See *Nietzsche's Jewish Problem*, 152–55.

82. Nietzsche remarked to Overbeck that the *Anti-Semitic Correspondence* is not available to the general public and is only sent to "reliable party comrades" (24 March 1887, Nr. 820, KSB 8.48).

83. Four of the five individuals listed here are known writers of anti-Semitic works. The exception is August Ebrard, a moderate Protestant theologian and professor at the University of Zurich. Why his name is included is a mystery. See *Nietzsche's Jewish Problem*, 156–57.

84. For example, in a letter to Elisabeth from June 1887 (Nr. 855, KSB 8.83).

85. In a letter to Georg Brandes (15 October 1887, Nr. 925, KSB 8.166).

86. It is not certain that Nietzsche sent anything like the draft version of this letter. Nietzsche often wrote much more harshly—and perhaps honestly—in drafts or in his notebooks than in his actual letters or his published writings.

87. Quite possibly Nietzsche learned of Förster's continued involvement from reading the *Anti-Semitic Correspondence* he received from Fritsch earlier in the year, which may account for his second, more angry letter to the anti-Semitic publisher.

88. Nietzsche refers here to Paul Heinrich Widemann, a friend of Köselitz and a student of Nietzsche, who went on to write the volume *Erkennen und Sein: Lösung des Problems des Idealen und Realen* (1885). Widemann was a close friend of Schmeitzner, and it was evidently Widemann who convinced Schmeitzner, who founded a publishing house in Chemnitz in 1874, to acquire the rights for all Nietzsche's works, even those earlier books he had published with Fritzsch. He also was the editor for the first year of *Schmeitzner's International Monthly*.

89. Krummel, "Dokumentation," 483–44.

90. In this letter, he expresses relief that the liberal era of government is over and that "finally the liberal Jewish establishment is coming to an end." Schmeitzner's letter is printed in Malcolm B. Brown, "Friedrich Nietzsche und sein Verleger Ernst Schmeitzner: Eine Darstellung ihrer Beziehung," *Archiv für Geschichte des Buchwesens* 28 (1987): 284. Schmeitzner is referring to the end of Bismarck's rule with the National Liberal Party, which was often identified with Jewish interests by anti-Semites because of prominent Jewish party members. It is unlikely that Nietzsche did not learn about Schmeitzner's anti-Semitism from Köselitz.

91. Franz Overbeck and Heinrich Köselitz, *Briefwechsel*, ed. David M. Hoffmann et al. (Berlin: de Gruyter, 1998), 47. Although Overbeck does not mention the journal by name, he is referring to Wilhelm Marr's *Anti-Semitic Notebooks*, which was supposed to appear bimonthly, but ceased publication after three issues because of the lack of interest.

92. The book to which Nietzsche is referring is *Dawn*, which was published in the summer of 1881. Nietzsche continues in his postcard: "But we need not be mean to each other! I remain with heartfelt wishes *always* your F. N." (Nr. 117, KSB 6.93–94). Quite obviously "party literature," in combination with the mention of Wagner, Schopenhauer, and Dühring, indicates Nietzsche had knowledge of Schmeitzner's anti-Semitic proclivities and publications.

93. Schmeitzner calls him "the father" of the journal in a letter to Nietzsche in May 1882 (Nr. 121, KGB III 2.253).

94. See David Leopold, "The Hegelian Antisemitism of Bruno Bauer," *History of European Ideas* 25 (1999): 179–206.

95. Douglas Moggach, *The Philosophy and Politics of Bruno Bauer* (Cambridge: Cambridge University Press, 2003), 186. See also Douglas Moggach, "Bruno Bauer," *The Stanford Encyclopedia of*

Philosophy (Spring 2010 Edition), ed. Edward N. Zalta [http://plato.stanford.edu/archives/spr2010/entries/bauer/]; and Zumbini, *Die Wurzeln des Bösen*, who notes that Bauer was close to Hermann Wagener, the social conservative editor of the *Kreuzzeitung*, and that Bauer composed all the entries on Jews and Judaism for Wegener's *Staats- und Gesellschaftslexikon*, including "Judaism in Foreign Lands" [*Das Judenthum in der Fremde*], which appeared in 1863 as a separate book (444).

96. The subtitle changed from "Journal for General and National Culture and Its Literature" to "Journal for the General Association Combatting Judaism [*alliance antijuive universelle*]."

97. Widemann's uncle was also Schmeitzner's attorney.

98. A frequent claim of the anti-Semitic movement was that Germany was in a state of emergency because of Jewish control of the financial world, the press, and cultural affairs.

99. Franz Overbeck and Heinrich Köselitz, *Briefwechsel*, ed. David M. Hoffmann et al. (Berlin: de Gruyter, 1998), 47–48.

100. Overbeck appears to be using the term in scare quotes to indicate its meaning as "anti-Jewish" and to distinguish it from the crude, political anti-Semitism that he and Nietzsche unequivocally oppose.

101. Overbeck, *Erinnerungen*, 77–79.

102. Overbeck was responsible for introducing Nietzsche to the theological writings of Paul de Lagarde, in particular to his piece *On the Relationship of the German State to Theology, Church, and Religion* (1873); Overbeck tells Lagarde in a letter from 1 February 1873 that he has shared it with his colleague, "the philologist Nietzsche." Cited from Andreas Urs Sommer, "Zwischen Agitation, Religionsstiftung und 'hoher Politik': Paul de Lagarde und Friedrich Nietzsche," *Nietzscheforschung* 4 (1998): 169–94; here 177.

103. Nietzsche had read Renan's works at a relatively early date. In notebooks written in preparation for his first *Untimely Meditation*, he suggests Renan's biography of Jesus was greater and more elegant than David Strauß's work on the same topic from 1835 to 1836 (Nachlass 1873, 27[1] and 1874, 34[37], KSA 7.587, 804). And it is evident that he read Renan again in the mid-1870s in preparation for *Human, All Too Human*. Most of his preoccupation with Renan, however, occurs in the 1880s. He disagrees with his Christian piety and his naïve psychology, but he does learn a great deal from him about the early history of Christianity.

104. Especially important for Nietzsche were the *Prolegomena to the History of Israel* (1882) and the *Sketch of the History of Israel and Judah* (1884), both of which are found with extensive marginal markings in Nietzsche's library.

105. Some scholars believe that in his last two years Nietzsche uses "Jewish" and "Christian" interchangeably. But a careful reading of the actual texts belies this claim. Nietzsche was quite aware of when—and why—he was using "Jewish" in his published writings of the last two years.

106. It is revealing that Kaufmann translates the phrase "furchteinflössender Logik" as "awe-inspiring logic," rather than "fear-inspiring logic," thus ascribing to Nietzsche a much more favorable impression of the Jewish instinct than the German should allow. Friedrich Nietzsche, *The Portable Nietzsche*, trans. Walter Kaufmann (New York: Viking, 1954), 592. See also Hubert Cancik, " 'Judentum in zweiter Potenz': Ein Beitrag zur Interpretation von Friedrich Nietzsches 'Der Antichrist,' " in *"Mit unsrer Macht ist nichts getan...": Festschrift für Dieter Schellong zum 65. Geburtstag*, 55–70 (Frankfurt: Haag + Herchen, 1993); here 64.

107. Michael Ahlsdorf, *Nietzsches Juden: Ein Philosoph formt sich ein Bild* (Aachen: Shaker, 1997), points to Max Müller as a possible source for the tenacity of the Jews, and Nietzsche was familiar with Müller's writings on religion, as evidenced in his notebooks from the 1870s. For a general discussion of this motif, see Ahlsdorf, 119–28.

108. Wellhausen, *Prolegomena*, 359.

109. In writing about the Gospels, for example, Nietzsche asserts "one is among Jews" and continues: "*Race* is required for it. In Christianity, as the art of holy lying, the whole of Judaism, a schooling and technique pursued with the utmost seriousness for hundreds of years, attains its ultimate perfection. The Christian, that *ultima ratio* of the lie, is the Jew once more—even *thrice* more" (AC 44, KSA 6.219).

110. Nietzsche could be drawing on many sources in this claim, among them Overbeck in his inaugural lecture in 1871: *Ueber Entstehung und Recht einer rein historischen Betrachtung der Neutestamentlichen Schriften in der Theologie*, Antritts-Vorlesung gehalten in der Aula zu Basel am 6. Juni 1870 (Basel: Schweighauserische Verlagsbuchhandlung, 1871), 8, or Paul de Lagarde, *Schriften für das deutsche Volk*, vol. 1: *Deutsche Schriften* (Munich: Lebmann, 1940), 67–68.

111. In describing the conceptual universe of Christianity, Nietzsche remarks: "The whole fatality was possible only because there was already in the world a related, racially-related megalomania, the *Jewish*: once the chasm between Jews and Jewish Christians opened up, the latter were left with no alternative but to employ *against* the Jews the very self-preservative procedures counseled by the Jewish instinct, while the Jews had previously employed them only against everything *non*-Jewish. The Christian is only a Jew of a '*freer*' confession" (AC 44, KSA 220–21).

112. See Hal Flemings, *Examining Criticisms of the Bible* (Bloomington, IN: AuthorHouse, 2008), 73–76.

Chapter 7. The Evolution Question

1. George Bernard Shaw, *Man and Superman: A Comedy and a Philosophy* (New York: Brentano's, 1905), xxxii and 220.

2. The popular superhero was a product of the 1930s, created in 1933 and first put in a comic book in 1938.

3. The word is used fairly consistently to contrast with other types of "men" in other works. In *Twilight of the Idols* (GD, Streifzüge eines Unzeitgemässen 37, KSA 6.136), for example, it seems to be synonymous with "higher man." In *Ecce Homo*, Nietzsche states that he employs the term to designate "a type that has turned out extremely well, in antithesis to 'modern' men, to 'good' men, to Christians and other nihilists" (EH, Warum ich so gute Bücher schreibe 1, KSA 6.300).

4. See, for example, the useful source Claire Richter, *Nietzsche et les théories biologiques contemporaines* (Paris: Mercure de France, 1911).

5. In the same passage, Nietzsche rejects an interpretation that relies on the " 'hero cult' of that great unconscious and involuntary counterfeiter Carlyle."

6. For example, in the last section of the preface to *On the Genealogy of Morals* (GM, Vorrede 8, KSA 5.255–56).

7. These citations are taken from an anonymous (Gl. is the identifier of the reviewer) review of the two texts written by Wilamowitz-Möllendorff against Nietzsche's *Birth of Tragedy*. The review appeared in *Allgemeiner literarischer Anzeiger für das evangelische Deutschland* 11 (January–June 1873): 64–65; reprinted in *Rezensionen und Reaktionen zu Nietzsches Werken, 1872–1889*, ed. Hauke Reich (Berlin: de Gruyter, 2013), 142.

8. P[aul] Michaelis, "Zur Genealogie der Moral," *Die Nationalzeitung* 41, no. 164 (2 March 1888): 1–3; reprinted in *Rezensionen und Reaktionen zu Nietzsches Werken, 1872–1889*, 671.

9. Martin Heidegger, *Nietzsche*, ed. David Farrel Krell, vol. 3 (San Francisco, CA: Harper & Row, 1987), 46.

10. Heidegger, *Nietzsche*, p. 280.

11. Walter Kaufmann, *Nietzsche: Philosopher, Psychologist, Antichrist*, 4th ed. (Princeton, NJ: Princeton University Press, 1974), 310.

12. Anticipating this resurgence of interest in Nietzsche and evolution was the pioneering essay from Werner Stegmaier, "Darwin, Darwinismus, Nietzsche: Zum Problem der Evolution," *Nietzsche-Studien* 16 (1987): 264–87. Stegmaier attempts to sort out various issues that had previously been confounded and understands Nietzsche's utterances as part of an ongoing dialogue with contemporaries. He errs in finding Nietzsche a consistent adherent of Darwin, as someone who differentiates Darwin from his putative "school" (Rée, Spencer, Haeckel), but he does a better job than previous commentators of pointing out what is at stake in Nietzsche's anti-Darwinian passages.

13. Gregory Moore, *Nietzsche, Biology and Metaphor* (Cambridge: Cambridge University Press, 2002); John Richardson, *Nietzsche's New Darwinism* (Oxford: Oxford University Press, 2004); Edith

Düsing, *Nietzsches Denkweg: Theologie—Darwinismus—Nihilismus* (Munich: Fink, 2006); Dirk R. Johnson, *Nietzsche's Anti-Darwinism* (Cambridge: Cambridge University Press, 2010).

14. Moore, *Nietzsche, Biology and Metaphor*, 14. Moore also notes that "Nietzsche's 'biologism' was generally recognised right up until 1945" (6).

15. Catherine Wilson's claim in "Darwin and Nietzsche: Selection, Evolution, and Morality," *Journal of Nietzsche Studies* 44 (2013): 354–70, that Nietzsche is "much closer to the view of the modern, neo-Darwinian biologist than were the nineteenth-century Darwinians" (367) may be accurate, but it does not contradict the contention that Nietzsche depended to a large degree on nineteenth-century sources to gain an understanding of Darwin in particular and evolution in general.

16. In an interesting recent study, Richardson argues that Nietzsche was greatly influenced by Darwin and that many of his notions are more coherent if considered an extension of Darwinism. The main difficulty with this study is that Richardson is forced to make assumptions about Nietzsche's views that often appear to run counter to his express statements. He treats, for example, the will to power as "a product or element of natural selection," although he admits that this account of will to power is nowhere articulated in Nietzsche's writings (65). For comments on Richardson's book, see Hartwig Frank, "Nietzsches System nach John Richardson," *Nietzsche-Studien* 34 (2005): 409–19; and Patrick Forber, "Nietzsche Was No Darwinian," *Philosophy and Phenomenological Research* 75 (2007): 369–82.

17. Ernst Mayr, *The Growth of Biological Thought: Diversity, Evolution, and Inheritance* (Cambridge, MA: Harvard University Press, 1982), 343–93.

18. For early accounts of Nietzsche's acquaintance with the biological theories of his time, see Richter, *Nietzsche et les theories biologiques contemporaines*; and Charles Andler, *Nietzsche: Sa vie et sa pensée* (Paris: Librairie Gallimard, 1958), 1:464–75. Andler's massive work was originally published in six volumes from 1920 to 1931. In general, Nietzsche's connections with the thought of his time are better recognized in the first third of the twentieth century than in the first four decades after the Second World War.

19. Friedrich Albert Lange, *Geschichte des Materialismus und Kritik seiner Bedeutung in der Gegenwart*, 2 vols., 3rd ed. (Iserloh: Baedeker, 1908), 2:240–309.

20. See, in particular, George Stack, *Lange and Nietzsche* (Berlin: de Gruyter, 1983); and Jörg Salaquarda, "Nietzsche und Lange," *Nietzsche-Studien* 7 (1978): 236–53.

21. Significantly, Nietzsche would similarly call for experiments to prove Darwin in a note from the early 1880s: "The age of experiments! Darwin's assertions should be proven—through experiments! Likewise the origin of higher organisms from lower. Experiments for thousands of years must be undertaken! Apes educated to become men!" (Nachlass 1881, 11[177], KSA 9.508).

22. Dieter Henke, "Nietzsches Darwinismuskritik aus der Sicht gegenwärtiger Evolutionsforschung," *Nietzsche-Studien* 13 (1984): 189–210, maintains that contemporary researchers in evolution also cannot avoid positing an internal mechanism (196).

23. Lange, *Geschichte des Materialismus*, 2:247.

24. Lange, *Geschichte des Materialismus*, 2:268–69.

25. Lange, *Geschichte des Materialismus*, 2:276.

26. Curt Paul Janz, *Friedrich Nietzsche: Biographie*, 3 vols., 2nd rev. ed. (Munich: Hanser, 1993), 1:317–21.

27. *Die Veränderungen der Thierwelt in der Schweiz seit Anwesenheit des Menschen*. Mit in den Text gedruckten Holzschnitten (Basel: Schweighauserische Verlagsbuchhandlung, 1875).

28. See Peter J. Bowler, *Evolution: The History of an Idea*, rev. ed. (Berkeley: University of California Press, 1983).

29. Emil Du Bois-Reymond, *Darwin versus Galiani* (Berlin: August Hirschwald, 1876), 11.

30. Mayr, *Growth of Biological Thought*, 405. Moore writes in a similar vein: "The theory of natural selection had little impact on late nineteenth-century biology, not only because its explanatory power was less convincing without a genetic model of heredity, but also because it was formulated in an intellectual climate that offered better support to rival concepts of organic development—such as those of Lamarck—which circumvented and subverted Darwin's more radical proposals" (25).

31. Ludwig Rütimeyer, *Die Grenzen der Thierwelt: Eine Betrachtung zu Darwin's Lehre* (Basel: Schweighauserische Verlagsbuchhandlung, 1868), 60.

32. Ludwig Rütimeyer, "Charles Darwin," in *Gesammelte Kleine Schriften*, vol. 2 (Basel: Verlag von Georg & Cie, 1898), 371–86; here 382.

33. Elisabeth Förster-Nietzsche, *Das Leben Friedrich Nietzsche's*, 2 vols. (Leipzig: Naumann, 1895–1904) 2.2: 521.

34. Erik Nordenskiöld, *Die Geschichte der Biologie: Ein Überblick*, trans. Guido Schneider (Jena: Gustav Fischer, 1926), 367–68.

35. Charles Darwin, *The Origin of Species* (New York: Gramercy Books, 1979), 62. The more complete title of Darwin's book was *On the Origin of Species by Means of Natural Selection, or the Preservation of Favoured Races in the Struggle for Life*.

36. See Lynn K. Nyhart, *Biology Takes Form: Animal Morphology and the German Universities, 1800–1900* (Chicago: University of Chicago Press, 1995), 117–20.

37. Karl Ernst von Baer, "Ueber Darwins Lehre," in *Studien aus dem Gebiete der Naturwissenschaften* (Braunschweig: Friedrich Vieweg und Sohn, 1886), 249. Parenthetical citations in the next paragraph refer to this essay by Baer.

38. Du Bois-Reymond, *Darwin versus Galiani*, 23. Du Bois-Reymond, in supporting Darwin's hypothesis of natural selection, is critical of Baer's attempt to smuggle purposiveness into scientific explanation.

39. Nietzsche could have known of Kölliker through Lange's discussion, *Geschichte des Materialismus*, 2:262–63.

40. For a fuller discussion of Kölliker's objections to Darwinism, see Nyhart, *Biology Takes Form*, 121–28.

41. Albert Kölliker, *Über die Darwin'sche Schöpfungstheorie* (Leipzig: Wilhelm Engelmann, 1864), 13.

42. Kölliker, *Über die Darwin'sche Schöpfungstheorie*, 15.

43. Michael Skowron, "Evolution und Wiederkunft: Nietzsche und Darwin zwischen Natur und Kultur," in *Nietzsche, Darwin und die Kritik der Politischen Theologie*, ed. Volker Gerhardt and Renate Reschke (Berlin: Akademie Verlag, 2010), 45–64, points out that neither Nietzsche nor Darwin used the term "evolution" very often; indeed, Nietzsche seems to have abandoned it altogether after his early years, quite possibly to avoid the teleological implications associated with the term (45–50).

44. See Janz, *Friedrich Nietzsche*, 1:533–34.

45. Alfred Kelly, *The Descent of Darwin: The Popularization of Darwinism in Germany, 1860–1914* (Chapel Hill: University of North Carolina Press, 1981), 7.

46. Philip G. Fothergill, *Historical Aspects of Organic Evolution* (London: Hollis and Carter, 1952), 121.

47. Kelly, *The Descent of Darwin*, 59.

48. In *Der alte und der neue Glaube* (Bonn: Emil Strauß, 1873), Strauß openly opposes the Social Democrats since their advocacy for the abolition of private property would undermine the family, which represents "the foundation of morality and culture" (285). Parenthetical citations in the following three paragraphs refer to Strauß's book.

49. Ernst Mayr notes that neither Kant nor Goethe was really an evolutionary thinker, although their writings do evidence "the steady approach toward evolutionary thought" (327).

50. There is no longer a consensus on how greatly Schopenhauer influenced Nietzsche even in his early years. Some studies have argued rather convincingly that Nietzsche was not quite as influenced by Schopenhauer as previous scholarship has contended. See, for example, Charles Senn Taylor, "Nietzsche Schopenhauerianism," *Nietzsche-Studien* 17 (1988): 45–73.

51. We will see more examples of optimistic conclusions drawn from Darwinism in Chapter 9, along with the pessimistic conclusions that often sought a remedy in eugenics.

52. Strauß, *Der alte und der neue Glaube*, 241.

53. Rütimeyer, *Die Grenzen der Thierwelt*, 71.

54. Regarding Nietzsche's early views of Hartmann, see Federico Gerratana, "Der Wahn Jenseits des Menschen: Zur frühen E. v. Hartmann-Rezeption Nietzsches (1869–1874)," *Nietzsche-Studien* 17 (1988): 391–433. See also Janz, *Friedrich Nietzsche*, 1:562–64.

55. Strauß, *Der alte und der neue Glaube*, 218.

56. See Jörg Salaquarda, "Studien zur *Zweiten Unzeitgemäßen Betrachtung*," *Nietzsche-Studien* 13 (1984): 1–45; esp. 32–33.

57. Eduard von Hartmann, *Philosophie des Unbewussten*, 9th ed. (Berlin: Carl Duncker, 1882), 2:222–51.

58. Anon [Eduard von Hartmann], *Das Unbewusste vom Standpunkt der Physiologie und Descendenztheorie* (Berlin: Carl Duncker, 1872), 20.

59. Lange, *Geschichte des Materialismus*, 2:245.

60. A more detailed account of Nietzsche's early Darwin reception can be found in Düsing, *Nietzsches Denkweg*, 200–254.

61. Peter J. Bowler, *The Eclipse of Darwinism: Anti-Darwinian Evolution Theories in the Decades around 1900* (Baltimore: Johns Hopkins University Press, 1983). Mayr offers a slightly different categorization with six variations: (1) "a built-in capacity for or drive towards increasing perfection (autogenetic theories)"; (2) "the effect of use and disuse, combined with an inheritance of acquired characters"; (3) "direct induction by the environment"; (4) "saltationism (mutationism)"; (5) "random (stochastic) differentiation"; and (6) "direction (order) imposed on random variation by natural selection." Important for our purposes is Mayr's observation that "each of them was held by numerous supporters from the time of Darwin (or even Lamarck) to the evolutionary synthesis" (360–61).

62. Sören Reuter in "'Dieser Lehre gegenüber ist der Darwinismus eine Philosophie für Fleischerburschen'. Grundzüge einer möglichen Darwin-Rezeption Nietzsches," in *Nietzsche, Darwin und die Kritik der Politischen Theologie*, ed. Volker Gerhardt and Renate Reschke (Berlin: Akademie Verlag, 2010), 83–104, examines the mediation of Darwin to Nietzsche in the philosophical, mostly neo-Kantian, tradition. He therefore downplays the actual scientists whom Nietzsche read and focuses instead on writers like Otto Caspari and Otto Liebmann, with whom Nietzsche was familiar, and who dealt to a certain extent with implications of Darwin's theory for philosophical topics. Reuter's assertions that Nietzsche conceived of his thought as a "commentary" to Darwinism (102), and that he altered his fundamental views very little after his exposure to works he read in the 1880s (104), are, however, not persuasive.

63. Kelly, *The Descent of Darwin*, 23 and 30–31.

64. In his notebook, Nietzsche wrote: "The struggle for existence is not the important principle!" (Nachlass 1875, 12[22], KSA 8.257). As we shall see, Nietzsche would often repeat this thought in his later writings.

65. This aphorism comes from the fifth "book" of *The Gay Science*. The first four "books" were published in 1882; Nietzsche added the fifth in 1887.

66. Wilhelm Roux, *Der Kampf der Theile im Organismus* (Leipzig: Wilhelm Engelmann, 1881); William Henry Rolph, *Biologische Probleme zugleich als Versuch zur Entwicklung einer rationellen Ethik*, 2nd expanded ed. (Leipzig: Wilhelm Engelmann, 1884); Carl von Nägeli, *Mechanisch-physiologische Theorie der Abstammungslehre* (Munich: Oldenbourg, 1884). Nietzsche's library contains the second, expanded edition of Rolph's book.

67. Karl Semper, *Die natürlichen Existenzbedingungen der Thiere*, 2 vols. (Leipzig: Brockhaus, 1880).

68. See Bowler, *The Eclipse of Darwinism*, 67.

69. Richard Schacht, "Nietzsche and Lamarckism," *Journal of Nietzsche Studies* 44 (2013): 264–80, is the latest in a series of scholars who have tried to connect Nietzsche with Lamarck's theories, in my view, unsuccessfully. The citations he produces as evidence are certainly not conclusive and can be accounted for very easily without recourse to the inheritance of acquired characteristics.

70. Richter speculates that Nietzsche's antipathy to Haeckel stems from Rütimeyer's negative assessment (*Nietzsche et les theories biologiques contemporaines*, 17).

71. Roux, *Der Kampf der Theile im Organismus*, 69.

72. Francis Darwin, ed., *The Life and Letters of Charles Darwin, Including an Autobiographical Chapter* (New York: D. Appleton, 1899), 2:419. It is a bit unclear how much of Roux Darwin actually understood, however. His full comment, which appeared in a letter to George John Romanes on 16 April 1881, makes it apparent that Darwin's German was not fluent enough to follow everything Roux wrote: "He is manifestly a well-read physiologist and pathologist, and from his position a good anatomist. It is full of reasoning, and this in German is very difficult to me, so that I have only skimmed through each page; here and there reading with a little more care. As far as I can imperfectly judge, it is the most important book on Evolution, which has appeared for some time." Later in the letter, he states that he "may be *wholly* mistaken about its value" and remarks that Roux makes "a gigantic oversight in never considering plants" (420).

73. After stating that science is on its way to finding a way of talking about the affects and feelings, Nietzsche adds: "Aber es bleibt eine Bilderrede" ["But it remains only speaking in images"] (Nachlass 1881, 11[128], KSA 9.487).

74. For a detailed discussion of Nietzsche's reception of Roux, see Wolfgang Müller-Lauter, "Der Organismus als innerer Kampf: Der Einfluß von Wilhelm Roux auf Friedrich Nietzsche," *Nietzsche-Studien* 7 (1978): 189–223. This intricate piece of research is available in English as "The Organism as Inner Struggle: Wilhelm Roux's Influence on Nietzsche," in *Nietzsche: His Philosophy of Contradictions and the Contradictions of His Philosophy*, trans. David J. Parent (Urbana: University of Illinois Press, 1999), 161–82, 230–41.

75. Rolph, *Biologische Probleme*, vi.

76. Rolph, *Biologische Probleme*, 96.

77. Nietzsche's note includes the reference "Rolph, Biologische Probleme 1881," which is somewhat strange since evidence from his library indicates that he read—and read very thoroughly—the revised edition from 1884. See Max Oehler, *Nietzsches Bibliothek* (Weimar: Gesellschaft der Freunde des Nietzsche-Archivs, 1942), 26; and *Nietzsches persönliche Bibliothek*, ed. Giuliano Campioni et al. (Berlin: de Gruyter, 2001), 504–5.

78. See Greg Moore, "Beiträge zur Quellenforschung," *Nietzsche-Studien* 27 (1998): 535–61.

79. Rolph, *Biologische Probleme*, 76.

80. Rolph, *Biologische Probleme*, 97.

81. *Nietzsches persönliche Bibliothek*, 565–66.

82. Michael Skowron, "Nietzsches 'Anti-Darwinismus,'" *Nietzsche-Studien* 37 (2008): 160–94, claims that the prefix "anti-" is not exclusively one of opposition, but also one of juxtaposition and overcoming (164)—although the actual passages in which Nietzsche writes about Darwin suggest more an opposition than anything else.

83. For example: "What definite value can the *domestication of the human* being have? or does a domestication really have a definitive value? There is good reason to deny it. Darwin's school makes a great effort to convince us of the opposite: it wants the *effects of domestication* to be deep, even fundamental" (Nachlass 1888, 14[133], KSA 13.315). Or in another passage, the association of "Darwin's school" with progress (Nachlass 1888, 14[123], KSA 13.304).

84. Herbert Spencer, *Data of Ethics* (London: Williams and Norgate, 1879), 11, 20. Parenthetical notations in this paragraph and the next are from Spencer's book.

85. Spencer, *Data of Ethics*, 133. Spencer does have differences with Mill's utilitarian thought, and he cites a letter he wrote explaining his opinions (57–58). In essence, the objection he has to utilitarianism is that "it recognizes no more developed form of Morality—does not see that it has reached but the initial state of Moral Science" (58).

86. Daniel Dennett, *Darwin's Dangerous Idea: Evolution and the Meanings of Life* (New York: Simon & Schuster, 1995), observes that Nietzsche targets the historical naïveté and the "Panglossian optimism" of Social Darwinists like Spencer (462).

87. For a good discussion of Nietzsche's reception of Spencer, see Moore, *Nietzsche, Biology and Metaphor*, 62–72. Dirk Johnson considers the *Genealogy* in its entirety to be a response to Darwin. In general, he overestimates Nietzsche's preoccupation with Darwin and his ability to distinguish Darwin from other English thinkers. Parts of the *Genealogy* clearly criticize what Nietzsche considered English

psychology, but it seems apparent Nietzsche is referring to Rée and Spencer with these remarks as much as Darwin.

88. Rolph, *Biologische Probleme*, 38. Nietzsche's marginal note to these comments in Rolph are "good." Parenthetical references in this paragraph are from Rolph's book.

89. Also: "The social conditions contradict in their primary demands the natural drives of animals as well as men, who are in no way destined for or suitable for social life" (214).

90. Nietzsche also wrote "good" in response to this passage in the margins.

91. Richter (*Nietzsche et les theories biologiques contemporaines*, 26) claims that Nietzsche had read a pamphlet by Nägeli from 1865 concerning evolution, and that he had probably done so after reading Oscar Schmidt's *Descendenzlehre und Darwinismus* [Evolutionary Theory and Darwinism] (Leipzig: Brockhaus, 1873). There is no evidence, however, that Nietzsche ever read anything except Nägeli's book from 1884, and although a copy of Schmidt was found in his library, we find no references to Schmidt and no clear indication that he appropriated his thought.

92. Bowler thinks the customary negative judgment of Nägeli to be too harsh since Nägeli himself contributed significantly to what would eventually become genetic theory, and since Mendel himself might not have harbored goals that coincide with modern genetic research. See Peter J. Bowler, *The Mendelian Revolution: The Emergence of Hereditarian Concepts in Modern Science and Society* (Baltimore: Johns Hopkins University Press, 1989), 84.

93. See Bowler, *The Eclipse of Darwinism*, 149.

94. Nägeli, *Mechanisch-physiologische Theorie der Abstammungslehre*, 284–337.

95. Nägeli, *Mechanisch-physiologische Theorie der Abstammungslehre*, 231.

96. In another note, Nietzsche dismisses Darwin as an afterthought to Hegel and Lamarck, indicating that Darwin really represents the continuation of a teleological tradition (Nachlass 1885, 34[73], KSA 11.442). Darwin as a consequence of Hegel is again taken up in *The Gay Science*, when the German philosopher is credited with establishing that one type emerges from another, and that Hegel therefore anticipates the great scientific achievements in Europe, Darwinism in particular: "for without Hegel there is no Darwin" (FW 357, KSA 3.598). Werner Stegmaier in "'ohne Hegel kein Darwin': Kontextuelle Interpretation des Aphorismus 357 aus dem V. Buch der *Fröhlichen Wissenschaft*," in *Nietzsche, Darwin und die Kritik der Politischen Theologie*, ed. Volker Gerhardt and Renate Reschke (Berlin: Akademie Verlag, 2010), 65–82, finds this mention of Darwin to be "the most positive" (65) in Nietzsche's published writings, but whether it is positive or not will depend on how Nietzsche is characterizing Hegel as well as how he regards the topic "what is German," which is the title of aphorism 357.

97. For correspondences between Nägeli's book and passages in Nietzsche, see Andrea Orsucci, "Beiträge zur Quellenforschung," *Nietzsche-Studien* 22 (1993): 371–402.

98. See Andreas Urs Sommer, "Nietzsche mit und gegen Darwin in den Schriften von 1888," in *Nietzsche, Darwin und die Kritik der Politischen Theologie*, ed. Volker Gerhardt and Renate Reschke (Berlin: Akademie Verlag, 2010), 31–44; here 32–39.

99. Rolph, *Biologische Probleme*, 82.

100. Eugen Dühring, *Cursus der Philosophie als streng wissenschaftlicher Weltanschauung und Lebensgestaltung* (Leipzig: Erich Koschny, 1875), 112, 119.

101. Although, of course, Paul Rée, who was influenced by the English, is apparently included in this grouping.

Chapter 8. The Cosmological Question

1. The original version of *The Gay Science* from 1882 contained four books and 342 aphorisms; book five (aphorisms 343 to 383) was added in 1887.

2. Bernd Magnus, *Nietzsche's Existential Imperative* (Bloomington: Indiana University Press, 1978), 38.

3. *Nietzsches Philosophie der ewigen Wiederkehr des Gleichen* (Berlin: Verlag Die Runde, 1935).

4. Oskar Becker, "Nietzsches Beweise für seine Lehre von der ewigen Wiederkunft," *Blätter für deutsche Philosophie* 9 (1936): 368–87. Reprinted in his *Dasein und Dawesen: Gesammelte philosophische Aufsätze* (Pfullingen: Neske, 1963), 41–66.

5. The quotation marks are Heidegger's.

6. Martin Heidegger, *Nietzsche*, vol. 2: *The Eternal Recurrence of the Same*, trans. David Farrell Krell (San Francisco, CA: Harper & Row, 1984), 111.

7. Heidegger, *Nietzsche*, 2:112.

8. Heidegger, *Nietzsche*, 2:114.

9. Heidegger, *Nietzsche*, 2:114.

10. Mihailo Djurić, "Die antiken Quellen der Wiederkunftslehre," *Nietzsche-Studien* 8 (1979): 1–16; here 7–8.

11. See Mircea Eliade, *The Myth of Eternal Return or, Cosmos and History*, trans. Willard R. Trask (Princeton, NJ: Princeton University Press, 1954).

12. Henri Lichtenberger, *La Philosophie de Nietzsche*, 4th ed. (Paris: Germer Baillière, 1901), 189. Lichtenberg observes that the connection to Heine was already noted in an article in the *Frankfurter Zeitung* on 18 April 1899. His discussion of sources for eternal recurrence, which also includes references to Blanqui and Le Bon, was not included in the first edition in 1898, but was added in subsequent editions.

13. Arthur Berthold, ed., *Bücher und Wege zu Büchern*, unter Mitwirkung von Elisab. Foerster-Nietzsche, Peter Jessen, und Philipp Rath (Berlin: W. Spemann, 1900), 440. Max Oehler, *Nietzsches Bibliothek* (Weimar: Gesellschaft der Freunde des Nietzsche-Archivs, 1942). The Oehler bibliography lists only Heine's *Neue Gedichte* (1844), a volume that is found in Nietzsche's library in Weimar. The updated and corrected listing contains both the *Neue Gedichte* and the *Letzte Gedichte und Gedanken*, which was published as a supplement to Heine's collected writings in 1869. See Guiliano Campioni et al., eds., *Nietzsches persönliche Bibliothek* (Berlin: de Gruyter, 2003), 282.

14. Heine converted to Protestantism in 1825, but he has been considered Jewish by almost all scholars and critics.

15. Heinrich Heine, *Sämtliche Werke*, ed. Manfred Windfuhr, vol. 7/1, *Reisebilder III/IV*, ed. Alfred Opitz (Hamburg: Hoffmann und Campe, 1986), 328–29. The version in *Letzte Gedichte und Gedanken* (Hamburg: Hoffmann und Campe, 1869), 277–78, differs slightly from the passage as it was originally written. Maria's response, for example, is "Let us be good friends."

16. See Klaus Pabel, *Heines "Reisebilder": Ästhetisches Bedürfnis und politisches Interesse am Ende der Kunstperiode* (Munich: Fink, 1977), 210–14.

17. Auguste Blanqui, "L'éternité par les astres: hypothèse astronomique," in *Instructions pour une prise d'armes, l'éternité par les astres, hypothèse astronomique et autre textes*, ed. Miguel Abensour and Valentin Pelosse (Paris: Société encyclopédique française, 1972), 167–69.

18. Blanqui, "L'éternité par les astres," 140.

19. If we consider Nietzsche's aversion to the Commune, there is an irony that he and the president of the Commune articulate similar cosmological theories.

20. Blanqui, "L'éternité par les astres," 159.

21. Blanqui, "L'éternité par les astres," 164.

22. Cited in the introduction to *Gustave Le Bon: The Man and His Works*, ed. Alice Widener (Indianapolis: Liberty Press, 1979), 16.

23. Gustave Le Bon, *L'homme et les sociétés: leurs origines et leur histoire* (Paris: Jean-Michel Place, 1988), 2:420.

24. Nietzsche uses the word energy [*Energie*] frequently, but he appears to prefer the notion of force [*Kraft*] when he is writing about scientific issues. The usual use of the German word *Energie* in his writings is connected with human attributes and refers to something more akin to "vitality" than to the scientific notion of energy. Nietzsche was writing in a period of transition in vocabulary: energy replaced force, which was seen as somewhat ambiguous, in the middle of the nineteenth century. See Stephen G. Brush, *The Temperature of History: Phases of Science and Culture in the Nineteenth Century* (New York: Burt Franklin & Co., 1978), 10.

25. See Robin Small, *Nietzsche in Context* (Aldershot: Ashgate, 2001), 135–52.

26. Friedrich Albert Lange, *Geschichte des Materialismus und Kritik seiner Bedeutung in der Gegenwart* (Iserlohn: J. Baedeker, 1875), 2:225. We can be certain that Nietzsche read the first edition of

Lange's work in 1866. Whether he read the second (1873 and 1875) or third edition (1877) is uncertain, but it seems clear that he read at least the fourth edition from 1882, since his library contains the 1887 imprint of this edition. The text was expanded greatly from the first to the second edition, but remained the same in subsequent editions except for differences in pagination. Jörg Salaquarda, "Nietzsche und Lange," *Nietzsche-Studien* 7 (1978): 236–60, claims Nietzsche did not see the second edition since he does not acknowledge the positive remark Lange made about *The Birth of Tragedy* in the first volume of the second edition (240). The remark appeared on page 133–34, in note 44: "The Apollonian nature of the Socratic direction of thought has been recently strongly emphasized in an unusual fashion in *Nietzsche, the Birth of Tragedy Out of the Spirit of Music* (Leipzig 1872)." George J. Stack, *Lange and Nietzsche* (Berlin: Walter de Gruyter, 1983), believes, however, that Nietzsche was familiar with editions published in the 1870s. Nietzsche could very well have missed the reference to his first book since the note sections in Lange are separated from the text and included at the end of each chapter, and since his name was not included in the index.

27. Lange prefers the word force [*Kraft*] to energy [*Energie*] as well, which explains perhaps Nietzsche's preference.

28. Lange, *Geschichte des Materialismus*, 2:214–15.

29. H[ermann von] Helmholtz, *Über die Erhaltung der Kraft* (Berlin: G. Reimer, 1847), 4; it is cited in Lange, *Geschichte des Materialismus*, 2:216. The italics do not appear in the original and must have been added by Lange.

30. Lange, *Geschichte des Materialismus*, 2:218.

31. Balfour Stewart, *The Conservation of Energy* (London: H. S. King & Co., 1874; German version, Leipzig: Brockhaus, 1875).

32. Arthur Schopenhauer, *The World as Will and Representation*, trans. E. F. J. Payne (Indian Hills, CO: Falcon's Wing Press, 1958), 1:273–74.

33. The second volume of the second edition of the *History of Materialism* appeared only in 1875, well after Nietzsche had written his first *Untimely Meditation*.

34. David Friedrich Strauß, *Der alte and der neue Glaube* (Bonn: Emil Strauß, 1873), 166.

35. Strauß, *Der alte and der neue Glaube*, 227.

36. Nietzsche is citing a passage that occurs in Eduard von Hartmann, *Philosophie des Unbewussten*, 9th ed. (Berlin: Carl Duncker, 1882), 2:401.

37. For a concise discussion of his inadequacies in dealing with thermodynamics, the reader should consult Arthur Danto, *Nietzsche as Philosopher* (New York: Columbia University Press, 1980), 203–9.

38. For a detailed recounting of the history of thermodynamics, especially as it relates to Nietzsche, see Paolo D'Iorio, "Cosmologie de l'Éternel Retour," *Nietzsche-Studien* 24 (1995): 62–123.

39. R[udolph] Clausius, *Abhandlung über die mechanische Wärmetheorie* (Braunschweig: Vieweg, 1864); retitled in the 2nd edition from 1876: *Die mechanische Wärmetheorie*.

40. O[tto] Caspari, *Die Thomson'sche Hypothese von der endlichen Temperaturausgleichung im Weltall, beleuchtet vom philosophischen Gesichtspunkte* (Stuttgart: August Horster, 1874).

41. Lange, *Geschichte des Materialismus* (1866), 2:378, 397.

42. As noted above, it is unclear whether Nietzsche read the second or third edition, although we can be certain he read later editions.

43. Lange, *Geschichte des Materialismus* (1875), 2:227–28.

44. Lange, *Geschichte des Materialismus* (1875), 2:227.

45. Lange, *Geschichte des Materialismus* (1875), 2:522.

46. See Stack, *Lange and Nietzsche*, 25–50.

47. Related in Curt Paul Janz, *Friedrich Nietzsche: Biographie*, 3 vols., 2nd rev. ed. (Munich: Carl Hanser, 1993), 1:124.

48. Janz, *Friedrich Nietzsche*, 1:319.

49. Lichtenberger, *La Philosophie de Nietzsche*, 179–80.

50. Lou Salomé, *Nietzsche*, trans. and ed. Siegfried Mandel (Urbana: University of Illinois Press, 1988), 86.

51. For example, in a letter to Erwin Rohde in July 1882, Nietzsche writes: "In autumn I am going to the University of Vienna and beginning a new course of studies" (Nr. 267, KSB 6.226). At one point, the three were also contemplating continuing their studies in Munich or Paris.

52. The German should read "All-Organismus," but the Colli-Montinari edition does not have the "-us" in this instance, although "Organismus" is otherwise spelled correctly in the passage.

53. Caspari, *Die Thomson'sche Hypothese*, 10.

54. Caspari, *Die Thomson'sche Hypothese*, 46.

55. Lange, *Geschichte des Materialismus* (1875), 2:212–13. See also the discussion in Stack, *Lange and Nietzsche*, 37–44. The term also occurs in J[ohann] G[ustav] Vogt, *Die Kraft: Eine real-monistische Weltanschauung* (Leipzig: Haus & Tischler, 1878), 21–22, in his discussion of the differentiation of "force-substance" in the origins of the universe; and in Otto Schmitz-Dumont, *Die Einheit der Naturkräften und die Deutung ihrer gemeinsamen Formel* (Berlin: Carl Duncker, 1881), 7, as part of the central thesis of the book.

56. See George J. Stack, "Nietzsche and Boscovich's Natural Philosophy," *Pacific Philosophical Quarterly* 62 (1981): 69–87; here p. 70.

57. Had he delved into Schelling, he might have been attracted to Schelling's views of dynamic forces in nature and his proximity at times to Leibniz. We should also note that Feuerbach and perhaps Strauß might not fit well with the most prominent names of German idealism. But Nietzsche could well be finding in all of them the same sort of dualistic structure and ultimate reliance on consciousness that he otherwise repudiates.

58. There are no books written by Büchner in Nietzsche's library. His name does not appear in any correspondence or in published writings. Nietzsche does refer to him twice in his notebooks in connection with his preparation for the first two *Untimely Meditations*. He is called a "classicist of the mob" [*Klassiker des Pöbels*] (Nachlass 1873, 27[30], KSA 7.596) and "the evil force-man" [*der böse Kraftmensch*] in one entry, and, in the other, "that fanatic friend of matter" [*jener fanatische Freund des Stoffs*] (Nachlass 1873–74, 30[20], KSA 7.740).

59. Directly after Nietzsche's explanation of forces and force centers quoted above in the note from 1888, he writes the following: "This conception is not without qualification a mechanistic one; for if it were, then it would not produce an unending recurrence of identical cases, but rather a final condition. *Because* the world has not yet attained it, mechanism must be considered by us an incomplete and merely preliminary hypothesis" (Nachlass 1888, 14[188], KSA 13.375).

60. Nietzsche makes only a few references to monism in his writings, but in all cases he means the theological concept, not the notion related to cosmology.

61. For example, in JGB 12, KSA 5.27.

62. Compare the notebook entry: "A plurality of forces, connected through a common alimentation process, we call 'life'" (Nachlass 1883–1884, 24[14], KSA 10.650).

63. Lange, *Geschichte des Materialismus* (1866), 2:373.

64. Greg Whitlock, "Roger Boscovich, Benedict de Spinoza and Friedrich Nietzsche: The Untold Story," *Nietzsche-Studien* 25 (1996): 200–220; Keith Ansell Pearson, "Nietzsche's Brave New World of Force: Thoughts on Nietzsche's 1873 'Time Atom Theory' Fragment & on the Influence of Boscovich on Nietzsche," *Pli* 9 (2000): 6–35; Matthew Tones and John Mandalios, "Nietzsche's Actuality: Boscovich and the Extremities of Becoming," *Journal of Nietzsche Studies* 46 (2015): 308–27. For a view that points to differences between Nietzsche and Boscovich, see Robin Small, "Boscovich Contra Nietzsche," *Philosophy and Phenomenological Research* 46 (1986): 419–35.

65. Luca Crescenzi, "Verzeichnis der von Nietzsche aus der Universitätsbibliothek in Basel entliehenen Bücher (1860–1879)," *Nietzsche-Studien* 23 (1994): 388–442.

66. The note occurs in Lange, *Geschichte des Materialismus* (1875), 2:291 (footnote 21). The material on Boscovich is in Gustav Theodor Fechner, *Ueber die physikalischen und philosophischen Atomenlehre* (Leipzig: Hermann Mendelssohn, 1864), 229–31 and 239–44.

67. In the article "Nietzsche and Boscovich's Natural Philosophy," Stack indicates incorrectly that Nietzsche learned about Boscovich from his reading of Lange (71). In his book *Lange and Nietzsche*, however, he (224–26) recognizes that Nietzsche could not have originally learned about Boscovich

from Lange, since he recognizes Boscovich is absent in the 1866 edition of *The History of Materialism*. He assumes Nietzsche discovered him through Fechner—although he supplies no evidence for this assumption; indeed, Lange footnotes Fechner in his second edition, so Nietzsche could not have made the Boscovich connection through Lange's first edition. It appears subsequent scholars have ignored Stack's insights on the differences in the first and second editions of his work and simply repeated Stack's erroneous assumption about Fechner.

68. In a letter to Köselitz in September of 1883, Nietzsche mentions parenthetically his preoccupation with atomic theory in the 1870s, stating that he had read at that time the "Jesuit Boscovich," who had demonstrated mathematically "that the assumption of material atomic points was a *useless* hypothesis for the strictest science of mechanism," but he adds that for the "praxis of research it is a matter of indifference" (Nr. 460, KSB 6.442). This letter suggests two things: (1) that Nietzsche's preoccupation with Boscovich in the 1870s had to do with his interests in antiquity; Nietzsche specifically mentions Epicurus before his parenthetical comment; and (2) that Nietzsche did not read Boscovich again in the 1880s; his knowledge of Boscovich appears to be the same in 1883 as it was in 1886, when he is mentioned in *Beyond Good and Evil*.

69. See Peter Poellner, *Nietzsche and Metaphysics* (Oxford: Clarendon Press, 1995), 46–57.

70. Köselitz did not agree with this judgment. See Frederick R. Love, *Nietzsche's Saint Peter: Genesis and Cultivation of an Illusion* (Berlin: de Gruyter, 1981), 187–88.

71. See Charles Andler, *Nietzsche sa vie et sa pensée*, 3 vols. (Paris: Gallimard, 1958), 2:421–24, Small, *Nietzsche in Context*, 136–39; and Helge S. Kragh, *Entropic Creation: Religious Contexts of Thermodynamics and Cosmology* (London: Routledge, 2008), 121. Andler's study was originally published in six volumes from 1920 to 1931. Perhaps since he was closer to the works and theories with which Nietzsche was engaged, Andler is much better at situating Nietzsche in the discourses of his time than many of the philosophical interpretations that appeared in mid-century. Martin Bauer, "Zur Genealogie von Nietzsches Kraftbegriff: Nietzsches Auseinandersetzung mit J. G. Vogt," *Nietzsche-Studien* 13 (1984): 211–27, denies that Vogt was a source for eternal recurrence, but only, it seems, because he believes there is no source (217). In general, Bauer's discussion places Vogt in the context of recurrence and nowhere mentions a possible connection with will to power.

72. Vogt, *Die Kraft*, 11, 90.

73. Kragh points out that "Vogt argued for an eternal succession of worlds rather than an endless repetition of the same world" (121).

74. Vogt, *Die Kraft*, 19.

75. See Vogt, *Die Kraft*, 21; Bauer, "Zur Genealogie von Nietzsches Kraftbegriff," 223–24.

76. Otto Caspari, *Der Zusammenhang der Dinge: Gesammelte philosophische Aufsätze* (Breslau: Eduard Trewendt, 1881), 1. The essay "Die Philosophie im Bunde mit der Naturforschung" appeared originally in *Kosmos* 1 (1877): 4–16.

77. Caspari, *Zusammenhang*, 36.

78. Friedrich Kuntze, "Ein Brief Maxwells an Schmitz-Dumont," *Kant-Studien* 33 (1928): 336–41.

79. Otto Schmitz-Dumont, *Die mathematischen Elemente der Erkenntnistheorie: Grundriss einer Philosophie der mathematischen Wissenschaften* (Berlin: Duncker, 1878); *Die Einheit der Naturkräfte und die Deutung ihrer gemeinsamen Formel* (Berlin: Duncker, 1881).

80. Schmitz-Dumont, *Die Einheit*, 158. He maintains further, as do other dynamists, that both force and matter are functions of human beings and our perspective on the world, rather than realities. Atoms do not exist without thinking; they disappear without thought, since they are our impressions (165).

81. Schmitz-Dumont, *Die Einheit*, 6.

82. Although Schmitz-Dumont was relatively unknown in his own time and completely forgotten today, he did correspond at one point with the illustrious mathematical physicist James Clerk Maxwell, whose work on electromagnetism earned him merited celebrity. Schmitz-Dumont evidently sent him a letter explaining his theory of a single unifying repelling force acting inversely as the square of distance, and in Maxwell's polite response, which brings up several objections, the Scottish scientist notes the

affinity between Schmitz-Dumont and Boscovich. Friedrich Kunze reproduces this letter (37–38) in "Ein Brief Maxwells an Schmitz-Dumont," *Kant-Studien* 33 (1928): 336–41.

83. Schmitz-Dumont, *Die Einheit*, 93.

84. Nikolaos Loukidelis and Christopher Brinkmann, "Leibnizian Ideas in Nietzsche's Philosophy: On Force, Monads, Perspectivism, and the Subject," in *Nietzsche and the Problem of Subjectivity*, ed. João Constâncio, Maria João Mayer Branco, and Bartholomew Ryan (Berlin: de Gruyter, 2015), 95–109; here 99–100; Rudolf Steiner, *The Secret Stream: Christian Rosenkreutz and Rosicrucianism* (Great Barrington, MA: Anthroposophic Press, 2000), 255 (footnote 8). Steiner reports that the winner of the contest was Gustav Widenmann [*sic*] (1812–1876), but it appears that the correct name is Widemann. I was unable to determine whether Widemann was related to Paul Heinrich Widemann, a friend of Heinrich Köselitz, who edited Ernst Schmeitzner's *International Monthly* in its initial year. Schmeitzner's lawyer was Widemann's father, but I was unable to find his first name. Since Köselitz suggested many books to Nietzsche, it is not out of the question that he was the one who recommended Drossbach to him. Rüdiger W. Schmidt, "Nietzsches Drossback-Lektüre: Bemerkungen zum Ursprung des literarischen Projekts 'Der Wille zur Macht,'" *Nietzsche-Studien* 17 (1988): 465–77, also suggests that Drossbach could have been recommended to him by Köselitz (470–71). Drossbach evidently also sponsored a significant prize in the 1880s from the Freie Deutsche Hochstift (Schmidt, 471). There is no mention of Drossbach in Nietzsche's correspondence or in his published or unpublished writings.

85. Drossbach's reflections could very well have had an impact on aphorism 11 in *Beyond Good and Evil*, where Nietzsche critiques Kant for introducing a faculty for synthetic judgments (JGB 11, KSA 5.24–26).

86. Maximilian Drossbach, *Ueber die scheinbaren und die wirklichen Ursachen des Geschehens in der Welt* (Halle: Pfeffer, 1884), 11. Parenthetical references in this paragraph refer to Drossbach's book.

87. For an excellent account of Nietzsche's reception of neo-Kantianism, especially as regards the biological sciences, see Christian J. Emden, *Nietzsche's Naturalism: Philosophy and the Life Sciences in the Nineteenth Century* (Cambridge: Cambridge University Press, 2014).

Chapter 9. The Eugenics Question

1. See Christian J. Emden, *Nietzsche's Naturalism: Philosophy and the Life Sciences in the Nineteenth Century* (Cambridge: Cambridge University Press, 2014).

2. Johann Peter Eckermann, *Gespräche mit Goethe in den letzten Jahren seines Lebens*, 3 vols. (Leipzig: Brockhaus, 1885), 2:63 (2 April 1829).

3. See Daniel Pick, *Faces of Degeneration: A European Disorder, c. 1848–c. 1918* (Cambridge: Cambridge University Press, 1989), 45–48.

4. B[énedict] A[ugustin] Morel, *Traité des dégénérescences physiques, intellectuelles et morales de l'espèce humaine* (Paris: J. B. Baillière, 1857), 5.

5. Morel, *Traité des dégénérescences physiques*, 47–48.

6. See Eric T. Carlson, "Medicine and Degeneration: Theory and Praxis," in *Degeneration: The Dark Side of Progress*, ed. J. Edward Chamberlin and Sander L. Gilman (New York: Columbia University Press, 1985), 121–44; here 121–23.

7. Morel, *Traité des dégénérescences physiques*, 682.

8. Morel, *Traité des dégénérescences physiques*, 685–93.

9. Morel, *Traité des dégénérescences physiques*, 4.

10. Charles Darwin, *The Descent of Man* (Amherst, NY: Prometheus Books, 1998), 133. Parenthetical citations in this paragraph refer to this edition of Darwin's *Descent*.

11. Alfred R. Wallace, "The Origin of Human Races and the Antiquity of Man Deduced from the Theory of 'Natural Selection,'" *Journal of the Anthropological Society of London*, 2 (1864): clvii–clxxxvii; here clxii. There is no evidence that Nietzsche was familiar firsthand with Wallace's speech, but the main themes could have come to his attention from page 156 of Charles Féré's *Sensation et mouvement* (Paris: Félix Alcan, 1887).

12. Wallace, "The Origin of Human Races," clxii.

13. Wallace, "The Origin of Human Races," clxv.
14. Wallace, "The Origin of Human Races," clxvii.
15. Wallace, "The Origin of Human Races," clxix–clxx.
16. E. Ray Lankester, *Degeneration: A Chapter in Darwinism* (London: Macmillan, 1880), 41–50.
17. Lankester, *Degeneration*, 58–59.
18. Lankester, *Degeneration*, 60.
19. Lankester, *Degeneration*, 59–62.
20. Anon. [William R. Greg], "On the Failure of 'Natural Selection' in the Case of Man," *Fraser's Magazine* 78 (1868): 353–62; here 356.
21. Anon., "On the Failure of 'Natural Selection,'" 358.
22. Eugene S. Talbot, *Degeneracy: Its Causes, Signs, and Results* (London: Walter Scott, 1898), 26.
23. Th[éodule-Armand] Ribot, *Heredity: A Psychological Study of Its Phenomena, Laws, Causes, and Consequences* (London: Henry S. King, 1875), 286.
24. Ribot, *Heredity*, 303.
25. Eduard Reich, *Die Fortpflanzung und Vermehrung des Menschen aus dem Gesichtspunkte der Physiologie und Bevölkerungslehre betrachtet* (Jena: Hermann Costenoble, 1880), 230–31; Nietzsche owned a copy of Reich's earlier, two-volume handbook on hygiene, *System der Hygiene* (Leipzig: Fleischer, 1870–71).
26. Herbert Spencer, *The Study of Sociology* (New York: D. Appleton, 1874), 369.
27. Nietzsche used the word "decadence" before he read Bourget, but in the sense of a general decline, not as a characteristic of contemporary life, and not in the sense of degeneration. See, for example, his letter to Overbeck in September 1881 (Nr. 146, KSB 6.127), where Nietzsche writes that he has suffered "a general decline [*decadence*]," in part because of the bad weather.
28. Gregory Moore, in *Nietzsche, Biology, Metaphor* (Cambridge: Cambridge University Press, 2002), asserts that decadence "was conceived in biological terms" "from the very beginning" (120).
29. See Bettina Wahrig-Schmidt, "'Irgendwie, jedenfalls physiologisch': Friedrich Nietzsche, Alexandre Herzen (fils) and Charles Féré 1888," *Nietzsche-Studien* 17 (1988): 434–64; and Hans Erich Lampl, "Ex oblivion: Das Féré-Palimpsest," *Nietzsche-Studien* 15 (1986): 225–49.
30. Nietzsche's note in obvious preparation for the composition of *Ecce Homo* is instructive in this regard. He opposes a classical to a romantic pessimism, associating the latter with Schopenhauer, de Vigny, Dostoevsky, Leopardi, Pascal, and all great nihilistic religions (Brahmanism, Buddhism, and Christianity). Then, referring to himself in the third person, he cites the spontaneity of his "physiological *vision*" as a contrast (Nachlass 1888, 14[25], KSA 13.229–30).
31. See also Nachlass 1882–1883, 4[171], KSA 10.162.
32. See notebook entries such as those appearing in the Nachlass 1888, 15[31–37], KSA 13.426–431. It appears Nietzsche developed many of these thoughts in reading Féré, whom he may in part be referencing in some of these notes.
33. Carlson, "Medicine and Degeneration," 130–33.
34. We should note, however, that Nietzsche slips back into the usual notion of causality in discussing alcohol when he considers it the cause of decline, rather than regarding its abuse as one of the effects of something already declining.
35. Anon., "On the Failure of 'Natural Selection,'" 361.
36. Plato, *The Collected Dialogues*, ed. Edith Hamilton and Huntington Cairns (Princeton, NJ: Princeton University Press, 1961), 699 (Rep 460c).
37. Plutarch, "Lycurgus," trans. John Dryden, http://classics.mit.edu/Plutarch/lycurgus.html.
38. Ernst Haeckel, *Natürliche Schöpfungsgeschichte*, 4th improved ed. (Berlin: Georg Reimer, 1873), 152–56. By 1873, the discussion of artificial selection was much expanded from the original edition from 1868. The casualties in the Franco-Prussian War may have accounted for Haeckel's increased interest in military affairs as they relate to evolution.
39. For example, Nachlass 1881, 11[299], KSA 9.556. See also Moore, *Nietzsche, Biology, Metaphor*, 9.
40. Emden, *Nietzsche's Naturalism*, 41.

41. Meta von Salis-Marschlins claims to have mentioned a theory from Ribot, and perhaps the author himself, to Nietzsche in a conversation in 1887. See *Begegnungen mit Nietzsche*, ed. Sander L. Gilman (Bonn: Bouvier, 1985), 578.

42. Ribot, *Heredity*, 290.

43. Ribot, *Heredity*, 293–94.

44. Féré, *Sensation et mouvement*, 158.

45. Féré, *Sensation et mouvement*, 161.

46. Henry W. Holland, "Heredity," *Atlantic Monthly* 52 (1883): 447–52. Ultimately, Holland disagrees with Galton's plea for eugenics because it contradicts eighteen hundred years of compassion for the downtrodden, weak, and unfortunate members of society.

47. Sander L. Gilman, "Nietzsche's Reading on the Dionysian: From Nietzsche's Library," *Nietzsche-Studien* 6 (1977): 292–94.

48. Marie-Luise Haase, "Friedrich Nietzsche liest Francis Galton," *Nietzsche-Studien* 18 (1989): 633–58.

49. These are the only two mentions of Galton in Nietzsche's correspondence.

50. *Begegnungen*, 479–80.

51. See Richard Frank Krummel, "Josef Paneth über seine Begegnung mit Nietzsche in der Zarathustra-Zeit," *Nietzsche-Studien* 17 (1988): 478–95.

52. Francis Galton, *Hereditary Genius: An Inquiry into Its Laws and Consequences* (London: Macmillan, 1869).

53. For an account of Galton's life, see Nicholas Wright Gillham, *Sir Francis Galton: From African Exploration to the Birth of Eugenics* (Oxford: Oxford University Press, 2001); and Ruth Schwartz Cowan, *Sir Francis Galton and the Study of Heredity in the Nineteenth Century* (New York: Garland, 1985).

54. Holland, "Heredity," 447.

55. See Giuliano Campioni et al., eds., *Nietzsches persönliche Bibliothek* (Berlin: de Gruyter, 2003), 170–71. In the discussion in the introduction, Erdmann Gottreich Christaller is credited with authorship (18), but in the alphabetical listing (170–71), authorship of the pamphlet is falsely ascribed to his father, the missionary and linguist Johann Gottlieb Christaller (1827–1895), who was instrumental in the initial study of West African languages. It is unknown how Nietzsche came upon this pamphlet, which he never mentions in his writings. Possibly Nietzsche saw it referenced in Karl Bleibtreu's *Revolution of Literature [Revolution der Literatur]* (1886).

56. Anon. [Erdmann Gottreich Christaller], *Die Aristokratie des Geistes als Lösung der sozialen Frage: Ein Grundriss der natürlichen und der vernünftigen Zuchtwahl in der Menschheit* (Leipzig: Wilhelm Friedrich, n.d. [1885]), 4. Parenthetical references in this section refer to Christaller's book.

57. Nietzsche marked this passage with "NB."

58. Christaller must have read only the first volume of this three-volume work, since volumes two and three appeared in 1885 and 1894, respectively.

59. For example, in aphorism 61 in *Beyond Good and Evil* (JGB 61, KSA 5.80).

60. The most recent and most thoroughly researched attempt to divorce Nietzsche from the more pernicious aspects of eugenics is the monograph by Gerd Schank, *"Rasse" und "Züchtung" bei Nietzsche* (Berlin: de Gruyter, 2000).

61. The connection between an overabundance of nourishment and the production of monstrosities was a consequence of Nietzsche's reading of William Henry Rolph's *Biologische Probleme zugleich als Versuch zur Entwicklung einer rationellen Ethik*, as discussed in Chapter 7.

62. See my monograph, *Nietzsche's Jewish Problem: Between Anti-Semitism and Anti-Judaism* (Princeton, NJ: Princeton University Press, 2016), 195–203.

63. These remarks appear to contrast with other passages in Nietzsche's writings, where he seems to disdain pure races and advocates the mixing of races. But, again, Nietzsche's "positive eugenics" have nothing to do with race as it was defined in his time; rather, the hierarchy Nietzsche is advocating would appear to be simply natural, rather than racial.

64. Lampl asserts that in this aphorism, Nietzsche racialized a passage from *Sensation et mouvement* by Charles Féré ("Ex oblivion," 254).

65. For a history of eugenics in Germany, see Peter Weingart, Jürgen Kroll, and Kurt Bayertz, *Rasse, Blut und Gene: Geschichte der Eugenik und Rassenhygiene in Deutschland* (Frankfurt: Suhrkamp, 1988); and Paul Weindling, *Health, Race and German Politics Between National Unification and Nazism, 1870–1945* (Cambridge: Cambridge University Press, 1989).

66. George Bernard Shaw, *Man and Superman: A Comedy and a Philosophy* (New York: Brentano's, 1905), xxiv, 185–86.

Concluding Remarks

1. My own modest and inadequate study on this topic was published as "The Birth of Psychoanalysis from the Spirit of Enmity: Nietzsche and Psychology in the Nineteenth Century," in *Nietzsche and Depth Psychology*, ed. Jacob Golomb, Weaver Santaniello, and Ronald Lehrer (Albany: SUNY Press, 1999), 149–69.

2. See Bettina Wahrig-Schmidt, "'Irgendwie, jedenfalls physiologisch': Friedrich Nietzsche, Alexandre Herzen (fils) and Charles Féré 1888," *Nietzsche-Studien* 17 (1988): 434–64; and Hans Erich Lampl, "Ex oblivion: Das Féré-Palimpsest," *Nietzsche-Studien* 15 (1986): 225–49. See also Michael Cowan, "'Nichts ist so sehr zeitgemäss als Willensschwäche': Nietzsche and the Psychology of the Will," *Nietzsche-Studien* 34 (2005): 48–74.

3. Christian J. Emden, *Nietzsche's Naturalism: Philosophy and the Life Sciences in the Nineteenth Century* (Cambridge: Cambridge University Press, 2014), does an excellent job of placing Nietzsche within the neo-Kantian discourse of his times.

4. The popularity of *On the Genealogy of Morals* among philosophical commentators in recent years is very much related to the fact that it, unlike most of Nietzsche's oeuvre, consists of three more or less cohesive essays. There have been more book-length accounts of the *Genealogy* over the past two decades than studies of all his aphoristic works combined.

Index

Addresses to the German Nation (Fichte), 76
Aesthetic Education (Schiller), 410–11
"Against Darwinism" (Nietzsche), 342–43
Agassiz, Louis, 332
alcohol, and degeneration, 17, 117, 124, 411, 426–27, 481n23, 503n34
Altenstein, Karl von, 30
Andler, Charles, 493n18, 501n71
Andreas-Salomé, Lou, 12, 175, 189–90, 192, 209, 211, 217, 242, 280–81, 289, 385; description of Paul Rée by, 186–87n40, and Nietzsche, 487n44
Antichrist, The (Nietzsche), 110, 171, 280, 425–26, 459, 487n52; on the creation of a higher human being, 442; on eugenics, 445; Jewish history in, 306–12
"Anti-Darwin" (Nietzsche), 355–58
Antifeminists, The (Dohm), 174–75
anti-Semites' Petition (1881–82), 13, 278, 289, 290, 490n81
Anti-Semitic Catechism (Fritsch), 292
Anti-Semitic Correspondence, 244, 291–92, 482n43, 489–90n81
Anti-Semitic Notebooks, 490n91
anti-Semitism, 14, 108, 219, 241, 243, 260–61, 285, 287–95, 302, 307, 309, 311–12, 454, 488n64, 489n69; in Berlin, 299; Nietzsche's vehement opposition to political anti-Semitism, 15, 288–90; as an obsession for Nietzsche, 294; as opposed to anti-Judaism, 295–301. *See also* Jewish Question; Wagner, Richard, anti-Semitism of
Archeology of Knowledge, The (Foucault), 6
Aristocracy of the Spirit as a Solution to the Social Question (Christaller), 18, 434–41; definition of intelligence using evolutionary terms in, 435–36
Aristotle, 205, 323
Arndt, Ernst Moritz, 76, 77
Arnold, Matthew, 433

Atlantic Monthly, 432, 433
Auerbach, Bertold, 270, 465n53
Austria, 75–76, 85, 86, 138, 198, 229, 279, 467n3; Nietzsche's visit to, 284
Austro-Prussian War (1866), 86, 88, 91, 263

Baer, Karl Ernst von, 326–27; response to Darwin, 327–28
Baeumler, Alfred, 260
Baillie, Joanna, 198
Bakunin, Mikhail, 159, 472n27
Barbarossa. *See* Friedrich I (Barbarossa)
Basel, 9, 23, 41, 90, 93, 112, 128, 159, 198, 230, 396; University of, 8, 11, 20, 27, 29, 44, 48, 49, 52, 78, 91, 95, 125, 188, 194, 204, 220, 222, 240, 269, 290, 324–25, 340, 385, 397
Bastiat, Claude Frédéric, 471n15
Baudelaire, Charles, 421
Bauer, Bruno, 295, 470n59, 490–91n95
Bayreuth, 20, 161–62
"Bayreuth Work" (Wolzogen), 232
Bayreuther Blätter, 104, 108, 225, 226, 228, 230, 232, 244, 281, 289; coverage of Nueva Germania in, 229, 232–35; types of articles printed in, 223–24
Bebel, August, 127, 159, 187, 477n43
Becker, Oskar, 366
Beger, August, 39–40
Bentham, Jeremy, 433
Berlin, 126, 130–31, 185, 263, 269–70, 289, 365, 385; University of, 21, 68, 204, 341, 343, 351
Berlin Anti-Semitism Controversy, 288, 299
Bernays, Jacob, 262–63, 485n26
Beyond Good and Evil (Nietzsche), 12–13, 16, 114, 181, 204, 253, 293, 303, 369, 404; on breeding, 442; castigation of "absolute religions" in, 446; on causality, 423; characterization of philosophy in, 7; concept of the "good European" in, 246; on controlled procreation, 443–44, 451–52; on the cosmological dimension of the will to power, 396–97;

Beyond Good and Evil (Nietzsche) (*continued*) on eternal recurrence and the will to power, 393–94; on grammar, 423; on great philosophy as a "personal confession," 356; identification of the English with mediocrity and Christian morality in, 416–17; on the instinct for self-preservation, 344–45; poor sales of, 114; preface to, 180; reference to Boscovich in, 397–98; on the role of education and *Bildung*, 72–73; treatment of women in, 210–14

Biedermann, Karl, 89

Bildung, 9, 21–22, 24, 25, 29–52 *passim*, 55, 61, 68, 69, 81, 93, 95, 109, 144, 284, 378, 464n32; goal of, 34–36; Nietzsche on the role of education and *Bildung*, 72–73; Nietzsche's adherence to the concept of, 24, 466n61; and obedience, 51

Biological Problems as Well as an Attempt to Develop a Rational Ethic (Rolph), 15, 340, 341, 349–51, 496n77, 504n61

"Birth of the Tragic Concept, The" (Nietzsche), 95

Birth of Tragedy, The (Nietzsche), 1, 10, 19, 22, 23, 47, 52, 57–58, 96, 140, 160, 162, 269–70, 274, 283, 317, 368, 409, 458, 459; and the German tradition of the veneration of Greece (German classicism), 97–98; and the greatness of tragic art, 144–45; indirect references to the Women's Question in, 207; on the inverse relationship between madness and optimism, 423; as Nietzsche's first "Wagnerian" publication, 95–96, 468n30, 468–69n31, 469n32; Nietzsche's reinterpretation of, 422–23; and the Paris Commune, 142–44; on Socratism, 267–68

Bischoffsheim, Raphael Louis, 274

Bismarck, Otto von, 10, 14, 30, 32–33, 76, 85, 86, 107–8, 113, 120, 127, 130, 133–34, 155, 167, 219, 254, 278, 294, 299; Nietzsche's attack on, 111–12; Nietzsche's views concerning, 84

Blackwell, Elizabeth, 187, 477n42

Blanqui, Auguste, 370–72, 390

Böcklin, Arnold, 324

Bois-Reymond, Emil du, 24, 325, 328, 340

Bonaparte, Napoleon, 75, 85, 120–21, 249

Bonn, 78, 185; University of, 8, 15, 25, 41, 46, 48, 49, 69, 74, 77, 84, 85, 128, 130, 262, 322, 384, 385, 401

Boscovich, Ruggiero Giuseppe, 17, 397–99, 500–501n67; Nietzsche's preoccupation with, 501n68

Bourget, Charles, 421

Bowler, Peter, 338, 497n92

Brandes, Georg, 115, 242, 256, 470n59, 485n8

Brenner, Albert, 197

Brentano, Lujo, 474n52

Breuer, Josef, 487n50

Brinton, Crane, 261

Brobjer, Thomas H., 25, 462n13, 473n41

Brockhaus, Ottile, 269

Browning, Elizabeth Barrett, 198

Brücke, Ernst Wilhelm von, 285, 432

Büchner, Ludwig, 375, 394, 404, 500n58

Bülow, Hans von, 462n2, 470n59

Bünger, Peter, 473n44

Burckhardt, Jacob, 27, 188, 194, 324, 381, 470n59

Burgard, Peter, 180

Capital (Marx), 440

capitalism, 11, 132, 153–54, 157, 159; aggressive capitalism, 148–49; Förster's disdain for, 169; Nietzsche's disdain for, 172; Second Empire capitalism, 151; Wagner's disdain for, 150

Carnot, Sadi, 381

Case of Wagner, The (Nietzsche), 116, 117, 122–23, 224

Caspari, Otto, 17, 382, 387–88, 391, 400, 404, 407; on an alternative to materialism, 400–401

Changes in the Animal World in Switzerland Since the Presence of Man (Rütimeyer), 324

Christaller, Erdmann Gottreich, 434–40, 504n55, 504n58; proposed remedy of for society's ills, 438–39; on the subaltern class, 439–40; and the term "people of the herd," 437

Christianity, 12, 18, 26, 61, 103, 107, 111, 118–19, 121, 124, 135, 170, 172, 178, 182, 209, 246–47, 254, 272–73, 285, 297, 301, 334–35, 396, 426, 446; civilizing influence of, 249; as a degenerative movement, 424–27; Nietzsche on the conceptual universe of Christianity, 492n111; Nietzsche's disdain for, 251, 302–12, 367; Nietzsche's identification of with socialism, 170–71; Nietzsche's view of the Oriental and the feminine inherent in, 210–11

Clausius, Rudolf Julius, 381–83, 399

Colonial Question, the, 13–14, 454; Förster, Nietzsche, and Wagner on colonization, 223–29, 248; German nationalism and colonialism, 220–23; and "great politics," 252–59; Nietzsche and colonial discourse, 218–20; Nietzsche on the inherent superiority of

Europe, 248–49; Nietzsche's advocacy of European world domination, 251–52; Nietzsche's concept of the "good European," 245–52, 483n48. *See also* Nueva Germania
Communist Manifesto (Marx), 126, 150
Congress of Vienna (1814–15), 75, 77, 120
Cornaro, Luigi, 424
Corssen, Wilhelm, 384–85
Cosmological Question, the, 16, 360–407, 501n71; and ancient and contemporary discourses on recurrence, 364–74; attraction of Nietzsche to philosophers of natural science, 395; and "heat death," 17, 383–84, 394; and the importance of eternal recurrence, 360–64; influence of Lange on Nietzsche's thought concerning, 498–99n26, 499n27; Nietzsche on energy and force, 498n24, 500n59; Nietzsche's early reflections on recurrence, 374–79; Nietzsche's neo-Kantian reflections on, 404; Nietzsche's views on the laws of thermodynamics, 16–17, 374–75, 380–92 *passim*; Vogt's influence on Nietzsche concerning, 399–400
cretinism, 411
"Culture of Men, A" (Nietzsche), 207
Curtius, Georg, 49
Customs Union, 75–76
Cuvier, Georges, 332
Czolbe, Heinrich, 384

Darwin, Charles, 15–17, 286, 315–17, 320, 322–46, 350–58, 400, 412–14, 416–20, 431, 432, 457; influence of on Nietzsche, 493n16; lack of fluency in German, 496n72; view of natural selection, 414
Darwinism, 315–17, 320–37 *passim*, 355, 356, 358, 400, 416, 419, 429, 442; alternatives to, 338–41, 346–48; treatment of in the works of Strauß and Hartmann, 329–38. *See also* Nägeli, Carl von, as an alternative to Darwin; Rolph, William Henry, as an alternative to Darwin; Roux, Wilhelm, as an alternative to Darwin
"Darwinism and Teleology" (Lange), 322
Data of Ethics, The (Spencer), 343–45, 347–49, 496n85
David Strauß, the Confessor and Writer (Nietzsche), 1, 101, 330, 336
Dawn (Nietzsche), 72, 152, 174, 210, 247, 253; attitude toward Jews in, 275–76
De origine et situ Germanorum (Tacitus), 81

degeneration, 12, 117, 146, 170, 171, 215, 226–28, 233, 246, 268, 277, 312, 339, 354, 411–27, 450, 452, 503n28; hypotheses of, 17. *See also* alcohol, and degeneration; Eugenics Question, and the discourse of degeneration; Eugenics Question, eugenic remedies for degeneration; Eugenics Question, Nietzsche on degeneration
Dégénérescence et criminalité (Féré), 422, 431, 456
democracy, 20, 89, 108, 141, 144, 149, 428; Nietzsche's views of, 168, 217, 249, 251; parliamentary democracy, 112, 183; social democracy, 136, 167, 232, 246
Denmark, 76
Derrida, Jacques, 179–80, 182, 183
Descent of Man (Darwin), 321, 412, 413, 418
Destruction of Reason, The (Lukács), 148–49
Deussen, Marie, née Volkmar, 486n33
Deussen, Paul, 69, 84, 486n33
Deutsche Colonien (Förster), 231
Devrient, Eduard, 330
d'Holbach, Baron, 370
Dilthey, Wilhelm, 61–62, 204
"Dionysian Worldview, The" (Nietzsche), 95, 100–101
Dionysian/Apollonian duality, 39, 97, 269
Discorsi sulla vita sobria (Cornaro), 424
discourse analysis, 6
discourses, 6; Nietzsche's use and understanding of, 6–7
"Diverse Sighs" (Nietzsche), 208
Djurić, Mihailo, 368
Dohm, Hedwig, 174–75, 190
Döllinger, Ignaz, 327
Drossbach, Maximilian, 17, 402–6, 502n84
Druskowitz, Helene, 198–200; founding of women's reviews (*The Holy Struggle* and *The Call to Feud*) by, 200
Duchy of Saxe-Meiningen, 77
Dühring, Eugen, 12, 129, 141, 160, 169, 187, 199, 224, 288, 290, 292, 295, 446; advocacy of socialism by, 291; on the English and Darwinism, 356; influence of in socialist circles, 476n40
Dumont, Léon, 4

Ebrard, August, 292, 490n83
Ecce Homo (Nietzsche), 2, 7, 28, 79, 111, 218, 255, 369, 459; anti-German sentiments in, 121–24, 223; comments on his mother and sister in, 209–10; passages about Wagner in, 116–17, 271–72; remarks on the overman in,

Ecce Homo (Nietzsche) (*continued*)
315–18; treatment of women in, 215–16; views on anti-Semitism in, 290–91
Eckermann, Johann Peter, 410
Education Question, the, 8–9, 19–74, 465n43, 465n52; and the central role of the German language instruction, 44–46; and the connection of elite education with job training, 9; and the disadvantages of historical education, 52–57, 61–67, 466nn65–66; and education that fosters genius, 34–35, 464n35; and the expansion of education, 29–37; and the narrowing of education (specialization), 38–42; Nietzsche's contribution to the discussion concerning secondary-school education, 41–42; Nietzsche's critique of the expansion of education, 31–34, 149; Nietzsche's critique of the *Gymnasium* and the university, 42–51; Nietzsche's critique of teachers, 36; and Nietzsche's cultural objective, 22–23; Nietzsche's discontent for the spread of educational opportunities among the masses, 35–36; and Nietzsche's "education contortion," 72; Nietzsche's later writings concerning, 72–74; Nietzsche's lectures concerning, 24–25, 464n20; and Nietzsche's personal experience with educational institutions, 25–29, 48–49; Nietzsche's repudiation of the concept of *Volksbildung*, 36–37; Nietzsche's use of the Socratic dialogue method in framing his lectures concerning education, 25; Nietzsche's use of the term *Bildungsanstalten* in his lectures on educational institutions, 29–30; and the paradigm of anti-institutional education, 67–68; and the renewed emphasis on classical antiquity, 46–47; and the widening of *Bildung*, 30, 33–35. *See also* historical learning, and cultural criticism; historical pedagogy, types of; "On the Future of our Educational Institutions"
"Egoism versus Altruism" (Spencer), 347–48
Eichhorn, Friedrich, 31
Eiser, Otto, 103; treatment of Nietzsche by, 486n29
"Elegy Written in a Country Churchyard" (Gray), 436
Eliot, George, 198
Engelmann, Wilhelm, 469n32
Engels, Friedrich, 148, 159, 163, 291; and the notion of the state "withering away," 474n51

England, 31, 125, 130, 188, 204, 257, 349, 356; relationship with Europe, 251; as a traditional colonial power, 221
Enlightenment, the, 70, 99, 316
"Ennoblement through degeneration" (Nietzsche), 339–40
"Éperons: Les Style de Nietzsche" (Derrida), 179, 182
Ermanaric, 83–84
"Ermanaric's Death" (Nietzsche), 84
Essai sur l'inégalité des races humaines (Gobineau), 224, 287
Essais de psychologie contemporaine (Bourget), 421
eternal recurrence, 7, 16–17, 66, 209, 317, 337, 360–92, 393–97 *passim*, 399, 404, 406–7, 457; alternatives to, 387–88; ancient and contemporary (during Nietzsche's time) discourses on, 364–74; and the idea of "force center," 390; importance of, 360–64; Le Bon's principles of, 373; Nietzsche's early reflections on recurrence, 374–79. *See also* thermodynamics, and eternal recurrence
ethics, biological nature of, 349
Eucken, Rudolf, 24, 46, 463n18
Eugenics Question, the, 17–18, 286–87, 408–53, 504n46, 504n63; and the aristocracy of the spirit, 434–41; and the concept of breeding, 442, 448–49; and the concept of negative eugenics, 445–46; and controlled procreation, 442–44, 451–52; and the discourse of degeneration, 411–12, 417–21; eugenic remedies for degeneration, 427–33; Nietzsche on degeneration, 421–27; Nietzsche on race and eugenics, 452–53; Nietzschean eugenics, 440–53 *passim*; Nietzsche's fascination with eugenic solutions, 18; and the shift from culture to biology, 408–11. *See also* Evolution Question, evolution and degeneration
Evans, Richard, 186, 188
Evolution Question, the, 15–16, 313–59, 366, 373, 382, 384, 393, 412, 425, 427, 430, 432, 442, 446, 448, 452, 457, 495n62; Darwinism in the works of Strauß and Hartmann, 329–38; and degeneration, 417–21; English optimism concerning evolution, 413–17; influence of Darwin on Nietzsche, 493n16; Nietzsche on moral indifference and Darwinism, 335–36; Nietzsche's decisive turn against Darwinism, 340–41; Nietzsche's early contact with evolutionary theory, 322–29; Nietzsche's lack of direct contact with Darwin's writings, 321;

Nietzsche's specific attacks on Darwin, 354–59; Nietzsche's use of the term "Darwinism," 330; and the "overman" hypothesis, 16, 313–18, 358–59; the roots of Nietzsche's anti-Darwinism, 358, 496nn82–83. *See also* Nägeli, Carl von, as an alternative to Darwin; Rolph, William Henry, as an alternative to Darwin; Roux, Wilhelm, as an alternative to Darwin

"Expeditions of an Untimely Man" (Nietzsche), 2

Falk, Adalbert, 32
Faust (Goethe), 142
Fechner, Gustav Theodor, 397
Féré, Charles, 422, 456; negative eugenics of, 431
Festspiele in Bayreuth, 1, 102–3, 272
Feuerbach, Ludwig, 394, 500n57
Fichte, Johann Gottlieb, 26, 76, 394
"First Love" (Turgenev), 191
"Five Prefaces to Five Unwritten Books" (Nietzsche), 270–71, 429
Force: A Real Monistic Perspective (Vogt), 399–400
Force and Matter (Büchner), 375, 394
Forgotten Fatherland (Macintyre), 231
Förster, Bernhard, 13, 156, 169, 209, 239, 242, 482n36; anti-Semitism of, 261, 278, 282, 288, 289, 293; as a colonialist, 220, 221, 223–30; death of, 232, 235; on Frantz's call for a progressive income tax, 480n10. *See also* Nueva Germania
Foucault, Michel, 6
"Four Great Errors, The" (Nietzsche), 423–24
"Fragments to an expanded form of the 'Birth of Tragedy'" (Nietzsche), 144
France, 31, 32, 64, 76, 77, 91, 92, 95, 116, 125, 130, 138–40, 188, 198, 221, 222, 254, 257, 261, 420. *See also* Franco-Prussian War (1870–71); Paris Commune and Communards
Franco-Prussian War (1870–71), 23, 48, 76, 86, 90, 468n25, 503n38; patriotic spirit of Prussia during, 96, 222; Prussian victory in, 32, 99, 125, 330; socialist opposition to, 127
fraternities, German nationalist (*Burschenschaften*), 51, 84, 120
Frauenstädt, Julius, 264
French Revolution, 96, 135, 184, 213, 438
Freud, Sigmund, 159, 203, 285, 432
Freytag, Gustav, 131
Friedrich I (Barbarossa), 83

Friedrich III, 79
Friedrich Wilhelm IV, 80
Fritsch, Theodor, 292–93, 295, 296
Fritzsch, Ernst, 161–62, 469n32
Fürth, 264
"Future of the North German Middle States, The" (Treitschke), 86
Fynn, Emily, 192, 477–78n56

Galton, Francis, 18, 203, 286, 414, 431–32, 450, 504n46; coining of the word "eugenics" by, 433
Gay Science, The (Nietzsche), 2, 16, 72, 110, 152, 157, 392; on the corruption of societies, 225–26; on Darwin, 497n96; on eternal recurrence, 361–62; on the instinct for self-preservation, 344; praise for Napoleon in, 249; treatment of women in, 214–15
General German Women's Association, 184, 186
General German Workers' Association, 127, 137
German Question, the, 10–11, 75–124, 454; conceptualization of in nonpolitical terms, 97, German unity as the solution to, 101–2; and Germanness, 76; Nietzsche's attitude toward the practical aspects of, 88–89; Nietzsche's rethinking of the question "What is German?" 102–14; rejection of German jingoism by Nietzsche, 10, 114; as simultaneous with the demise of the Holy Roman Empire, 75; and the small German solution to, 85–86; and Wagner, culture, and German values, 89–102. *See also* National Liberal Party; Nietzsche, Friedrich, anti-German tirades of
German Wars of Liberation, 76, 81–82; Nietzsche's views on, 120–21
Germans, diversity of, 113–14
Germany, 22–23, 75–76, 491n98; "Founders' Age" of, 114, 125–26; population increase in, 126. *See also* Second Reich
Germany: A Winter's Tale (Heine), 83
Gersdorff, Carl von, 11, 23, 86, 94, 130–37, 139, 273, 322; importance of Lassalle to, 133; opinion of Jews, 263–64; opinion of Nietzsche's *Philology of the Future*, 269–70; opinion of the Paris Commune, 138
Geyer, Ludwig, 117
Gillot, Henrik, 189
Glagau, Otto, 273
Glasenapp, Carl Friedrich, 232
Gobineau, Joseph Arthur, 224, 265, 287, 289, 302
Goethe, Johann Wolfgang von, 22, 70, 80, 97, 99, 100, 106, 111, 121, 224, 235, 251, 332–33,

Goethe, Johann Wolfgang von (*continued*)
340, 369; and romanticism, 409–10; at the University of Leipzig, 185–86
Goldman, Emma, 177–78
"good European" concept, 13, 237, 245–52, 483n48; and the "children of the future," 250; as a Nietzschean alternative to nationalism, 246; as a project for the future, 247; qualities of the good European, 246–47
Görres, Joseph, 76
Gray, Thomas, 436
"great politics," 13–14, 245, 252–58, 483–84n55; and the colonial imagination, 257–58; negative view of, 254
"Great Politics and What They Cost" (Nietzsche), 253
"Great Politics of the German Cabinets, 1871–1914" (various authors), 252
"Greatest Weight, The" (Nietzsche), 361–62
Greece, 52; persistence of Greek antiquity in Nietzsche's thought, 66–67, 84; slavery as a necessary component of Greek society, 143
"Greek Music Drama, The" (Nietzsche), 95
Griechische Schulgrammatik (Koch), 28
Growth of Biological Thought (Mayr), 493n30
Gutzkow, Karl, 465n53
Gymnasium, 9, 24, 30, 35, 39, 40, 42, 463n14; essential duty/role of, 45, 65; Nietzsche's critique of the *Gymnasium* and the university, 42–51. *See also* Naumburg Cathedral Gymnasium

Haeckel, Ernst, 324, 340, 400, 429–30; and the concept of "artificial selection," 443; interest of in military affairs, 503n38
Handbook of Anti-Semitism, The (Fritsch), 292
Hanover, 85, 86
Härtle, Heinrich, 260
Hartmann, Eduard von, 24, 52, 339, 369, 466n62, 466n71; Nietzsche's attack on, 63–64, 336–38; Nietzsche's satirical comments on, 378–79
Hayek, Friedrich, 148
Hegel, G. W. F., 54, 68, 70, 106, 122, 351, 369, 394, 410, 497n96; historical culture and Hegelianism, 56; Nietzsche's attack on, 62–63
Heidegger, Martin, 16, 318–19, 365–67; establishment of rigid parameters for philosophical discussion by and their effect on Nietzsche, 366–67
Heine, Heinrich, 16, 83, 116, 262, 368–69; conversion of to Protestantism, 498n14; on eternal recurrence, 369–70; Nietzsche's opinion of, 369
Helmholtz, Hermann von, 24, 375
Heraclitus, 16, 367–68
Hereditary Genius (Galton), 433
Heredity (Ribot), 420, 430–31
Herzen, Alexander, 195
Hessen, 85, 86
historical learning, and cultural criticism, 61–67; and the abuses of history in the unified German state, 61, 64; and Nietzsche's attack on modernity, 64–65
historical pedagogy, types of: antiquarian history, 59–60; critical history, 60–61; monumental history, 58–59
History of Creation (Haeckel), 429–30
History of Materialism (Lange), 15, 16, 31, 129, 159, 322–23, 340, 377, 382–84, 394, 396, 397; as the chief source of Nietzsche's scientific knowledge, 374–75
History of the Social-Political Parties in Germany (Joerg), 135–37
Hödel, Max, 471n3
Höffding, Harald, 4
Hoffmann von Fallersleben, August Heinrich, 76–77
Holland, Henry W., 432, 504n46
Holy Roman Empire, 75, 83
"Homer and Classical Philology" (Nietzsche), 24
Human, All Too Human (Nietzsche), 11, 19, 72, 104, 154, 158, 176, 274; aphorisms devoted to socialism in, 165–67; attack on Bismarck in, 111–12; concept of the "good European" in, 245–46; dedication of to Voltaire, 230; discussion of women in Greece in, 207; on heightened social and community spirit, 336; influence of socialistic ideals on, 473n39; original conception of, 198; "Original German" aphorism in, 106; preoccupation with "great politics" in, 252–53; treatment of women in, 207–11, 213, 215, 217
Humboldt, Wilhelm von, 21, 49
"Hymn to Friendship" (Nietzsche), 103

Ibsen, Henrik, 213
Idea of the Realgymnasium, The (Beger), 39–40
Ideas: The Book of Le Grand (Heine), 368
"Idylls of Messina" (Nietzsche), 294
imperialism, as the highest state of capitalism, 148
"Impossible Class, The" (Nietzsche), 155–56
In Rank and File (Spielhagen), 131–35, 473n37

Inquiries into Human Faculty and Its Development (Galton), 203, 286, 432, 433
International Monthly, 294–95, 490n88, 502n84
Irigaray, Luce, 179, 182, 183

Jahn, Otto, 130; and the "battle of philologists," 485n23
Janz, Curt Paul, 3
Jaspers, Karl, 462n14
Jensen, Anthony K., 461n6
Jewish Question, the, 14–15, 126, 260–312, 454, 484n2; accusation against Nietzsche of being anti-Semitic, 484n6; ambivalent attitude of Nietzsche toward the Jews, 279–80, 287, 486nn36–37; and anti-Semitism versus anti-Judaism, 295–301; and the genealogy of Jewish slave morality, 301–6; and Jewish hegemony/dominion due to their financial prowess, 277–78; and Jewish history in *The Antichrist*, 306–12; the Jewish Question addressed in *Beyond Good and Evil*, 278–79; and Jewish stereotypes, 282–83; modification of Nietzsche's views on, 273–76, Nietzsche's admiration of Jews in the face of persecution, 276–77, 491n107; Nietzsche's anti-Jewish thought during his Wagnerian period, 265–71; Nietzsche's anti-Jewish views prior to his relationship with Wagner, 264–65; Nietzsche's anti-Semitic associations, 287–95; Nietzsche's aversion to anti-Semitism, 296–98; Nietzsche's displeasure at being associated with anti-Semitism, 292–93; Nietzsche's early experiences with Jews and Judaism, 261–65; Nietzsche's familiarity with Jews and Judaism, 14; Nietzsche's Jewish friends and acquaintances, 280–87; Nietzsche's post-Wagnerian ambivalence toward Jewry, 271–80, 486n35; Nietzsche's proposed solution to, 286–87; Nietzsche's use of the term "Misojuden," 288, 488n68; Nietzsche's relationship to political anti-Semitism, 15, 288–89; and Socratism, 39, 98, 268
Jewish Question, The (Bauer), 295
Jews, association of with accumulating wealth, 151, 227, 264, 266, 271, 282, 287, 488n62
Joerg, Joseph Edmund, 135–37
Johann of Saxony, 85
Joule, James Prescott, 374, 376, 382
Journey from Munich to Genoa (Heine), 368
Judaism in Music (Wagner), 14, 265–66, 269
Judeo-Christian tradition, 333–34, 379, 409; and the conception of genesis and the afterlife, 379; doctrine of, 258; ethics and morality of, 255, 423, 425; heritage of, 249, 254, 424; value system of, 254–55

Kant, Immanuel, 4, 54, 106, 122, 332–33, 374, 377, 384, 395, 402
Kaufmann, Walter, 178, 216, 261, 314, 491n106; on the rejection of biologism, 319–20
Keller, Gottfried, 324, 470n59
Kelly, Alfred, 331
Kinkel, Gottfried, 190
Kirchhoff, Gustav, 377–78
Klingbeil, Julius, 235
Klopstock, Friedrich Gottlieb, 26
Knortz, Karl, 115
Koch, Ernst, 28
Kofman, Sarah, 179, 475n20
Kohler, Josef, 5–6
Kölliker, Rudolf Albert, 328–29, 340
Korn, Philipp Anton, 186
Körner, Theodor, 81–82
Köselitz, Heinrich, 114, 187, 190, 194, 199, 236, 244, 274, 282, 294, 295, 298, 300, 317, 374, 381, 398, 470n62, 473n40, 476n41, 477n42, 490n88, 502n84
Kosmos: Journal for a Unified Worldview on the Basis of Evolutionary Theory, 400
Krug, Gustav, 80–82, 270
Kulturkampf (cultural struggle), 32–33; and the Catholic Church, 32
Kürbitz, E., 231

Lachner, Franz, 330
Lagarde, Paul de, 107–8, 221, 290, 293; negative evaluation of the Apostle Paul, 301
Lamarck, Jean-Baptiste, 321, 323, 332
Lamarckism, 339, 340, 352
Lange, Friedrich, 221–22, 231; promotion of "pure Germanness" by, 221
Lange, Friedrich Albert, 15, 16, 31, 129, 159, 168, 326, 327, 340, 351, 355, 374–77, 390, 395–97, 399, 400; and Darwinism, 322–23, 328, 338; on "heat death," 17, 382–84, 394
Lange und Nietzsche (Stack), 498–99n26, 500 501n67
Lankester, E. Ray, 417–18
Laplace, Pierre-Simon de, 371, 374, 377, 384
Lassalle, Ferdinand, 11, 37, 87, 127, 133–37, 145, 159, 160, 171, 286, 471n15; break with Marx and Engels, 163; Nietzsche's reluctant admiration for, 488n61

Last Poems and Thoughts of H. Heine (ed. Strodtmann), 369, 498n13, 498n15
Law as a Cultural Phenomenon (Kohler), 5
League for the Protection of Mothers, 175
Le Bon, Gustav, 372–74; on biological determinism, 373; on eternal recurrence, 373
Lecky, William, 4
Leclerc, Georges-Louis, 411
Leibniz, Gottfried Wilhelm, 4, 106, 122, 387, 389, 395, 403, 404, 500n57
Leipzig, 11, 14, 49, 78, 114, 137, 159, 161, 184–85, 264–65; Battle of, 82; University of, 10, 14, 46, 48, 74, 85, 128, 130, 138, 171, 263, 290, 311, 343, 384, 385, 399
Lenin, Vladimir, 148
Les Maladies de la volonté (Ribot), 456
Lessing, Theodor, 100, 133, 264, 269, 340, 485n25
L'éternité par les astres (Blanqui), 370–72
Levy, Leopold Moritz, 486n33
L'homme et les sociétés: leur origines et leur histoire (Le Bon), 372–73
"Libel Trial" (Nietzsche), 282
liberalism, 96, 135, 136, 186, 291, 373; of John Stuart Mill, 433; national liberalism, 134, 467n16
Lichtenberger, Henri, 368, 385, 498n12
Liebknecht, Wilhelm, 127
Liebmann, Otto, 4
Life of Jesus, The (Strauß), 331, 491n103
Lipiner, Siegfried, relationship with Nietzsche, 283–85, 485n8, 487n52, 487n55
Lipschitz, Rudolf, 262
Lohengrin (Wagner), 90
Lombroso, Cesare, 426–27
Lonsbach, Richard Maximillian, 484n1
Louvre, the, arson of, 139–40, 160
Love and Women (H. Stöcker), 175, 177
Löwith, Karl, 365
Lüderitz, Adolf, 219
Lukács, Georg, 148–49
Luther, Martin, 99, 100, 106–7, 118–20, 224, 274, 305
"Luther's Marriage" (Wagner), 118

Macintyre, Ben, 231
Magnus, Bernd, 365
Maltzan, Hermann von, 244
Man and Superman (Shaw), 313, 319
Mansuroff, Madame de, 193
Marine Lover of Friedrich Nietzsche (Irigaray), 179

Marr, Wilhelm, 266, 269, 288, 289, 302, 303, 490n91
Marti, Urs, 473n38
Marx, Karl, 54, 126, 129, 135, 143, 148, 150, 153, 154, 159, 163, 262, 440; and freedom from wage labor as a solution to the Social Question, 472n30; response to *The Jewish Question* (Bauer), 295
Marxists, 11, 148–49
Mass Psychology and Ego Analysis (Freud), 372
"Master of the Earth, The" (Nietzsche), 250
Mastersingers of Nuremberg, The (Wagner), 90
Mathematical Elements of Epistemology, The (Schmitz-Dumont), 401
May Laws (1872), 32
Mayer, Julius Robert, 374–75, 382
Mayr, Ernst, 325, 494n49, 494n61
Mazzini, Giuseppe, 141, 161, 162, 195
Mechanical-Physiological Theory of Organic Evolution, A (Nägeli), 16, 340, 351–52
Mehring, Franz, 148
Memoirs of an Idealist (Meysenbug), 195–97
Mendel, Gregor, 351
Mendelssohn, Felix, 122, 266
Metternich, Klemens von, *Realpolitik* of, 120
Meyer, Conrad Ferdinand, 199
Meyerbeer, Giacomo, 48, 95, 266, 270, 465–66n56
Meysenbug, Malwida von, 12, 159, 175, 192, 193, 199, 206, 281, 471n6; correspondence with Nietzsche, 194–95; opinion of Nietzsche, 206; plan of for establishing a coeducational school, 197–98; relationship with Nietzsche, 194–98, 200–201
Mill, John Stuart, 12, 159, 205, 212, 213, 345, 433, 455; Nietzsche's opinion of, 202–3; on women, 201–4, 212
Modern Attempts at a Substitute for Religion (Druskowitz), 199
modernity, 38, 220, 227, 245, 246, 255; conservative criticism of, 45, 64, 461n1; education as a counteraction to, 24; "Jewish modernity," 270, 288; manifestations of, 64, 126, 154, 236; and the Social Question, 152–54; wayward modernity, 24, 66
Moleschott, Jacob, 404
Mommsen, Tycho, 44, 46
monism, 395, 400, 500n60; dynamic monism, 397–402, 404, 406, 407
Moore, Gregory, 320, 493n30, 503n28
Morel, Bénédict-Augustin, 17, 411–12, 427
Mosengel, Adolf, 91–92, 468n24

Mother Earth, 177, 178
Müller, Max, 491n107
Mushacke, Eduard, 185, 470n58, 485n27
Mushacke, Hermann, 86, 185, 264
Music of the Future, 269
mutation theory, 339

Nachtigal, Gustav, 219
Nägeli, Carl von, 16, 340; as an alternative to Darwin, 351–54; belief of in spontaneous generation, 352; and the concept of micelles, 352
Nathan the Wise (Lessing), 264
National Liberal Party, 14, 32, 88, 127, 299, 490n90; and Nietzsche, 84–86, 103–4, 109–10, 168, 171, 472n22
National Socialism/National Socialists/Nazis, 108, 260, 288, 313, 314, 319, 484n56, 484n2
nationalism, 10–11, 47, 75–114, 120, 217, 245; German nationalism and colonialism, 220–23, 236, 258; and Nietzsche, 13, 222
Natural Conditions of Existence as They Affect Animal Life, The (Semper), 340
natural selection, 15–16, 321, 323, 325–58 *passim*, 412–13, 418–19, 427–31, 442, 446–47; Darwin's view of, 414; Wallace's role in the theory of, 414–16. *See also* Evolution Question
Naumburg, 8, 78, 80, 128, 130, 184, 209, 231, 241–42, 261, 262, 283
Naumburg Cathedral Gymnasium, 8, 21, 25–26, 46, 81, 262
Neue Gedichte (Heine), 498n13
"Newer Ethics, The" (H. Stöcker), 177–78
"New-World Conception" (Nietzsche), 391–92
Nielsen, Rosalie, 161–62, 474nn49–50
Nietzsche, Carl Ludwig, 26
Nietzsche (Förster-Nietzsche), Elisabeth, 4, 13, 27, 79, 112, 171, 190, 220, 223, 231, 232, 235, 250, 261, 282, 326, 369, 384–85, 393; and her brother's re-enlistment in the military, 91–92, 468n25; relationship with her brother, 209, 239–44, 289–90, 293, 487n44; on the women in Nietzsche's life, 191–92
Nietzsche, Franziska, 26, 78, 84, 128, 141, 209–10, 237, 241, 242, 262, 283, 464n22, 484n3
Nietzsche, Friedrich, 454–56, 462n8, 500n51; abhorrence of for journalism, 239; and the anarchist tradition, 112; animus of toward the press, 38–39; "aristocratic radicalism" of, 112, 470n59; borrowing of from contemporary sources, 6, 459–60; bragging of, 470nn62–63; classical studies of, 84; and the concept of "posthumous man," 2, 3, 218; as a dialogical thinker, 461n6; discussion of historical issues by, 457–58; disdain of for the masses, 36; disdain of for parliamentary democracy, 112–13; disenchantment of with the teaching profession, 71–72; education of, 8, 21, 25–29, 262; on Europeanness and European identity, 10, 246–48, 255; excellence of as a teacher, 28–29, 49; as a faculty member at Basel, 49; as a "feminist," 12; financial situation of, 240; on genius, 34–35; on German unity, 64; on the Gospels, 491n109; as the heir of a German "Grecophilia," 22; on human/animal consciousness and relationships to history, 54–56; on the human sciences, 61–62; indebtedness of to contemporary sources, 5–6; interchangeable use of the terms "Jewish" and "Christian" by, 491n105; international reputation of, 115; involvement of in the discourses of his time, 3–4, 218–19, 454–56; on Jews and the press, 39, 266–67; lack of firsthand knowledge of modern philosophy, 8; library of, 8, 462n14, 498n13, 500n58; loyalties of for Prussia, 10; and materialism, 31–32; as a member of Franconia, 49, 51, 84, 120, 464n20; as a member of the Wagner Society, 230; military service of, 87–88, 91–94, 468n25; nationality of, 77–79, 116, 463n7; on opera, 160; on the opposition between history and life, 57–58; at Pforta boarding school, 25–27, 84, 262, 384; as a philologist, 8–9; physical illnesses of, 93; political beliefs of, 84–85, 109–13, 252–59, 467n16, 471n6, 472n22; as a poor student in mathematics, 384; preoccupation of with patriotic topics, 83–84; pre-university days of, 81–82; on priestly "parasitism," 311; on the primacy of physiology over all other matters, 257; Prussian and Germanic phase of, 79–89; rejection of all forms of modern government by, 109–10; relationship with his sister, 242–43, 289–90, 489n78; relationship with Lipiner, 283–85, 485n8, 487n52, 487n55; relationship with Meyerbeer, 465–66n56; relationship with Paul Rée, 487nn44–45; on the "religion of joy," 176, 475n9; self-designation of as a "good European," 113; sensitivity to his lack of readers, 2, 114–15; sensitivity to and obsession with weather and climate, 121, 236–37; sources of for Marxist theory,

Nietzsche, Friedrich (*continued*)
473n41; as a student at Bonn, 48–49; as a supporter of the new Reich, 10; on the task of "great politics," 252–59; as an "untimely" thinker, 1–3, 219, 461n1; on the unhistorical and the superhistorical, 55–56, 361; at the University of Leipzig, 185–86; works published after his mental breakdown, 459. *See also* eternal recurrence; Nietzsche, Friedrich, anti-German tirades of; Nietzsche, Friedrich, and the concept of a ruling class; Nietzsche, Friedrich, concern of with culture; Nietzsche, Friedrich, and the nature of his writings; Nietzsche, Friedrich, relationship with Wagner; Nueva Germania, Nietzsche's involvement in; will to power

Nietzsche, Friedrich, anti-German tirades of, 114–24; attacks on the German Reformation, 118–20; attacks on the German Wars of Liberation, 120–21; climax of his anti-German sentiments reached in *Ecce Homo*, 121–24, 223; derogatory references of to the German state, 30; and his lack of readership in Germany, 114–16

Nietzsche, Friedrich, and the concept of a ruling class, 13–14, 114, 146, 147, 255, 440–45; domination of, 252, 483n51; and eugenics, 454; Jewish assimilation into, 312, 488n62; mention of in his notebooks, 483n50; training of, 251

Nietzsche, Friedrich, concern of with culture, 29, 47, 89–90, 92–93, 140–41; on "cultural Philistinism," 101–2; on culture and money in contemporary society, 32; and the establishment of the "Germania" cultural club, 80–81, 467n12; and Greece as a paradigm for cultural excellence, 52, 66–67; Nietzsche's cultural objective (the renaissance of German culture), 22–23, 50–51; Nietzsche's reevaluation of noted individuals in the German cultural tradition, 105–7; position of concerning the *Kulturkampf* (cultural struggle), 32–33; on the relationship between the state and culture, 48; and the Wagnerian program for German cultural renaissance, 1, 10, 47, 196, 336

Nietzsche, Friedrich, and the nature of his writings, 7–8; importance of contextualization in understanding his approach to philosophy, 8; refusal of to distinguish between the abstract and the historical, the philosophical and the mundane, 7

Nietzsche, Friedrich, relationship with Wagner, 1, 14, 19–21, 118, 481n17; adaptation of Wagner's views by Nietzsche, 10; attacks of on Wagner, 116–18; enormous influence of Wagner on Nietzsche, 90–91; and nationalism, 10; Nietzsche's break with Wagner, 10, 102–4, 271–73; as a relationship not of equals, 20–21

Nietzsche and the Feminine (ed. Burgard), 179, 180, 182

Nietzsche and Metaphor (Kofman), 179

Nietzsche, Biology and Metaphor (Moore), 320–21

Nietzsche contra Wagner (Nietzsche), 20, 116, 222, 224, 272, 459

Nietzsche et la scène philosophique (Kofman), 179

Nietzsche myth, the: contributions of early Nietzsche scholarship to, 4; contributions of his sister to, 4; and the myth of Polish nobility, 79, 116, 129, 467n8

Nietzsche's Jewish Problem: Between Anti-Semitism and Anti-Judaism (Holub), 484–85n7

Nobiling, Karl Eduard, 471n3

nobility, 158, 448–49; English nobility, 279; German nobility, 426; lower levels of, 132–33; in the Middle Ages, 438; the "new" nobility, 441–42; and politics, 110

North German Confederation, 86

Nueva Germania, 13, 156, 220, 221, 225, 237, 454; coverage of in the *Bayreuther Blätter*, 232, 233; financial problems of, 244–45; history of, 229–35, 240–41; Nietzsche's sources of information concerning, 234–35. *See also* Nueva Germania, Nietzsche's involvement in

Nueva Germania, Nietzsche's involvement in, 236–45; ambivalent attitudes toward the colony, 243–44; and Nietzsche's attention to colonial affairs in Paraguay, 238–39; Nietzsche's decline to make a financial investment in, 239–42; and Nietzsche's doubts concerning the business dealings of Förster, 244–45; and Nietzsche's obsession with climate, 236–37; reasons other than climate that Nietzsche did not move to Paraguay, 237–38

Oberlin College, 188, 477n45
Oberrealschulen, 41
Oehler, Richard, 260
"Of the People of Israel" (Nietzsche), 276
Oken, Lorenz, 351

Old Faith and the New, The (Strauß), 52, 101, 330, 377; main themes of, 331–32
Oliver, Kelly, 179
"On Great Politics" (Nietzsche), 253
"On Little Old and Young Women" (Nietzsche), 173–74
On the Advantage and Disadvantage of History for Life (Nietzsche), 1, 22, 52–57, 64, 66, 337–38; and the idea of eternal recurrence, 360–61, 368
On the Apparent and Real Causes of Occurrences in the World (Drossbach), 402–4
"On the Conservation of Energy" (Helmholtz), 375
"On the Future of Marriage" (Nietzsche), 449–51
"On the Future of our Educational Institutions" (Nietzsche), 9, 23–52, 55–59 *passim*, 61, 63–65, 67, 71, 74, 78, 81, 84, 120, 136–37, 140, 149, 150, 455
On the Genealogy of Morals (Nietzsche), 5, 114, 141, 146, 205, 296; on alcohol, 426; on "English psychologists," 356; on grammar, 423; on the legal customs surrounding debt, 5–6; popularity of, 505n4; prominent role of Judaism in, 302–3; on rancor in anti-Semites and anarchists, 291; as a response to Darwin, 496–97n87
"On the Higher Man" (Nietzsche), 482–83n47
"On the Lack of Noble Manners" (Nietzsche), 157
On the Nature of the Comets (Zöllner), 290
"On the Old Problem: 'What Is German?'" (Nietzsche), 106
On the Origin of Species (Darwin), 15, 321, 322, 412
On the Physical and Philosophical Doctrine of Atoms (Fechner), 397
On the Present Situation in the German Reich (de Lagarde), 108
On the Relationship of the German State to Theology, Church, and Religion (de Lagarde), 107–8
"On the Vision and the Riddle" (Nietzsche), 362–63
"On Women" (Schopenhauer), 205–6
On Women's Emancipation (Teichmüller), 204
Opera and Drama (Wagner), 95
orthogenesis, 339
"Other Dance Song, The" (Nietzsche), 176–77
Otto-Peters, Louise, 184–85
"Our Views" (Treitschke), 288

"Over Fifty Years" (Nietzsche), 82–83
Overbeck, Franz, 103, 112, 114, 194, 198, 220, 240, 286, 294, 305, 490n91; concern about Schmeitzner's publication of anti-Semitic materials, 298–300; as a specialist in early Christian theology, 301
Overbeck, Ida, 282
overman, concept of, 16, 313–18; comments on in *Ecce Homo*, 315–18; in the context of evolutionary theory, 358–59; and the "willed overman," 359; in *Zarathustra*, 416
"Overman, The" (Nietzsche), 359

Pädagogium, 9, 27–28, 43, 71, 74, 91
Paneth, Joseph, 203, 285–87, 294, 295, 300, 432, 433, 485n8, 488n58
Parerga and Paralipomena (Schopenhauer), 34, 205
Paris Commune and the Communards, 11, 37, 127, 137–43, 160, 172, 331, 370; Gersdorff's opinion of, 138; Nietzsche's reaction to, 138–42
Parsifal (Wagner), 90, 103, 104, 272, 446
Pasha, Mehmed Emin (Isaak Eduard Schnitzer), 234
"Peoples and Fatherlands" (Nietzsche), 293, 457
Pernerstorfer circle, the, 283, 284, 285
Pessimistic Cardinal Principles: A Vademecum for the Most Free Spirits (Druskowitz), 200
Peters, Carl, 219, 234
Philology of the Future (Wilamowitz), 269–70
"Philosophy in Union with Scientific Research" (Caspari), 400
Philosophy of the Unconscious (Hartmann), 52, 337, 378
Pinder, Wilhelm, 80, 81, 263
Plato, 164, 169, 186, 205, 207, 323, 428–29
Plutarch, 429
politics, 86–89; conventional politics, 130; as the domain of the nobility, 110; German global politics, 220; "iron and blood" politics, 254; politics of revenge, 254–55. *See also* "great politics"; Nietzsche, Friedrich, political beliefs of
Problematic Characters (Spielhagen), 131
Prometheus Unbound (Lipiner), 283
prostitution, 18, 426, 448–49, 450, 477n43, 479n84
Prussia, 23, 30, 32, 91, 94, 125–26, 138, 277–78; educational reform in, 21, 41; gaining of additional territories by, 77–78; Nietzsche's opinions concerning, 79–89; unification of

Prussia (*continued*)
Germany under the auspices of Prussia, 75–76, 85, 86, 88, 108. *See also* Franco-Prussian War (1870)
Prussian Saxony, 10, 14, 77, 79, 261
Psychological Observations (Rée), 280–81
Psychology of the Crowd, The (Le Bon), 372
Pure Germanness (Lange), 480n13

"Question of power, not justice, A" (Nietzsche), 162–63
Quintessence of Socialism, The (Schäffle), 129, 159, 473n43

Rand, Ayn, 148
Ranke, Leopold von, 26
Real and Apparent World, The (Teichmüller), 205
Realschulen, 9, 24, 27, 29, 35, 39–43, 463n14; controversy surrounding, 40–41; increased legitimacy of, 39–40; *Realschulen* of the Second Order, 41
Rée, Georg, 281–82
Rée, Paul, 12, 189, 197, 261, 280–83, 345; Nietzsche's feelings toward, 281–82, 487n44; planned travel of to Vienna, 281, 385
Reich, Eduard, 420, 503n25
"Religion and Art" (Wagner), 226
Reminiscences of Parsifal (Förster), 228–29, 231, 293
Renaissance, the, 118–19, 121, 247, 249, 359, 470n65; the "new Renaissance," 175
Renan, Ernest, 301, 307, 491n103
Republic (Plato), 207
Reuter, Richard, 107, 108
Reuter, Sören, 495n62
Revue philosophique, 456
Rhinegold, The (Wagner), 150
Ribot, Théodule-Armand, 420, 430–31, 456
Richard Wagner in Bayreuth (Nietzsche), 1–2, 19, 224, 271, 376
Richter, Clair, 495n7, 497n91
Ring of the Nibelungs (Wagner), 90, 150
Ritschl, Friedrich, 27, 49, 78, 92, 130, 263; and the "battle of philologists," 485n23
Ritschl, Sophie, née Guttentag, 92, 263
Rochefoucauld, François de La, 207–8
Röder-Wiederhold, Louise, 190
Rohde, Erwin, 20, 89, 92, 94, 98, 161, 196, 204, 283; on Jewish arrogance, 270; trip to Paris of with Nietzsche, 385
Rolph, William Henry, 4, 15–16, 340, 356, 496n77; as an alternative to Darwin, 343–45, 349–51; critique of Spencer, 350–51

Roman Catholicism, 32, 106, 119, 127
Roos, Richard, 261
Rosenberg, Alfred, 260
Rousseau, Jean-Jacques, 70, 161, 170
Roux, Wilhelm, 340, 496n72, 496n74; as an alternative to Darwin, 341–43; as the founder of experimental embryology, 341
Ruskin, John, 433
Rütimeyer, Ludwig, 15, 324–25, 430; contribution of to Darwin's reputation, 325–26

Salaquarda, Jörg, 498–99n26
Salis-Marschlins, Meta von, 193–94, 198, 478n62, 504n41; Nietzsche's disparaging comments on, 194, 478nn60–61
Saxony, 77–79, 86–87, 89, 127; as an ally of Austria, 85; as an ally of France, 77; anti-Semitism in, 14–15
Schacht, Richard, 495n69
Schaerer, Santiago, 235
Schäffle, Albert Eberhard Friedrich, 129, 159
Schelling, Friedrich, 327, 394, 500n57
Schiller, Friedrich, 22, 80, 97, 410–11; Nietzsche's attack on, 106, 469n47
Schirnhofer, Resa von, 190–92, 432, 477n52, 478n58
Schlechta, Karl, 261
Schlegel, Friedrich, 370
Schliemann, Heinrich, 410
Schmeitzner, Ernst, 230–31, 261, 278, 290, 294, 381, 490n90
Schmidt, Auguste, 184–85
Schmidt, Johann Kaspar. *See* Stirner, Max
Schmidt, Julian, 471n15
Schmitz-Dumont, Otto, 17, 501n80, 501–2n82; argument of against the dualism of matter and force, 401–2
Schnitzer, Carl Oscar Theodor, 234
Schopenhauer, Arthur, 1, 3, 4, 8, 19–21, 25, 31, 49, 52, 56, 63, 94, 95, 106, 111, 116, 121, 122, 131, 132, 143, 177, 186, 251, 264, 286, 322, 331, 334, 337, 340, 405, 446, 456, 484n6; emphasis of on genius in his philosophy, 34, 47; on historical knowledge, 376–77; influence of on Nietzsche, 494n50; Nietzsche's consideration of as an educator, 68–71; on the notion of will, 60; opinion of women, 197, 205–6, 209, 212
Schopenhauer as Educator (Nietzsche), 9, 19, 20, 68–71, 94–95, 150; identification of the three fundamental types of human beings in, 161
Schubert, Max, 231–32

Schulpforta, 8, 15, 21, 25, 27–28, 46, 74, 77, 79–84 *passim*, 90, 128, 130, 262, 263, 269, 384
Schulze-Delitzsch, Franz Hermann, 471n15
Second Reich/Second Empire, 1, 3, 9–11, 14, 21, 22, 32, 44, 47, 52, 56, 57, 64, 67, 74, 75, 77, 78, 86, 95, 97, 104, 107, 110, 118, 124, 127, 149, 216, 220–22, 248, 252, 254, 255, 258, 266, 332, 336; and capitalism, 151; cultural enthusiasm during, 102; elections in, 113; and the example of Greek civilization, 67; historical optimism of, 10, 56–57, 94, 101–2, 379; jingoism of, 10, 114; Judeophobic discourse of, 271; modern culture of, 47; Nietzsche's view of, 473–74n46; perils of, 108; population increase during, 126
Semper, Karl, 340
Sensation et mouvement (Féré), 422, 431
Seydlitz, Reinhart von, 115, 284
Shaw, George Bernard, 313, 319, 452
"Siegfried Idyll" (Wagner), 118
slavery: and the genealogy of Jewish slave morality, 301–6; as a necessary component of Greek society, 143; Nietzsche's views on, 143–47, 172n30; as the prerequisite for the production of great art, 145
Social Democracy, 11, 167
Social Democratic Party of Germany (SPD), 128
Social Democratic Workers' Party of Germany (SDAP), 11, 127–28
Social Question, the, 11–12, 37, 125–72, 472n30; definition of, 126; as a facet of modernity, 152–53; moderation of Nietzsche's views on social issues during his aphoristic period, 152–58; Nietzsche's ambivalence toward, 137–38; Nietzsche's hatred of the *nouveaux riches*, 149; Nietzsche's idea of emigration as an alternative to the plight of the proletariat, 156–57; and Nietzsche's interest in the Fourth Estate, 11, 130–37, 462n15, 472n27; Nietzsche's negative view of revolutionary activities, 141–42; Nietzsche's views on slavery, 143–47; Nietzsche's views on workers and capitalists, 147–58, 172; readings that informed Nietzsche concerning the Social Question, 129–37; and the rise of the German working class, 125–29; and the social structure of "Alexandrian culture," 142–43, 160. *See also* socialism
socialism, 158–72 *passim*, 473n39; Nietzsche on the relationship between socialism and justice, 164–65, 169; and Nietzsche's attack on the National Liberals, 168; Nietzsche's evaluation of tied to his Wagnerian partisanship, 161–62; Nietzsche's identification of socialism with Christianity, 170–71; Nietzsche's objections to, 158–61, 167–69, 171–72; Nietzsche's post-Wagnerian view of, 162–64; Nietzsche's sustained consideration of socialism in eight points, 165–67; Nietzsche's view of socialism as "reactionary," 164; Nietzsche's view of the Socialist Laws, 167–68
"Socialism" (Mill), 159
Socialist Laws (1878), 11, 37, 128, 147, 163, 471n4, 476n40; Nietzsche's view of, 167–68
Socialist Workers' Party of Germany (SAPD), 128
Socrates, 22, 427, 428. *See also* Socratism
Socrates and Greek Tragedy (Nietzsche), 96
"Socrates and Tragedy" (Nietzsche), 39, 95, 142, 266–68
Socratism, 99, 100, 113, 142, 266–67; and the Jewish Question, 39, 98, 268
Solalinde, Cirilio, 240–41
"Song of the Germans, The" (Fallersleben), 76–77
Song of the Nibelungs, 83
Spencer, Herbert, 17, 343–51; on egoism and altruism, 347–48; on evolution, 345–47; Nietzsche's attack on, 348–49; Rolph's critique of, 350–51; and the "survival of the fittest" concept, 412
Spielhagen, Friedrich, 84, 131–35; fame of in Russia, 131
Spir, Afrikan, 4
Spitteler, Carl, 199
Stack, George, 498–99n26, 500–501n67
Stanley, Henry Morton, 234
Stegmaier, Werner, 492n12
Stein, Heinrich von, 76, 232
Steinschneider, Moritz, 488n64
Stephani, Eduard, 87
Stewart, Balfour, 376
Stirner, Max, 112, 139
Stöcker, Adolf, 112, 288, 289
Stöcker, Helene, 175–77
Strauß, David Friedrich, 10, 52, 56, 101, 102, 129, 394, 430; and Darwinism, 330–34; Nietzsche's attacks on, 19, 56, 129, 334–35, 491n103; on scientific theories, 377–78
Strindberg, August, 115
Strodtmann, Adolf, 369
"Struggle for the Gymnasium, The" (Eucken), 24
Struggle of the Parts in the Organism, The (Roux), 15, 340

Study of Sociology, The (Spencer), 345
Subjection of Women, The (Mill), 12, 159, 202; German translation of, 203
Sully, James, 4
"Sunday in Nueva Germania, A" (Förster-Nietzsche), 235
Sybel, Heinrich von, 48, 85, 203–4
System of Nature (d'Holbach), 370

Tacitus, 81
Taine, Hippolyte, 115, 470n59
Talbot, Eugene, 420
Tannhäuser (Wagner), 90
Teichmüller, Gustav, 203, 204–5, 212
Theory of Natural Philosophy (Boscovich), 397
thermodynamics, 16–17, 374–75; and eternal recurrence, 380–92 *passim*
Thomson, William (Lord Kelvin), 382, 387, 394
"Thomson Hypothesis, The" (Caspari), 382
"Thornton on Labour and Its Claims" (Mill), 159
Three English Women Writers (Druskowitz), 198
Thus Spoke Zarathustra (Nietzsche), 12, 16, 114, 244, 314, 392, 416, 470n63; "anti-Semitic interpretation" of, 292; basic conception of, 380; on the "good European," 483n48; Nietzsche's infamous "whip" remark concerning women in, 173, 176–77, 191–92, 211, 475n11
"Time Atomism Fragment" (Nietzsche), 397
Traditions of Manu/Law Book of Manu, Nietzsche's fascination with, 171, 444–45
Traité des dégénérescences de l'espèce humaine (Morel), 17, 411
Travel Pictures (Heine), 368–69
Treitschke, Heinrich von, 24, 40, 41, 44, 46, 84, 102, 204, 288; and the beginnings of anti-Semitism in Berlin, 299; and the nationalist movement, 86; political tracts of, 290; as a proponent of colonial expansion, 220
Tristan and Isolde (Wagner), 90
Turgenev, Ivan, 191
Twilight of the Idols (Nietzsche), 2, 7, 73, 182, 355, 426, 444, 492n3; on the confusion of cause and effect, 42–24; on Socrates, 427; on the "spiritualization of sensuality," 255; the "Workers Question" section of, 146–47

Ueberweg, Friedrich, 384
Unity of Natural Forces, The (Schmitz-Dumont), 401
Untimely Meditations (Nietzsche), 1, 3, 23, 47, 99, 165, 207, 466n74; attack on Strauß in, 19, 56, 129; attack on von Hartmann in, 24; on historical thought and education in the Second Reich, 9; subtext of, 52

Value of Life, The (Dühring), 290, 446
"Value of Work, The" (Nietzsche), 154–55
Victory of Judaism over Germanism Considered from a Non-Confessional Perspective, The (Marr), 266, 288, 303
Vischer-Bilfinger, Wilhelm, 27, 78, 91, 139, 468n25
vivisection, 220, 224, 228, 290, 480n9
Vogt, Johannes Gustav, 17, 399–400
Volksbildung (general education), 33, 36–37, 48, 136–37, 217; as the antithesis of *Bildung*, 36
Volksschule, 48
Voltaire, 230

Wächter, Karl Georg von, 87
Wagner, Cosima, 14, 39, 90, 92, 139–40, 161, 222, 267, 273, 281; animus of toward the French, 468n26; conversion of to Protestantism, 272; marriages of, 462n2; on Nietzsche and socialism, 473–74n46; and religion, 486n31. See also *Birth of Tragedy*, as Nietzsche's first "Wagnerian" publication
Wagner, Richard, 1, 2, 7, 12, 19–21, 31, 47, 80, 106–8, 116, 121, 136, 140, 142, 159, 162, 172, 195, 220, 222, 230, 231, 251, 269, 271, 274, 284, 287, 289, 290, 293, 294, 311, 330, 331, 334, 408, 409, 446, 454, 470n59; anticapitalism of, 150; anti-Semitism of, 14, 118, 151, 265–68, 273, 281, 285, 302, 303; and colonization, 223–29, 232–34; on the decay of the arts in non-German countries, 100; embrace of Christianity by, 272, 469n44; essay of on Beethoven, 96–100; French influence on, 116–17; and German nationalism, 222–23, 480–81n15; "German nature" of, 113–14; and the German question, 89–102, 104–5; Germanness of in his creative works, 90; Jewish origins of, 117, 122; relationship of to revolution, 472n27; on vegetarianism, 226. See also *Birth of Tragedy*, as Nietzsche's first "Wagnerian" publication; Nietzsche, Frederick, relationship with Wagner
Wagner und Nietzsche zur Zeit ihrer Freundschaft (Förster-Nietzsche), 474n50
Wallace, Alfred Russel, 341, 413, 418–20, 429, 502n11; as co-discoverer of the natural selection theory, 414–416
Weber, Carl Moritz, 8

Wellhausen, Julius, 301, 307; as the authority for the "developmental" hypothesis, 310
"What Is German?" (Wagner), 90, 104
"What Is the Fatherland of the Germans?" (Arndt), 76
"What the Germans Lack" (Nietzsche), 124
"Why I Am a Destiny" (Nietzsche), 2–3
Widemann, Paul Heinrich, 295, 490n88, 502n84
Wilamowitz-Moellendorff, Ulrich von, 269–70, 317, 485n26
Wilhelm I, assassination attempts on, 127–28, 167, 471n3
Wilhelm II, 112
Wilhelm Meister's Apprenticeship (Goethe), 215
will to power, 16, 200, 250, 350, 358, 392–407; cosmological dimension of, 396–97; and eternal recurrence, 393–94; prominence of in Nietzsche's thought, 392–93; as the vital force in organic life, 353, 392–405 *passim*
Will to Power, The (Nietzsche), 171, 250, 364, 451; as the largest collection of Nietzsche's notebook entries, 458–59
Wilson, Catherine, 493n15
Winckelmann, Johann Joachim, 22, 97, 410
Wisner, Heinrich von Morgenstern de, 231
Wolf, Friedrich August, 46–47, 143
Wolzogen, Hans von, 224, 232, 281; support of for Nueva Germania, 233–34
"Woman and Child" (Nietzsche), 177, 207, 209, 457

Woman and Socialism/ Woman in the Past, Present, and Future (Bebel), 187, 476n41
Womanizing Nietzsche (Oliver), 179
Women's Educational Organization, 185
Women's Question, the, 12–13, 173–217, 460, 476n26; central motifs of Nietzsche concerning, 216–17; claiming Nietzsche for feminism, 174–78; men writing on the women's question, 201–6; Nietzsche's early reflections on, 206–11; Nietzsche's later reflections on, 211–17; and Nietzsche's relationship with his sister and mother, 209, 242–43, 479n85; Nietzsche's women friends, 189–201 *passim*; and philosophical feminism's views on Nietzsche, 178–84; popularity of Nietzsche among feminists, 183–84; strategies of feminists to diminish misogynist sentiments in Nietzsche, 179–83; the women's movement and Nietzsche, 184–88
Workers' Question, The: Its Significance for the Present and the Future (Lange), 129, 159, 168
World as Will and Representation, The (Schopenhauer), 34, 68, 376
Wuttke, Heinrich, 87

Zimmern, Helen, 193
Zöllner, Johann, 290, 489n80
Zurich, 129, 190, 192, 198; as a destination for Jewish Russian women, 189; University of, 12, 193, 195, 215

Acknowledgments

My work on this book started over twenty-five years ago. At that time, I was a member of the German faculty at the University of California, Berkeley. I entered into a contract to publish a short volume on Nietzsche with the understanding that it would be a preliminary study to something larger and more scholarly, and that initial monograph appeared in 1995 (*Friedrich Nietzsche*, Twayne World Authors Series 857). In the intervening years, I also published several essays on Nietzsche, three of which are shorter versions of chapters in this book; they have been revised, updated, and expanded for inclusion in the present study: "Nietzsche and the Women's Question" *German Quarterly* 68.1 (1995): 67–71; "Nietzsche's Colonialist Imagination: Nueva Germania, Good Europeanism, and Great Politics," in *The Imperialist Imagination: German Colonialism and Its Legacy*, ed. Sara Friedrichsmeyer, Sara Lennox, and Susanne Zantop (Ann Arbor: University of Michigan Press, 1998), 33–49; and "Dialectic of the Biological Enlightenment: Nietzsche, Degeneration, and Eugenics," in *Practicing Progress: The Promise and Limitations of Enlightenment*, Festschrift for John McCarthy, ed. Richard Schade and Dieter Sevin (Amsterdam: Rodopi, 2007), 173–85.

I was sidetracked from my work on Nietzsche—indeed, from most of my scholarly endeavors—when I took up a series of administrative positions at various institutions of higher education: Dean of the Undergraduate Division at Berkeley, Provost and Vice Chancellor for Academic Affairs at the University of Tennessee in Knoxville, and Chancellor at the University of Massachusetts Amherst. In these posts, I would sometimes joke that *Beyond Good and Evil* should be required reading for any administrator, but I would be stretching the truth if I claimed that my role in administration afforded me additional insights into Nietzsche and his thought. The postponement of the project by many years after its initial stages, however, did give me the opportunity to return to the material and look at it from a fresh perspective. I believe I came to understand Nietzsche better as a human being struggling with the issues confronting him in the nineteenth century, to grasp his quirks and inadequacies as an individual, as well as his strengths and virtues. Temporal distance sometimes helps a scholar to attain a dispassionate perspective, and I hope that it has assisted me in presenting a full and balanced account of matters that are frequently subject to partisan debate.

A project such as this one, whose completion has spanned many decades, owes a great deal to a great many people. I cannot possibly name them all here, and since I do not want to exclude anyone who deserves recognition, I will refrain from individual names. But I do want to acknowledge that the high intellectual level of discourse among colleagues at Berkeley, both inside and outside the German Department, was tremendously important for my development as a scholar and writer. I am also enormously grateful to Ohio State University for enabling me to come to Columbus as the Ohio Eminent Scholar in German. The resources that position has provided for me have made my transition from academic administration back into the faculty a seamless process, and have made work on this project and my entire intellectual life much easier. I am also grateful to my colleagues at OSU, in particular the faculty in Germanic Languages and Literatures, for their support and friendship. I would be remiss if I did not extend thanks to various employees in the University Library; research in the humanities has changed so much during the past quarter of a century, and the librarians at Ohio State patiently introduced me to innovations that have fostered the completion of this study. I also owe a large debt of gratitude to various editors and employees at the University of Pennsylvania Press. Their patience, professionalism, and attention to detail have contributed to a much-improved study. No words can express what I owe to my three wonderful daughters, two of whom are now teenagers, and the other a ten-year-old who imagines herself a good deal older than she is. Over the past five years, when I returned to my scholarly life, they have given me so much pleasure and helped me to keep things in proper perspective. My wife Sabine, to whom I dedicate this book, has celebrated with me in good times and supported me during some very difficult moments. I don't know how I would have survived to write this book without her.

Lightning Source UK Ltd.
Milton Keynes UK
UKHW040725160119
335322UK00008B/313/P